GABRIEL MANTZ

# THE COMPLETE WORLD CUP 1976-1986

British Library Cataloguing in Publication Data
A catalogue record for this book is available from the British Library

ISBN: 978-1-86223-286-0

Copyright © 2013, SOCCER BOOKS LIMITED (01472 696226)
72 St. Peter's Avenue, Cleethorpes, N.E. Lincolnshire, DN35 8HU, England
Web site   www.soccer-books.co.uk
e-mail   info@soccer-books.co.uk

All rights are reserved. No part of this publication may be reproduced, stored in a retrieval system or transmitted, in any form or by any means, electronic, mechanical, photocopying, recording, or otherwise, without the prior written permission of Soccer Books Limited.

**Printed in the UK by 4Edge**

Dear Readers

Following our publication last year which presented a complete statistical record for the FIFA World Cup from the first tournament held in Uruguay in 1930 to the tenth tournament in West Germany in 1974, this second volume continues the story and contains statistics from 1978 through to 1986.

The eleventh finals tournament was held in Argentina in 1978 with 16 teams in four groups once again competing for the trophy. From 1982 onwards, the number of teams participating in the final tournament was increased to 24, duly increasing the number of matches played and increasing the magnitude of the tournament as a whole. The number of teams which entered the qualifying tournament also increased from edition to edition with the World Championship encompassing increasingly more and more countries on all continents.

After the 1974, the qualification process was adjusted so that more and more colourful and 'exotic' teams made their first appearances in the final tournaments (Tunisia, Cameroon, Iran, Kuwait, New Zealand, Honduras, Canada etc.). Though perhaps less capable than some of the bigger countries whose teams did not qualify, the qualification process was now more 'fair', allowing a wider geographical spread of countries to reach football's biggest tournament and making it a truer World Cup. In many cases these 'minnows' were often able to surprise the stronger countries, winning some unexpected results and demonstrating that the difference in value between the established teams and the newcomers was becoming increasingly smaller.

As might be expected, the three final tournaments of 1978, 1982 and 1986 saw traditionally strong teams winning as Argentina (twice) and Italy triumphed. However, these tournaments are also remembered as much for the great teams which didn't win the trophy yet whose quality of play is still remembered today: Holland in 1978, Brazil in 1982 and France in both 1982 and 1986. Also, the period 1978-1986 was dominated by the emergence and development of the probably best player in the football history since Pelé: Diego Armando Maradona! A brilliant player with a great career often dogged by controversy that probably culminated in the World Cup title in 1986, but unfortunately finished in less admirable terms during the 1990s. But that is another story... And we saw many other great players such as Michel Platini, Karl-Heinz Rummenigge, Zico, Socrates, Paolo Rossi and last but not least Gary Lineker!

In this second volume about past editions of the World Cup, you will find complete statistics (with team line-ups including the full names of players) of all matches played in the FIFA World Cup 1978, 1982 and 1986, both in qualifying rounds and the final tournaments themselves. As was the case in volume one, this book also lists the names of the coaches of the national teams, data about referees who officiated in the final tournaments and, of course, all final tournament squads for the teams who qualified.

Volume One, covering the World Cup from 1930 to 1974 is still available from Soccer Books Limited, as are other publications covering all the tournaments up to and including the 2010 World Cup. Details of these World Cup and many other statistical titles are listed on the back cover of this book.

The Author

## FIFA COUNTRY CODES – AFRICA

| | | | |
|---|---|---|---|
| Algeria | ALG | Libya | LBY |
| Angola | ANG | Madagascar | MAD |
| Benin | BEN | Malawi | MWI |
| Botswana | BOT | Mali | MLI |
| Burkina Faso | BFA | Mauritania | MTN |
| Burundi | BDI | Mauritius | MRI |
| Cameroon | CMR | Morocco | MAR |
| Cape Verde Islands | CPV | Mozambique | MOZ |
| Central African Republic | CTA | Namibia | NAM |
| Chad | CHA | Niger | NIG |
| Comoros Islands | COM | Nigeria | NGA |
| Congo | CGO | Rwanda | RWA |
| Djibouti | DJI | São Tome e Principe | STP |
| Egypt | EGY | Senegal | SEN |
| Equatorial Guinea | EQG | Seychelles | SEY |
| Eritrea | ERI | Sierra Leone | SLE |
| Ethiopia | ETH | Somalia | SOM |
| Gabon | GAB | South Africa | RSA |
| Gambia | GAM | Sudan | SUD |
| Ghana | GHA | Swaziland | SWZ |
| Guinea | GUI | Tanzania | TAN |
| Guinea-Bissau | GNB | Togo | TOG |
| Ivory Coast | CIV | Tunisia | TUN |
| Kenya | KEN | Uganda | UGA |
| Lesotho | LES | Zambia | ZAM |
| Liberia | LBR | Zimbabwe | ZIM |

## FIFA COUNTRY CODES – ASIA

| | | | |
|---|---|---|---|
| Afghanistan | AFG | Maldives | MDV |
| Australia | AUS | Mongolia | MGL |
| Bahrain | BHR | Myanmar | MYA |
| Bangladesh | BAN | Nepal | NEP |
| Bhutan | BHU | Korea D.P.R. | PRK |
| Brunei | BRU | Oman | OMA |
| Cambodia | CAM | Pakistan | PAK |
| China P.R. | CHN | Palestine | PAL |
| Chinese Taipei/Taiwan | TPE | Philippines | PHI |
| Guam | GUM | Qatar | QAT |
| Hong Kong | HKG | Saudi Arabia | KSA |
| India | IND | Singapore | SIN |
| Indonesia | IDN | Korea Republic | KOR |
| Iran | IRN | Sri Lanka | SRI |
| Iraq | IRQ | Syria | SYR |
| Japan | JPN | Tajikistan | TJK |
| Jordan | JOR | Thailand | THA |
| Kuwait | KUW | Timor-Leste | TLS |
| Kyrgyzstan | KGZ | Turkmenistan | TKM |
| Laos | LAO | United Arab Emirates | UAE |
| Lebanon | LIB | Uzbekistan | UZB |
| Macau | MAC | Vietnam | VIE |
| Malaysia | MAS | Yemen | YEM |

## FIFA COUNTRY CODES – EUROPE

| Country | Code | Country | Code |
|---|---|---|---|
| Albania | ALB | Latvia | LVA |
| Andorra | AND | Liechtenstein | LIE |
| Armenia | ARM | Lithuania | LTU |
| Austria | AUT | Luxembourg | LUX |
| Azerbaijan | AZE | Macedonia | MKD |
| Belarus | BLR | Malta | MLT |
| Belgium | BEL | Moldova | MDA |
| Bosnia-Herzegovina | BIH | Montenegro | MNE |
| Bulgaria | BUL | Northern Ireland | NIR |
| Croatia | CRO | Norway | NOR |
| Cyprus | CYP | Poland | POL |
| Czech Republic | CZE | Portugal | POR |
| Denmark | DEN | Republic of Ireland | IRL |
| England | ENG | Romania | ROU |
| Estonia | EST | Russia | RUS |
| Faroe Islands | FRO | San Marino | SMR |
| Finland | FIN | Scotland | SCO |
| France | FRA | Serbia | SRB |
| Georgia | GEO | Slovakia | SVK |
| Germany | GER | Slovenia | SVN |
| Greece | GRE | Spain | ESP |
| Holland | NED | Sweden | SWE |
| Hungary | HUN | Switzerland | SUI |
| Iceland | ISL | Turkey | TUR |
| Israel | ISR | Ukraine | UKR |
| Italy | ITA | Wales | WAL |
| Kazakhstan | KAZ | | |

## FIFA COUNTRY CODES – NORTH, CENTRAL AMERICA & CARIBBEAN

| Country | Code | Country | Code |
|---|---|---|---|
| Anguilla | AIA | Haiti | HAI |
| Antigua & Barbuda | ATG | Honduras | HON |
| Aruba | ARU | Jamaica | JAM |
| Bahamas | BAH | Martinique | MTQ |
| Barbados | BRB | Mexico | MEX |
| Belize | BLZ | Montserrat | MSR |
| Bermuda | BER | Netherlands Antilles | ANT |
| British Virgin Islands | VGB | Nicaragua | NIC |
| Canada | CAN | Panama | PAN |
| Cayman Islands | CAY | Puerto Rico | PUR |
| Costa Rica | CRC | Saint Lucia | LCA |
| Cuba | CUB | Saint Kitts and Nevis | SKN |
| Dominica | DMA | Saint Martin | SMT |
| Dominican Republic | DOM | St. Vincent and the Grenadines | VIN |
| El Salvador | SLV | Sint Maarten | SXM |
| French Guiana | GYF | Suriname | SUR |
| Grenada | GRN | Trinidad & Tobago | TRI |
| Guadeloupe | GPE | Turks and Caicos Islands | TCA |
| Guatemala | GUA | United States of America | USA |
| Guyana | GUI | US Virgin Islands | VIR |

## FIFA COUNTRY CODES – SOUTH AMERICA

| | | | |
|---|---|---|---|
| Argentina | **ARG** | Ecuador | **ECU** |
| Bolivia | **BOL** | Paraguay | **PAR** |
| Brazil | **BRA** | Peru | **PER** |
| Chile | **CHI** | Uruguay | **URU** |
| Colombia | **COL** | Venezuela | **VEN** |

## FIFA COUNTRY CODES – OCEANIA

| | | | |
|---|---|---|---|
| American Samoa | **ASA** | Samoa | **SAM** |
| Cook Islands | **COK** | Solomon Islands | **SOL** |
| Fiji | **FIJ** | Tahiti | **TAH** |
| New Caledonia | **NCL** | Tonga | **TGA** |
| New Zealand | **NZL** | Vanuatu | **VAN** |

## OBSOLETE COUNTRY CODES

| | | | |
|---|---|---|---|
| Czechoslovakia | **TCH** | South Vietnam | **VSO** |
| Dahomey | **DAH** | South Yemen | **SYE** |
| Dutch East Indies | **DEI** | Upper Volta | **UPV** |
| East Germany | **GDR** | Soviet Union | **URS** |
| North Yemen | **NYE** | West Germany | **GER** |
| Rhodesia | **RHO** | Yugoslavia | **YUG** |
| Saar | **SAA** | Zaire | **ZAI** |

## SUMMARY

| | |
|---|---|
| Editorial | 3 |
| FIFA Country Codes | 4 |
| Summary | 7 |
| **1978**, Argentina | 8 |
|     *Qualifiers* | |
|         Europe | 9 |
|         South America | 34 |
|         Intercontinental Play-offs | 41 |
|         North, Central America and Caribbean | 42 |
|         Africa | 60 |
|         Asia & Oceania | 76 |
|     *Final Tournament* | 93 |
|     *Squads* | 110 |
| **1982**, Spain | 118 |
|     *Qualifiers* | |
|         Europe | 119 |
|         South America | 156 |
|         North, Central America and Caribbean | 163 |
|         Africa | 181 |
|         Asia & Oceania | 198 |
|         *Final Tournament* | 217 |
|         *Squads* | 240 |
| **1986**, Mexico | 252 |
|     *Qualifiers* | |
|         Europe | 253 |
|         South America | 289 |
|         North, Central America and Caribbean | 301 |
|         Africa | 313 |
|         Asia | 330 |
|         Oceania | 350 |
|         Intercontinental Play-offs | 354 |
|     *Final Tournament* | 355 |
|     *Squads* | 378 |

# 1978, ARGENTINA
(Argentina '78)

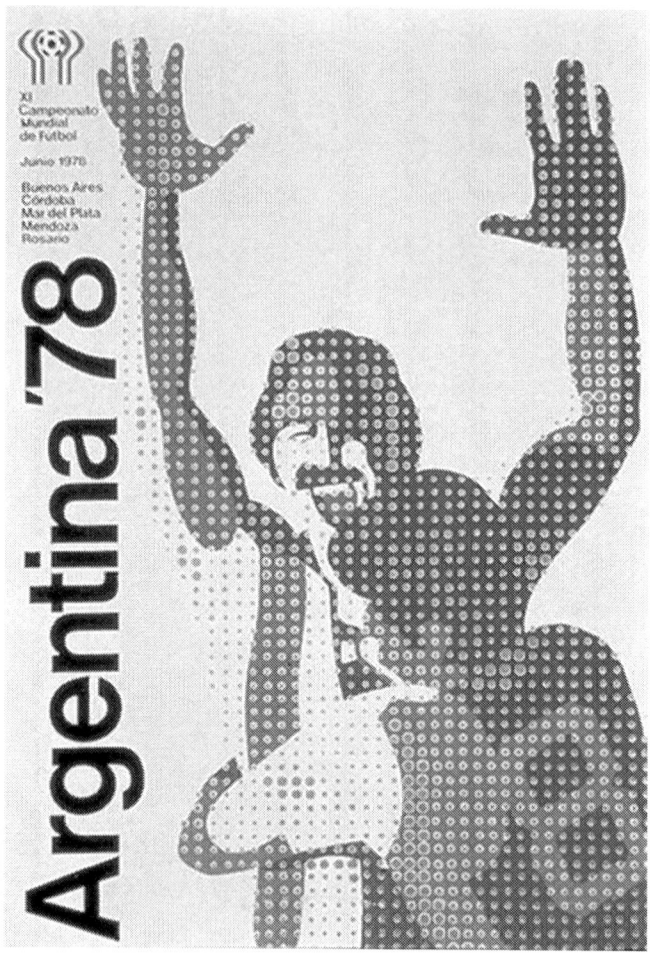

# WORLD CUP 1978 QUALIFIERS

A total of 107 teams entered the 1978 FIFA World Cup qualification rounds, competing for a total of 16 spots in the final tournament. Argentina, as the hosts, and West Germany, as the defending champions, qualified automatically, leaving 14 spots open for competition.

The 16 spots available in the 1978 FIFA World Cup were distributed among the continental zones as follows:
- Europe: 9 or 10 places, 1 of them went to automatic qualifier West Germany, while 9 places were contested by 31 teams. The team winning the ninth qualifying group advanced to the intercontinental play-offs against a team from South America.
- South America: 3 or 4 places, 1 of them went to automatic qualifier Argentina, while the other 3 places were contested by 9 teams. The team coming third in the second qualifying round advanced to the intercontinental play-offs against a team from Europe.
- North, Central America and Caribbean: 1 place, contested by 17 teams.
- Africa: 1 place, contested by 26 teams.
- Asia and Oceania: 1 place, contested by 22 teams.

There were some big surprises in the qualifiers when England (who had finished second in their group behind Italy on goal difference only), failed to qualify for the second World Cup in succession. Czechoslovakia (the reigning European champions!), Yugoslavia and the Soviet Union also failed to qualify. Austria qualified for the first time since 1958, while France, Spain and Hungary qualified for the first time since 1966. In South America, Argentina's greatest rivals, Uruguay, failed to defeat Bolivia so missed out on the finals and, elsewhere, both Iran and Tunisia qualified for their first-ever finals tournament.

## EUROPE

### GROUP 1

| Date | Venue | Match | Result |
|---|---|---|---|
| 23.05.1976 | Limassol | Cyprus - Denmark | 1-5(1-3) |
| 16.10.1976 | Porto | Portugal - Poland | 0-2(0-0) |
| 27.10.1976 | København | Denmark – Cyprus | 5-0(0-0) |
| 31.10.1976 | Warszawa | Poland – Cyprus | 5-0(3-0) |
| 17.11.1976 | Lisboa | Portugal - Denmark | 1-0(0-0) |
| 05.12.1976 | Limassol | Cyprus - Portugal | 1-2(0-1) |
| 01.05.1977 | København | Denmark - Poland | 1-2(0-1) |
| 15.05.1977 | Limassol | Cyprus - Poland | 1-3(1-2) |
| 21.09.1977 | Chorzów | Poland - Denmark | 4-1(2-0) |
| 09.10.1977 | København | Denmark - Portugal | 2-4(1-2) |
| 29.10.1977 | Chorzów | Poland - Portugal | 1-1(1-0) |
| 16.11.1977 | Faro | Portugal - Cyprus | 4-0(2-0) |

**FINAL STANDINGS**

| | | | | | | | | | |
|---|---|---|---|---|---|---|---|---|---|
| 1. | **Poland** | 6 | 5 | 1 | 0 | 17 | - | 4 | 11 |
| 2. | Portugal | 6 | 4 | 1 | 1 | 12 | - | 6 | 9 |
| 3. | Denmark | 6 | 2 | 0 | 4 | 14 | - | 12 | 4 |
| 4. | Cyprus | 6 | 0 | 0 | 6 | 3 | - | 24 | 0 |

Poland qualified for the Final Tournament.

23.05.1976, Tsirion Stádio, Limassol; Attendance: 5,000
Referee: Nikolai Dudin (Bulgaria)
**CYPRUS - DENMARK** **1-5(1-3)**
**CYP:** Dimos Konstantinou (Fanos Stylianou), Yiannis Mertakkas, Nicos Patikkis, Stavros Stylianou, Stefanos Lysandrou, Gregory Savva, Stefanis Michael, Markos Markou, Sotiris Kaiafas (20.Andros Miamiliotis), Nicos Charalambous, Andreas Kanaris. Trainer: Costas Talianos (Greece).
**DEN:** Benno Larsen, Johnny Hansen, Henning Munk Jensen (Cap), Per Røntved, Niels Tune Hansen, Morten Olsen, Heino Hansen, Ole Rasmussen, Allan Rodenkam Simonsen, Henning Jensen, Lars Bastrup. Trainer: Kurt Børge Nielsen.
**Goals**: 1-0 Stefanis Michael (10), 1-1 Allan Rodenkam Simonsen (11), 1-2 Niels Tune Hansen (15), 1-3 Ole Rasmussen (18), 1-4 Lars Bastrup (50), 1-5 Lars Bastrup (75).

16.10.1976, Estádio das Antas, Porto; Attendance: 40,000
Referee: Michel Kitabdjian (France)
**PORTUGAL - POLAND** **0-2(0-0)**
**POR:** Manuel Galrinho Bento, Artur Manuel Soares Correia (66.Mário Jorge Moinhos de Matos), Rui Gouveia Pinto Rodrigues, Fernando António José Freitas Alexandrino, Minervino José Lopes Pietra, António José da Conceiçao Oliveira „Toni" (Cap) (46.Celso Luís de Matos), Octávio Joaquim Coelho Machado, João António Ferreira Resende Alves, Tamagnini Manuel Gomes Baptista „Nené", Manuel José Tavares Fernandes, António Luís Alves Ribeiro Oliveira. Trainer: José Maria Carvalho Pedroto.
**POL:** Zygmunt Kukla, Krzysztof Rześny, Władysław Żmuda, Henryk Maculewicz, Wojciech Rudy, Henryk Kasperczak, Kazimierz Deyna (Cap), Bogdan Masztaler, Grzegorz Lato, Andrzej Szarmach, Stanisław Terlecki (76.Zbigniew Boniek). Trainer: Jacek Gmoch.
**Goals**: 0-1 Grzegorz Lato (49), 0-2 Grzegorz Lato (77).

27.10.1976, Idrætsparken, København; Attendance: 5,000
Referee: Nikola Dudin (Bulgaria)
**DENMARK – CYPRUS** **5-0(0-0)**
**DEN:** Benno Larsen, Johnny Hansen, Henning Munk Jensen (Cap), Per Røntved, Flemming Ahlberg, Morten Olsen, Ole Bjørnmose, Benny Nielsen, Ove Flindt Bjerg, Henning Jensen, Jørgen Kristensen. Trainer: Kurt Børge Nielsen.
**CYP:** Georgios Pantziaras, Kallis Konstantinou, Nicos Patikkis, Christos Lillos, Stavros Stylianou, Stefanis Michael, Andros Miamiliotis (75.Christakis Mavris), Markos Markou, Sotiris Kaiafas (55.Andreas Konstantinou I), Gregory Savva, Andreas Kanaris. Trainer: Panikos Krystallis.
**Goals**: 1-0 Benny Nielsen (55), 2-0 Henning Jensen (60 penalty), 3-0 Henning Jensen (65), 4-0 Per Røntved (68 penalty), 5-0 Jørgen Kristensen (75).

31.10.1976, Stadion Dziesięciolecia, Warszawa; Attendance: 60,000
Referee: György Müncz (Hungary)
**POLAND – CYPRUS** **5-0(3-0)**
**POL:** Zygmunt Kukla, Henryk Maculewicz, Władysław Żmuda, Henryk Kasperczak, Zbigniew Boniek, Kazimierz Deyna (Cap), Bogdan Masztaler (46.Włodzimierz Mazur), Andrzej Szarmach, Stanisław Terlecki, Janusz Sybis, Włodzimierz Lubański. Trainer: Jacek Gmoch.
**CYP:** Georgios Pantziaras, Nicos Patikkis, Loukas Papaloukas, Christos Lillos, Stefanis Michael (70.Georgios Aristidou), Stavros Stylianou, Kallis Konstantinou, Gregory Savva, Sotiris Kaiafas (80.Christakis Mavris), Markos Markou, Andreas Kanaris. Trainer: Panikos Krystallis.
**Goals**: 1-0 Kazimierz Deyna (24 penalty), 2-0 Andrzej Szarmach (25), 3-0 Kazimierz Deyna (40), 4-0 Zbigniew Boniek (58), 5-0 Stanisław Terlecki (77).

17.11.1976, Estádio da Luz, Lisboa; Attendance: 35,000
Referee: Abdelkader Aouissi (Algeria)
**PORTUGAL - DENMARK**      **1-0(0-0)**
**POR:** João Francisco Fonseca Santos, Artur Manuel Soares Correia, Humberto Manuel de Jesus Coelho (Cap) (46.João Gonçalves Laranjeira), José de Jesus Mendes, António Carlos de Sousa Laranjeira Lima „Taí", João António Ferreira Resende Alves, Celso Luís de Matos, Fernando Albino de Sousa Chalana, Tamagnini Manuel Gomes Baptista „Nené", Vítor Manuel Ferreira Baptista, António Luís Alves Ribeiro Oliveira (46.Manuel José Tavares Fernandes). Trainer: José Maria Carvalho Pedroto.
**DEN:** Birger Jensen, Johnny Hansen, Henning Munk Jensen (Cap), Per Røntved, Flemming Ahlberg, Ole Bjørnmose (John Andersen), Heino Hansen, Ove Flindt Bjerg (Ulrik Le Fevre), Allan Rodenkam Simonsen, Niels-Christian Holmstrøm, Jørgen Kristensen. Trainer: Kurt Børge Nielsen.
**Goal:** 1-0 Manuel José Tavares Fernandes (70).

05.12.1976, Tsirion Stádio, Limassol; Attendance: 10,000
Referee: Constantin Ghiţă (Romania)
**CYPRUS - PORTUGAL**      **1-2(0-1)**
**CYP:** Georgios Pantziaras, Nicos Patikkis, Loukas Papaloukas (46.Christos Lillos), Stavros Stylianou, Stefanis Michael, Kallis Konstantinou, Markos Markou (46.Georgios Aristidou), Christakis Mavris, Andreas Konstantinou I, Andros Miamiliotis, Sotiris Kaiafas. Trainer: Panikos Krystallis.
**POR:** Manuel Galrinho Bento, Artur Manuel Soares Correia, João Gonçalves Laranjeira, José de Jesus Mendes, Augusto Soares Inácio, Francisco Mário Pinto da Silva (80.António José da Conceiçao Oliveira „Toni"), Albertino Eduardo Ferreira Ventura Pereira, Octávio Joaquim Coelho Machado, Fernando Albino de Sousa Chalana, Manuel José Tavares Fernandes, Tamagnini Manuel Gomes Baptista „Nené" (Cap). Trainer: José Maria Carvalho Pedroto.
**Goals:** 0-1 Fernando Albino de Sousa Chalana (36), 1-1 Stavros Stylianou (74 penalty), 1-2 Tamagnini Manuel Gomes Baptista „Nené" (76).

01.05.1977, Idrætsparken, København; Attendance: 48,000
Referee: Anders Mattson (Finland)
**DENMARK - POLAND**      **1-2(0-1)**
**DEN:** Birger Jensen, Johnny Hansen, Henning Munk Jensen (Cap) (60.Lars Larsen), Per Røntved, Flemming Ahlberg, Heino Hansen (80.Jan Sørensen), Ole Bjørnmose, Jan Højland, Allan Rodenkam Simonsen, Ove Flindt Bjerg, Flemming Lund. Trainer: Kurt Børge Nielsen.
**POL:** Jan Tomaszewski, Marek Dziuba, Władysław Żmuda, Henryk Wieczorek, Wojciech Rudy (24.Czesław Boguszewicz), Henryk Kasperczak, Kazimierz Deyna (Cap), Bogdan Masztaler, Grzegorz Lato, Włodzimierz Lubański (88.Zbigniew Boniek), Andrzej Szarmach. Trainer: Jacek Gmoch.
**Goals:** 0-1 Włodzimierz Lubański (7), 1-1 Allan Rodenkam Simonsen (49), 1-2 Włodzimierz Lubański (84).

15.05.1977, Tsirion Stádio, Limassol; Attendance: 8,000
Referee: Moshe Ashkenazi (Israel)
**CYPRUS - POLAND**      **1-3(1-2)**
**CYP:** Georgios Pantziaras, Nicos Patikkis, Andreas Pastellidis, Stefanis Michael, Stavros Stylianou, Kallis Konstantinou, Takis Antoniou, Gregory Savva, Sotiris Kaiafas (60.Lakis Gavalas), Fivos Vrachimis (52.Christakis Mavris), Andreas Kanaris. Trainer: Panikos Krystallis.
**POL:** Jan Tomaszewski, Henryk Wawrowski, Henryk Maculewicz (88.Adam Nawałka), Władysław Żmuda, Jerzy Ludyga, Henryk Kasperczak, Kazimierz Deyna (Cap), Bogdan Masztaler, Grzegorz Lato, Andrzej Szarmach, Stanisław Terlecki (67.Włodzimierz Mazur). Trainer: Jacek Gmoch.
**Goals:** 1-0 Takis Antoniou (14), 1-1 Grzegorz Lato (28), 1-2 Stanisław Terlecki (40), 1-3 Włodzimierz Mazur (82).

21.09.1977, Stadion Śląski, Chorzów; Attendance: 92,500
Referee: Nicolae Rainea (Romania)
**POLAND - DENMARK** **4-1(2-0)**
**POL:** Jan Tomaszewski, Henryk Wawrowski, Władysław Żmuda, Henryk Maculewicz, Wojciech Rudy, Henryk Kasperczak, Kazimierz Deyna (Cap) (71.Zbigniew Boniek), Bogdan Masztaler (87.Adam Nawałka), Grzegorz Lato, Włodzimierz Lubański, Andrzej Szarmach. Trainer: Jacek Gmoch.
**DEN:** Per Poulsen, John Andersen (56.Jan Sørensen), Flemming Mortensen, Henning Munk Jensen (Cap), Per Røntved, Flemming Ahlberg, Ove Flindt Bjerg, Allan Hansen (56.Heino Hansen), Kristen Nygaard, Flemming Lund, Jørgen Kristensen. Trainer: Kurt Børge Nielsen.
**Goals**: 1-0 Bogdan Masztaler (27), 2-0 Grzegorz Lato (38), 3-0 Kazimierz Deyna (62), 3-1 Kristen Nygaard (66 penalty), 4-1 Andrzej Szarmach (81).

09.10.1977, Idrætsparken, København; Attendance: 23,300
Referee: Azim Zade (Soviet Union)
**DENMARK - PORTUGAL** **2-4(1-2)**
**DEN:** Per Poulsen, Johnny Hansen, Henning Munk Jensen (Cap), Per Røntved, Flemming Mortensen, Heino Hansen, Niels Tune Hansen, Kristen Nygaard, Flemming Lund, Torsten Andersen, Jørgen Kristensen (79.Allan Hansen). Trainer: Kurt Børge Nielsen.
**POR:** Manuel Galrinho Bento, Gabriel Azevedo Mendes, Humberto Manuel de Jesus Coelho (Cap), João Gonçalves Laranjeira, Alfredo Manuel Ferreira Silva Murça, Octávio Joaquim Coelho Machado, António José da Conceiçao Oliveira „Toni", João António Ferreira Resende Alves, Tamagnini Manuel Gomes Baptista „Nené" (46.Manuel José Tavares Fernandes), Rui Manuel Trindade Jordão, Fernando Albino de Sousa Chalana (69.Rodolfo dos Reis Ferreira). Trainer: Júlio Cernadas Pereira „Juca".
**Goals**: 0-1 Rui Manuel Trindade Jordão (13), 0-2 Tamagnini Manuel Gomes Baptista „Nené" (33), 1-2 Per Røntved (37 penalty), 1-3 Manuel José Tavares Fernandes (61), 1-4 Octávio Joaquim Coelho Machado (78), 2-4 Allan Hansen (87).

29.10.1977, Stadion Śląski, Chorzów; Attendance: 80,000
Referee: Walter Eschweiler (West Germany)
**POLAND - PORTUGAL** **1-1(1-0)**
**POL:** Jan Tomaszewski, Henryk Wawrowski, Władysław Żmuda, Henryk Maculewicz, Wojciech Rudy, Henryk Kasperczak, Kazimierz Deyna (Cap) (84.Jan Erlich), Adam Nawałka, Bogdan Masztaler (38.Zbigniew Boniek), Grzegorz Lato, Andrzej Szarmach. Trainer: Jacek Gmoch.
**POR:** Manuel Galrinho Bento, Gabriel Azevedo Mendes, Humberto Manuel de Jesus Coelho (Cap), João Gonçalves Laranjeira, Alfredo Manuel Ferreira Silva Murça, Octávio Joaquim Coelho Machado, António José da Conceiçao Oliveira „Toni", João António Ferreira Resende Alves, Fernando Albino de Sousa Chalana (61.Arsénio Rodrigues Jardim „Seninho"), Manuel José Tavares Fernandes, António Luís Alves Ribeiro Oliveira. Trainer: Júlio Cernadas Pereira „Juca".
**Goals**: 1-0 Kazimierz Deyna (38), 1-1 Manuel José Tavares Fernandes (61).

16.11.1977, Estádio São Luis, Faro; Attendance: 13,000
Referee: Michal Jursa (Czechoslovakia)
**PORTUGAL - CYPRUS** **4-0(2-0)**
**POR:** Manuel Galrinho Bento, Artur Manuel Soares Correia, Humberto Manuel de Jesus Coelho (Cap), João Gonçalves Laranjeira, Alfredo Manuel Ferreira Silva Murça (46.Francisco António Lucas Vital), Minervino José Lopes Pietra (78.Francisco „Chico" Delfim Dias Faria), António José da Conceiçao Oliveira „Toni", João António Ferreira Resende Alves, Arsénio Rodrigues Jardim „Seninho", Manuel José Tavares Fernandes, Fernando Albino de Sousa Chalana. Trainer: Júlio Cernadas Pereira „Juca".
**CYP:** Georgios Pantziaras, Nicos Patikkis, Michalakis Kolokasis, Nicos Pantziaras, Kallis Konstantinou, Stefanis Michael, Nicos Charalambous, Gregory Savva, Kypros Damianou (76.Christakis Mavris), Petros Theofanous, Andreas Kanaris. Trainer: Andreas Lazarides.
**Goals**: 1-0 Arsénio Rodrigues Jardim „Seninho" (8), 2-0 Fernando Albino de Sousa Chalana (16), 3-0 Francisco António Lucas Vital (72), 4-0 Manuel José Tavares Fernandes (83).

## GROUP 2

| | | | |
|---|---|---|---|
| 13.06.1976 | Helsinki | Finland - England | 1-4(1-2) |
| 22.09.1976 | Helsinki | Finland - Luxembourg | 7-1(3-0) |
| 13.10.1976 | London | England - Finland | 2-1(1-0) |
| 16.10.1976 | Luxembourg | Luxembourg - Italy | 1-4(0-2) |
| 17.11.1976 | Roma | Italy - England | 2-0(1-0) |
| 30.03.1977 | London | England - Luxembourg | 5-0(1-0) |
| 26.05.1977 | Luxembourg | Luxembourg - Finland | 0-1(0-1) |
| 08.06.1977 | Helsinki | Finland - Italy | 0-3(0-1) |
| 12.10.1977 | Luxembourg | Luxembourg - England | 0-2(0-1) |
| 15.10.1977 | Torino | Italy - Finland | 6-1(3-0) |
| 16.11.1977 | London | England - Italy | 2-0(1-0) |
| 03.12.1977 | Roma | Italy - Luxembourg | 3-0(2-0) |

### FINAL STANDINGS

| | | | | | | | | | |
|---|---|---|---|---|---|---|---|---|---|
| 1. | **Italy** | 6 | 5 | 0 | 1 | 18 | - | 4 | 10 |
| 2. | England | 6 | 5 | 0 | 1 | 15 | - | 4 | 10 |
| 3. | Finland | 6 | 2 | 0 | 4 | 11 | - | 16 | 4 |
| 4. | Luxembourg | 6 | 0 | 0 | 6 | 2 | - | 22 | 0 |

Italy qualified for the Final Tournament.

13.06.1976, Olympiastadion, Helsinki; Attendance: 24,336
Referee: Alfred Delcourt (Belgium)
**FINLAND - ENGLAND** **1-4(1-2)**
**FIN:** Göran Enckelman, Erkki Vihtilä, Arto Tolsa, Ari Mäkynen, Esko Ranta, Pertti Jantunen, Jouko Suomalainen (65.Seppo Pyykkö), Esa Heiskanen, Olavi Rissanen, Aki Heiskanen, Matti Paatelainen (Cap). Trainer: Aulis Rytkönen.
**ENG:** Raymond Neal Clemence, Colin Todd, Michael Dennis Mills, Philip Brian Thompson, Paul Edward Madeley, Trevor John Cherry, Kevin Joseph Keegan, Michael Roger Channon, Stuart James Pearson, Trevor David Brooking, Gerald Charles James Francis (Cap). Manager: Donald Revie.
**Goals:** 0-1 Stuart James Pearson (14), 1-1 Matti Paatelainen (28), 1-2 Kevin Joseph Keegan (30), 1-3 Michael Roger Channon (56), 1-4 Kevin Joseph Keegan (60).

22.09.1976, Olympiastadion, Helsinki; Attendance: 4,555
Referee: Svein Inge Thime (Norway)
**FINLAND - LUXEMBOURG** **7-1(3-0)**
**FIN:** Göran Enckelman,Teppo Heikkinen, Erkki Vihtilä, Ari Mäkynen, Esko Ranta, Pertti Jantunen, Esa Heiskanen (53.Jyrki Nieminen), Miikka Toivola, Olavi Rissanen, Aki Heiskanen, Matti Paatelainen (Cap) (75.Seppo Pyykkö). Trainer: Aulis Rytkönen.
**LUX:** Raymond Zender, Jeannot Schaul, Jean-Louis Margue, Joseph Hansen, René Flenghi (46.Gilbert Zender), Louis Pilot (Cap), Nibio Orioli, Gilbert Dresch, Nicolas Braun, Paul Philipp, Gilbert Dussier. Trainer: Gilbert Legrand.
**Goals:** 1-0 Aki Heiskanen (15), 2-0 Esa Heiskanen (22), 3-0 Esa Heiskanen (27), 4-0 Olavi Rissanen (51), 4-1 Gilbert Zender (52), 5-1 Teppo Heikkinen (54), 6-1 Olavi Rissanen (61), 7-1 Ari Mäkynen (82 penalty).

13.10.1976, Wembley Stadium, London; Attendance: 92,000
Referee: Ulf Helmer Johan Eriksson (Sweden)
**ENGLAND - FINLAND** **2-1(1-0)**
**ENG:** Raymond Neal Clemence, Colin Todd, Kevin Thomas Beattie, Philip Brian Thompson, Brian Greenhoff, Raymond Colin Wilkins, Kevin Joseph Keegan (Cap), Michael Roger Channon, Joseph Royle, Trevor David Brooking (73.Michael Dennis Mills), Dennis Tueart (73.Gordon Alec Hill). Manager: Donald Revie.
**FIN:** Göran Enckelman, Teppo Heikkinen, Erkki Vihtilä, Ari Mäkynen, Esko Ranta, Pertti Jantunen (61.Esa Heiskanen), Jouko Suomalainen (67.Seppo Pyykkö), Miikka Toivola, Jyrki Nieminen, Aki Heiskanen, Matti Paatelainen (Cap). Trainer: Aulis Rytkönen.
**Goals:** 1-0 Dennis Tueart (4), 1-1 Jyrki Nieminen (48), 2-1 Joseph Royle (52).

16.10.1976, Stade Municipal, Luxembourg; Attendance: 9,000
Referee: Ernst Dörflinger (Switzerland)
**LUXEMBOURG - ITALY** **1-4(0-2)**
**LUX:** Raymond Zender, Jeannot Schaul, Robert Da Grava, Léon Mond, Louis Pilot (Cap), Jean-Louis Margue, Jeannot Krecke, Gilbert Dresch, Nibio Orioli (62.Paul Langers), Gilbert Dussier, Nicolas Braun. Trainer: Gilbert Legrand.
**ITA:** Dino Zoff, Marco Tardelli, Francesco Rocca, Patrizio Sala, Roberto Mozzini, Giacinto Facchetti, Franco Causio, Fabio Capello, Francesco Graziani, Giancarlo Antognoni, Roberto Bettega. Trainers: Fulvio Bernardini - Enzo Bearzot.
**Goals:** 0-1 Francesco Graziani (24), 0-2 Roberto Bettega (44), 0-3 Giancarlo Antognoni (50), 0-4 Roberto Bettega (81), 1-4 Nicolas Braun (86).

17.11.1976, Stadio Olimpico, Roma; Attendance: 70,718
Referee: Abraham Klein (Israel)
**ITALY - ENGLAND** **2-0(1-0)**
**ITA:** Dino Zoff, Antonello Cuccureddu, Marco Tardelli, Romeo Benetti II, Claudio Gentile, Giacinto Facchetti, Franco Causio, Fabio Capello, Francesco Graziani, Giancarlo Antognoni, Roberto Bettega. Trainers: Fulvio Bernardini - Enzo Bearzot.
**ENG:** Raymond Neal Clemence, David Thomas Clement (75.Kevin Thomas Beattie), Michael Dennis Mills, Brian Greenhoff, Roy Leslie McFarland, Emlyn Walter Hughes, Kevin Joseph Keegan (Cap), Michael Roger Channon, Stanley Bowles, Trevor John Cherry, Trevor David Brooking. Manager: Donald Revie.
**Goals:** 1-0 Giancarlo Antognoni (36), 2-0 Roberto Bettega (77).

30.03.1977, Wembley Stadium, London; Attendance: 81,718
Referee: Paul Bonett (Malta)
**ENGLAND - LUXEMBOURG** **5-0(1-0)**
**ENG:** Raymond Neal Clemence, John Gidman, Trevor John Cherry, Raymond Kennedy, David Victor Watson, Emlyn Walter Hughes, Kevin Joseph Keegan (Cap), Michael Roger Channon, Joseph Royle (46.Paul Mariner), Trevor John Francis, Gordon Alec Hill. Manager: Donald Revie.
**LUX:** Raymond Zender, Jean-Louis Margue, Louis Pilot (Cap), Léon Mond, Jean Zuang, Roger Fandel, Marcel Di Domenico (76.Nibio Orioli), Gilbert Dresch, Nicolas Braun, Paul Philipp, Gilbert Dussier. Trainer: Gilbert Legrand.
**Goals:** 1-0 Kevin Joseph Keegan (10), 2-0 Trevor John Francis (58), 3-0 Raymond Kennedy (63), 4-0 Michael Roger Channon (69), 5-0 Michael Roger Channon (81 penalty).
**Sent off:** Gilbert Dresch (86).

26.05.1977, Stade Municipal, Luxembourg; Attendance: 1,700
Referee: Ole Amundsen (Denmark)
**LUXEMBOURG - FINLAND** **0-1(0-1)**
**LUX:** Raymond Zender, Marcel Barthel (51.Nibio Orioli), Roger Fandel, Léon Mond, Louis Pilot (Cap), Jean Zuang, Romain Michaux, Jeannot Krecke (46.Jean-Louis Margue), Gilbert Dussier, Marcel Di Domenico, Nicolas Braun. Trainer: Gilbert Legrand.
**FIN:** Göran Enckelman, Teppo Heikkinen, Erkki Vihtilä, Arto Tolsa, Esko Ranta, Pertti Jantunen, Jouko Suomalainen, Miikka Toivola (62.Jyrki Nieminen), Olavi Rissanen, Aki Heiskanen (78.Kai Haaskivi), Matti Paatelainen (Cap). Trainer: Aulis Rytkönen.
**Goal:** 0-1 Aki Heiskanen (58).

08.06.1977, Olympiastadion, Helsinki; Attendance: 17,539
Referee: Robert Héliès (France)
**FINLAND - ITALY** **0-3(0-1)**
**FIN:** Göran Enckelman, Teppo Heikkinen, Erkki Vihtilä, Arto Tolsa, Esko Ranta, Pertti Jantunen, Jouko Suomalainen, Miikka Toivola (51.Jyrki Nieminen), Olavi Rissanen, Aki Heiskanen (69.Markku Närvä), Matti Paatelainen (Cap). Trainer: Aulis Rytkönen.
**ITA:** Dino Zoff, Marco Tardelli, Claudio Gentile, Romeo Benetti II, Roberto Mozzini, Giacinto Facchetti, Franco Causio (46.Claudio Sala), Renato Zaccarelli, Francesco Graziani, Giancarlo Antognoni, Roberto Bettega. Trainers: Fulvio Bernardini - Enzo Bearzot.
**Goals:** 0-1 Claudio Gentile (8), 0-2 Roberto Bettega (56), 0-3 Romeo Benetti II (81).

12.10.1977, Stade Municipal, Luxembourg; Attendance: 10,621
Referee: Alojzy Jarguz (Poland)
**LUXEMBOURG - ENGLAND** **0-2(0-1)**
**LUX:** Jeannot Moes, Marcel Barthel, Roger Fandel (82.Joseph Zangerle), Léon Mond, Nicolas Rohmann, Paul Philipp (Cap), Romain Michaux, Jean Zuang, Gilbert Dussier, Nicolas Braun (80.Marcel Di Domenico), Vinicio Monacelli. Trainer: Gilbert Legrand.
**ENG:** Raymond Neal Clemence, Trevor John Cherry, David Victor Watson (69.Kevin Thomas Beattie), Emlyn Walter Hughes (Cap), Raymond Kennedy, Ian Robert Callaghan, Terence McDermott (65.Trevor John Whymark), Raymond Colin Wilkins, Trevor John Francis, Paul Mariner, Gordon Alec Hill. Manager: Ronald Greenwood.
**Goals:** 0-1 Raymond Kennedy (31), 0-2 Paul Mariner (90).

15.10.1977, Stadio Comunale, Torino; Attendance: 62,888
Referee: Nikolai Dudin (Bulgaria)
**ITALY - FINLAND** **6-1(3-0)**
**ITA:** Dino Zoff, Marco Tardelli, Claudio Gentile, Romeo Benetti II, Roberto Mozzini, Giacinto Facchetti, Franco Causio, Renato Zaccarelli, Francesco Graziani, Giancarlo Antognoni, Roberto Bettega. Trainer: Enzo Bearzot.
**FIN:** Göran Enckelman, Jouko Suomalainen (7.Reijo Vaittinen), Erkki Vihtilä, Ari Mäkynen, Esko Ranta, Pertti Jantunen, Kai Haaskivi, Miikka Toivola, Heikki Suhonen, Aki Heiskanen (61.Teppo Heikkinen), Matti Paatelainen (Cap). Trainer: Aulis Rytkönen.
**Goals:** 1-0 Roberto Bettega (29), 2-0 Roberto Bettega (38), 3-0 Francesco Graziani (45), 4-0 Roberto Bettega (59), 5-0 Roberto Bettega (62), 5-1 Kai Haaskivi (67), 6-1 Renato Zaccarelli (71).

16.11.1977, Wembley Stadium, London; Attendance: 92,500
Referee: Károly Palotai (Hungary)
**ENGLAND - ITALY**                                                                                  **2-0(1-0)**
**ENG:** Raymond Neal Clemence, Philip George Neal, Trevor John Cherry, Raymond Colin Wilkins, David Victor Watson, Emlyn Walter Hughes (Cap), Kevin Joseph Keegan (83.Trevor John Francis), Steven James Coppell, Robert Dennis Latchford (75.Stuart James Pearson), Trevor David Brooking, Peter Simon Barnes. Manager: Ronald Greenwood.
**ITA:** Dino Zoff, Marco Tardelli, Claudio Gentile, Romeo Benetti II, Roberto Mozzini, Giacinto Facchetti (83.Antonello Cuccureddu), Franco Causio, Renato Zaccarelli, Francesco Graziani (46.Claudio Sala), Giancarlo Antognoni, Roberto Bettega. Trainer: Enzo Bearzot.
**Goals**: 1-0 Kevin Joseph Keegan (11), 2-0 Trevor David Brooking (80).

03.12.1977, Stadio Olimpico, Roma; Attendance: 80,000
Referee: Dušan Maksimović (Yugoslavia)
**ITALY - LUXEMBOURG**                                             **3-0(2-0)**
**ITA:** Dino Zoff, Antonello Cuccureddu, Marco Tardelli (46.Aldo Maldera III), Romeo Benetti II, Claudio Gentile, Lionello Manfredonia, Franco Causio, Renato Zaccarelli, Francesco Graziani, Giancarlo Antognoni, Roberto Bettega. Trainer: Enzo Bearzot.
**LUX:** Jeannot Moes, Marcel Barthel, Roger Fandel, Léon Mond, Nicolas Rohmann, Jean Zuang, Romain Michaux (46.Jean-Louis Margue), Marcel Di Domenico, Gilbert Dussier, Paul Philipp (Cap), André Zwally. Trainer: Gilbert Legrand.
**Goals**: 1-0 Roberto Bettega (4), 2-0 Francesco Graziani (11), 3-0 Franco Causio (56).

## GROUP 3

| Date | Venue | Match | Result |
|---|---|---|---|
| 31.10.1976 | Izmir | Turkey - Malta | 4-0(1-0) |
| 17.11.1976 | Dresden | East Germany - Turkey | 1-1(1-1) |
| 05.12.1976 | Valletta | Malta - Austria | 0-1(0-0) |
| 02.04.1977 | Valletta | Malta - East Germany | 0-1(0-0) |
| 17.04.1977 | Wien | Austria - Turkey | 1-0(1-0) |
| 30.04.1977 | Salzburg | Austria - Malta | 9-0(5-0) |
| 24.09.1977 | Wien | Austria - East Germany | 1-1(1-1) |
| 12.10.1977 | Leipzig | East Germany - Austria | 1-1(0-1) |
| 29.10.1977 | Potsdam | East Germany - Malta | 9-0(3-0) |
| 30.10.1977 | Izmir | Turkey - Austria | 0-1(0-0) |
| 16.11.1977 | Izmir | Turkey - East Germany | 1-2(0-1) |
| 27.11.1977 | Valletta | Malta - Turkey | 0-3(0-2) |

### FINAL STANDINGS

| | | | | | | | | |
|---|---|---|---|---|---|---|---|---|
| 1. **Austria** | 6 | 4 | 2 | 0 | 14 | - | 2 | 10 |
| 2. East Germany | 6 | 3 | 3 | 0 | 15 | - | 4 | 9 |
| 3. Turkey | 6 | 2 | 1 | 3 | 9 | - | 5 | 5 |
| 4. Malta | 6 | 0 | 0 | 6 | 0 | - | 27 | 0 |

Austria qualified for the Final Tournament.

31.10.1976, "Kemal Atatürk" Stadı, Izmir; Attendance: 68,034
Referee: Michal Jursa (Czechoslovakia)
**TURKEY - MALTA** **4-0(1-0)**
**TUR:** Şenol Güneş, Turgay Semercioğlu, Alpaslan Eratlı, İsmail Arca, Ali Yavaş, Kemal Batmaz, Mehmet Özgül (Necmi Perekli), Fatih Terim, Ali Kemal Denizci, İsa Ertürk, Cemil Turan (Necati Özçağlayan). Trainer: Coşkun Özarı.
**MLT:** Alfred Mizzi, Edwin Farrugia, Albert Carter-Mizzi (46.George Ciantar), Edward Darmanin, John Holland, Sonny Gouder (46.Dennis Fenech), Chris Vella, William Vassallo (Cap), George Xuereb, Raymond Xuereb, Vincent Magro. Trainer: Johnny Calleja.
**Goals**: 1-0 Mehmet Özgül (22), 2-0 Cemil Turan (54), 3-0 Cemil Turan (57), 4-0 Cemil Turan (75).

17.11.1976, Dynamo Stadion, Dresden; Attendance: 18,000
Referee: Patrick Partridge (England)
**EAST GERMANY - TURKEY** **1-1(1-1)**
**DDR:** Jürgen Croy, Udo Schmuck (48.Hans-Jürgen Dörner), Gerd Kische, Konrad Weise, Klaus Müller, Reinhard Häfner, Reinhard Lauck (Cap) (71.Dieter Riedel), Hartmut Schade, Joachim Streich, Peter Kotte, Gert Heidler. Trainer: Georg Buschner.
**TUR:** Şenol Güneş, Turgay Semercioğlu, Alpaslan Eratlı, Erol Togay, Fatih Terim, Kadir Özcan, Ali Yavaş (5.Necati Özçağlayan), Mehmet Özgül, Ali Kemal Denizci, İsa Ertürk, Cemil Turan. Trainer: Doğan Andaç.
**Goals**: 1-0 Peter Kotte (3 penalty), 1-1 Cemil Turan (31 penalty).

05.12.1976, Empire Stadium, Gzira; Attendance: 7,368
Referee: Hédi Séoudi (Tunisia)
**MALTA - AUSTRIA** **0-1(0-0)**
**MLT:** Alfred Mizzi, Lawrence Borg, Edwin Farrugia, John Holland, Edward Darmanin, Frank Micallef, Vincent Magro, William Vassallo (Cap), George Xuereb, Raymond Xuereb (75.Chris Vella), Carlo Seychell (68.David Azzopardi). Trainer: Johnny Calleja.
**AUT:** Friedrich Koncilia, Robert Sara, Peter Persidis, Bruno Pezzey, Heinrich Strasser, Roland Hattenberger, Josef Hickersberger, Herbert Oberhofer, Josef Stering (46.Herbert Prohaska), Johann Krankl, Walter Schachner (81.Hans Pirkner). Trainer: Helmut Senekowitsch.
**Goal**: 0-1 Johann Krankl (57).

02.04.1977, Empire Stadium, Gzira; Attendance: 6,279
Referee: Bruno Dellabruna (Switzerland)
**MALTA - EAST GERMANY** **0-1(0-0)**
**MLT:** Robert Gatt, George Ciantar, Edwin Farrugia, John Holland, Edward Darmanin (Cap), Frank Micallef, Vincent Magro, David Azzopardi, George Xuereb (74.Emanuel Leli Fabri), Raymond Xuereb, Carlo Seychell. Trainer: Johnny Calleja.
**DDR:** Hans-Ulrich Grapenthin, Hans-Jürgen Dörner (Cap), Gerd Kische, Konrad Weise, Lothar Kurbjuweit, Reinhard Häfner, Gert Heidler (53.Hartmut Schade), Reinhard Lauck, Hans-Jürgen Riediger, Joachim Streich, Martin Hoffmann. Trainer: Georg Buschner.
**Goal**: 0-1 Joachim Streich (55).

17.04.1977, Prater Stadion, Wien; Attendance: 60,000
Referee: Viktor Jarkov (Soviet Union)
**AUSTRIA - TURKEY** **1-0(1-0)**
**AUT:** Friedrich Koncilia, Robert Sara, Peter Persidis, Bruno Pezzey, Gerhard Breitenberger, Roland Hattenberger, Josef Hickersberger, Herbert Prohaska, Josef Stering, Johann Krankl, Walter Schachner. Trainer: Helmut Senekowitsch.
**TUR:** Şenol Güneş, Turgay Semercioğlu, Alpaslan Eratlı, Erol Togay, Fatih Terim, Necati Özçağlayan, Mehmet Özgül (75.Hüseyin Nuri Tok), Nıko Kovı (70.Cem Pamiroğlu), Ali Kemal Denizci, Engin Verel, Cemil Turan. Trainer: Metin Türel.
**Goal**: 1-0 Walter Schachner (42).

30.04.1977, Lehen Stadion, Salzburg; Attendance: 17,000
Referee: Alojzy Jarguz (Poland)
**AUSTRIA - MALTA** **9-0(5-0)**
**AUT:** Friedrich Koncilia, Robert Sara, Peter Persidis, Bruno Pezzey, Heinrich Strasser, Josef Hickersberger, Roland Hattenberger, Herbert Prohaska, Josef Stering (78.Peter Koncilia), Johann Krankl, Walter Schachner (46 Hans Pirkner). Trainer: Helmut Senekowitsch.
**MLT:** Robert Gatt, George Ciantar, Edwin Farrugia, John Holland, Mario Schembri, Edward Darmanin (Cap), Vincent Magro, Emanuel Leli Fabri, Raymond Xuereb, Frank Micallef, Carlo Seychell (46.George Xuereb). Trainer: Johnny Calleja.
**Goals**: 1-0 Johann Krankl (9), 2-0 Johann Krankl (12), 3-0 Johann Krankl (18), 4-0 Johann Krankl (20), 5-0 Josef Stering (30), 6-0 Johann Krankl (53), 7-0 Hans Pirkner (65), 8-0 Johann Krankl (66), 9-0 Josef Stering (69).
**Sent off**: Edwin Farrugia (67).

24.09.1977, Prater Stadion, Wien; Attendance: 72,000
Referee: Thomas Reynolds (Wales)
**AUSTRIA - EAST GERMANY** **1-1(1-1)**
**AUT:** Friedrich Koncilia, Robert Sara, Eduard Krieger, Bruno Pezzey, Gerhard Breitenberger, Roland Hattenberger, Josef Hickersberger, Kurt Jara (76.Herbert Prohaska), Josef Stering, Wilhelm Kreuz, Johann Krankl. Trainer: Helmut Senekowitsch.
**DDR:** Jürgen Croy, Hans-Jürgen Dörner (Cap), Gerd Kische, Konrad Weise, Gerd Weber, Reinhard Häfner, Hartmut Schade, Lutz Lindemann, Gert Heidler (73.Hans-Jürgen Riediger), Peter Kotte (46.Jürgen Sparwasser), Martin Hoffmann. Trainer: Georg Buschner.
**Goals**: 1-0 Wilhelm Kreuz (8), 1-1 Martin Hoffmann (39).

12.10.1977, Zentralstadion, Leipzig; Attendance: 95,000
Referee: Ian Foote (Scotland)
**EAST GERMANY - AUSTRIA** **1-1(0-1)**
**DDR:** Jürgen Croy, Hans-Jürgen Dörner (Cap), Gerd Kische, Konrad Weise, Gerd Weber, Reinhard Häfner, Hartmut Schade, Lutz Lindemann, Wolfram Löwe, Peter Kotte (56.Hans-Jürgen Riediger), Martin Hoffmann (87.Jürgen Sparwasser). Trainer: Georg Buschner.
**AUT:** Friedrich Koncilia, Robert Sara, Eduard Krieger, Bruno Pezzey, Gerhard Breitenberger, Roland Hattenberger, Herbert Prohaska (88.Erich Obermayer), Josef Hickersberger, Kurt Jara, Josef Stering, Wilhelm Kreuz. Trainer: Helmut Senekowitsch.
**Goals**: 0-1 Roland Hattenberger (43), 1-1 Wolfram Löwe (51).

29.10.1977, „Karl Liebknecht" Stadion, Babelsberg; Attendance: 15,000
Referee: Jaffar Namdar (Iran)
**EAST GERMANY - MALTA** **9-0(3-0)**
**DDR:** Jürgen Croy, Hans-Jürgen Dörner (Cap), Gerd Kische, Konrad Weise, Gerd Weber, Reinhard Häfner, Jürgen Pommerenke (46.Joachim Streich), Hartmut Schade, Hans-Jürgen Riediger, Jürgen Sparwasser, Martin Hoffmann. Trainer: Georg Buschner.
**MLT:** Alfred Debono I, Lawrence Borg, George Ciantar (68.Emanuel Farrugia), Anton Camilleri, John Holland, Frank Micallef (34.Edward Darmanin), Vincent Magro, William Vassallo (Cap), George Xuereb, Raymond Xuereb, David Azzopardi. Trainer: Johnny Calleja.
**Goals**: 1-0 Martin Hoffmann (2), 2-0 Martin Hoffmann (44), 3-0 Martin Hoffmann (84), 4-0 Hartmut Schade (38), 5-0 Jürgen Sparwasser (52), 6-0 Gerd Weber (56), 7-0 Joachim Streich (63 penalty), 8-0 Joachim Streich (79), 9-0 Joachim Streich (82).

30.10.1977, "Kemal Atatürk" Stadı, Izmir; Attendance: 72,000
Referee: John Robertson Proudfoot Gordon (Scotland)
**TURKEY - AUSTRIA** **0-1(0-0)**
**TUR:** Eser Özaltındere, Turgay Semercioğlu, Erol Togay, Fatih Terim, Erdoğan Arica, Engin Verel, Volkan Yayim, Sedat III Özden (76.İsa Ertürk), Ali Kemal Denizci, Cemil Turan, Mustafa Denizli (17.Gökmen Özdenak). Trainer: Metin Türel.
**AUT:** Friedrich Koncilia, Robert Sara, Eduard Krieger, Bruno Pezzey, Gerhard Breitenberger, Roland Hattenberger, Herbert Prohaska, Kurt Jara, Josef Stering, Wilhelm Kreuz, Johann Krankl. Trainer: Helmut Senekowitsch.
**Goal**: 0-1 Herbert Prohaska (71).

16.11.1977, "Kemal Atatürk" Stadı, Izmir; Attendance: 10,000
Referee: Alberto Michelotti (Italy)
**TURKEY - EAST GERMANY** **1-2(0-1)**
**TUR:** Eser Özaltındere (46.Rasim Erten), Turgay Semercioğlu, Erol Togay, Fatih Terim, Erdoğan Arica, Volkan Yayim, İsa Ertürk, Önder Mustafaoğlu, Öner Kılıç, Cemil Turan (73.Sedat III Özden), Mustafa Denizli. Trainer: Metin Türel.
**DDR:** Jürgen Croy, Hans-Jürgen Dörner (Cap), Gerd Kische, Konrad Weise, Gerd Weber, Reinhard Häfner, Lutz Lindemann, Hartmut Schade, Hans-Jürgen Riediger, Joachim Streich (55.Jürgen Pommerenke), Martin Hoffmann (88.Jürgen Sparwasser). Trainer: Georg Buschner.
**Goals**: 0-1 Hartmut Schade (30), 0-2 Martin Hoffmann (62), 1-2 Volkan Yayim (81).

27.11.1977, Empire Stadium, Gzira; Attendance: 2,246
Referee: Mohamed Larache (Morocco)
**MALTA - TURKEY** **0-3(0-2)**
**MLT:** Charles Sciberras, Oliver Losco, Emanuel Farrugia, John Holland, Edward Darmanin, David Azzopardi, Vincent Magro, William Vassallo (Cap), George Xuereb (46.Chris Vella), Louis Arpa, Carlo Seychell. Trainer: Johnny Calleja.
**TUR:** Eser Özaltındere, Turgay Semercioğlu, Erdoğan Arica, Erol Togay (80.Güngör Tekin), Necati Özçağlayan, Engin Verel, Önder Mustafaoğlu, Volkan Yayim (75.Mustafa Denizli), Ali Kemal Denizci, Cemil Turan, Sedat III Özden. Trainer: Metin Türel.
**Goals**: 0-1 Sedat III Özden (21), 0-2 Cemil Turan (36), 0-3 Sedat III Özden (48).

# GROUP 4

| | | | | |
|---|---|---|---|---|
| 05.09.1976 | Reykjavík | Iceland - Belgium | | 0-1(0-0) |
| 08.09.1976 | Reykjavík | Iceland - Holland | | 0-1(0-1) |
| 13.10.1976 | Rotterdam | Holland - Northern Ireland | | 2-2(0-1) |
| 10.11.1976 | Liège | Belgium - Northern Ireland | | 2-0(1-0) |
| 26.03.1977 | Antwerpen | Belgium - Holland | | 0-2(0-1) |
| 11.06.1977 | Reykjavík | Iceland - Northern Ireland | | 1-0(1-0) |
| 31.08.1977 | Nijmegen | Holland - Iceland | | 4-1(3-0) |
| 03.09.1977 | Bruxelles | Belgium - Iceland | | 4-0(2-0) |
| 21.09.1977 | Belfast | Northern Ireland - Iceland | | 2-0(0-0) |
| 12.10.1977 | Belfast | Northern Ireland - Holland | | 0-1(0-0) |
| 26.10.1977 | Amsterdam | Holland - Belgium | | 1-0(1-0) |
| 16.11.1977 | Belfast | Northern Ireland- Belgium | | 3-0(1-0) |

### FINAL STANDINGS

| | | | | | | | | | |
|---|---|---|---|---|---|---|---|---|---|
| 1. | Holland | 6 | 5 | 1 | 0 | 11 | - | 3 | 11 |
| 2. | Belgium | 6 | 3 | 0 | 3 | 7 | - | 6 | 6 |
| 3. | Northern Ireland | 6 | 2 | 1 | 3 | 7 | - | 6 | 5 |
| 4. | Iceland | 6 | 1 | 0 | 5 | 2 | - | 12 | 2 |

Holland qualified for the Final Tournament.

05.09.1976, Laugardalsvöllur Stadium, Reykjavík; Attendance: 9,580
Referee: John Carpenter (Republic of Ireland)
**ICELAND - BELGIUM** **0-1(0-0)**
**ISL:** Árni Stefánsson, Ólafur Sigurvinsson, Jón Pétursson, Marteinn Geirsson, Jóhannes Eðvaldsson (Cap), Gísli Torfason, Guðgeir Leifsson, Ásgeir Sigurvinsson, Teitur Þórðarson, Guðmundur Þorbjörnsson (46.Ingi Björn Albertsson), Árni Sveinsson (75.Ásgeir Elíasson). Trainer: Anthony Knapp (England).
**BEL:** Christian Piot, Eric Gerets, Michel Renquin, Erwin Vandendaele, Maurice Martens, Ludo Coeck, François Vander Elst, René Verheyen, Williy Wellens (60.Rudi Haleydt), Paul Courant (75.Julien Cools), Jacques Teugels. Trainer: Guy Thys.
**Goal:** 0-1 François Vander Elst (72).

08.09.1976, Laugardalsvöllur Stadium, Reykjavík; Attendance: 10,210
Referee: Patrick Mullan (Scotland)
**ICELAND - HOLLAND** **0-1(0-1)**
**ISL:** Árni Stefánsson, Ólafur Sigurvinsson, Jón Pétursson, Marteinn Geirsson, Jóhannes Eðvaldsson (Cap), Gísli Torfason, Guðgeir Leifsson, Ásgeir Sigurvinsson, Teitur Þórðarson, Matthías Hallgrímsson, Ásgeir Elíasson. Trainer: Anthony Knapp (England).
**NED:** Jan Ruiter, Wilhelmus Antonius van de Kerkhof, Adrianus Ambrosus Cornelus van Kraay, Wilhelmus Gerardus Rijsbergen, Rudolf Jozef Krol (Cap), Wilhelmus Marinus Anthonius Jansen, Wilhelmus Martinus Leonardus Johannes van der Kuylen, Arend Haan, Reinier Lambertus van de Kerkhof, Geertruida Maria Geels (60.Cornelis Kist), Robert Pieter Rensenbrink. Trainer: Johannes Zwartkruis.
**Goal:** 0-1 Geertruida Maria Geels (42).

13.10.1976, Feyenoord Stadion, Rotterdam; Attendance: 56,000
Referee: Ángel Franco Martínez (Spain)
**HOLLAND - NORTHERN IRELAND**     **2-2(0-1)**
**NED:** Edouard Treijtel, Wilhelmus Antonius van de Kerkhof (46.Reinier Lambertus van de Kerkhof), Adrianus Ambrosus Cornelus van Kraay, Wilhelmus Gerardus Rijsbergen, Rudolf Jozef Krol, Wilhelmus Marinus Anthonius Jansen, Johannes Jacobus Neeskens, Arend Haan, Geertruida Maria Geels (60.Wilhelmus Martinus Leonardus Johannes van der Kuylen), Johannes Hendrik Cruijff (Cap), Robert Pieter Rensenbrink. Trainer: Johannes Zwartkruis.
**NIR:** Patrick Anthony Jennings, James Michael Nicholl, Thomas A. Jackson, Patrick James Rice, Alan Hunter, Bryan Hamilton, George Best, Samuel Baxter McIlroy, Roland Christopher McGrath (Derek William Spence), David McCreery, Trevor Anderson. Manager: Robert Dennis Blanchflower.
**Goals:** 0-1 Roland Christopher McGrath (4), 1-1 Rudolf Jozef Krol (64), 2-1 Johannes Hendrik Cruijff (66), 2-2 Derek William Spence (88).

10.11.1976, Stade Sclessin, Liège; Attendance: 25,081
Referee: Adolf Prokop (East Germany)
**BELGIUM - NORTHERN IRELAND**     **2-0(1-0)**
**BEL:** Christian Piot, Eric Gerets, Hugo Broos, Erwin Vandendaele, Michel Renquin, François Vander Elst, Ludo Coeck, Paul Courant, Julien Cools, Roger Van Gool, Raoul Lambert. Trainer: Guy Thys.
**NIR:** Patrick Anthony Jennings, James Michael Nicholl, Patrick James Rice (80.Samuel Nelson), Thomas A. Jackson, Alan Hunter, Bryan Hamilton, George Best, Samuel Baxter McIlroy, Roland Christopher McGrath, David McCreery, Trevor Anderson. Manager: Robert Dennis Blanchflower.
**Goals:** 1-0 Roger Van Gool (28), 2-0 Raoul Lambert (53).

26.03.1977, Stade Boschuil, Antwerpen; Attendance: 48,343
Referee: Sergio Gonella (Italy)
**BELGIUM - HOLLAND**     **0-2(0-1)**
**BEL:** Christian Piot, Alfons Bastijns, Hugo Broos, Ludo Coeck, Jozef Volders, Julien Cools, François Vander Elst, René Verheyen, Roger Van Gool (46.Jan Ceulemans), Paul Courant, Williy Wellens. Trainer: Guy Thys.
**NED:** Pieter Schrijvers, Willem Johannes Laurens Suurbier, Wilhelmus Gerardus Rijsbergen, Rudolf Jozef Krol, Hugo Hermanus Hovenkamp, Wilhelmus Antonius van de Kerkhof, Cornelis Kist (65.Wilhelmus Martinus Leonardus Johannes van der Kuylen), Johannes Jacobus Neeskens, John Nicolaas Rep, Johannes Hendrik Cruijff (Cap), Robert Pieter Rensenbrink. Trainer: Johannes Zwartkruis.
**Goals:** 0-1 John Nicolaas Rep (19), 0-2 Johannes Hendrik Cruijff (65).

11.06.1977, Laugardalsvöllur Stadium, Reykjavík; Attendance: 10,269
Referee: Rudolf Glöckner (East Germany)
**ICELAND - NORTHERN IRELAND**     **1-0(1-0)**
**ISL:** Sigurður Dagsson, Ólafur Sigurvinsson, Janus Guðlaugsson, Marteinn Geirsson, Jóhannes Eðvaldsson (Cap), Gísli Torfason, Guðgeir Leifsson, Ingi Björn Albertsson, Ásgeir Sigurvinsson, Teitur Þórðarson, Guðmundur Þorbjörnsson (65.Atli Eðvaldsson). Trainer: Anthony Knapp (England).
**NIR:** Patrick Anthony Jennings, Patrick James Rice, Samuel Nelson, James Michael Nicholl, Alan Hunter, Bryan Hamilton, Roland Christopher McGrath, Samuel Baxter McIlroy, Thomas A. Jackson (Derek William Spence), David McCreery, Trevor Anderson (Gerard Joseph Armstrong). Manager: Robert Dennis Blanchflower.
**Goal:** 1-0 Ingi Björn Albertsson (33).

31.08.1977, de Goffert Stadion, Nijmegen; Attendance: 25,000
Referee: Martti Hirviniemi (Finland)
**HOLLAND - ICELAND** **4-1(3-0)**
**NED:** Jan van Beveren, Willem Johannes Laurens Suurbier, Wilhelmus Gerardus Rijsbergen (65.Jorgen Karel Eduard Dusbaba), Rudolf Jozef Krol (Cap), Hugo Hermanus Hovenkamp, Wilhelmus Antonius van de Kerkhof, Wilhelmus Marinus Anthonius Jansen, Willem van Hanegem, John Nicolaas Rep, Geertruida Maria Geels, Reinier Lambertus van de Kerkhof. Trainer: Johannes Zwartkruis.
**ISL:** Sigurður Dagsson, Ólafur Sigurvinsson, Janus Guðlaugsson, Marteinn Geirsson, Gísli Torfason, Hörður Hilmarsson, Guðgeir Leifsson, Ingi Björn Albertsson (46.Ásgeir Elíasson), Teitur Þórðarson (72.Matthías Hallgrímsson), Ásgeir Sigurvinsson (Cap), Árni Sveinsson. Trainer: Anthony Knapp (England).
**Goals**: 1-0 Willem van Hanegem (15), 2-0 Geertruida Maria Geels (17), 3-0 John Nicolaas Rep (23), 3-1 Ásgeir Sigurvinsson (66 penalty), 4-1 Geertruida Maria Geels (90).

03.09.1977, Parc Astrid, Bruxelles; Attendance: 5,807
Referee: Svein Inge Thieme (Norway)
**BELGIUM - ICELAND** **4-0(2-0)**
**BEL:** Jean-Marie Pfaff, Gilbert Van Binst, Hugo Broos, Walter Meeuws, Maurice Martens, Julien Cools, François Vander Elst, René Vandereycken, Raoul Lambert, Paul Courant, Jan Ceulemans. Trainer: Guy Thys.
**ISL:** Árni Stefánsson, Ólafur Sigurvinsson, Janus Guðlaugsson, Marteinn Geirsson, Gísli Torfason, Hörður Hilmarsson, Guðgeir Leifsson, Atli Eðvaldsson, Matthías Hallgrímsson (51.Guðmundur Þorbjörnsson), Ásgeir Sigurvinsson (Cap), Ásgeir Elíasson. Trainer: Anthony Knapp (England).
**Goals**: 1-0 Gilbert Van Binst (14), 2-0 Maurice Martens (19 penalty), 3-0 Paul Courant (59), 4-0 Raoul Lambert (66).

21.09.1977, Windsor Park, Belfast; Attendance: 15,000
Referee: Henning-Lund Sørensen (Denmark)
**NORTHERN IRELAND - ICELAND** **2-0(0-0)**
**NIR:** Patrick Anthony Jennings, Patrick James Rice, James Michael Nicholl, Samuel Nelson, Alan Hunter, David McCreery, Roland Christopher McGrath, George Best, Samuel Baxter McIlroy, Martin Hugh Michael O'Neill, Trevor Anderson. Manager: Robert Dennis Blanchflower.
**ISL:** Sigurður Dagsson, Viðar Halldórsson, Janus Guðlaugsson, Marteinn Geirsson, Jóhannes Eðvaldsson (Cap), Jón Gunnlaugsson, Guðgeir Leifsson, Atli Eðvaldsson, Matthías Hallgrímsson (65.Ólafur Danívalsson), Árni Sveinsson, Ásgeir Elíasson (46.Kristinn Björnsson). Trainer: Anthony Knapp (England).
**Goals**: 1-0 Roland Christopher McGrath (62), 2-0 Samuel Baxter McIlroy (76).

12.10.1977, Windsor Park, Belfast; Attendance: 30,000
Referee: Antonio José da Silva Garrido (Portugal)
**NORTHERN IRELAND - HOLLAND** **0-1(0-0)**
**NIR:** Patrick Anthony Jennings, Patrick James Rice, Samuel Nelson, James Michael Nicholl, Alan Hunter, Martin Hugh Michael O'Neill, Samuel Baxter McIlroy, George Best, David McCreery, Roland Christopher McGrath, Trevor Anderson. Manager: Robert Dennis Blanchflower.
**NED:** Jan Jongbloed, Willem Johannes Laurens Suurbier, Wilhelmus Gerardus Rijsbergen (50.Jorgen Karel Eduard Dusbaba), Rudolf Jozef Krol (Cap), Hugo Hermanus Hovenkamp, Wilhelmus Marinus Anthonius Jansen, Wilhelmus Antonius van de Kerkhof, Willem van Hanegem, John Nicolaas Rep, Johannes Hendrik Cruijff (71.Wilhelmus Martinus Leonardus Johannes van der Kuylen), Reinier Lambertus van de Kerkhof. Trainer: Ernst Happel (Austria).
**Goal**: 0-1 Wilhelmus Antonius van de Kerkhof (74).

26.10.1977, Olympisch Stadion, Amsterdam; Attendance: 65,000
Referee: Patrick Partridge (England)
**HOLLAND - BELGIUM**  **1-0(1-0)**
**NED:** Jan Jongbloed, Willem Johannes Laurens Suurbier, Jorgen Karel Eduard Dusbaba, Rudolf Jozef Krol, Hugo Hermanus Hovenkamp, Wilhelmus Marinus Anthonius Jansen (13.Willem van Hanegem), Wilhelmus Antonius van de Kerkhof, Johannes Jacobus Neeskens, Reinier Lambertus van de Kerkhof (63.Geertruida Maria Geels), Johannes Hendrik Cruijff (Cap), Robert Pieter Rensenbrink. Trainer: Ernst Happel (Austria).
**BEL:** Jean-Marie Pfaff, Eric Gerets, Walter Meeuws, Hugo Broos, Jean Thissen (62.François Vander Elst), Michel Renquin, Julien Cools, Ludo Coeck, René Vandereycken, Roger Van Gool, Raoul Lambert. Trainer: Guy Thys.
**Goal**: 1-0 Reinier Lambertus van de Kerkhof (2).

16.11.1977, Windsor Park, Belfast; Attendance: 8,000
Referee: Georges Konrath (France)
**NORTHERN IRELAND- BELGIUM**  **3-0(1-0)**
**NIR:** Patrick Anthony Jennings, Patrick James Rice, Samuel Nelson, James Michael Nicholl, Alan Hunter (54.Christopher James Nicholl), Samuel Baxter McIlroy, Roland Christopher McGrath, David McCreery, Gerard Joseph Armstrong, David Charles Stewart, Trevor Anderson. Manager: Robert Dennis Blanchflower.
**BEL:** Jean-Marie Pfaff, Eric Gerets, Hugo Broos, Walter Meeuws, Michel Renquin, Julien Cools, Ludo Coeck, Frank Vercauteren, Raymond Mommens, Williy Wellens, Jan Ceulemans. Trainer: Guy Thys.
**Goals**: 1-0 Gerard Joseph Armstrong (42), 2-0 Roland Christopher McGrath (58), 3-0 Gerard Joseph Armstrong (74).

# GROUP 5

| | | | | |
|---|---|---|---|---|
| 09.10.1976 | Sofia | Bulgaria - France | 2-2(1-2) |
| 17.11.1976 | Paris | France - Republic of Ireland | 2-0(0-0) |
| 30.03.1977 | Dublin | Republic of Ireland - France | 1-0(1-0) |
| 01.06.1977 | Sofia | Bulgaria - Republic of Ireland | 2-1(1-0) |
| 12.10.1977 | Dublin | Republic of Ireland - Bulgaria | 0-0 |
| 16.11.1977 | Paris | France - Bulgaria | 3-1(1-0) |

## FINAL STANDINGS

| | | | | | | | | |
|---|---|---|---|---|---|---|---|---|
| 1. **France** | 4 | 2 | 1 | 1 | 7 | - | 4 | 5 |
| 2. Bulgaria | 4 | 1 | 2 | 1 | 5 | - | 6 | 4 |
| 3. Republic of Ireland | 4 | 1 | 1 | 2 | 2 | - | 4 | 3 |

France qualified for the Final Tournament.

09.10.1976, „Vasil Levski" National Stadium, Sofia; Attendance: 58,000
Referee: Ian Foote (Scotland)
**BULGARIA - FRANCE** **2-2(1-2)**
**BUL:** Toshko Krastev, Nikolai Grancharov, Ivan Tishanski, Tsonio Vasilev, Kiril Stankov, Hristo Bonev (Cap), Borislav Dimitrov (52.Atanas Aleksandrov), Pavel Panov, Voin Voinov, Kiril Milanov, Georgi Denev (46.Chavdar Tsvetkov). Trainers: Hristo Mladenov - Ioncho Arsov.
**FRA:** Dominique Baratelli, Gérard Janvion, Christian Lopez, Marius Trésor (Cap), Maxime Bossis, Dominique Bathenay, Christian Synaeghel, Michel Platini, Jean Gallice, Bernard Lacombe, Didier Six (61.Olivier Rouyer). Trainer: Michel Hidalgo.
**Goals:** 0-1 Michel Platini (37), 1-1 Hristo Bonev (45), 1-2 Bernard Lacombe (40), 2-2 Pavel Panov (68).

17.11.1976, Stade Parc des Princes, Paris; Attendance: 43,437
Referee: Dušan Maksimović (Yugoslavia)
**FRANCE - REPUBLIC OF IRELAND** **2-0(0-0)**
**FRA:** Dominique Baratelli, Gérard Janvion, Christian Lopez, Marius Trésor (Cap), Maxime Bossis, Dominique Bathenay, Raymond Kéruzoré, Michel Platini, Dominique Rocheteau, Bernard Lacombe (71.Olivier Rouyer), Didier Six. Trainer: Michel Hidalgo.
**IRL:** Michael Kearns, Patrick Martin Mulligan, James Paul Holmes, Michael Paul Martin, David Anthony O'Leary, Gerard Anthony Daly, John Michael Giles (Cap), William Brady, Francis Anthony Stapleton (62.Michael Anthony Walsh), Stephen Derek Heighway, Daniel Joseph Givens. Trainer: John Michael Giles.
**Goals:** 1-0 Michel Platini (47), 2-0 Dominique Bathenay (88).

30.03.1977, Lansdowne Road, Dublin; Attendance: 48,000
Referee: Erich Linemayr (Austria)
**REPUBLIC OF IRELAND - FRANCE** **1-0(1-0)**
**IRL:** Michael Kearns, Patrick Martin Mulligan, Michael Paul Martin, David Anthony O'Leary, James Paul Holmes, Gerard Anthony Daly, John Michael Giles (Cap), William Brady, Daniel Joseph Givens, Raymond Christopher Patrick Treacy, Stephen Derek Heighway. Trainer: John Michael Giles.
**FRA:** André Rey, Gérard Janvion, Patrice Rio, Christian Lopez (Cap), Thierry Tusseau, Dominique Bathenay, Michel Platini, Christian Synaeghel, Olivier Rouyer, Bernard Lacombe, Dominique Rocheteau. Trainer: Michel Hidalgo.
**Goal:** 1-0 William Brady (11).

01.06.1977, „Vasil Levski" National Stadium, Sofia; Attendance: 55,000
Referee: Nikolaos Zlatanos (Greece)
**BULGARIA - REPUBLIC OF IRELAND**                                           **2-1(1-0)**
**BUL:** Rumiancho Goranov, Borislav Dimitrov, Kiril Ivkov (Cap), Tsonio Vasilev, Nikolai Arabov, Todor Barzov (61.Andrei Jeliazkov), Radoslav Zdravkov (53.Atanas Aleksandrov), Krasimir Borisov, Kiril Milanov, Pavel Panov, Chavdar Tsvetkov. Trainers: Hristo Mladenov - Ioncho Arsov.
**IRL:** Michael Kearns, Patrick Martin Mulligan, Michael Paul Martin, David Anthony O'Leary, James Paul Holmes, William Brady, Gerard Anthony Daly (79.Noel Campbell), Francis Anthony Stapleton, John Michael Giles (Cap), Stephen Derek Heighway, Daniel Joseph Givens. Trainer: John Michael Giles.
**Goals:** 1-0 Pavel Panov (14), 1-1 Daniel Joseph Givens (46), 2-1 Andrei Jeliazkov (76).
**Sent off:** Michael Paul Martin (82), Noel Campbell (82).

12.10.1977, Lansdowne Road, Dublin; Attendance: 25,000
Referee: Sergio Gonella (Italy)
**REPUBLIC OF IRELAND - BULGARIA**                                    **0-0**
**IRL:** Gerald Joseph Peyton, Patrick Martin Mulligan, David Anthony O'Leary, Mark Thomas Lawrenson, James Paul Holmes, Gerard Anthony Daly, John Michael Giles (Cap), William Brady, Daniel Joseph Givens, Francis Anthony Stapleton, Stephen Derek Heighway. Trainer: John Michael Giles.
**BUL:** Stefan Staikov, Tsonio Vasilev (72.Nikolai Grancharov), Boris Angelov, Kiril Ivkov (Cap), Nikolai Arabov, Georgi Bonev, Angel Kolev, Vanio Kostov, Pavel Panov, Spas Djevizov, Chavdar Tsvetkov (54.Atanas Aleksandrov). Trainers: Hristo Mladenov - Ioncho Arsov.

16.11.1977, Stade Parc des Princes, Paris; Attendance: 44,860
Referee: Charles George Rainier Corver (Holland)
**FRANCE - BULGARIA**                                                                 **3-1(1-0)**
**FRA:** André Rey, Gérard Janvion, Patrice Rio, Marius Trésor (Cap), Maxime Bossis, Jean-Marc Guillou, Michel Platini, Dominique Bathenay, Dominique Rocheteau (70.Christian Dalger), Bernard Lacombe, Didier Six. Trainer: Michel Hidalgo.
**BUL:** Rumiancho Goranov, Tsonio Vasilev, Boris Angelov, Kiril Ivkov (46.Chavdar Tsvetkov), Georgi Bonev, Hristo Bonev (Cap), Nikolai Arabov, Vanio Kostov, Atanas Aleksandrov, Angel Stankov, Angel Kolev (54.Voin Voinov). Trainers: Hristo Mladenov - Ioncho Arsov.
**Goals:** 1-0 Dominique Rocheteau (38), 2-0 Michel Platini (63), 2-1 Chavdar Tsvetkov (85), 3-1 Christian Dalger (89).

# GROUP 6

| | | | | |
|---|---|---|---|---|
| 16.06.1976 | Stockholm | Sweden - Norway | | 2-0(2-0) |
| 08.09.1976 | Oslo | Norway - Switzerland | | 1-0(0-0) |
| 09.10.1976 | Basel | Switzerland - Sweden | | 1-2(1-1) |
| 08.06.1977 | Stockholm | Sweden - Switzerland | | 2-1(0-0) |
| 07.09.1977 | Oslo | Norway - Sweden | | 2-1(1-0) |
| 30.10.1977 | Bern | Switzerland - Norway | | 1-0(1-0) |

## FINAL STANDINGS

| | | | | | | | |
|---|---|---|---|---|---|---|---|
| 1. Sweden | 4 | 3 | 0 | 1 | 7 - 4 | | 6 |
| 2. Norway | 4 | 2 | 0 | 2 | 3 - 4 | | 4 |
| 3. Switzerland | 4 | 1 | 0 | 3 | 3 - 5 | | 2 |

Sweden qualified for the Final Tournament.

16.06.1976, Råsunda Stadion, Stockholm; Attendance: 30,631
Referee: Charles George Reinier Corver (Holland)
**SWEDEN - NORWAY** **2-0(2-0)**
**SWE:** Ronnie Carl Hellström, Mats Werner, Kent Karlsson, Björn Nordqvist, Björn Andersson, Staffan Tapper, Anders Linderoth, Ove Grahn, Conny Torstensson, Thomas Sjöberg, Roland Sandberg (35.Jan Mattsson). Trainer: Georg Ericson.
**NOR:** Tom Rüsz Jacobsen, Helge Karlsen, Jan Birkelund, Svein Grøndalen, Trond Pedersen, Tor Egil Johansen, Svein Kvia, Boye Skistad, Helge Skuseth (47.Bjørn Tronstad), Tom Lund, Gabriel Høyland. Trainer: Kjell Schau Andreassen – Nils Arne Eggen.
**Goals**: 1-0 Björn Andersson (27), 2-0 Thomas Sjöberg (41).

08.09.1976, Ullevaal Stadion, Oslo; Attendance: 15,024
Referee: Francis Rion (Belgium)
**NORWAY - SWITZERLAND** **1-0(0-0)**
**NOR:** Tom Rüsz Jacobsen, Tore Kordahl, Helge Karlsen, Jan Birkelund, Svein Grøndalen, Stein Thunberg, Roger Albertsen, Svein Kvia, Jan Hansen, Odd Iversen, Tom Lund. Trainer: Kjell Schau Andreassen – Nils Arne Eggen.
**SUI:** Erich Burgener, Serge Trinchero, Jörg Stohler, Lucio Bizzini (54.Gilbert Guyot), Jakob Brechbühl (78.Hans-Jörg Pfister), Umberto Barberis, Jakob Kuhn, René Botteron, Daniel Jeandupeux, Fritz Künzli, Kurt Müller. Trainer: René Hüssy.
**Goal**: 1-0 Tom Lund (75).

09.10.1976, St. Jakob Stadion, Basel; Attendance: 30,000
Referee: Hilmi Ok (Turkey)
**SWITZERLAND - SWEDEN** **1-2(1-1)**
**SUI:** Erich Burgener (77.Karl Grob), Serge Trinchero, Jakob Brechbühl, Lucio Bizzini, Pierre-Albert Chapuisat, Jean-Marie Conz, Umberto Barberis, René Botteron, Josef Küttel (62.Kurt Müller), Walter Seiler, Daniel Jeandupeux. Trainer: Miroslav Blažević (Yugoslavia).
**SWE:** Ronnie Carl Hellström, Björn Andersson, Kent Karlsson, Björn Nordqvist, Hans Borg, Bo Börjesson, Anders Linderoth, Conny Torstensson, Torbjörn Nilsson (69.Olle Nordin), Thomas Sjöberg, Benny Wendt (82.Anders Ljungberg). Trainer: Georg Ericson.
**Goals**: 0-1 Bo Börjesson (29), 1-1 Serge Trinchero (39 penalty), 1-2 Thomas Sjöberg (73).

08.06.1977, Råsunda Stadion, Stockholm; Attendance: 43,269
Referee: Malcolm Wright (Northern Ireland)
**SWEDEN - SWITZERLAND** **2-1(0-0)**
**SWE:** Ronnie Carl Hellström, Björn Andersson (83.Magnus Andersson), Roy Andersson, Björn Nordqvist, Jörgen Augustsson, Hans Borg, Bo Börjesson, Anders Linderoth, Lennart Larsson, Thomas Sjöberg, Benny Wendt. Trainer: Georg Ericson.
**SUI:** Erich Burgener, Pierre-Albert Chapuisat, Jakob Brechbühl, Lucio Bizzini, Serge Trinchero (46.Arthur von Wartburg), Umberto Barberis, Otto Demarmels, René Botteron, Claudio Sulser (60.Kurt Müller), Rudolf Elsener, Peter Risi. Trainer: Roger Vonlanthen.
**Goals:** 1-0 Thomas Sjöberg (69), 2-0 Bo Börjesson (77), 2-1 Peter Risi (80).

07.09.1977, Ullevaal Stadion, Oslo; Attendance: 23,065
Referee: Adolf Prokop (East Germany)
**NORWAY - SWEDEN** **2-1(1-0)**
**NOR:** Geir Karlsen, Helge Karlsen, Svein Grøndalen, Jan Birkelund, Trond Pedersen, Tom Lund, Rune Ottesen, Tor Egil Johansen, Stein Thunberg (88.Tom Jacobsen), Odd Iversen (88.Ole Johnny Henriksen), Pål Jacobsen. Trainer: Kjell Schau Andreassen – Nils Arne Eggen.
**SWE:** Ronnie Carl Hellström, Roland Andersson, Roy Andersson, Björn Nordqvist, Hans Borg, Bo Börjesson (38.Thomas Sjöberg), Anders Linderoth, Eine Fredriksson, Conny Torstensson, Ralf Edström (28.Lennart Larsson), Benny Wendt. Trainer: Georg Ericson.
**Goals:** 1-0 Rune Ottesen (34), 1-1 Thomas Sjöberg (57), 2-1 Odd Iversen (68).

30.10.1977, Wankdorf Stadion, Bern; Attendance: 11,000
Referee: Valentin Lipatov (Soviet Union)
**SWITZERLAND - NORWAY** **1-0(1-0)**
**SUI:** Erich Burgener, Pierre-Albert Chapuisat, Charles In-Albon, Serge Trinchero, Lucio Bizzini, Umberto Barberis, André Meyer, René Botteron, Rudolf Elsener, Claudio Sulser (72.Kurt Müller), Roland Schönenberger (64.Marc Schnyder). Trainer: Roger Vonlanthen.
**NOR:** Geir Karlsen, Svein Grøndalen, Helge Karlsen (65.Tore Kordahl), Jan Birkelund, Trond Pedersen (72.Steinar Aase), Rune Ottesen, Tor Egil Johansen, Stein Thunberg, Pål Jacobsen, Odd Iversen, Tom Lund. Trainer: Kjell Schau Andreassen – Nils Arne Eggen.
**Goal:** 1-0 Claudio Sulser (29).

# GROUP 7

| | | | | |
|---|---|---|---|---|
| 13.10.1976 | Praha | Czechoslovakia - Scotland | | 2-0(0-0) |
| 17.11.1976 | Glasgow | Scotland - Wales | | 1-0(1-0) |
| 30.03.1977 | Wrexham | Wales - Czechoslovakia | | 3-0(1-0) |
| 21.09.1977 | Glasgow | Scotland - Czechoslovakia | | 3-1(2-0) |
| 12.10.1977 | Liverpool | Wales - Scotland | | 0-2(0-0) |
| 16.11.1977 | Praha | Czechoslovakia - Wales | | 1-0(1-0) |

## FINAL STANDINGS

| | | | | | | | | |
|---|---|---|---|---|---|---|---|---|
| 1. Scotland | 4 | 3 | 0 | 1 | 6 | - | 3 | 6 |
| 2. Czechoslovakia | 4 | 2 | 0 | 2 | 4 | - | 6 | 4 |
| 3. Wales | 4 | 1 | 0 | 3 | 3 | - | 4 | 2 |

Scotland qualified for the Final Tournament.

13.10.1976, Stadion Sparta, Praha; Attendance: 38,000
Referee: Alberto Michelotti (Italy)
**CZECHOSLOVAKIA - SCOTLAND**     **2-0(0-0)**
**TCH:** Alexander Vencel, Pavel Biroš, Anton Ondruš (Cap), Jozef Čapkovič (68.Ladislav Jurkemik), Koloman Gögh (13.Ján Kozák), Jaroslav Pollák, Karel Dobiaš, Antonín Panenka, Marián Masný, Zdeněk Nehoda, Ladislav Petráš. Trainer: Václav Ježek.
**SCO:** Alan Roderick Rough, Daniel Fergus McGrain, William Donachie, Martin McLean Buchan, Gordon McQueen, Archibald Gemmill (Cap), Donald Sanderson Masson (68.Richard Asa Hartford), Bruce David Rioch, Kenneth Mathieson Dalglish (56.Kenneth Burns), Joseph Jordan, Andrew Mullen Gray. Manager: William Esplin Ormond.
**Goals**: 1-0 Antonín Panenka (48), 2-0 Ladislav Petráš (50).
**Sent off**: Anton Ondruš (76).

17.11.1976, Hampden Park, Glasgow; Attendance: 63,233
Referee: Ferdinand Biwersi (West Germany)
**SCOTLAND - WALES**     **1-0(1-0)**
**SCO:** Alan Roderick Rough, Daniel Fergus McGrain, William Donachie, John Henderson Blackley, Gordon McQueen, Archibald Gemmill (Cap), Kenneth Burns, Bruce David Rioch (67.Richard Asa Hartford), Edwin Gray (84.William H. Pettigrew), Kenneth Mathieson Dalglish, Joseph Jordan. Manager: William Esplin Ormond.
**WAL:** William David Davies, Malcolm Edward Page, Joseph Patrick Jones, Leighton Phillips, Ian Peter Evans, Arfon Trevor Griffiths, Michael Reginald Thomas, Brian Flynn, Terence Charles Yorath, John Benjamin Toshack, Leighton James (76.Alan Thomas Curtis). Manager: Michael Smith.
**Goal**: 1-0 Ian Peter Evans (15 own goal).

30.03.1977, The Racecourse Stadium, Wrexham; Attendance: 18,022
Referee: Antonio José da Silva Garrido (Portugal)
**WALES - CZECHOSLOVAKIA**     **3-0(1-0)**
**WAL:** William David Davies, Roderick John Thomas, Joseph Patrick Jones, Leighton Phillips, Ian Peter Evans, John Francis Mahoney, Peter Anthony Sayer, Brian Flynn, Terence Charles Yorath, Nicholas Simon Deacy, Leighton James. Manager: Michael Smith.
**TCH:** Alexander Vencel, Jan Pivarník, Ladislav Jurkemik, Pavel Biroš, Koloman Gögh, Jaroslav Pollák (Cap), Karel Dobiaš, Antonín Panenka, Marián Masný, Zdeněk Nehoda, Jozef Móder (46.Miroslav Gajdůšek). Trainer: Václav Ježek.
**Goals**: 1-0 Leighton James (27), 2-0 Nicholas Simon Deacy (65), 3-0 Leighton James (75).

21.09.1977, Hampden Park, Glasgow; Attendance: 85,000
Referee: Francis Jean Joseph Elisa Rion (Belgium)
**SCOTLAND - CZECHOSLOVAKIA** **3-1(2-0)**
**SCO:** Alan Roderick Rough, William Pullar Jardine, Daniel Fergus McGrain, Thomas Forsyth, Gordon McQueen, Donald Sanderson Masson, Bruce David Rioch (Cap), Richard Asa Hartford, William McClure Johnston, Kenneth Mathieson Dalglish, Joseph Jordan. Manager: Alistair MacLeod.
**TCH:** Pavol Michalík, Miroslav Pauřik, Jozef Čapkovič, Karel Dvořák, Koloman Gögh, Karel Dobiaš (69.Peter Gallis), Jaroslav Pollák (Cap), Jozef Móder (46.Ľubomír Knapp), Miroslav Gajdůšek, Marián Masný, Zdeněk Nehoda. Trainer: Václav Ježek.
**Goals:** 1-0 Joseph Jordan (19), 2-0 Richard Asa Hartford (35), 3-0 Kenneth Mathieson Dalglish (54), 3-1 Miroslav Gajdůšek (82).

12.10.1977, Anfield Road, Liverpool (England); Attendance: 50,850
Referee: Robert Charles Paul Wurtz (France)
**WALES - SCOTLAND** **0-2(0-0)**
**WAL:** William David Davies, Roderick John Thomas, Joseph Patrick Jones, David Edward Jones, Leighton Phillips, John Francis Mahoney, Peter Anthony Sayer (75.Nicholas Simon Deacy), Brian Flynn, Terence Charles Yorath, John Benjamin Toshack, Michael Reginald Thomas. Manager: Michael Smith.
**SCO:** Alan Roderick Rough, William Pullar Jardine (57.Martin McLean Buchan), William Donachie, Thomas Forsyth, Gordon McQueen, Donald Sanderson Masson (Cap), Richard Asa Hartford, Luigi Macari, William McClure Johnston, Kenneth Mathieson Dalglish, Joseph Jordan. Manager: Alistair MacLeod.
**Goals:** 0-1 Donald Sanderson Masson (79 penalty), 0-2 Kenneth Mathieson Dalglish (87).

16.11.1977, Stadion Sparta, Praha; Attendance: 22,383
Referee: Adolf Prokop (East Germany)
**CZECHOSLOVAKIA - WALES** **1-0(1-0)**
**TCH:** Zdeněk Hruška, Jozef Barmoš, Jan Fiala (67.Zdeněk Prokeš), Rostislav Vojáček (Cap), Koloman Gögh, Ivan Bilský, Karel Jarůšek, Miroslav Gajdůšek, Marián Masný (87.Ján Kozák), Karel Kroupa, Zdeněk Nehoda. Trainer: Václav Ježek.
**WAL:** William David Davies, Roderick John Thomas, Joseph Patrick Jones, David Edward Jones, Leighton Phillips, John Francis Mahoney, Donato Nardiello, Brian Flynn, Terence Charles Yorath, John Benjamin Toshack, Michael Reginald Thomas (73.Nicholas Simon Deacy). Manager: Michael Smith.
**Goal:** 1-0 Zdeněk Nehoda (12).

# GROUP 8

| | | | | |
|---|---|---|---|---|
| 10.10.1976 | Sevilla | Spain - Yugoslavia | 1-0(0-0) |
| 16.04.1977 | Bucureşti | Romania - Spain | 1-0(1-0) |
| 08.05.1977 | Zagreb | Yugoslavia - Romania | 0-2(0-2) |
| 26.10.1977 | Madrid | Spain - Romania | 2-0(0-0) |
| 13.11.1977 | Bucureşti | Romania - Yugoslavia | 4-6(3-2) |
| 30.11.1977 | Beograd | Yugoslavia - Spain | 0-1(0-0) |

### FINAL STANDINGS

| | | | | | | | | |
|---|---|---|---|---|---|---|---|---|
| 1. | Spain | 4 | 3 | 0 | 1 | 4 - 1 | 6 |
| 2. | Romania | 4 | 2 | 0 | 2 | 7 - 8 | 4 |
| 3. | Yugoslavia | 4 | 1 | 0 | 3 | 6 - 8 | 2 |

Spain qualified for the Final Tournament.

10.10.1976, Estadio „Ramón Sánchez Pizjuán", Sevilla; Attendance: 19,217
Referee: Károly Palotai (Hungary)
**SPAIN - YUGOSLAVIA**        **1-0(0-0)**
**ESP:** Miguel Ángel González Suárez, José Luis Capón González, Miguel Bernardo Bianquetti „Migueli", Ignacio „Iñaki" Cortabarría Arrabategui, José Antonio Camacho Alfaro, Ángel María Villar Llona, José Martínez Sánchez „Pirri" (Cap), Vicente Del Bosque González (28.Juan Enrique Gómez González „Juanito"), Enrique Castro González „Quini", Carlos Alonso González „Santillana", José Ignacio Churruca Sistiaga (70.José Francisco Rojo Arroitia „Chechu Rojo I"). Trainer: Ladislao Kubala.
**YUG:** Ratko Svilar, Luka Peruzović, Džemal Hadžiabdić, Branko Oblak (Cap), Josip Katalinski, Vladislav Bogićević, Slaviša Žungul (70.Borislav Đorđević), Dražen Mužinić, Danilo Popivoda, Jure Jerković, Ivan Šurjak. Trainer: Ivan Toplak.
**Goal:** 1-0 José Martínez Sánchez „Pirri" (86 penalty).

16.04.1977, Stadionul Steaua, Bucureşti; Attendance: 18,500
Referee: John Robertson Proudfoot Gordon (Scotland)
**ROMANIA - SPAIN**        **1-0(1-0)**
**ROU:** Cristian Gheorghe, Florin Cheran, Alexandru Sătmăreanu II, Ştefan Sameş (62.Ioan Bruno Grigore), Iosif Vigu, Ion Dumitru (Cap), Ladislau Bölöni, Anghel Iordănescu, Zoltan Crişan (77.Ilie Balaci), Dudu Georgescu, Constantin Zamfir. Trainer: Ştefan Kovács.
**ESP:** Miguel Ángel González Suárez, José Luis Capón González, Gregorio de Benito Rubio, José Martínez Sánchez „Pirri" (Cap), José Antonio Camacho Alfaro, Eugenio Leal Vargas, Ángel María Villar Llona, Juan Manuel Asensi Ripoll, José Ignacio Churruca Sistiaga, Juan Enrique Gómez González „Juanito", Rubén Andres Cano Martínez Sáez. Trainer: Ladislao Kubala.
**Goal:** 1-0 Gregorio de Benito Rubio (6 own goal).

08.05.1977, Maksimir Stadion, Zagreb; Attendance: 45,000
Referee: Menachem Ashkenazi (Israel)
**YUGOSLAVIA - ROMANIA**        **0-2(0-2)**
**YUG:** Ivan Katalinić, Ivan Buljan (46.Dušan Savić), Dražen Mužinić, Luka Peruzović, Josip Katalinski, Ivan Šurjak, Danilo Popivoda, Branko Oblak, Dušan Bajević (46.Zoran Filipović), Jure Jerković, Dragan Džajić (Cap). Trainer: Ivan Toplak.
**ROU:** Cristian Gheorghe, Florin Cheran (Cap), Ştefan Sameş, Alexandru Sătmăreanu II, Iosif Vigu, Mihai Romilă II, Ladislau Bölöni, Anghel Iordănescu, Zoltan Crişan (81.Ilie Balaci), Dudu Georgescu, Constantin Zamfir. Trainer: Ştefan Kovács.
**Goals:** 0-1 Dudu Georgescu (37), 0-2 Anghel Iordănescu (47).

26.10.1977, Estadio „Vicente Calderón", Madrid; Attendance: 50,000
Referee: Robert Charles Paul Wurtz (France)
**SPAIN - ROMANIA** **2-0(0-0)**
**ESP:** Luis Miguel Arkonada Echarre, Antonio Benítez Fernández (86.Marcelino Pérez Ayllón), Miguel Bernardo Bianquetti „Migueli", José Martínez Sánchez „Pirri" (Cap), José Antonio Camacho Alfaro, Eugenio Leal Vargas, Juan Manuel Asensi Ripoll, José Ignacio Churruca Sistiaga (56.Jesús María Satrústegui Azpiroz), Juan Enrique Gómez González „Juanito", Rubén Andres Cano Martínez Sáez, Daniel Ruiz-Bazan Justa „Dani". Trainer: Ladislao Kubala.
**ROU:** Cristian Gheorghe, Florin Cheran, Ştefan Sameş, Alexandru Sătmăreanu II, Iosif Vigu, Ion Dumitru (Cap), Ilie Balaci (64.Cornel Dinu), Ladislau Bölöni, Zoltan Crişan, Dudu Georgescu, Anghel Iordănescu (86.Mihai Romilă II). Trainer: Ştefan Kovács.
**Goals:** 1-0 Eugenio Leal Vargas (74), 2-0 Rubén Andres Cano Martínez Sáez (83).

13.11.1977, Stadionul Steaua, Bucureşti; Attendance: 30,000
Referee: Alfred Delcourt (Belgium)
**ROMANIA - YUGOSLAVIA** **4-6(3-2)**
**ROU:** Dumitru Moraru, Florin Cheran, Ştefan Sameş, Alexandru Sătmăreanu II (46.Vasile Dobrău), Iosif Vigu, Ion Dumitru (Cap) (64.Mihai Romilă II), Ladislau Bölöni, Anghel Iordănescu, Zoltan Crişan, Dudu Georgescu, Constantin Zamfir. Trainer: Ştefan Kovács.
**YUG:** Petar Borota, Dražen Mužinić, Mario Boljat, Aleksandar Trifunović, Nenad Stojković, Jusuf Hatunić, Slaviša Žungul (60.Momčilo Vukotić), Dušan Nikolić (65.Velimir Zajec), Zoran Filipović, Ivan Šurjak (Cap), Safet Sušić. Selection comittee: Marko Valok – Stevan Vilotić – Gojko Zec.
**Goals:** 1-0 Iosif Vigu (2), 1-1 Safet Sušić (14), 1-2 Dražen Mužinić (18), 2-2 Anghel Iordănescu (40), 3-2 Ladislau Bölöni (43), 3-3 Safet Sušić (51), 3-4 Safet Sušić (62), 4-4 Dudu Georgescu (67), 4-5 Aleksandar Trifunović (79), 4-6 Zoran Filipović (90).

30.11.1977, Crvena zvezda Stadion, Beograd; Attendance: 80,000
Referee: Kenneth Howard Burns (England)
**YUGOSLAVIA - SPAIN** **0-1(0-0)**
**YUG:** Ivan Katalinić, Dražen Mužinić, Mario Boljat, Aleksandar Trifunović, Nenad Stojković, Jusuf Hatunić, Danilo Popivoda (64.Vahid Halilhodžić), Sead Sušić (46.Momčilo Vukotić), Miodrag Kustudić, Ivan Šurjak (Cap), Safet Sušić. Selection comittee: Marko Valok – Stevan Vilotić – Gojko Zec.
**ESP:** Miguel Ángel González Suárez, Marcelino Pérez Ayllón, Miguel Bernardo Bianquetti „Migueli", José Martínez Sánchez „Pirri" (Cap) (13.Antonio Olmo Ramírez), José Antonio Camacho Alfaro, Isidoro San José Pozo Sánchez, Eugenio Leal Vargas, Juan Manuel Asensi Ripoll, Julio Cardeñosa Rodríguez, Juan Enrique Gómez González „Juanito" (75.Daniel Ruiz-Bazan Justa „Dani"), Rubén Andres Cano Martínez Sáez. Trainer: Ladislao Kubala.
**Goal:** 0-1 Rubén Andres Cano Martínez Sáez (71).

# GROUP 9

| | | | | |
|---|---|---|---|---|
| 09.10.1976 | Athína | Greece - Hungary | 1-1(0-0) |
| 24.04.1977 | Moskva | Soviet Union - Greece | 2-0(1-0) |
| 30.04.1977 | Budapest | Hungary - Soviet Union | 2-1(1-0) |
| 10.05.1977 | Thessaloníki | Greece - Soviet Union | 1-0(0-0) |
| 18.05.1977 | Tbilisi | Soviet Union - Hungary | 2-0(2-0) |
| 28.05.1977 | Budapest | Hungary - Greece | 3-0(2-0) |

### FINAL STANDINGS

| | | | | | | | | |
|---|---|---|---|---|---|---|---|---|
| 1. Hungary | 4 | 2 | 1 | 1 | 6 | - | 4 | 5 |
| 2. Soviet Union | 4 | 2 | 0 | 2 | 5 | - | 3 | 4 |
| 3. Greece | 4 | 1 | 1 | 2 | 2 | - | 6 | 3 |

Hungary qualified for the Intercontinental Play-offs.

09.10.1976, Karaïskáki Stádio, Peiraiás; Attendance: 25,255
Referee: Franz Wöhrer (Austria)
**GREECE - HUNGARY**                                                                   **1-1(0-0)**
**GRE:** Vasílis Konstantinou, Harálambos Intzoglou, Giánnis Kyrástas, Anthimos Kapsís, Pantelis Nikolaou, Dimítris Nikoloudis, Stavros Sarafis, Dimítris Domazos, Mihális Kritikopoulos, Dimítris Papaïoánnou (Cap), Giórgos Delikaris (58.Konstantinos Davourlis). Trainer: Lakis Petropoulos.
**HUN:** László Kovács, Péter Török (46.János Nagy III), László Bálint, Zoltán Kereki, József Tóth, Tibor Nyilasi, Zoltán Ebedli, Sándor Pintér, László Pusztai (55.István Magyar), László Fazekas, Béla Várady. Trainer: Lajos Baróti.
**Goals**: 1-0 Dimítris Papaïoánnou (68), 1-1 Zoltán Kereki (84).

24.04.1977, Lenin Stadium, Moskva; Attendance: 50,000
Referee: Jean Dubach (Switzerland)
**SOVIET UNION - GREECE**                                    **2-0(1-0)**
**URS:** Vladimir Astapovskiy, Anatoliy Konikov, Shota Khinchagashvili, Evgeniy Lovchev, Sergey Olshanskiy, Vladimir Troshkin, Leonid Buryak, David Kipiani, Vladimir Fëdorov (Vladimir Onishchenko), Aleksandr Minaev (Aleksandr Maksimenkov), Oleg Blokhin (Cap). Trainer: Nikita Simonyan.
**GRE:** Vasílis Konstantinou, Giánnis Kyrástas, Konstantinos Iosifidis (79.Mihális Kritikopoulos), Giórgos Firos, Anthimos Kapsís, Hrístos Terzanidis, Stavros Sarafis (61.Dimítris Nikoloudis), Giórgos Delikaris, Giórgos Koudas (Cap), Hrístos Ardizoglou, Ilías Galakos. Trainer: Lakis Petropoulos.
**Goals**: 1-0 Anatoliy Konikov (26), 2-0 David Kipiani (77).

30.04.1977, Népstadion, Budapest; Attendance: 70,000
Referee: Heinz Aldinger (West Germany)
**HUNGARY - SOVIET UNION**                                **2-1(1-0)**
**HUN:** Sándor Gujdár, Győző Martos, László Bálint, Zoltán Kereki, József Tóth, Tibor Nyilasi (51.Péter Török), Sándor Pintér, Sándor Zombori, László Pusztai, István Kovács, Béla Várady (80.László Fazekas). Trainer: Lajos Baróti.
**URS:** Vladimir Astapovskiy, Anatoliy Konikov, Shota Khinchagashvili, Evgeniy Lovchev, Seilda Bayshakov, Viktor Kruglov (Vladimir Troshkin), Leonid Buryak, Oleg Dolmatov (David Kipiani), Vladimir Fëdorov, Aleksandr Minaev, Oleg Blokhin (Cap). Trainer: Nikita Simonyan.
**Goals**: 1-0 Tibor Nyilasi (44), 2-0 Zoltán Kereki (66), 2-1 David Kipiani (88).

10.05.1977, Kaftatzógleio Stádio, Thessaloníki; Attendance: 32,000
Referee: Cesare Gussoni (Italy)
**GREECE - SOVIET UNION**                     **1-0(0-0)**
**GRE:** Vasílis Konstantinou, Giánnis Kyrástas, Konstantinos Iosifidis, Pantelis Nikolaou, Giórgos Firos, Angelos Anastasiadis, Hrístos Terzanidis, Giórgos Koudas (Cap), Giórgos Delikaris (68.Dimítris Nikoloudis), Hrístos Ardizoglou, Dimítris Papaïoánnou (89.Théodoros Pallas). Trainer: Lakis Petropoulos.
**URS:** Yuriy Degtyarev, Anatoliy Konikov, Viktor Matvienko, Shota Khinchagashvili, Seilda Bayshakov, Vladimir Troshkin, Leonid Buryak (Aleksandr Maksimenkov), Vladimir Onishchenko, Aleksandr Minaev (Vladimir Fëdorov), David Kipiani, Oleg Blokhin (Cap). Trainer: Nikita Simonyan.
**Goal:** 1-0 Dimítris Papaïoánnou (56).

18.05.1977, Dinamo Stadium, Tbilisi; Attendance: 75,000
Referee: John Keith Taylor (England)
**SOVIET UNION - HUNGARY**              **2-0(2-0)**
**URS:** Yuriy Degtyarev, Anatoliy Konikov (Cap), Viktor Matvienko, Shota Khinchagashvili, Aleksandr Novikov, Vladimir Troshkin, Leonid Buryak, Vladimir Onishchenko, Aleksandr Maksimenkov (Aleksandr Minaev), David Kipiani, Oleg Blokhin. Trainer: Nikita Simonyan.
**HUN:** Sándor Gujdár, Győző Martos, László Bálint, Zoltán Kereki, József Tóth, Tibor Nyilasi, Sándor Pintér, Sándor Zombori (79.László Fazekas), László Pusztai (46.Péter Török), István Kovács, Béla Várady. Trainer: Lajos Baróti.
**Goals:** 1-0 Leonid Buryak (3), 2-0 László Bálint (14 own goal).

28.05.1977, Népstadion, Budapest; Attendance: 70,000
Referee: Johannes Beck (Holland)
**HUNGARY - GREECE**                         **3-0(2-0)**
**HUN:** Sándor Gujdár, Győző Martos, László Bálint, Zoltán Kereki, József Tóth, Tibor Nyilasi, Sándor Pintér, Sándor Zombori (74.Péter Török), László Pusztai, István Kovács (84.László Fazekas), Béla Várady. Trainer: Lajos Baróti.
**GRE:** Vasílis Konstantinou, Giánnis Kyrástas (77.Konstantinos Eleftherakis), Giórgos Firos, Konstantinos Iosifidis, Pantelis Nikolaou, Angelos Anastasiadis, Giórgos Koudas, Hrístos Terzanidis, Dimítris Papaïoánnou (Cap), Antónis Antoniadis, Hrístos Ardizoglou. Trainer: Lakis Petropoulos.
**Goals:** 1-0 László Pusztai (13), 2-0 Tibor Nyilasi (15), 3-0 László Fazekas (88).

# SOUTH AMERICA

## FIRST ROUND

### SUBGROUP A

| | | | | |
|---|---|---|---|---|
| 20.02.1977 | Bogotá | Colombia - Brazil | | 0-0 |
| 24.02.1977 | Bogotá | Colombia - Paraguay | | 0-1(0-1) |
| 06.03.1977 | Asunción | Paraguay - Colombia | | 1-1(0-0) |
| 09.03.1977 | Rio de Janeiro | Brazil - Colombia | | 6-0(4-0) |
| 13.03.1977 | Asunción | Paraguay - Brazil | | 0-1(0-0) |
| 20.03.1977 | Rio de Janeiro | Brazil - Paraguay | | 1-1(1-0) |

**FINAL STANDINGS**

| | | | | | | | | |
|---|---|---|---|---|---|---|---|---|
| 1. | Brazil | 4 | 2 | 2 | 0 | 8 - 1 | 6 |
| 2. | Paraguay | 4 | 1 | 2 | 1 | 3 - 3 | 4 |
| 3. | Colombia | 4 | 0 | 2 | 2 | 1 - 8 | 2 |

Brazil qualified for the Second Round.

20.02.1977, Estadio „Nemesio Camacho" 'El Campín', Bogotá; Attendance: 55,439
Referee: Miguel Angel Comesaña (Argentina)
**COLOMBIA - BRAZIL** **0-0**
**COL:** Luis Geronimo López, Arturo Rafael Segovia, José de los Reyes Zárate, Henry Caicedo (89.Gabriel Berdugo), Oscar Emilio Bolaño, Eduardo Julián Retat, Osvaldo Antonio Calero, Diego Edison Umaña, Willington José Ortíz, Eduardo Emilio Vilarete, Jorge Ramón Cáceres. Trainer: Blagoje Vidinić (Yugoslavia).
**BRA:** Émerson Leão, José Maria Rodrigues Alves "Zé Maria I", João Justino Amaral dos Santos "Amaral I", Rigoberto Costa "Beto Fuscão", Wladimir Rodrigues dos Santos, Givanildo José de Oliveira (77.Luís Carlos Melo Lopes "Caçapava"), Paulo Roberto Falcão, Arthur Antunes Coimbra "Zico", Roberto Rivelino, Gilberto Alves "Gil" (72.Valdomiro Vaz Franco), Carlos Roberto de Oliveira "Roberto Dinamite". Trainer: Osvaldo Brandão.

24.02.1977, Estadio „Nemesio Camacho" 'El Campín', Bogotá; Attendance: 45,838
Referee: Augusto Orozco Guerrero (Peru)
**COLOMBIA - PARAGUAY** **0-1(0-1)**
**COL:** Luis Geronimo López, Arturo Rafael Segovia, José de los Reyes Zárate, Henry Caicedo (28.Gabriel Berdugo), Oscar Emilio Bolaño, Eduardo Julián Retat, Abraham Jorge Amado, Diego Edison Umaña, Willington José Ortíz, Eduardo Emilio Vilarete (66.Juan Moreno), Jorge Ramón Cáceres. Trainer: Blagoje Vidinić (Yugoslavia).
**PAR:** José de la Cruz Benítez, Juan Gualberto Espínola, Hugo Julián Benítez Isasi, Secundino Aifuch Osorio, José Domingo Insfrán, Alcides Sosa Ovelar, Carlos de los Santos Jara Saguier, Hugo Enrique Kiese Wisner, Adolfo Lazzarini Osorio (46.Osvaldo Aquino), Apolinar Paniagua (70.Eladio Vera Arías), Pedro Alcides Bareiro Molinas. Trainer: Ramón Rodríguez.
**Goal:** 0-1 Carlos de los Santos Jara Saguier (26).

06.03.1977, Estadio Defensores del Chaco, Asunción; Attendance: 30,154
Referee: Roque Tito Cerullo Giuliano (Uruguay)
**PARAGUAY - COLOMBIA**     **1-1(0-0)**
**PAR:** José de la Cruz Benítez, Juan Gualberto Espínola, Hugo Julián Benítez Isasi, Secundino Aifuch Osorio, José Domingo Insfrán, Carlos de los Santos Jara Saguier, Alcides Sosa Ovelar, Osvaldo Aquino, Carlos José Báez Vargas (Adolfo Lazzarini Osorio), Apolinar Paniagua (Eladio Vera Arías), Pedro Alcides Bareiro Molinas. Trainer: Ramón Rodríguez.
**COL:** Luis Geronimo López, Arturo Rafael Segovia, Luis Eduardo Soto, José de los Reyes Zárate, Oscar Emilio Bolaño, Eduardo Julián Retat, Osvaldo Antonio Calero, Diego Edison Umaña (Abraham Jorge Amado), Willington José Ortíz, Eduardo Emilio Vilarete, Juan Moreno (Alfonso López). Trainer: Blagoje Vidinić (Yugoslavia).
**Goals:** 0-1 Eduardo Vilarete (58), 1-1 Carlos de los Santos Jara Saguier (90).

09.03.1977, Estádio „Jornalista Mário Filho" (Maracanã), Rio de Janeiro; Attendance: 132,764
Referee: Ángel Norberto Coerezza (Argentina)
**BRAZIL - COLOMBIA**     **6-0(4-0)**
**BRA:** Émerson Leão, José Maria Rodrigues Alves "Zé Maria I", Luís Edmundo Pereira, Carlos Alberto Tôrres, Francisco das Chagas Marinho (61.Édino Nazareth Filho "Edinho"), Antônio Carlos Cerezo "Toninho Cerezo", Arthur Antunes Coimbra "Zico", Roberto Rivelino, Gilberto Alves "Gil" (72.João Soares Almeida Filho "Joãozinho I"), Carlos Roberto de Oliveira "Roberto Dinamite", Paulo César Lima. Trainer: Cláudio de Morais „Coutinho".
**COL:** Luis Geronimo López, Arturo Rafael Segovia, José de los Reyes Zárate, Gabriel Berdugo, Oscar Emilio Bolaño, Osvaldo Antonio Calero (33.Abraham Jorge Amado), Eduardo Julián Retat, Diego Edison Umaña, Willington José Ortíz (46.Juan Moreno), Eduardo Emilio Vilarete, Jorge Ramón Cáceres. Trainer: Blagoje Vidinić (Yugoslavia).
**Goals:** 1-0 Carlos Roberto de Oliveira "Roberto Dinamite" (15), 2-0 Arthur Antunes Coimbra "Zico" (25), 3-0 Carlos Roberto de Oliveira "Roberto Dinamite" (31), 4-0 Francisco das Chagas Marinho (41), 5-0 Francisco das Chagas Marinho (55), 6-0 Roberto Rivelino (85).
**Sent off:** Arthur Antunes Coimbra "Zico" / José de los Reyes Zárate.

13.03.1977, Estadio Defensores del Chaco, Asunción; Attendance: 40,490
Referee: Luis Pestarino (Argentina)
**PARAGUAY - BRAZIL**     **0-1(0-0)**
**PAR:** José de la Cruz Benítez, Alicio Ignacio Solalinde Miers, Hugo Julián Benítez Isasi, Secundino Aifuch Osorio, José Domingo Insfrán, Alcides Sosa Ovelar, Carlos de los Santos Jara Saguier, Hugo Enrique Kiese Wisner, Juvencio Osorio Maldonado, Adolfo Lazzarini Osorio, Pedro Alcides Bareiro Molinas (Eladio Vera Arías). Trainer: Ramón Rodríguez.
**BRA:** Émerson Leão, José Maria Rodrigues Alves "Zé Maria I" (Marco Antônio Feliciano), Luís Edmundo Pereira, Carlos Alberto Tôrres, Francisco das Chagas Marinho, Antônio Carlos Cerezo "Toninho Cerezo", Paulo Roberto Falcão, Roberto Rivelino, Gilberto Alves "Gil", Carlos Roberto de Oliveira "Roberto Dinamite", Paulo César Lima. Trainer: Cláudio Pècego de Moraes Coutinho.
**Goal:** 0-1 José Domingo Isfran (59 own goal).

20.03.1977, Estádio „Jornalista Mário Filho" (Maracanã), Rio de Janeiro; Attendance: 94,947
Referee: Ramón Ivannoe Barreto Ruíz (Uruguay)
**BRAZIL - PARAGUAY**     **1-1(1-0)**
**BRA:** Émerson Leão, Francisco das Chagas Marinho, Carlos Alberto Tôrres, Édino Nazareth Filho "Edinho", Marco Antônio Feliciano, Antônio Carlos Cerezo "Toninho Cerezo" (62.Carlos Alberto Gomes "Pintinho"), Paulo Roberto Falcão, Roberto Rivelino, Valdomiro Vaz Franco, Carlos Roberto de Oliveira "Roberto Dinamite", Paulo César Lima. Trainer: Cláudio Pècego de Moraes Coutinho.
**PAR:** José de la Cruz Benítez, Alicio Ignacio Solalinde Miers, Hugo Julián Benítez Isasi, Secundino Aifuch Osorio, José Domingo Insfrán, Alcides Sosa Ovelar, Carlos de los Santos Jara Saguier, Sabino Gerardo González Aquino, Adolfo Lazzarini Osorio (62.Juan Gualberto Espínola), Apolinar Paniagua (79.Arecio Colmán), Carlos José Báez Vargas. Trainer: Ramón Rodríguez.

**Goals**: 1-0 Carlos Roberto de Oliveira "Roberto Dinamite" (6 penalty), 1-1 Carlos José Báez Vargas (54).

## SUBGROUP B

| | | | | |
|---|---|---|---|---|
| 09.02.1977 | Caracas | Venezuela - Uruguay | 1-1(0-1) |
| 27.02.1977 | La Paz | Bolivia - Uruguay | 1-0(0-0) |
| 06.03.1977 | Caracas | Venezuela - Bolivia | 1-3(0-1) |
| 13.03.1977 | La Paz | Bolivia - Venezuela | 2-0(2-0) |
| 17.03.1977 | Montevideo | Uruguay - Venezuela | 2-0(1-0) |
| 27.03.1977 | Montevideo | Uruguay - Bolivia | 2-2(1-1) |

### FINAL STANDINGS

| | | | | | | | | |
|---|---|---|---|---|---|---|---|---|
| 1. | Bolivia | 4 | 3 | 1 | 0 | 8 - 3 | 7 |
| 2. | Uruguay | 4 | 1 | 2 | 1 | 5 - 4 | 4 |
| 3. | Venezuela | 4 | 0 | 1 | 3 | 2 - 8 | 1 |

Bolivia qualified for the Second Round.

09.02.1977, Estadio Nacional „Brígido Iriarte", Caracas; Attendance: 5,000
Referee: Guillermo Velásquez Ramírez (Colombia)
**VENEZUELA - URUGUAY**      **1-1(0-1)**
VEN: Santiago Romero, Omar Ochoa, Fréderic Ellie Arlet, Carlos Betancourt, William Salas, Carlos Enrique Marín (Cap) (85.Nabor Fuenmayor), José Ricardo Moss, Ramón Echenáusi, Rafael Iriarte, Vicente Flores, José Mora (40.Iván García). Trainer: Dan Georgiadis (Greece).
URU: Rodolfo Sergio Rodríguez, Sergio Ramírez, Alfredo De los Santos, Rafael Villazán, Juan Vicente Morales, Juan Ramón Carrasco Torres, Pedro Graffigna, Alfonso Darío Pereyra Bueno (77.Lorenzo Unanue), Laddy Nittder Pizzani (59.Alberto Raúl Santelli), Fernando Morena Belaro, Washington Olivera. Trainer: Juan Eduardo Hohberg.
**Goals**: 0-1 Washington Olivera (5), 1-1 Carlos Enrique Marín (83).

27.02.1977, Estadio "Libertador Simón Bolívar", La Paz; Attendance: 20,306
Referee: Romualdo Arppi Filho (Brazil)
**BOLIVIA - URUGUAY**      **1-0(0-0)**
BOL: Carlos Conrado Jiménez Hurtado, Jorge Campos, Jaime Lima Guardia, Pablo Baldivieso Fernández, Jaime Rimazza Vargas, Raúl Morales Gonzáles, Carlos Aragonés Espinosa, Eduardo Angulo Torme, Mario Ovidio Mezza Soruco, Porfirio Jiménez (73.Jesús Reynaldo Hurtado), Miguel Aguilar. Trainer: Wilfredo Camacho.
URU: Rodolfo Sergio Rodríguez, Sergio Ramírez, Alfredo De los Santos, Francisco Salomón, Juan Vicente Morales, Juan Ramón Carrasco Torres (61.Lorenzo Unanue), Pedro Graffigna, Alfonso Darío Pereyra Bueno, Waldemar Barreto Victorino, Fernando Morena Belaro, Washington Olivera (61.Miguel Rosifredo Caillava). Trainer: Juan Eduardo Hohberg.
**Goal**: 1-0 Porfirio Jiménez (48).

06.03.1977, Estadio Nacional „Brígido Iriarte", Caracas; Attendance: 5,034
Referee: Juan Ambrosio Silvagno Cavanna (Chile)
**VENEZUELA - BOLIVIA** **1-3(0-1)**
**VEN:** Santiago Romero, Carlos Enrique Marín, Fréderic Ellie Arlet, Carlos Betancourt (59.José Betancourt Toro), William Salas, Nabor Fuenmayor, José Ricardo Moss, Ramón Echenáusi, José Enrique Chiazzaro, Rafael Iriarte, Vicente Flores (38.Edgar Soto). Trainer: Dan Georgiadis (Greece).
**BOL:** Carlos Conrado Jiménez Hurtado, Jorge Campos, Jaime Rimazza Vargas, Jaime Lima Guardia, Pablo Baldivieso Fernández, Arturo Saucedo Landa (59.Raúl Morales Gonzáles), Carlos Aragonés Espinosa, Eduardo Angulo Torme (62.Erwin Romero Escudero), Mario Ovidio Mezza Soruco, Porfirio Jiménez, Miguel Aguilar. Trainer: Wilfredo Camacho.
**Goals**: 0-1 Mario Ovidio Mezza Soruco (7), 0-2 Porfirio Jiménez (76), 0-3 Miguel Aguilar (80), 1-3 Rafael Iriarte (87).

13.03.1977, Estadio „Libertador Simón Bolívar", La Paz; Attendance: 21,217
Referee: Edison Pérez Nuñez (Peru)
**BOLIVIA - VENEZUELA** **2-0(2-0)**
**BOL:** Carlos Conrado Jiménez Hurtado, Jorge Campos, Jaime Lima Guardia, Pablo Baldivieso Fernández, Jaime Rimazza Vargas, Raúl Morales Gonzáles (61.Arturo Saucedo Landa), Eduardo Angulo Torme, Carlos Aragonés Espinosa, Mario Ovidio Mezza Soruco (61.Erwin Romero Escudero), Porfirio Jiménez, Miguel Aguilar. Trainer: Wilfredo Camacho.
**VEN:** Andrés Jiménez, Carlos Enrique Marín, Fréderic Ellie Arlet, José Betancourt Toro (46.Carlos Betancourt), William Salas, José Ricardo Moss, Ramón Echenáusi, Rafael Iriarte (46.Iván García), Vicente Flores, Edgar Soto, José Enrique Chiazzaro. Trainer: Dan Georgiadis (Greece).
**Goals**: 1-0 Porfirio Jiménez (17), 2-0 Carlos Aragonés Espinosa (43).

17.03.1977, Estadio Centenario, Montevideo; Attendance: 4,383
Referee: Armando Nunes Castanheiras da Rosa Marques (Brazil)
**URUGUAY - VENEZUELA** **2-0(1-0)**
**URU:** Rodolfo Sergio Rodríguez, Sergio Ramírez, Raúl Moller, Martin Taborda, Manuel Santana, Miguel Rosifredo Caillava, Pedro Graffigna (65.Juan José Duarte), Lorenzo Unanue, Laddy Nittder Pizzani, Alberto Raúl Santelli (69.Juan Ramón Carrasco Torres), Washington Olivera. Trainer: Raúl Bentancor.
**VEN:** Santiago Romero, Carlos Enrique Marín, Fréderic Ellie Arlet, José Betancourt Toro, Carlos Betancourt, José Ricardo Moss, Ramón Echenáusi, Gerardo Vielma, Rafael Iriarte, José Enrique Chiazzaro, Vicente Flores (84.Edgar Soto). Trainer: Dan Georgiadis (Greece).
**Goals**: 1-0 Laddy Nittder Pizzani (11), 2-0 Laddy Nittder Pizzani (83).

27.03.1977, Estadio Centenario, Montevideo; Attendance: 7,477
Referee: Arturo Andrés Ithurralde (Argentina)
**URUGUAY - BOLIVIA** **2-2(1-1)**
**URU:** Rodolfo Sergio Rodríguez, Eduardo del Capellán, Raúl Moller, Martin Taborda, Manuel Santana, Lorenzo Unanue, Pedro Graffigna (77.Juan Muhlethaler), Alfonso Darío Pereyra Bueno, Laddy Nittder Pizzani, Alberto Raúl Santelli, Jorge Rodríguez Cantero. Trainer: Raúl Bentancor.
**BOL:** Carlos Conrado Jiménez Hurtado, Jorge Campos, Jaime Lima Guardia, Pablo Baldivieso Fernández, Jaime Rimazza Vargas, Eduardo Angulo Torme, Arturo Saucedo Landa (46.Raúl Morales Gonzáles), Erwin Romero Escudero, Carlos Aragonés Espinosa, Porfirio Jiménez, Miguel Aguilar. Trainer: Wilfredo Camacho.
**Goals**: 1-0 Alfonso Darío Pereyra Bueno (23), 1-1 Miguel Aguilar (25), 2-1 Alfonso Darío Pereyra Bueno (49), 2-2 Miguel Aguilar (59).

# SUBGROUP C

| | | | | |
|---|---|---|---|---|
| 20.02.1977 | Quito | Ecuador - Peru | | 1-1(0-1) |
| 27.02.1977 | Guayaquil | Ecuador - Chile | | 0-1(0-1) |
| 06.03.1977 | Santiago | Chile - Peru | | 1-1(1-0) |
| 12.03.1977 | Lima | Peru - Ecuador | | 4-0(1-0) |
| 20.03.1977 | Santiago | Chile - Ecuador | | 3-0(2-0) |
| 26.03.1977 | Lima | Peru - Chile | | 2-0(0-0) |

## FINAL STANDINGS

| | | | | | | | | |
|---|---|---|---|---|---|---|---|---|
| 1. Peru | 4 | 2 | 2 | 0 | 8 | - | 2 | 6 |
| 2. Chile | 4 | 2 | 1 | 1 | 5 | - | 3 | 5 |
| 3. Ecuador | 4 | 0 | 1 | 3 | 1 | - | 9 | 1 |

Peru qualified for the Second Round.

20.02.1977, Estadio Olimpico „Atahualpa", Quito; Attendance: 39,576
Referee: Agomar Martins Rohrig (Brazil)
**ECUADOR - PERU**      **1-1(0-1)**
**ECU:** Carlos Omar Delgado, Washington Méndez, Fausto Rubén Carrera, Fernando Villena, Fausto Klinger, Luis Augusto Granda (Luis Cristóbal Mantilla), José Voltaire Villafuerte, Juan Carlos Gómez (60.José Fabián Pazymiño), Jorge Vinicio Ron, Angel Luis Liciardi, Wilson Nieves. Trainer: Ernesto Guerra.
**PER:** Ramón Quiroga Arancibia, Eleazar Soria, Julio Meléndez, Héctor Eduardo Chumpitaz González, Rubén Toribio Díaz Rivas, Alfredo Quesada Farfas, José Manuel Velásquez Castillo, Juan José Muñante López (60.Oswaldo Felipe Ramírez Salcedo), Hugo Alejandro Sotil Yerén, Teófilo Juan Cubillas Arizaga (46.Percy Rojas Montero), Juan Carlos Oblitas Saba. Trainer: Marcos Calderón Medrano.
**Goals**: 0-1 Juan Carlos Oblitas Saba (42), 1-1 José Fabián Pazymiño (89).

27.02.1977, Estadio Modelo, Guayaquil; Attendance: 51,200
Referee: Jorge Eduardo Romero (Argentina)
**ECUADOR - CHILE**      **0-1(0-1)**
**ECU:** Carlos Omar Delgado, Washington Méndez, Fausto Rubén Carrera, Carlos German Campoverde, Fausto Klinger, José Daniel Tenorio, José Voltaire Villafuerte (Luis Augusto Granda), Juan Carlos Gómez, Jorge Vinicio Ron, Angel Luis Liciardi (60.José Fabián Pazymiño), Wilson Nieves. Trainer: Ernesto Guerra.
**CHI:** Adolfo Nef Sanhueza, Daniel Díaz, Elías Ricardo Figueroa Brander, Alberto Fernando Ralph Quintano, Enzo Sergio Escobar Olivares, Carlos Enzo Reinoso Valdenegro, Roberto Hodge Rivera, Ignacio Prieto Urrejola (Mario del Transito Soto Benavides), Sergio Ahumada Bacho, Osvaldo Castro Pelayos, Miguel Angel Gamboa Pedemonte. Trainer: Caupolicán Peña.
**Goal**: 0-1 Miguel Angel Gamboa Pedemonte (33).

06.03.1977, Estadio Nacional, Santiago; Attendance: 67,983
Referee: José Faville Neto (Brazil)
**CHILE - PERU**     **1-1(1-0)**
**CHI:** Adolfo Nef Sanhueza, Daniel Díaz, Elías Ricardo Figueroa Brander, Alberto Fernando Ralph Quintano, Enzo Sergio Escobar Olivares, Carlos Enzo Reinoso Valdenegro, Roberto Hodge Rivera, Ignacio Prieto Urrejola (40.Sergio Ahumada Bacho), Luis Miranda (67.Mario del Transito Soto Benavides), Osvaldo Castro Pelayos, Miguel Angel Gamboa Pedemonte. Trainer: Caupolicán Peña.
**PER:** Ramón Quiroga Arancibia, Eleazar Soria, Julio Meléndez, Héctor Eduardo Chumpitaz González, Rubén Toribio Díaz Rivas, José Manuel Velásquez Castillo, Alfredo Quesada Farías, Teófilo Juan Cubillas Arizaga (18.Hugo Alejandro Sotil Yerén), Juan José Muñante López, Percy Rojas Montero (67.Alejandro Luces), Juan Carlos Oblitas Saba. Trainer: Marcos Calderón Medrano (30).
**Goals:** 1-0 Sergio Ahumada Bacho (42), 1-1 Juan José Muñante López (73).

12.03.1977, Estadio Nacional, Lima; Attendance: 43,319
Referee: Luis Barrancos Álvarez (Bolivia)
**PERU - ECUADOR**     **4-0(1-0)**
**PER:** Ramón Quiroga Arancibia, Eleazar Soria, Julio Meléndez, Héctor Eduardo Chumpitaz González, Rubén Toribio Díaz Rivas, Alfredo Quesada Farías, José Manuel Velásquez Castillo, Juan José Muñante López, Percy Rojas Montero (68.Augusto Palacios), Hugo Alejandro Sotil Yerén (58.Alejandro Luces), Juan Carlos Oblitas Saba. Trainer: Marcos Calderón Medrano.
**ECU:** Eduardo García, Washington Méndez, Fausto Rubén Carrera, Fernando Villena, Fausto Klinger, Luis Augusto Granda, José Voltaire Villafuerte, Ecuador Figueroa (Luis Cristóbal Mantilla), José Fabián Pazymiño, Jorge Vinicio Ron, Wilson Nieves. Trainer: Ernesto Guerra.
**Goals:** 1-0 José Manuel Velásquez Castillo (19), 2-0 Juan Carlos Oblitas Saba (48), 3-0 Juan Carlos Oblitas Saba (50), 4-0 Alejandro Luces (63).

20.03.1977, Estadio Nacional, Santiago; Attendance: 15,571
Referee: Vicente Llobregat Vicedo (Venezuela)
**CHILE - ECUADOR**     **3-0(2-0)**
**CHI:** Adolfo Nef Sanhueza, Mario Enrique Galindo Calixto, Elías Ricardo Figueroa Brander, Alberto Fernando Ralph Quintano, Enzo Sergio Escobar Olivares, Manuel Antonio Rojas Zuniga (Sergio Ahumada Bacho), Rodolfo del Rosario Dubó Segovia, Héctor Pinto, Carlos Enzo Reinoso Valdenegro, Osvaldo Castro Pelayos (Julio Crisosto), Pedro Pinto. Trainer: Caupolicán Peña.
**ECU:** Walter Pinillos, Jesús Emilio Ortiz, Fausto Rubén Carrera, Fausto Klinger, Donald Iván Caicedo, Luis Augusto Granda (Ecuador Figueroa), José Voltaire Villafuerte, Juan Carlos Gómez, José Fabián Pazymiño (Wilson Nieves), Jorge Vinicio Ron, Luis Cristóbal Mantilla. Trainer: Ernesto Guerra.
**Goals:** 1-0 Elías Ricardo Figueroa Brander (29), 2-0 Osvaldo Castro Pelayos (40), 3-0 Elías Ricardo Figueroa Brander (55).

27.03.1977, Estadio Nacional, Lima; Attendance: 52,000
Referee: Arnaldo David César Coelho (Brazil)
**PERU - CHILE**     **2-0(0-0)**
**PER:** Ramón Quiroga Arancibia, José Navarro Aramburu, Julio Meléndez, Héctor Eduardo Chumpitaz González, Rubén Toribio Díaz Rivas, Alfredo Quesada Farías, José Manuel Velásquez Castillo, Percy Rojas Montero (60.Oswaldo Felipe Ramírez Salcedo), Juan José Muñante López (64.Alejandro Luces), Hugo Alejandro Sotil Yerén, Juan Carlos Oblitas Saba. Trainer: Marcos Calderón Medrano.
**CHI:** Leopoldo Manuel Vallejos Bravo, Daniel Díaz, Elías Ricardo Figueroa Brander, Alberto Fernando Ralph Quintano, Enzo Sergio Escobar Olivares, Héctor Pinto, Eddio Inostroza, Rodolfo del Rosario Dubó Segovia (Sergio Ahumada Bacho), Carlos Enzo Reinoso Valdenegro, Jorge Américo Spedaletti, Osvaldo Castro Pelayos (Pedro Pinto). Trainer: Caupolicán Peña.
**Goals:** 1-0 Hugo Alejandro Sotil Yerén (49), 2-0 Juan Carlos Oblitas Saba (55).

# SECOND ROUND

| | | | | |
|---|---|---|---|---|
| 10.07.1977 | Cali | Brazil - Peru | | 1-0(0-0) |
| 14.07.1977 | Cali | Brazil - Bolivia | | 8-0(4-0) |
| 17.07.1977 | Cali | Peru - Bolivia | | 5-0(2-0) |

### FINAL STANDINGS

| | | | | | | | | |
|---|---|---|---|---|---|---|---|---|
| 1. | **Brazil** | 2 | 2 | 0 | 0 | 9 - 0 | 4 |
| 2. | **Peru** | 2 | 1 | 0 | 1 | 5 - 1 | 2 |
| 3. | **Bolivia** | 2 | 0 | 0 | 2 | 0 - 13 | 0 |

Brazil and Peru qualified for the Final Tournament.
Bolivia qualified for the Intercontinental Play-offs.

10.07.1977, Estadio „Pascal Guerrero", Cali; Attendance: 50,345
Referee: Miguel Ángel Francisco Comesaña (Argentina)
**BRAZIL - PERU** **1-0(0-0)**
**BRA:** Émerson Leão, José Maria Rodrigues Alves "Zé Maria I", Luís Edmundo Pereira, Édino Nazareth Filho "Edinho", José Rodrigues Neto, Antônio Carlos Cerezo "Toninho Cerezo", Paulo Isidoro de Jesus (46.Dirceu José Guimarães „Dirceu II"), Roberto Rivelino, Gilberto Alves "Gil", Carlos Roberto de Oliveira "Roberto Dinamite", Paulo César Lima. Trainer: Cláudio Pècego de Moraes Coutinho.
**PER:** Ramón Quiroga Arancibia, José Navarro Aramburu, Julio Meléndez, Héctor Eduardo Chumpitaz González, Rubén Toribio Díaz Rivas, Alfredo Quesada Farías, José Manuel Velásquez Castillo, Teófilo Juan Cubillas Arizaga, Juan José Muñante López, Hugo Alejandro Sotil Yerén (61.Percy Rojas Montero), Juan Carlos Oblitas Saba. Trainer: Marcos Calderón Medrano.
**Goal**: 1-0 Gilberto Alves "Gil" (53).

14.07.1977, Estadio „Pascal Guerrero", Cali; Attendance: 38,037
Referee: Juan Ambrosio Silvagno Cavanna (Chile)
**BRAZIL - BOLIVIA** **8-0(4-0)**
**BRA:** Émerson Leão, José Maria Rodrigues Alves "Zé Maria I", Luís Edmundo Pereira, João Justino Amaral dos Santos "Amaral I", José Rodrigues Neto, Antônio Carlos Cerezo "Toninho Cerezo", Arthur Antunes Coimbra "Zico" (Marcelo de Oliveira Santos), Roberto Rivelino, Gilberto Alves "Gil", Carlos Roberto de Oliveira "Roberto Dinamite" (José Reinaldo da Lima "Reinaldo I"), Dirceu José Guimarães „Dirceu II". Trainer: Cláudio Pècego de Moraes Coutinho.
**BOL:** Carlos Conrado Jiménez Hurtado (12.Ismael Peinado Lino), Windsor Del Llano Suárez, Jaime Rimazza Vargas, Jaime Lima Guardia, Pablo Baldivieso Fernández, Raúl Morales Gonzáles (66.Arturo Saucedo Landa), Carlos Aragonés Espinosa, Eduardo Angulo Torme, Erwin Romero Escudero, Porfirio Jiménez, Miguel Aguilar. Trainer: Wilfredo Camacho.
**Goals**: 1-0 Arthur Antunes Coimbra "Zico" (3), 2-0 Arthur Antunes Coimbra "Zico" (10), 3-0 Carlos Roberto de Oliveira "Roberto Dinamite" (22), 4-0 Arthur Antunes Coimbra "Zico" (27), 5-0 Gilberto Alves "Gil" (54), 6-0 Arthur Antunes Coimbra "Zico" (60), 7-0 Antônio Carlos Cerezo "Toninho Cerezo" (69), 8-0 Marcelo de Oliveira Santos (89).

17.07.1977, Estadio „Pascal Guerrero", Cali; Attendance: 32,511
Referee: Ramón Ivanoe Barreto Ruíz (Uruguay)
**PERU - BOLIVIA** 5-0(2-0)
**PER:** Ramón Quiroga Arancibia, José Navarro Aramburu, Julio Meléndez, Héctor Eduardo Chumpitaz González, Rubén Toribio Díaz Rivas, José Manuel Velásquez Castillo, Julio Aparicio, Teófilo Juan Cubillas Arizaga (61.Oswaldo Felipe Ramírez Salcedo), Juan José Muñante López, Hugo Alejandro Sotil Yerén (46.Percy Rojas Montero), Juan Carlos Oblitas Saba. Trainer: Marcos Calderón Medrano.
**BOL:** Ismael Peinado Lino, Jorge Campos, Jaime Rimazza Vargas, Jaime Lima Guardia, Pablo Baldivieso Fernández, Windsor Del Llano Suárez, Carlos Aragonés Espinosa (57.Raúl Morales Gonzáles), Eduardo Angulo Torme, Erwin Romero Escudero, Porfirio Jiménez, Miguel Aguilar. Trainer: Wilfredo Camacho.
**Goals:** 1-0 Teófilo Juan Cubillas Arizaga (32), 2-0 Teófilo Juan Cubillas Arizaga (44), 3-0 José Manuel Velásquez Castillo (64), 4-0 Percy Rojas Montero (75), 5-0 José Manuel Velásquez Castillo (89).

## INTERCONTINENTAL PLAY-OFFS

| | | | |
|---|---|---|---|
| 29.10.1977 | Budapest | Hungary - Bolivia | 6-0(5-0) |
| 30.11.1977 | La Paz | Bolivia - Hungary | 2-3(1-2) |

### FINAL STANDINGS

| | | | | | | | | |
|---|---|---|---|---|---|---|---|---|
| 1. **Hungary** | 2 | 2 | 0 | 0 | 9 | - | 2 | 4 |
| 2. Bolivia | 2 | 0 | 0 | 2 | 2 | - | 9 | 0 |

Hungary qualified for the Final Tournament.

29.10.1977, Népstadion, Budapest; Attendance: 65,000
Referee: Ramón Ivanoe Barreto Ruíz (Urug)
**HUNGARY - BOLIVIA** 6-0(5-0)
**HUN:** Sándor Gujdár, Péter Török, István Kocsis, Zoltán Kereki, József Tóth, Tibor Nyilasi (79.László Nagy), Sándor Pintér, Sándor Zombori, László Fazekas (69.László Pusztai), András Törőcsik, Béla Várady. Trainer: Lajos Baróti.
**BOL:** Arturo Galarza Mayereger, Windsor Del Llano Suárez, Víctor Jaime Villalon, Pablo Baldivieso Fernández, René Domingo Tarritolay Tester, Carlos Aragonés Espinosa, Erwin Romero Escudero, Eduardo Angulo Torme, Mario Ovidio Mezza Soruco (79.Freddy Vargas Orozco), Luis Fernando Bastida Pascual (46.Juan Carlos Sánchez Frias), Miguel Aguilar. Trainer: Wilfredo Camacho.
**Goals:** 1-0 Tibor Nyilasi (12), 2-0 András Törőcsik (19), 3-0 Sándor Zombori (21), 4-0 Béla Várady (27), 5-0 Sándor Pintér (40), 6-0 László Nagy (81).

30.11.1977, Estadio „Libertador Simón Bolívar", La Paz; Attendance: 26,983
Referee: Charles George Rainier Corver (Holland)
**BOLIVIA - HUNGARY** 2-3(1-2)
**BOL:** Luis Galarza Mayereger, Jorge Campos, Windsor Del Llano Suárez, Víctor Jaime Villalon, René Domingo Tarritolay Tester, Carlos Aragonés Espinosa, Erwin Romero Escudero, Eduardo Angulo Torme (30.Erwin Espinoza), Mario Ovidio Mezza Soruco, Luis Fernando Bastida Pascual (46.Juan Carlos Sánchez Frias), Miguel Aguilar. Trainer: Wilfredo Camacho.
**HUN:** Sándor Gujdár, Győző Martos, István Kocsis, Zoltán Kereki, József Tóth, István Halász, Sándor Pintér, Sándor Zombori, László Fazekas (69.László Pusztai), András Törőcsik, Béla Várady (69.László Nagy). Trainer: Lajos Baróti.
**Goals:** 0-1 András Törőcsik (38), 0-2 István Halász (43), 1-2 Carlos Aragonés Espinosa (45 penalty), 1-3 Windsor Del Llano Suárez (80 own goal), 2-3 Carlos Aragonés Espinosa (90).

# NORTH, CENTRAL AMERICA & CARIBBEAN

## NORTH AMERICAN ZONE

| 24.09.1976 | Vancouver | Canada - United States | 1-1(0-1) |
| 03.10.1976 | Los Angeles | United States - Mexico | 0-0 |
| 10.10.1976 | Vancouver | Canada - Mexico | 1-0(1-0) |
| 15.10.1976 | Puebla | Mexico - United States | 3-0(2-0) |
| 20.10.1976 | Seattle | United States - Canada | 2-0(0-0) |
| 27.10.1976 | Toluca | Mexico - Canada | 0-0 |

### FINAL STANDINGS

| | | | | | | | | |
|---|---|---|---|---|---|---|---|---|
| 1. Mexico | 4 | 1 | 2 | 1 | 3 | - | 1 | 4 |
| 2. Canada | 4 | 1 | 2 | 1 | 2 | - | 3 | 4 |
| United States | 4 | 1 | 2 | 1 | 3 | - | 4 | 4 |

Mexico qualified for the CONCACAF Zone Final.

24.09.1976, Empire Stadium, Vancouver; Attendance: 15,543
Referee: Marco Antonio Dorantes García (Mexico)
**CANADA - UNITED STATES**                                                   **1-1(0-1)**
**CAN:** Anthony Chursky, Robert Iarusci, Brian Robinson, Robert Lenarduzzi, Bruce Alec Wilson, James Douglas, Robert Bolitho, Carmine Marcantonio, John Kerr, Leslie Parsons, Gary Thompson. Trainer: Eckhard Krautzun (West Germany).
**USA:** Arnold Mausser, David D'Errico, Robert Smith, Steve Pecher, James Pollihan, Alexander Skotarek, John Mason, Allan Trost (Cap), Michael Harold Flater, Frederic Grgurev, Boris Bandov. Trainer: Walter Chyzowich.
**Goals:** 0-1 Boris Bandov (8), 1-1 Robert Bolitho (77).
**Sent off:** Steve Pecher (72).

03.10.1976, Memorial Coliseum, Los Angeles; Attendance: 31,171
Referee: Dante Maglio (Canada)
**UNITED STATES - MEXICO**                                                   **0-0**
**USA:** Arnold Mausser, Neil Cohen (80.Santiago Formoso), David D'Errico, Alexander Skotarek, James Pollihan, Samuel Bick (58.Steven Ralbovsky), Allan Trost (Cap), Dennis Wit, Michael Harold Flater, Frederic Grgurev, Boris Bandov. Trainer: Walter Chyzowich.
**MEX:** Francisco Castrejón Ramírez, Manuel Nájera Siller, Eduardo Ramos Escobedo, Javier Sánchez Galindo, Arturo Vázquez Ayala, Antonio de la Torre Villalpando, Hugo Dávila Godiñez, Javier Rubén Cárdenas Martínez, Pedro Damián Alvarez Alvarado (58.Rubén Anguiano Aguilar), José Alfredo Jiménez Ramírez, Leonardo Cuéllar Rivera. Trainer: Ignacio Tréllez.

10.10.1976, Empire Stadium, Vancouver; Attendance: 17,939
Referee: Toros Kibritjan (United States)
**CANADA - MEXICO**                                                        **1-0(1-0)**
**CAN:** Anthony Chursky, Brian Robinson (24.Silvano Lenarduzzi), Robert Iarusci, Robert Lenarduzzi, Bruce Alec Wilson, John Kerr, Robert Bolitho, James Douglas, Brian Gant, Brian Budd (16.Leslie Parsons), Gary Thompson. Trainer: Eckhard Krautzun (West Germany).
**MEX:** Francisco Castrejón Ramírez, Manuel Nájera Siller, Eduardo Ramos Escobedo, Javier Sánchez Galindo, Arturo Vázquez Ayala, Antonio de la Torre Villalpando, Hugo Dávila Godiñez, Javier Rubén Cárdenas Martínez, Rubén Anguiano Aguilar, José Alfredo Jiménez Ramírez (46.José de Jesús Aceves

Padilla), Leonardo Cuéllar Rivera. Trainer: Ignacio Tréllez.
**Goal**: 1-0 Leslie Parsons (32).

15.10.1976, Estadio Cuauhtémoc, Puebla; Attendance: 35,000
Referee: Werner John Henry Winsemann (Canada)
**MEXICO - UNITED STATES**  **3-0(2-0)**
**MEX:** Francisco Castrejón Ramírez, Manuel Nájera Siller, Eduardo Ramos Escobedo, Javier Sánchez Galindo, Arturo Vázquez Ayala, Antonio de la Torre Villalpando, Hugo Dávila Godiñez, Francisco Javier Solís Cruz (59.Rubén Anguiano Aguilar), Pedro Damián Alvarez Alvarado (75.Rafael Chávez Rodríguez), José de Jesús Aceves Padilla, Leonardo Cuéllar Rivera. Trainer: Ignacio Tréllez.
**USA:** Arnold Mausser, Robert Smith, Steve Pecher, Alexander Skotarek, Santiago Formoso, David D'Errico, Allan Trost (Cap), Dennis Wit (69.Steven Ralbovsky), Michael Harold Flater, Julius Veee (46.Frederic Grgurev), Boris Bandov. Trainer: Walter Chyzowich.
**Goals**: 1-0 Francisco Javier Solís Cruz (28), 2-0 Pedro Damián Alvarez Alvarado (40), 3-0 Hugo Dávila Godiñez (83 penalty).

20.10.1976, Kingdome Stadium, Seattle; Attendance: 17,675
Referee: Lamberto Mario Rubio Vásquez (Mexico)
**UNITED STATES - CANADA**  **2-0(0-0)**
**USA:** Arnold Mausser, Robert Smith, Steve Pecher, Alexander Skotarek, James Pollihan, David D'Errico, Allan Trost (Cap), Miro Rys (76.Michael Harold Flater), Julius Veee, Fred Grgurev, Boris Bandov. Trainer: Walter Chyzowich.
**CAN:** Anthony Chursky, Silvano Lenarduzzi, Robert Iarusci, Robert Lenarduzzi, Bruce Alec Wilson, John Kerr, Robert Bolitho, James Douglas, Lloyd Glenn Johnson, Leslie Parsons, Gary Thompson (Brian Budd). Trainer: Eckhard Krautzun (West Germany).
**Goals**: 1-0 Miro Rys (55), 2-0 Julius Veee (81).

27.10.1976, Estadio "Luis Gutiérrez Dosal", Toluca; Attendance: 26,719
Referee: Henry Richard Landauer (United States)
**MEXICO - CANADA**  **0-0**
**MEX:** Francisco Castrejón Ramírez, Manuel Nájera Siller, Eduardo Ramos Escobedo, Javier Sánchez Galindo, Arturo Vázquez Ayala, Antonio de la Torre Villalpando, Hugo Dávila Godiñez, Francisco Javier Solís Cruz, Luis Montoya Ortíz, José de Jesús Aceves Padilla (58.José Alfredo Jiménez Ramírez), Leonardo Cuéllar Rivera (52.Javier Rubén Cárdenas Martínez). Trainer: Ignacio Tréllez.
**CAN:** Anthony Chursky, Robert Iarusci, Silvano Lenarduzzi, Robert Lenarduzzi, Bruce Alec Wilson, John Kerr, Robert Bolitho (58.Daryl Samson), Garry Ayre, Wesley McLeod, Lloyd Glenn Johnson, Brian Budd (76.Gary Thompson). Trainer: Eckhard Krautzun (West Germany).

**PLAY-OFF**

22.12.1976, Stade "Sylvio Cator", Port-au-Prince (Haiti); Attendance: 32,869
Referee: Guillermo Ramírez Velásquez (Colombia)
**CANADA – UNITED STATES**  **3-0(1-0)**
**CAN:** Zeljko Bilecki, Brian Robinson, Robert Iarusci, Silvano Lenarduzzi, Bruce Alec Wilson, John Kerr (Robert Bolitho), Robert Lenarduzzi, Garry Ayre, Victor Kodelja (Brian Gant), Brian Budd, Wesley McLeod. Trainer: Eckhard Krautzun (West Germany).
**USA:** Arnold Mausser, Robert Smith, Alexander Skotarek (Cap), Steve Pecher, James Pollihan, Steven Ralbovsky, Allan Trost (46.Daniel Counce), Michael Harold Flater, Frederic Grgurev (46.Santiago Formoso), Julius Veee, Boris Bandov. Trainer: Walter Chyzowich.
**Goals**: 1-0 Brian Budd (21), 2-0 Robert Lenarduzzi (80), 3-0 Robert Bolitho (87).
**Sent off**: Steve Pecher (60).
Canada qualified for the CONCACAF Zone Final.

# CENTRAL AMERICAN ZONE

| | | | |
|---|---|---|---|
| 04.04.1976 | Ciudad de Panama | Panama - Costa Rica | 3-2(0-1) |
| 02.05.1976 | Ciudad de Panama | Panama - El Salvador | 1-1(0-1) |
| 11.07.1976 | San José | Costa Rica - Panama | 3-0(3-0) |
| 01.08.1976 | San Salvador | El Salvador - Panama | 4-1(2-0) |
| 17.09.1976 | Ciudad de Panama | Panama - Guatemala | 2-4(2-0) |
| 26.09.1976 | Cd. de Guatemala | Guatemala - Panama | 7-0(3-0) |
| 01.12.1976 | San Salvador | El Salvador - Costa Rica | 1-1(1-0) |
| 05.12.1976 | San José | Costa Rica - Guatemala | 0-0 |
| 08.12.1976 | Cd. de Guatemala | Guatemala - El Salvador | 3-1(2-1) |
| 12.12.1976 | Cd. de Guatemala | Guatemala - Costa Rica | 1-1(0-0) |
| 15.12.1976 | San José | Costa Rica - El Salvador | 1-1(1-0) |
| 19.12.1976 | San Salvador | El Salvador - Guatemala | 2-0(2-0) |

## FINAL STANDINGS

| | | | | | | | | |
|---|---|---|---|---|---|---|---|---|
| 1. | Guatemala | 6 | 3 | 2 | 1 | 15 - 6 | 8 |
| 2. | El Salvador | 6 | 2 | 3 | 1 | 10 - 7 | 7 |
| 3. | Costa Rica | 6 | 1 | 4 | 1 | 8 - 6 | 6 |
| 4. | Panama | 6 | 1 | 1 | 4 | 7 - 21 | 3 |

Guatemala and El Salvador qualified for the CONCACAF Zone Final.

04.04.1976, Estadío de la Revolución, Ciudad de Panamá; Attendance: 3,477
Referee: Carlos León Cedillos (Honduras)
**PANAMA - COSTA RICA**                                                                 **3-2(0-1)**
**PAN**: Edelberto Aguirre Tejera, Morales de León, Nivaldo Acuña, Manlio Bernal, Luis Ortega, Virgilio Vázquez, Héctor Néstor Hernández, Luis Ernesto Tapia, Simeon Escobar, Agustín Sánchez, Normando Navarro (*Substitutes*: Frederico Ponce, Héctor Avila Bonilla). Trainer: Renato Panay (Chile).
**CRC**: Víctor Eduardo Monge Rojas, Alfonso Estupiñán Quiróz, José María Agüero Araya, Bolívar Quirós Saens, Enrique Argüello Vásquez, Mario Antonio Barrantes Quesada, Gerardo Chavarría, Asdrúbal Paniagua Ramírez, Alberto Ovares Cruz, Javier Jiménez Báez, William Salgado Sanchez (Jesús Manuel López). Trainer: José Etchegoyen (Uruguay).
**Goals**: 0-1 Javier Jiménez (34), 1-1 Agustín Sánchez (52), 2-1 Agustín Sánchez (63), 3-1 Frederico Ponce (75), 3-2 Mario Barrantes (86).

02.05.1976, Estadio de la Revolución, Ciudad de Panamá; Attendance: 7,345
Referee: Luis Alberto Rojas (Costa Rica)
**PANAMA - EL SALVADOR**                                                                 **1-1(0-1)**
**PAN**: Edelberto Aguirre Tejera, Morales de León, Nivaldo Acuña, Pablo Aguilar, Roberto Mahoney, Luis Ortega, Virgilio Vázquez, Héctor Néstor Hernández, Luis Ernesto Tapia, Agustín Sánchez, Frederico Ponce (*Substitutes*: Héctor Avila Bonilla). Trainer: Renato Panay (Chile).
**SLV**: Tomás Ernesto Pineda Nieto, Guillermo Rodríguez Bou, Luis Rivas Ortíz, Francisco José Jovel Cruz, Carlos Humberto Recinos Ortíz, Víctor Manuel Valencia Mejía, Eduardo Valdéz, César Acevedo, Ismael Díaz, Luis Baltazar Ramírez Zapata, David Arnoldo Cabrera (José Luis Rugamas Portillo). Trainer: Aurelio Pinto Beltrão (Brazil).
**Goals**: 0-1 Luis Baltazar Ramírez Zapata (16), 1-1 Virgilio Vázquez (50 penalty).
**Sent off**: Luis Ortega (60), José Luis Rugamas Portillo (60).

11.07.1976, Estadío "Ricardo Saprissa", San José; Attendance: 20,336
Referee: Valentin Gazo Álvarez (Nicaragua)
**COSTA RICA - PANAMA** **3-0(3-0)**
**CRC**: Marco Antonio Rojas Porras (Víctor Eduardo Monge Rojas), Alexis Alfaro, Alfonso Brenes Rivera, Frederico Méndez Rios, Mario Esquivel Castro, José Manuel Rojas Ramírez, Johnny Alvarado Cascante, Hernán Morales Martínez, Alfredo Piedra Gutiérrez (Francisco Hernández Ramírez), Carlos Solano Fernández, Javier Jiménez Báez. Trainer: José Etchegoyen (Uruguay).
**PAN**: Edelberto Aguirre Tejera, Morales de León, Nivaldo Acuña, Rafael Torres, Héctor Avila Bonilla, Sánchez Cáceres, Virgilio Vázquez, Luis Ernesto Tapia, Héctor Néstor Hernández, Agustín Sánchez, Frederico Ponce (*Substitutes*: Daniel Montillo Ruíz, Pablo Aguillar). Trainer: Renato Panay (Chile).
**Goals**: 1-0 Johnny Alvarado Cascante (11), 2-0 Johnny Alvarado Cascante (22), 3-0 Javier Jiménez (44).
**Sent off**: Nivaldo Acuña (72).

01.08.1976, Estadio Cuscatlán, San Salvador; Attendance: 36,440
Referee: Lamberto Vázquez (México)
**EL SALVADOR - PANAMA** **4-1(2-0)**
**SLV**: Tomás Ernesto Pineda Nieto, Guillermo Rodríguez Bou, Francisco José Jovel Cruz, Ramón Alfredo Fagoaga Romero, Carlos Humberto Recinos Ortíz, Eduardo Valdéz, Víctor Manuel Valencia Mejía, Werner Antonio Solís Miranda, Felix Pineda Flores, Luis Baltazar Ramírez Zapata, Ismael Díaz (Silvio Romero Aquino). Trainer: Aurelio Pinto Beltrão (Brazil).
**PAN**: Edelberto Aguirre Tejera, Luis Quíroz, Eduardo Macea, Manlio Bernal, Oscar Rodríguez, Virgilio Vázquez, Héctor Néstor Hernández, Luis Ernesto Tapia, Daniel Montillo Ruíz, Oscar Molinar, Selin González. Trainer: Renato Panay (Chile).
**Goals**: 1-0 Luis Baltazar Ramírez Zapata (7), 2-0 Luis Baltazar Ramírez Zapata (14), 3-0 Silvio Romero Aquino (69), 4-0 Luis Baltazar Ramírez Zapata (78), 4-1 Héctor Néstor Hernández (88).

17.09.1976, Estadio de la Revolución, Ciudad de Panamá; Attendance: 10,167
Referee: Carlos Manuel Álvarez Morales (Costa Rica)
**PANAMA - GUATEMALA** **2-4(2-0)**
**PAN**: Jaime Bernal (77.Oscar Molinar), Héctor Avila Bonilla, Francisco Zamora, Rodrigo Ortíz, Eduardo Macea, Luis Ernesto Tapia, Oscar Rodríguez, Virgilio Vázquez, Frederico Ponce, Daniel Montillo Ruíz, Agustín Sánchez. Trainer: Renato Panay (Chile).
**GUA**: Julio Rodolfo García Guzman, Julio Roberto Gómez Rendón, Allan Kenny Wellmann, Luis Alberto Valle Melgar, Sergio Estuardo Rivera Hernández, Benjamín Eduardo Monterroso Díaz (Peter Sandoval Mercing), Jorge Hurtarte, Edgar René Bolanos Galdamaz, Félix Alfonso McDonald Sarmiento (Oscar Enrique Sánchez Rivas), Selvin Valentine Pennant Taylor, Julio César Anderson Quiroga. Trainer: Carlos Cavagnaro (Argentina).
**Goals**: 1-0 Allan Kenny Wellmann (9 own goal), 2-0 Daniel Montillo Ruíz (25), 2-1 Selvin Valentine Pennant Taylor (51), 2-2 Oscar Enrique Sánchez Rivas (56), 2-3 Oscar Enrique Sánchez Rivas (63), 2-4 Julio César Anderson Quiroga (88).

26.09.1976, Estadio „Mateo Flores", Ciudad de Guatemala; Attendance: 20,010
Referee: Desiderio Avendano Ruíz (El Salvador)
**GUATEMALA - PANAMA** **7-0(3-0)**
**GUA**: Julio Rodolfo García Guzman, Julio Roberto Gómez Rendón, Allan Kenny Wellmann, Luis Alberto Valle Melgar, Sergio Estuardo Rivera Hernández, Benjamín Eduardo Monterroso Díaz (Peter Sandoval Mercing), Jorge Hurarte, Edgar René Bolanos Galdamaz, Oscar Enrique Sánchez Rivas, Selvin Valentine Pennant Taylor, Julio César Anderson Quiroga (Félix Alfonso McDonald Sarmiento). Trainer: Carlos Cavagnaro (Argentina).
**PAN**: Eduardo Medrano, Héctor Avila Bonilla, Francisco Zamora, Eduardo Macea, Rodrigo Ortíz, Luis Váldez (46.Alcides Contreras; 83.Tomás Valencia), Oscar Molinar, Virgilio Vázquez, Frederico Ponce, Daniel Montillo Ruíz, Agustín Sánchez. Trainer: Renato Panay (Chile).
**Goals**: 1-0 Oscar Enrique Sánchez Rivas (2), 2-0 Selvin Valentine Pennant Taylor (4), 3-0 Selvin

Valentine Pennant Taylor (40), 4-0 Oscar Enrique Sánchez Rivas (53), 5-0 Félix Alfonso McDonald Sarmiento (62), 6-0 Oscar Enrique Sánchez Rivas (68), 7-0 Peter Sandoval Mercing (69).

01.12.1976, Estadío Cuscatlán, San Salvador; Attendance: 40,868
Referee: Romulo Méndez Moliná (Guatemala)
**EL SALVADOR - COSTA RICA** **1-1(1-0)**
**SLV:** Omar Barillas, Jorge Alberto Pena, Francisco José Jovel Cruz, Ramón Alfredo Fagoaga Romero, Wilfredo Penate Calderón, Werner Antonio Solís Miranda, Víctor Manuel Valencia Mejía, José Norberto Huezo Montoya, Felix Pineda Flores, Luis Baltazar Ramírez Zapata, David Arnoldo Cabrera. Trainer: Aurelio Pinto Beltrão (Brazil).
**CRC:** Marco Antonio Rojas Porras, Alfonso Estupiñán Quiróz, Frederico Méndez Rios, Alfonso Brenes Rivera, Mario Esquivel Castro, Johnny Alvarado Cascante, José Manuel Rojas Ramírez, Gerardo Chavarría, Hernán Morales Martínez, Carlos Solano Fernández, Javier Jiménez Báez (Alfredo Piedra Gutiérrez). Trainer: José Etchegoyen (Uruguay).
**Goals:** 1-0 David Arnoldo Cabrera (27), 1-1 Javier Jiménez (78).
**Sent off:** Alfredo Piedra Gutiérrez.

05.12.1976, Estadio Nacional de la Sabana, San José; Attendance: 19,596
Referee: Alfonso Archundia Gonzáles (Mexico)
**COSTA RICA - GUATEMALA** **0-0**
**CRC:** Marco Antonio Rojas Porras, Javier Masís Figueroa, Frederico Méndez Rios, Alfonso Brenes Rivera, Mario Esquivel Castro, Hernán Morales Martínez, José Manuel Rojas Ramírez, Gerardo Chavarría, Francisco Hernández Ramírez (46.Gerardo Solano), Carlos Solano Fernández (Víctor Acuña), Javier Jiménez Báez. Trainer: José Etchegoyen (Uruguay).
**GUA:** Ricardo Antonio Piccinini Alburez, Leonardo Carlos McNish Pérez, Carlos Alfonso Monterroso, Allan Kenny Wellmann, Sergio Estuardio Rivera Hernández, Jorge Hurtarte, Benjamín Eduardo Monterroso Díaz (Julio César Anderson Quiroga), Edgar René Bolaños Galdámez (Luis Alberto Valle Melgar), René Arturo Morales, Selvin Valentine Pennant Taylor, Oscar Enrique Sánchez Rivas. Trainer: Carlos Enrique Wellmann.

08.12.1976, Estadio „Mateo Flores", Ciudad de Guatemala; Attendance: 30,535
Referee: Luis Paulino Siles Calderón (Costa Rica)
**GUATEMALA - EL SALVADOR** **3-1(2-1)**
**GUA:** Ricardo Antonio Piccinini Alburez, Leonardo Carlos McNish Pérez (Julio Roberto Gómez Rendón), Allan Kenny Wellmann, Carlos Alfonso Monterroso, Sergio Estuardo Rivera Hernández, Jorge Hurarte, Benjamín Eduardo Monterroso Díaz, Edgar René Bolaños Galdámez, René Arturo Morales (Julio César Anderson Quiroga), Selvin Valentine Pennant Taylor, Oscar Enrique Sánchez Rivas. Trainer: Carlos Enrique Wellmann.
**SLV:** Omar Barillas, Jorge Alberto Pena, Francisco José Jovel Cruz, Wilfredo Penate Calderón, Ramón Alfredo Fagoaga Romero, Víctor Manuel Valencia Mejía, Felix Pineda Flores (Juan Ramón Martínez), José Norberto Huezo Montoya (Eduardo Valdéz), Luis Baltazar Ramírez Zapata, Werner Antonio Solís Miranda, David Arnoldo Cabrera. Trainer: Aurelio Pinto Beltrão (Brazil).
**Goals:** 0-1 Víctor Manuel Valencia Mejía (14 penalty), 1-1 Leonardo Carlos McNish Pérez (19), 2-1 Benjamín Eduardo Monterroso Díaz (30), 3-1 Oscar Enrique Sánchez Rivas (80).

**12.12.1976**, Estadio „Mateo Flores", Ciudad de Guatemala; Attendance: 24,363
Referee: José Manuel Andino Pinel (Honduras)
**GUATEMALA - COSTA RICA**                                 **1-1(0-0)**
**GUA:** Ricardo Antonio Piccinini Alburez, Julio Roberto Gómez Rendón, Carlos Alfonso Monterroso, Allan Kenny Wellmann, Luis René Villavicencio, Jorge Hurarte, Edgar René Bolaños Galdámez, Benjamín Eduardo Monterroso Díaz, Félix Alfonso McDonald Sarmiento (Peter Sandoval Mercing), Selvin Valentine Pennant Taylor, Oscar Enrique Sánchez Rivas. Trainer: Carlos Enrique Wellmann.
**CRC:** Marco Antonio Rojas Porras, Javier Masís Figueroa, Frederico Méndez Rios, Alfonso Brenes Rivera, Mario Esquivel Castro, Gerardo Chavarría, José Manuel Rojas Ramírez, Hernán Morales Martínez (Johnny Alvarado Cascante), Edgar Marín Levy (William Fischer Salgado), Carlos Solano Fernández, Javier Jiménez Báez. Trainer: José Etchegoyen (Uruguay).
**Goals:** 1-0 Peter Sandoval Mercing (77), 1-1 William Fischer Salgado (89).
**Sent off:** José Manuel Rojas Ramírez (15).

**15.12.1976**, Estadío Nacional de la Sabana, San José; Attendance: 16,310
Referee: Juan Ramón Vivar (Guatemala)
**COSTA RICA - EL SALVADOR**                            **1-1(1-0)**
**CRC:** Marco Antonio Rojas Porras, Javier Masís Figueroa, Frederico Méndez Rios, Alfonso Brenes Rivera, Mario Esquivel Castro, William Fischer Salgado, Hernán Morales Martínez, Johnny Alvarado Cascante (Gerardo Chavarría), Alfredo Piedra Gutiérrez, Carlos Solano Fernández, Javier Jiménez Báez. Trainer: José Etchegoyen (Uruguay).
**SLV:** Mauricio Humberto Castillo, Jorge Alberto Pena, Francisco José Jovel Cruz, Ramón Alfredo Fagoaga Romero, Wilfredo Penate Calderón, José Luis Rugamas Portillo (José Norberto Huezo Montoya), Eduardo Valdéz, Víctor Manuel Valencia Mejía, Jorge Alberto González Barillas, David Arnoldo Cabrera, Luis Baltazar Ramírez Zapata (Felix Pineda Flores). Trainer: Aurelio Pinto Beltrão (Brazil).
**Goals:** 1-0 Javier Masís Figueroa (40), 1-1 Luis Baltazar Ramírez Zapata (75).
**Sent off:** Felix Pineda Flores.

**19.12.1976**, Estadio Cuscatlán, San Salvador; Attendance: 61,449
Referee: Alfonso Archundia Gonzáles (Mexico)
**EL SALVADOR - GUATEMALA**                          **2-0(2-0)**
**SLV:** Mauricio Humberto Castillo, Jorge Alberto Pena, Miguel Ángel Viscarra, Wilfredo Penate Calderón, Francisco José Jovel Cruz, Víctor Manuel Valencia Mejía, Juan Ramón Martínez, Eduardo Valdéz (Werner Antonio Solís Miranda), Luis Baltazar Ramírez Zapata, José Norberto Huezo Montoya, David Arnoldo Cabrera. Trainer: Aurelio Pinto Beltrão (Brazil).
**GUA:** Ricardo Antonio Piccinini Alburez, Julio Roberto Gómez Rendón, Allan Kenny Wellmann (Luis Alberto Valle Melgar), Carlos Alfonso Monterroso, Luis René Villavicencio, Jorge Hurarte, Benjamín Eduardo Monterroso Díaz, Edgar René Bolaños Galdámez, René Arturo Morales (Félix Alfonso McDonald Sarmiento), Selvin Valentine Pennant Taylor, Oscar Enrique Sánchez Rivas. Trainer: Carlos Enrique Wellmann.
**Goals:** 1-0 David Arnoldo Cabrera (1), 2-0 Víctor Manuel Valencia Mejía (12).

# CARIBBEAN ZONE

## SUBGROUP A – ROUND 1

04.07.1976　Georgetown　　Guyana - Suriname　　　　2-0(1-0)
29.08.1976　Paramaribo　　Suriname - Guyana　　　　3-0(2-0)

### FINAL STANDINGS

| | | | | | | | | |
|---|---|---|---|---|---|---|---|---|
| 1. Suriname | 2 | 1 | 0 | 1 | 3 | - | 2 | 2 |
| 2. Guyana | 2 | 1 | 0 | 1 | 2 | - | 3 | 2 |

Suriname qualified for the Second Round.

04.07.1976, Bourda Oval, Georgetown; Attendance: 12,000
Referee: Felix Gray (Trinidad and Tobago)
**GUYANA - SURINAME**　　　　　　　　　　　　　　**2-0(1-0)**
**GUY**: Wendell Sandiford, Clive Fraser, Earl ONeal, David Woodford, Gregory Thorne, Maurice Enmore, Keith Layne, Terence Nichols, Vibert Butts (70.Walter Prince), Rudolphe Hunte (70.Patrick Barton), Keith Niles.
**SUR:** Edmund Franklin Leilis, Siegfried George Brondenstein, Remie Jacques Olmberg, Kenneth Frank Borgia, Paul Rudolph Valdink, Paul Rubén Corte, Rinaldo Wensley Bundel, Frits Lambertus Purperhart, Humphrey Castillion, Errol Rudolph Emmanuelson, Trimo Anton Kasyo. Trainer: Ollie Camps.
**Goals**: 1-0 Vibert Butts (9), 2-0 Keith Niles (72).

29.08.1976, Natsjonalstadion, Paramaribo; Attendance: 13,598
Referee: Rudolphe Wooding (Trinidad and Tobago)
**SURINAME - GUYANA**　　　　　　　　　　　　　　**3-0(2-0)**
**SUR:** Edmund Franklin Leilis, Wilfred Frederik Garden, Remie Jacques Olmberg, Ewout Leefland, Siegfried George Brondenstein, Roy Glenn George, Arnold Robert Zebeda, Rinaldo Stanley Entingh (Humphrey Castillion), Henry Playfaire, Ramon Burgzorg, Errol Rudolph Emmanuelson. Trainer: Ollie Camps.
**GUY**: Wendell Sandiford, Clive Fraser, Gregory Thorne, Earl ONeal, David Woodford, Maurice Enmore, Keith Layne, Walter Devonish, Rudolphe Hunte, Keith Smart, Keith Niles (Patrick Barton).
**Goals**: 1-0 Henry Playfaire (1), 2-0 Roy Glenn George (35), 3-0 Roy Glenn George (53).

| | | | | | | | | | |
|---|---|---|---|---|---|---|---|---|---|
| 15.08.1976 | Bridgetown | | Barbados – Trinidad and Tobago | | | | | 2-1(0-0) | |
| 31.08.1976 | Port-of-Spain | | Trinidad and Tobago - Barbados | | | | | 1-0(1-0) | |

## FINAL STANDINGS

| | | | | | | | | |
|---|---|---|---|---|---|---|---|---|
| 1. | Barbados | 2 | 1 | 0 | 1 | 2 | - | 2 | 2 |
| | Trinidad and Tobago | 2 | 1 | 0 | 1 | 2 | - | 2 | 2 |

15.08.1976, National Stadium, Bridgetown; Attendance: 5,000
Referee: Josephius Steeman (Surinam)
**BARBADOS – TRINIDAD AND TOBAGO** **2-1(0-0)**
**BRB**: Charles Williams, Michael Edmee, Clarence Alleyne, Malcolm White, Ricardo Goddard, Eric Alleyne, Victor Clarke, Tennyson Sandiford, Gerald Goddard, Dennis Harewood, Elson Searle.
**TRI**: Kelvin Barclay, Renwick Williams, Russell Tesheira, Selris Figaro, Steve Pierre, Everald Cummings, Kendal Walkes, Michael Grayson, Steve David, Keith Aqui, Godfrey Harris. Trainer: Edgar Vidale.
**Goals**: 1-0 Victor Clarke (47), 2-0 Victor Clarke (54 penalty), 2-1 Steve David (83).

31.08.1976, Port of Spain; Attendance: 15,978
Referee: Theodorus Koetsier (Netherlands Antilles)
**TRINIDAD AND TOBAGO - BARBADOS** **1-0(1-0)**
**TRI**: Kelvin Barclay, Everald Cummings, Russell Tesheira, Selris Figaro, Ramon Moraldo, Steve Pierre, Leon Carpette, Anthony Douglas, Leroy de Leon, Steve David, Noel Llewellyn. Trainer: Edgar Vidale.
**BRB**: Charles Williams, Michael Edmee, Malcolm White, Ricardo Goddard, Clarence Alleyne, Victor Clarke, Dennis Harewood, Gerald Goddard, Tennyson Sandiford, Eric Alleyne, Elson Searle.
**Goal**: 1-0 Anthony Douglas (35).

## PLAY-OFF

14.09.1976, National Stadium, Bridgetown; Attendance: 4,188
Referee: Ramón Calderón (Cuba)
**BARBADOS - TRINIDAD AND TOBAGO** **1-3(1-1)**
**BRB**: Charles Williams, Michael Edmee, Malcolm White, Clarence Alleyne, Darnley Carter, Eric Alleyne, Victor Clarke, Ivor Went, Hubert Shepherd, Gerald Goddard, Elson Searle.
**TRI**: Kelvin Barclay, Anthony Russell, Russell Tesheira, Selris Figaro, Steve Pierre, Anthony Douglas, Leroy de Leon, Noel Llewellyn, Leon Carpette, Everald Cummings, Warren Archibald. Trainer: Edgar Vidale.
**Goals**: 0-1 Noel Llewellyn (3), 1-1 Victor Clarke (26), 1-2 Leon Carpette (74), 1-3 Warren Archibald (85).
Trinidad and Tobago qualified for the Second Round.

# SUBGROUP A – ROUND 2

| 14.11.1976 | Paramaribo | Suriname - Trinidad and Tobago | 1-1(1-1) |
|---|---|---|---|
| 28.11.1976 | Port-of-Spain | Trinidad and Tobago - Suriname | 2-2(1-1) |

### FINAL STANDINGS

| | | | | | | | | | |
|---|---|---|---|---|---|---|---|---|---|
| 1. | Suriname | 2 | 0 | 2 | 0 | 3 | - | 3 | 2 |
| | Trinidad and Tobago | 2 | 0 | 2 | 0 | 3 | - | 3 | 2 |

14.11.1976, Natsjonalstadion, Paramaribo; Attendance: 12,656
Referee: John Chandler (United States)
**SURINAME - TRINIDAD AND TOBAGO**      **1-1(1-1)**
**SUR:** Edmund Franklin Leilis, Siegfried Rustenberg, Wilfred Frederik Garden, Siegfried George Brondenstein, Remie Jacques Olmberg, Kenneth Frank Borgia (Henry Playfaire), Rinaldo Stanley Entingh, Arnold Robert Zebeda, Errol Rudolph Emmanuelson, Roy Glenn George, Humphrey Castillion (Delando Righters). Trainer: Ollie Camps.
**TRI:** Earl Carter, Steve Pierre, Ramon Moraldo, Selris Figaro, Leroy Spann, Leroy de Leon, Noel Llewellyn, Steve David, Warren Archibald (58.Kendall Walkes), Anthony Russell, Everald Cummings. Trainer: Edgar Vidale.
**Goals**: 1-0 Roy Glenn George (2), 1-1 Steve David (9).

28.11.1976, Queens Park Oval, Port of Spain; Attendance: 23,000
Referee: Vicente Llobregat Vicedo (Venezuela)
**TRINIDAD AND TOBAGO - SURINAME**      **2-2(1-1)**
**TRI:** Earl Carter, Russell Tesheira, Ramon Moraldo, Selris Figaro, Leon Carpette (62.Leroy Spann), Everald Cummings, Leroy de Leon, Steve Pierre, Noel Llewellyn, Steve David, Warren Archibald. Trainer: Edgar Vidale.
**SUR:** Edmund Franklin Leilis, Siegfried Rustenberg, Wilfred Frederik Garden, Remie Jacques Olmberg, Siegfried George Brondenstein (88.Milton Lieveld), Roy Glenn George, Arnold Robert Zebeda, Rinaldo Stanley Entingh, Henry Playfaire, Errol Rudolph Emmanuelson, Humphrey Castillion (66.Delando Righters). Trainer: Ollie Camps.
**Goals**: 1-0 Selris Figaro (29 penalty), 1-1 Remie Jacques Olmberg (44), 2-1 Noel Llewellyn (64), 2-2 Rinaldo Stanley Entingh (83).

### PLAY-OFF

18.12.1976, Estadio National, Cayenne (French Guiana); Attendance: 23,331
Referee: Vicente Llobregat Vicedo (Venezuela)
**SURINAME - TRINIDAD AND TOBAGO**      **3-2(0-0,2-2)**
**SUR:** Edmund Franklin Leilis, Siegfried Rustenberg (Milton Lieveld), Wilfred Frederik Garden, Siegfried George Brondenstein, Remie Jacques Olmberg, Paul Rubén Corte, Rinaldo Stanley Entingh, Arnold Robert Zebeda, Errol Rudolph Emmanuelson, Roy Glenn George, Delando Righters (Ramón Burgzorg). Trainer: Ollie Camps.
**TRI:** Kelvin Barclay, Russell Tesheira, Steve Pierre (Anthony Russell), Raymond Moraldo, Selris Figaro, Leroy de Leon (Leroy Spann), Anthony Douglas, Everald Cummings, Ronald la Forest, Steve David, Noel Llewellyn. Trainer: Edgar Vidale.
**Goals**: 0-1 Steve David, 1-1 Roy Glenn George (60), 1-2 Steve David (70), 2-2 Roy Glenn George (80), 3-2 Remie Jacques Olmberg (107 penalty).
Suriname qualified for the CONCACAF Zone Final.

# SUBGROUP B – PRELIMINARY ROUND

02.04.1976  Santo Domingo     Dominican Republic - Haiti     0-3(0-3)
17.04.1976  Port-au-Prince    Haiti - Dominican Republic     3-0(2-0)

### FINAL STANDINGS

| | | | | | | | | |
|---|---|---|---|---|---|---|---|---|
| 1. | Haiti | 2 | 2 | 0 | 0 | 6 - 0 | 4 |
| 2. | Dominican Republic | 2 | 0 | 0 | 2 | 0 - 6 | 0 |

Haiti qualified for the First Round.

02.04.1976, Estadio Olímpico „Juan Pablo Duarte", Santo Domingo; Attendance: 14,684
Referee: Michael Wuertz (United States)
**DOMINICAN REPUBLIC - HAITI**                                              **0-3(0-3)**
**DOM**: Herman Mejía, Padron Herminio, Ramón Rodríguez, Juan Trinidad, Andreas Barrientos, José de Jesús Pichardo, Francisco Arias, José Salcedo Ramírez, Luis Cornelio, Manuel Delgado, Ramón Martínez Mota.
**HAI:** Wilner Piquant, Louidor Labissiere, Ernst Jean-Joseph, Arsène Auguste, Frantz Mathieu, Claude Barthélemy, Joseph Leandre, Jean-Marie Jean-Baptiste, Philippe Vorbe, Leintz Domingue (Jean-Michel Malenkov), Pierre Bayonne (Roger Saint-Vil). Trainer: Antoine Tassy.
**Goals**: 0-1 Arsène Auguste (2), 0-2 Pierre Bayonne (29), 0-3 Jean-Marie Jean-Baptiste (32).

17.04.1976, Stade „Sylvio Cator", Port-au-Prince; Attendance: 19,478
Referee: Luis Villarejo Ramírez (Puerto Rico)
**HAITI - DOMINICAN REPUBLIC**                                              **3-0(2-0)**
**HAI:** Henri Francillon, Louidor Labissiere, Ernst Jean-Joseph, Arsène Auguste, Frantz Mathieu, Philippe Vorbe, William Baudin, Jean-Michel Malenkov, Jean-Marie Jean-Baptiste, Leintz Domingue, Pierre Bayonne. Trainer: Antoine Tassy.
**DOM**: Herman Mejía, Padron Herminio, Ramón Rodríguez, Juan Trinidad, Andreas Barrientos, José de Jesús Pichardo, Francisco Arias, Manuel Delgado, José Salcedo Ramírez, Ramón Martínez Mota.
**Goals**: 1-0 Pierre Bayonne (32), 2-0 Leintz Domingue (44), 3-0 Pierre Bayonne (63).

# SUBGROUP B – ROUND 1

30.07.1976　Oranjestad　　Netherlands Antilles - Haiti　　1-2(0-2)
14.08.1976　Port-au-Prince　Haiti - Netherlands Antilles　　7-0(4-0)

### FINAL STANDINGS

| | | | | | | | |
|---|---|---|---|---|---|---|---|
| 1. Haiti | 2 | 2 | 0 | 0 | 9 - 1 | 4 |
| 2. Netherlands Antilles | 2 | 0 | 0 | 2 | 1 - 9 | 0 |

Haiti qualified for the Second Round.

30.07.1976, Wilhelminastadion, Aruba; Attendance: 5,332
Referee: Kenneth Chaplin (Jamaica)
**NETHERLANDS ANTILLES - HAITI**　　　　　　　　　　**1-2(0-2)**
**ANT:** Jubert Eugenio Richardson, Reynold Randolph Anthony Becker, Carlos Ignacio Zimmerman, Peter Paul Engles, Henricus Maria Josephus Stelt, Hyacintho Nelson Tromp (E. Tromp), Erroll Maximino St. Jago, Thomas Kwidama, Mario Grigorio Bislip (Monico Eleuterio Ruíz), Felix Angelino Pérez, Nesidelio Ismael Ridderstap.
**HAI:** Wilner Piquant, Louidor Labissiere, Ernst Jean-Joseph, Frantz Mathieu, Jean-Claude Désir, Joseph Leandre, Leintz Domingue, Pierre Bayonne, Carlo Brevil, Jean-Marie Jean-Baptiste (William Baudin), Emmanuel Sanon. Trainer: Antoine Tassy.
**Goals**: 0-1 Emmanuel Sanon (27), 0-2 Emmanuel Sanon (39), 1-2 Monico Eleuterio Ruíz (84).
**Sent off**: William Baudin (50).

14.08.1976, Stade „Sylvio Cator", Port-au-Prince; Attendance: 10,646
Referee: José María Luis Montane Bosch (Puerto Rico)
**HAITI - NETHERLANDS ANTILLES**　　　　　　　　　　**7-0(4-0)**
**HAI:** Wilner Piquant, Louidor Labissiere, Ernst-Jean Joseph, Frantz Mathieu, Jean-Claude Désir, Joseph Leandre, Carlo Brevil, Jean-Marie Jean-Baptiste (46.Philippe Vorbe), Emmanuel Sanon, Pierre Bayonne, Leintz Domingue. Trainer: Antoine Tassy.
**ANT:** Jubert Eugenio Richardson, Reynold Randolph Anthony Becker, Carlos Ignacio Zimmerman, Isaac Bernabela, Hyacintho Nelson Tromp, Felix Angelino Pérez, Henricus Maria Josephus Stelt, Erroll Maximino St. Jago, Thomas Kwidama, Monico Eleuterio Ruíz, Mario Grigorio Bislip.
**Goals**: 1-0 Leintz Domingue (5), 2-0 Emmanuel Sanon (27), 3-0 Louidor Labissiere (30), 4-0 Leintz Domingue (41), 5-0 Carlo Brevil (50), 6-0 Pierre Bayonne (56), 7-0 Emmanuel Sanon (79).

| | | | | | | | |
|---|---|---|---|---|---|---|---|
| 15.08.1976 | Kingston | Jamaica - Cuba | | | | | 1-3(0-1) |
| 29.08.1976 | Havanna | Cuba - Jamaica | | | | | 2-0(1-0) |

## FINAL STANDINGS

| | | | | | | | | |
|---|---|---|---|---|---|---|---|---|
| 1. | Cuba | 2 | 2 | 0 | 0 | 5 - 1 | 4 |
| 2. | Jamaica | 2 | 0 | 0 | 2 | 1 - 5 | 0 |

Cuba qualified for the Second Round.

15.08.1976, National Stadium, Kingston; Attendance: 13,000
Referee: José Lizandro Freundt de la Puente (Dominican Republic)
**JAMAICA - CUBA** **1-3(0-1)**
**JAM:** Orville Anthony Edwards, Ralston Horace Moore, Errol Theophilus Barrett, Carl Alexander Brown, Calvin Clifton Stewart, David Eddison Bernard, Carlton James Smith, Clarence William Prendes (70.Andred Recardo Andrews), Rowland Rennison Phillips (55.George Adolphus Henry), Herbert George Gordon, Wesley Luke Whitley.
**CUB:** José Francisco Reinoso Zayas, Luis Holmaza Odelín, Antonio Garcés Segura, René Bonora Puertas, José Luis Elejal de Gorostiza, Andrés Roldán Cordero, Francisco Farinas Gutiérrez, Dagoberto Lara Soriano, Miguel Rivero Bonilla, Augustín Pérez Castillo, Carlos Loredo Pérez (71.Carlos Montenegro Almenares). Trainer: Sergio Pedrón.
**Goals:** 0-1 Miguel Rivero Bonilla (29), 0-2 Dagoberto Lara Soriano (50), 1-2 Carl Alexander Brown (65), 1-3 Francisco Farinas Gutiérrez (75).

29.08.1976, Estadio Latin-Americano, La Habana; Attendance: 30,000
Referee: Pastor Octavio Basilio (Dominican Republic)
**CUBA - JAMAICA** **2-0(1-0)**
**CUB:** José Francisco Reinoso Zayas, Lorenzo Sotomayor Fernández, René Bonora Puertas, Luis Holmaza Odelín (Luis Hernández Heres), Antonio Garcés Segura, Carlos Loredo Pérez, José Luis Elejal de Gorostiza, Francisco Farinas Gutiérrez, Jorge Rafael Masso Mustelier, Andrés Roldán Cordero, Augustín Pérez Castillo (Roberto Pereira Hernández). Trainer: Sergio Pedrón.
**JAM:** Orville Anthony Edwards, Ralston Horace Moore, Errol Theophilus Barrett, Carl Alexander Brown, Calvin Clifton Stewart, David Eddison Bernard, Martin Woodstock, Lorne Garfield Donaldson, Herbert George Gordon, Clarence William Prendes, Rowland Rennison Phillips.
**Goals:** 1-0 Francisco Farinas Gutiérrez (42), 2-0 Augustín Pérez Castillo (77).
**Sent off:** Sergio Pedrón.

# SUBGROUP B – ROUND 2

| 28.11.1976 | Havanna | Cuba - Haiti | 1-1(1-0) |
| 11.12.1976 | Port-au-Prince | Haiti - Cuba | 1-1(0-0) |

## FINAL STANDINGS

| | | | | | | | | |
|---|---|---|---|---|---|---|---|---|
| 1. | Cuba | 2 | 0 | 2 | 0 | 2 - 2 | 2 |
| | Haiti | 2 | 0 | 2 | 0 | 2 - 2 | 2 |

28.11.1976, Estadio Latino-Americano, La Habana; Attendance: 25,593
Referee: Karl Stewart (Jamaica)
**CUBA - HAITI** 1-1(1-0)
**CUB:** José Francisco Reinoso Zayas, Antonio Garcés Segura, Jorge Rafael Masso Mustelier, Regino Delgado Robau, Carlos Loredo Pérez, René Bonora Puertas, Francisco Farinas Gutiérrez, Luis Holmaza Odelín, Luis Manuel Sánchez Téllez, Andrés Roldán Cordero, Ramón Núñez Armas. Trainer: Sergio Pedrón.
**HAI:** Henri Francillon, Louidor Labissiere, Wilner Nazaire, Arsène Auguste, Frantz Mathieu (33.Charles Vorbe), Jean-Marie Jean-Baptiste, Eduard Antoine, Philippe Vorbe (38.Jean-Michel Malenkov), Leintz Dominigue, Emmanuel Sanon, Jean-Claude Désir. Trainer: Antoine Tassy.
**Goals**: 1-0 Ramón Núñez Armas (1), 1-1 Emmanuel Sanon (54).

11.12.1976, Stade „Sylvio Cator", Port-au-Prince; Attendance: 20,000
Referee: José María Luis Montane Bosch (Puerto Rico)
**HAITI - CUBA** 1-1(0-0)
**HAI:** Wilner Piquant, Frantz Mathieu, Wilner Nazaire, Ernst Jean-Joseph, Arsène Auguste, Eduard Antoine, Jean-Claude Désir, Jean-Marie Jean-Baptiste (Philippe Vorbe), Leintz Domingue, Jean-Michel Malenkov (Charles Vorbe), Emmanuel Sanon. Trainer: Antoine Tassy.
**CUB:** José Francisco Reinoso Zayas, Luis Holmaza Odelín, Antonio Garcés Segura, René Bonora Puertas, Andrés Roldán Cordero, Lazaro Amado Povea, Ramón Núñez Armas (Roberto Pereira Hernández), Francisco Farinas Gutiérrez (Augustín Pérez Castillo), Regino Delgado Robau, Jorge Rafael Masso Mustelier, Carlos Loredo Pérez. Trainer: Sergio Pedrón.
**Goals**: 0-1 Andrés Roldán Cordero (79), 1-1 Emmanuel Sanon (81).
**Sent off**: Jorge Rafael Masso Mustelier (85).

## PLAY-OFF

29.12.1976, Ciudad Estadio de la Revolución, de Panamá (Panama); Attendance: 27,812
Referee: Mario Antonio Dorantes (Mexico)
**HAITI - CUBA** 2-0(0-0)
**HAI:** Henri Francillon, Leintz Domingue, Ernst Jean-Joseph, Arsène Auguste, Wilner Nazaire, Jean-Claude Désir, Carlo Brevil, Philippe Vorbe, Eduard Antoine, Emmanuel Sanon, Pierre Bayonne. Trainer: Antoine Tassy.
**CUB:** José Francisco Reinoso Zayas, Luis Holmaza Odelín, Antonio Garcés Segura, René Bonora Puertas, José Luis Elejal de Gorostiza, Andrés Roldán Cordero, Lazaro Amado Poves, Francisco Farinas Gutiérrez, Regino Delgado Robau, Carlos Loredo Pérez, Roberto Pereira Hernández. Trainer: Sergio Pedrón.
**Goals**: 1-0 Leintz Domingue (63), 2-0 Jean-Claude Désir (83 penalty).
Haiti qualified for the CONCACAF Zone Final.

# CONCACAF ZONE FINAL

| | | | |
|---|---|---|---|
| 08.10.1977 | Monterrey | Guatemala – Suriname | 3-2(2-1) |
| 08.10.1977 | Monterrey | Canada – El Salvador | 1-2(0-1) |
| 09.10.1977 | Ciudad de México | Mexico – Haiti | 4-1(1-0) |
| 12.10.1977 | Ciudad de México | Canada – Suriname | 2-1(1-1) |
| 12.10.1977 | Ciudad de México | Mexico – El Salvador | 3-1(1-1) |
| 12.10.1977 | Monterrey | Guatemala – Haiti | 1-2(0-2) |
| 15.10.1977 | Monterrey | Mexico – Suriname | 8-1(3-1) |
| 16.10.1977 | Ciudad de México | El Salvador – Haiti | 0-1(0-1) |
| 16.10.1977 | Ciudad de México | Canada – Guatemala | 2-1(2-0) |
| 19.10.1977 | Ciudad de México | Mexico – Guatemala | 2-1(1-1) |
| 20.10.1977 | Monterrey | El Salvador – Suriname | 3-2(1-0) |
| 20.10.1977 | Monterrey | Canada – Haiti | 1-1(0-0) |
| 22.10.1977 | Monterrey | Mexico – Canada | 3-1(2-1) |
| 23.10.1977 | Ciudad de México | Guatemala – El Salvador | 2-2(0-1) |
| 23.10.1977 | Ciudad de México | Haiti – Suriname | 1-0(1-0) |

08.10.1977, Estadio Tecnológico, Monterrey (Mexico); Attendance: 42,000
Referee: Michael Wuertz (USA)
**GUATEMALA - SURINAME**      **3-2(2-1)**
**GUA**: Julio Rodolfo García Guzmán, Julio Roberto Gómez Rendón, Allan Kenny Wellmann, Edgar René Bolaños Galdámez, Sergio Estuardo Rivera Hernández, Luis Alberto Valle Melgar, Benjamín Eduardo Monterroso Díaz (72.Mario René Alfaro Noriega), Félix Alfonso McDonald Sarmiento, Oscar Enrique Sánchez Rivas (58.José Emilio Nazareno Mitrovich), Edgar Hernán González, Julio César Anderson Quiroga. Trainer: Carlos Enrique Wellmann.
**SUR**: Edmund Franklin Leilis, Roy Vandenburg, Wilfred Frederik Garden, Remie Jacques Olmberg, Roy Glenn George, Siegfried George Brondenstein, Fritz Lambertus Purperhart, Delando Righters, Rinaldo Stanley Entingh, Errol Rudolph Emmanuelson, Edwin Reiner Schal (72.John Castillon). Trainer: Alexander Bratwaite.
**Goals**: 0-1 Edwin Reiner Schal (2), 1-1 Félix Alfonso McDonald Sarmiento (16), 2-1 Félix Alfonso McDonald Sarmiento (38), 2-2 Delano Righters (55), 3-2 Mario René Alfaro Noriega (85).

08.10.1977, Estadio Tecnológico, Monterrey (Mexico); Attendance: 42,000
Referee: Luis Pestarino (Argentina)
**CANADA – EL SALVADOR**      **1-2(0-1)**
**CAN**: Zeljko Bilecki, John McGrane, Silvano Lenarduzzi, Garry Ayre, Bruce Wilson, Robert Bolitho (81.Leslie Parsons), Eugene Strenicer, Brian Reginald Gant, Victor Kodelja, Ike MacKay, Peter Roe (72.Brian Budd). Trainer: Eckhard Krautzun (West Germany).
**SLV**: Alberto Fay Dessent, Francisco José Jovel Cruz, Carlos Humberto Recinos Ortíz, Ramón Alfredo Fagoaga Romero, Jorge Alberto Peña, José Norberto Huezo Montoya (89.Héctor Alcides Pichioni), Sergio Alfredo Rivera, Juan Alberto Quinteros, Jorge Alberto González Barillas (73.Eduardo Valdéz), Mario Helmer Rosas, Luis Baltazar Ramírez Zapata. Trainer: Juan Ricardo Faccio (Uruguay).
**Goals**: 0-1 Luis Baltazar Ramírez Zapata (43), 0-2 Luis Baltazar Ramírez Zapata (83), 1-2 Brian Budd (86)

09.10.1977, Estadio Azteca, Ciudad de México; Attendance: 108,000
Referee: Ramón Ivannoe Barreto Ruíz (Uruguay)
**MEXICO – HAITI**      **4-1(1-0)**
**MEX**: Francisco Castrejón Ramírez, Manuel Nájera Siller, Carlos Gómez Casillas, Eduardo Ramos Escobedo, Arturo Vázquez Ayala, Antonio de la Torre Villalpando, Rafael Chávez Rodríguez (65.Javier Rubén Cárdenas Martínez), Leonardo Cuéllar Rivera, Cristóbal Ortega Martínez, José Alfredo Jiménez Ramírez (46.Víctor Rangel Ayala), Hugo Sánchez Márquez. Trainer: José Antonio Roca García.
**HAI**: Henri Francillon, Pierre Bayonne, Ernst Jean-Joseph, Frantz Mathieu, Arsène Auguste, Eduard Antoine (67.Louidor Labissiere), Wilner Nazaire (51.Gérard Romulus), Jean-Claude Désir, Guy Dorsainville, Emmanuel Sanon, Leintz Domingue. Trainer: Josef Piontek (West Germany).
**Goals**: 1-0 Hugo Sánchez Márquez (30), 2-0 Víctor Rangel Ayala (46), 3-0 Víctor Rangel Ayala (65), 3-1 Arsène Auguste (78), 4-1 Víctor Rangel Ayala (82).

12.10.1977, Estadio Azteca, Ciudad de México (Mexico); Attendance: 90,000
Referee: Luis Paulino Siles Calderón (Costa Rica)
**CANADA – SURINAME**      **2-1(1-1)**
**CAN**: Anthony Chursky (46.Zeljko Bilecki), Robert Iarusci, Silvano Lenarduzzi, Garry Ayre, Bruce Wilson, Robert Lenarduzzi, Eugene Strenicer, Milovan Bakic, Victor Kodelja (46.Brian Budd), Leslie Parsons, Ike MacKay. Trainer: Eckhard Krautzun (West Germany).
**SUR**: Errol de Mees, Roy Vandenburg, Wilfred Frederik Garden, Remie Jacques Olmberg, Siegfried George Brondenstein, Roy Glenn George, Arnold Robert Zebeda (Fritz Lambertus Purperhart), Rinaldo Stanley Entingh, Delando Righters, Edwin Reiner Schal, Paul Rubén Corte (John Castillon). Trainer: Alexander Bratwaite.
**Goals**: 1-0 Leslie Parsons (33), 1-1 Remie Jacques Olmberg (39 penalty), 2-1 Milovan Bakic (75).

12.10.1977, Estadio Azteca, Ciudad de México; Attendance: 110,000
Referee: Toros Kibritjan (United States)
**MEXICO – EL SALVADOR**      **3-1(1-1)**
**MEX**: José Pilar Reyes Requenes, Manuel Nájera Siller, Carlos Gómez Casillas, Eduardo Ramos Escobedo, Arturo Vázquez Ayala, Antonio de la Torre Villalpando, Javier Rubén Cárdenas Martínez (80.José Luis Real Casilla), Leonardo Cuéllar Rivera, Cristóbal Ortega Martínez (60.Raúl Isiordia Ayón), Víctor Rangel Ayala, Hugo Sánchez Márquez. Trainer: José Antonio Roca García.
**SLV**: Alberto Fay Dessent, Francisco José Jovel Cruz, Carlos Humberto Recinos Ortíz, Ramón Alfredo Fagoaga Romero, Jorge Alberto Peña, José Norberto Huezo Montoya, Sergio Alfredo Rivera, Juan Alberto Quinteros, Luis Baltazar Ramírez Zapata, Mario Helmer Rosas (67.Eduardo Valdéz), Jorge Alberto González Barillas (30.Víctor Manuel Mejía Valencia). Trainer: Juan Ricardo Faccio (Uruguay).
**Goals**: Javier Rubén Cárdenas Martínez (36), Víctor Rangel Ayala (59), Víctor Rangel Ayala (90).

12.10.1977, Estadio Tecnológico, Monterrey (Mexico); Attendance: 13,465
Referee: Luis Pestarino (Argentina)
**GUATEMALA – HAITI**      **1-2(0-2)**
**GUA**: Ricardo Antonio Piccinini Alburez, Julio Roberto Gómez Rendón, Allan Kenny Wellmann, Edgar René Bolaños Galdamez, Sergio Estuardo Rivera Hernández, Luis Alberto Valle Melgar, Benjamín Eduardo Monterroso Díaz, Félix Alfonso McDonald Sarmiento, Oscar Enrique Sánchez Rivas (Julio César Anderson Quiroga), Edgar Hernán González (José Emilio Nazareno Mitrovich), Juan Bautista Rozotto. Trainer: Carlos Enrique Wellmann.
**HAI**: Henri Francillon, Pierre Bayonne, Frantz Mathieu, Ernst Jean-Joseph, Arsène Auguste, Eduard Antoine, Gérard Romulus, Jean-Claude Désir, Leintz Domingue (Jean-Marie Jean-Baptiste), Guy Dorsainville, Emmanuel Sanon. Trainer: Josef Piontek (West Germany).
**Goals**: 0-1 Leintz Domingue (20 penalty), 0-2 Pierre Bayonne (44), 1-2 José Emilio Nazareno Mitrovich (58).

15.10.1977, Estadio Tecnológico, Monterrey; Attendance: 52,000
Referee: José Luis Valverde Salazar (Costa Rica)
**MEXICO – SURINAME**                                                     **8-1(3-1)**
**MEX**: José Pilar Reyes Requenes, René Trujillo Caloca, Carlos Gómez Casillas, Eduardo Ramos Escobedo, Arturo Vázquez Ayala, José Luis Real Casilla, Manuel Guillén Espinoza, Francisco Javier Solís Cruz (54.Rafael Chávez Rodríguez), Raúl Isiordia Ayón, Víctor Rangel Ayala (54.José Alfredo Jiménez Ramírez), Hugo Sánchez Márquez. Trainer: José Antonio Roca García.
**SUR**: Edmund Franklin Leilis, Siegfried Rustenberg (78.Delano Righters), Wilfred Frederik Garden, Ewout Leefland, Siegfried George Brondenstein, Fritz Lambertus Purperhart, Remie Jacques Olmberg, Arnold Robert Zebeda (51.John Castillon), Rinaldo Stanley Entingh, Edwin Reiner Schal, Errol Rudolph Emmanuelson. Trainer: Alexander Bratwaite.
**Goals**: 0-1 Remie Jacques Olmberg (23 penalty), 1-1 Víctor Rangel Ayala (25), 2-1 Raúl Isiordia Ayón (37), 3-1 Hugo Sánchez Márquez (39), 4-1 Raúl Isiordia Ayón (49), 5-1 José Alfredo Jiménez Ramírez (73), 6-1 José Alfredo Jiménez Ramírez (84), 7-1 Rafael Chávez Rodríguez (86), 8-1 Hugo Sánchez Márquez (90).

16.10.1977, Estadio Azteca, Ciudad de México (Mexico); Attendance: 25,000
Referee: Ramón Ivannoe Barreto Ruíz (Uruguay)
**CANADA – GUATEMALA**                                                    **2-1(2-0)**
**CAN**: Anthony Chursky, Robert Iarusci, Silvano Lenarduzzi, Garry Ayre, Bruce Wilson, Robert Lenarduzzi, Eugene Strenicer, Robert Bolitho, Milovan Bakic (Brian Reginald Gant), Leslie Parsons, Ike MacKay (Gary Thompson). Trainer: Eckhard Krautzun (West Germany).
**GUA**: Julio Rodolfo García Guzmán, Luis Alberto Valle Melgar (50.René Cordero Toledo), Edgar René Bolaños Galdámez, Julio Roberto Gómez Rendón, Allan Kenny Wellmann, Juan Bautista Rozotto (46.Mario René Alfaro Noriega), Félix Alfonso McDonald Sarmiento, Benjamín Eduardo Monterroso Díaz, Sergio Estuardo Rivera Hernández, Oscar Enrique Sánchez Rivas, José Emilio Nazareno Mitrovich. Trainer: Carlos Enrique Wellmann.
**Goals**: 1-0 Leslie Parsons (21), 2-0 Robert Lenarduzzi (34), 2-1 Mario René Alfaro Noriega (78).

16.10.1977, Estadio Azteca, Ciudad de México (Mexico); Attendance: 53,978
Referee: Ramón Calderón Castro (Cuba)
**EL SALVADOR – HAITI**                                                   **0-1(0-1)**
**SLV**: Alberto Fay Dessent, Francisco José Jovel Cruz, Ramón Alfredo Fagoaga Romero, Jorge Alberto Peña, Wilfredo Penate Calderón, Carlos Humberto Recinos Ortíz, Sergio Alfredo Rivera, José Norberto Huezo Montoya, Jorge Alberto González Barillas, Mario Helmer Rosas (David Arnoldo Cabrera), Silvio Romero Aquino (Eduardo Valdéz). Trainer: Juan Ricardo Faccio (Uruguay).
**HAI**: Henri Francillon, Pierre Bayonne, Frantz Mathieu, Ernst Jean-Joseph, Arsène Auguste, Eduard Antoine, Gérald Romulus, Jean-Claude Désir (Daniel Cadet), Leintz Domingue, Guy Dorsainville (Louidor Labissiere), Emmanuel Sanon. Trainer: Josef Piontek (West Germany).
**Goal**: 0-1 Emmanuel Sanon (24).

19.10.1977, Estadio Azteca, Ciudad de México; Attendance: 110,000
Referee: Luis Pestarino (Argentina)
**MEXICO – GUATEMALA**                                                    **2-1(1-1)**
**MEX**: Francisco Castrejón Ramírez, Manuel Nájera Siller, Carlos Gómez Casillas, Eduardo Ramos Escobedo, Arturo Vázquez Ayala, Antonio de la Torre Villalpando, Javier Rubén Cárdenas Martínez (72.José Luis Real Casilla), Leonardo Cuéllar Rivera, Cristóbal Ortega Martínez, Víctor Rangel Ayala (82.José de Jesús Aceves Padilla), Hugo Sánchez Márquez. Trainer: José Antonio Roca García.
**GUA**: Julio Rodolfo García Guzmán, Edgar René Bolaños Galdámez, Benjamín Eduardo Monterroso Díaz, Sergio Estuardo Rivera Hernández, Juan José Pérez Monge, Eduardo Salguero Ruíz, Julio Roberto Gómez Rendón, Leonardo Carlos McNish Pérez (68.Juan Bautista Rozzotto), Mario René Alfaro Noriega, José Emilio Nazareno Mitrovich, Julio César Anderson Quiroga. Trainer: Carlos Enrique Wellmann.
**Goals**: 1-0 Arturo Vázquez Ayala (37 penalty), 1-1 José Emilio Nazareno Mitrovich (44), 2-1 Javier Rubén Cárdenas Martínez (54).

20.10.1977, Estadio Tecnológico, Monterrey (Mexico); Attendance: 30,000
Referee: José Luis Valverde Salazar (Costa Rica)
**CANADA – HAITI**                                                                           **1-1(0-0)**
**CAN:** Anthony Chursky, Robert Iarusci, Silvano Lenarduzzi, Garry Ayre, Bruce Wilson, Robert Lenarduzzi, Eugene Strenicer (76.Robert Bolitho), Milovan Bakic, John McGrane, Leslie Parsons, Ike MacKay (59.Gary Thompson). Trainer: Eckhard Krautzun (West Germany).
**HAI:** Henri Francillon, Pierre Bayonne (62.Josué Constant), Frantz Mathieu, Ernst Jean-Joseph, Arsène Auguste, Eduard Antoine, Gérard Romulus (66.Guy Dorsainville), Louidor Labissiere, Leintz Domingue, Emmanuel Sanon, Daniel Cadet. Trainer: Josef Piontek (West Germany).
**Goals**: 0-1 Guy Dorsainville (78), 1-1 Milovan Bakic (90).

20.10.1977, Estadio Azteca, Ciudad de México (Mexico); Attendance: 34,476
Referee: Carlyle Crockwell (Bermuda)
**EL SALVADOR – SURINAME**                          **3-2(1-0)**
**SLV**: Alberto Fay Dessent, Francisco José Jovel Cruz, Ramón Alfredo Fagoaga Romero, Luis Felipe Romero (66.Guillermo Rodríguez Bou), Jorge Alberto Peña, José Norberto Huezo Montoya, Víctor Manuel Mejía Valencia, Juan Alberto Quinteros (56.Sergio Alfredo Rivera), Mario Helmer Rosas, Jorge Alberto González Barillas, David Arnoldo Cabrera. Trainer: Juan Ricardo Faccio (Uruguay).
**SUR**: Errol de Mees, Roy Vandenburg (Harold Forster), Wilfred Frederik Garden, Remie Jacques Olmberg, Siegfried George Brondenstein, Roy Glenn George, Fritz Lambertus Purperhart, Delano Righters (Paul Rubén Corte), Rinaldo Stanley Entingh, Errol Rudolph Emmanuelson, Edwin Reiner Schal. Trainer: Alexander Bratwaite.
**Goals**: 1-0 Jorge Alberto González Barillas (42), 1-1 Errol Rudolph Emmanuelson (58), 2-1 Mario Helmer Rosas (77), 3-1 Mario Helmer Rosas (87), 3-2 Remie Jacques Olmberg (89 penalty).

22.10.1977, Estadio Tecnológico, Monterrey; Attendance: 55,000
Referee: Rudolph Moses (Netherlands Antilles)
**MEXICO – CANADA**                                               **3-1(2-1)**
**MEX:** Francisco Castrejón Ramírez, Manuel Nájera Siller, Alfredo Tena Garduño, Javier Guzmán Colin, Arturo Vázquez Ayala, Antonio de la Torre Villalpando, Francisco Javier Solís Cruz (46.José de Jesús Aceves Padilla), Leonardo Cuéllar Rivera, Raúl Isiordia Ayón, José Alfredo Jiménez Ramírez, Hugo Sánchez Márquez (75.Cristóbal Ortega Martínez). Trainer: José Antonio Roca García.
**CAN:** Anthony Chursky, Robert Iarusci, Silvano Lenarduzzi, Garry Ayre, Bruce Richardson Twamley (60.John McGrane), Robert Bolitho, Milovan Bakic, Brian Reginald Gant (88.Eugene Strenicer), Peter Roe, Leslie Parsons, Gary Thompson. Trainer: Eckhard Krautzun (West Germany).
**Goals**: 0-1 Leslie Parsons (9), 1-1 Javier Guzmán (39), 2-1 Javier Guzmán (44), 3-1 Hugo Sánchez Márquez (65).
**Sent off**: Peter Roe (34).

23.10.1977, Estadio Azteca, Ciudad de México (Mexico); Attendance: 18,630
Referee: Carlos Roberto Ortíz Pérez (Honduras)
**HAITI – SURINAME**                                                 **1-0(1-0)**
**HAI**: Henri Francillon, Ernst Jean-Joseph, Pierre Bayonne, Frantz Mathieu, Arsène Auguste, Eduard Antoine, Gérald Romulus (Josué Constant), Daniel Cadet, Louidor Labissiere (Jean-Marie Jean-Baptiste), Guy Dorsainville, Leintz Domingue. Trainer: Josef Piontek (West Germany).
**SUR**: Errol de Mees, Harold Forster, Wilfred Frederik Garden, Remie Jacques Olmberg, Siegfried George Brondenstein, Roy Glenn George (Fritz Lambertus Purperhart), Paul Rubén Corte, Delano Righters, Edwin Reiner Schal, John Castillon (Arnold Robert Zebeda), Rinaldo Stanley Entingh. Trainer: Alexander Bratwaite.
**Goal**: 1-0 Leintz Domingue (7).

23.10.1977, Estadio Tecnológico, Monterrey (Mexico); Attendance: 21,483
Referee: José Lizandri Freundt De la Puente (Dominican Republic)
**GUATEMALA – EL SALVADOR** **2-2(0-1)**
**GUA:** Ricardo Antonio Piccinini Alburez, Sergio Estuardo Rivera Hernández, Benjamín Eduardo Monterroso Díaz, Allan Kenny Wellmann, Oswaldo Morales Pinzón, Juan Bautista Rozotto (35.Eduardo Salguero Ruíz), Julio Roberto Gómez Rendón, Juan José Pérez Monge, Edgar Hernán González (21.Luis Alberto Valle Melgar), Félix Alfonso McDonald Sarmiento, Julio César Anderson Quiroga. Trainer: Carlos Enrique Wellmann.
**SLV:** Alberto Fay Dessent, Francisco José Jovel Cruz, Guillermo Rodríguez Bou, Ramón Alfredo Fagoaga Romero, Wilfredo Penate Calderón, Jorge Alberto González Barillas (87.Werner Antonio Solís Miranda), Sergio Alfredo Rivera, Juan Alberto Quinteros, José Norberto Huezo Montoya, Mario Helmer Rosas (63.David Arnoldo Cabrera), Luis Baltazar Ramírez Zapata. Trainer: Juan Ricardo Faccio (Uruguay).
**Goals:** 0-1 Mario Helmer Rosas (42), 1-1 Sergio Estuardo Rivera Hernández (63), 2-1 Sergio Estuardo Rivera Hernández (78), 2-2 José Norberto Huezo Montoya (84).

### FINAL STANDINGS

| | | | | | | | | | |
|---|---|---|---|---|---|---|---|---|---|
| 1. | **Mexico** | 5 | 5 | 0 | 0 | 20 | - | 5 | 10 |
| 2. | Haiti | 5 | 3 | 1 | 1 | 6 | - | 6 | 7 |
| 3. | El Salvador | 5 | 2 | 1 | 2 | 8 | - | 9 | 5 |
| 4. | Canada | 5 | 2 | 1 | 2 | 7 | - | 8 | 5 |
| 5. | Guatemala | 5 | 1 | 1 | 3 | 8 | - | 10 | 3 |
| 6. | Suriname | 5 | 0 | 0 | 5 | 6 | - | 17 | 0 |

Mexico qualified for the Final Tournament.

# AFRICA

## PRELIMINARY ROUND

| 07.03.1976 | Freetown | Sierra Leone – Niger | 5-1(1-1) |
|---|---|---|---|
| 21.03.1976 | Niamey | Niger – Sierra Leone | 2-1(1-1) |

### FINAL STANDINGS

| | | | | | | | | |
|---|---|---|---|---|---|---|---|---|
| 1. | Sierra Leone | 2 | 1 | 0 | 1 | 6 - 3 | 2 |
| 2. | Niger | 2 | 1 | 0 | 1 | 3 - 6 | 2 |

Sierra Leone qualified for the First Round.

07.03.1976, National Stadium, Freetown; Attendance: 4,250
Referee: Aguiahr Komla Barto (Togo)
**SIERRA LEONE - NIGER** **5-1(1-1)**
**SLE**: Frank Jongo Williams, Edward Campbell, Abu Bangoura, Albert Conteh (57.Christian Cole), Umaru Sesay, Ibrahim Jalloh, Kama Dumbuya, William Sango, Brima Kamara, Wasieu Sounmonu, Ade Swarray (46.Samuel Turay). Trainer: Stephen Bio.
**NIG**: Damane Mahamane Salaou, Moussa Sani Dari, Ali Hamani, Mahamadou Islam Hali (46.Omar Abdou), Issa Amadou, Yaye Yacouba, Boukari Adamou, Harouna Tondi, Momoud Ousmane (46.Morou Adamou), Moussa Kamfideni, Sanda Seydou.
**Goals**: 0-1 Boukari Adamou (17), 1-1 Kama Dumbuya (37), 2-1 Wasieu Sounmonu (57), 3-1 Wasieu Sounmonu (66), 4-1 Kama Dumbaya (68), 5-1 Samuel Turay (70).

21.03.1976, Stade National, Niamey; Attendance: 1,641
Referee: Thompson Shakirudeen Badru (Nigeria)
**NIGER – SIERRA LEONE** **2-1(1-1)**
**NIG**: Damane Mahamane Salaou, Moussa Sani Dari, Momoud Ousmane, Damano Salaou, Issa Amadou, Yaye Yacouba, Alidou Zibo, Boukari Adamou, Moussa Kamfideni, Sanda Seydou, Harouna Tondi.
**SLE**: Frank Jongo Williams, Edward Campbell, Abu Bangoura, Albert Conteh, Umaru Sesay, Ibrahim Jalloh, Brima Kamara, William Sango, Kama Dumbuya, Wasieu Sounmonu, Ade Swarray. Trainer: Stephen Bio.
**Goals**: 1-0 Sanda Seydou (36), 1-1 William Sango (37), 2-1 Moussa Kamfideni (52).

| 13.03.1976 | Ouagadougou | Upper Volta – Mauritania | 1-1(0-0) |
|---|---|---|---|
| 28.03.1976 | Nouakchott | Mauritania – Upper Volta | 0-2(0-1) |

### FINAL STANDINGS

| | | | | | | | | |
|---|---|---|---|---|---|---|---|---|
| 1. | Upper Volta | 2 | 1 | 1 | 0 | 3 - 1 | 3 |
| 2. | Mauritania | 2 | 0 | 1 | 1 | 1 - 3 | 1 |

Upper Volta qualified for the First Round.

13.03.1976, Stade Municipal, Ouagadougou; Attendance: 3,323
Referee: Amadou Mamoudou (Niger)
**UPPER VOLTA – MAURITANIA** **1-1(0-0)**
**UPV**: Sidiki Diarra, Modeste Dah Sehira, Zakaria Sanou, Alassane Guiré, Tewinde Compaoré, Ladji Coulibaly, Hubert Hien, Jean-Baptiste Ilboudo, Joseph Kaboré, Zakaria Sanou, Dramana Koné. Trainer: Otto Pfister (West Germany).

**MTN**: Mamadou N'Daw, Lam Papa Malick, Diakkaté Cheikhatou, Bouya Ba Oumar, Gagny Coulibaly, Ould Nagy Sid El Moctar, Brahim Ould MBarreck, Abdoulaye Fayé, D'Jibril N'Diaye, Ahmed Mohammed Cheikhatou, Ould Ahmed Abdoulaye Fall.
**Goals**: 1-0 Joseph Kaboré (44 penalty), 1-1 Abdoulaye Fayé (68 penalty).

28.03.1976, Stade National, Nouackchott; Attendance: 1,782
Referee: Mody Ba (Mali)
**MAURITANIA – UPPER VOLTA** 0-2(0-1)
**MTN**: *No line-up available.*
**UPV**: Sidiki Diarra, Modeste Dah Sehira, Alassane Guiré, Tewinde Compaoré, Ladji Coulibaly, René Nikiema, Corneille Nignan, Jo Ouattara, Kouligo Zoma, Dramana Koné, Gaucher. Trainer: Otto Pfister (West Germany).
**Goals**: 0-1 Kouligo Zoma (32), 0-2 Joseph Ouattara (57).

## FIRST ROUND

## SUBGROUP A

| 01.04.1976 | Alger | Algeria - Libya | 1-0(0-0) |
| 16.04.1976 | Tripoli | Libya - Algeria | 0-0 |

### FINAL STANDINGS

| | | | | | | | | | |
|---|---|---|---|---|---|---|---|---|---|
| 1. | Algeria | 2 | 1 | 1 | 0 | 1 | - | 0 | 3 |
| 2. | Libya | 2 | 0 | 1 | 1 | 0 | - | 1 | 1 |

Algeria qualified for the Second Round.

01.04.1976, Stade du 5$^{ème}$ Juillet, Alger; Attendance: 20,267
Referee: Jean Dubach (Switzerland)
**ALGERIA - LIBYA** 1-0(0-0)
**ALG**: Abdenour Kaoua, Mohammed Khedis, Abdelmalek Ali Messaoud, Zoubir Maaziz, Djemal Keddou, Abdelaziz Safsafi, Abdelkader Ighili, Rachid Omar Betrouni, Mohammed Griche, Aissa Draoui, Mourad Naim (Hocine Rabet). Trainer: Rachid Mekhloufi.
**LBY**: Rajab El Fitouri, Younis Musbah Shangar, El Mehdi El Kherief (Nadji El Ghadi), Ali Mersal, Buhloul El Hashemi, Abdulgader Touhami, Aboubaker El Amami, Ali Mohammad (Messoud Rabti), Tahir Saad Khair El Fezzani, Ali El Essaoud, Hussein Sherif. Trainer: Mohammed El Khamisi.
**Goal**: 1-0 Rachid Omar Betrouni (83).

16.04.1976, Stade du 11$^{ème}$ Juin, Tripoli; Attendance: 30,000
Referee: Emilio Carlos Guruceta Muro (Spain)
**LIBYA - ALGERIA** 0-0
**LBY**: Rajab El Fitouri, Younis Musbah Shangar, Nadji El Ghadi, Abdulgader Touhami, Buhloul El Hashemi, Ali Mersal, Ali Mohammad, Tahir Saad Khair El Fezzani, Aboubaker El Amami, Ali El Essaoud, Hussein Sherif. Trainer: Mohammed El Khamisi.
**ALG**: Abdenour Kaoua, Mohammed Khedis, Abdelmalek Ali Messaoud, Zoubir Maaziz, Djemal Keddou, Abdelaziz Safsafi, Rachid Omar Betrouni, Abdelkader Ighili, Mohammed Griche, Aissa Draoui, Houari Ouali. Trainer: Rachid Mekhloufi.

| | | | | | | | | |
|---|---|---|---|---|---|---|---|---|
| 12.12.1976 | Casablanca | Morocco – Tunisia | | | | | | 1-1(1-0) |
| 09.01.1977 | Tunis | Tunisia - Morocco | | | | | | 1-1(1-0,1-1) |
| | | | | | | | | 4-2 pen |

### FINAL STANDINGS

| | | | | | | | |
|---|---|---|---|---|---|---|---|
| 1. Tunisia | 2 | 0 | 2 | 0 | 2 | - 2 | 2 |
| 2. Morocco | 2 | 0 | 2 | 0 | 2 | - 2 | 2 |

Tunisia qualified for the Second Round.

12.12.1976, Stade Pere Jego, Casablanca; Attendance: 13,056
Referee: Franz Wöhrer (Austria)
**MOROCCO – TUNISIA** **1-1(1-0)**
**MAR**: Mohamed Hazzaz, Mustapha Fetoui, Tahir Arraed, Larbi Ihardane, Abdallah Semmate, Mohamed Ahmed Mouhou, Abdelghani Lakhal (46.Boubaker Bouazzaoui), Abdelmajid Shaira, Mohamed Ahmed Faras, Kamal Smiri, Hassan Amcharrat (88.Azzeddine Amanallah). Trainer: Virgil Mărdărescu (Romania).
**TUN**: Sadouk Sassi, Mokhtar Dhouib, Ali Kaabi, Khaled Mokhtar Gasmi, Omar Jebaili, Néjib Ghommidh, Témime Lahzami, Khemais Labidi, Mohamed Ali Akid, Tarak Dhiab, Abderraouf Ben Aziza (46.Mohammed Néjib Limam). Trainer: Abdelmajid Chetali.
**Goals**: 1-0 Abdelghani Lakhal (35), 1-1 Tarak Dhiab (56).

09.01.1977, Stade Olympique d'El Menzah, Tunis; Attendance: 44,500
Referee: Walter Hungerbuhler (Switzerland)
**TUNISIA - MOROCCO** **1-1(1-0,1-1,1-1)**
**4-2 on penalties**
**TUN**: Sadouk Sassi, Mokhtar Dhouib, Ali Kaabi, Khaled Mokhtar Gasmi, Omar Jebaili, Néjib Ghommidh, Témime Lahzami, Khemais Labidi, Mohamed Ali Akid (73.Abderraouf Ben Aziza), Tarak Dhiab, Mohammed Néjib Limam (91.Ouadda Moncef). Trainer: Abdelmajid Chetali.
**MAR**: Mohamed Hazzaz, Ahmed Dallahi, Ahmed Larbi Megrouah, Larbi Ihardane, Abdelkrim Merry, Houcine Anafal (66.Mohamed Bousati), Abdelghani Lakdhal (46.Guezzar Redouane), Mustapha Tahar Arraed, Mohamed Ahmed Faras, Mohamed Ahmed Mouhou, Kamal Smiri. Trainer: Virgil Mărdărescu (Romania).
**Goals**: 1-0 Khemais Labidi (34), 1-1 Mustapha Tahar Arraed (55).

| | | | | |
|---|---|---|---|---|
| 17.10.1976 | Lomé | Togo - Senegal | | 1-0(0-0) |
| 31.10.1976 | Dakar | Senegal - Togo | | 1-1(0-0) |

### FINAL STANDINGS

| | | | | | | | |
|---|---|---|---|---|---|---|---|
| 1. Togo | 2 | 1 | 1 | 0 | 2 | - 1 | 3 |
| 2. Senegal | 2 | 0 | 1 | 1 | 1 | - 2 | 1 |

Togo qualified for the Second Round.

17.10.1976, Stade "Général Eyadema", Lomé; Attendance: 5,173
Referee: Benjamin Kwabena Dwomoh (Ghana)
**TOGO - SENEGAL** **1-0(0-0)**
**TOG**: Yaovi Assogba, Ramanou Apampa, Kossivi Dokou, Sakibou Issa, Messan Hounkpati, Kodzovi Vinan, Alirou Rachidou, Lobo Adamah, Eza Lawson, Anani Afanou, Tabania Ametepe (*Substitution*: Kosock DEnagno Doussor).
**SEN**: Amady Diop, Moustapha N'Diaye, Ali Ibrahim Ba N'Diaye, Oumar Diop, Amadou Diakhou Gayé, Abdoulaye Ba, Yamougor Seck, Mousse Diousse (Cheikh Fam), Birame N'Gom, Seydou Ba, Abdoulaye Sène.
**Goal**: 1-0 Alirou Rachidou (87).

31.10.1976, Stade "Demba Diop", Dakar; Attendance: 7,000
Referee: Abdel Ali Naciri (Morocco)
**SENEGAL - TOGO** **1-1(0-0)**
**SEN:** Amady Diop, Moustapha N'Diaye, Ali Ibrahim Ba N'Diaye, Amadou Diakhou Gayé, Oumar Diop, Abdoulaye Ba, Thierno M'Boup (55.Yamougor Seck), Diadjiliou Diallo, Serigne Youssoupha Thiam (70.Bleck), Seydou Ba, Abdoulaye Sène.
**TOG:** Komi Kudadze, Sakibou Issa, Ramanou Apampa, Kossivi Dokou, Kodzovi Vinan, GBale Ahamadah, Messan Hounkpati, Alirou Rachidou, Anani Afanou, Kosock Denagno Doussor, Tabania Ametepe.
**Goals:** 0-1 Anani Afanou (58), 1-1 Abdoulaye Ba (63).

| | | | |
|---|---|---|---|
| 10.10.1976 | Accra | Ghana - Guinea | 2-1(0-0) |
| 31.10.1976 | Conakry | Guinea - Ghana | 2-1(0-0) |

### FINAL STANDINGS

| | | | | | | | | |
|---|---|---|---|---|---|---|---|---|
| 1. | Ghana | 2 | 1 | 0 | 1 | 3 - 3 | | 2 |
| | Guinea | 2 | 1 | 0 | 1 | 3 - 3 | | 2 |

10.10.1976, City Sports Stadium, Accra; Attendance: 10,000
Referee: Theodore Koudou Poll (Ivory Coast)
**GHANA - GUINEA** **2-1(0-0)**
**GHA:** Samuel Ampeh, Enoch Asumadu (46.Isaac Paha Jr.), Ofei Ansah, Awuley Quaye, James Dadzie, Isaac Eshun (60.Opoku Afriyle), Ibrahim Kassum, Emmanuel Quarshie, Daniel Kwasi Owusu, Abdul Razak Ahmed, Mohammed Ahmed.
**GUI:** Abdoulaye Keïta Sylla, Jacob Bangoura, Ibrahim Fofana, Chérif Soulemane, Djibrill Diarra, Naby Laye Camara, Morciré Sylla, Youssuf Camara, Mamadou Aliou Keïta, Ali Ibrahim P. Keïta, Bangally Sylla.
**Goals:** 0-1 Youssuf Camara (52), 1-1 Ibrahim Kassum (57), 2-1 Opoku Afriyle (83).

31.10.1976, Stade 28$^{\text{ème}}$ Septembre, Conakry; Attendance: 20,000
Referee: Abdelkader Aouissi (Algeria)
**GUINEA - GHANA** **2-1(0-0)**
**GUI:** Abdoulaye Keïta Sylla, Morciré Sylla, Chérif Soulemane, Djibrill Diarra, Ibrahim Fofana, Ousmane Thiam Tollo (46.Seydouba Sylla), Youssuf Camara, Mamadou Aliou Keïta, Naby Laye Camara, Ali Ibrahim P. Keïta (46.Bangally Condé), Bangally Sylla.
**GHA:** Samuel Ampeh, Enoch Asumadu, Ofei Ansah (Isaac Paha Jr.), Awuley Quaye, James Dadzie, Adolph Armah, Ibrahim Kassum, Emmanuel Quarshie, Daniel Kwasi Owusu (46.Willie Klutse), Afriye Opoku, Mohammed Ahmed.
**Goals:** 1-0 Naby Laye Camara (51), 1-1 Ofei Ansah (59), 2-1 Mamadou Aliou Keïta (56).

## PLAY-OFF

16.01.1977, Stade "Géneral Eyadema", Lomé (Togo); Attendance: 13,482
Referee: Youssou N'Diaye (Senegal)
**GUINEA - GHANA**                                                    **2-0(2-0)**
**GUI**: Mamado Sano, Moussa Camara, Ibrahim Fofana, Morciré Sylla, Djibrill Diarra, Ali Ibrahim K. Keïta, Ali Ibrahim P. Keïta, Bengally Sylla, Naby Laye Camara, Aboubacar Ousmane Badara Bangoura, Seydouba Sylla.
**GHA**: Samuel Ampeh, Enoch Asumadu, Ofei Ansah, Awuley Quaye, James Dadzie, Adolph Armah (35.Emmanuel Quarshie), Ibrahim Kassum, Karim Abdul Razak Tanko, George Alhassan (60.Robert Hammond), Daniel Kwasi Owusu, Mohammed Ahmed.
**Goals**: 1-0 Naby Laye Camara (3), 2-0 Seydouba Sylla (31).
Guinea qualified for the Second Round.

## SUBGROUP B

Zaire qualified for the Second Round (Central African Republic withdrew).

| 16.10.1976 | Freetown | Sierra Leone - Nigeria | 0-0 |
| 30.10.1976 | Lagos | Nigeria – Sierra Leone | 6-2(4-0) |

### FINAL STANDINGS

| | | | | | | | | |
|---|---|---|---|---|---|---|---|---|
| 1. | Nigeria | 2 | 1 | 1 | 0 | 6 - 2 | 3 |
| 2. | Sierra Leone | 2 | 0 | 1 | 1 | 2 - 6 | 1 |

Nigeria qualified for the Second Round.

16.10.1976, Kington Sports Ground, Freetown; Attendance: 5,173
Referee: Etrue Joel Turkson (Ghana)
**SIERRA LEONE - NIGERIA**                                                    **0-0**
**SLE**: Frank Jongo Williams, Edward Campbell, Abu Bangoura, Mohammed Sama, Buba Kamara, Ibrahim Jalloh, Abdul Muckni, William Songo, Brima Kamara, Ismail Dyfan, Augustus Lawson (*Substitutes*: Wasieu Sounmonu, Abdul Rahim). Trainer: Stephen Bio.
**NGA**: Emmanuel Okala, Patrick Ekeji, Samuel Ojebode, Muda Lawal, Christian Chukwu, Godwin Odiye, Baba Otu Mohammed, Alloysius Atuegbu, Thompson Usiyen, Kelechi Emeteole (42.Segun Odegbami), Kunle Awesu (70.Haruna Ilerika). Trainer: Tihomir Jelisavčić (Yugoslavia).

30.10.1976, Surulere Stadium, Lagos; Attendance: 25,996
Referee: Gration Matovu (Tanzania)
**NIGERIA – SIERRA LEONE**                                                    **6-2(4-0)**
**NGA**: Emmanuel Okala, Patrick Ekeji, Samuel Ojebode, Christian Madu (46.Muda Lawal), Christian Chukwu, Godwin Odiye, Segun Odegbami, Alloysius Atuegbu, Thompson Usiyen (Solomon Oriakhi), Kelechi Emeteole, Kunle Awesu. Trainer: Tihomir Jelisavčić (Yugoslavia).
**SLE**: Frank Jongo Williams (32.Idrissa Bangoura), Edward Campbell, Abu Bangoura, Mohammed Sama, Buba Kamara, Ibrahim Jalloh, Danid Eamara, Wasieu Sounmonu, Albert Conteh, Ismail Dyfan, Augustus Lawson. Trainer: Stephen Bio.
**Goals**: 1-0 Segun Odegbami (25), 2-0 Alloysius Atuegbu (28), 3-0 Alloysius Atuegbu (34), 4-0 Thompson Usiyen (40), 5-0 Kelechi Emeteole (63), 5-1 Ismail Dyfan (74), 6-1 Kunle Awesu (77), 6-2 Mohammed Sama (88 penalty).

| 17.10.1976 | Brazzaville | Congo - Cameroon | 2-2(0-2) |
| 31.10.1976 | Yaoundé | Cameroon - Congo | 1-2(1-1) |

### FINAL STANDINGS

| | | | | | | | | |
|---|---|---|---|---|---|---|---|---|
| 1. Congo | 2 | 1 | 1 | 0 | 4 | - | 3 | 3 |
| 2. Cameroon | 2 | 0 | 1 | 1 | 3 | - | 4 | 1 |

Congo qualified for the Second Round.

17.10.1976, Stade de la Revolution, Brazzaville; Attendance: 17,367
Referee: Winston Gumboh (Zambia)
**CONGO - CAMEROON**                                              **2-2(0-2)**
**CGO**: François N'Guedi, Martial Lassyz (63.Kimbouala Bakala), Gaston N'Ganga Muivi, Gabriel Alphonse N'Dengaki (46.Basile N'Gollo), Joseph Mounoundzi, Bienvenu Kimbembé, Jonas Bagamboula M'Bemba, Dominique M'Bamba, Joseph Wamba, Jean-Jacques N'Domba, Sébastien Lackou. Trainer: Maurice Ondzolet & Paulin Ayina.
**CMR**: Thomas N'Kono, Jacques Ename, Jean Marie Tsebo, Paul N'Lend, François N'Doumbé Lea, Raphael Ayissi, René Emana (72.Guy Jacques Manga), Grégoire M'Bida, Roger Milla, Jean Manga Onguéné (71.Franklin N'Go), Jean Daniel Eboué.
**Goals**: 0-1 Roger Milla (11), 0-2 Jean Manga Onguéné (35), 1-2 Joseph Mounoundzi (66 penalty), 2-2 Joseph Wamba (76).

31.10.1976, Stade du "Président Ahmadu Ahdjo", Yaoundé; Attendance: 26,050
Referee: Housainou N'Jai (Gambia)
**CAMEROON - CONGO**                                              **1-2(1-1)**
**CMR**: Thomas N'Kono, Pierre Many, Jean Marie Tsebo, Paul N'Lend, Raphael Ayissi, Grégoire M'Bida, René Emana, François N'Doumbé Lea, Jean Manga Onguéné, Jean Daniel Eboué (64.Guy Jacques Manga), Roger Milla.
**CGO**: François N'Guedi, Kimbouala Bakala, Gaston N'Ganga Muivi, Gabriel Alphonse N'Dengaki, Joseph Mounoundzi, Dominique M'Bamba, Daniel Ebomoa, Bienvenu Kimbembé, Jonas Bagamboula M'Bemba, Jean-Jacques N'Domba (75.Louis Massamba), Sébastien Lackou. Trainer: Paulin Ayina.
**Goals**: 1-0 Roger Milla (7), 1-1 Daniel Ebomoa (19), 1-2 Jean-Jacques NDoumba (52).
**Sent off**: François N'Guedi (82).
*Please note*: the match was interrupted after 82 mins and awarded 2-0 to Congo.


| 04.09.1976 | Ouagadougou | Upper Volta – Ivory Coast | 1-1(0-1) |
| 26.09.1976 | Abidjan | Ivory Coast – Upper Volta | 2-0(2-0) |

### FINAL STANDINGS

| | | | | | | | | |
|---|---|---|---|---|---|---|---|---|
| 1. Ivory Coast | 2 | 1 | 1 | 0 | 3 | - | 1 | 3 |
| 2. Upper Volta | 2 | 0 | 1 | 1 | 1 | - | 3 | 1 |

Ivory Coast qualified for the Second Round.

04.09.1976, Stade de Magadougou, Ouagadougou; Attendance: 5,418
Referee: Youssou NDiaye (Senegal)
**UPPER VOLTA – IVORY COAST**                                     **1-1(0-1)**
**UPV**: Sidiki Diarra, Modeste Dah Sehira (Laurent Banadi), Adama Ouédraogo, Alassane Guiré, Tewinde Compaoré, Ladji Coulibaly, René Nikiema, Corneille Nignan, Joseph Kaboré, Kouligo Zoma, Paul Yaméogo. Trainer: Otto Pfister (West Germany).

**CIV**: Néstor Bodo Akakou, Philbert Dié Foneye, Severin Zogbo Tapé, Paul Bouabré Koko, Koffi Ignace Kouadio, Amadou Lazane, Jérôme Lebri Manahou (75.Zoko Ackbala), Anatole Opeli (75.Kangali Kouadio), Leon Goua G'Bize, Gaston Bawa, Kouman Kobenan. Trainer: Gérard Gabo.
**Goals**: 0-1 Gaston Bawa (36), 1-1 Joseph Kaboré (70).

26.09.1976, Stade "Félix Houphouet Boigny", Abidjan, Attendance: 5,960
Referee: Hamad Diagne (Guinea)
**IVORY COAST – UPPER VOLTA**     **2-0(2-0)**
**CIV**: Koffi Ignace Kouadio, Severin Zogbo Tapé, Leopold Bridji, Bebe Koffi Konan, Adama Konaté, Amadou Lazane, Lucien Kouamé, Anatole Odelouri, Leon Goua G'Bize (57.Gaston Bawa), Kobenan Kouman, Maxine Traoré (70.Zoko Ackbala). Trainer: Gérard Gabo.
**UPV**: Sidiki Diarra, Modeste Dah Sehira (53.Pierre Sanou), Alassane Guiré, Adama Ouédraogo, Laurent Banadi, Tewinde Compaoré, Louis Dahourou, René Nikiema, Joseph Kaboré, Kouligo Zoma, Paul Yaméogo (75.Deme Arouna). Trainer: Otto Pfister (West Germany).
**Goals**: 1-0 Lucien Kouamé (17), 2-0 Kouman Kobenan (34).
**Sent off**: Abatole Odelouri (85).

## SUBGROUP C

| 29.10.1976 | Cairo | Egypt - Ethiopia | 3-0(2-0) |
| 14.11.1976 | Addis Abeba | Ethiopia - Egypt | 1-2(1-1) |

### FINAL STANDINGS

| | | | | | | | | |
|---|---|---|---|---|---|---|---|---|
| 1. | Egypt | 2 | 2 | 0 | 0 | 5 | - 1 | 4 |
| 2. | Ethiopia | 2 | 0 | 0 | 2 | 1 | - 5 | 0 |

Egypt qualified for the Second Round.

29.10.1976, Nasser Stadium, Cairo; Attendance: 20,000
Referee: Gianfranco Menegali (Italy)
**EGYPT - ETHIOPIA**     **3-0(2-0)**
**EGY**: Hassan Ali Hassan Hussein, Mohammed Salah El Din, Mohammed Moustafa Hassan Younis, Fathi Mabrouk Hanafi, Shaker Mohammed Mahmoud Abdel Fattah, Mohamed Maher Hammam Bedair Abu Kheir, Farouk Fouad Gaafar, Omar Abdallah Omer, Mahmoud Ibrahim El Khateeb, Mokhtar Ali Mokhtar, Adel El Bably Aouad Allah. Trainer: Burkhard Pape (West Germany).
**ETH**: Wondimu Teklu, Haile Selassie Alemayehu, Ahmed Buker, Asrat Haile, Asfaw Bayu, Kibrom Medhin, Berhane Mulugeta, Ali Mohammed, Hailu Goshu, Solomon Shiferahu, Tekalinge Kasahun.
**Goals**: 1-0 Mahmoud Ibrahim El Khateeb (4), 2-0 Mahmoud Ibrahim El Khateeb (19), 3-0 Mahmoud Ibrahim El Khateeb (77).
**Sent off**: Tekalinge Kasahun (76).

14.11.1976, National Stadium, Addis Abeba; Attendance: 50,000
Referee: Robert Charles Paul Wurtz (France)
**ETHIOPIA - EGYPT**     **1-2(1-1)**
**ETH**: Wondimu Teklu, Haile Selassie Alemayehu, Ahmed Buker (Arefaine Mitiku), Asrat Haile (Simyon Tesfaye), Ali Mohammed, Asfaw Bayu, Amanuel Gebru, Berhane Mulugeta, Tekalinge Kasahun, Hailu Goshu, Solomon Shiferahu.
**EGY**: Hassan Ali Hassan Hussein, Mohammed Salah El Din, Mohammed Moustafa Hassan Younis, Fathi Mabrouk Hanafi, Shaker Mohammed Mahmoud Abdel Fattah, Mohamed Maher Hammam Bedair Abu Kheir, Farouk Fouad Gaafar, Moustafa Ahmed Abdou Ali, Mahmoud Ibrahim El Khateeb, Mokhtar Ali Mokhtar, Adel El Bably Aouad Allah (Gamal Abdel Azim). Trainer: Burkhard Pape (West Germany).
**Goals**: 0-1 Mahmoud Ibrahim El Khateeb (12), 1-1 Tekalinge Kassahun (40), 1-2 Mahmoud Ibrahim El Khateeb (73).

Kenya qualified for the Second Round (Sudan withdrew).

Uganda qualified for the Second Round (Tanzania withdrew).

| | | | | |
|---|---|---|---|---|
| 09.05.1976 | Lusaka | Zambia - Malawi | | 4-0(2-0) |
| 30.05.1976 | Blantyre | Malawi - Zambia | | 0-1(0-0) |

## FINAL STANDINGS

| | | | | | | | | |
|---|---|---|---|---|---|---|---|---|
| 1. | Zambia | 2 | 2 | 0 | 0 | 5 - 0 | 4 |
| 2. | Malawi | 2 | 0 | 0 | 2 | 0 - 5 | 0 |

Zambia qualified for the Second Round.

09.05.1976, 7$^{th}$ April Stadium, Lusaka; Attendance: 16,000
Referee: K. Muambe-Kabwe (Zaire)
**ZAMBIA - MALAWI**  **4-0(2-0)**
**ZAM:** Abraham Nkole, Ackim Mulamata, Kaiser Kalambo, Dickson Chama, Ackim Musenge, James Mwale (Boniface Simutowe), Moses Simwala, Jani Simulambo, Bernard Chanda, Alexander Chola, Willie Phiri. Trainer: Ante Buselić (Yugoslavia).
**MWI**: Boniface Maganga, Henry Tewesa, Mosted Sichinga, Stephen Phiri, Robert Banda, Jack Chamangwana, Konok Munde, Kinnah Phiri, Peter Nyama, Damiano Malalefula (46.Topsy Msuku), Zorro Msiska (46.Elwyn Mwafurilwa).
**Goals**: 1-0 Willie Phiri (12), 2-0 Bernard Chanda (40), 3-0 Willie Phiri (75), 4-0 Jack Chamangwana (88 own goal).

30.05.1976, Kamasu Stadium, Blantyre; Attendance: 8,230
Referee: Charles Randrianaly (Madagascar)
**MALAWI - ZAMBIA**  **0-1(0-0)**
**MWI**: Boniface Maganga, Henry Tewesa, Jack Chamangwana, Mosted Sichinga, Elwyn Mwafurilwa, Robert Banda, Kanok Munde, Topsy Msuku, Kinnah Phiri, Peter Nyama, Eliam Mika (*Substitution*: Stephen Phiri).
**ZAM:** Abraham Nkole, Ackim Mulamata, Kaiser Kalambo, Dickson Chama, Ackim Musenge, Bernard Chanda, Moses Simwala, Jani Simulambo, Alexander Chola, Willie Phiri, Obby Kapita. Trainer: Ante Buselić (Yugoslavia).
**Goal**: 0-1 Obby Kapita (48).

# SECOND ROUND

## SUBGROUP A

| 06.02.1977 | Tunis | Tunisia - Algeria | 2-0(0-0) |
|---|---|---|---|
| 28.02.1977 | Alger | Algeria - Tunisia | 1-1(1-0) |

### FINAL STANDINGS

| | | | | | | | | |
|---|---|---|---|---|---|---|---|---|
| 1. | Tunisia | 2 | 1 | 1 | 0 | 3 - 1 | 3 |
| 2. | Algeria | 2 | 0 | 1 | 1 | 1 - 3 | 1 |

Tunisia qualified for the Third Round.

06.02.1977, Stade Olympique d'El Menzah, Tunis; Attendance: 50,000
Referee: Antoine Queudeville (Luxembourg)
**TUNISIA - ALGERIA**     **2-0(0-0)**
**TUN:** Sadouk Sassi, Mokhtar Dhouib, Ali Kaabi, Khaled Mokhtar Gasmi (23.Kamel El Chébli), Omar Jebaili, Néjib Ghommidh, Témime Lahzami, Khemais Labidi, Mohamed Ali Akid, Tarak Dhiab, Mohammed Agrebi Ben Rehaiem (46.Mohammed Néjib Limam). Trainer: Abdelmajid Chetali.
**ALG:** Mehdi Cerbah, Mohammed Khedis, Rabah Menguelti, Abdelmalek Ali Messaoud, Zoubir Maaziz, Abdelaziz Safsafi, Omar Bertrouni, Abdel Kader Ighili, Mohammed Griche (70.Nabil Guasmi), Aissa Draoui, Hocine Rabet (58.Ali Ben Cheikh). Trainer: Rachid Mekhloufi.
**Goals:** 1-0 Mohamed Ali Akid (56), 2-0 Ali Kaabi (73).

28.02.1977, Stade du 5ème Juillet, Alger; Attendance: 80,000
Referee: Paul Bonett (Malta)
**ALGERIA - TUNISIA**     **1-1(1-0)**
**ALG:** Mehdi Cerbah, Mohammed Khedis, Abdelmalek Ali Messaoud, Mohammed Guendouz, Djemal Keddou, Abdelaziz Safsafi, Omar Bertrouni, Ali Ben Cheikh, Mokhrane Baileche, Aissa Draoui (Djemal Tlemçani), Moustapha Dahleb. Trainer: Rachid Mekhloufi.
**TUN:** Sadouk Sassi, Mokhtar Dhouib, Ali Kaabi, Mohsen Jendoubi Labidi, Kamel El Chébli, Khaled Mokhtar Gasmi, Témime Lahzami (Mohammed Agrebi Ben Rehaiem), Khemais Labidi, Mohamed Ali Akid (Omar Jebaili), Tarak Dhiab, Mohammed Néjib Limam. Trainer: Abdelmajid Chetali.
**Goals:** 1-0 Mohammed Guendouz (34), 1-1 Omar Jebaili (89).


| 13.02.1977 | Lomé | Togo - Guinea | 0-2(0-1) |
|---|---|---|---|
| 27.02.1977 | Conakry | Guinea - Togo | 2-1(2-0) |

### FINAL STANDINGS

| | | | | | | | | |
|---|---|---|---|---|---|---|---|---|
| 1. | Guinea | 2 | 2 | 0 | 0 | 4 - 1 | 4 |
| 2. | Togo | 2 | 0 | 0 | 2 | 1 - 4 | 0 |

Guinea qualified for the Third Round.

13.02.1977, Stade "Général Eyadema", Lomé; Attendance: 7,976
Referee: Félix Balloux (Ivory Coast)
**TOGO - GUINEA**     **0-2(0-1)**
**TOG:** Komi Kudadze, Kponton Sanvee, Kossivi Dokou, Sakibou Issa, Messan Hounkpati, G'Bale Ahamadah, Alirou Rachidou, Anani Afanou, Aykoué Ajavon, Koamivi Konou, Kpatcha Kabia.
**GUI:** Abdoulaye Keïta Sylla, Moussa Camara, Ibrahim Fofana, Djibrill Diarra, Morciré Sylla, Ousmane Thiam Tollo, Seydouba Sylla (46.Chérif Soulemane), Naby Laye Camara, Aboubacar Ousmane Badara Bangoura, Ali Ibrahim P. Keïta, Bengally Sylla.

**Goals**: 0-1 Aboubacar Ousmane Badara Bangoura (15), 0-2 Chérif Soulemane (84).

27.02.1977, Stade du 28ème Septembre, Conakry; Attendance: 11,892
Referee: Tanor Dieng (Senegal)
**GUINEA - TOGO**  **2-1(2-0)**
**GUI**: Abdoulaye Keïta Sylla, Moussa Camara, Ibrahim Fofana, Sandipe Beinurd, Morciré Sylla, Ousmane Thiam Tollo, Seydouba Sylla (46.Ali Ibrahim K. Keïta), Naby Laye Camara, Ali Ibrahim P. Keïta (82.Amara Touré), Chérif Soulemane, Bengally Sylla.
**TOG**: Komi Koudadze, Kponton Sanvee, Ohin Anyakon, Ramanou Apampa (11.Sakibou Issa), Messan Hounkpati, Koffi Fiaty, Alirou Rachirou, Dossou Vasseho, Kodjovi Adokpa, Kosock Denagno Doussor, Tabania Ametepé.
**Goals**: 1-0 Naby Laye Camara (36), 2-0 Ousmane Thiam Tollo (40 penalty), 2-1 Tabania Ametepé (55).

## SUBGROUP B

Nigeria qualified for the Third Round (Zaire withdrew).

| | | | |
|---|---|---|---|
| 13.02.1977 | Bouaké | Ivory Coast - Congo | 3-2(2-1) |
| 27.02.1977 | Brazzaville | Congo – Ivory Coast | 1-3(1-2) |

### FINAL STANDINGS

| | | | | | | | | |
|---|---|---|---|---|---|---|---|---|
| 1. | Ivory Coast | 2 | 2 | 0 | 0 | 6 | - 3 | 4 |
| 2. | Congo | 2 | 0 | 0 | 2 | 3 | - 6 | 0 |

Ivory Coast qualified for the Third Round.

13.02.1977, Stade Municipal, Bouaké; Attendance: 3,600
Referee: Benjamin Kwabena Dwomoh (Ghana)
**IVORY COAST - CONGO**  **3-2(2-1)**
**CIV**: Néstor Bodo Akakou, Severin Zogbo Tapé, Laurent Tapé, Jean-Baptiste Akassou Akran, Adama Konaté, Lazane Amadou Ouattara (15.Daniel Kouassi Apessika), Jérôme Lebri Manahou, Irie Bi Toh, Léon Goua G'Bize, Kobenan Kouman, Maxime Lacina Traoré (60.Kangah Kouadio). Trainer: Gérard Gabo.
**CGO**: Paul Tandou, Martial Lassyz, Gaston N'Ganga Muivi, Gabriel Alphonse N'Dengaki, Joseph Mounoundzi, Bienvenu Kimbembé, Jonas Bagamboula M'Bemba, Jean-Jacques N'Domba, Daniel Ebomoa (59.Dominique MBama), Paul Moukila, Sébastian Lackou. Trainer: Paulin Ayina.
**Goals**: 1-0 Léon Goua G'Bize (10), 2-0 Jérôme Lebri Manahou (20), 2-1 Jonas Bagamboula MBemba (36), 3-1 Kobenan Kouman (81), 3-2 Jean-Jacques NDomba (89).

27.02.1977, Stade de la Revolution, Brazzaville; Attendance: 70,000
Referee: Festus Okubule (Nigeria)
**CONGO – IVORY COAST**  **1-3(1-2)**
**CGO**: Justin Vohayemade, Martial Lassyz, Gaston N'Ganga Muivi, Gabriel Alphonse N'Dengaki, Antoine Bisseyou, Bienvenu Kimbembé, Joseph Mounoundzi, Jonas Bagamboula M'Bemba, Paul Moukila (13.Pierre Lingongo), Jean-Jacques N'Domba, Sébastian Lackou. Trainer: Paulin Ayina.
**CIV**: Néstor Bodo Akakou, Philibert Dié Foneye, Severin Zogbo Tapé, Ignace Guidi, Jean-Baptiste Akassou Akran, Laurent Madou Zahuie, Pascal Miezan Aka, Jérôme Lebri Manahou, Léon Goua G'Bize, Kobenan Kouman, Maxime Lacina Traoré. Trainer: Gérard Gabo.
**Goals**: 0-1 Kobenan Kouman (10), 1-1 Pierre Lingongo (23), 1-2 Pascal Miezan (38), 1-3 Léon Goua G'Bize (82).

# SUBGROUP C

| 06.02.1977 | Nairobi | Kenya - Egypt | 0-0 |
| 27.02.1977 | Cairo | Egypt - Kenya | 1-0(1-0) |

### FINAL STANDINGS

| | | | | | | | | |
|---|---|---|---|---|---|---|---|---|
| 1. Egypt | 2 | 1 | 1 | 0 | 1 | - | 0 | 3 |
| 2. Kenya | 2 | 0 | 1 | 1 | 0 | - | 1 | 1 |

Egypt qualified for the Third Round.

06.02.1977, City Stadium, Nairobi; Attendance: 8,337
Referee: Mohammed Ahmewd Jama (Somalia)
**KENYA - EGYPT** **0-0**
**KEN**: Mohammed Magogo, James Ojiambo (75.Maurice Goodwin), Joseph Oygando (54.James Ogolla), Edward Kiiwa, Martin Ochieng, Edward Wamalwa, Allen Thigo, Binzi M'Wakoto, Charles Ochieng, Babu Makokech, Aggrey Lukoye. Trainer: Raymond Ernest Wood (England).
**EGY**: Hassan Ali Hassan Hussein, Fathi Mabrouk Hanafi, Ahmed Abdel Bakhi Abohlika, Farouk Fouad Gaafar, Mohamed Maher Hammam Bedair Abu Kheir, Hassan Ali Shehata, Mohammed Hussein Hamdi Ibrahim Nour, Moustafa Ahmed Abdou Ali, Mokhtar Ali Mokhtar (77.Taher Mohammed Mamdouh El Rasik El Sheik), Osama Mohammed Hassan Ali Khalil (77.Ibrahim Youssef Awad Allah), Adel El Bably Aouad Allah. Trainer: Dušan Ninković (Yugoslavia).

27.02.1977, Nasser Stadium, Cairo; Attendance: 70,000
Referee: Youssef Mohammed El Ghoul (Libya)
**EGYPT - KENYA** **1-0(1-0)**
**EGY**: Ahmed Ikramy El Shahat, Ahmed Abdel Bakhi Abohlika, Mohammed Moustafa Hassan Younis, Fathi Mabrouk Hanafi, Shaker Mohammed Mahmoud Abdel Fattah, Mohamed Maher Hammam Bedair Abu Kheir, Farouk Fouad Gaafar, Hassan Ali Shehata, Moustafa Ahmed Abdou Ali, Mahmoud Ibrahim El Khateeb, Osama Mohammed Hassan Ali Khalil. Trainer: Dušan Ninković (Yugoslavia).
**KEN**: Mohammed Magogo, James Ojiambo, Martin Ochieng, Edward Kiiwa, James Ogolla, Edward Wamalwa, Babu Makokech, Allen Thigo, Charles Ochieng, Gerald Imbo, Abdallah Gazahi. Trainer: Raymond Ernest Wood (England).
**Goal**: 1-0 Osama Mohammed Hassan Ali Khalil (13).


| 13.02.1977 | Kampla | Uganda - Zambia | 1-0(0-0) |
| 27.02.1977 | Ndola | Zambia - Uganda | 4-2(2-1,3-2) |

### FINAL STANDINGS

| | | | | | | | | |
|---|---|---|---|---|---|---|---|---|
| 1. Zambia | 2 | 1 | 0 | 1 | 4 | - | 3 | 2 |
| 2. Uganda | 2 | 1 | 0 | 1 | 3 | - | 4 | 2 |

Zambia qualified for the Third Round.

13.02.1977, Nakivubo Stadium, Kampala; Attendance: 11,940
Referee: Ismael Kemal (Ethiopia)
**UGANDA - ZAMBIA** **1-0(0-0)**
**UGA**: George Mukasa, Ahmad Doka, Samuel Musenze, Thomas L'Wanga, James Kirunda, Timothy Ayieko, Leo Adera, Edward Semwanga, Ahmed Nasur Abdullah (63.Polly Ouma), Moses N'Sereko, Dennis Obua. Trainer: Peter Okee.

**ZAM**: Emmanuel Mwape, Edwin MBaso, Kaiser Kalambo, Robert Lutoba, Ackim Musenge, Simutowe Boniface, Moses Simwala, Jani Simulambo, Godfrey Chitalu (74.Brighton Sinyangwe), Alexander Chola, Willie Phiri. Trainer: Ante Buselić (Yugoslavia).
**Goal**: 1-0 Polly Ouma (73).

27.02.1977, Dag Hammerskjoeld Stadium, Ndola; Attendance: 30,000
Referee: Gration Hemans Matovu (Tanzania)
**ZAMBIA - UGANDA**　　　　　　　　　　　　　　　　　　　　　**4-2(2-1,3-2)**
**ZAM**: Emmanuel Mwape, Edwin MBaso, Kaiser Kalambo, Robert Lutoba, Ackim Musenge, Bernard Chanda, Jani Simulambo, Burton Mugala (33.Godfrey Chitalu), Alexander Chola, Brighton Sinyangwe (65.Moses Simwala), Willie Phiri., Trainer: Brightwell Banda.
**UGA**: George Mukasa, Wilson NSobya, Ahmed Doka, Ashe Mukasa, Thomas L'Wanga, Francis Kulabigwo, Moses N'Sereko, Edward Semwanga, Polly Ouma, Ahmed Nasur Abdullah (46.Leo Adera), Dennis Obua. Trainer: Peter Okee.
**Goals**: 0-1 Ahmed Nasur Abdullah (14), 1-1 Alexander Chola (28), 2-1 Bernard Chanda (34), 2-2 Dennis Obua (74), 3-2 Godfrey Chitalu (85), 4-2 Godfrey Chitalu (106).

# THIRD ROUND

## SUBGROUP A

| | | | |
|---|---|---|---|
| 05.06.1977 | Conakry | Guinea - Tunisia | 1-0(0-0) |
| 19.06.1977 | Tunis | Tunisia - Guinea | 3-1(1-1) |

### FINAL STANDINGS

| | | | | | | | | |
|---|---|---|---|---|---|---|---|---|
| 1. | Tunisia | 2 | 1 | 0 | 1 | 3 | - 2 | 2 |
| 2. | Guinea | 2 | 1 | 0 | 1 | 2 | - 3 | 2 |

Tunisia qualified for the African Zone Final.

05.06.1977, Stade du 28$^{ème}$ Septembre, Conakry; Attendance: 25,000
Referee: Mohammed Larache (Morocco)
**GUINEA - TUNISIA**　　　　　　　　　　　　　　　　　　　　**1-0(0-0)**
**GUI**: Abdoulaye Keïta Sylla, Moussa Camara, Ibrahim Fofana, Djibrill Diarra, Morcilé Sylla, Ismael Sylla, Amara Touré, Aboubacar Ousmane Badara Bangoura (Ali Ibrahim K. Keïta), Naby Laye Camara, Chérif Soulemane, Bengally Sylla.
**TUN**: Sadouk Sassi, Mokhtar Dhouib, Ali Kaabi, Mohsen Jendoubi Labidi, Kamel El Chébli, Néjib Ghommidh, Témime Lahzami (Mohammed Néjib Limam), Mohammed Agrebi Ben Rehaiem, Khemais Labidi (Omar Jebaili), Tarak Dhiab, Mohamed Ali Akid. Trainer: Abdelmajid Chetali.
**Goal**: 1-0 Bengally Sylla (77).

19.06.1977, Stade Olympique d'El Menzah, Tunis; Attendance: 35,248
Referee: Hussein Fahmy Bahig (Egypt)
**TUNISIA - GUINEA**　　　　　　　　　　　　　　　　　　　　**3-1(1-1)**
**TUN**: Sadouk Sassi, Mokhtar Dhouib, Ali Kaabi, Kamel El Chébli, Khaled Mokhtar Gasmi, Néjib Ghommidh, Tarek Dhiab, Mohammed Agrebi Ben Rehaiem, Mohamed Ali Akid (23.Moncef Khouini), Témime Lahzami, Mohammed Néjib Limam (71.Khemais Labidi). Trainer: Abdelmajid Chetali.
**GUI**: Abdoulaye Keïta Sylla, Moussa Camara, Ibrahim Fofana (46.Chérif Soulemane), Djibrill Diarra, Morcilé Sylla, Ismael Sylla, Amara Touré, Chérif Keïta (63.Bangaly Kombé), Naby Laye Camara, Sekou Sylla, Bangally Sylla.
**Goals**: 1-0 Mohammed Néjib Limam (9), 1-1 Ismael Sylla (11), 2-1 Témime Lahzami (59), 3-1 Moncef Khouini (62).

# SUBGROUP B

| 10.07.1977 | Lagos | Nigeria – Ivory Coast | 4-0(3-0) |
|---|---|---|---|
| 25.07.1977 | Bouaké | Ivory Coast - Nigeria | 2-2(1-0) |

### FINAL STANDINGS

| | | | | | | | | |
|---|---|---|---|---|---|---|---|---|
| 1. Nigeria | 2 | 1 | 1 | 0 | 6 | - | 2 | 3 |
| 2. Ivory Coast | 2 | 0 | 1 | 1 | 2 | - | 6 | 1 |

Nigeria qualified for the African Zone Final.

10.07.1977, National Stadium, Lagos; Attendance: 29,815
Referee: Lawrence Chaya (Zambia)
**NIGERIA – IVORY COAST** **4-0(3-0)**
**NGA:** Emmanuel Okala, Patrick Ekeji, Samuel Ojebode, Muda Lawal, Christian Chukwu, Godwin Odiye, Segun Odegbami, Alloysius Atuegbu, Thompson Usiyen, Godwin Iwelumo, Adokie Amiesimaka. Trainer: Tihomir Jelisavčić (Yugoslavia).
**CIV:** Kouadio Koffi, Philibert Dié Feneye, Severin Zogbo Tapé, Paul Bouabré Koko (40.Camille Naounou Bobu), Jean-Baptiste Akassou Akran, Lazane Amadou Ouattara (70.Jérôme Lebri Manahou), Paul Bahona, Daniel Kouassi Apessika, Léon Goua G'Bize, Kobenan Kouman, Maxime Lacina Traoré. Trainer: Gérard Gabo.
**Goals:** 1-0 Thompson Usiyen (7), 2-0 Godwin Iwelumo (18), 3-0 Thompson Usiyen (30), 4-0 Samuel Ojebode (56 penalty).

25.07.1977, Stade Municipal, Bouaké; Attendance: 2,040
Referee: Youssou N'Diaye (Senegal)
**IVORY COAST - NIGERIA** **2-2(1-0)**
**CIV:** Néstor Bodo Akakou, Severin Zogbo Tapé, Gaston Adjoukoua, Ignace Guidi, Jean-Baptiste Akassou Akran, Laurent Madon Zahuie, Lucien Konassi Kouamé (75.Maxime Lacina Traoré), Pascal Miezan Aka, Jérôme Lebri Manahou, Kobenan Kouman, Ya Senon Honoré (46.Léon Goua G'Bize). Trainer: Gérard Gabo.
**NGA:** Emmanuel Okala, Patrick Ekeji, Samuel Ojebode, Muda Lawal, Christian Chukwu, Godwin Odiye, Segun Odegbami, Alloysius Atuegbu, Thompson Usiyen (Christopher Ogu), Godwin Iwelumo, Adokie Amiesimaka. Trainer: Tihomir Jelisavčić (Yugoslavia).
**Goals:** 1-0 Jérôme Lebri Manahou (37), 2-0 Jérôme Lebri Manahou (58), 2-1 Segun Odegbami (74), 2-2 Adokie Amiesimaka (89).

# SUBGROUP C

| | | | |
|---|---|---|---|
| 15.07.1977 | Cairo | Egypt - Zambia | 2-0(1-0) |
| 31.07.1977 | Lusaka | Zambia - Egypt | 0-0 |

## FINAL STANDINGS

| | | | | | | | | |
|---|---|---|---|---|---|---|---|---|
| 1. Egypt | 2 | 1 | 1 | 0 | 2 | - | 0 | 3 |
| 2. Zambia | 2 | 0 | 1 | 1 | 0 | - | 2 | 1 |

Egypt qualified for the African Zone Final.

15.07.1977, Nasser Stadium, Cairo; Attendance: 35,746
Referee: Alberto Michelotti (Italy)
**EGYPT - ZAMBIA**  **2-0(1-0)**
**EGY**: Abdel Ahmed Hussein, Mohammed Salah El Din, Mohammed Kuyafat El Sayed El Siagy, Saber El Maniawy, Sa'ad Mohammed Saleit, Farouk Fouad Gaafar, Omar Abdallah Omer, Mohamed Maher Hammam Bedair Abu Kheir, Ismael Mahmoud Abdel Moniem El Khoaga, Osama Mohammed Hassan Ali Khalil, Mohammed Abdallah Hamama. Trainer: Dušan Ninković (Yugoslavia).
**ZAM**: Vincent Chileshe, Edwin MBaso, Kaiser Kalambo, Robert Lutoba, Ackim Musenge, Willie Phiri, Simon Kaushi, Jani Simulambo, Bernard Chanda, Alexander Chola, Brighton Sinyangwe. Trainer: Brightwell Banda.
**Goals**: 1-0 Farouk Fouad Gaafar (29), 2-0 Mohamed Maher Hammam Bedair Abu Kheir (49).

31.07.1977, 7$^{th}$ April Stadium, Lusaka; Attendance: 30,165
Referee: John Robertson Proudfoot Gordon (Scotland)
**ZAMBIA - EGYPT**  **0-0**
**ZAM**: Vincent Chileshe, Edwin MBaso, Kaiser Kalambo, Robert Lutoba, Ackim Musenge, Willie Phiri, Alexander Chola, Bernard Chanda, Godfrey Chitalu (Jani Simulambo), Brighton Sinyangwe, Patrick Phiri (Simon Kausli). Trainer: Brightwell Banda.
**EGY**: Ahmed Ikramy El Shahat, Mohammed Salah El Din, Moustapha Osman Galab, Mohammed Kuyafat El Sayed El Siagy, Mohamed Maher Hammam Bedair Abu Kheir, Sa'ad Mohammed Saleit, Gamal Abdel Azim, Mohamed Maher Hammam Bedair Abu Kheir (46.Ibrahim Youssef Awad Allah), Ismael Mahmoud Abdel Moniem El Khoaga, Osama Mohammed Hassan Ali Khalil, Adel El Bably Aouad Allah. Trainer: Dušan Ninković (Yugoslavia).

# AFRICAN ZONE FINAL

| | | | |
|---|---|---|---|
| 25.09.1977 | Tunis | Tunisia - Nigeria | 0-0 |
| 08.10.1977 | Lagos | Nigeria - Egypt | 4-0(1-0) |
| 21.10.1977 | Cairo | Egypt - Nigeria | 3-1(2-0) |
| 12.11.1977 | Lagos | Nigeria - Tunisia | 0-1(0-0) |
| 25.11.1977 | Cairo | Egypt - Tunisia | 3-2(1-0) |
| 11.12.1977 | Tunis | Tunisia - Egypt | 4-1(2-0) |

## FINAL STANDINGS

| | | | | | | | | |
|---|---|---|---|---|---|---|---|---|
| 1. | Tunisia | 4 | 2 | 1 | 1 | 7 - 4 | 5 |
| 2. | Egypt | 4 | 2 | 0 | 2 | 7 - 11 | 4 |
| 3. | Nigeria | 4 | 1 | 1 | 2 | 5 - 4 | 3 |

Tunisia qualified for the Final Tournament.

25.09.1977, Stade Olympique d'El Menzah, Tunis; Attendance: 38,229
Referee: John Carpenter (Republic of Ireland)
**TUNISIA - NIGERIA**     **0-0**
**TUN**: Sadouk Sassi, Mokhtar Dhouib, Ali Kaabi, Khaled Mokhtar Gasmi, Omar Jebaili, Néjib Ghommidh (46.Khemais Labidi), Témime Lahzami, Mohammed Agrebi Ben Rehaiem, Ali Manai, Tarak Dhiab, Mohamed Ali Akid (61.Mohammed Néjib Limam). Trainer: Abdelmajid Chetali.
**NGA**: Emmanuel Okala, Patrick Ekeji, Samuel Ojebode, Muda Lawal, Christian Chukwu, Godwin Odiye, Segun Odegbami, Alloysius Atuegbu, Johnny N'Wadioha (66.Emmanuel Obasuyi), Godwin Iwelumo, Adokie Amiesimaka. Trainer: Tihomir Jelisavčić (Yugoslavia).

08.10.1977, National Stadium, Lagos; Attendance: 25,932
Referee: César da Luz Correia (Portugal)
**NIGERIA - EGYPT**     **4-0(1-0)**
**NGA**: Emmanuel Okada, Johnny N'Wadioha, Annas Ahmed, Samuel Ojebode, Muda Lawal, Christian Chukwu, Godwin Odiye, Segun Odegbami, Alloysius Atuegbu, Godwin Iwelumo, Adokie Amiesimaka. Trainer: Tihomir Jelisavčić (Yugoslavia).
**EGY**: Ahmed Ikramy El Shahat, Mohammed Salah El Din, Mohammed Kuyafat El Sayed El Siagy, Moustapha Osman Galab, Mohammed Moustafa Hassan Younis, Mohamed Maher Hammam Bedair Abu Kheir, Farouk Fouad Gaafar, Mohammed Saleit Sa'ad, Hassan Ali Shehata, Osama Mohammed Hassan Ali Khalil, Mosaad Mustafa Mohammed Nour. Trainer: Dušan Ninković (Yugoslavia).
**Goals**: 1-0 Christian Chukwu (24), 2-0 Segun Odegbami (54), Segun Odegbami (67), 4-0 Johnny N'Wadioha (74).

21.10.1977, Nasser Stadium, Cairo; Attendance: 90,000
Referee: Emmanuel Platopoulos (Greece)
**EGYPT - NIGERIA**     **3-1(2-0)**
**EGY**: Ahmed Ikramy El Shahat, Mohammed Salah El Din, Sami Mansour, Mohammed Moustafa Hassan Younis, Mohamed Maher Hammam Bedair Abu Kheir, Farouk Fouad Gaafar, Sa'ad Mohammed Saleit, Hassan Ali Shehata, Moustafa Ahmed Abdou Ali, Osama Mohammed Hassan Ali Khalil, Mokhtar Ali Mokhtar. Trainer: Dušan Ninković (Yugoslavia).
**NGA**: Emmanuel Okala, Patrick Ekeji, Samuel Ojebode, Muda Lawal, Christian Chukwu, Godwin Odiye, Segun Odegbami, Alloysius Atuegbu, Johnny N'Wadioha, Godwin Iwelumo, Adokie Amiesimaka. Trainer: Tihomir Jelisavčić (Yugoslavia).
**Goals**: 1-0 Moustafa Ahmed Abdou Ali (11), 2-0 Moustafa Ahmed Abdou Ali (27), 2-1 George Iwelumo (75), 3-1 Mokhtar Ali Mokhtar (90).

12.11.1977, National Stadium, Lagos; Attendance: 80,000
Referee: Ernst Dorflinger (Switzerland)
**NIGERIA - TUNISIA**  **0-1(0-0)**
**NGA:** Emmanuel Okala, Patrick Ekeji, Samuel Ojebode, Muda Lawal, Christian Chukwu, Godwin Odiye, Segun Odegbami, Alloysius Atuegbu, Johnny N'Wadioba, Kelechi Emeteole (Emmanuel Obasuyi), Adokie Amiesimaka (Rufus Ejele). Trainer: Tihomir Jelisavčić (Yugoslavia).
**TUN:** Sadouk Sassi, Ali Kaabi (46.Néjib Ghommidh), Mokhtar Dhouib, Khaled Mokhtar Gasmi, Kamal El Chébli, Khemais Labidi, Témime Lahzami, Mohammed Agrebi Ben Rehaiem, Tarek Dhiab, Mohamed Ali Akid (58.Abderraouf Ben Aziza), Mohammed Néjib Limam. Trainer: Abdelmajid Chetali.
**Goal:** 0-1 Godwin Odiye (61 own goal).

25.11.1977, Nasser Stadium, Cairo; Attendance: 120,000
Referee: Hilmi Ok (Turkey)
**EGYPT - TUNISIA**  **3-2(1-0)**
**EGY:** Ahmed Ikramy El Shahat, Mohammed Salah El Din (12.Maher Moustafa Hamman), Mohammed Moustafa Hassan Younis, Sami Mansour, Farouk Fouad Gaafar, Mohamed Maher Hammam Bedair Abu Kheir, Hassan Ali Shehata, Sa'ad Mohammed Saleit, Moustafa Ahmed Abdou Ali, Mokhtar Ali Mokhtar, Osama Mohammed Hassan Ali Khalil (72.Mahmoud Ibrahim El Khateeb). Trainer: Dušan Ninković (Yugoslavia).
**TUN:** Sadouk Sassi, Mokhtar Dhouib, Ali Kaabi, Omar Jebaili, Khaled Mokhtar Gasmi, Néjib Ghommidh, Tarek Dhiab, Kemais Labidi (57.Abderraouf Ben Aziza), Mohamed Ali Akid, Mohammed Agrebi Ben Rehaim, Mohammed Néjib Limam (46.Témime Lahzami). Trainer: Abdelmajid Chetali.
**Goals:** 1-0 Farouk Fouad Gaafar (26 penalty), 2-0 Moustafa Ahmed Abdou Ali (52), 2-1 Abderraouf Ben Aziza (80), 3-1 Mahmoud Ibrahim El Khateeb (83), 4-1 Mohamed Ali Akid (86).

11.12.1977, Stade Olympique d'El Menzah, Tunis; Attendance: 42,850
Referee: Gianfranco Menegali (Italy)
**TUNISIA - EGYPT**  **4-1(2-0)**
**TUN:** Sadouk Sassi, Mokhtar Dhouib, Ali Kaabi, Khaled Mokhtar Gasmi, Kamel El Chédli, Néjib Ghommidh, Témime Lahzami, Mohammed Agrebi Ben Rehaiem (70.Khemais Labidi), Mohamed Ali Akid, Tarek Dhiab, Mohammed Néjib Limam (60.Abderraouf Ben Aziza). Trainer: Abdelmajid Chetali.
**EGY:** Ahmed Ikramy El Shahat (65.Thabet El Batal), Ahmed Abdel Bakhi Abohlika, Mohammed Moustafa Hassan Younis, Sami Mansour, Mohamed Maher Hammam Bedair Abu Kheir, Hassan Ali Shehata, Moustafa Ahmed Abdou Ali (70.Osama Mohammed Hassan Ali Khalil), Sa'ad Mohammed Saleit, Mahmoud Ibrahim El Khateeb, Taher Mohammed Mamdouh El Rasik El Sheik, Mokhtar Ali Mokhtar. Trainer: Dušan Ninković (Yugoslavia).
**Goals:** 1-0 Mohamed Ali Akid (14), 2-0 Témime Lahzami (41), 3-0 Abderraouf Ben Aziza (65), 4-0 Khemais Labidi (75), 4-1 Ahmed Abdel Bakhi Abohlika (80).

# ASIA / OCEANIA

## GROUP 1

Sri Lanka withdrew

| | | | | |
|---|---|---|---|---|
| 27.02.1977 | Singapore | Singapore - Thailand | | 2-0(0-0) |
| 28.02.1977 | Singapore | Hong Kong - Indonesia | | 4-1(0-1) |
| 01.03.1977 | Singapore | Malaysia - Thailand | | 6-4(4-1) |
| 02.03.1977 | Singapore | Singapore - Hong Kong | | 2-2(1-1) |
| 03.03.1977 | Singapore | Indonesia - Malaysia | | 0-0 |
| 05.03.1977 | Singapore | Hong Kong - Thailand | | 2-1(1-0) |
| 06.03.1977 | Singapore | Singapore - Malaysia | | 1-0(1-0) |
| 07.03.1977 | Singapore | Thailand - Indonesia | | 3-2(3-1) |
| 08.03.1977 | Singapore | Hong Kong - Malaysia | | 1-1(1-1) |
| 09.03.1977 | Singapore | Singapore - Indonesia | | 0-4(0-3) |

### FINAL STANDINGS

| | | | | | | | | |
|---|---|---|---|---|---|---|---|---|
| 1. | Hong Kong | 4 | 2 | 2 | 0 | 9 - 5 | 6 |
| 2. | Singapore | 4 | 2 | 1 | 1 | 5 - 6 | 5 |
| 3. | Malaysia | 4 | 1 | 2 | 1 | 7 - 6 | 4 |
| 4. | Indonesia | 4 | 1 | 1 | 2 | 7 - 7 | 3 |
| 5. | Thailand | 4 | 1 | 0 | 3 | 8 - 12 | 2 |

27.02.1977, National Stadium, Singapore; Attendance: 50,445
Referee: Anton Boskovic (Australia)
**SINGAPORE - THAILAND**     **2-0(0-0)**
**SIN**: Eric Paine (Edmund Wee), Ibrahim Haslir, Robert Sim, Samad Allapitchay, Suriamurthy Rajagopal, Mohamed Gulam (Lim Teng Sal), Abidin Zainul, M. Kumar, Mohamed Hussein Noh, Dollah Kassim, Kim Song Quah. Trainer: Choo Seng Quee.
**THA**: Chaiwat Phroman, Yamsang Surasak, Yamsang Pituk, Amnaj Chalermchavalet, Pallop Makramthong, Surin Chaikitti, Sompong Nantapraparsil, Weerayudth Sawaddi, Jesdapon Na Phatalung, Vidthaya Laohakul, Chirdsak Chaibutr (Niwat Sesawasdi). Trainer: Peter Schnittger (West Germany).
**Goals**: 1-0 Kim Song Quah (48), 2-0 Suriamurthy Rajagopal (77).

28.02.1977, National Stadium, Singapore; Attendance: 31,991
Referee: Jafar Namdar (Iran)
**HONG KONG - INDONESIA**     **4-1(0-1)**
**HKG**: Chu Kwok Kuen, Chan Sai Kau, Choi York Yee (Lee Kwai Hong), Chung Chor Wai, Kwok Ka Ming, Lai Sun Cheung, Lau Wing Yip, Leung Nang Yan, Poon Cheung Wong, Tang Hung Cheong (Wun Chee Keung), Tsang Ting Fai. Trainer: Franz van Balkom (Holland).
**IDN**: Ronny Paslah, Simson Rumah Passal (Wahju Hidajat), Auri Johannis, Suaeb Rizal, Lisza Ojong, Nobon Andraawanty, Waskito Kaihun, Abdillah D'Junaidy, Herry Riswanto, Iswadi, Faizal Andi Lala (Andjas Asmara).
**Goals**: 0-1 Waskito Kainun (11), 1-1 Chung Chor Wai (61), 2-1 Wun Chee Keung (65), 3-1 Kwok Ka-Ming (69), 4-1 Lau Wing Yip (79).

01.03.1977, National Stadium, Singapore; Attendance: 42,460
Referee: Alex Vaz (India)
**MALAYSIA - THAILAND** **6-4(4-1)**
**MAS**: Ramasamy Arumugan, Mohammed Jamal Nasir Abdul Jalil, Soh Chin Aun, Yahya Jusoh (Khalid Hadji Ali), Santokh Singh, Shukor Salleh, Wan Mohammed Wan Rashid (Abdullah Ali), Wong Choon Wah, Ali Isa Bakar, James Wong Chye Fook, Keong Yip Chee. Trainer: Datuk Kuppan.
**THA**: Chaiwat Phroman, Yamsang Pituk (Surapon Thammasucharit), Yamsang Surasak, Amnaj Chalermchavalet, Surin Chaikitti, Pallop Makramthong, Sompong Nantapraparsil (Weerayudth Sawaddi), Niwat Sesawasdi, Jesdapon Na Phatalung, Vidthaya Laohakul, Chirdsak Chaibutr. Trainer: Peter Schnittger (West Germany).
**Goals**: 1-0 Wong Choon Wah (17), 2-0 Ali Isa Bakar (18), 2-1 Jesdapon Na Phatalung (27), 3-1 Ali Isa Bakar (31), 4-1 Wong Choon Wah (42), 5-1 Wong Choon Wah (50), 6-1 Wong Choon Wah (62), 6-2 Jesdapon Na Phatalung (71), 6-3 Weerayudth Sawaddi (87), 6-4 Niwat Sesawasdi (88).

02.03.1977, National Stadium, Singapore; Attendance: 63,049
Referee: Ronald Harries (New Zealand)
**SINGAPORE - HONG KONG** **2-2(1-1)**
**SIN**: Eric Paine, Ibrahim Haslir, Samad Allapitchay, Syed Mutalib, Robert Sim, Abidin Zainul, M. Kumar, Dollah Kassim, Mohamed Hussein Noh (Nasir Jalil), Suriamurthy Rajagopal, Kim Song Quah. Trainer: Choo Seng Quee.
**HKG**: Chu Kwok Kuen, Chan Sai Kau, Chung Chor Wai, Kwok Ka Ming, Lai Sun Cheung, Lau Wing Yip, Lee Kwai Hong, Poon Cheung Wong, Tang Hung Cheong, Tsang Ting Fai, Wun Chee Keung. Trainer: Franz van Balkom (Holland).
**Goals**: 0-1 Wun Chee Keung (20), 1-1 Kim Song Quah (37), 1-2 Wun Chee Keung (52), 2-2 Dollah Kassim (59).

03.03.1977, National Stadium, Singapore; Attendance:
Referee: Toshio Asami (Japan)
**INDONESIA - MALAYSIA** **0-0**
**IDN**: Ronny Paslah, Wahju Hidajat, Auri Johannis, Iman Suhatman, Lisza Ojong, Nobon Andraawanty, Iswadi, Abdillah D'Junaidy, Herry Riswanto, Roland Hermanus Pattinasarany, Hadi Ismanto (Waskito Kainun).
**MAS**: Ramasamy Arumugan, Mohammed Jamal Nasir Abdul Jalil, Soh Chin Aun, Abdullah D. Davandran, Santokh Singh, Shukor Salleh, Wan Mohammed Wan Rashid (Reduan Abdullah Ali), Wong Choon Wah, Ali Isa Bakar, James Wong Chye Fook, Keong Yip Chee. Trainer: Datuk Kuppan.

05.03.1977, National Stadium, Singapore; Attendance: 30,106
Referee: Kim Joo-Won (South Korea)
**HONG KONG - THAILAND** **2-1(1-0)**
**HKG**: Chu Kwok Kuen, Chan Sai Kau, Chung Chor Wai, Kwok Ka Ming, Lai Sun Cheung, Lau Wing Yip, Leung Nang Yan, Poon Cheung Wong, Tang Hung Cheong, Tsang Ting Fai, Choi York Yee. Trainer: Franz van Balkom (Holland).
**THA**: Chaiwat Phroman, Yamsang Pituk, Yamsang Surasak, Amnaj Chalermchavalet, Surin Chaikitti, Pallop Makramthong, Somboon Suparapop, Niwat Sesawasdi, Jesdapon Na Phatalung, Vidthaya Laohakul, Chirdsak Chaibutr. Trainer: Peter Schnittger (West Germany).
**Goals**: 1-0 Kwok Ka Ming (50), 1-1 Vidthaya Laohakul (55), 2-1 Chung Chor Wai (70).

06.03.1977, National Stadium, Singapore; Attendance: 63,124
Referee: Toshio Asami (Japan)
**SINGAPORE - MALAYSIA** **1-0(1-0)**
**SIN**: Eric Paine, Ibrahim Haslir, Syed Mutalib, Samad Allapitchay, Robert Sim, Abidin Zainul, M. Kumar (Mohamed Gulam), Suriamurthy Rajagopal (Nasir Jalil), Dollah Kassim, Mohamed Hussein Noh, Kim Song Quah. Trainer: Choo Seng Quee.
**MAS**: Ramasamy Arumugan, Yahya Jusoh, Soh Chin Aun, Abdullah D. Davandran, Santokh Singh, Shukor Salleh (Wan Mohammed Wan Rashid), Wong Choon Wah, Keong Yip Chee, Ali Isa Bakar, James Wong Chye Fook, Abdullah Ali. Trainer: Datuk Kuppan.
**Goal**: 1-0 Mohamed Hussein Noh (31).

07.03.1977, National Stadium, Singapore; Attendance: 22,988
Referee: Alex Vaz (India)
**THAILAND - INDONESIA** **3-2(3-1)**
**THA**: Chaiwat Phroman, Paisan, Yamsang Pituk, Pallop Makramthong, Amnaj Chalermchavalet, Somboon Suparapop, Surin Chaikitti, Niwat Sesawasdi, Jesdapon Na Phatalung, Vidthaya Laohakul, Chirdsak Chaibutr (Sompon Jarnyavisut). Trainer: Peter Schnittger (West Germany).
**IDN**: Ronny Paslah, Wahju Hidajat, Auri Johannis, Iman Suhatman (Suaeb Rizal), Lisza Ojong, Roland Hermanus Pattinasarany, Waskito Kainun, Abdillah D'Junaidy, Jaya Hartono (Nobon Andraawanty), Herry Riswanto, Faizal Andi Lala.
**Goals**: 1-0 Chirdsak Chaibutr (27), 2-0 Na Phatalung Jesdapon (29), 3-0 Niwat Sesawasdi (35), 3-1 Herry Riswanto (43), 3-2 Abdillah D'Junaidy (70)

08.03.1977, National Stadium, Singapore; Attendance: 48,804
Referee: Ronald Harries (New Zealand)
**HONG KONG - MALAYSIA** **1-1(1-1)**
**HKG**: Chu Kwok Kuen, Chan Sai Kau, Tsang Ting Fai, Sze Kin Hai, Au Wing Hung, Kwok Ka Ming (12.Fung Chi Ming), Lai Sun Cheung, Tang Hung Cheong, Chung Chor Wai, Wun Chee Keung, Leung Nang Yan. Trainer: Franz van Balkom (Holland).
**MAS**: Ramasamy Arumugan, Mohammed Jamal Nasir Abdul Jalil (Bakri Ibni), Soh Chin Aun, Yahya Jusoh, Abdullah D. Davandran, Santokh Singh, Wong Choon Wah, Ali Isa Bakar (Khalid Hadji Ali), Keong Yip Chee, Abdullah Ali, Reduan Abdullah Ali. Trainer: Datuk Kuppan.
**Goals**: 1-0 Fung Chi Ming (15), 1-1 Ali Isa Bakar (75).

09.03.1977, National Stadium, Singapore; Attendance: 45,160
Referee: Kim Joo Won (South Korea)
**SINGAPORE - INDONESIA** **0-4(0-3)**
**SIN**: Edmund Wee, Ibrahim Haslir, Lim Teng Sai, Syed Mutalib (Suresh Anandan), Robert Sim, Mohamed Gulam, Abidin Zainul, Mohamed Hussein Noh, Nasir Jalil, Dollah Kassim, Tang Chew Kam (Suriamurthy Rajagopal). Trainer: Choo Seng Quee.
**IDN**: Ronny Paslah, Wahju Hidajat (Iman Suhatman), Auri Johannis, Suaeb Rizal, Lisza Ojong, Andjas Asmara, Hadi Ismanto, Abdillah D'Junaidy, Iswadi, Roland Hermanus Pattinasarany, Faizal Andi Lala.
**Goals**: 0-1 Roland Hermanus Pattinasarany (4), 0-2 Andjas Asmara (11), 0-3 Faizal Andi Lala (22), 0-4 Iswadi (48).

## PLAY-OFF

12.03.1977, National Stadium, Singapore; Attendance: 60,248
Referee: Anton Boskovic (Australia)
**SINGAPORE – HONG KONG**　　　　　　　　　　　　　　　**0-1(0-1)**
**SIN**: Eric Paine, Ibrahim Haslir, Samad Allapitchay, Lim Teng Sai, Robert Sim, Abidin Zainul, Mohamed Gulam, Mohamed Hussein Noh, Dollah Kassim, Kim Song Quah, Nasir Jalil (Suriamurthy Rajagopal). Trainer: Choo Seng Quee.
**HKG**: Chu Kwok Kuen, Chung Chor Wai, Fung Chi Ming, Choi York Yee, Kwok Ka Ming, Lau Wing Yip, Wu Kwok Hung (Leung Nang Yan), Poon Cheung Wong, Tang Hung Cheong, Tsang Ting Fai, Chan Sai Kau. Trainer: Franz van Balkom (Holland).
**Goal**: 0-1 Lau Wing Yip (34).
Hong Kong qualified for the Asian Zone Final.

## GROUP 2

North Korea withdrew.

| Date | Venue | Match | Score |
|---|---|---|---|
| 27.02.1977 | Tel Aviv | Israel – South Korea | 0-0 |
| 06.03.1977 | Tel Aviv | Israel - Japan | 2-0(1-0) |
| 10.03.1977 | Tel Aviv | Japan - Israel | 0-2(0-1) |
| 20.03.1977 | Seoul | South Korea - Israel | 3-1(1-0) |
| 26.03.1977 | Tokio | Japan – South Korea | 0-0 |
| 03.04.1977 | Seoul | South Korea - Japan | 1-0(0-0) |

### FINAL STANDINGS

| | | | | | | | | | |
|---|---|---|---|---|---|---|---|---|---|
| 1. | South Korea | 4 | 2 | 2 | 0 | 4 | - | 1 | 6 |
| 2. | Israel | 4 | 2 | 1 | 1 | 5 | - | 3 | 5 |
| 3. | Japan | 4 | 0 | 1 | 3 | 0 | - | 5 | 1 |

South Korea qualified for the Asian Zone Final.

27.02.1977, National Stadium, Ramat-Gan, Tel Aviv; Attendance: 24,400
Referee: Brian McGinley (Scotland)
**ISRAEL – SOUTH KOREA**　　　　　　　　　　　　　　　**0-0**
**ISR**: Yosef Sorinov, Eli Leventhal, Haim Bar, Avi Cohen I, Meir Nimni (Yaacov Cohen), Uri Malmilian, Itzhak Shum (Daniel Neumann), Mordechai Spiegler, Moshe Schweitzer, Gideon Damti, Viktor Peretz. Trainer: David Schweitzer.
**KOR**: Kim Hwang-Ho, Choi Jong-Deok, Hwang Jae-Man, Cho Young-Jeung, Park Sung-Hwa, Kim Kang-Nam, Kim Sung-Nam, Young-Moo Lee, Cha Bum-Kun, Huh Jung-Moo (Shin Hyun-Ho), Park Yong-Joo (Kim Jin-Kook). Trainer: Choi Jung-Min.

06.03.1977, National Stadium, Ramat-Gan, Tel Aviv; Attendance: 9,300
Referee: Michel Kitabdjian (France)
**ISRAEL - JAPAN**　　　　　　　　　　　　　　　**2-0(1-0)**
**ISR**: Yosef Sorinov, Eli Leventhal, Haim Bar, Avi Cohen I, Moshe Leon, Uri Malmilian, Yaron Oz, Mordechai Spiegler, Gideon Damti, Oded Machnes, Viktor Peretz (Rifat Turk). Trainer: David Schweitzer.
**JPN**: Mitsuhisa Taguchi, Shigemi Ishii, Hiroshi Ochiai, Eijun Kiyokumo, Kazuo Saito, Nobuo Fujishima, Nobuo Kawakami, Yasuhiko Okudera, Yoshikazu Nagai, Akira Nishino, Hiroyuki Usui (Keizo Imai). Trainer: Hiroshi Ninomiya.
**Goals**: 1-0 Oded Machnes (43), 2-0 Haim Bar (57).

10.03.1977, National Stadium, Ramat-Gan, Tel Aviv; Attendance: 7,300
Referee: Achille Verbecke (France)
**JAPAN - ISRAEL**　　　　　　　　　　　　　　　　　　　　　　　　　　**0-2(0-1)**
**JPN:** Mitsuhisa Taguchi, Shigemi Ishii, Eijun Kiyokumo, Masaaki Yokotani, Hiroshi Ochiai, Kazuo Saito (Hideki Maeda), Nobuo Fujishima, Akira Nishino, Yoshikazu Nagai, Hiroyuki Usui (Kunishige Kamamoto), Yasuhiko Okudera. Trainer: Hiroshi Ninomiya.
**ISR:** Yosef Sorinov, Eli Leventhal, Haim Bar, Avi Cohen I, Moshe Leon, Uri Malmilian, Yaron Oz, Mordechai Spiegler, Gideon Damti, Oded Machnes (Yehosua Feigenbaum), Viktor Peretz. Trainer: David Schweitzer.
**Goals:** 0-1 Oded Machnes (41), 0-2 Viktor Peretz (52).

20.03.1977, Municipal Stadium, Seoul; Attendance: 38,718
Referee: Koh Guan Kiat (Malaysia)
**SOUTH KOREA - ISRAEL**　　　　　　　　　　　　　　　　　　　　　　**3-1(1-0)**
**KOR:** Kim Hwang-Ho, Cho Young-Jeung, Hwang Jae-Man, Choi Jong-Deok, Park Sung-Hwa, Kim Kang-Nam (2.Park Sang-In), Kim Sung-Nam, Young-Moo Lee, Cha Bum-Kun, Huh Jung-Moo, Kim Jin-Kook. Trainer: Choi Jung-Min.
**ISR:** Yosef Sorinov, Eli Leventhal, Haim Bar, Avi Cohen I, Moshe Leon, Yehosua Feigenbaum, Yaron Oz (46.Uri Malmilian), Mordechai Spiegler (46.Yaacov Cohen), Moshe Schweitzer, Gideon Damti, Viktor Peretz. Trainer: David Schweitzer.
**Goals**: 1-0 Cha Bum-Kun (22), 1-1 Uri Malmilian (76), 2-1 Park Sang-In (87), 3-1 Choi Jong-Deok (88).

26.03.1977, Yoyoki National Stadium, Tokyo; Attendance: 9,266
Referee: Sivapalan Kathiravale (Malaysia)
**JAPAN – SOUTH KOREA**　　　　　　　　　　　　　　　　　　　　　　　**0-0**
**JPN:** Mitsuhisa Takuchi, Hiroshi Ochiai, Shigemi Ishii, Eijun Kiyokumo, Kazuo Saito, Akira Nishino, Nobuo Fujishima, Kunishige Kamamoto, Yasuhiko Okudera, Yoshikazu Nagai, Hiroyuki Usui (Hideki Maeda). Trainer: Hiroshi Ninomiya.
**KOR:** Kim Hwang-Ho, Choi Jong-Deok, Hwang Jae-Man, Park Sung-Hwa, Cho Young-Jeung, Young-Moo Lee (70.Cho Kwang-Rae), Kim Sung-Nam (70.Shin Hyun-Ho), Park Sang-In, Cha Bum-Kun, Huh Jung-Moo. Trainer: Choi Jung-Min.

03.04.1977, National Stadium, Seoul; Attendance: 35,000
Referee: Zainal Abidin Abu Bakar (Malaysia)
**SOUTH KOREA - JAPAN**　　　　　　　　　　　　　　　　　　　　　　　**1-0(0-0)**
**KOR:** Kim Hwang-Ho, Choi Jong-Deok, Kim Ho-Kon, Cho Young-Jeung, Park Sung-Hwa, Hwang Jae-Man, Cho Kwang-Rae (Park Sang-In), Kim Sung-Nam, Lee Young-Moo, Cha Bum-Kun, Huh Jung-Moo. Trainer: Choi Jung-Min.
**JPN:** Mitsuhisa Takuchi, Hiroshi Ochiai, Kazuo Saito, Eijun Kiyokumo, Nobuo Fujishima, Kunishige Kamamoto, Shigemi Ishii (Masaaki Yokotani), Akira Nishino, Yoshikazu Nagai, Yasuhiko Okudera, Hiroyuki Usui (Hideki Maeda). Trainer: Hiroshi Ninomiya.
**Goal**: 1-0 Cha Bum-Kun (83 penalty).

# GROUP 3

Iraq withdrew
| | | | |
|---|---|---|---|
| 12.11.1976 | Jeddah | Saudi Arabia - Syria | 2-0(1-0) |
| 26.11.1976 | Damascus | Syria – Saudi Arabia | 2-1(1-1) |
| 07.01.1977 | Riyadh | Saudi Arabia - Iran | 0-3(0-1) |
| 28.01.1977 | Damascus | Syria - Iran | 0-1(0-0) |
| 06.04.1977 | | Iran - Syria | 2-0* |
| 22.04.1977 | Shiraz | Iran – Saudi Arabia | 2-0(1-0) |

### FINAL STANDINGS

| | | | | | | | |
|---|---|---|---|---|---|---|---|
| 1. Iran | 4 | 4 | 0 | 0 | 8 - 0 | | 8 |
| 2. Saudi Arabia | 4 | 1 | 0 | 3 | 3 - 7 | | 2 |
| 3. Syria | 4 | 1 | 0 | 3 | 2 - 6 | | 2 |

Iran qualified for the Asian Zone Final.

12.11.1976, Malaz Stadium, Riyadh; Attendance: 19,750
Referee: Ernst Dörflinger (Switzerland)
**SAUDI ARABIA - SYRIA** **2-0(1-0)**
**KSA**: Youssef Yahya Abdel Rawas, Mohammed Balkair Swalik, Ibrahim Tahseen, Essa Hamdan Al Dosary, Khalid Abdallah Al Tourki, Rasheed Abdel Rahman Al Jamman, Essa Kalifah Al Dosary, Wahidi Goher Al Mohammed, Saad Ibrahim Al Sadhan, Saoud Mohammed Jassem Bo Saeed, Samir Sultan Al Fahad. Trainer: William Harry McGarry (England).
**SYR**: Saif Shaher, Riad Mohammed Asfahany, Ibrahim Mouhallami, Ahmed Kaddour, Shaker Kaskim, Abdoulghani Tatich, Marwan Khalifa Khouri, Nabil Nano, Souheil Loutfi, Samir Said, Birgikli Haythem. Trainer: Karkouli Lutfi.
**Goals**: 1-0 Samir Sultan Al Fahad (22), 2-0 Saoud Mohammed Jassem Bo Saeed (54).

26.11.1976, Al Abbasiyin Stadium, Damascus; Attendance: 5,000
Referee: Doğan Babacan (Turkey)
**SYRIA – SAUDI ARABIA** **2-1(1-1)**
**SYR**: Ahmed Kall, Riad Mohammed Asfahany, Ibrahim Mouhallami, Abdul Fattah Hawa, Abdoulghani Tatich, Shaker Kaskim, Marwan Khalifa Khouri, Katbe Abdul Rahman, Souheil Loutfi, Samir Said, Birgikli Haythem. Trainer: Karkouli Lutfi.
**KSA**: Youssef Yahya Abdel Rawas, Mohammed Balkair Swalik, Rasheed Abdel Rahman Al Jamman, Othman Marzouq Al Fairoz Mubarak, Ibrahim Tahseen, Wahidi Goher Al Mohammed, Essa Hamdan Al Dosary, Essa Kalifah Al Dosary, Saoud Mohammed Jassem Bo Saeed, Khalid Abdallah Al Tourki, Samir Sultan Al Fahad (*Substitution*: Mohammed Abdul Ghani). Trainer: William Harry McGarry (England).
**Goals**: 1-0 Katbe Abdul Rahman (36), 1-1 Mohammed Abdul Ghani (44), 2-1 Khuri Marwan (82).

07.01.1977, Malaz Stadium, Riyadh; Attendance: 30,000
Referee: Erich Linemayr (Austria)
**SAUDI ARABIA - IRAN** **0-3(0-1)**
**KSA**: Youssef Yahya Abdel Rawas, Ibrahim Tahseen, Essa Kalifah Al Dosary, Essa Hamdan Al Dosary (58.Samir Sultan Al Fahad), Othman Marzouq Al Fairoz Mubarak (70.Naji Khalaf), Saoud Mohammed Jassem Bo Saeed, Mohammed Balkair Swalik, Fouda Abdulla, Shidkhan Saeed, Al Jamal Nasser, Naif Marzouq Al Makdali. Trainer: William Harry McGarry (England).
**IRN**: Nasser Hejazi, Andranik Eskandarian, Hassan Nazari, Meerfakhraei Suhamudeen, Hossein Kazerani, Ali Parvin, Mohammad Sadeghi, Iraj Danaeifard, Gholam Hossein Mazloomi (87.Ghafour Jahani), Hassan Roshan, Alireza Khorshidi. Trainer: Heshmatollah Mohajerani.
**Goals**: 0-1 Gholam Hossein Mazloomi (16), 0-2 Hassan Roshan (62), 0-3 Gholam Hossein Mazloomi

(78).

28.01.1977, Al Abbasiyin Stadium, Damascus; Attendance: 22,000
Referee: Georges Konrath (France)
**SYRIA - IRAN**                                              **0-1(0-0)**
**SYR**: Shaher Saif, Riad Mohammed Asfahany, Abdul Fattah Hawa, Mahmoud Toughli, Ibrahim Mouhallami, Georges Nasri, Abdoulghani Tatich, Katbe Abdul Rahman, Abdul Mowlah, Berzaghli Abdolqadir, Marwan Khalifa Khouri. Trainer: Karkouli Lutfi.
**IRN**: Nasser Hejazi, Andranik Eskandarian, Hassan Nazari, Nasrollah Abdollahi, Hossein Kazerani (56.Meerfakhraei Suhamudeen), Ali Parvin, Mohammad Sadeghi, Ebrahim Ghasempour (80.Mahmood Haqeeqian), Gholam Hossein Mazloomi, Hassan Roshan, Alireza Khorshidi. Trainer: Heshmatollah Mohajerani.
**Goal**: 0-1 Ali Parvin.

06.04.1977
**IRAN - SYRIA**                                              **2-0***
*Syria withdrew, the match was awarded as win (2-0) for Iran.*

22.04.1977, Tajgozari Stadium, Shiraz; Attendance: 20,000
Referee: Ernst Dörflinger (Switzerland)
**IRAN – SAUDI ARABIA**                                       **2-0(1-0)**
**IRN**: Behzad Nabavi, Ali Reza Ghesghayan, Nasser Musallami, Mohammad Ali Shojaei, Mehdi Dinvarzadeh, Hussain Hussaini, Mohsin Yousifi, Hossein Faraki, Muslim Khani, Abdulrazzaq Khadimpeer (78.Maees Minasian), Hamid Alidoosti (46.Habib Shareefi). Trainer: Heshmatollah Mohajerani.
**KSA**: Salim Abdul Rahman Aly Marwan, Ibrahim Tahseen (52.Hamid Subhi), Ahmed Tofari, Jassim Anbar, Salim Abdullah, Essa Kalifah Al Dosary, Adris Aden, Khalid Abdallah Al Tourki, Saoud Mohammed Jassem Bo Saeed (46.Ibrahim Mubarak), Abdulla Al Fooda, Saad Ibrahim Al Sadhan. Trainer: William Harry McGarry (England).
**Goals**: 1-0 Mohsin Yousifi (10), 2-0 Habib Shareefi (84).

## GROUP 4

United Arab Emirates withdrew.

| Date | Venue | Match | Result |
|---|---|---|---|
| 11.03.1977 | Doha | Kuwait - Bahrain | 2-0(2-0) |
| 13.03.1977 | Doha | Qatar - Bahrain | 2-0(1-0) |
| 15.03.1977 | Doha | Qatar - Kuwait | 0-2(0-1) |
| 17.03.1977 | Doha | Kuwait - Bahrain | 2-1(1-0) |
| 19.03.1977 | Doha | Qatar - Bahrain | 0-3(0-1) |
| 21.03.1977 | Doha | Qatar - Kuwait | 1-4(0-3) |

### FINAL STANDINGS

| | | | | | | | | |
|---|---|---|---|---|---|---|---|---|
| 1. | Kuwait  | 4 | 4 | 0 | 1 | 10 - 2 | 8 |
| 2. | Bahrain | 4 | 1 | 0 | 3 | 4 - 6  | 2 |
| 3. | Qatar   | 4 | 1 | 0 | 3 | 3 - 9  | 2 |

Kuwait qualified for the Asian Zone Final.

11.03.1977, Khalifa International Stadium, Doha (Qatar); Attendance: 4,000
Referee: Patrick Partridge (England)
**KUWAIT - BAHRAIN**     **2-0(2-0)**
**KUW**: Ahmed Khuder Al Tarabulsi, Hussain Mohammad Ahmed Al Kandari, Abdullah Yousuf Mayouf, Mahboub Juma Mahboub Mubarak, Ibrahim Mohammed Al Duraihem, Farouk Ibrahim Al Awadhi Al Saleh (46.Saoud Khalid Bo Hamad), Saed Mohammed Abdul Aziz Al Houti, Hamad Khalid Bo Hamad, Fatih Kamil Fayyaz Matar Marzouq, Faisal Ali Al Dakhil (65.Abdul Aziz Saoud Al Anbari), Jassem Jamal Yaqoub Sultan. Trainer: Mário Jorge Lobo Zagallo (Brazil).
**BHR**: Hamoud Sultan Mazkoor, Faisal Mohammed, Nazeer Al Derzi, Jawhar Al Mass, Hamad Saleh Nayem, Mohamed Jassim Abbas, Mohammed Al Zayyani, Ibrahim Zowayed, Mohammed Bahram, Fouad Abou Shaqr, Ibrahim Al Farhan.
**Goals**: 1-0 Jassem Jamal Yaqoub Sultan (40), 2-0 Abdul Aziz Saoud Al Anbari (62).

13.03.1977, Khalifa International Stadium, Doha; Attendance: 3,000
Referee: Walter Hungerbühler (Switzerland)
**QATAR - BAHRAIN**     **2-0(1-0)**
**QAT**: Mohammed Sami Wafah, Anbar Basheer Abubakr, Sulaiman Hassan Kashmeer, Salman Almas Jumah, Anbar Mubarak Al Ali, Ahmad Omar Shaker, Majed Mohammad Majed, Hassan Abdul Rahman Abdullah Al Qadi, Mansour Muftah Faraj Bekhit, Hassan Matar Sayed Al Suwaidi, Abdullah Ahmad Hassan. Trainer: Frank Wignall (England).
**BHR**: Hamoud Sultan Mazkoor, Abdullah Bader, Jawhar Al Mass, Nazeer Al Derzi, Faisal Mohammed, Hamad Saleh Nayem, Ibrahim Zowayed, Mohamed Jassim Abbas, Mohammed Bahram, Ibrahim Al Farhan, Fouad Abou Shaqr.
**Goals**: 1-0 Mansour Muftah Faraj Bekhit (40), 2-0 Hassan Matar Sayed Al Suwaidi (62).

15.03.1977, Khalifa International Stadium, Doha; Attendance: 4,000
Referee: Klaus Ohmsen (West Germany)
**QATAR - KUWAIT**     **0-2(0-1)**
**QAT**: Mohammed Sami Wafah, Anbar Basheer Abubakr, Anbar Mubarak Al Ali, Sulaiman Hassan Kashmeer, Maqboul Abdullah Jumah, Ahmad Omar Shaker (79.Mohammed Taher Mohammed), Mohammed Ghanem Heji Al Remihy, Abdullah Ahmad Hassan, Hassan Abdul Rahman Abdullah Al Qadi, Mansour Muftah Faraj Bekhit, Hassan Matar Sayed Al Suwaidi. Trainer: Frank Wignall (England).
**KUW**: Ahmed Khuder Al Tarabulsi, Hussain Mohammad Ahmed Al Kandari, Abdullah Yousuf Mayouf, Mahboub Juma Mahboub Mubarak, Ibrahim Mohammed Al Duraihem, Farouk Ibrahim Al Awadhi Al Saleh, Saed Mohammed Abdul Aziz Al Houti, Hamad Khalid Bo Hamad (72.Saoud Khalid Bo Hamad), Jassem Jamal Yaqoub Sultan, Fatih Kamil Fayyaz Matar Marzouq (74.Faisal Ali Al Dakhil), Abdul Aziz Saoud Al Anbari. Trainer: Mário Jorge Lobo Zagallo (Brazil).
**Goals**: 0-1 Jassem Jamal Yaqoub Sultan (28), 0-2 Abdul Aziz Saoud Al Anbari (68).

17.03.1977, Khalifa International Stadium, Doha (Qatar); Attendance: 2,000
Referee: Riccardo Lattanzi (Italy)
**KUWAIT - BAHRAIN**     **2-1(1-0)**
**KUW**: Ahmed Khuder Al Tarabulsi, Hussain Mohammad Ahmed Al Kandari, Abdullah Yousuf Mayouf, Ibrahim Mohammed Al Duraihem, Redah Abdullah Mohammed MaRafi, Farouk Ibrahim Al Awadhi Al Saleh (67.Saleh Abdul Razzak Al Asfoor), Saed Mohammed Abdul Aziz Al Houti (64.Saoud Khalid Bo Hamad), Hamad Khalid Bo Hamad, Fatih Kamil Fayyaz Matar Marzouq, Jassem Jamal Yaqoub Sultan, Abdul Aziz Saoud Al Anbari. Trainer: Mário Jorge Lobo Zagallo (Brazil).
**BHR**: Hamoud Sultan Mazkoor, Nazeer Al Derzi, Faisal Mohammed, Mohammed Al Zayyani, Jawhar Al Mass, Hamad Saleh Nayem, Abdullah Bader, Ibrahim Zowayed, Fouad Abou Shaqr, Ibrahim Al Farhan, Mohammed Fahad.
**Goals**: 1-0 Abdul Aziz Saoud Al Anbari (33), 2-0 Ibrahim Mohammed Al Duraihem (56), 2-1 Fouad Abou Shaqr (73).

19.03.1977, Khalifa International Stadium, Doha; Attendance: 2,000
Referee: Patrick Partridge (England)
**QATAR - BAHRAIN**                                                                                                 **0-3(0-1)**
**QAT**: Mohammed Sami Wafah, Anbar Basheer Abubakr, Anbar Mubarak Al Ali, Sulaiman Hassan Kashmeer, Maqboul Abdullah Jumah, Mohammed Ghanem Heji Al Remihy, Ahmed Fostoq, Abdullah Ahmad Hassan, Hassan Abdul Rahman Abdullah Al Qadi, Mansour Muftah Faraj Bekhit, Hassan Matar Sayed Al Suwaidi. Trainer: Frank Wignall (England).
**BHR**: Hamoud Sultan Mazkoor, Jawhar Al Mass, Nazeer Al Derzi, Mohammed Al Zayyani, Abdullah Bader, Hamad Saleh Nayem, Ibrahim Zowayed, Mohammed Fahad, Fouad Abou Shaqr, Ibrahim Al Farhan, Yousef Sharida.
**Goals**: 0-1 Fouad Abou Shaqr (32), 0-2 Mohammed Al Zayyani (57), 0-3 Ibrahim Al Farhan (73 penalty).

21.03.1977, Khalifa International Stadium, Doha; Attendance: 2,000
Referee: Riccardo Lattanzi (Italy)
**KUWAIT - QATAR**                                                                                 **4-1(3-0)**
**KUW**: Ahmed Khuder Al Tarabulsi, Hussain Mohammad Ahmed Al Kandari, Abdullah Yousuf Mayouf, Mahboub Juma Mahboub Mubarak, Ibrahim Mohammed Al Duraihem, Farouk Ibrahim Al Awadhi Al Saleh, Saed Mohammed Abdul Aziz Al Houti (46.Saoud Khalid Bo Hamad), Hamad Khalid Bo Hamad, Fatih Kamil Fayyaz Matar Marzouq (63.Faisal Ali Al Dakhil), Jassem Jamal Yaqoub Sultan, Abdul Aziz Saoud Al Anbari. Trainer: Mário Jorge Lobo Zagallo (Brazil).
**QAT**: Mohammed Sami Wafah (27.Hussein Abdullah Mohammed), Anbar Basheer Abubakr, Anbar Mubarak Al Ali, Sulaiman Hassan Kashmeer, Maqboul Abdullah Jumah, Ahmad Omar Shaker, Mohammed Ghanem Heji Al Remihy (68.Abdullah Ahmad Hassan), Said Abdullah Najm Al Solaiti, Hassan Abdul Rahman Abdullah Al Qadi, Hassan Matar Sayed Al Suwaidi, Mansour Muftah Faraj Bekhit. Trainer: Frank Wignall (England).
**Goals**: 1-0 Jassem Jamal Yaqoub Sultan (10), 2-0 Abdullah Yousuf Mayouf (16), 3-0 Farouk Ibrahim Al Awadhi Al Saleh (20), 4-0 Hamad Khalid Bo Hamad (60), 4-1 Anbar Basheer Abubakr (82).

# GROUP 5

| | | | |
|---|---|---|---|
| 13.03.1977 | Suva | Australia - Taiwan | 3-0(2-0) |
| 16.03.1977 | Suva | Taiwan - Australia | 1-2(1-1) |
| 20.03.1977 | Auckland | New Zealand - Taiwan | 6-0(4-0) |
| 23.03.1977 | Auckland | Taiwan - New Zealand | 0-6(0-2) |
| 27.03.1977 | Sydney | Australia - New Zealand | 3-1(0-1) |
| 30.03.1977 | Auckland | New Zealand - Australia | 1-1(1-1) |

## FINAL STANDINGS

| | | | | | | | | |
|---|---|---|---|---|---|---|---|---|
| 1. Australia | 4 | 3 | 1 | 0 | 9 | - | 3 | 7 |
| 2. New Zealand | 4 | 2 | 1 | 1 | 14 | - | 4 | 5 |
| 3. Taiwan | 4 | 0 | 0 | 4 | 1 | - | 17 | 0 |

Australia qualified for the Asian Zone Final.

13.03.1977, Ba Sports, Suva (Fiji); Attendance: 4,000
Referee: Watana Promasakhanaskolnakorn (Thailand)
**AUSTRALIA - TAIWAN** **3-0(2-0)**
**AUS**: Todd Clarke, George Harris, Peter Frederick Wilson, Colin Bennett, Harry Williams, James Rooney, Agenor Muniz, Gary Byrne, Attila Abonyi, Peter Ollerton, John Kosmina. Trainer: James Shoulder (England).
**TPE**: Chen Hung-chiang, Choa Chen-chung, Hsu Chih-hsiang, Chen Chun-ming, Jong Chien-wu, Fang Shin-sing, Chang Kuo-chi, Lo Chin-tsong, Lee Fu-tsai, Lin Tsun-tien, You Cheng-kung (*Substitutes*: Lee Down-jia, Chow Tson-fu). Trainer: Lew Pak.
**Goals**: 1-0 James Rooney (8), 2-0 Attila Abonyi (16), 3-0 James Rooney (46).

16.03.1977, Ba Sports, Suva (Fiji); Attendance: 2,000
Referee: Vijit Getkaew (Thailand)
**TAIWAN - AUSTRALIA** **1-2(1-1)**
**TPE**: Chen Hung-chiang, Choa Chen-chung, Hsu Chih-hsiang, Jong Chien-wu, Fang Shin-sing, Chow Tson-fu (59.Lin Tsin-Tien), Chang Kuo-chi, Lo Chin-tsong, Fu Po-Tsun, Lee Fu-tsai, You Cheng-kung (79.Chang Jen-lin). Trainer: Lew Pak.
**AUS**: Todd Clarke, Peter Stone, Peter Frederick Wilson, Colin Bennett, George Harris, Agenor Muniz, Gary Byrne, James Rooney, Attie Abonyi, Peter Ollerton (Johnatan Nyskohus), John Kosmina. Trainer: James Shoulder (England).
**Goals**: 1-0 Fang Shin-sing (29), 1-1 John Kosmina (35), 1-2 Attila Abonyi (58).

20.03.1977, Newmarket Park, Auckland; Attendance: 5,000
Referee: Govindasamy Suppiah (Singapore)
**NEW ZEALAND - TAIWAN** **6-0(4-0)**
**NZL**: Kevin Curtin, Anthony Sibley, John Houghton, Adrian Coroon Elrick, Ronald Armstrong, Brian Alfred Turner (60.Warren Fleet), Steven Paul Sumner, David Taylor, Clive Campbell, Keith Nelson, Kevin Weymouth. Trainer: Walter Cyril Joseph Hughes.
**TPE**: Chen Hung-chiang, Hsu Chih-hsiang, Lee Fu-tsai, Jong Chien-wu, Chow Tson-fu, Fang Shin-sing, Lo Chih-tsong, Chang Kuo-chi, Choa Chen-chung, Chen Chun-ming (46.Lee Down-jia), Lin Tsun-tien. Trainer: Lew Pak.
**Goals**: 1-0 Keith Nelson (3), 2-0 Keith Nelson (6), 3-0 Clive Campbell (16), 4-0 David Taylor (42), 5-0 Keith Nelson (60), 6-0 Kevin Weymouth (73).

23.03.1977, Newmarket Park, Auckland; Attendance: 3,000
Referee: Harpajan Sing Dhillon (Singapore)
**TAIWAN - NEW ZEALAND**                                             **0-6(0-2)**
**TPE**: Chen Hung-chiang, Hsu Chih-hsiang, Lee Fu-tsai, Jong Chien-wu, Chow Tson-fu, Fang Shin-sing, Lo Chih-tsong, Chang Kuo-chi, Choa Chen-chung, Lin Tsun-tien, You Chen-kung. Trainer: Lew Pak.
**NZL**: Kevin Curtin, Anthony Sibley (46.Ian Park), John Houghton, Adrian Coroon Elrick, Ronald Armstrong, Brian Alfred Turner, Steven Paul Sumner, David Taylor, Clive Campbell, Keith Nelson, Kevin Weymouth. Trainer: Walter Cyril Joseph Hughes.
**Goals**: 0-1 Keith Nelson (10), 0-2 Steven Paul Sumner (15), 0-3 Steven Paul Sumner (51), 0-4 Steven Paul Sumner (55), 0-5 Ronald Armstrong (71), 0-6 Keith Nelson (74).

27.03.1977, Cricket Ground, Sydney; Attendance: 12,250
Referee: Cham Tam Sun (Hong Kong)
**AUSTRALIA - NEW ZEALAND**                                          **3-1(0-1)**
**AUS**: Todd Clarke, George Harris, Peter Frederick Wilson, Colin Bennett, Harry Williams, Agenor Muniz (67.David Harding), Gary Byrne, James Rooney, Attila Abonyi, Peter Ollerton, John Kosmina. Trainer: James Shoulder (England).
**NZL**: Kevin Curtin, Anthony Sibley, John Houghton, Adrian Coroon Elrick, Ronald Armstrong, Brian Alfred Turner, Steven Paul Sumner, David Taylor, Clive Campbell (65.Glenn Laurence Dods), Keith Nelson, Kevin Weymouth (82.Ian Park). Trainer: Walter Cyril Joseph Hughes.
**Goals**: 0-1 Keith Nelson (4), 1-1 Peter Ollerton (60), 2-1 John Kosmina (72), 3-1 Peter Ollerton (85).

30.03.1977, Newmarket Park, Auckland; Attendance: 11,000
Referee: Cheung Kwok Kui (Hong Kong)
**NEW ZEALAND - AUSTRALIA**                                          **1-1(1-1)**
**NZL**: Kevin Curtin, Anthony Sibley, John Houghton, Adrian Coroon Elrick, Ronald Armstrong, Brian Alfred Turner, Steven Paul Sumner, David Taylor, Glenn Laurence Dods, Keith Nelson, Kevin Weymouth (Ian Park). Trainer: Walter Cyril Joseph Hughes.
**AUS**: Todd Clarke, George Harris, Peter Frederick Wilson, Colin Bennett, Harry Williams, David Harding, James Rooney, Gary Byrne, John Kosmina, Peter Ollerton, Attila Abonyi. Trainer: James Shoulder (England).
**Goals**: 1-0 Peter Ollerton (18), 1-1 Keith Nelson (34).

# ASIAN ZONE FINAL

| | | | |
|---|---|---|---|
| 19.06.1977 | Hong Kong | Hong Kong - Iran | 0-2(0-1) |
| 26.06.1977 | Hong Kong | Hong Kong – South Korea | 0-1(0-0) |
| 03.07.1977 | Pusan | South Korea - Iran | 0-0 |
| 10.07.1977 | Adelaide | Australia - Hong Kong | 3-0(1-0) |
| 14.08.1977 | Melbourne | Australia - Iran | 0-1(0-0) |
| 27.08.1977 | Sydney | Australia – South Korea | 2-1(0-1) |
| 02.10.1977 | Hong Kong | Hong Kong - Kuwait | 1-3(1-1) |
| 09.10.1977 | Seoul | South Korea - Kuwait | 1-0(0-0) |
| 16.10.1977 | Sydney | Australia - Kuwait | 1-2(0-1) |
| 23.10.1977 | Seoul | South Korea - Australia | 0-0 |
| 28.10.1977 | Tehran | Iran - Kuwait | 1-0(0-0) |
| 30.10.1977 | Hong Kong | Hong Kong - Australia | 2-5(0-3) |
| 05.11.1977 | Kuwait City | Kuwait – South Korea | 2-2(0-1) |
| 11.11.1977 | Tehran | Iran – South Korea | 2-2(0-1) |
| 12.11.1977 | Kuwait City | Kuwait - Hong Kong | 4-0(3-0) |
| 18.11.1977 | Tehran | Iran - Hong Kong | 3-0(3-0) |
| 19.11.1977 | Kuwait City | Kuwait – Australia | 1-0(0-0) |
| 25.11.1977 | Tehran | Iran – Australia | 1-0(0-0) |
| 03.12.1977 | Kuwait City | Kuwait - Iran | 1-2(1-0) |
| 04.12.1977 | Seoul | South Korea - Hong Kong | 5-2(2-0) |

## FINAL STANDINGS

| | | | | | | | | |
|---|---|---|---|---|---|---|---|---|
| 1. | Iran | 8 | 6 | 2 | 0 | 12 - 3 | 14 |
| 2. | South Korea | 8 | 3 | 4 | 1 | 12 - 8 | 10 |
| 3. | Kuwait | 8 | 4 | 1 | 3 | 13 - 8 | 9 |
| 4. | Australia | 8 | 3 | 1 | 4 | 11 - 8 | 7 |
| 5. | Hong Kong | 8 | 0 | 0 | 8 | 5 - 26 | 0 |

Iran qualified for the Final Tournament.

19.06.1977, Government Stadium, Hong Kong; Attendance: 28,000
Referee: Cezare Gussoni (Italy)
**HONG KONG - IRAN**     **0-2(0-1)**
HKG: Chu Kwok Kuen, Poon Cheung Wong, Choi York Yee, Chan Saei Kawo, Tsang Ting Fai, Leung Nang Yan (77.Lee Kwai Hong), Woo Kok Hong, Sze Kin Hai (69.Tang Hong Jung), Kwok Ka Ming, Lau Wing Yip, Chung Chor Wai. Trainer: Franz van Balkom (Holland).
IRN: Nasser Hejazi, Habib Khabiri, Hassan Nazari, Nasrollah Abdollahi, Hossein Kazerani, Ali Parvin, Mohammad Sadeghi, Ebrahim Ghasempour, Mohammad Reza Adelkhani (46.Iraj Danaeifard), Hassan Roshan, Ghafour Jahani. Trainer: Heshmatollah Mohajerani.
**Goals**: 0-1 Hossein Kazerani (22), 0-2 Ghafour Jahani (77).

26.06.1977, Government Stadium, Hong Kong; Attendance: 26,952
Referee: Ferdinand Biwersi (West Germany)
**HONG KONG – SOUTH KOREA**     **0-1(0-0)**
HKG: Chu Kwok Kuen, Chan Fat Chi, Lai Sun Cheung (70.Chi Kang Lun), Tsang Ting Fai, Chan Sai Kau (70.Au Wing Hung), Leung Nang Yan, Wu Kwok Hung, Kwok Ka Ming, Lee Kwai Hong, Chung Chor Wai, Lau Wing Yip. Trainer: Franz van Balkom (Holland).
KOR: Kim Hwang-Ho, Kim Ho-Kon, Hwang Jae-Man, Choi Jong-Deok, Park Sung-Hwa, Cho Young-Jeung, Kim Kang-Nam, Kim Sung-Nam, Lee Hoe-Taik (46.Choi Jong-Deok), Cha Bum-Kun, Kim Jin-Kook. Trainer: Choi Jung-Min.
**Goal**: 0-1 Cha Bum-Kun (81).

03.07.1977, Kudok Municipal Stadium, Pusan; Attendance: 14,882
Referee: Ian Foote (Scotland)
**SOUTH KOREA - IRAN**      **0-0**
**KOR:** Byun Ho-Yung, Kim Ho-Kon, Cho Young-Jeung, Park Sung-Hwa, Hwang Jae-Man, Park Sang-In, Cha Bum-Kun, Cho Kwang-Rae, Lee Hoe-Taik (46.Kim Jae-Han), Huh Jung-Moo, Kim Jin-Kook. Trainer: Choi Jung-Min.
**IRN:** Nasser Hejazi, Andranik Eskandarian, Hassan Nazari, Nasrollah Abdolahi, Hossein Kazerani, Ali Parvin, Ebrahim Ghasempour, Iraj Danaeifard, Ghafour Jahani (67.Hossein Faraki), Hassan Roshan, Mohammad Sadeghi. Trainer: Heshmatollah Mohajerani.

10.07.1977, Hindmarsh Stadium, Adelaide; Attendance: 14,000
Referee: Walter Hungerbühler (Switzerland)
**AUSTRALIA - HONG KONG**      **3-0(1-0)**
**AUS:** Allan Maher, George Harris, Peter Frederick Wilson, Colin Bennett, Harry Williams, Murray Barnes, David Harding, James Rooney, John Kosmina, Peter Ollerton, Johnatan Nyskohus. Trainer: James Shoulder (England).
**HKG:** Chu Kwok Kuen, Chan Fat Chi (65.Chung Chor Wai), Choi York Yee, Lai Sun Cheung, Chan Sai Kau, Tsang Ting Fai, Lee Kwai Hong, Wu Kwok Hung, Kwok Ka Ming, Cheung Ka Ping, Lau Wing Yip (46.Sze Kin Hai). Trainer: Franz van Balkom (Holland).
**Goals:** 1-0 John Kosmina (27), 2-0 Murray Barnes (46), 3-0 John Kosmina (84).

14.08.1977, Olympic Park, Melbourne; Attendance: 17,000
Referee: Franz Wöhrer (Austria)
**AUSTRALIA - IRAN**      **0-1(0-0)**
**AUS:** Allan Maher, George Harris, Colin Bennett, Peter Frederick Wilson, Harry Williams, Murray Barnes, David Harding, James Rooney, John Kosmina, Peter Ollerton, Johnatan Nyskohus (71.Peter Sharne). Trainer: James Shoulder (England).
**IRN:** Nasser Hedjazi, Hassan Nazari, Hossein Kazerani, Nasrollah Abdolahi, Andranik Eskandarian, Hassan Nayebagha, Ali Parvin, Ibrahim Ghassempour (80.Habib Khabiri), Mohammed Sadeghi, Hassan Roshan, Ghafour Jahani. Trainer: Heshmatollah Mohajerani.
**Goal:** 0-1 Hassan Roshan (68).

27.08.1977, Sports Ground, Sydney; Attendance: 8,719
Referee: Johannes Nicolaas Ignatius „Jan" Keizer (Holland)
**AUSTRALIA – SOUTH KOREA**      **2-1(0-1)**
**AUS:** Allan Maher, George Harris (62.Gary Byrne), Peter Frederick Wilson, Colin Bennett, Harry Williams, Murray Barnes, David Harding, James Rooney, John Kosmina, Peter Ollerton, Johnatan Nyskohus (62.Attila Abonyi). Trainer: James Shoulder (England).
**KOR:** Byun Ho-Yung (66.Kim Hwang-Ho), Choi Jong-Deok (80.Kim Jin-Kook), Kim Ho-Kon, Cho Young-Jeung, Park Sung-Hwa, Kang Byung-Chan, Huh Jung-Moo, Cho Kwang-Rae, Park Sang-In, Cha Bum-Kun, Kim Jae-Han. Trainer: Choi Jung-Min.
**Goals:** 0-1 Cha Bum-Kun (23), 1-1 John Kosmina (63), 2-1 John Kosmina (82).

02.10.1977, Government Stadium, Hong Kong; Attendance: 25,000
Referee: Ángel Franco Martínez (Spain)
**HONG KONG - KUWAIT** **1-3(1-1)**
**HKG**: Ma Pit Hung, Chan Fat Chi, Chan Sai Kau, Chee Yat Por, Chung Chor Wai (66.Wun Chee Keung), Fung Chi Ming (69.Cheung Ka Ping), Kwok Ka Ming, Lai Sun Cheung, Sze Kin Hai, Tsang Ting Fai, Wu Kwok Hung. Trainer: Franz van Balkom (Holland).
**KUW**: Ahmed Khuder Al Tarabulsi, Ibrahim Mohammed Al Duraihem (81.Redah Abdullah Mohammed Ma'Rafi), Mahboub Juma Mahboub Mubarak, Abdullah Yousuf Mayouf, Hussain Mohammad Ahmed Al Kandari, Saed Mohammed Abdul Aziz Al Houti (46.Saoud Khalid Bo Hamad), Farouk Ibrahim Al Awadhi Al Saleh, Hamad Khalid Bo Hamad, Jassem Jamal Yaqoub Sultan (77.Fatih Kamil Fayyaz Matar Marzouq), Abdul Aziz Saoud Al Anbari, Faisal Ali Al Dakhil. Trainer: Mário Jorge Lobo Zagallo (Brazil).
**Goals**: 0-1 Faisal Ali Al Dakhil (11), 1-1 Chung Chor Wai (25), 1-2 Saud Bo Hamad (64), 1-3 Jassem Jamal Yaqoub Sultan (72).

09.10.1977, National Stadium, Seoul; Attendance: 13,000
Referee: Giulio Sciacci (Italy)
**SOUTH KOREA - KUWAIT** **1-0(0-0)**
**KOR**: Byun Ho-Yung, Choi Jong-Deok, Kim Ho-Kon, Cho Young-Jeung, Park Sung-Hwa, Cho Kwang-Rae, Kim Kang-Nam, Kim Sung-Nam, Cha Bum-Kun, Park Sang-In, Kim Jae-Han. Trainer: Choi Jung-Min.
**KUW**: Ahmed Khuder Al Tarabulsi, Sultan Yaqoub Sultan, Mahboub Juma Mahboub Mubarak, Saed Mohammed Abdul Aziz Al Houti, Hamad Khalid Bo Hamad, Hussain Mohammad Ahmed Al Kandari (Redah Abdullah Mohammed Ma'Rafi), Abdullah Yousuf Mayouf, Mahboub Juma Mahboub Mubarak, Jassem Jamal Yaqoub Sultan, Faisal Ali Al Dakhil (Fatih Kamil Fayyaz Matar Marzouq), Abdul Aziz Saoud Al Anbari. Trainer: Mário Jorge Lobo Zagallo (Brazil).
**Goal**: 1-0 Park Sang-In (49).

16.10.1977, Cricket Ground, Sydney; Attendance: 12,015
Referee: Michel Vautrot (France)
**AUSTRALIA - KUWAIT** **1-2(1-1)**
**AUS**: Allan Maher, Colin John Curran, Peter Frederick Wilson, Colin Bennett, Harry Williams, Murray Barnes, David Harding (Peter Stone), James Rooney, Adrian Alston, John Kosmina, Peter Ollerton (Attila Abonyi). Trainer: James Shoulder (England).
**KUW**: Ahmad Al Tarabolsi, Hussain Mohammad Ahmed Al Kandari, Adnan Abdullah, Abdullah Yousuf Mayouf, Farouk Ibrahim Al Awadhi Al Saleh (85.Saoud Khalid Bo Hamad), Saed Mohammed Abdul Aziz Al Houti, Hamad Khalid Bo Hamad, Fatih Kamil Fayyaz Matar Marzouq, Faisal Ali Al Dakhil, Jassem Jamal Yaqoub Sultan, Abdul Aziz Saoud Al Anbari. Trainer: Mário Jorge Lobo Zagallo (Brazil).
**Goals**: 1-0 James Rooney (40), 1-1 Fatih Kamil Fayyaz Matar Marzouq (41 penalty), 1-2 Abdul Aziz Saoud Al Anbari (49).

23.10.1977, National Stadium, Seoul; Attendance: 20,000
Referee: Ulf Helmer Johan Eriksson (Sweden)
**SOUTH KOREA - AUSTRALIA** **0-0**
**KOR**: Kim Hee-Cheon, Choi Jong-Deok, Cho Young-Jeung (53.Kim Hee-Tae), Park Sung-Hwa, Kim Ho-Kon, Huh Jung-Moo, Park Sang-In, Kim Kang-Nam, Park Jong-Won (80.Lee Young-Moo), Kim Jae-Han, Cha Bum-Kun. Trainer: Choi Jung-Min.
**AUS**: Allan Maher, Colin John Curran, Peter Frederick Wilson, Colin Bennett, George Harris, Gary Byrne, James Rooney (62.Gary Marocchi), Peter Stone, John Kosmina, Peter Ollerton (67.Adrian Alston), Attila Abonyi. Trainer: James Shoulder (England).

28.10.1977, Ayramehr Stadium, Tehran; Attendance: 110,000
Referee: Clive Thomas (Wales)
**IRAN - KUWAIT** **1-0(0-0)**
**IRN**: Nasser Hejazi, Hassan Nazari, Hussain Kazarani, Nasrollah Abdolahi, Andranik Eskandarian, Hassan Nayebagha, Mohammad Sadeghi, Ebrahim Ghasempour, Ali Parvin, Mohammad Reza Adelkhani, Ghafour Jahani. Trainer: Heshmatollah Mohajerani.
**KUW**: Ahmed Khuder Al Tarabulsi, Sultan Yacoub Sultan, Abdullah Yousuf Mayouf, Ibrahim Mohammed Al Duraihem, Mahboub Juma Mahboub Mubarak, Saed Mohammed Abdul Aziz Al Houti, Hamad Khalid Bo Hamad (68.Badr Abdul Hamid Bo Abbas), Saoud Khalid Bo Hamad, Jassem Jamal Yaqoub Sultan, Abdul Aziz Saoud Al Anbari, Faisal Ali Al Dakhil. Trainer: Mário Jorge Lobo Zagallo (Brazil).
**Goal**: 1-0 Ghafour Jahani (48).

30.10.1977, Government Stadium, Hong Kong; Attendance: 8,000
Referee: Alexis Ponnet (Belgium)
**HONG KONG - AUSTRALIA** **2-5(0-3)**
**HKG**: Ma Pit Hung, Chan Sai Kau, Choi York Yee (30.Lai Sun Cheung), Tsang Ting Fai, Lee Kwai Hong, Kwok Ka Ming, Tang Hung Cheong, Wu Kwok Hung, Chung Chor Wai, Wun Chee Keung (46.Cheung Ka Ping), Sze Kin Hai. Trainer: Franz van Balkom (Holland).
**AUS**: Allan Maher, Colin John Curran (75.Gary Marocchi), Peter Frederick Wilson, Colin Bennett, George Harris, Gary Byrne, James Rooney, Peter Stone, John Kosmina (75.Johnatan Nyskohus), Peter Ollerton, Attila Abonyi. Trainer: James Shoulder (England).
**Goals**: 0-1 Peter Ollerton (18), 0-2 Peter Ollerton (21), 0-3 Peter Ollerton (26), 0-4 Attila Abonyi (59 penalty), 1-4 Tang Hung Cheong (60), 2-4 Chung Chor Wai (80), 2-5 Colin Bennett (86).

05.11.1977, National Stadium, Kuwait City; Attendance: 33,342
Referee: Jean Dubach (Switzerland)
**KUWAIT – SOUTH KOREA** **2-2(0-1)**
**KUW**: Ahmed Khuder Al Tarabulsi, Hussain Mohammad Ahmed Al Kandari, Abdullah Yousuf Mayouf, Adnan Abdullah Ghuloum Dashti (46.Redah Abdullah Mohammed Ma'Rafi), Ibrahim Mohammed Al Duraihem, Farouk Ibrahim Al Awadhi Al Saleh, Saed Mohammed Abdul Aziz Al Houti (46.Hamad Khalid Bo Hamad), Abdul Aziz Saoud Al Anbari, Fatih Kamil Fayyaz Matar Marzouq, Badr Abdul Hamid Bo Abbas, Faisal Ali Al Dakhil. Trainer: Mário Jorge Lobo Zagallo (Brazil).
**KOR**: Byun Ho-Yung, Choi Jong-Deok, Kim Ho-Kon, Cho Young-Jeung, Park Sung-Hwa, Huh Jung-Moo, Kim Kang-Nam (61.Kim Hee-Tae), Cha Bum-Kun, Park Jong-Won, Park Sang-In, Kim Jae-Han (33.Lee Young-Moo). Trainer: Choi Jung-Min.
**Goals**: 0-1 Cha Bum-Kun (18), 1-1 Faisal Ali Al Dakhil (48), 2-1 Badr Abdul Hamid Bo Abbas (78), 2-2 Choi Jong-Deok (82).

11.11.1977, Ayramehr Stadium, Tehran; Attendance: 80,000
Referee: Patrick Partridge (England)
**IRAN – SOUTH KOREA** **2-2(0-1)**
**IRN**: Nasser Hejazi, Hassan Nazari, Hussain Kazarani, Nasrollah Abdolahi, Andranik Eskandarian, Ali Parvin, Mohammad Sadeghi (86.Iraj Danaeifard), Ebrahim Ghasempour, Hassan Roshan, Mohammad Reza Adelkhani, Ghafour Jahani (68.Gholam Hossein Mazloomi). Trainer: Heshmatollah Mohajerani.
**KOR**: Byun Ho-Yung, Choi Jong-Deok, Hwang Jae-Man, Cho Young-Jeung, Park Sung-Hwa, Cho Kwang-Rae, Lee Young-Moo, Park Sang-In, Cha Bum-Kun, Park Jong-Won, Kim Jae-Han. Trainer: Choi Jung-Min.
**Goals**: 0-1 Lee Young-Moo (29), 1-1 Hassan Roshan (55), 2-1 Hassan Roshan (57), 2-2 Lee Young-Moo (87).

12.11.1977, National Stadium, Kuwait City; Attendance: 25,000
Referee: Albert Victor (Luxembourg)
**KUWAIT - HONG KONG** **4-0(3-0)**
**KUW**: Ahmed Khuder Al Tarabulsi, Ibrahim Mohammed Al Duraihem, Abdullah Yousuf Mayouf (30.Adnan Abdullah Ghuloum Dashti), Saed Mohammed Abdul Aziz Al Houti, Redah Abdullah Mohammed Ma'Rafi (62.Hussain Mohammad Ahmed Al Kandari), Farouk Ibrahim Al Awadhi Al Saleh, Hamad Khalid Bo Hamad, Badr Abdul Hamid Bo Abbas, Faisal Ali Al Dakhil, Fatih Kamil Fayyaz Matar Marzouq, Abdul Aziz Saoud Al Anbari. Trainer: Mário Jorge Lobo Zagallo (Brazil).
**HKG**: Chu Kwok Kuen, Chan Fat Chi, Tsang Ting Fai, Cheng Yun Hue, Lai Sun Cheung, Leung Nang Yan, Lee Kwai Hong, Tang Hung Cheong, Kwok Ka Ming, Cheung Ka Ping, Lau Wing Yip. Trainer: Franz van Balkom (Holland).
**Goals**: 1-0 Faisal Ali Al Dakhil (3), 2-0 Faisal Ali Al Dakhil (17), 3-0 Abdul Aziz Saoud Al Anbari (45), 4-0 Fatih Kamil Fayyaz Matar Marzouq (80).

18.11.1977, Ayramehr Stadium, Tehran; Attendance: 50,000
Referee: Marjan Raus (Yugoslavia)
**IRAN - HONG KONG** **3-0(3-0)**
**IRN**: Mansour Rasheedi, Hassan Nazari (70.Mahmoud Ibrahimzadeh), Hussain Kazarani, Nasrollah Abdolahi, Andranik Eskandarian, Ali Parvin, Hassan Nayebagha, Ebrahim Ghasempour, Iraj Danaeifard (60.Alireza Azizi), Alireza Khorshidi, Ghafour Jahani. Trainer: Heshmatollah Mohajerani.
**HKG**: Chu Kwok Kuen, Chan Fat Chi, Tsang Ting Fai, Choi York Yee, Poon Cheung Wong, Kwok Ka Ming, Leung Nang Yan, Tang Hung Cheong, Lee Kwai Hong, Cheung Ka Ping, Lau Wing Yip. Trainer: Franz van Balkom (Holland).
**Goals**: 1-0 Ghafour Jahani (3), 2-0 Hussain Kazarani (19), 3-0 Ghafour Jahani (35).

19.11.1977, National Stadium, Kuwait City; Attendance: 25,000
Referee: Josef Bucek (Austria)
**KUWAIT – AUSTRALIA** **1-0(0-0)**
**KUW**: Ahmed Khuder Al Tarabulsi, Hussain Mohammad Ahmed Al Kandari, Adnan Abdullah Ghuloum Dashti (46.Hamad Khalid Bo Hamad), Abdullah Yousuf Mayouf, Saed Mohammed Abdul Aziz Al Houti, Abbas Hussein Bo Abbas, Farouk Ibrahim Al Awadhi Al Saleh, Fatih Kamil Fayyaz Matar Marzouq, Redah Abdullah Mohammed Ma'Rafi, Faisal Ali Al Dakhil (88.Badr Abdul Hamid Bo Abbas), Abdul Aziz Saoud Al Anbari. Trainer: Mário Jorge Lobo Zagallo (Brazil).
**AUS**: Allan Maher, Colin John Curran, David Jones, Colin Bennett, George Harris, Gary Byrne, James Rooney, Peter Stone, John Kosmina, Peter Ollerton, Attila Abonyi (69.Johnatan Nyskohus). Trainer: James Shoulder (England).
**Goal**: 1-0 Faisal Ali Al Dakhil (51).
**Sent off**: John Kosmina (56).

25.11.1977, Ayramehr Stadium, Tehran; Attendance: 84,000
Referee: Michel Kitabdjian (France)
**IRAN – AUSTRALIA** **1-0(0-0)**
**IRN**: Nasser Hedjazi, Hassan Nazari, Hossein Kazerani, Nasrollah Abdolahi, Andranik Eskandarian, Hassan Nayebagha, Ali Parvin, Ibrahim Ghassempour, Mohammed Sadeghi, Ghafour Jahani, Mohammed Reza Adelkhani. Trainer: Heshmatollah Mohajerani.
**AUS**: Allan Maher, Gary Byrne, Peter Frederick Wilson, Colin Bennett, Colin John Curran, Gary Marocchi, James Rooney, Peter Stone, Adrian Alston, Peter Ollerton, Attila Abonyi (Johnatan Nyskohus). Trainer: James Shoulder (England).
**Goal**: 1-0 Ghafour Jahani (44).

03.12.1977, Al Kuwait Club Stadium, Kuwait City; Attendance: 22,000
Referee: Malcom Wright (Northern Ireland)
**KUWAIT - IRAN** **1-2(1-0)**
**KUW**: Ahmed Khuder Al Tarabulsi, Ibrahim Mohammed Al Duraihem, Abdullah Yousuf Mayouf, Adnan Abdullah Ghuloum Dashti, Redah Abdullah Mohammed Ma'Rafi, Saed Mohammed Abdul Aziz Al Houti, Badr Abdul Hamid Bo Abbas, Farouk Ibrahim Al Awadhi Al Saleh, Fatih Kamil Fayyaz Matar Marzouq, Abdul Aziz Saoud Al Anbari, Faisal Ali Al Dakhil. Trainer: Mário Jorge Lobo Zagallo (Brazil).
**IRN**: Bahram Mavaddat, Hassan Nazari, Mohammad Ali Shojaei, Mostafa Mussalami, Habib Khabiri, Mahmood Haqeeqian (70.Ali Reza Ghesghayan), Behtash Fariba, Ebrahim Ghasempour, Hossein Faraki, Hussain Fedakar, Hameed Alidoosti. Trainer: Heshmatollah Mohajerani.
**Goals**: 1-0 Faisal Ali Al Dakhil (14), 1-1 Fariba Behtash (48), 1-2 Habib Khabiri (59).

04.12.1977, Kudok Municipal Stadium, Pusan; Attendance: 15,184
Referee: Heinz Aldinger (West Germany)
**SOUTH KOREA - HONG KONG** **5-2(2-0)**
**KOR**: Kim Hwang-Ho, Kim Ho-Kon, Hwang Jae-Man, Cho Young-Jeung, Park Sung-Hwa, Cho Kwang-Rae, Kim Sung-Nam, Huh Jung-Moo, Park Sang-In, Cha Bum-Kun, Kim Jae-Han. Trainer: Choi Jung-Min.
**HKG**: Chu Kwok Kuen, Chan Fat Chi, Cheng Yun Hue, Lai Sun Cheung, Chan Sai Kau, Tang Hung Cheong (Leung Nang Yan), Kwok Ka Ming, Cheung Ka Ping, Tsang Ting Fai, Lee Kwai Hong (Sze Kin Hai), Lau Wing Yip. Trainer: Franz van Balkom (Holland).
**Goals**: 1-0 Kim Ho-Kon (22), 2-0 Huh Jung-Moo (43), 2-1 Kwok Ka Ming (47), 3-1 Kim Jae-Han (76), 3-2 Fat Chi Chan (77), 4-2 Kim Jae-Han (81), 5-2 Kim Jae-Han (89).

# WORLD CUP 1978
# THE FINAL TOURNAMENT

The 11th edition of the FIFA World Cup, was held in Argentina between 1st and 25th June 1978, Argentina having been chosen as the host nation by FIFA in London, England on 6th July 1966. The format of the final tournament was the same as in 1974 except that FIFA introduced the dreaded penalty shoot-out to determine the winner in games in the event of a draw after 120 minutes!

The 16 teams were placed first into four seeding pots:
Pot 1:
Argentina, West Germany, Holland, Brazil.
Pot 2:
Italy, Sweden, Mexico, Peru.
Pot 3:
Hungary, Poland, Scotland, Spain.
Pot 4:
Austria, France, Iran, Tunisia.

The 16 teams were then drawn in following groups:

| GROUP 1 | GROUP 2 |
|---|---|
| Argentina | West Germany |
| Hungary | Poland |
| Italy | Tunisia |
| France | Mexico |

| GROUP 3 | GROUP 4 |
|---|---|
| Brazil | Holland |
| Sweden | Iran |
| Austria | Peru |
| Spain | Scotland |

The teams finishing first and second in each group were qualified for the second round.

The venues:
Buenos Aires (Estadio Monumental „Antonio Vespucio Liberti" - Capacity: 76,000)
Buenos Aires (Estadio „José Amalfitani", Buenos Aires - 49,540)
Córdoba (Estadio Chateau Carreras - 46,083)
Mar del Plata (Estadio „José María Minella"- 43,542)
Mendoza (Estadio Parque „General San Martín" - 34,875)
Rosario (Estadio "Gigante de Arroyito" - 41,654)

    The biggest surprise in the first round was in Group 3, where Austria topped the group ahead of Brazil. Austria, lead by Prohaska and Krankl, unexpectedly beat both Spain and Sweden before losing to Brazil who, surprisingly, managed only to draw against the other two teams. In Group 4, Peru unexpectedly defeated Scotland (whose overconfident manager, Ally McLeod, had predicted his team would become World Champions!) and Holland took the top spot despite losing to the Scots in the last group game. The hosts, Argentina, were unimpressive but progressed to the next round thanks largely to refereeing lapses.
    In the second round, although Austria themselves failed to progress to the semi-finals, they nonetheless defeated the reigning champions, West Germany, in the final game which meant the Germans also failed to progress. The semi-finals line-up consisted of Argentina, Brazil, Italy and Holland.

The Final itself was between Holland, the beaten finalists from 1974, and the host country, Argentina, and could best be described as a controversial fixture. The hosts attempted to use gamesmanship to unsettle the Dutch, firstly taking to the field late and then questioning the legality of a plaster cast on the wrist of René van de Kerkhof! In a game which saw further questionable refereeing decisions (with more than 50 free-kicks awarded against the Dutch team, many unfairly), Mario Kempes opened the scoring for the hosts in the first half. However, Nanninga equalised for the Dutch just a few minutes from the end of normal time and, in the $90^{th}$ minute, Rensenbrink missed a chance to win the trophy, firing a shot against the post. In extra-time, the Argentinian team rallied and Kempes gave the hosts the lead before Bertoni scored the third to seal the victory as Holland pushed forward in search of an equaliser.

## GROUP 1

| | | | |
|---|---|---|---|
| 02.06.1978 | Mar del Plata | Italy - France | 2-1(1-1) |
| 02.06.1978 | Buenos Aires | Argentina – Hungary | 2-1(1-1) |
| 06.06.1978 | Mar del Plata | Italy - Hungary | 3-1(2-0) |
| 06.06.1978 | Buenos Aires | Argentina - France | 2-1(1-0) |
| 10.06.1978 | Mar del Plata | France - Hungary | 3-1(3-1) |
| 10.06.1978 | Buenos Aires | Italy - Argentina | 1-0(0-0) |

### FINAL STANDINGS

| | | | | | | | | |
|---|---|---|---|---|---|---|---|---|
| 1. | **Italy** | 3 | 3 | 0 | 0 | 6 | - 2 | 6 |
| 2. | **Argentina** | 3 | 2 | 0 | 1 | 4 | - 3 | 4 |
| 3. | **France** | 3 | 1 | 0 | 2 | 5 | - 5 | 2 |
| 4. | **Hungary** | 3 | 0 | 0 | 3 | 3 | - 8 | 0 |

02.06.1978, Estadio „José María Minella", Mar del Plata; Attendance: 42,373
Referee: Nicolae Rainea (Romania)
**ITALY - FRANCE**     **2-1(1-1)**
**ITA:** Dino Zoff, Claudio Gentile, Antonio Cabrini, Romeo Benetti II, Mauro Bellugi, Gaetano Scirea, Franco Causio, Marco Tardelli, Paolo Rossi, Giancarlo Antognoni (46.Renato Zaccarelli), Roberto Bettega. Trainer: Enzo Bearzot.
**FRA:** Jean-Paul Bertrand-Demanes, Gérard Janvion, Patrice Rio, Marius Trésor (Cap), Maxime Bossis, Henri Michel, Jean-Marc Guillou, Michel Platini, Christian Dalger, Bernard Lacombe (75.Marc Berdoll), Didier Six (76.Olivier Rouyer). Trainer: Michel Hidalgo.
**Goals**: 0-1 Bernard Lacombe (1), 1-1 Paolo Rossi (29), 2-1 Renato Zaccarelli (54).
**Cautions**: Marco Tardelli / Henri Michel, Michel Platini.

02.06.1978, Estadio Monumental „Antonio Vespucio Liberti", Buenos Aires; Attendance: 71,615
Referee: Antonio José da Silva Garrido (Portugal)
**ARGENTINA – HUNGARY**     **2-1(1-1)**
**ARG:** Ubaldo Matildo Fillol, Jorge Mario Olguín, Luis Adolfo Galván, Daniel Alberto Passarella (Cap), Alberto César Tarantini, Osvaldo César Ardiles, Américo Rubén Gallego, José Daniel Valencia (75.Norberto Osvaldo Alonso), René Orlando Houseman (67.Ricardo Daniel Bertoni), Leopoldo Jacinto Luque, Mario Alberto Kempes. Trainer: César Luis Menotti.
**HUN:** Sándor Gujdár, Péter Török (46.Győző Martos), István Kocsis, Zoltán Kereki, József Tóth, Tibor Nyilasi, Sándor Pintér, Sándor Zombori, Károly Csapó, András Törőcsik, László Nagy. Trainer: Lajos Baróti.
**Goals**: 0-1 Károly Csapó (9), 1-1 Leopoldo Jacinto Luque (15), 2-1 Ricardo Daniel Bertoni (84).
**Cautions**: Daniel Alberto Passarella / Tibor Nyilasi, András Törőcsik.
**Sent off**: András Törőcsik (87), Tibor Nyilasi (90).

06.06.1978, Estadio „José María Minella", Mar del Plata; Attendance: 35,000
Referee: Ramón Ivannoe Barreto Ruíz (Uruguay)
**ITALY - HUNGARY** **3-1(2-0)**
**ITA:** Dino Zoff, Claudio Gentile, Antonio Cabrini (79.Antonello Cuccureddu), Romeo Benetti II, Mauro Bellugi, Gaetano Scirea, Franco Causio, Marco Tardelli, Paolo Rossi, Giancarlo Antognoni, Roberto Bettega (83.Francesco Graziani). Trainer: Enzo Bearzot.
**HUN:** Ferenc Mészáros, Győző Martos, István Kocsis, Zoltán Kereki, József Tóth, Károly Csapó, Sándor Pintér, Sándor Zombori, László Pusztai, László Fazekas (46.András Tóth), László Nagy (46.István Halász). Trainer: Lajos Baróti.
**Goals:** 1-0 Paolo Rossi (34), 2-0 Roberto Bettega (35), 3-0 Romeo Benetti II (61), 3-1 András Tóth (81 penalty).
**Cautions:** Sándor Zombori, Győző Martos.

06.06.1978, Estadio Monumental „Antonio Vespucio Liberti", Buenos Aires; Attendance: 77,216
Referee: Jean Dubach (Switzerland)
**ARGENTINA - FRANCE** **2-1(1-0)**
**ARG:** Ubaldo Matildo Fillol, Jorge Mario Olguín, Luis Adolfo Galván, Daniel Alberto Passarella (Cap), Alberto César Tarantini, Osvaldo César Ardiles, Américo Rubén Gallego, José Daniel Valencia (64.Norberto Osvaldo Alonso; 71.Oscar Alberto Ortíz), René Orlando Houseman, Leopoldo Jacinto Luque, Mario Alberto Kempes. Trainer: César Luis Menotti.
**FRA:** Jean-Paul Bertrand-Demanes (55.Dominique Baratelli), Patrick Battiston, Christian Lopez, Marius Trésor (Cap), Maxime Bossis, Michel Platini, Henri Michel, Dominique Bathenay, Dominique Rocheteau, Bernard Lacombe, Didier Six. Trainer: Michel Hidalgo.
**Goals:** 1-0 Daniel Alberto Passarella (45 penalty), 1-1 Michel Platini (60), 2-1 Leopoldo Jacinto Luque (73).
**Cautions:** Didier Six.

10.06.1978, Estadio „José María Minella", Mar del Plata; Attendance: 28,000
Referee: Arnaldo David Cesar Coelho (Brazil)
**FRANCE - HUNGARY** **3-1(3-1)**
**FRA:** Dominique Dropsy, Gérard Janvion, Christian Lopez, Marius Trésor (Cap), François Bracci, Jean Petit, Dominique Bathenay, Claude Papi (46.Michel Platini), Dominique Rocheteau (75.Didier Six), Marc Berdoll, Olivier Rouyer. Trainer: Michel Hidalgo.
**HUN:** Sándor Gujdár, Győző Martos, László Bálint, Zoltán Kereki, József Tóth, Tibor Nyilasi, Sándor Pintér, Sándor Zombori, László Pusztai, András Törőcsik, László Nagy (73.Károly Csapó). Trainer: Lajos Baróti.
**Goals:** 1-0 Christian Lopez (23), 2-0 Marc Berdoll (38), 3-0 Dominique Rocheteau (42), 3-1 Sándor Zombori (42).

10.06.1978, Estadio Monumental „Antonio Vespucio Liberti", Buenos Aires; Attendance: 71,712
Referee: Abraham Klein (Israel)
**ITALY - ARGENTINA** **1-0(0-0)**
**ITA:** Dino Zoff, Claudio Gentile, Antonio Cabrini, Romeo Benetti II, Mauro Bellugi (6.Antonello Cuccureddu), Gaetano Scirea, Franco Causio, Marco Tardelli, Paolo Rossi, Giancarlo Antognoni (73.Renato Zaccarelli), Roberto Bettega. Trainer: Enzo Bearzot.
**ARG:** Ubaldo Matildo Fillol, Jorge Mario Olguín, Luis Adolfo Galván, Daniel Alberto Passarella (Cap), Alberto César Tarantini, Osvaldo César Ardiles, Américo Rubén Gallego, José Daniel Valencia, Ricardo Daniel Bertoni, Oscar Alberto Ortíz, Mario Alberto Kempes (72.René Orlando Houseman). Trainer: César Luis Menotti.
**Goal:** 1-0 Roberto Bettega (67).
**Cautions:** Romeo Benetti II.

# GROUP 2

| | | | | |
|---|---|---|---|---|
| 01.06.1978 | Buenos Aires | West Germany - Poland | | 0-0 |
| 02.06.1978 | Rosario | Tunisia - Mexico | | 3-1(0-1) |
| 06.06.1978 | Rosario | Poland - Tunisia | | 1-0(1-0) |
| 06.06.1978 | Córdoba | West Germany - Mexico | | 6-0(4-0) |
| 10.06.1978 | Rosario | Poland - Mexico | | 3-1(1-0) |
| 10.06.1978 | Córdoba | West Germany - Tunisia | | 0-0 |

## FINAL STANDINGS

| | | | | | | | | |
|---|---|---|---|---|---|---|---|---|
| 1. | Poland | 3 | 2 | 1 | 0 | 4 - 1 | | 5 |
| 2. | West Germany | 3 | 1 | 2 | 0 | 6 - 0 | | 4 |
| 3. | Tunisia | 3 | 1 | 1 | 1 | 3 - 2 | | 3 |
| 4. | Mexico | 3 | 0 | 0 | 3 | 2 - 12 | | 0 |

01.06.1978, Estadio Monumental „Antonio Vespucio Liberti", Buenos Aires; Attendance: 77,000
Referee: Angel Norberto Coerezza (Argentina)
**WEST GERMANY - POLAND** **0-0**
**GER:** Josef Maier, Hans-Hubert Vogts (Cap), Rolf Rüssmann, Manfred Kaltz, Herbert Zimmermann, Rainer Bonhof, Erich Beer, Heinz Flohe, Rüdiger Abramczik, Klaus Fischer, Hans Müller. Trainer: Helmut Schön.
**POL:** Jan Tomaszewski, Henryk Maculewicz, Jerzy Gorgoń, Władysław Żmuda, Antoni Szymanowski, Adam Nawałka, Kazimierz Deyna (Cap), Bogdan Masztaler (84.Henryk Kasperczak), Grzegorz Lato, Włodzimierz Lubański (79.Zbigniew Boniek), Andrzej Szarmach. Trainer: Jacek Gmoch.

02.06.1978, Estadio "Gigante de Arroyito", Rosario; Attendance: 17,396
Referee: John Robertson Proudfoot Gordon (Scotland)
**TUNISIA - MEXICO** **3-1(0-1)**
**TUN:** Mokhtar Naili, Mokhtar Dhouib, Mohsen Jendoubi Labidi, Ali Kaabi, Omar Jebaili, Néjib Ghommidh, Tarak Dhiab, Mohammed Agrebi Ben Rehaiem, Témime Lahzami (Cap) (88.Khemais Labidi), Mohamed Ali Akid, Abderraouf Ben Aziza (81.Slah Karoui).
**MEX:** José Pilar Reyes Requenes, Jesús Martínez Díez, Alfredo Tena Garduño, Eduardo Ramos Escobedo, Arturo Vázquez Ayala, Antonio de la Torre Villalpando, Guillermo Mendizábal Sánchez (67.Gerardo Lugo Gómez), Leonardo Cuéllar Rivera, Raúl Isiordia Ayón, Víctor Rangel Ayala, Hugo Sánchez Márquez. Trainer: José Antonio Roca García.
**Goals**: 0-1 Arturo Vázquez Ayala (45 penalty), 1-1 Ali Kaabi (55), 2-1 Néjib Ghommidh (79), 3-1 Mokhtar Dhouib (87).

06.06.1978, Estadio „Gigante de Arroyito", Rosario; Attendance: 15,000
Referee: Angel Franco Martínez (Spain)
**POLAND - TUNISIA** **1-0(1-0)**
**POL:** Jan Tomaszewski, Henryk Maculewicz, Jerzy Gorgoń, Władysław Żmuda, Antoni Szymanowski, Adam Nawałka, Kazimierz Deyna (Cap), Henryk Kasperczak, Grzegorz Lato, Włodzimierz Lubański (76. Zbigniew Boniek), Andrzej Szarmach (60.Andrzej Iwan). Trainer: Jacek Gmoch.
**TUN:** Mokhtar Naili, Mokhtar Dhouib, Omar Jebaili, Mohsen Jendoubi Labidi, Ali Kaabi, Néjib Ghommidh, Khaled Mokhtar Gasmi, Tarak Dhiab, Mohammed Agrebi Ben Rehaiem, Témime Lahzami (Cap), Mohamed Ali Akid.
**Goal**: 1-0 Grzegorz Lato (42).

06.06.1978, Estadio Chateau Carreras, Córdoba; Attendance: 35,258
Referee: Farouk Bouzo (Syria)
**WEST GERMANY - MEXICO** **6-0(4-0)**
**GER:** Josef Maier, Hans-Hubert Vogts (Cap), Rolf Rüssmann, Manfred Kaltz, Bernhard Dietz, Rainer Bonhof, Heinz Flohe, Hans Müller, Karl-Heinz Rummenigge, Klaus Fischer, Dieter Müller. Trainer: Helmut Schön.
**MEX:** José Pilar Reyes Requenes (40.Pedro Soto Moreno), Jesús Martínez Díez, Alfredo Tena Garduño, Eduardo Ramos Escobedo, Arturo Vázquez Ayala (Cap), Antonio de la Torre Villalpando, Guillermo Mendizábal Sánchez, Leonardo Cuéllar Rivera, Enrique López Zarza (46.Gerardo Lugo Gómez), Víctor Rangel Ayala, Hugo Sánchez Márquez. Trainer: José Antonio Roca García.
**Goals:** 1-0 Dieter Müller (14), 2-0 Hans Müller (29), 3-0 Karl-Heinz Rummenigge (38), 4-0 Heinz Flohe (44), 5-0 Karl-Heinz Rummenigge (71), 6-0 Heinz Flohe (89).
**Cautions:** Rainer Bonhof / Arturo Vázquez Ayala.

10.06.1978, Estadio "Gigante de Arroyito", Rosario; Attendance: 22,651
Referee: Jaffar Namdar (Iran)
**POLAND - MEXICO** **3-1(1-0)**
**POL:** Jan Tomaszewski, Antoni Szymanowski, Jerzy Gorgoń, Władysław Żmuda, Wojciech Rudy (85.Henryk Maculewicz), Henryk Kasperczak, Kazimierz Deyna (Cap), Zbigniew Boniek, Bogdan Masztaler, Grzegorz Lato, Andrzej Iwan (76.Włodzimierz Lubański). Trainer: Jacek Gmoch.
**MEX:** Pedro Soto Moreno, Ignacio Flores Ocaranza, Rigoberto Cisneros Dueñas, Carlos Gómez Casillas, Arturo Vázquez Ayala, Antonio de la Torre Villalpando, Javier Rubén Cárdenas Martínez (46.Guillermo Mendizábal Sánchez), Leonardo Cuéllar Rivera, Cristóbal Ortega Martínez, Víctor Rangel Ayala, Hugo Sánchez Márquez. Trainer: José Antonio Roca García.
**Goals:** 1-0 Zbigniew Boniek (43), 1-1 Víctor Rangel Ayala (51), 2-1 Kazimierz Deyna (56), 3-1 Zbigniew Boniek (84).

10.06.1978, Estadio Chateau Carreras, Córdoba; Attendance: 30,667
Referee: César Guerrero Orozco (Peru)
**WEST GERMANY - TUNISIA** **0-0**
**GER:** Josef Maier, Hans-Hubert Vogts (Cap), Rolf Rüssmann, Manfred Kaltz, Bernhard Dietz, Rainer Bonhof, Heinz Flohe, Hans Müller, Karl-Heinz Rummenigge, Klaus Fischer, Dieter Müller. Trainer: Helmut Schön.
**TUN:** Mokhtar Naili, Mokhtar Dhouib, Mohsen Jendoubi Labidi, Ali Kaabi, Omar Jebaili, Khaled Mokhtar Gasmi, Néjib Ghommidh, Tarak Dhiab, Mohammed Agrebi Ben Rehaiem, Mohamed Ali Akid (63.Abderraouf Ben Aziza), Témime Lahzami (Cap).
**Cautions:** Hans Müller / Tarak Dhiab.

# GROUP 3

| 03.06.1978 | Buenos Aires | Austria - Spain | 2-1(1-1) |
|---|---|---|---|
| 03.06.1978 | Mar del Plata | Sweden - Brazil | 1-1(1-1) |
| 07.06.1978 | Buenos Aires | Austria - Sweden | 1-0(1-0) |
| 07.06.1978 | Mar del Plata | Brazil - Spain | 0-0 |
| 11.06.1978 | Buenos Aires | Spain - Sweden | 1-0(0-0) |
| 11.06.1978 | Mar del Plata | Brazil - Austria | 1-0(1-0) |

## FINAL STANDINGS

| | | | | | | | | |
|---|---|---|---|---|---|---|---|---|
| 1. | **Austria** | 3 | 2 | 0 | 1 | 3 - 2 | 4 |
| 2. | **Brazil** | 3 | 1 | 2 | 0 | 2 - 1 | 4 |
| 3. | Spain | 3 | 1 | 1 | 1 | 2 - 2 | 3 |
| 4. | Sweden | 3 | 0 | 1 | 2 | 1 - 3 | 1 |

03.06.1978, Estadio „José Amalfitani", Buenos Aires; Attendance: 49,317
Referee: Károly Palotai (Hungary)
**AUSTRIA - SPAIN**                                                **2-1(1-1)**
**AUT:** Friedrich Koncilia, Robert Sara, Erich Obermayer, Bruno Pezzey, Gerhard Breitenberger, Herbert Prohaska, Josef Hickersberger (67.Heribert Weber), Wilhelm Kreuz, Kurt Jara, Walter Schachner (79.Hans Pirkner), Johann Krankl. Trainer: Helmut Senekowitsch.
**ESP:** Miguel Ángel González Suárez, Marcelino Pérez Ayllón, Miguel Bernardo Bianquetti „Migueli", José Martínez Sánchez „Pirri" (Cap), Jesús Antonio De la Cruz Gallego, Juan Manuel Asensi Ripoll, Isidoro San José Pozo Sánchez, Julio Cardeñosa Rodríguez (46.Eugenio Leal Vargas), Daniel Ruiz-Bazan Justa „Dani", Rubén Andres Cano Martínez Sáez, Carlos Rexach Cerdá (60.Enrique Castro González „Quini"). Trainer: Ladislao Kubala.
**Goals**: 1-0 Walter Schachner (10), 1-1 Daniel Ruiz-Bazan Justa „Dani" (21), 2-1 Johann Krankl (76).

03.06.1978, Estadio „José María Minella", Mar del Plata; Attendance: 32,569
Referee: Clive Thomas (Wales)
**SWEDEN - BRAZIL**                                        **1-1(1-1)**
**SWE:** Ronnie Carl Hellström, Hans Borg, Roy Andersson, Björn Nordqvist (Cap), Ingemar Erlandsson, Lennart Larsson (79.Ralf Edström), Anders Linderoth, Bo Göran Larsson, Staffan Tapper, Thomas Sjöberg, Benny Wendt. Trainer: Georg Ericson.
**BRA:** Émerson Leão, Antônio Dias dos Santos "Toninho", José Oscar Bernardi, João Justino Amaral dos Santos "Amaral I", Édino Nazareth Filho "Edinho", Antônio Carlos Cerezo "Toninho Cerezo" (87.Dirceu José Guimarães „Dirceu II"), João Batista da Silva, Roberto Rivelino (Cap), Arthur Antunes Coimbra "Zico", Gilberto Alves "Gil" (66.Manoel Resende de Matos Cabral "Nelinho"), José Reinaldo da Lima "Reinaldo I". Trainer: Cláudio Pècego de Moraes Coutinho.
**Goals**: 1-0 Thomas Sjöberg (37), 1-1 José Reinaldo da Lima "Reinaldo I" (45).
**Cautions**: José Oscar Bernardi.

07.06.1978,; Attendance: 46,000
Referee: Charles George Reinier Corver (Holland)
**AUSTRIA - SWEDEN**                                     **1-0(1-0)**
**AUT:** Friedrich Koncilia, Robert Sara, Erich Obermayer, Bruno Pezzey, Gerhard Breitenberger, Herbert Prohaska, Josef Hickersberger, Eduard Krieger (71.Heribert Weber), Kurt Jara, Wilhelm Kreuz, Johann Krankl. Trainer: Helmut Senekowitsch.
**SWE:** Ronnie Carl Hellström, Hans Borg, Roy Andersson, Björn Nordqvist (Cap), Ingemar Erlandsson, Lennart Larsson, Staffan Tapper (36.Conny Torstensson), Anders Linderoth (60.Ralf Edström), Bo Göran Larsson, Thomas Sjöberg, Benny Wendt. Trainer: Georg Ericson.
**Goal**: 1-0 Johann Krankl (43 penalty).

07.06.1978, Estadio „José María Minella", Mar del Plata; Attendance: 34,771
Referee: Sergio Gonella (Italy)
**BRAZIL - SPAIN**     **0-0**
**BRA:** Émerson Leão (Cap), Antônio Dias dos Santos "Toninho", José Oscar Bernardi, João Justino Amaral dos Santos "Amaral I", Édino Nazareth Filho "Edinho", Manoel Resende de Matos Cabral "Nelinho" (71.Gilberto Alves "Gil"), João Batista da Silva, Antônio Carlos Cerezo "Toninho Cerezo", Arthur Antunes Coimbra "Zico" (83.Jorge Pinto Mendonça), José Reinaldo da Lima "Reinaldo I", Dirceu José Guimarães „Dirceu II". Trainer: Cláudio Pècego de Moraes Coutinho.
**ESP:** Miguel Ángel González Suárez, Marcelino Pérez Ayllón, Miguel Bernardo Bianquetti „Migueli" (51.Antonio Biosca Pérez), Antonio Olmo Ramírez, Francisco Javier Álvarez „Uría" (79.Antonio Guzmán Nuñez), Isidoro San José Pozo Sánchez, Juan Manuel Asensi Ripoll (Cap), Eugenio Leal Vargas, Juan Enrique Gómez González „Juanito", Carlos Alonso González „Santillana", Julio Cardeñosa Rodríguez. Trainer: Ladislao Kubala.
**Cautions**: Eugenio Leal Vargas.

11.06.1978, Estadio "José Amalfitani", Buenos Aires; Attendance: 46,765
Referee: Ferdinand Biwersi (West Germany)
**SPAIN - SWEDEN**     **1-0(0-0)**
**ESP:** Miguel Ángel González Suárez, Marcelino Pérez Ayllón, Antonio Olmo Ramírez (46.José Martínez Sánchez „Pirri"), Antonio Biosca Pérez, Francisco Javier Álvarez „Uría", Isidoro San José Pozo Sánchez, Juan Manuel Asensi Ripoll (Cap), Eugenio Leal Vargas, Julio Cardeñosa Rodríguez, Juan Enrique Gómez González „Juanito", Carlos Alonso González „Santillana". Trainer: Ladislao Kubala.
**SWE:** Ronnie Carl Hellström, Hans Borg, Roy Andersson, Björn Nordqvist (Cap), Ingemar Erlandsson, Lennart Larsson, Bo Göran Larsson, Olle Nordin, Torbjörn Nilsson, Thomas Sjöberg (67.Anders Linderoth), Ralf Edström (59.Benny Wendt). Trainer: Georg Ericson.
**Goal**: 1-0 Juan Manuel Asensi Ripoll (76).
**Cautions**: Hans Borg.

11.06.1978, Estadio „José María Minella", Mar del Plata; Attendance: 35,221
Referee: Robert Charles Paul Wurtz (France)
**BRAZIL - AUSTRIA**     **1-0(1-0)**
**BRA:** Émerson Leão (Cap), Antônio Dias dos Santos "Toninho", José Oscar Bernardi, João Justino Amaral dos Santos "Amaral I", José Rodrigues Neto, João Batista da Silva, Antônio Carlos Cerezo "Toninho Cerezo" (71.Francisco Jezuíno Avanzi "Chicão I"), Dirceu José Guimarães „Dirceu II", Gilberto Alves "Gil", Jorge Pinto Mendonça (84.Arthur Antunes Coimbra "Zico"), Carlos Roberto de Oliveira "Roberto Dinamite". Trainer: Cláudio Pècego de Moraes Coutinho.
**AUT:** Friedrich Koncilia, Robert Sara, Erich Obermayer, Bruno Pezzey, Gerhard Breitenberger, Herbert Prohaska, Josef Hickersberger (61.Heribert Weber), Eduard Krieger (82.Günther Happich), Kurt Jara, Wilhelm Kreuz, Johann Krankl. Trainer: Helmut Senekowitsch.
**Goal**: 1-0 Carlos Roberto de Oliveira "Roberto Dinamite" (40).

# GROUP 4

| | | | |
|---|---|---|---|
| 03.06.1978 | Córdoba | Peru - Scotland | 3-1(1-1) |
| 03.06.1978 | Mendoza | Holland - Iran | 3-0(1-0) |
| 07.06.1978 | Córdoba | Scotland - Iran | 1-1(1-0) |
| 07.06.1978 | Mendoza | Peru - Holland | 0-0 |
| 11.06.1978 | Córdoba | Peru - Iran | 4-1(3-1) |
| 11.06.1978 | Mendoza | Scotland - Holland | 3-2(1-1) |

## FINAL STANDINGS

| | | | | | | | | |
|---|---|---|---|---|---|---|---|---|
| 1. | Peru | 3 | 2 | 1 | 0 | 7 - 2 | 5 |
| 2. | Holland | 3 | 1 | 1 | 1 | 5 - 3 | 3 |
| 3. | Scotland | 3 | 1 | 1 | 1 | 5 - 6 | 3 |
| 4. | Iran | 3 | 0 | 1 | 2 | 2 - 8 | 1 |

03.06.1978, Estadio Chateau Carreras, Córdoba; Attendance: 37,792
Referee: Ulf Helmer Johan Eriksson (Sweden)
**PERU - SCOTLAND**     **3-1(1-1)**
**PER:** Ramón Quiroga Arancibia, Jaime Eduardo Duarte Huerta, Rodolfo Manzo Audante, Héctor Eduardo Chumpitaz González (Cap), Rubén Toribio Díaz Rivas, José Manuel Velásquez Castillo, César Augusto Cueto Villa (82.Percy Rojas Montero), Teófilo Juan Cubillas Arizaga, Juan José Muñante López, Guillermo La Rosa Laguna (62.Hugo Alejandro Sotil Yerén), Juan Carlos Oblitas Saba. Trainer: Marcos Calderón Medrano.
**SCO:** Alan Roderick Rough, Stuart Robert Kennedy, Martin McLean Buchan, Thomas Forsyth, Kenneth Burns, Donald Sanderson Masson (70.Archibald Gemmill), Bruce David Rioch (Cap) (70.Luigi Macari), Richard Asa Hartford, William McClure Johnston, Kenneth Mathieson Dalglish, Joseph Jordan. Manager: Alistair MacLeod.
**Goals:** 0-1 Joseph Jordan (15), 1-1 César Augusto Cueto Villa (42), 2-1 Teófilo Juan Cubillas Arizaga (71), 3-1 Teófilo Juan Cubillas Arizaga (77).
**Cautions:** José Manuel Velásquez Castillo.

03.06.1978, Estadio Parque „General San Martín", Mendoza; Attendance: 33,431
Referee: Alfonso González Archundia (Mexico)
**HOLLAND - IRAN**     **3-0(1-0)**
**NED:** Jan Jongbloed, Willem Johannes Laurens Suurbier, Rudolf Jozef Krol (Cap), Wilhelmus Gerardus Rijsbergen, Wilhelmus Antonius van de Kerkhof, Wilhelmus Marinus Anthonius Jansen, Johannes Jacobus Neeskens, Arend Haan, John Nicolaas Rep, Reinier Lambertus van de Kerkhof (70.Dirk Jacobus Willem Nanninga), Robert Pieter Rensenbrink. Trainer: Ernst Happel (Austria).
**IRN:** Nasser Hejazi, Hassan Nazari, Nasrollah Abdollahi, Hossein Kazerani, Andranik Eskandarian, Ali Parvin (Cap), Ebrahim Ghasempour, Mohammad Sadeghi, Hassan Nayebagha, Ghafour Jahani, Hossein Faraki (51.Hassan Roshan).Trainer: Heshmatollah Mohajerani.
**Goals**: 1-0 Robert Pieter Rensenbrink (40 penalty), 2-0 Robert Pieter Rensenbrink (62), 3-0 Robert Pieter Rensenbrink (78 penalty).
**Cautions**: Andranik Eskandarian

07.06.1978, Estadio Chateau Carreras, Córdoba; Attendance: 7,938
Referee: Youssou N'Diaye (Senegal)
**SCOTLAND - IRAN**     **1-1(1-0)**
**SCO:** Alan Roderick Rough, William Pullar Jardine, William Donachie, Martin McLean Buchan (57.Thomas Forsyth), Kenneth Burns, Archibald Gemmill (Cap), Luigi Macari, Richard Asa Hartford, John Neilson Robertson, Kenneth Mathieson Dalglish (73.Joseph Montgomery Harper), Joseph Jordan. Manager: Alistair MacLeod.

**IRN**: Nasser Hejazi, Hassan Nazari, Nasrollah Abdollahi, Hossein Kazerani, Andranik Eskandarian, Ali Parvin (Cap), Ebrahim Ghasempour, Mohammad Sadeghi, Iraj Danaeifard (89.Hassan Nayebagha), Ghafour Jahani, Hossein Faraki (83.Hassan Roshan). Trainer: Heshmatollah Mohajerani.
**Goals**: 1-0 Andranik Eskandarian (43 own goal), 1-1 Iraj Danaeifard (60).
**Cautions**: Andranik Eskandarian

07.06.1978, Estadio Parque „General San Martín", Mendoza; Attendance: 28,125
Referee: Adolf Prokop (East Germany)
**PERU - HOLLAND**     **0-0**
**PER**: Ramón Quiroga Arancibia, Jaime Eduardo Duarte Huerta, Rodolfo Manzo Audante, Héctor Eduardo Chumpitaz González (Cap), Rubén Toribio Díaz Rivas, César Augusto Cueto Villa, José Manuel Velásquez Castillo, Teófilo Juan Cubillas Arizaga, Juan José Muñante López, Guillermo La Rosa Laguna (62.Hugo Alejandro Sotil Yerén), Juan Carlos Oblitas Saba. Trainer: Marcos Calderón Medrano.
**NED**: Jan Jongbloed, Willem Johannes Laurens Suurbier, Rudolf Jozef Krol (Cap), Wilhelmus Gerardus Rijsbergen, Jan Poortvliet, Wilhelmus Antonius van de Kerkhof, Johannes Jacobus Neeskens (70.Dirk Jacobus Willem Nanninga), Wilhelmus Marinus Anthonius Jansen, Arend Haan, Reinier Lambertus van de Kerkhof (46.John Nicolaas Rep), Robert Pieter Rensenbrink. Trainer: Ernst Happel (Austria).
**Cautions**: Juan José Muñante López / Reinier Lambertus van de Kerkhof.

11.06.1978, Estadio Chateau Carreras, Córdoba; Attendance: 21,000
Referee: Alojzy Jarguz (Poland)
**PERU - IRAN**     **4-1(3-1)**
**PER**: Ramón Quiroga Arancibia, Jaime Eduardo Duarte Huerta, Rodolfo Manzo Audante (67.Germán Carlos Leguía Dragó), Héctor Eduardo Chumpitaz González (Cap), Rubén Toribio Díaz Rivas, José Manuel Velásquez Castillo, César Augusto Cueto Villa, Teófilo Juan Cubillas Arizaga, Juan José Muñante López, Guillermo La Rosa Laguna (60.Hugo Alejandro Sotil Yerén), Juan Carlos Oblitas Saba. Trainer: Marcos Calderón Medrano.
**IRN**: Nasser Hejazi, Hassan Nazari, Nasrollah Abdollahi, Hossein Kazerani, Javad Allahverdi, Ali Parvin (Cap), Ebrahim Ghasempour, Mohammad Sadeghi, Iraj Danaeifard, Hossein Faraki (52.Ghafour Jahani), Hassan Roshan (66.Behtash Fariba). Trainer: Heshmatollah Mohajerani.
**Goals**: 1-0 José Manuel Velásquez Castillo (2), 2-0 Teófilo Juan Cubillas Arizaga (36 penalty), 3-0 Teófilo Juan Cubillas Arizaga (39 penalty), 3-1 Hassan Roshan (41), 4-1 Teófilo Juan Cubillas Arizaga (79).
**Cautions**: Hassan Nazari.

11.06.1978, Estadio Parque „General San Martín", Mendoza; Attendance: 35,130
Referee: Erich Linemayr (Austria)
**SCOTLAND - HOLLAND**     **3-2(1-1)**
**SCO**: Alan Roderick Rough, Stuart Robert Kennedy, William Donachie, Martin McLean Buchan, Thomas Forsyth, Archibald Gemmill, Bruce David Rioch (Cap), Graeme James Souness, Richard Asa Hartford, Kenneth Mathieson Dalglish, Joseph Jordan. Manager: Alistair MacLeod.
**NED**: Jan Jongbloed, Willem Johannes Laurens Suurbier, Rudolf Jozef Krol (Cap), Wilhelmus Gerardus Rijsbergen (44.Pieter Wildschut), Jan Poortvliet, Wilhelmus Antonius van de Kerkhof, Johannes Jacobus Neeskens (10.Johannes Boskamp), Wilhelmus Marinus Anthonius Jansen, Reinier Lambertus van de Kerkhof, John Nicolaas Rep, Robert Pieter Rensenbrink. Trainer: Ernst Happel (Austria).
**Goals**: 0-1 Robert Pieter Rensenbrink (34 penalty), 1-1 Kenneth Mathieson Dalglish (44), 2-1 Archibald Gemmill (46 penalty), 3-1 Archibald Gemmill (68), 3-2 John Nicolaas Rep (71).
**Cautions**: Archibald Gemmill.

# SECOND ROUND

## GROUP A

| | | | | |
|---|---|---|---|---|
| 14.06.1978 | Buenos Aires | West Germany - Italy | 0-0 | |
| 14.06.1978 | Córdoba | Holland - Austria | 5-1(3-0) | |
| 18.06.1978 | Córdoba | West Germany - Holland | 2-2(1-1) | |
| 18.06.1978 | Buenos Aires | Italy - Austria | 1-0(1-0) | |
| 21.06.1978 | Buenos Aires | Holland - Italy | 2-1(0-1) | |
| 21.06.1978 | Córdoba | Austria – West Germany | 3-2(0-1) | |

### FINAL STANDINGS

| | | | | | | | | |
|---|---|---|---|---|---|---|---|---|
| 1. | Holland | 3 | 2 | 1 | 0 | 9 - 4 | 5 |
| 2. | Italy | 3 | 1 | 1 | 1 | 2 - 2 | 3 |
| 3. | West Germany | 3 | 0 | 2 | 1 | 4 - 5 | 2 |
| 4. | Austria | 3 | 1 | 0 | 2 | 4 - 8 | 2 |

14.06.1978, Estadio Monumental „Antonio Vespucio Liberti", Buenos Aires; Attendance: 67,547
Referee: Dušan Maksimović (Yugoslavia)
**WEST GERMANY - ITALY**     **0-0**
**GER:** Josef Maier, Hans-Hubert Vogts (Cap), Rolf Rüssmann, Manfred Kaltz, Bernhard Dietz, Rainer Bonhof, Heinz Flohe (68.Erich Beer), Herbert Zimmermann (53.Harald Konopka), Karl-Heinz Rummenigge, Klaus Fischer, Bernd Hölzenbein. Trainer: Helmut Schön.
**ITA:** Dino Zoff, Claudio Gentile, Antonio Cabrini, Romeo Benetti II, Mauro Bellugi, Gaetano Scirea, Franco Causio, Marco Tardelli, Paolo Rossi, Giancarlo Antognoni (46.Renato Zaccarelli), Roberto Bettega. Trainer: Enzo Bearzot.

14.06.1978, Estadio Chateau Carreras, Córdoba; Attendance: 15,000
Referee: John Robertson Proudfoot Gordon (Scotland)
**HOLLAND - AUSTRIA**     **5-1(3-0)**
**NED:** Pieter Schrijvers, Jan Poortvliet, Rudolf Jozef Krol (Cap), Ernestus Wilhelmus Johannes Brandts (65.Adrianus Ambrosus Cornelus van Kraay), Pieter Wildschut, Wilhelmus Marinus Anthonius Jansen, Wilhelmus Antonius van de Kerkhof, Arend Haan, Reinier Lambertus van de Kerkhof (60.Dirk Hendrikus Schoenaker), John Nicolaas Rep, Robert Pieter Rensenbrink. Trainer: Ernst Happel (Austria).
**AUT:** Friedrich Koncilia, Robert Sara, Erich Obermayer, Bruno Pezzey, Gerhard Breitenberger, Herbert Prohaska, Josef Hickersberger, Eduard Krieger, Kurt Jara, Wilhelm Kreuz, Johann Krankl. Trainer: Helmut Senekowitsch.
**Goals:** 1-0 Ernestus Wilhelmus Johannes Brandts (6), 2-0 Robert Pieter Rensenbrink (35 penalty), 3-0 John Nicolaas Rep (36), 4-0 John Nicolaas Rep (53), 4-1 Erich Obermayer (80), 5-1 Wilhelmus Antonius van de Kerkhof (82).

18.06.1978, Estadio Chateau Carreras, Córdoba; Attendance: 40,750
Referee: Ramón Ivannoe Barreto Ruíz (Uruguay)
**WEST GERMANY - HOLLAND** **2-2(1-1)**
**GER:** Josef Maier, Hans-Hubert Vogts (Cap), Rolf Rüssmann, Manfred Kaltz, Bernhard Dietz, Rainer Bonhof, Erich Beer, Bernd Hölzenbein, Rüdiger Abramczik, Dieter Müller, Karl-Heinz Rummenigge. Trainer: Helmut Schön.
**NED:** Pieter Schrijvers, Jan Poortvliet, Rudolf Jozef Krol (Cap), Ernestus Wilhelmus Johannes Brandts, Pieter Wildschut (80.Dirk Jacobus Willem Nanninga), Wilhelmus Marinus Anthonius Jansen, Wilhelmus Antonius van de Kerkhof, Arend Haan, Reinier Lambertus van de Kerkhof, John Nicolaas Rep, Robert Pieter Rensenbrink. Trainer: Ernst Happel (Austria).
**Goals**: 1-0 Rüdiger Abramczik (3), 1-1 Arend Haan (27), 2-1 Dieter Müller (70), 2-2 Reinier Lambertus van de Kerkhof (84).
**Cautions**: Josef Maier / Dirk Jacobus Willem Nanninga, Wilhelmus Antonius van de Kerkhof
**Sent off**: Dirk Jacobus Willem Nanninga (88).

18.06.1978, Estadio Monumental „Antonio Vespucio Liberti", Buenos Aires; Attendance: 50,000
Referee: Francis Jean Joseph Elisa Rion (Belgium)
**ITALY - AUSTRIA** **1-0(1-0)**
**ITA:** Dino Zoff, Claudio Gentile, Antonio Cabrini, Romeo Benetti II, Mauro Bellugi (46.Antonello Cuccureddu), Gaetano Scirea, Franco Causio, Marco Tardelli, Paolo Rossi, Renato Zaccarelli, Roberto Bettega (71.Francesco Graziani). Trainer: Enzo Bearzot.
**AUT:** Friedrich Koncilia, Robert Sara, Erich Obermayer, Bruno Pezzey, Heinrich Strasser, Eduard Krieger, Herbert Prohaska, Wilhelm Kreuz, Josef Hickersberger, Walter Schachner (63.Hans Pirkner), Johann Krankl. Trainer: Helmut Senekowitsch.
**Goal**: 1-0 Paolo Rossi (13).

21.06.1978, Estadio Monumental „Antonio Vespucio Liberti", Buenos Aires; Attendance: 67,433
Referee: Ángel Franco Martínez (Spain)
**HOLLAND - ITALY** **2-1(0-1)**
**NED:** Pieter Schrijvers (20.Jan Jongbloed), Jan Poortvliet, Rudolf Jozef Krol (Cap), Ernestus Wilhelmus Johannes Brandts, Wilhelmus Marinus Anthonius Jansen, Johannes Jacobus Neeskens, Wilhelmus Antonius van de Kerkhof, Arend Haan, Reinier Lambertus van de Kerkhof, John Nicolaas Rep (65.Adrianus Ambrosus Cornelus van Kraay), Robert Pieter Rensenbrink. Trainer: Ernst Happel (Austria).
**ITA:** Dino Zoff, Antonello Cuccureddu, Antonio Cabrini, Romeo Benetti II (77.Francesco Graziani), Claudio Gentile, Gaetano Scirea, Franco Causio (46.Claudio Sala), Marco Tardelli, Paolo Rossi, Renato Zaccarelli, Roberto Bettega. Trainer: Enzo Bearzot.
**Goals**: 0-1 Ernestus Wilhelmus Johannes Brandts (10 own goal), 1-1 Ernestus Wilhelmus Johannes Brandts (49), 2-1 Arend Haan (74).
**Cautions**: John Nicolaas Rep, Arend Haan / Romeo Benetti II, Antonio Cabrini, Marco Tardelli.

21.06.1978, Estadio Chateau Carreras, Córdoba; Attendance: 46,500
Referee: Abraham Klein (Israel)
**AUSTRIA – WEST GERMANY** **3-2(0-1)**
**AUT:** Friedrich Koncilia, Robert Sara, Erich Obermayer, Bruno Pezzey, Heinrich Strasser, Herbert Prohaska, Josef Hickersberger, Wilhelm Kreuz, Eduard Krieger, Walter Schachner (72.Franz Oberacher), Johann Krankl. Trainer: Helmut Senekowitsch.
**GER:** Josef Maier, Hans-Hubert Vogts (Cap), Rolf Rüssmann, Manfred Kaltz, Bernhard Dietz, Rainer Bonhof, Erich Beer (46.Hans Müller), Bernd Hölzenbein, Rüdiger Abramczik, Dieter Müller (61.Klaus Fischer), Karl-Heinz Rummenigge. Trainer: Helmut Schön.
**Goals**: 0-1 Karl-Heinz Rummenigge (19), 1-1 Hans-Hubert Vogts (60 own goal), 2-1 Johann Krankl (66), 2-2 Bernd Hölzenbein (68), 3-2 Johann Krankl (88).
**Cautions**: Robert Sara, Herbert Prohaska / Rüdiger Abramczik.

# GROUP B

| | | | | |
|---|---|---|---|---|
| 14.06.1978 | Mendoza | Brazil - Peru | 3-0(1-0) |
| 14.06.1978 | Rosario | Argentina – Poland | 2-0(1-0) |
| 18.06.1978 | Mendoza | Poland - Peru | 1-0(0-0) |
| 18.06.1978 | Rosario | Argentina - Brazil | 0-0 |
| 21.06.1978 | Mendoza | Brazil - Poland | 3-1(1-1) |
| 21.06.1978 | Rosario | Argentina - Peru | 6-0(2-0) |

## FINAL STANDINGS

| | | | | | | | | |
|---|---|---|---|---|---|---|---|---|
| 1. | Argentina | 3 | 2 | 1 | 0 | 8 - 0 | 5 |
| 2. | Brazil | 3 | 2 | 1 | 0 | 6 - 1 | 5 |
| 3. | Poland | 3 | 1 | 0 | 2 | 2 - 5 | 2 |
| 4. | Peru | 3 | 0 | 0 | 3 | 0 - 10 | 0 |

14.06.1978, Estadio Parque „General San Martín", Mendoza; Attendance: 31,278
Referee: Nicolae Rainea (Romania)
**BRAZIL - PERU** 3-0(1-0)
**BRA:** Émerson Leão (Cap), Antônio Dias dos Santos "Toninho", José Oscar Bernardi, João Justino Amaral dos Santos "Amaral I", José Rodrigues Neto, João Batista da Silva, Antônio Carlos Cerezo "Toninho Cerezo" (76.Francisco Jezuíno Avanzi "Chicão I"), Dirceu José Guimarães „Dirceu II", Gilberto Alves "Gil" (70.Arthur Antunes Coimbra "Zico"), Jorge Pinto Mendonça, Carlos Roberto de Oliveira "Roberto Dinamite". Trainer: Cláudio Pècego de Moraes Coutinho.
**PER:** Ramón Quiroga Arancibia, Jaime Eduardo Duarte Huerta, Rodolfo Manzo Audante, Héctor Eduardo Chumpitaz González (Cap) , Rubén Toribio Díaz Rivas (11.José Navarro Aramburu), José Manuel Velásquez Castillo, César Augusto Cueto Villa, Juan José Muñante López, Teófilo Juan Cubillas Arizaga, Guillermo La Rosa Laguna, Juan Carlos Oblitas Saba (46.Percy Rojas Montero). Trainer: Marcos Calderón Medrano.
**Goals:** 1-0 Dirceu José Guimarães „Dirceu II" (15), 2-0 Dirceu José Guimarães „Dirceu II" (28), 3-0 Arthur Antunes Coimbra "Zico" (73).
**Cautions:** Carlos Roberto de Oliveira "Roberto Dinamite" / José Manuel Velásquez Castillo.

14.06.1978, Estadio „Gigante de Arroyito", Rosario; Attendance: 37,091
Referee: Ulf Helmer Johan Eriksson (Sweden)
**ARGENTINA – POLAND** 2-0(1-0)
**ARG:** Ubaldo Matildo Fillol, Jorge Mario Olguín, Luis Adolfo Galván, Daniel Alberto Passarella (Cap), Alberto César Tarantini, Osvaldo César Ardiles, Américo Rubén Gallego, José Daniel Valencia (46.Julio Ricardo Villa), Ricardo Daniel Bertoni, René Orlando Houseman (83.Oscar Alberto Ortíz), Mario Alberto Kempes. Trainer: César Luis Menotti.
**POL:** Jan Tomaszewski, Henryk Maculewicz, Antoni Szymanowski, Władysław Żmuda, Adam Nawałka, Henryk Kasperczak, Kazimierz Deyna (Cap), Zbigniew Boniek, Bogdan Masztaler (65.Włodzimierz Mazur), Grzegorz Lato, Andrzej Szarmach. Trainer: Jacek Gmoch.
**Goals:** 1-0 Mario Alberto Kempes (16), 2-0 Mario Alberto Kempes (71).
**Cautions:** Américo Rubén Gallego / Henryk Maculewicz.

18.06.1978, Estadio Parque „General San Martín", Mendoza; Attendance: 35,288
Referee: Patrick Partridge (England)
**POLAND - PERU** 1-0(0-0)
**POL:** Zygmunt Kukla, Antoni Szymanowski, Władysław Żmuda, Jerzy Gorgoń, Henryk Maculewicz, Adam Nawałka, Kazimierz Deyna (Cap), Zbigniew Boniek (86.Włodzimierz Lubański), Bogdan Masztaler (46.Henryk Kasperczak), Grzegorz Lato, Andrzej Szarmach. Trainer: Jacek Gmoch.
**PER:** Ramón Quiroga Arancibia, Jaime Eduardo Duarte Huerta, Rodolfo Manzo Audante, Héctor Eduardo Chumpitaz González (Cap), José Navarro Aramburu, César Augusto Cueto Villa, Alfredo

Quesada Farías, Teófilo Juan Cubillas Arizaga, Juan José Muñante López (46.Percy Rojas Montero), Guillermo La Rosa Laguna (74.Hugo Alejandro Sotil Yerén), Juan Carlos Oblitas Saba. Trainer: Marcos Calderón Medrano.
**Goal**: 1-0 Andrzej Szarmach (65).
**Cautions**: Jerzy Gorgoń, Zbigniew Boniek / Rodolfo Manzo Audante, Ramón Quiroga Arancibia.

18.06.1978, Estadio „Gigante de Arroyito", Rosario; Attendance: 37,326
Referee: Károly Palotai (Hungary)
**ARGENTINA - BRAZIL**          **0-0**
**ARG**: Ubaldo Matildo Fillol, Jorge Mario Olguín, Luis Adolfo Galván, Daniel Alberto Passarella (Cap), Alberto César Tarantini, Osvaldo César Ardiles (46.Julio Ricardo Villa), Américo Rubén Gallego, Mario Alberto Kempes, Ricardo Daniel Bertoni, Leopoldo Jacinto Luque, Oscar Alberto Ortíz (60.Norberto Osvaldo Alonso). Trainer: César Luis Menotti.
**BRA**: Émerson Leão (Cap), Antônio Dias dos Santos "Toninho", José Oscar Bernardi, João Justino Amaral dos Santos "Amaral I", José Rodrigues Neto (34.Édino Nazareth Filho "Edinho"), João Batista da Silva, Francisco Jezuíno Avanzi "Chicão I", Dirceu José Guimarães „Dirceu II", Gilberto Alves "Gil", Jorge Pinto Mendonça (67.Arthur Antunes Coimbra "Zico"), Carlos Roberto de Oliveira "Roberto Dinamite". Trainer: Cláudio Pècego de Moraes Coutinho.
**Cautions**: Julio Ricardo Villa / Francisco Jezuíno Avanzi "Chicão I", Édino Nazareth Filho "Edinho", Arthur Antunes Coimbra "Zico".

21.06.1978, Estadio „Parque General San Martín", Mendoza; Attendance: 39,586
Referee: Juan Ambrosio Silvagno Cavanna (Chile)
**BRAZIL - POLAND**          **3-1(1-1)**
**BRA**: Émerson Leão (Cap), Manoel Resende de Matos Cabral "Nelinho", José Oscar Bernardi, João Justino Amaral dos Santos "Amaral I", Antônio Dias dos Santos "Toninho", João Batista da Silva, Antônio Carlos Cerezo "Toninho Cerezo" (78.Roberto Rivelino), Arthur Antunes Coimbra "Zico" (7.Jorge Pinto Mendonça), Dirceu José Guimarães „Dirceu II", Gilberto Alves "Gil", Carlos Roberto de Oliveira "Roberto Dinamite". Trainer: Cláudio Pècego de Moraes Coutinho.
**POL**: Zygmunt Kukla, Antoni Szymanowski, Władysław Żmuda, Jerzy Gorgoń, Henryk Maculewicz, Adam Nawałka, Kazimierz Deyna (Cap), Zbigniew Boniek, Henryk Kasperczak (65.Włodzimierz Lubański), Grzegorz Lato, Andrzej Szarmach. Trainer: Jacek Gmoch.
**Goals**: 1-0 Manoel Resende de Matos Cabral "Nelinho" (13), 1-1 Grzegorz Lato (45), 2-1 Carlos Roberto de Oliveira "Roberto Dinamite" (57), 3-1 Carlos Roberto de Oliveira "Roberto Dinamite" (63).
**Cautions**: Jorge Pinto Mendonça, Antônio Carlos Cerezo "Toninho Cerezo".

21.06.1978, Estadio „Gigante de Arroyito", Rosario; Attendance: 38,000
Referee: Robert Charles Paul Wurtz (France)
**ARGENTINA - PERU**          **6-0(2-0)**
**ARG**: Ubaldo Matildo Fillol, Jorge Mario Olguín, Luis Adolfo Galván, Daniel Alberto Passarella (Cap), Alberto César Tarantini, Omar Rubén Larrosa, Américo Rubén Gallego (86.Miguel Ángel Oviedo), Mario Alberto Kempes, Ricardo Daniel Bertoni (65.René Orlando Houseman), Leopoldo Jacinto Luque, Oscar Alberto Ortíz. Trainer: César Luis Menotti.
**PER**: Ramón Quiroga Arancibia, Jaime Eduardo Duarte Huerta, Rodolfo Manzo Audante, Héctor Eduardo Chumpitaz González (Cap), Roberto Rojas Tardío, Alfredo Quesada Farías, José Manuel Velásquez Castillo (51.Raúl Enrique Gorriti Dragó), César Augusto Cueto Villa, Juan José Muñante López, Teófilo Juan Cubillas Arizaga, Juan Carlos Oblitas Saba. Trainer: Marcos Calderón Medrano.
**Goals**: 1-0 Mario Alberto Kempes (21), 2-0 Alberto César Tarantini (43), 3-0 Mario Alberto Kempes (49), 4-0 Leopoldo Jacinto Luque (50), 5-0 René Orlando Houseman (67), 6-0 Leopoldo Jacinto Luque (72).
**Cautions**: Alfredo Quesada Farías, José Manuel Velásquez Castillo.

## 3rd PLACE PLAY-OFF

24.06.1978, Estadio Monumental „Antonio Vespucio Liberti", Buenos Aires; Attendance: 69,659
Referee: Abraham Klein (Israel)
**BRAZIL - ITALY**                                                                                                                                                   **2-1(0-1)**
**BRA:** Émerson Leão (Cap), Manoel Resende de Matos Cabral "Nelinho", José Oscar Bernardi, João Justino Amaral dos Santos "Amaral I", José Rodrigues Neto, João Batista da Silva, Antônio Carlos Cerezo "Toninho Cerezo" (65.Roberto Rivelino), Dirceu José Guimarães „Dirceu II", Gilberto Alves "Gil" (46.José Reinaldo da Lima "Reinaldo I"), Jorge Pinto Mendonça, Carlos Roberto de Oliveira "Roberto Dinamite". Trainer: Cláudio Pècego de Moraes Coutinho.
**ITA:** Dino Zoff, Claudio Gentile, Antonello Cuccureddu, Antonio Cabrini, Patrizio Sala, Gaetano Scirea, Franco Causio, Aldo Maldera III, Paolo Rossi, Giancarlo Antognoni (78.Claudio Sala), Roberto Bettega. Trainer: Enzo Bearzot.
**Goals**: 0-1 Franco Causio (38), 1-1 Manoel Resende de Matos Cabral "Nelinho" (64), 2-1 Dirceu José Guimarães „Dirceu II" (71).
**Cautions**: Manoel Resende de Matos Cabral "Nelinho", João Batista da Silva / Claudio Gentile.

## FINAL

25.06.1978, Estadio Monumental „Antonio Vespucio Liberti", Buenos Aires; Attendance: 71,483
Referee: Sergio Gonella (Italy)
**ARGENTINA - HOLLAND**                                                                                                                                   **3-1(1-0,1-1)**
**ARG:** Ubaldo Matildo Fillol, Jorge Mario Olguín, Luis Adolfo Galván, Daniel Alberto Passarella (Cap), Alberto César Tarantini, Osvaldo César Ardiles (66.Omar Rubén Larrosa), Américo Rubén Gallego, Mario Alberto Kempes, Ricardo Daniel Bertoni, Leopoldo Jacinto Luque, Oscar Alberto Ortíz (74.René Orlando Houseman). Trainer: César Luis Menotti.
**NED:** Jan Jongbloed, Jan Poortvliet, Rudolf Jozef Krol (Cap), Ernestus Wilhelmus Johannes Brandts, Wilhelmus Marinus Anthonius Jansen (75.Willem Johannes Laurens Suurbier), Wilhelmus Antonius van de Kerkhof, Johannes Jacobus Neeskens, Arend Haan, Reinier Lambertus van de Kerkhof, John Nicolaas Rep (58.Dirk Jacobus Willem Nanninga), Robert Pieter Rensenbrink. Trainer: Ernst Happel (Austria).
**Goals**: 1-0 Mario Alberto Kempes (38), 1-1 Dirk Jacobus Willem Nanninga (82), 2-1 Mario Alberto Kempes (105), 3-1 Ricardo Daniel Bertoni (115).
**Cautions**: Omar Rubén Larrosa, Osvaldo César Ardiles / Rudolf Jozef Krol, Willem Johannes Laurens Suurbier, Johannes Jacobus Neeskens.

## WORLD CUP 1978 FINAL RANKING

| # | Team | P | W | D | L | GF | - | GA | Pts |
|---|------|---|---|---|---|----|---|----|-----|
| 1. | **Argentina** | 7 | 5 | 1 | 1 | 15 | - | 4 | 11 |
| 2. | Holland | 7 | 3 | 2 | 2 | 15 | - | 10 | 8 |
| 3. | Brazil | 7 | 4 | 3 | 0 | 10 | - | 3 | 11 |
| 4. | Italy | 7 | 4 | 1 | 2 | 9 | - | 6 | 9 |
| 5. | Poland | 6 | 3 | 1 | 2 | 6 | - | 6 | 7 |
| 6. | West Germany | 6 | 1 | 4 | 1 | 10 | - | 5 | 6 |
| 7. | Austria | 6 | 3 | 0 | 3 | 7 | - | 10 | 6 |
| 8. | Peru | 6 | 2 | 1 | 3 | 7 | - | 12 | 5 |
| 9. | Tunisia | 3 | 1 | 1 | 1 | 3 | - | 2 | 3 |
| 10. | Spain | 3 | 1 | 1 | 1 | 2 | - | 2 | 3 |
| 11. | Scotland | 3 | 1 | 1 | 1 | 5 | - | 5 | 3 |
| 12. | France | 3 | 1 | 0 | 2 | 5 | - | 5 | 2 |
| 13. | Sweden | 3 | 0 | 1 | 2 | 1 | - | 3 | 1 |
| 14. | Iran | 3 | 0 | 1 | 2 | 2 | - | 8 | 1 |
| 15. | Hungary | 3 | 0 | 0 | 3 | 3 | - | 8 | 0 |
| 16. | Mexico | 3 | 0 | 0 | 3 | 2 | - | 12 | 0 |

## WORLD CUP 1978 AWARDS

**GOLDEN BALL (best player of the World Cup final tournament)**
Mario Alberto Kempes (Argentina)

**GOLDEN BOOT (best goalscorer)**
Mario Alberto Kempes (Argentina)

**BEST YOUNG PLAYER**
Antonio Cabrini (Italy)

**FIFA FAIR-PLAY TROPHY**
Argentina

# GOALSCORERS

**6 goals:** Mario Alberto Kempes (Argentina)
**5 goals:** Robert Pieter Rensenbrink (Holland)
Teófilo Juan Cubillas Arizaga (Peru)
**4 goals:** Leopoldo Jacinto Luque (Argentina)
Johann Krankl (Austria)
**3 goals:** Dirceu José Guimarães „Dirceu II", Carlos Roberto de Oliveira "Roberto Dinamite" (Brazil),
John Nicolaas Rep (Holland)
Paolo Rossi (Italy)
Karl-Heinz Rummenigge (West Germany)
**2 goals:** Ricardo Daniel Bertoni (Argentina), Manoel Resende de Matos Cabral "Nelinho" (Brazil), Arend Haan, Ernestus Wilhelmus Johannes Brandts (Holland), Roberto Bettega (Italy), Zbigniew Boniek, Grzegorz Lato (Poland), Archibald Gemmill (Scotland), Heinz Flohe, Dieter Müller (West Germany)
**1 goal:** René Orlando Houseman, Daniel Alberto Passarella, Alberto César Tarantini (Argentina), Erich Obermayer, Walter Schachner (Austria), José Reinaldo da Lima "Reinaldo I", Arthur Antunes Coimbra "Zico" (Brazil), Marc Berdoll, Bernard Lacombe, Christian Lopez, Michel Platini, Dominique Rocheteau (France), Reinier Lambertus van de Kerkhof, Wilhelmus Antonius van de Kerkhof, Dirk Jacobus Willem Nanninga (Holland), Károly Csapó, András Tóth, Sándor Zombori (Hungary), Iraj Danaeifard, Hassan Roshan (Iran), Romeo Benetti II, Franco Causio, Renato Zaccarelli (Italy), Víctor Rangel Ayala, Arturo Vázquez Ayala (Mexico), César Augusto Cueto Villa, José Manuel Velásquez Castillo (Peru), Kazimierz Deyna, Andrzej Szarmach (Poland), Kenneth Mathieson Dalglish, Joseph Jordan (Scotland), Juan Manuel Asensi Ripoll, Daniel Ruiz-Bazan Justa „Dani" (Spain), Thomas Sjöberg (Sweden), Mokhtar Dhouib, Néjib Ghommidh, Ali Kaabi (Tunisia), Rüdiger Abramczik, Bernd Hölzenbein, Hans Müller (West Germany)

Own goals:
3 Andranik Eskandarian (Iran), against Scotland
Ernestus Wilhelmus Johannes Brandts (Holland), against Italy
Hans-Hubert Vogts (West Germany), against Austria

Total number of goals scored: **102**
Average goals per match: **2.68**
Total number of penalty kicks awarded: **13**
Total number of penalty kicks scored: **12**

# LIST OF REFEREES

| Name | DOB | Country | M |
|---|---|---|---|
| Abraham Klein | 29.03.1934 | Israel | 3 |
| Robert Charles Paul Wurtz | 16.11.1941 | France | 2 |
| Károly Palotai | 11.09.1935 | Hungary | 2 |
| Sergio Gonella | 23.05.1933 | Italy | 2 |
| Nicolae Rainea | 19.11.1933 | Romania | 2 |
| John Robertson Proudfoot Gordon | 02.02.1930 | Scotland | 2 |
| Angel Franco Martínez | 31.10.1938 | Spain | 2 |
| Ulf Helmer Johan Eriksson | 26.05.1942 | Sweden | 2 |
| Ramón Ivannoe Barreto Ruíz | 14.09.1939 | Uruguay | 2 |
| Angel Norberto Coerezza | 24.10.1933 | Argentina | 1 |
| Erich Linemayr | 24.01.1933 | Austria | 1 |
| Francis Jean Joseph Elisa Rion | 10.06.1933 | Belgium | 1 |
| Arnaldo David Cesar Coelho | 15.01.1943 | Brazil | 1 |
| Juan Ambrosio Silvagno Cavanna | 29.07.1934 | Chile | 1 |
| Adolf Prokop | 02.02.1939 | East Germany | 1 |
| Patrick Partridge | 30.06.1933 | England | 1 |
| Charles George Reinier Corver | 16.01.1936 | Holland | 1 |
| Jaffar Namdar | 11.07.1934 | Iran | 1 |
| Alfonso González Archundia | 14.06.1934 | Mexico | 1 |
| César Guerrero Orozco | 14.04.1930 | Peru | 1 |
| Alojzy Jarguz | 19.03.1934 | Poland | 1 |
| Antonio José da Silva Garrido | 03.12.1932 | Portugal | 1 |
| Youssou N'Diaye | 20.06.1932 | Senegal | 1 |
| Jean Dubach | 28.02.1930 | Switzerland | 1 |
| Farouk Bouzo | 03.03.1938 | Syria | 1 |
| Clive Thomas | 22.06.1936 | Wales | 1 |
| Ferdinand Biwersi | 24.06.1934 | West Germany | 1 |
| Dušan Maksimović | 06.01.1940 | Yugoslavia | 1 |

# WORLD CUP 1978 – THE SQUADS

## ARGENTINA

| Nr | Name | DOB | Club |
|---|---|---|---|
| | **Goalkeepers** | | |
| 3 | Héctor Rodolfo Baley | 16.11.1950 | CA Huracán Buenos Aires |
| 5 | Ubaldo Matildo Fillol | 21.07.1950 | CA River Plate Buenos Aires |
| 13 | Ricardo Antonio La Volpe Guarchoni | 06.02.1952 | CA San Lorenzo de Almagro |
| | **Defenders** | | |
| 7 | Luis Adolfo Galván | 24.02.1948 | CA Talleres de Córdoba |
| 11 | Daniel Pedro Killer | 21.12.1949 | Racing Club de Avellaneda |
| 15 | Jorge Mario Olguín | 17.05.1952 | CA San Lorenzo de Almagro |
| 18 | Rubén Oscar Pagnanini | 31.01.1949 | CA Independiente Avellaneda |
| 19 | Daniel Alberto Passarella | 25.05.1953 | CA River Plate Buenos Aires |
| 20 | Alberto César Tarantini | 03.12.1955 | *Unattached* |
| | **Midfielders** | | |
| 1 | Norberto Osvaldo Alonso | 04.01.1953 | CA River Plate Buenos Aires |
| 2 | Osvaldo César Ardiles | 03.08.1952 | CA Huracán Buenos Aires |
| 6 | Américo Rubén Gallego | 25.04.1955 | CA Newell's Old Boys Rosario |
| 8 | Rubén Galván | 07.04.1952 | CA Independiente Avellaneda |
| 12 | Omar Rubén Larrosa | 18.11.1947 | CA Independiente Avellaneda |
| 16 | Oscar Alberto Ortíz | 08.04.1953 | CA River Plate Buenos Aires |
| 17 | Miguel Ángel Oviedo | 12.10.1950 | CA Talleres de Córdoba |
| 21 | José Daniel Valencia | 03.10.1955 | CA Talleres de Córdoba |
| 22 | Julio Ricardo Villa | 18.08.1952 | Racing Club de Avellaneda |
| | **Forwards** | | |
| 4 | Ricardo Daniel Bertoni | 14.03.1955 | CA Independiente Avellaneda |
| 9 | René Orlando Houseman | 19.07.1953 | CA Huracán Buenos Aires |
| 10 | Mario Alberto Kempes | 15.07.1954 | CF Valencia (ESP) |
| 14 | Leopoldo Jacinto Luque | 03.05.1949 | CA River Plate Buenos Aires |
| **Trainer:** | César Luis Menotti | 05.11.1938 | |

## AUSTRIA

| Nr | Name | DOB | Club |
|---|---|---|---|
| | **Goalkeepers** | | |
| 1 | Friedrich Koncilia | 25.02.1948 | SSW Innsbruck |
| 21 | Erwin Fuchsbichler | 27.03.1952 | VÖEST Linz |
| 22 | Hubert Baumgartner | 25.02.1955 | FK Austria Wien |
| | **Defenders** | | |
| 2 | Robert Sara | 09.06.1946 | FK Austria Wien |
| 3 | Erich Obermayer | 23.01.1953 | FK Austria Wien |
| 4 | Gerhard Breitenberger | 14.10.1954 | VÖEST Linz |
| 5 | Bruno Pezzey | 03.02.1955 | SSW Innsbruck |
| 14 | Heinrich Strasser | 26.10.1948 | FC Admira/Wacker Wien |
| 15 | Heribert Weber | 28.06.1955 | SK Sturm Graz |
| 16 | Peter Persidis | 08.03.1947 | SK Rapid Wien |
| | **Midfielders** | | |
| 6 | Roland Hattenberger | 07.12.1948 | VfB Stuttgart (GER) |
| 7 | Josef Hickersberger | 27.04.1948 | TSV Fortuna Düsseldorf (GER) |
| 8 | Herbert Prohaska | 08.08.1955 | FK Austria Wien |
| 11 | Kurt Jara | 14.10.1950 | MSV Duisburg (GER) |
| 12 | Eduard Krieger | 16.12.1946 | Club Brugge KV (BEL) |
| 13 | Günther Happich | 28.01.1952 | Wiener Sport-Club |
| 20 | Ernst Baumeister | 22.01.1957 | FK Austria Wien |
| | **Forwards** | | |
| 9 | Hans Krankl | 14.02.1953 | SK Rapid Wien |
| 10 | Wilhelm Kreuz | 29.05.1949 | SC Feyenoord Rotterdam (NED) |
| 17 | Franz Oberacher | 24.03.1954 | SSW Innsbruck |
| 18 | Walter Schachner | 01.02.1957 | DSV Alpine Donawitz |
| 19 | Hans Pirkner | 25.03.1946 | FK Austria Wien |
| **Trainer:** | Helmut Senekowitsch | 22.10.1933 | |

## BRAZIL

| Nr | Name | DOB | Club |
|---|---|---|---|
| **Goalkeepers** | | | |
| 1 | Émerson Leão | 11.07.1949 | SE Palmeiras São Paulo |
| 12 | Carlos Roberto Gallo | 04.03.1956 | AA Ponte Preta Campinas |
| 22 | Valdir de Arruda Peres | 02.01.1951 | São Paulo FC |
| **Defenders** | | | |
| 2 | Antônio Dias dos Santos "Toninho" | 07.06.1948 | CR Flamengo Rio de Janeiro |
| 3 | José Oscar Bernardi | 20.06.1954 | AA Ponte Preta Campinas |
| 4 | João Justino Amaral dos Santos "Amaral I" | 25.12.1954 | SC Corinthians Paulista São Paulo |
| 6 | Édino Nazareth Filho "Edinho" | 05.06.1955 | Fluminense FC Rio de Janeiro |
| 13 | Manoel Resende de Matos Cabral "Nelinho" | 26.07.1950 | Cruzeiro EC Belo Horizonte |
| 14 | Abel Carlos da Silva Braga | 01.09.1952 | CR Vasco da Gama Rio de Janeiro |
| 15 | José Fernando Polozzi | 01.10.1955 | AA Ponte Preta Campinas |
| 16 | José Rodrigues Neto | 01.12.1949 | Botafogo de FR Rio de Janeiro |
| **Midfielders** | | | |
| 5 | Antônio Carlos Cerezo "Toninho Cerezo" | 21.04.1955 | Atlético Mineiro Belo Horizonte |
| 8 | Arthur Antunes Coimbra "Zico" | 03.03.1953 | CR Flamengo Rio de Janeiro |
| 11 | Dirceu José Guimarães | 15.06.1952 | CR Vasco da Gama Rio de Janeiro |
| 17 | João Batista da Silva | 08.03.1955 | SC Internacional Porto Alegre |
| 21 | Francisco Jezuíno Avanzi "Chicão I" | 30.01.1949 | São Paulo FC |
| **Forwards** | | | |
| 7 | José Sérgio Presti "Zé Sérgio" | 08.03.1957 | São Paulo FC |
| 9 | José Reinaldo da Lima "Reinaldo I" | 11.01.1957 | Atlético Mineiro Belo Horizonte |
| 10 | Roberto Rivelino | 01.01.1946 | Fluminense FC Rio de Janeiro |
| 18 | Gilberto Alves "Gil" | 24.12.1950 | Botafogo de FR Rio de Janeiro |
| 19 | Jorge Pinto Mendonça | 06.06.1954 | SE Palmeiras São Paulo |
| 20 | Carlos Roberto de Oliveira "Roberto Dinamite" | 13.04.1954 | CR Vasco da Gama Rio de Janeiro |
| **Trainer:** Cláudio Pècego de Moraes Coutinho | | 05.01.1939 | |

## FRANCE

| Nr | Name | DOB | Club |
|---|---|---|---|
| **Goalkeepers** | | | |
| 1 | Dominique Baratelli | 26.12.1947 | OGC Nice |
| 21 | Jean-Paul Bertrand-Demanes | 23.05.1952 | FC Nantes |
| 22 | Dominique Dropsy | 09.12.1951 | Racing Club Strasbourg |
| **Defenders** | | | |
| 2 | Patrick Battiston | 12.03.1957 | FC Metz |
| 3 | Maxime Bossis | 26.06.1955 | FC Nantes |
| 4 | Gérard Janvion | 21.08.1953 | AS Saint-Étienne |
| 5 | François Bracci | 03.11.1951 | Olympique de Marseille |
| 6 | Christian Lopez | 15.03.1953 | AS Saint-Étienne |
| 7 | Patrice Rio | 15.08.1948 | FC Nantes |
| 8 | Marius Trésor | 15.01.1950 | Olympique de Marseille |
| **Midfielders** | | | |
| 9 | Dominque Bathenay | 13.02.1954 | AS Saint-Étienne |
| 10 | Jean-Marc Guillou | 20.12.1945 | OGC Nice |
| 11 | Henri Michel | 28.10.1947 | FC Nantes |
| 12 | Claude Papi | 16.04.1949 | SEC Bastia |
| 13 | Jean Petit | 25.09.1949 | AS Monaco |
| 15 | Michel Platini | 21.06.1955 | AS Nancy-Lorraine |
| **Forwards** | | | |
| 14 | Marc Berdoll | 06.04.1953 | Olympique de Marseille |
| 16 | Christian Dalger | 19.12.1949 | AS Monaco |
| 17 | Bernard Lacombe | 15.08.1952 | Olympique Lyonnais |
| 18 | Dominique Rocheteau | 14.01.1955 | AS Saint-Étienne |
| 19 | Didier Six | 21.08.1954 | Racing Club Lens |
| 20 | Olivier Rouyer | 01.12.1955 | AS Nancy-Lorraine |
| **Trainer:** Michel Hidalgo | | 22.03.1933 | |

## HOLLAND

| Nr | Name | DOB | Club |
|---|---|---|---|
| | **Goalkeepers** | | |
| 1 | Pieter Schrijvers | 15.12.1946 | AFC Ajax Amsterdam |
| 8 | Jan Jongbloed | 25.11.1940 | Roda JC Kerkrade |
| 19 | Willem Doesburg | 28.10.1943 | Sparta Rotterdam |
| | **Defenders** | | |
| 2 | Jan Poortvliet | 21.09.1955 | PSV Eindhoven |
| 4 | Adrie van Kraay | 01.08.1953 | PSV Eindhoven |
| 5 | Rudolf Jozef Krol | 24.03.1949 | AFC Ajax Amsterdam |
| 7 | Pieter Wildschut | 25.10.1957 | FC Twente Enschede |
| 15 | Hugo Hermanus Hovenkamp | 05.10.1950 | AZ'67 Alkmaar |
| 17 | Wilhelmus Gerardus Rijsbergen | 18.01.1952 | SC Feyenoord Rotterdam |
| 20 | Willem Johannes Laurens Suurbier | 16.01.1945 | FC Schalke 04 Gelsenkirchen (GER) |
| 22 | Ernestus Wilhelmus Johannes Brandts | 03.02.1956 | PSV Eindhoven |
| | **Midfielders** | | |
| 3 | Dirk Hendrikus Schoenaker | 30.11.1952 | AFC Ajax Amsterdam |
| 6 | Wilhelmus Marinus Anthonius Jansen | 28.10.1946 | SC Feyenoord Rotterdam |
| 9 | Arend Haan | 16.11.1948 | RSC Anderlecht Bruxelles (BEL) |
| 11 | Wilhelmus Antonius van de Kerkhof | 16.09.1951 | PSV Eindhoven |
| 13 | Johannes Jacobus Neeskens | 15.09.1951 | FC Barcelona (ESP) |
| 14 | Johannes Boskamp | 21.10.1948 | RWD Molenbeek (BEL) |
| | **Forwards** | | |
| 10 | Reinier Lambertus van de Kerkhof | 16.09.1951 | PSV Eindhoven |
| 12 | Robert Pieter Rensenbrink | 03.07.1947 | RSC Anderlecht Bruxelles (BEL) |
| 16 | John Nicolaas Rep | 25.11.1951 | SEC Bastia (FRA) |
| 18 | Dirk Jacobus Willem Nanninga | 17.01.1949 | Roda JC Kerkrade |
| 21 | Heinricus Carolus Gerardus Lubse | 23.09.1951 | PSV Eindhoven |
| **Trainer:** | Ernst Happel (AUT) | 29.11.1925 | |

## HUNGARY

| Nr | Name | DOB | Club |
|---|---|---|---|
| | **Goalkeepers** | | |
| 1 | Sándor Gujdár | 08.11.1951 | Budapesti Honvéd SE |
| 21 | Ferenc Mészáros | 11.04.1950 | Vasas SC Budapest |
| 22 | László Kovács | 24.04.1951 | Videoton SC Székesfehérvár |
| | **Defenders** | | |
| 2 | Péter Török | 18.04.1951 | Vasas SC Budapest |
| 3 | István Kocsis | 06.10.1949 | Budapesti Honvéd SE |
| 4 | József Tóth | 02.12.1951 | Újpesti Dózsa SC |
| 6 | Zoltán Kereki | 13.07.1953 | Szombathelyi Haladás VSE |
| 12 | Győző Martos | 15.12.1949 | Ferencvárosi TC |
| 14 | László Bálint | 01.02.1948 | Ferencvárosi TC |
| 15 | Tibor Rab | 02.10.1955 | Ferencvárosi TC |
| | **Midfielders** | | |
| 5 | Sándor Zombori | 31.10.1951 | Vasas SC Budapest |
| 8 | Tibor Nyilasi | 18.01.1955 | Ferencvárosi TC |
| 10 | Sándor Pintér | 18.07.1950 | Budapesti Honvéd SE |
| 13 | Károly Csapó | 23.02.1952 | Tatabányai Bányász SC |
| 16 | István Halász | 12.10.1951 | Tatabányai Bányász SC |
| 18 | László Nagy | 21.10.1949 | Újpesti Dózsa SC |
| 20 | Ferenc Fülöp | 22.02.1955 | MTK Budapest |
| | **Forwards** | | |
| 7 | László Fazekas | 15.10.1947 | Újpesti Dózsa SC FC |
| 9 | András Törőcsik | 01.05.1955 | Újpesti Dózsa SC FC |
| 11 | Béla Várady | 12.04.1953 | Vasas SC Budapest |
| 17 | László Pusztai | 01.03.1946 | Ferencvárosi TC |
| 19 | András Tóth | 05.09.1949 | Újpesti Dózsa SC |
| **Trainer:** | Lajos Baróti | 19.08.1914 | |

## IRAN

| Nr | Name | DOB | Club |
|---|---|---|---|
| | **Goalkeepers** | | |
| 1 | Nasser Hejazi | 14.12.1949 | Shahbaz Tehran FC |
| 12 | Bahram Mavaddat | 30.01.1950 | Sepahan Tehran FC |
| 22 | Mohammad Reza Rasoul Korbekandi | 27.01.1953 | Zob Ahan FC Isfahan |
| | **Defenders** | | |
| 5 | Javad Allahverdi | 16.07.1954 | Persepolis Tehran FC |
| 11 | Ali Reza Ghesghayan | 27.02.1954 | Bargh Shiraz FC |
| 14 | Hassan Nazari | 19.08.1955 | Taj Tehran FC |
| 15 | Andranik Eskandarian | 31.12.1951 | Taj Tehran FC |
| 19 | Mohammad Ali Shojaei | 23.03.1953 | Sepahan Tehran FC |
| 20 | Nasrollah Abdollahi | 02.09.1951 | Shahbaz Tehran FC |
| 21 | Hossein Kazerani | 13.04.1947 | Pas Tehran FC |
| | **Midfielders** | | |
| 2 | Iraj Danaeifard | 19.03.1951 | Taj Tehran FC |
| 6 | Hassan Nayebagha | 17.09.1950 | Homa Tehran FC |
| 7 | Ali Parvin | 12.10.1946 | Persepolis Tehran FC |
| 8 | Ebrahim Ghasempour | 24.08.1956 | Shahbaz Tehran FC |
| 9 | Mohammad Sadeghi | 17.03.1951 | Pas Tehran FC |
| | **Forwards** | | |
| 3 | Behtash Fariba | 11.02.1955 | Pas Tehran FC |
| 4 | Majid Bishkar | 06.08.1956 | Rastakhiz Tehran FC |
| 10 | Hassan Roshan | 02.06.1955 | Taj Tehran FC |
| 13 | Hamid Majd Teymouri | 03.06.1953 | Shahbaz Tehran FC |
| 16 | Nasser Nouraei | 09.07.1956 | Homa Tehran FC |
| 17 | Ghafour Jahani | 18.06.1950 | Malavan Bandar Anzali FC |
| 18 | Hossein Faraki | 19.04.1956 | Pas Tehran FC |
| **Trainer:** | Heshmatollah Mohajerani | 11.12.1938 | |

## ITALY

| Nr | Name | DOB | Club |
|---|---|---|---|
| | **Goalkeepers** | | |
| 1 | Dino Zoff | 28.02.1942 | FC Juventus Torino |
| 12 | Paolo Conti | 01.04.1950 | AS Roma |
| 22 | Ivano Bordon | 13.04.1951 | Internazionale FC Milano |
| | **Defenders** | | |
| 2 | Mauro Bellugi | 07.02.1950 | FC Bologna |
| 3 | Antonio Cabrini | 08.10.1957 | FC Juventus Torino |
| 4 | Antonello Cuccureddu | 04.10.1949 | FC Juventus Torino |
| 5 | Claudio Gentile | 27.09.1953 | FC Juventus Torino |
| 6 | Aldo Maldera | 14.10.1953 | Milan AC |
| 7 | Lionello Manfredonia | 27.11.1956 | SS Lazio Roma |
| 8 | Gaetano Scirea | 25.05.1953 | FC Juventus Torino |
| | **Midfielders** | | |
| 9 | Giancarlo Antognoni | 01.04.1954 | AC Fiorentina Firenze |
| 10 | Romeo Benetti | 20.10.1945 | FC Juventus Torino |
| 11 | Eraldo Pecci | 12.04.1955 | Torino Calcio |
| 13 | Patrizio Sala | 16.06.1955 | Torino Calcio |
| 14 | Marco Tardelli | 24.09.1954 | FC Juventus Torino |
| 15 | Renato Zaccarelli | 18.01.1951 | Torino Calcio |
| 16 | Franco Causio | 01.02.1949 | FC Juventus Torino |
| 17 | Claudio Sala | 08.09.1947 | Torino Calcio |
| | **Forwards** | | |
| 18 | Roberto Bettega | 27.12.1950 | FC Juventus Torino |
| 19 | Francesco Graziani | 16.12.1952 | Torino Calcio |
| 20 | Paolo Pulici | 27.04.1950 | Torino Calcio |
| 21 | Paolo Rossi | 23.09.1956 | Lanerossi Vicenza |
| **Trainer:** | Vincenzo „Enzo" Bearzot | 26.09.1927 | |

## MEXICO

| Nr | Name | DOB | Club |
|---|---|---|---|
| | **Goalkeepers** | | |
| 1 | José Pilar Reyes Requenes | 12.10.1955 | Tigres de la UA de Nuevo León |
| 22 | Pedro Soto Moreno | 22.10.1952 | CF América Ciudad de México |
| | **Defenders** | | |
| 2 | Manuel Nájera Siller | 20.12.1952 | CD Universidad de Guadalajara |
| 3 | Alfredo Tena Garduño | 21.11.1956 | CF América Ciudad de México |
| 4 | Eduardo Ramos Escobedo | 08.11.1949 | CD Guadalajara |
| 5 | Arturo Vázquez Ayala | 26.06.1949 | Club UNAM Ciudad de México |
| 12 | Jesús Martínez Díez | 07.06.1952 | CF América Ciudad de México |
| 13 | Rigoberto Cisneros Dueñas | 15.08.1953 | Deportivo Toluca FC |
| 14 | Carlos Gómez Casillas | 16.08.1952 | CSD León |
| 15 | Ignacio Flores Ocaranza | 31.07.1953 | CDSC Cruz Azul Ciudad de México |
| | **Midfielders** | | |
| 6 | Guillermo Mendizábal Sánchez | 08.10.1954 | CDSC Cruz Azul Ciudad de México |
| 7 | Antonio de la Torre Villalpando | 21.09.1951 | CF América Ciudad de México |
| 10 | Cristóbal Ortega Martínez | 25.07.1956 | CF América Ciudad de México |
| 16 | Javier Cárdenas Martínez | 08.12.1952 | Deportivo Toluca FC |
| 17 | Leonardo Cuéllar Rivera | 14.01.1952 | Club UNAM Ciudad de México |
| 18 | Gerardo Lugo Gómez | 13.03.1955 | CF Atlante Ciudad de México |
| | **Forwards** | | |
| 8 | Enrique López Zarza | 25.10.1957 | Club UNAM Ciudad de México |
| 9 | Víctor Rangel Ayala | 11.03.1957 | CD Guadalajara |
| 11 | Hugo Sánchez Márquez | 11.07.1958 | Club UNAM Ciudad de México |
| 19 | Hugo René Rodríguez Corona | 14.03.1959 | Club Santos Laguna Torreón |
| 20 | Mario Medina Rojas | 02.09.1952 | Deportivo Toluca FC |
| 21 | Raúl Isiordia Ayón | 22.12.1952 | Atlético Español FC Cdad. de México |
| | Trainer: José Antonio Roca García | 24.05.1928 | |

## PERU

| Nr | Name | DOB | Club |
|---|---|---|---|
| | **Goalkeepers** | | |
| 1 | Ottorino Sartor Espinoza | 18.09.1945 | ID Colegio Nacional de Iquitos |
| 13 | Juan José Cáceres Palomares | 27.12.1949 | Club Alianza Lima |
| 21 | Ramón Quiroga Arancibia | 23.07.1950 | Club Sporting Cristal Lima |
| | **Defenders** | | |
| 2 | Jaime Eduardo Duarte Huerta | 27.02.1955 | Club Alianza Lima |
| 3 | Rodolfo Manzo Audante | 05.06.1949 | Club CD Municipal Lima |
| 4 | Héctor Eduardo Chumpitaz González | 12.04.1944 | Club Sporting Cristal Lima |
| 5 | Rubén Toribio Díaz Rivas | 17.04.1952 | Club Sporting Cristal Lima |
| 14 | José Navarro Aramburu | 24.09.1948 | Club Sporting Cristal Lima |
| 22 | Roberto Rojas Tardío | 26.10.1955 | Club Alianza Lima |
| | **Midfielders** | | |
| 6 | José Manuel Velásquez Castillo | 04.06.1952 | Club Alianza Lima |
| 8 | César Augusto Cueto Villa | 16.06.1952 | Club Alianza Lima |
| 10 | Teófilo Juan Cubillas Arizaga | 08.03.1949 | Club Alianza Lima |
| 15 | Germán Carlos Leguía Dragó | 02.01.1954 | Club CD Municipal Lima |
| 16 | Raúl Enrique Gorriti Dragó | 10.10.1956 | Club Sporting Cristal Lima |
| 17 | Alfredo Quesada Farías | 22.09.1949 | Club Sporting Cristal Lima |
| 18 | Ernesto Labarthe Flores | 02.06.1956 | Sport Boys Association Callao |
| | **Forwards** | | |
| 7 | Juan José Muñante López | 12.07.1948 | Club UNAM Cd. de México (MEX) |
| 9 | Percy Rojas Montero | 16.09.1949 | Club Sporting Cristal Lima |
| 11 | Juan Carlos Oblitas Saba | 16.02.1951 | Sporting Cristal Lima |
| 12 | Roberto Orlando Mosquera Vera | 21.06.1956 | Club Sporting Cristal Lima |
| 19 | Guillermo La Rosa Laguna | 06.06.1952 | Club Alianza Lima |
| 20 | Hugo Alejandro Sotil Yerén | 08.03.1949 | Club Alianza Lima |
| | Trainer: Marcos Calderón Medrano | 11.07.1928 | |

## POLAND

| Nr | Name | DOB | Club |
|---|---|---|---|
| | **Goalkeepers** | | |
| 1 | Jan Tomaszewski | 09.01.1948 | ŁKS Łódź |
| 21 | Zygmunt Kukla | 21.01.1948 | FKS Stal Mielec |
| 22 | Zdzisław Kostrzewa | 26.10.1955 | Zagłębie Sosnowiec |
| | **Defenders** | | |
| 3 | Henryk Maculewicz | 24.04.1950 | Wisła Kraków |
| 4 | Antoni Szymanowski | 13.01.1951 | Wisła Kraków |
| 6 | Jerzy Gorgoń | 18.07.1949 | KS Górnik Zabrze |
| 9 | Władysław Żmuda | 06.06.1954 | KS Śląsk Wrocław |
| 10 | Wojciech Rudy | 24.10.1952 | Zagłębie Sosnowiec |
| 13 | Janusz Kupcewicz | 09.12.1955 | KS Arka Gdynia |
| 14 | Mirosław Justek | 23.09.1948 | Lech Poznań |
| 20 | Roman Wójcicki | 08.01.1958 | KS Odra Opole |
| | **Midfielders** | | |
| 5 | Adam Nawałka | 23.10.1957 | Wisła Kraków |
| 8 | Henryk Kasperczak | 10.07.1946 | FKS Stal Mielec |
| 11 | Bohdan Masztaler | 19.09.1949 | ŁKS Łódź |
| 12 | Kazimierz Deyna | 23.10.1947 | KP Legia Warszawa |
| 15 | Marek Kusto | 29.04.1954 | KP Legia Warszawa |
| 18 | Zbigniew Boniek | 03.03.1956 | RTS Widzew Łódź |
| | **Forwards** | | |
| 2 | Włodzimierz Mazur | 18.04.1954 | Zagłębie Sosnowiec |
| 7 | Andrzej Iwan | 10.11.1959 | Wisła Kraków |
| 16 | Grzegorz Lato | 08.04.1950 | FKS Stal Mielec |
| 17 | Andrzej Szarmach | 03.10.1950 | FKS Stal Mielec |
| 19 | Włodzimierz Lubański | 28.02.1947 | KSC Lokeren (BEL) |
| **Trainer:** | Jacek Gmoch | 13.01.1939 | |

## SCOTLAND

| Nr | Name | DOB | Club |
|---|---|---|---|
| | **Goalkeepers** | | |
| 1 | Alan Roderick Rough | 25.11.1951 | Partick Thistle FC Glasgow |
| 12 | James Anton Blyth | 02.02.1955 | Coventry City FC (ENG) |
| 20 | Robert Brown Clark | 26.09.1945 | Aberdeen FC |
| | **Defenders** | | |
| 2 | William Pullar Jardine | 31.12.1948 | Glasgow Rangers FC |
| 3 | William Donachie | 05.10.1951 | Manchester City FC (ENG) |
| 4 | Martin McLean Buchan | 06.03.1949 | Manchester United FC (ENG) |
| 5 | Gordon McQueen | 26.06.1952 | Manchester United FC (ENG) |
| 13 | Stuart Robert Kennedy | 31.05.1953 | Aberdeen FC |
| 14 | Thomas Forsyth | 23.01.1949 | Glasgow Rangers FC |
| 22 | Kenneth Burns | 23.09.1953 | Nottingham Forest FC (ENG) |
| | **Midfielders** | | |
| 6 | Bruce David Rioch | 06.09.1947 | Derby County FC (ENG) |
| 7 | Donald Sanderson Masson | 26.08.1949 | Derby County FC (ENG) |
| 10 | Richard Asa Hartford | 24.10.1950 | Manchester City FC (ENG) |
| 11 | William McClure Johnston | 19.12.1946 | West Bromwich Albion FC (ENG) |
| 15 | Archibald Gemmill | 24.03.1947 | Nottingham Forest FC (ENG) |
| 18 | Graeme James Souness | 06.05.1953 | Liverpool FC (ENG) |
| | **Forwards** | | |
| 8 | Kenneth Mathieson Dalglish | 04.03.1951 | Liverpool FC (ENG) |
| 9 | Joseph Jordan | 15.12.1951 | Manchester United FC (ENG) |
| 16 | Luigi "Lou" Macari | 07.06.1949 | Manchester United FC (ENG) |
| 17 | Derek Joseph Johnstone | 04.11.1953 | Glasgow Rangers FC |
| 19 | John Neilson Robertson | 20.01.1953 | Nottingham Forest FC (ENG) |
| 21 | Joseph Montgomery Harper | 11.01.1948 | Aberdeen FC |
| **Trainer:** | Alistair MacLeod | 26.02.1931 | |

## SPAIN

| Nr | Name | DOB | Club |
|---|---|---|---|
| **Goalkeepers** | | | |
| 1 | Luis Miguel Arkonada Echarre | 26.06.1954 | Real Sociedad San Sebastián |
| 13 | Miguel Ángel González Suárez | 24.12.1947 | Real Madrid CF |
| 22 | Francisco Javier González „Urrutikoetxea" | 17.02.1952 | RCD Español Barcelona |
| **Defenders** | | | |
| 2 | Jesús Antonio De la Cruz Gallego | 07.05.1947 | FC Barcelona |
| 5 | Miguel Bernardo Bianquetti „Migueli" | 19.12.1951 | FC Barcelona |
| 6 | Antonio Biosca Pérez | 08.12.1949 | Real Betis Balompié Sevilla |
| 16 | Antonio Olmo Ramírez | 18.01.1954 | FC Barcelona |
| 17 | Marcelino Pérez Ayllón | 13.08.1955 | Club Atlético de Madrid |
| 18 | José Martínez Sánchez „Pirri" | 11.03.1945 | Real Madrid CF |
| **Midfielders** | | | |
| 3 | Francisco Javier Álvarez „Uría" | 01.02.1950 | Real Sporting Gijón CF |
| 4 | Juan Manuel Asensi Ripoll | 23.09.1949 | FC Barcelona |
| 11 | Julio Cardeñosa Rodríguez | 27.10.1949 | Real Betis Balompié Sevilla |
| 12 | Antonio Guzmán Nuñez | 02.12.1953 | AD Rayo Vallecano de Madrid |
| 14 | Eugenio Leal Vargas | 13.05.1953 | Club Atlético de Madrid |
| 21 | Isidoro San José Pozo Sánchez | 27.10.1956 | Real Madrid CF |
| **Forwards** | | | |
| 7 | Daniel Ruiz-Bazan Justa „Dani" | 28.06.1951 | Athletic Club de Bilbao |
| 8 | Juan Enrique Gómez González „Juanito" | 10.11.1954 | Real Madrid CF |
| 9 | Enrique Castro González „Quini" | 23.09.1949 | Real Sporting Gijón CF |
| 10 | Carlos Alonso González „Santillana" | 23.08.1952 | Real Madrid CF |
| 15 | Rafael Carlos Pérez González „Marañón" | 23.07.1948 | RCD Español Barcelona |
| 19 | Carlos Rexach Cerdá | 13.01.1947 | FC Barcelona |
| 20 | Rubén Andres Cano Martínez Sáez | 05.02.1951 | Club Atlético de Madrid |
| **Trainer:** | Ladislao Kubala (HUN) | 10.06.1927 | |

## SWEDEN

| Nr | Name | DOB | Club |
|---|---|---|---|
| **Goalkeepers** | | | |
| 1 | Ronnie Carl Hellström | 21.02.1949 | 1.FC Kaiserslautern (GER) |
| 12 | Göran Hagberg | 08.11.1947 | Östers IF Växjö |
| 17 | Jan Möller | 17.09.1953 | Malmö FF |
| **Defenders** | | | |
| 2 | Hans Borg | 04.08.1953 | TSV Eintracht Braunschweig (GER) |
| 3 | Roy Andersson | 02.08.1949 | Malmö FF |
| 4 | Björn Nordqvist | 06.10.1942 | IFK Göteborg |
| 5 | Ingemar Erlandsson | 16.11.1957 | Malmö FF |
| 13 | Magnus Andersson | 23.04.1958 | Malmö FF |
| 19 | Kent Karlsson | 25.11.1945 | IFK Eskilstuna |
| 20 | Roland Andersson | 28.03.1950 | Malmö FF |
| **Midfielders** | | | |
| 6 | Staffan Tapper | 10.07.1948 | Malmö FF |
| 7 | Anders Linderoth | 21.03.1950 | Olympique de Marseille (FRA) |
| 8 | Bo Göran Larsson | 05.05.1944 | Malmö FF |
| 10 | Thomas Sjöberg | 06.07.1952 | Malmö FF |
| 14 | Roland Åhman | 31.01.1957 | Örebro SK |
| 18 | Olle Nordin | 23.11.1949 | IFK Göteborg |
| **Forwards** | | | |
| 9 | Lennart Larsson | 09.07.1953 | FC Schalke 04 Gelsenkirchen (GER) |
| 11 | Benny Wendt | 04.11.1950 | 1.FC Kaiserslautern (GER) |
| 15 | Torbjörn Nilsson | 09.07.1954 | IFK Göteborg |
| 16 | Conny Torstensson | 28.08.1949 | FC Zürich (SUI) |
| 21 | Sanny Åslund | 29.08.1952 | AIK Stockholm |
| 22 | Ralf Edström | 07.10.1952 | IFK Göteborg |
| **Trainer:** | Georg Ericson | 18.12.1919 | |

## TUNISIA

| Nr | Name | DOB | Club |
|---|---|---|---|
| **Goalkeepers** | | | |
| 1 | Sadok Sassi "Attouga" | 15.11.1945 | Club Africain Tunis |
| 21 | Lamine Ben Aziza | 10.11.1952 | Étoile Sportive du Sahel |
| 22 | Mokhtar Naili | 03.09.1953 | Club Africain Tunis |
| **Defenders** | | | |
| 2 | Mokhtar Dhouib | 23.03.1952 | Club Sportif Sfaxien |
| 3 | Ali Kaabi | 15.11.1953 | Club Olympique des Transports Tunis |
| 5 | Mohsen Jendoubi Labidi | 15.01.1954 | Stade Tunisien |
| 17 | Ridha El Louze | 27.04.1953 | Sfax Railways Sports |
| 18 | Kamel El Chébli | 09.03.1954 | Club Africain Tunis |
| 20 | Omar Jebaili | 24.12.1956 | Avenir Sportif de La Marsa |
| **Midfielders** | | | |
| 4 | Khaled Mokhtar Gasmi | 08.04.1953 | Club Athlétique Bizertin |
| 6 | Néjib Ghommidh | 12.03.1953 | Club Africain Tunis |
| 8 | Mohammed Agrebi Ben Rehaiem | 20.03.1951 | Club Sportif Sfaxien |
| 10 | Tarak Dhiab | 15.07.1954 | Espérance Sportive de Tunis |
| 12 | Khemais Labidi | 30.08.1950 | Jeunesse Sportive Kairouanaise |
| **Forwards** | | | |
| 7 | Témime Lahzami | 01.01.1949 | Al-Ittihad Jeddah (KSA) |
| 9 | Mohamed Ali Akid | 05.07.1949 | Club Sportif Sfaxien |
| 11 | Abderraouf Ben Aziza | 23.09.1953 | Étoile Sportive du Sahel |
| 13 | Mohammed Néjib Limam | 12.06.1953 | Stade Tunisien |
| 14 | Slah Karoui | 11.09.1951 | Étoile Sportive du Sahel |
| 15 | Mohamed Ben Mouza | 05.04.1954 | Club Africain Tunis |
| 16 | Ohman Chehaibi | 23.12.1954 | Jeunesse Sportive Kairouanaise |
| 19 | Mokhtar Hasni | 19.03.1952 | RAA La Louviére (BEL) |
| **Trainer:** Abdelmajid Chetali | | 04.07.1939 | |

## WEST GERMANY

| Nr | Name | DOB | Club |
|---|---|---|---|
| **Goalkeepers** | | | |
| 1 | Josef „Sepp" Maier | 28.02.1944 | FC Bayern München |
| 21 | Rudolf Kargus | 15.08.1952 | Hamburger SV |
| 22 | Dieter Burdenski | 26.11.1950 | SV Werder Bremen |
| **Defenders** | | | |
| 2 | Hans-Hubert „Berti" Vogts | 30.12.1946 | Borussia VfL Mönchengladbach |
| 3 | Bernard Dietz | 22.03.1948 | MSV Duisburg |
| 4 | Rolf Rüssmann | 13.10.1950 | FC Schalke 04 Gelsenkirchen |
| 5 | Manfred Kaltz | 06.01.1953 | Hamburger SV |
| 8 | Herbert Zimmermann | 01.07.1954 | 1.FC Köln |
| 12 | Hans-Georg Schwarzenbeck | 03.04.1948 | FC Bayern München |
| 13 | Harald Konopka | 18.11.1952 | 1.FC Köln |
| **Midfielders** | | | |
| 6 | Rainer Bonhof | 29.03.1952 | Borussia VfL Mönchengladbach |
| 10 | Heinz Flohe | 28.01.1948 | 1.FC Köln |
| 15 | Erich Beer | 09.12.1946 | Hertha BSC Berlin |
| 16 | Bernhard Cullmann | 01.11.1949 | 1.FC Köln |
| 18 | Gerhard Zewe | 13.06.1950 | TSV Fortuna Düsseldorf |
| 20 | Hansi Müller | 27.07.1957 | VfB Stuttgart |
| **Forwards** | | | |
| 7 | Rüdiger Abramczik | 18.02.1956 | FC Schalke 04 Gelsenkirchen |
| 9 | Klaus Fischer | 27.12.1949 | FC Schalke 04 Gelsenkirchen |
| 11 | Karl-Heinz Rummenigge | 25.09.1955 | FC Bayern München |
| 14 | Dieter Müller | 01.04.1954 | 1.FC Köln |
| 17 | Bernd Hölzenbein | 09.03.1946 | SG Eintracht Frankfurt |
| 19 | Ronald Worm | 07.10.1953 | MSV Duisburg |
| **Trainer:** Helmut Schön | | 15.09.1915 | |

# 1982, SPAIN
(Copa Mundial de Fútbol – España 82)

# WORLD CUP 1982 QUALIFIERS

For the first time, the World Cup finals expanded from 16 to 24 teams. This allowed the presence of more teams in the final tournament, especially from Africa and Asia.

A total of 109 teams entered the 1982 FIFA World Cup qualification rounds, competing for a total of 24 spots in the final tournament. Spain, as the hosts, and Argentina, as the defending champions, qualified automatically, leaving 22 spots open for competition. The 22 spots available were distributed among the continental zones as follows:
- Europe: 13 places, contested by 33 teams including Israel;
- South America: 3, contested by 9 teams;
- North, Central America and Caribbean: 2 places, contested by 15 teams.
- Africa: 2 place, contested by 29 teams.
- Asia and Oceania: 2 places, contested by 21 teams.

A total of 103 teams played at least in the qualifiers. Once again, some of the big teams failed to qualify, notably Holland (losing finalists in the two previous series), Sweden, Uruguay and Mexico.

## EUROPE

### GROUP 1

| 04.06.1980 | Helsinki | Finland - Bulgaria | 0-2(0-1) |
| 03.09.1980 | Tiranë | Albania - Finland | 2-0(2-0) |
| 24.09.1980 | Helsinki | Finland - Austria | 0-2(0-1) |
| 19.10.1980 | Sofia | Bulgaria - Albania | 2-1(1-0) |
| 15.11.1980 | Wien | Austria - Albania | 5-0(3-0) |
| 03.12.1980 | Sofia | Bulgaria - West Germany | 1-3(0-2) |
| 06.12.1980 | Tiranë | Albania - Austria | 0-1(0-1) |
| 01.04.1981 | Tiranë | Albania - West Germany | 0-2(0-1) |
| 29.04.1981 | Hamburg | West Germany - Austria | 2-0(2-0) |
| 13.05.1981 | Sofia | Bulgaria - Finland | 4-0(1-0) |
| 24.05.1981 | Lahti | Finland - West Germany | 0-4(0-3) |
| 28.05.1981 | Wien | Austria - Bulgaria | 2-0(1-0) |
| 17.06.1981 | Linz | Austria - Finland | 5-1(2-0) |
| 02.09.1981 | Kotka | Finland - Albania | 2-1(0-0) |
| 23.09.1981 | Bochum | West Germany - Finland | 7-1(2-1) |
| 14.10.1981 | Wien | Austria - West Germany | 1-3(1-2) |
| 14.10.1981 | Tiranë | Albania - Bulgaria | 0-2(0-0) |
| 11.11.1981 | Sofia | Bulgaria - Austria | 0-0 |
| 18.11.1981 | Dortmund | West Germany - Albania | 8-0(5-0) |
| 22.11.1981 | Düsseldorf | West Germany - Bulgaria | 4-0(1-0) |

#### FINAL STANDINGS

| | | | | | | | | | |
|---|---|---|---|---|---|---|---|---|---|
| 1. | **West Germany** | 8 | 8 | 0 | 0 | 33 | - | 3 | 16 |
| 2. | **Austria** | 8 | 5 | 1 | 2 | 16 | - | 6 | 11 |
| 3. | Bulgaria | 8 | 4 | 1 | 3 | 11 | - | 10 | 9 |
| 4. | Albania | 8 | 1 | 0 | 7 | 4 | - | 22 | 2 |
| 5. | Finland | 8 | 1 | 0 | 7 | 4 | - | 27 | 2 |

West Germany and Austria qualified for the Final Tournament.

04.06.1980, Olympiastadion, Helsinki; Attendance: 7,805
Referee: Brian Robert McGinlay (Scotland)
**FINLAND - BULGARIA** **0-2(0-1)**
**FIN:** Seppo Sairanen (8.Pekka Nurmio), Mikko Lampi, Arto Tolsa, Leo Houtsonen, Esko Ranta, Antti Ronkainen (65.Atik Ismail), Seppo Pyykkö, Miikka Toivola, Pasi Rautiainen, Tuomo Hakala, Jyrki Nieminen. Trainer: Esko Malm.
**BUL:** Hristo Hristov, Ivan Zafirov, Bojil Kolev, Valentin Maldjanski, Roman Karakolev, Georgi Dimitrov, Kostadin Kostadinov, Plamen Markov (87.Plamen Tsvetkov), Andrei Jeliazkov (Cap), Vanio Kostov, Chavdar Tsvetkov (87.Georgi Iliev). Trainer: Atanas Parjelov.
**Goals:** 0-1 Plamen Markov (28), 0-2 Kostadin Kostadinov (82).

03.09.1980, Stadiumi „Qemal Stafa", Tiranë; Attendance: 25,000
Referee: Emmanuel Platopoulos (Greece)
**ALBANIA - FINLAND** **2-0(2-0)**
**ALB:** Jani Kaçi, Millan Baçi, Safet Berisha, Kastriot Hysi, Muhedin Targaj, Ferit Rragami, Ferdinand Lleshi, Andrea Marko, Sefedin Braho, Vasillaq Zëri, Arben Minga (70.Dashnor Bajaziti). Trainer: Zyber Konçi.
**FIN:** Olli Isoaho, Aki Lahtinen, Arto Tolsa, Juha Helin (46.Hannu Turunen), Matti Ahonen, Vesa Pulliainen (46.Hannu Rajaniemi), Juha Dahllund, Seppo Pyykkö, Tuomo Hakala, Kari Virtanen, Juhani Himanka. Trainer: Esko Malm.
**Goals:** 1-0 Sefedin Braho (2), 2-0 Millan Baçi (18).

24.09.1980, Olympiastadion, Helsinki; Attendance: 8,099
Referee: Clive Thomas (Wales)
**FINLAND - AUSTRIA** **0-2(0-1)**
**FIN:** Olli Isoaho, Aki Lahtinen, Arto Tolsa, Leo Houtsonen, Esko Ranta, Kari Virtanen, Seppo Pyykkö, Juha Dahllund, Antti Ronkainen (60.Hannu Turunen), Ari Tissari, Hannu Rajaniemi (75.Ari Jalasvaara). Trainer: Esko Malm.
**AUT:** Friedrich Koncilia, Josef Pregesbauer, Erich Obermayer, Bruno Pezzey, Mario Zuenelli, Helmut Wartinger (54.Kurt Welzl), Roland Hattenberger, Kurt Jara, Walter Schachner, Herbert Prohaska, Johann Krankl. Trainer: Karl Stotz.
**Goals:** 0-1 Kurt Jara (13), 0-2 Kurt Welzl (77).

19.10.1980, „Vasil Levski" National Stadium, Sofia; Attendance: 16,700
Referee: Talal Tokat (Turkey)
**BULGARIA - ALBANIA** **2-1(1-0)**
**BUL:** Hristo Hristov, Ivan Zafirov, Borislav Dimitrov, Blagoi Blangev, Valentin Maldjanski, Georgi Dimitrov, Georgi Slavkov, Andrei Jeliazkov (Cap), Kostadin Kostadinov, Plamen Markov (51.Georgi Iliev), Rudji Kerimov. Trainer: Atanas Parjelov.
**ALB:** Jani Kaçi, Millan Baçi, Safet Berisha, Kastriot Hysi, Muhedin Targaj, Kreshnik Çipi, Vasillaq Zëri (58.Dashnor Bajaziti), Haxhi Ballgjini, Ferdinand Lleshi, Sefedin Braho, Ilir Përnaska. Trainer: Zyber Konçi.
**Goals:** 1-0 Andrei Jeliazkov (14), 2-0 Georgi Slavkov (51), 2-1 Ilir Përnaska (69).

15.11.1980, Prater Stadion, Wien; Attendance: 31,000
Referee: Rudolf Renggli (Switzerland)
**AUSTRIA - ALBANIA** **5-0(3-0)**
**AUT:** Herbert Feurer, Johann Dihanich, Erich Obermayer, Bruno Pezzey, Hans-Dieter Mirnegg, Roland Hattenberger, Herbert Prohaska, Kurt Jara, Kurt Welzl, Johann Krankl, Walter Schachner (82.Christian Keglevits). Trainer: Karl Stotz.
**ALB:** Jani Kaçi, Millan Baçi, Safet Berisha, Kastriot Hysi, Muhedin Targaj, Haxhi Ballgjini, Ferdinand Lleshi, Dashnor Bajaziti, Kreshnik Çipi, Sefedin Braho (61.Aleko Bregu), Ilir Përnaska. Trainer: Zyber Konçi.
**Goals:** 1-0 Bruno Pezzey (19), 2-0 Walter Schachner (26), 3-0 Walter Schachner (35), 4-0 Kurt Welzl (58), 5-0 Johann Krankl (86).

03.12.1980, „Vasil Levski" National Stadium, Sofia; Attendance: 50,000
Referee: Riccardo Lattanzi (Italy)
**BULGARIA - WEST GERMANY** **1-3(0-2)**
**BUL:** Hristo Hristov, Ivan Zafirov, Georgi Dimitrov (46.Georgi Slavkov), Tsonio Vasilev, Angel Rangelov, Georgi I. Iliev, Tsvetan Ionchev, Plamen Markov, Spas Djevizov, Andrei Jeliazkov (Cap), Radoslav Zdravkov (79.Rudji Kerimov). Trainer: Atanas Parjelov.
**GER:** Harald Schumacher, Manfred Kaltz, Ulrich Stielike, Karlheinz Förster, Bernhard Dietz (Cap), Hans-Peter Briegel, Felix Magath (72.Miroslav Votava), Hans Müller, Karl-Heinz Rummenigge, Horst Hrubesch, Klaus Allofs (72.Ronald Borchers). Trainer: Josef Derwall.
**Goals**: 0-1 Manfred Kaltz (14), 0-2 Manfred Kaltz (36 penalty), 0-3 Karl-Heinz Rummenigge (54), 1-3 Tsvetan Ionchev (66)

06.12.1980, Stadiumi „Qemal Stafa", Tiranë; Attendance: 25,000
Referee: László Pádár (Hungary)
**ALBANIA - AUSTRIA** **0-1(0-1)**
**ALB:** Jani Kaçi, Millan Baçi, Safet Berisha, Kastriot Hysi, Muhedin Targaj, Ferit Rragami, Ferdinand Lleshi, Andrea Marko (66.Ilir Lame), Sefedin Braho (58.Agustin Kola), Vasillaq Zëri, Ilir Përnaska. Trainer: Zyber Konçi.
**AUT:** Herbert Feurer, Heribert Weber, Erich Obermayer, Bruno Pezzey, Hans-Dieter Mirnegg, Roland Hattenberger, Herbert Prohaska, Kurt Jara, Kurt Welzl, Felix Gasselich (76.Ernst Baumeister), Walter Schachner (46.Gernot Jurtin). Trainer: Karl Stotz.
**Goal**: 0-1 Kurt Welzl (38).

01.04.1981, Stadiumi „Qemal Stafa", Tiranë; Attendance: 30,000
Referee: Antonín Vencel (Czechoslovakia)
**ALBANIA - WEST GERMANY** **0-2(0-1)**
**ALB:** Jani Kaçi, Muhedin Targaj, Safet Berisha, Kujtim Çoçoli, Kastriot Hysi, Ilir Lame, Uran Xhafa (74.Millan Baçi), Shyqyri Ballgjini, Ilir Përnaska, Arben Minga, Ferdinand Lleshi. Trainer: Loro Boriçi.
**GER:** Harald Schumacher, Manfred Kaltz, Ulrich Stielike, Karlheinz Förster (74.Wilfried Hannes), Bernhard Dietz (Cap), Bernd Schuster, Felix Magath, Hans Müller, Karl-Heinz Rummenigge, Horst Hrubesch, Klaus Allofs. Trainer: Josef Derwall.
**Goals**: 0-1 Bernd Schuster (9), 0-2 Bernd Schuster (71).

29.04.1981, Volksparkstadion, Hamburg; Attendance: 61,000
Referee: Charles George Rainier Corver (Holland)
**WEST GERMANY - AUSTRIA** **2-0(2-0)**
**GER:** Harald Schumacher, Manfred Kaltz, Ulrich Stielike, Karlheinz Förster, Hans-Peter Briegel, Bernd Schuster, Felix Magath, Paul Breitner, Hans Müller, Klaus Fischer (76.Karl Allgöwer), Karl-Heinz Rummenigge (Cap). Trainer: Josef Derwall.
**AUT:** Friedrich Koncilia, Bernd Krauss, Erich Obermayer, Bruno Pezzey, Hans-Dieter Mirnegg, Roland Hattenberger (69.Heribert Weber), Herbert Prohaska, Reinhold Hintermaier (69.Ernst Baumeister), Kurt Jara, Johann Krankl, Kurt Welzl. Trainer: Karl Stotz.
**Goals**: 1-0 Bernd Krauss (30 own goal), 2-0 Klaus Fischer (36).

13.05.1981, „Vasil Levski" National Stadium, Sofia; Attendance: 10,000
Referee: Eduard Sostarić (Yugoslavia)
**BULGARIA - FINLAND** **4-0(1-0)**
**BUL:** Georgi Velinov, Tsonio Vasilev, Veselin Balevski, Georgi Bonev, Georgi Dimitrov, Grigor Grigorov, Kostadin Kostadinov, Georgi Slavkov, Andrei Jeliazkov, Plamen Tsvetkov (46.Radoslav Zdravkov), Chavdar Tsvetkov. Trainer: Atanas Parjelov.
**FIN:** Olli Isoaho, Aki Lahtinen, Arto Tolsa, Reijo Vaittinen, Esa Pekonen (80.Kari Bergqvist), Jukka Ikäläinen, Juha Dahllund (63.Pasi Jaakonsaari), Seppo Pyykkö, Leo Houtsonen, Atik Ismail, Ari Valvee. Trainer: Esko Malm.
**Goals:** 1-0 Georgi Slavkov (10), 2-0 Georgi Slavkov (53), 3-0 Kostadin Kostadinov (55), 4-0 Chavdar Tsvetkov (90).

24.05.1981, Keskusurheilukenttä Stadion, Lahti; Attendance: 10,030
Referee: John Carpenter (Republic of Ireland)
**FINLAND - WEST GERMANY** **0-4(0-3)**
**FIN:** Olli Isoaho, Aki Lahtinen, Arto Tolsa (46.Juha Helin), Reijo Vaittinen, Leo Houtsonen, Jukka Ikäläinen, Kari Virtanen, Seppo Pyykkö, Petteri Kupiainen, Keijo Kousa, Ari Valvee (63.Atik Ismail). Trainer: Esko Malm.
**GER:** Harald Schumacher, Manfred Kaltz, Wilfried Hannes, Karlheinz Förster, Hans-Peter Briegel, Wolfgang Dremmler, Felix Magath (76.Karl Allgöwer), Paul Breitner, Hans Müller (82.Ronald Borchers), Klaus Fischer, Karl-Heinz Rummenigge (Cap). Trainer: Josef Derwall.
**Goals:** 0-1 Hans-Peter Briegel (25), 0-2 Klaus Fischer (37), 0-3 Manfred Kaltz (40), 0-4 Klaus Fischer (80).

28.05.1981, Prater Stadion, Wien; Attendance: 60,000
Referee: Patrick Partridge (England)
**AUSTRIA - BULGARIA** **2-0(1-0)**
**AUT:** Herbert Feurer, Johann Dihanich, Heribert Weber, Bruno Pezzey, Hans-Dieter Mirnegg, Herbert Prohaska, Roland Hattenberger, Kurt Jara, Kurt Welzl, Johann Krankl, Christian Keglevits (56.Walter Schachner). Trainer: Karl Stotz.
**BUL:** Hristo Hristov, Vencho Sabotinov, Veselin Balevski, Tsonio Vasilev, Valentin Maldjanski, Georgi Dimitrov, Radoslav Zdravkov (74.Kostadin Kostadinov), Georgi Slavkov, Andrei Jeliazkov, Grigor Grigorov (74.Plamen Markov), Chavdar Tsvetkov. Trainer: Atanas Parjelov.
**Goals:** 1-0 Johann Krankl (30 penalty), 2-0 Kurt Jara (88).

17.06.1981, Linzer Stadion, Linz; Attendance: 27,500
Referee: Alojzy Jarguz (Poland)
**AUSTRIA - FINLAND** **5-1(2-0)**
**AUT:** Herbert Feurer, Johann Dihanich, Bruno Pezzey, Heribert Weber, Hans-Dieter Mirnegg, Roland Hattenberger, Herbert Prohaska (80.Wilhelm Kreuz), Kurt Jara, Kurt Welzl (78.Walter Schachner), Johann Krankl, Gernot Jurtin. Trainer: Karl Stotz.
**FIN:** Olavi Huttunen, Aki Lahtinen, Juha Helin, Leo Houtsonen, Reijo Vaittinen, Kari Virtanen, Juha Dahllund, Jukka Ikäläinen, Hannu Turunen, Ari Valvee, Keijo Kousa (60.Hannu Rajaniemi). Trainer: Esko Malm.
**Goals:** 1-0 Herbert Prohaska (16), 2-0 Herbert Prohaska (18), 3-0 Johann Krankl (49), 4-0 Kurt Welzl (56), 5-0 Gernot Jurtin (65), 5-1 Ari Valvee (71).

02.09.1981, Urheilukeskus Stadion, Kotka; Attendance: 6,830
Referee: Ib Nielsen (Denmark)
**FINLAND - ALBANIA** 2-1(0-0)
**FIN:** Olli Isoaho, Aki Lahtinen, Juha Dahllund, Reijo Vaittinen, Esa Pekonen, Hannu Turunen, Leo Houtsonen, Seppo Pyykkö (79.Antti Ronkainen), Peter Utriainen, Keijo Kousa, Pasi Jaakonsaari. Trainer: Esko Malm.
**ALB:** Perlat Musta, Muhedin Targaj, Safet Berisha, Kujtim Çoçoli, Kastriot Hysi, Haxhi Ballgjini, Ilir Lame, Ferdinand Lleshi, Ilir Përnaska (13.Arben Minga), Roland Luçi (74.Ferit Rragami), Shyqyri Ballgjini. Trainer: Loro Boriçi.
**Goals:** 0-1 Muhedin Targaj (47 penalty), 1-1 Leo Houtsonen (61), 2-1 Keijo Kousa (85).

23.09.1981, Ruhrstadion, Bochum; Attendance: 46,000
Referee: Norbert Rolles (Luxembourg)
**WEST GERMANY - FINLAND** 7-1(2-1)
**GER:** Harald Schumacher, Manfred Kaltz, Ulrich Stielike, Bernd Förster, Hans-Peter Briegel, Wolfgang Dremmler, Felix Magath, Paul Breitner, Ronald Borchers, Klaus Fischer, Karl-Heinz Rummenigge (Cap). Trainer: Josef Derwall.
**FIN:** Olli Isoaho, Esa Pekonen, Juha Dahllund, Leo Houtsonen, Aki Lahtinen, Hannu Turunen, Jukka Ikäläinen (71.Jyrki Nieminen), Seppo Pyykkö, Peter Utriainen, Keijo Kousa, Pasi Jaakonsaari (71.Antti Ronkainen). Trainer: Esko Malm.
**Goals:** 1-0 Klaus Fischer (11), 1-1 Hannu Turunen (41), 2-1 Karl-Heinz Rummenigge (42), 3-1 Paul Breitner (54), 4-1 Karl-Heinz Rummenigge (60), 5-1 Paul Breitner (67), 6-1 Karl-Heinz Rummenigge (72), 7-1 Wolfgang Dremmler (83).

14.10.1981, Prater Stadion, Wien; Attendance: 72,000
Referee: Alexis Ponnet (Belgium)
**AUSTRIA - WEST GERMANY** 1-3(1-2)
**AUT:** Friedrich Koncilia, Johann Dihanich, Heribert Weber, Bruno Pezzey, Hans-Dieter Mirnegg, Herbert Prohaska, Reinhold Hintermaier (75.Maximilian Hagmayr), Roland Hattenberger, Kurt Jara, Johann Krankl, Walter Schachner. Trainer: Karl Stotz.
**GER:** Harald Schumacher, Manfred Kaltz, Ulrich Stielike, Karlheinz Förster, Hans-Peter Briegel, Wolfgang Dremmler, Paul Breitner, Felix Magath, Pierre Littbarski, Klaus Fischer, Karl-Heinz Rummenigge (Cap). Trainer: Josef Derwall.
**Goals:** 1-0 Walter Schachner (15), 1-1 Pierre Littbarski (17), 1-2 Felix Magath (20), 1-3 Pierre Littbarski (76).

14.10.1981, Stadiumi „Qemal Stafa", Tiranë; Attendance: 25,000
Referee: Adolf Prokop (East Germany)
**ALBANIA - BULGARIA** 0-2(0-0)
**ALB:** Perlat Musta, Millan Baçi, Safet Berisha, Kujtim Çoçoli, Muhedin Targaj, Ferit Rragami, Ilir Lame, Haxhi Ballgjini, Arben Minga, Vasillaq Zëri (75.Luan Seiti), Agustin Kola. Trainer: Loro Boriçi.
**BUL:** Georgi Velinov, Plamen Nikolov, Veselin Balevski, Georgi Dimitrov, Blagoi Blangev, Kiril Liubomirov, Kostadin Kostadinov, Georgi Slavkov, Plamen Tsvetkov (46.Plamen Markov), Andrei Jeliazkov (83.Vencho Sabotinov), Stoicho Mladenov. Trainer: Atanas Parjelov.
**Goals:** 0-1 Georgi Slavkov (49), 0-2 Stoicho Mladenov (84).

11.11.1981, "Vasil Levski" National Stadium, Sofia; Attendance: 55,000
Referee: Michel Vautrot (France)
**BULGARIA - AUSTRIA** **0-0**
**BUL:** Georgi Velinov, Plamen Nikolov, Veselin Balevski, Blagoi Blangev, Georgi Dimitrov, Kiril Liubomirov, Kostadin Kostadinov, Georgi Slavkov (61.Tsvetan Ionchev), Andrei Jeliazkov (46.Plamen Markov), Stoicho Mladenov, Chavdar Tsvetkov. Trainer: Atanas Parjelov.
**AUT:** Herbert Feurer, Bernd Krauss, Bruno Pezzey, Heribert Weber, Hans-Dieter Mirnegg (56.Johann Dihanich), Roland Hattenberger, Herbert Prohaska, Kurt Jara, Reinhold Hintermaier, Walter Schachner, Johann Krankl (73.Maximilian Hagmayr). Trainer: Karl Stotz.

18.11.1981, Westfalenstadion, Dortmund; Attendance: 40,000
Referee: Reidar Bjørnestad (Norway)
**WEST GERMANY - ALBANIA** **8-0(5-0)**
**GER:** Eike Immel, Manfred Kaltz (60.Lothar Herbert Matthäus), Ulrich Stielike, Karlheinz Förster, Hans-Peter Briegel, Wolfgang Dremmler, Paul Breitner, Felix Magath, Pierre Littbarski, Klaus Fischer, Karl-Heinz Rummenigge (Cap) (50.Jürgen Milewski). Trainer: Josef Derwall.
**ALB:** Perlat Musta (58.Ilir Luarasi), Muhedin Targaj, Safet Berisha, Kastriot Hysi, Agustin Kola, Ferdinand Lleshi, Ferit Rragami, Haxhi Ballgjini, Ardan Popa, Sefedin Braho, Roland Luçi. Trainer: Loro Boriçi.
**Goals**: 1-0 Karl-Heinz Rummenigge (5), 2-0 Karl-Heinz Rummenigge (19), 3-0 Klaus Fischer (32), 4-0 Manfred Kaltz (36), 5-0 Karl-Heinz Rummenigge (43), 6-0 Pierre Littbarski (52), 7-0 Paul Breitner (68 penalty), 8-0 Klaus Fischer (72).

22.11.1981, Rheinstadion, Düsseldorf; Attendance: 50,000
Referee: Erik Fredriksson (Sweden)
**WEST GERMANY - BULGARIA** **4-0(1-0)**
**GER:** Harald Schumacher, Manfred Kaltz, Wilfried Hannes, Karlheinz Förster, Hans-Peter Briegel, Wolfgang Dremmler, Paul Breitner, Felix Magath (56.Klaus Allofs), Horst Hrubesch, Klaus Fischer, Karl-Heinz Rummenigge (Cap). Trainer: Josef Derwall.
**BUL:** Georgi Velinov, Plamen Nikolov, Veselin Balevski, Georgi Bonev, Georgi Dimitrov, Ivan Iliev, Kostadin Kostadinov, Plamen Markov (46.Kiril Liubomirov), Stoicho Mladenov, Radoslav Zdravkov, Tsvetan Ionchev. Trainer: Atanas Parjelov.
**Goals**: 1-0 Klaus Fischer (4), 2-0 Karl-Heinz Rummenigge (49), 3-0 Manfred Kaltz (62 penalty), 4-0 Karl-Heinz Rummenigge (82).

# GROUP 2

| Date | City | Match | Score |
|---|---|---|---|
| 26.03.1980 | Nicosia | Cyprus - Republic of Ireland | 2-3(1-3) |
| 10.09.1980 | Dublin | Republic of Ireland - Holland | 2-1(0-0) |
| 11.10.1980 | Limassol | Cyprus - France | 0-7(0-4) |
| 15.10.1980 | Dublin | Republic of Ireland - Belgium | 1-1(1-1) |
| 28.10.1980 | Paris | France - Republic of Ireland | 2-0(1-0) |
| 19.11.1980 | Bruxelles | Belgium - Holland | 1-0(0-0) |
| 19.11.1980 | Dublin | Republic of Ireland - Cyprus | 6-0(4-0) |
| 21.12.1980 | Nicosia | Cyprus - Belgium | 0-2(0-1) |
| 18.02.1981 | Bruxelles | Belgium - Cyprus | 3-2(2-1) |
| 22.02.1981 | Groningen | Holland - Cyprus | 3-0(1-0) |
| 25.03.1981 | Rotterdam | Holland - France | 1-0(0-0) |
| 25.03.1981 | Bruxelles | Belgium - Republic of Ireland | 1-0(0-0) |
| 29.04.1981 | Paris | France - Belgium | 3-2(3-1) |
| 29.04.1981 | Nicosia | Cyprus - Holland | 0-1(0-1) |
| 09.09.1981 | Rotterdam | Holland - Republic of Ireland | 2-2(1-1) |
| 09.09.1981 | Bruxelles | Belgium - France | 2-0(1-0) |
| 14.10.1981 | Rotterdam | Holland - Belgium | 3-0(2-0) |
| 14.10.1981 | Dublin | Republic of Ireland - France | 3-2(3-1) |
| 18.11.1981 | Paris | France - Holland | 2-0(0-0) |
| 05.12.1981 | Paris | France - Cyprus | 4-0(2-0) |

## FINAL STANDINGS

| | | | | | | | | | |
|---|---|---|---|---|---|---|---|---|---|
| 1. | **Belgium** | 8 | 5 | 1 | 2 | 12 | - | 9 | 11 |
| 2. | **France** | 8 | 5 | 0 | 3 | 20 | - | 8 | 10 |
| 3. | Republic of Ireland | 8 | 4 | 2 | 2 | 17 | - | 11 | 10 |
| 4. | Holland | 8 | 4 | 1 | 3 | 11 | - | 7 | 9 |
| 5. | Cyprus | 8 | 0 | 0 | 8 | 4 | - | 29 | 0 |

Belgium and France qualified for the Final Tournament.

26.03.1980, GSP Stádio, Nicosia; Attendance: 10,000
Referee: Zvi Sharir (Israel)
**CYPRUS - REPUBLIC OF IRELAND**      **2-3(1-3)**
**CYP:** Fanos Stylianou, Andreas Papacostas, Fytos Neophytou, Stavros Papadopoulos, Stefanos Lysandrou, Nicos Pantziaras, Filippos Dimitriou (46.Marios Tsingis), Loizos Mavroudis, Sotiris Kaiafas, Andreas Kissonergis, Andreas Kanaris (75.Petros Theofanous). Trainer: Costas Taliano (Greece).
**IRL:** Gerald Joseph Peyton, Anthony Patrick Grealish, Augustine Ashley Grimes, Mark Thomas Lawrenson, David Anthony O'Leary, Gerard Anthony Daly, William Brady (Cap), Jeremiah Michael Murphy (72.Frank O'Brien), Stephen Derek Heighway (53.Gerard Joseph Ryan), Francis Anthony Stapleton, Paul Gerard McGee. Trainer: John Michael Giles.
**Goals:** 0-1 Paul Gerard McGee (8), 0-2 Mark Thomas Lawrenson (23), 1-2 Nicos Pantziaras (28), 1-3 Paul Gerard McGee (37), 2-3 Sotiris Kaiafas (73 penalty).

10.09.1980, Lansdowne Road, Dublin; Attendance: 25,000
Referee: Henning Lund-Sørensen (Denmark)
**REPUBLIC OF IRELAND - HOLLAND**    **2-1(0-0)**
**IRL:** Gerald Joseph Peyton, David Francis Langan, David Anthony O'Leary, Pierce O'Leary, Christopher William Gerard Hughton, Mark Thomas Lawrenson, Gerard Anthony Daly, Anthony Patrick Grealish, William Brady (Cap), Francis Anthony Stapleton, Daniel Joseph Givens. Trainer: Eoin Hand.
**NED:** Johannes Frederik Hiele, Hubertus Johannes Nicolaas Wijnstekers, Michael Antonius Bernardus van de Korput (46.Johannes Antonius Bernardus Metgod), Ronald Spelbos, Ernestus Wilhelmus Johannes Brandts, Dirk Hendrikus Schoenaker (63.Wilhelmus Antonius van de Kerkhof), Johannes Wilhelmus Peters (Cap), Franciscus Johannes Thijssen, Jan van Deinsen, Antoine van Mierlo, Simon Melkianus Tahamata. Trainer: Johannes Zwartkruis.
**Goals:** 0-1 Simon Melkianus Tahamata (57), 1-1 Gerard Anthony Daly (78), 2-1 Mark Thomas Lawrenson (84).

11.10.1980, Tsirion Stádio, Limassol; Attendance: 15,000
Referee: Bruno Galler (Switzerland)
**CYPRUS - FRANCE**    **0-7(0-4)**
**CYP:** Georgios Pantziaras, Andreas Papacostas, Dimitris Kizas, Klitos Erotokritou, Stavros Papadopoulos, Nicos Pantziaras, Marios Tsingis, Christakis Mavris (46.Stefanos Lysandrou), Sotiris Kaiafas (23.Petros Theofanous), Loizos Mavroudis, Andreas Kissonergis. Trainer: Costas Talianos (Greece).
**FRA:** Dominique Dropsy, Patrick Battiston, Léonard Specht, Henri Michel, Maxime Bossis, Jean-François Larios, Jean Amadou Tigana (51.Jean Petit), Michel Platini (Cap), Bruno Baronchelli (73.Atre Jacques „Zimako"), Bernard Lacombe, Didier Six. Trainer: Michel Hidalgo.
**Goals**: 0-1 Bernard Lacombe (4), 0-2 Michel Platini (14), 0-3 Michel Platini (23), 0-4 Jean-François Larios (40 penalty), 0-5 Jean-François Larios (76 penalty), 0-6 Didier Six (82), 0-7 Atre Jacques „Zimako" (87).

15.10.1980, Lansdowne Road, Dublin; Attendance: 40,000
Referee: Norbert Rolles (Luxembourg)
**REPUBLIC OF IRELAND - BELGIUM**    **1-1(1-1)**
**IRL:** Gerald Joseph Peyton, David Francis Langan, Kevin Bernard Moran, Mark Thomas Lawrenson, Christopher William Gerard Hughton, William Brady (Cap), Gerard Anthony Daly, Anthony Patrick Grealish, Francis Anthony Stapleton, Stephen Derek Heighway, Daniel Joseph Givens (58.Paul Gerard McGee). Trainer: Eoin Hand.
**BEL:** Jean-Marie Pfaff, Eric Gerets, Luc Millecamps (88.Michel De Wolf), Walter Meeuws, Michel Renquin, Wilfried Van Moer (84.Joseph Heyligen), Ludo Coeck, René Vandereycken, Albert Cluytens, Erwin Vandenbergh, Jan Ceulemans. Trainer: Guy Thys.
**Goals**: 0-1 Albert Cluytens (13), 1-1 Anthony Patrick Grealish (42).

28.10.1980, Stade Parc des Princes, Paris; Attendance: 44,800
Referee: Augusto Lamo Castillo (Spain)
**FRANCE - REPUBLIC OF IRELAND**    **2-0(1-0)**
**FRA:** Dominique Dropsy, Patrick Battiston, Léonard Specht, Christian Lopez, Maxime Bossis, Jean-François Larios, Jean Amadou Tigana, Michel Platini (Cap) (74.Jean Petit), Dominique Rocheteau, Bernard Lacombe (66.Atre Jacques „Zimako"), Didier Six. Trainer: Michel Hidalgo.
**IRL:** Gerald Joseph Peyton, David Francis Langan, Mark Thomas Lawrenson, Kevin Bernard Moran, Christopher William Gerard Hughton, Michael Paul Martin (78.Gerard Joseph Ryan), William Brady (Cap), Anthony Patrick Grealish, Stephen Derek Heighway, Francis Anthony Stapleton, Michael John Robinson. Trainer: Eoin Hand.
**Goals**: 1-0 Michel Platini (11), 2-0 Atre Jacques „Zimako" (77).

19.11.1980, Stade Heysel, Bruxelles; Attendance: 57,665
Referee: Elzar Azim Zade (Soviet Union)
**BELGIUM - HOLLAND** **1-0(0-0)**
**BEL:** Jean-Marie Pfaff, Eric Gerets, Luc Millecamps, Walter Meeuws, Michel Renquin, Wilfried Van Moer, Ludo Coeck, René Vandereycken, Albert Cluytens, Erwin Vandenbergh, Jan Ceulemans. Trainer: Guy Thys.
**NED:** Willem Doesburg, Hubertus Johannes Nicolaas Wijnstekers (20.Johannes Antonius Bernardus Metgod), Rudolf Jozef Krol (Cap), Ernestus Wilhelmus Johannes Brandts, Hugo Hermanus Hovenkamp, Johannes Wilhelmus Peters, Wilhelmus Antonius van de Kerkhof, Michael Antonius Bernardus van de Korput, Simon Melkianus Tahamata, Cornelis Thomas Henri Maria Tol (27.Reinier Lambertus van de Kerkhof), Cornelis Kist. Trainer: Johannes Zwartkruis.
**Goal**: 1-0 Erwin Vandenbergh (48 penalty).

19.11.1980, Lansdowne Road, Dublin; Attendance: 25,000
Referee: Eysteinn Guðmundsson (Iceland)
**REPUBLIC OF IRELAND - CYPRUS** **6-0(4-0)**
**IRL:** Gerald Joseph Peyton, David Francis Langan, Mark Thomas Lawrenson, Kevin Bernard Moran, Christopher William Gerard Hughton, Gerard Anthony Daly, William Brady (Cap), Anthony Patrick Grealish, Stephen Derek Heighway, Francis Anthony Stapleton, Michael John Robinson (74.Daniel Joseph Givens). Trainer: Eoin Hand.
**CYP:** Andreas Konstantinou II, Filippos Kalotheou, Loukis Louka, Stefanos Lysandrou, Nicos Pantziaras, Klitos Erotokritou, Fanis Theofanous, Yiannakis Yiangoudakis, Sotiris Kaiafas (46.Chrysanthos Lagos), Marios Tsingis, Andros Miamiliotis (63.Loizos Mavroudis). Trainer: Costas Talianos (Greece).
**Goals**: 1-0 Gerard Anthony Daly (10 penalty), 2-0 Gerard Anthony Daly (24), 3-0 Anthony Patrick Grealish (25), 4-0 Michael John Robinson (29), 5-0 Francis Anthony Stapleton (46), 6-0 Christopher William Gerard Hughton (63).

21.12.1980, Makareio Stádio, Nicosia; Attendance: 6,000
Referee: Robert Bonar Valentine (Scotland)
**CYPRUS - BELGIUM** **0-2(0-1)**
**CYP:** Andreas Konstantinou II, Nicos Patikkis, Costas Miamiliotis, Stefanos Lysandrou, Klitos Erotokritou, Nicos Pantziaras, Yiannakis Yiangoudakis, Christakis Mavris (Georgios Petrou), Sotiris Kaiafas (Filippos Dimitriou), Loizos Mavroudis, Andros Miamiliotis. Trainer: Costas Talianos (Greece).
**BEL:** Jean-Marie Pfaff, Eric Gerets, Luc Millecamps, Walter Meeuws, Gérard Plessers (72.Ludo Coeck), Wilfried Van Moer, René Vandereycken, Raymond Mommens, Albert Cluytens (78.Edouard Voordeckers), Erwin Vandenbergh, Jan Ceulemans. Trainer: Guy Thys.
**Goals**: 0-1 Erwin Vandenbergh (29), 0-2 Jan Ceulemans (69).

18.02.1981, Stade Heysel, Bruxelles; Attendance: 17,445
Referee: Arto Ravander (Finland)
**BELGIUM - CYPRUS** **3-2(2-1)**
**BEL:** Jean-Marie Pfaff, Eric Gerets, Ludo Coeck, Michel Renquin, Gérard Plessers (72.Frank Vercauteren), Albert Cluytens (72.Edouard Voordeckers), René Vandereycken, Raymond Mommens, Williy Wellens, Erwin Vandenbergh, Jan Ceulemans. Trainer: Guy Thys.
**CYP:** Andreas Konstantinou II, Loukis Louka, Klitos Erotokritou, Stefanos Lysandrou, Toumazos Toumazou, Nicos Pantziaras, Andros Miamiliotis (85.Marios Tsingis), Filippos Dimitriou, Fivos Vrachimis, Fanis Theofanous (85.Chrysanthos Lagos), Yiannakis Yiangoudakis. Trainer: Costas Talianos (Greece).
**Goals**: 1-0 Gérard Plessers (12), 2-0 Erwin Vandenbergh (17), 2-1 Stefanos Lysandrou (42), 2-2 Fivos Vrachimis (59), 3-2 Jan Ceulemans (67).

22.02.1981, Osterpark Stadion, Groningen; Attendance: 17,500
Referee: Howard William King (Wales)
**HOLLAND - CYPRUS** **3-0(1-0)**
**NED:** Willem Doesburg, Romeo Zondervan, Johannes Antonius Bernardus Metgod, Ronald Spelbos, Hugo Hermanus Hovenkamp, Petrus Wilhelmus Arntz (46.Dirk Jacobus Willem Nanninga), Franciscus Johannes Thijssen, Johannes Wilhelmus Peters (Cap), Jos Jonker, Cornelis Schapendonk, Cornelis Thomas Henri Maria Tol (57.Pierre Vermeulen). Trainer: Robert Baan.
**CYP:** Andreas Konstantinou II, Loukis Louka, Klitos Erotokritou, Stefanos Lysandrou, Toumazos Toumazou, Nicos Pantziaras, Andros Miamiliotis (Marios Tsingis), Filippos Dimitriou, Fivos Vrachimis (Chrysanthos Lagos), Fanis Theofanous, Yiannakis Yiangoudakis. Trainer: Costas Talianos (Greece).
**Goals:** 1-0 Hugo Hermanus Hovenkamp (15), 2-0 Kees Schapendonk (48), 3-0 Dirk Jacobus Willem Nanninga (58).

25.03.1981, Feyenoord Stadion, Rotterdam; Attendance: 58,000
Referee: Luigi Agnolin (Italy)
**HOLLAND - FRANCE** **1-0(0-0)**
**NED:** Pieter Schrijvers, Edo Ophof, Rudolf Jozef Krol (Cap), Jan Poortvliet, Hugo Hermanus Hovenkamp (46.Tscheu La Ling), Wilhelmus Antonius van de Kerkhof, Arnoldus Johannes Hyacinthus Mühren, Franciscus Johannes Thijssen, Johannes Wilhelmus Peters (65.Hubertus Jozef Margaretha Stevens), Reinier Lambertus van de Kerkhof, John Nicolaas Rep. Trainer: Robert Baan.
**FRA:** Dominique Dropsy, Gérard Janvion, Léonard Specht, Christian Lopez (Cap), Maxime Bossis, Jean-François Larios, Alain Giresse, Alain Moizan (77.Didier Christophe), Dominique Rocheteau, Bernard Lacombe (63.Atre Jacques „Zimako"), Didier Six. Trainer: Michel Hidalgo.
**Goal:** 1-0 Arnoldus Johannes Hyacinthus Mühren (47).

25.03.1981, Stade Heysel, Bruxelles; Attendance: 37,978
Referee: Raul Joaquim Fernandes Nazarre (Portugal)
**BELGIUM - REPUBLIC OF IRELAND** **1-0(0-0)**
**BEL:** Michel Preud´homme, Eric Gerets, Luc Millecamps, Walter Meeuws, Michel Renquin, Ludo Coeck (76.Williy Wellens), René Vandereycken, Raymond Mommens (84.Frank Vercauteren), Albert Cluytens, Erwin Vandenbergh, Jan Ceulemans. Trainer: Guy Thys.
**IRL:** James Martin McDonagh, David Francis Langan, Michael Paul Martin, Kevin Bernard Moran, Christopher William Gerard Hughton, Gerard Anthony Daly, Anthony Patrick Grealish, William Brady (Cap), Michael John Robinson, Francis Anthony Stapleton (71.Michael Anthony Walsh), Stephen Derek Heighway. Trainer: Eoin Hand.
**Goal:** 1-0 Jan Ceulemans (87).

29.04.1981, Stade Parc des Princes, Paris; Attendance: 44,954
Referee: Victoriano Sánchez Arminio (Spain)
**FRANCE - BELGIUM** **3-2(3-1)**
**FRA:** Dominique Dropsy, Gérard Janvion, Christian Lopez (Cap), Marius Trésor, Maxime Bossis, Jean Amadou Tigana, Alain Giresse, Bernard Genghini, Gérard Soler (71.Atre Jacques „Zimako"), Dominique Rocheteau, Didier Six. Trainer: Michel Hidalgo.
**BEL:** Michel Preud´homme, Eric Gerets, Luc Millecamps (17.Michel De Wolf), Walter Meeuws, Michel Renquin, Wilfried Van Moer, René Vandereycken, Frank Vercauteren (63.René Verheyen), Albert Cluytens, Erwin Vandenbergh, Jan Ceulemans. Trainer: Guy Thys.
**Goals:** 0-1 Erwin Vandenbergh (5), 1-1 Gérard Soler (14), 2-1 Didier Six (26), 3-1 Gérard Soler (31), 3-2 Jan Ceulemans (52).

29.04.1981, Makareio Stádio, Nicosia; Attendance: 7,500
Referee: Ivan Iosifov (Bulgaria)
**CYPRUS - HOLLAND**                                                                               **0-1(0-1)**
CYP: Georgios Pantziaras, Loukis Louka, Filippos Kalotheou, Stavros Papadopoulos, Klitos Erotokritou, Nicos Pantziaras, Pavlos Kounnas (46.Fanis Theofanous, 86.Chrysanthos Lagos), Filippos Dimitriou, Fivos Vrachimis, Yiannakis Yiangoudakis, Loizos Mavroudis. Trainer: Costas Talianos (Greece).
NED: Pieter Schrijvers, Hubertus Johannes Nicolaas Wijnstekers, Rudolf Jozef Krol (Cap), Hubertus Jozef Margaretha Stevens, Hugo Hermanus Hovenkamp, Johannes Antonius Bernardus Metgod, Wilhelmus Antonius van de Kerkhof, Arnoldus Johannes Hyacinthus Mühren, Tscheu La Ling, Cornelis van Kooten, John Nicolaas Rep (62.Simon Melkianus Tahamata). Trainer: Robert Baan.
Goal: 0-1 Cornelis van Kooten (29).

09.09.1981, Feyenoord Stadion, Rotterdam; Attendance: 48,000
Referee: Vojtěch Christov (Czechoslovakia)
**HOLLAND - REPUBLIC OF IRELAND**                     **2-2(1-1)**
NED: Pieter Schrijvers, Hubertus Johannes Nicolaas Wijnstekers, Rudolf Jozef Krol (Cap), Ernestus Wilhelmus Johannes Brandts, Michael Antonius Bernardus van de Korput, Franciscus Johannes Thijssen, Arnoldus Johannes Hyacinthus Mühren, John Nicolaas Rep, Geertruida Maria Geels (46.Johannes Wilhelmus Peters), Cornelis van Kooten, Tscheu La Ling (59.Reinier Lambertus van de Kerkhof). Trainer: Cornelis Bernardus Rijvers.
IRL: James Martin McDonagh, David Francis Langan, John Anthony Devine, Mark Thomas Lawrenson, David Anthony O'Leary, William Brady (Cap), Michael Paul Martin (74.Ronald Andrew Whelan), Anthony Patrick Grealish, Stephen Derek Heighway (61.Gerard Joseph Ryan), Michael John Robinson, Francis Anthony Stapleton. Trainer: Eoin Hand.
Goals: 1-0 Franciscus Johannes Thijssen (11), 1-1 Michael John Robinson (40), 2-1 Arnoldus Johannes Hyacinthus Mühren (64 penalty), 2-2 Francis Anthony Stapleton (71).

09.09.1981, Stade Heysel, Bruxelles; Attendance: 52,525
Referee: Károly Palotai (Hungary)
**BELGIUM - FRANCE**                                            **2-0(1-0)**
BEL: Jean-Marie Pfaff, Michel Renquin, Luc Millecamps, Walter Meeuws, Marc Baecke, Wilfried Van Moer (51.Marc Millecamps), Ludo Coeck, Frank Vercauteren, Alexander Czerniatynski, Erwin Vandenbergh, Jan Ceulemans. Trainer: Guy Thys.
FRA: Patrick Hiard, Gérard Janvion, Philippe Mahut, Christian Lopez, Maxime Bossis, Alain Moizan (60.Yannick Stopyra), Jean-François Larios, Alain Giresse, Atre Jacques „Zimako", Michel Platini (Cap), Didier Six. Trainer: Michel Hidalgo.
Goals: 1-0 Alexander Czerniatynski (25), 2-0 Erwin Vandenbergh (83).

14.10.1981, Feyenoord Stadion, Rotterdam; Attendance: 56,000
Referee: Brian McGinley (Scotland)
**HOLLAND - BELGIUM**                                        **3-0(2-0)**
NED: Johannes Franciscus van Breukelen, Michael Antonius Bernardus van de Korput, Rudolf Jozef Krol (Cap), Johannes Antonius Bernardus Metgod, Hugo Hermanus Hovenkamp, Franciscus Johannes Thijssen, Johannes Jacobus Neeskens, Arnoldus Johannes Hyacinthus Mühren, Tscheu La Ling, Cornelis van Kooten (46.Geertruida Maria Geels), John Nicolaas Rep. Trainer: Cornelis Bernardus Rijvers.
BEL: Jean-Marie Pfaff, Eric Gerets, Luc Millecamps, Walter Meeuws, Michel Renquin, Marc Millecamps, René Vandereycken, Eduard Snelders (62.Gérard Plessers), Frank Vercauteren, Alexander Czerniatynski, Edouard Voordeckers (46.Albert Cluytens). Trainer: Guy Thys.
Goals: 1-0 Johannes Antonius Bernardus Metgod (6), 2-0 Cornelis van Kooten (26), 3-0 Geertruida Maria Geels (54).
Sent off: Walter Meeuws (40).

14.10.1981, Lansdowne Road, Dublin; Attendance: 53,000
Referee: Ulf Eriksson (Sweden)
**REPUBLIC OF IRELAND - FRANCE** 3-2(3-1)
**IRL:** James Martin McDonagh, David Francis Langan, David Anthony O'Leary, Kevin Bernard Moran, Christopher William Gerard Hughton, Ronald Andrew Whelan, Michael Paul Martin, Mark Thomas Lawrenson, William Brady (Cap), Francis Anthony Stapleton (87.Daniel Joseph Givens), Michael John Robinson. Trainer: Eoin Hand.
**FRA:** Jean-Luc Castaneda, Maxime Bossis, Philippe Mahut (69.François Bracci), Christian Lopez, Gérard Janvion, René Girard, Jean-François Larios, Didier Christophe, Michel Platini (Cap), Alain Couriol, Bruno Bellone (63.Didier Six). Trainer: Michel Hidalgo.
**Goals:** 1-0 Philippe Mahut (5 own goal), 1-1 Bruno Bellone (9), 2-1 Francis Anthony Stapleton (25), 3-1 Michael John Robinson (39), 3-2 Michel Platini (83).

18.11.1981, Stade Parc des Princes, Paris; Attendance: 48,000
Referee: Antonio José da Silva Garrido (Portugal)
**FRANCE - HOLLAND** 2-0(0-0)
**FRA:** Jean-Luc Castaneda, Gérard Janvion, Christian Lopez, Marius Trésor, Maxime Bossis, Alain Giresse, Michel Platini (Cap) (75.Jean Amadou Tigana), Bernard Genghini, Dominique Rocheteau, Bernard Lacombe (69.Atre Jacques „Zimako"), Didier Six. Trainer: Michel Hidalgo.
**NED:** Johannes Franciscus van Breukelen, Hubertus Johannes Nicolaas Wijnstekers, Rudolf Jozef Krol (Cap), Michael Antonius Bernardus van de Korput (72.Tscheu La Ling), Jan Poortvliet, Johannes Wilhelmus Peters, Johannes Jacobus Neeskens, Johannes Antonius Bernardus Metgod (46.Simon Melkianus Tahamata), Arnoldus Johannes Hyacinthus Mühren, John Nicolaas Rep, Cornelis van Kooten. Trainer: Cornelis Bernardus Rijvers.
**Goals**: 1-0 Michel Platini (52), 2-0 Didier Six (82).

05.12.1981, Stade Parc des Princes, Paris; Attendance: 43,437
Referee: Edwin Borg (Malta)
**FRANCE - CYPRUS** 4-0(2-0)
**FRA:** Jean-Luc Castaneda, Gérard Janvion, Christian Lopez, Marius Trésor (Cap), Maxime Bossis, Alain Giresse, Jean Amadou Tigana, Bernard Genghini, Dominique Rocheteau, Bernard Lacombe, Didier Six (63.Bruno Bellone). Trainer: Michel Hidalgo.
**CYP:** Fanos Stylianou, Costas Miamiliotis, Klitos Erotokritou, Stefanos Lysandrou, Georgios Kezos, Filippos Dimitriou, Nicos Pantziaras, Fanis Theofanous, Yiannakis Yiangoudakis, Loizos Mavroudis, Fivos Vrachimis. Trainer: Costas Talianos (Greece).
**Goals**: 1-0 Dominique Rocheteau (25), 2-0 Bernard Lacombe (29), 3-0 Bernard Lacombe (82), 4-0 Bernard Genghini (86).

# GROUP 3

| Date | Venue | Match | Score |
|---|---|---|---|
| 02.06.1980 | Reykjavík | Iceland - Wales | 0-4(0-1) |
| 03.09.1980 | Reykjavík | Iceland - Soviet Union | 1-2(0-1) |
| 24.09.1980 | Izmir | Turkey - Iceland | 1-3(0-1) |
| 15.10.1980 | Cardiff | Wales - Turkey | 4-0(2-0) |
| 15.10.1980 | Moskva | Soviet Union - Iceland | 5-0(2-0) |
| 19.11.1980 | Cardiff | Wales - Czechoslovakia | 1-0(1-0) |
| 03.12.1980 | Praha | Czechoslovakia - Turkey | 2-0(2-0) |
| 25.03.1981 | Ankara | Turkey - Wales | 0-1(0-0) |
| 15.04.1981 | Istanbul | Turkey - Czechoslovakia | 0-3(0-0) |
| 27.05.1981 | Bratislava | Czechoslovakia - Iceland | 6-1(2-0) |
| 30.05.1981 | Wrexham | Wales - Soviet Union | 0-0 |
| 09.09.1981 | Reykjavík | Iceland - Turkey | 2-0(1-0) |
| 09.09.1981 | Praha | Czechoslovakia - Wales | 2-0(1-0) |
| 23.09.1981 | Reykjavík | Iceland - Czechoslovakia | 1-1(1-0) |
| 23.09.1981 | Moskva | Soviet Union - Turkey | 4-0(3-0) |
| 07.10.1981 | Izmir | Turkey - Soviet Union | 0-3(0-2) |
| 14.10.1981 | Swansea | Wales - Iceland | 2-2(1-0) |
| 28.10.1981 | Tbilisi | Soviet Union - Czechoslovakia | 2-0(1-0) |
| 18.11.1981 | Tbilisi | Soviet Union - Wales | 3-0(2-0) |
| 29.11.1981 | Bratislava | Czechoslovakia - Soviet Union | 1-1(1-1) |

## FINAL STANDINGS

| | | | | | | | | |
|---|---|---|---|---|---|---|---|---|
| 1. | Soviet Union | 8 | 6 | 2 | 0 | 20 - 2 | 14 |
| 2. | Czechoslovakia | 8 | 4 | 2 | 2 | 15 - 6 | 10 |
| 3. | Wales | 8 | 4 | 2 | 2 | 12 - 7 | 10 |
| 4. | Iceland | 8 | 2 | 2 | 4 | 10 - 21 | 6 |
| 5. | Turkey | 8 | 0 | 0 | 8 | 1 - 22 | 0 |

Soviet Union and Czechoslovakia qualified for the Final Tournament.

02.06.1980, Laugardalsvöllur Stadium, Reykjavík; Attendance: 10,254
Referee: Rolf Nyhus (Norway)
**ICELAND - WALES** **0-4(0-1)**
**ISL:** Þorsteinn Ólafsson, Sævar Jónsson (85.Árni Sveinsson), Trausti Haraldsson, Marteinn Geirsson (Cap), Siðurdur Halldórsson (85.Dýri Guðmundsson), Janus Guðlaugsson, Arnór Guðjohnsen, Atli Eðvaldsson, Pétur Pétursson, Karl Þórðarson, Guðmundur Þorbjörnsson. Trainer: Guðni Kjartansson.
**WAL:** William David Davies, Peter Nicholas, Joseph Patrick Jones, Paul Terence Price, Leighton Phillips, Terence Charles Yorath (75.William Byron Stevenson), David Charles Giles, Brian Flynn, Ian Patrick Walsh, Leighton James, Gordon John Davies (80.Carl Stephen Harris). Manager: Harold Michael England.
**Goals:** 0-1 Ian Patrick Walsh (45), 0-2 David Charles Giles (53), 0-3 Brian Flynn (61 penalty), 0-4 Ian Patrick Walsh (75).

03.09.1980, Laugardalsvöllur Stadium, Reykjavík; Attendance: 4,190
Referee: Oliver Donnelly (Northern Ireland)
**ICELAND - SOVIET UNION**     **1-2(0-1)**
**ISL:** Þorsteinn Bjarnason, Viðar Halldórsson, Örn Óskarsson, Marteinn Geirsson (Cap), Siðurdur Halldórsson, Magnús Bergs, Albert Guðmundsson, Árni Sveinsson, Sigurlás Þorleifsson (76.Kristján Olgeirsson), Pétur Ormslev (26.Sigurður Grétarsson), Guðmundur Þorbjörnsson. Trainer: Guðni Kjartansson.
**URS:** Rinat Dasaev, Tengiz Sulakvelidze, Aleksandr Chivadze, Vagiz Khidiyatullin, Oleg Romantzev (Cap), Sergey Shavlo (Khoren Oganesyan), Leonid Buryak, Vladimir Bessonov, Sergey Andreev, Yuriy Gavrilov, Oleg Blokhin (87.Sergey Rodionov). Trainer: Konstantin Beskov.
**Goals**: 0-1 Yuriy Gavrilov (35), 1-1 Árni Sveinsson (75), 1-2 Sergey Andreev (80).

24.09.1980, "Kemal Atatürk" Stadı, Izmir; Attendance: 18,506
Referee: Ioan Igna (Romania)
**TURKEY - ICELAND**     **1-3(0-1)**
**TUR:** Şenol Güneş, Turgay Semercioğlu, Cem Pamiroğlu, Erol Togay, Fatih Terim, Mustafa Turgat (46.Volkan Yayim), Necdet Ergün, Sedat III Özden, Sadullah Acele (46.Ayhan Akbin), Serdar Bali, Mustafa Denizli. Trainer: Sabri Kiraz.
**ISL:** Þorsteinn Bjarnason, Viðar Halldórsson, Trausti Haraldsson, Marteinn Geirsson (Cap), Siðurdur Halldórsson, Albert Guðmundsson, Janus Guðlaugsson, Guðmundur Þorbjörnsson (65.Sigurður Grétarsson), Teitur Þórðarson, Ásgeir Sigurvinsson, Atli Eðvaldsson. Trainer: Guðni Kjartansson.
**Goals**: 0-1 Janus Guðlaugsson (12), 0-2 Albert Guðmundsson (60), 1-2 Fatih Terim (72 penalty), 1-3 Teitur Þórðarson (81).

15.10.1980, Ninian Park, Cardiff; Attendance: 11,770
Referee: Torben Mansson (Denmark)
**WALES - TURKEY**     **4-0(2-0)**
**WAL:** William David Davies, Peter Nicholas, Joseph Patrick Jones, Paul Terence Price, Leighton Phillips, Terence Charles Yorath, David Charles Giles, Brian Flynn, Carl Stephen Harris, Ian Patrick Walsh, Leighton James. Manager: Harold Michael England.
**TUR:** Şenol Güneş, Turgay Semercioğlu, Cem Pamiroğlu, Hüsnü Özkara, Fatih Terim, Erhan Önal, Necdet Ergün, Güngör Şahinkaya, Tuncay Soyak, Sedat III Özden (80.Serdar Bali), Halil Ibrahim Eren. Trainer: Sabri Kiraz.
**Goals**: 1-0 Brian Flynn (19), 2-0 Leighton James (37 penalty), 3-0 Ian Patrick Walsh (79), 4-0 Leighton James (85).
**Sent off**: Tuncay Soyak (78).

15.10.1980, Lenin Stadium, Moskva; Attendance: 31,000
Referee: Aleksander Suchanek (Poland)
**SOVIET UNION - ICELAND**     **5-0(2-0)**
**URS:** Rinat Dasaev, Tengiz Sulakvelidze, Aleksandr Chivadze (Cap), Vagiz Khidiyatullin (76.Aleksandr Mirzoyan), Sergey Baltacha, Sergey Shavlo (61.Vadim Evtushenko), Aleksandr Tarkhanov, Vladimir Bessonov, Sergey Andreev, Yuriy Gavrilov, Khoren Oganesyan. Trainer: Konstantin Beskov.
**ISL:** Þorsteinn Bjarnason, Trausti Haraldsson, Örn Óskarsson, Marteinn Geirsson (Cap), Siðurdur Halldórsson, Albert Guðmundsson (66.Árni Sveinsson), Arnór Guðjohnsen (77.Sigurlás Þorleifsson), Viðar Halldórsson, Teitur Þórðarson, Ásgeir Sigurvinsson, Guðmundur Þorbjörnsson. Trainer: Guðni Kjartansson.
**Goals**: 1-0 Sergey Andreev (9), 2-0 Khoren Oganesyan (39), 3-0 Khoren Oganesyan (58), 4-0 Sergey Andreev (78), 5-0 Vladimir Bessonov (84).

19.11.1980, Ninian Park, Cardiff; Attendance: 20,175
Referee: Walter Eschweiler (West Germany)
**WALES - CZECHOSLOVAKIA** **1-0(1-0)**
**WAL:** William David Davies, Peter Nicholas, Kevin Ratcliffe, Paul Terence Price, Leighton Phillips, Terence Charles Yorath, Michael Reginald Thomas, David Charles Giles, Brian Flynn, Ian Patrick Walsh (49.Carl Stephen Harris), Jeremy Melvyn Charles. Manager: Harold Michael England.
**TCH:** Zdeněk Hruška, Jozef Barmoš, Libor Radimec, Rostislav Vojáček, Luděk Macela, Ján Kozák, Ladislav Jurkemik (72.Petr Janečka), Antonín Panenka, Marián Masný, Zdeněk Nehoda (Cap), Ladislav Vízek. Trainer: Jozef Vengloš.
**Goal:** 1-0 David Charles Giles (10).

03.12.1980, Stadion Strahov, Praha; Attendance: 8,500
Referee: Erik Fredriksson (Sweden)
**CZECHOSLOVAKIA - TURKEY** **2-0(2-0)**
**TCH:** Zdeněk Hruška, Jozef Barmoš, Ladislav Jurkemik, Rostislav Vojáček, Luděk Macela, Ján Kozák, Přemsyl Bičovský, Antonín Panenka, Petr Janečka, Zdeněk Nehoda (Cap), Ladislav Vízek. Trainer: Jozef Vengloš.
**TUR:** Şenol Güneş, Turgay Semercioğlu, Necati Özçağlayan, Zafer Bilgitay, Onur Alp Kayador, Sedat III Özden, Güngör Şahinkaya, Muzzaffer Atacan, Halil Ibrahim Eren, Bahtiyar Yorulmaz, İskender Gönen. Trainer: Özkan Sümer.
**Goals:** 1-0 Zdeněk Nehoda (13), 2-0 Zdeněk Nehoda (15).

25.03.1981, 19 Mayis Stadı, Ankara; Attendance: 35,000
Referee: Sándor Kuti (Hungary)
**TURKEY - WALES** **0-1(0-0)**
**TUR:** Şenol Güneş, Onur Alp Kayador, Muammer Birdal (Sedat Karaoğlu), Necati Özçağlayan, Hüsnü Özkara, Sedat III Özden, Güngör Şahinkaya, Volkan Yayim (76.Şevket Kesler), Necdet Ergün, Tuncay Mesçi, Halil Ibrahim Eren. Trainer: Özkan Sümer.
**WAL:** William David Davies, Peter Nicholas, Kevin Ratcliffe, Paul Terence Price, Leighton Phillips, Joseph Patrick Jones, Carl Stephen Harris (75.David Charles Giles), Terence Charles Yorath, Brian Flynn, Ian Patrick Walsh (58.Jeremy Melvyn Charles), Leighton James. Manager: Harold Michael England.
**Goal:** 0-1 Carl Stephen Harris (67).

15.04.1981, "Ali Sami Yen" Stadı, Istanbul; Attendance: 40,000
Referee: Roger Schoeters (Belgium)
**TURKEY - CZECHOSLOVAKIA** **0-3(0-0)**
**TUR:** Şenol Güneş, Onur Alp Kayador, Muammer Birdal, Zafer Bilgitay, Fatih Terim, Sedat III Özden, Halil Ibrahim Eren (77.Necdet Ergün), Erhan Önal, Tuncay Soyak (35.Mehmet Ekşi), İlyas Tüfekçi, Bahtiyar Yorulmaz. Trainer: Fethi Demircan.
**TCH:** Stanislav Seman, František Jakubec, Libor Radimec, Luděk Macela, Jozef Barmoš, Ján Kozák, Jan Berger, Petr Němec (84.Marián Masný), Petr Janečka, Zdeněk Nehoda (Cap), Ladislav Vízek. Trainer: Jozef Vengloš.
**Goals:** 0-1 Petr Janečka (59), 0-2 Ján Kozák (70), 0-3 Ladislav Vízek (81).

27.05.1981, Stadion Tehelné pole, Bratislava; Attendance: 25,000
Referee: Nikolaos Zlatanos (Greece)
**CZECHOSLOVAKIA - ICELAND** **6-1(2-0)**
**TCH:** Stanislav Seman, František Jakubec, Luděk Macela, Libor Radimec, Jozef Barmoš, Ján Kozák, Jan Berger, Antonín Panenka, Marián Masný, Zdeněk Nehoda (Cap) (74.Petr Janečka), Ladislav Vízek. Trainer: Jozef Vengloš.
**ISL:** Þorsteinn Bjarnason, Trausti Haraldsson, Þorgrímur Þráinsson, Magnús Bergs, Siðurdur Halldórsson, Janus Guðlaugsson, Atli Eðvaldsson, Arnór Guðjohnsen, Pétur Pétursson, Ásgeir Sigurvinsson (Cap), Árni Sveinsson. Trainer: Guðni Kjartansson.
**Goals**: 1-0 Ladislav Vízek (34), 2-0 Antonín Panenka (41 penalty), 2-1 Magnús Bergs (53), 3-1 Zdeněk Nehoda (71), 4-1 Ján Kozák (77), 5-1 Ján Kozák (78), 6-1 Petr Janečka (86).

30.05.1981, The Racecourse Stadium, Wrexham; Attendance: 29,366
Referee: Bruno Galler (Switzerland)
**WALES - SOVIET UNION** **0-0**
**WAL:** William David Davies, Joseph Patrick Jones, Kevin Ratcliffe, Leighton Phillips, Paul Terence Price, Peter Nicholas, Brian Flynn, Terence Charles Yorath, Ian Patrick Walsh (70.Jeremy Melvyn Charles), Michael Reginald Thomas, Carl Stephen Harris (75.David Charles Giles). Manager: Harold Michael England.
**URS:** Rinat Dasaev, Tengiz Sulakvelidze, Aleksandr Chivadze (Cap), Sergey Borovskiy, Sergey Baltacha, Khoren Oganesyan, Vladimir Bessonov, Leonid Buryak, Sergey Andreev, David Kipiani (84.Yuriy Gavrilov), Oleg Blokhin. Trainer: Konstantin Beskov.

09.09.1981, Laugardalsvöllur Stadium, Reykjavík; Attendance: 4,292
Referee: Kevin O'Sullivan (Republic of Ireland)
**ICELAND - TURKEY** **2-0(1-0)**
**ISL:** Guðmundur Baldursson, Sævar Jónsson, Örn Óskarsson, Marteinn Geirsson (Cap), Viðar Halldórsson, Magnús Bergs, Pétur Pétursson, Atli Eðvaldsson, Lárus Guðmundsson, Pétur Ormslev (70.Ómar Torfason), Sigurður Lárusson. Trainer: Guðni Kjartansson.
**TUR:** Şenol Güneş, Onur Alp Kayador, Zafer Bilgitay, Turgay Poyraz, Fatih Terim, Engin Verel (67.Riza Çalımbay), Halil Ibrahim Eren (46.Hüsnü Özkara), Sedat III Özden, Bahtiyar Yorulmaz, Ceyhun Güray, İlyas Tüfekçi. Trainer: Fethi Demircan.
**Goals**: 1-0 Lárus Guðmundsson (21), 2-0 Atli Eðvaldsson (65).

09.09.1981, Stadion Strahov, Praha; Attendance: 38,000
Referee: Franz Wöhrer (Austria)
**CZECHOSLOVAKIA - WALES** **2-0(1-0)**
**TCH:** Stanislav Seman, Přemysl Bičovský, Libor Radimec, Rostislav Vojáček, Jozef Barmoš, Ján Kozák, Ladislav Jurkemik, Jan Berger, Antonín Panenka (26.Werner Lička), Ladislav Vízek, Zdeněk Nehoda (Cap). Trainer: Jozef Vengloš.
**WAL:** William David Davies, William Byron Stevenson, Kevin Ratcliffe, Joseph Patrick Jones, Leighton Phillips (73.Ian Patrick Walsh), Brian Flynn, Peter Nicholas, Michael Reginald Thomas (62.Robert Mark James), Leighton James, Carl Stephen Harris, Alan Thomas Curtis. Manager: Harold Michael England.
**Goals**: 1-0 William David Davies (26 own goal), 2-0 Werner Lička (68).

23.09.1981, Laugardalsvöllur Stadium, Reykjavík; Attendance: 7,343
Referee: Kenneth Johnston Hope (Scotland)
**ICELAND - CZECHOSLOVAKIA** **1-1(1-0)**
**ISL:** Guðmundur Baldursson, Viðar Halldórsson, Örn Óskarsson, Marteinn Geirsson (Cap), Sævar Jónsson, Magnús Bergs (66.Sigurður Lárusson), Janus Guðlaugsson, Atli Eðvaldsson, Arnór Guðjohnsen, Ásgeir Sigurvinsson, Pétur Ormslev (76.Ragnar Margeirsson). Trainer: Guðni Kjartansson.
**TCH:** Stanislav Seman, Přemsyl Bičovský, Rostislav Vojáček, Libor Radimec, Jozef Barmoš, Ján Kozák, Jan Berger, Antonín Panenka (66.Petr Němec), Ladislav Vízek, Zdeněk Nehoda (Cap), Werner Lička (46.Marián Masný). Trainer: Jozef Vengloš.
**Goals:** 1-0 Pétur Ormslev (6), 1-1 Ján Kozák (78).

23.09.1981, Lenin Stadium, Moskva; Attendance: 41,500
Referee: Damir Matovinović (Yugoslavia)
**SOVIET UNION - TURKEY** **4-0(3-0)**
**URS:** Rinat Dasaev, Vladimir Lozinskiy, Aleksandr Chivadze (Cap), Sergey Baltacha, Anatoliy Demyanenko, Vitaliy Daraselia, Ramaz Shengeliya, Vladimir Bessonov, Leonid Buryak (46.Khoren Oganesyan), Yuriy Gavrilov, Oleg Blokhin (63.Sergey Andreev). Trainer: Konstantin Beskov.
**TUR:** Şenol Güneş, Turgay Semercioğlu, Turgay Poyraz (46.Sadık Aksöz), Hüsnü Özkara, Fatih Terim, Necati Özçağlayan, Mustafa Gedik, Ceyhun Güray, Bahtiyar Yorulmaz, Sedat III Özden, Şenol Çorlu. Trainer: Fethi Demircan.
**Goals:** 1-0 Aleksandr Chivadze (4), 2-0 Anatoliy Demyanenko (20), 3-0 Oleg Blokhin (26), 4-0 Ramaz Shengeliya (49).

07.10.1981, "Kemal Atatürk" Stadı, Izmir; Attendance: 62,150
Referee: Walter Eschweiler (West Germany)
**TURKEY - SOVIET UNION** **0-3(0-2)**
**TUR:** Şenol Güneş (39.Yaşar Duran), Erhan Altın, Süleyman Oktay, Hüsnü Özkara, Necati Özçağlayan, Mehmet Cüneyt Tanman, Fatih Terim, Sedat III Özden, Selçuk Yula, Bora Öztürk (58.İsa Ertürk), Sadık Aksöz. Trainer: Fethi Demircan.
**URS:** Rinat Dasaev, Vladimir Lozinskiy, Aleksandr Chivadze (Cap), Sergey Baltacha (75.Yuriy Susloparov), Anatoliy Demyanenko, Vitaliy Daraselia, Ramaz Shengeliya (46.Sergey Andreev), Vladimir Bessonov, Leonid Buryak, Yuriy Gavrilov, Oleg Blokhin. Trainer: Konstantin Beskov.
**Goals:** 0-1 Ramaz Shengeliya (17), 0-2 Oleg Blokhin (38), 0-3 Oleg Blokhin (54).

14.10.1981, Vetch Field, Swansea; Attendance: 20,000
Referee: Arto Ravander (Finland)
**WALES - ICELAND** **2-2(1-0)**
**WAL:** William David Davies, Kevin Ratcliffe, Joseph Patrick Jones, John Francis Mahoney, Peter Nicholas, Alan Thomas Curtis, Robert Mark James, Ian Patrick Walsh, Jeremy Melvyn Charles, Carl Stephen Harris (67.Ian James Rush), Leighton James. Manager: Harold Michael England.
**ISL:** Guðmundur Baldursson, Viðar Halldórsson, Örn Óskarsson, Marteinn Geirsson (Cap), Sævar Jónsson, Magnús Bergs, Janus Guðlaugsson, Atli Eðvaldsson, Arnór Guðjohnsen, Ásgeir Sigurvinsson, Pétur Ormslev. Trainer: Guðni Kjartansson.
**Goals:** 1-0 Robert Mark James (25), 1-1 Ásgeir Sigurvinsson (41), 2-1 Alan Thomas Curtis (54), 2-2 Ásgeir Sigurvinsson (61).

28.10.1981, Dinamo Stadium, Tbilisi; Attendance: 80,000
Referee: Michel Vautrot (France)
**SOVIET UNION - CZECHOSLOVAKIA** **2-0(1-0)**
**URS**: Rinat Dasaev, Tengiz Sulakvelidze, Aleksandr Chivadze (Cap) (55.Yuriy Susloparov), Sergey Borovskiy, Sergey Baltacha, Vitaliy Daraselia (80.Sergey Shavlo), Vladimir Bessonov, Leonid Buryak, Ramaz Shengeliya, Yuriy Gavrilov, Oleg Blokhin. Trainer: Konstantin Beskov.
**TCH**: Stanislav Seman, Přemsyl Bičovský, Rostislav Vojáček, Libor Radimec, Jozef Barmoš, Ján Kozák, Jan Berger, Ladislav Jurkemik, Ladislav Vízek (79.Werner Lička), Zdeněk Nehoda (Cap), Tomáš Kříž. Trainer: Jozef Vengloš.
**Goals**: 1-0 Ramaz Shengeliya (28), 2-0 Ramaz Shengeliya (46).

18.11.1981, Dinamo Stadium, Tbilisi; Attendance: 80,000
Referee: Johannes Nicolaas Ignatius Keizer (Holland)
**SOVIET UNION - WALES** **3-0(2-0)**
**URS**: Rinat Dasaev, Sergey Borovskiy, Yuriy Susloparov, Sergey Baltacha, Anatoliy Demyanenko, Vitaliy Daraselia, Tengiz Sulakvelidze, Leonid Buryak, Ramaz Shengeliya, Yuriy Gavrilov (71.Vladimir Gutzaev), Oleg Blokhin (Cap). Trainer: Konstantin Beskov.
**WAL**: William David Davies, Kevin Ratcliffe, Joseph Patrick Jones (85.Stephen John Lovell), Peter Nicholas, Leighton Phillips, Paul Terence Price, Alan Thomas Curtis, Brian Flynn, Ian James Rush, John Francis Mahoney (46.Michael Reginald Thomas), Leighton James. Manager: Harold Michael England.
**Goals**: 1-0 Vitaliy Daraselia (13), 2-0 Oleg Blokhin (18), 3-0 Yuriy Gavrilov (64).

29.11.1981, Stadion Tehelné pole, Bratislava; Attendance: 47,000
Referee: Clive Bradley White (England)
**CZECHOSLOVAKIA - SOVIET UNION** **1-1(1-1)**
**TCH**: Zdeněk Hruška, František Jakubec, Jan Fiala, Rostislav Vojáček, Jozef Barmoš, Ján Kozák, Přemsyl Bičovský, Antonín Panenka, Marián Masný, Zdeněk Nehoda (Cap), Tomáš Kříž (59.Ladislav Vízek). Trainer: Jozef Vengloš.
**URS**: Rinat Dasaev, Sergey Borovskiy, Yuriy Susloparov, Tengiz Sulakvelidze, Anatoliy Demyanenko, Andrey Bal, Vitaliy Daraselia, Leonid Buryak, Ramaz Shengeliya (74.Sergey Andreev), Yuriy Gavrilov, Oleg Blokhin (Cap). Trainer: Konstantin Beskov.
**Goals**: 0-1 Oleg Blokhin (14), 1-1 Rostislav Vojáček (34).

# GROUP 4

| Date | City | Match | Result |
|---|---|---|---|
| 10.09.1980 | London | England - Norway | 4-0(1-0) |
| 24.09.1980 | Oslo | Norway - Romania | 1-1(1-1) |
| 15.10.1980 | București | Romania - England | 2-1(1-0) |
| 29.10.1980 | Bern | Switzerland - Norway | 1-2(0-1) |
| 19.11.1980 | London | England - Switzerland | 2-1(2-0) |
| 28.04.1981 | Luzern | Switzerland - Hungary | 2-2(1-1) |
| 29.04.1981 | London | England - Romania | 0-0 |
| 13.05.1981 | Budapest | Hungary - Romania | 1-0(1-0) |
| 20.05.1981 | Oslo | Norway - Hungary | 1-2(0-0) |
| 30.05.1981 | Basel | Switzerland - England | 2-1(2-0) |
| 03.06.1981 | București | Romania - Norway | 1-0(0-0) |
| 06.06.1981 | Budapest | Hungary - England | 1-3(1-1) |
| 17.06.1981 | Oslo | Norway - Switzerland | 1-1(0-0) |
| 09.09.1981 | Oslo | Norway - England | 2-1(2-1) |
| 23.09.1981 | București | Romania - Hungary | 0-0 |
| 10.10.1981 | București | Romania - Switzerland | 1-2(0-0) |
| 14.10.1981 | Budapest | Hungary - Switzerland | 3-0(1-0) |
| 31.10.1981 | Budapest | Hungary - Norway | 4-1(1-1) |
| 11.11.1981 | Bern | Switzerland - Romania | 0-0 |
| 18.11.1981 | London | England - Hungary | 1-0(1-0) |

## FINAL STANDINGS

| | | | | | | | | | |
|---|---|---|---|---|---|---|---|---|---|
| 1. | **Hungary** | 8 | 4 | 2 | 2 | 13 | - | 8 | 10 |
| 2. | **England** | 8 | 4 | 1 | 3 | 13 | - | 8 | 9 |
| 3. | Romania | 8 | 2 | 4 | 2 | 5 | - | 5 | 8 |
| 4. | Switzerland | 8 | 2 | 3 | 3 | 9 | - | 12 | 7 |
| 5. | Norway | 8 | 2 | 2 | 4 | 8 | - | 15 | 6 |

Hungary and England qualified for the Final Tournament.

10.09.1980, Wembley Stadium, London; Attendance: 48,200
Referee: Marcel Van Langenhove (Belgium)
**ENGLAND - NORWAY** **4-0(1-0)**
ENG: Peter Leslie Shilton, Vivian Alexander Anderson, Kenneth Graham Sansom, Philip Brian Thompson (Cap), David Victor Watson, Bryan Robson, Eric Lazenby Gates, Terence McDermott, Paul Mariner, Anthony Stewart Woodcock, Graham Rix. Manager: Ronald Greenwood.
NOR: Tom Rüsz Jacobsen, Bjarne Berntsen, Tore Kordahl, Einar Jan Aas, Svein Grøndalen, Roger Albertsen, Åge Hareide, Arne Dokken, Arne Larsen Økland, Pål Jacobsen, Arne Erlandsen (83.Rune Ottesen). Trainer: Tor Røste Fossen.
Goals: 1-0 Terence McDermott (37), 2-0 Anthony Stewart Woodcock (66), 3-0 Terence McDermott (75 penalty), 4-0 Paul Mariner (85).

24.09.1980, Ullevaal Stadion, Oslo; Attendance: 22,600
Referee: Siegfried Kirschen (East Germany)
**NORWAY - ROMANIA** **1-1(1-1)**
NOR: Tom Rüsz Jacobsen, Bjarne Berntsen, Tore Kordahl, Einar Jan Aas, Svein Grøndalen, Åge Hareide, Rune Ottesen, Arne Dokken, Arne Larsen Økland, Pål Jacobsen, Hallvar Thoresen. Trainer: Tor Røste Fossen.
ROU: Vasile Iordache, Nicolae Negrilă, Ştefan Sameş, Costică Ştefănescu (Cap) (75.Alexandru Nicolae), Ion Munteanu II, Aurel Ţicleanu (69.Ilie Balaci), Aurel Beldeanu, Anghel Iordănescu, Zoltan Crişan, Rodion Gorun Cămătaru, Marcel Răducanu. Trainer: Valentin Stănescu.

**Goals**: 0-1 Anghel Iordănescu (10), 1-1 Åge Hareide (20).

15.10.1980, Stadionul 23 August, București; Attendance: 75,000
Referee: Ulf Eriksson (Sweden)
**ROMANIA - ENGLAND**     **2-1(1-0)**
**ROU**: Vasile Iordache, Nicolae Negrilă, Ştefan Sameş, Costică Ştefănescu (Cap), Ion Munteanu II, Aurel Ţicleanu, Aurel Beldeanu (71.Ion Dumitru), Anghel Iordănescu, Zoltan Crişan, Rodion Gorun Cămătaru, Marcel Răducanu. Trainer: Valentin Stănescu.
**ENG**: Raymond Neal Clemence, Philip George Neal, Kenneth Graham Sansom, Philip Brian Thompson (Cap), David Victor Watson, Bryan Robson, Graham Rix, Terence McDermott, Garry Birtles (65.Laurence Paul Cunningham), Anthony Stewart Woodcock, Eric Lazenby Gates (46.Steven James Coppell). Manager: Ronald Greenwood.
**Goals**: 1-0 Marcel Răducanu (35), 1-1 Anthony Stewart Woodcock (64), 2-1 Anghel Iordănescu (75 penalty).

29.10.1980, Wankdorf Stadion, Bern; Attendance: 14,000
Referee: Dušan Krchnak (Czechoslovakia)
**SWITZERLAND - NORWAY**     **1-2(0-1)**
**SUI**: Karl Engel, Jörg Stohler, Roger Wehrli, Heinz Lüdi, Heinz Hermann, Umberto Barberis, Gian-Piero Zappa (46.Rudolf Elsener), René Botteron, Peter Marti, Roland Schönenberger, Markus Tanner. Trainer: Léo Walker.
**NOR**: Tom Rüsz Jacobsen, Bjarne Berntsen, Tore Kordahl, Einar Jan Aas, Svein Grøndalen, Roger Albertsen, Åge Hareide, Rune Ottesen (63.Morten Vinje), Arne Dokken (53.Svein Mathisen), Pål Jacobsen, Hallvar Thoresen. Trainer: Tor Røste Fossen.
**Goals**: 0-1 Åge Hareide (5), 1-1 Umberto Barberis (49), 1-1 Svein Mathisen (79).

19.11.1980, Wembley Stadium, London; Attendance: 70,000
Referee: Johannes Nicolaas Ignatius Keizer (Holland)
**ENGLAND - SWITZERLAND**     **2-1(2-0)**
**ENG**: Peter Leslie Shilton, Philip George Neal, Kenneth Graham Sansom, Bryan Robson, David Victor Watson, Michael Dennis Mills (Cap), Steven James Coppell, Terence McDermott, Paul Mariner, Trevor David Brooking (82.Graham Rix), Anthony Stewart Woodcock. Manager: Ronald Greenwood.
**SUI**: Erich Burgener, Alain Geiger, Heinz Hermann, Heinz Lüdi (46.André Egli), Roger Wehrli, Hans-Jörg Pfister, Umberto Barberis, René Botteron, Markus Tanner, Roland Schönenberger (37.Peter Marti), Rudolf Elsener. Trainer: Léo Walker.
**Goals**: 1-0 Markus Tanner (22 own goal), 2-0 Paul Mariner (36), 2-1 Hans-Jörg Pfister (76).

28.04.1981, Allmend Stadion, Luzern; Attendance: 24,000
Referee: Ian M.D. Foote (Scotland)
**SWITZERLAND - HUNGARY**     **2-2(1-1)**
**SUI**: Erich Burgener, Gian-Piero Zappa, Herbert Hermann, André Egli, Heinz Hermann, Roger Wehrli, René Botteron, Umberto Barberis, Alfred Scheiwiler (77.Hanspeter Zwicker), Claudio Sulser, Rudolf Elsener. Trainer: Paul Wolfisberg.
**HUN**: Ferenc Mészáros, Győző Martos, László Bálint, Imre Garaba, József Tóth, Sándor Müller, Károly Csapó (75.Gábor Szántó), József Mucha (81.József Varga), László Fazekas, András Törőcsik, László Kiss. Trainer: Kálmán Mészöly.
**Goals**: 1-0 Claudio Sulser (31), 1-1 László Bálint (45), 2-1 Claudio Sulser (47), 2-2 Sándor Müller (64 penalty).
**Sent off**: Heinz Hermann (84).

29.04.1981, Wembley Stadium, London; Attendance: 62,500
Referee: Heinz Aldinger (West Germany)
**ENGLAND - ROMANIA** **0-0**
**ENG:** Peter Leslie Shilton, Vivian Alexander Anderson, Kenneth Graham Sansom, Bryan Robson, David Victor Watson (Cap), Russell Charles Osman, Raymond Colin Wilkins, Trevor David Brooking (70.Terence McDermott), Steven James Coppell, Trevor John Francis, Anthony Stewart Woodcock. Manager: Ronald Greenwood.
**ROU:** Vasile Iordache, Nicolae Negrilă, Ştefan Sameş, Costică Ştefănescu (Cap), Ion Munteanu II, Tudorel Stoica, Aurel Beldeanu, Anghel Iordănescu, Zoltan Crişan, Rodion Gorun Cămătaru, Ilie Balaci. Trainer: Valentin Stănescu.

13.05.1981, Népstadion, Budapest; Attendance: 60,000
Referee: Alexis Ponnet (Belgium)
**HUNGARY - ROMANIA** **1-0(1-0)**
**HUN:** Béla Katzirz, Győző Martos, László Bálint, Imre Garaba, József Tóth, Sándor Müller (78.Gábor Szántó), Tibor Nyilasi, József Varga, László Fazekas, László Kiss (74.Béla Bodonyi), András Törőcsik. Trainer: Kálmán Mészöly.
**ROU:** Vasile Iordache, Nicolae Negrilă, Nicolae Tilihoi, Costică Ştefănescu (Cap), Ion Munteanu II, Tudorel Stoica, Aurel Beldeanu, Anghel Iordănescu (69.Marcel Răducanu), Zoltan Crişan, Rodion Gorun Cămătaru, Ilie Balaci. Trainer: Valentin Stănescu.
**Goal**: 1-0 László Fazekas (18).

20.05.1981, Ullevaal Stadion, Oslo; Attendance: 23,000
Referee: Malcolm Moffatt (Northern Ireland)
**NORWAY - HUNGARY** **1-2(0-0)**
**NOR:** Jon Abrahamsen, Bjarne Berntsen (84.Svein Mathisen), Tore Kordahl, Einar Jan Aas, Trond Pedersen, Åge Hareide (81.Vidar Davidsen), Anders Giske, Tom Lund, Pål Jacobsen, Arne Larsen Økland, Hallvar Thoresen. Trainer: Tor Røste Fossen.
**HUN:** Béla Katzirz, Győző Martos, Attila Kerekes, Imre Garaba, József Tóth, Sándor Müller, Tibor Nyilasi, József Varga, László Fazekas, László Kiss András Törőcsik (66.Béla Bodonyi). Trainer: Kálmán Mészöly.
**Goals**: 1-0 Hallvar Thoresen (55), 1-1 László Kiss (77), 1-2 László Kiss (79).

30.05.1981, St. Jakob Stadion, Basel; Attendance: 40,000
Referee: Adolf Prokop (East Germany)
**SWITZERLAND - ENGLAND** **2-1(2-0)**
**SUI:** Erich Burgener, Gian-Piero Zappa, Heinz Lüdi, Herbert Hermann (88.Martin Weber), André Egli, Roger Wehrli, René Botteron, Umberto Barberis, Alfred Scheiwiler, Claudio Sulser, Rudolf Elsener (85.Ernie Maissen). Trainer: Paul Wolfisberg.
**ENG:** Raymond Neal Clemence, Michael Dennis Mills, Kenneth Graham Sansom, Raymond Colin Wilkins, David Victor Watson (80.Peter Simon Barnes), Russell Charles Osman, Steven James Coppell, Bryan Robson, Kevin Joseph Keegan (Cap), Paul Mariner, Trevor John Francis (36.Terence McDermott). Manager: Ronald Greenwood.
**Goals**: 1-0 Alfred Scheiwiler (28), 2-0 Claudio Sulser (30), 2-1 Terence McDermott (54).

03.06.1981, Stadionul 23 August, București; Attendance: 65,000
Referee: Erkan Göksel (Turkey)
**ROMANIA - NORWAY** **1-0(0-0)**
**ROU:** Cristian Gheorghe, Nicolae Negrilă, Ștefan Sameș, Costică Ștefănescu (Cap), Ion Munteanu II, Aurel Țicleanu, Aurel Beldeanu, Ilie Balaci (63.Cornel Țălnar), Zoltan Crișan, Rodion Gorun Cămătaru (89.Mircea Sandu), Marcel Răducanu. Trainer: Valentin Stănescu.
**NOR:** Roy Amundsen, Trond Pedersen, Einar Jan Aas, Tore Kordahl, Svein Grøndalen, Jan Hansen, Bjarne Berntsen, Anders Giske (75.Sverre Brandhaug), Svein Mathisen, Arne Larsen Økland (44.Vidar Davidsen), Arne Dokken. Trainer: Tor Røste Fossen.
**Goal**: 1-0 Aurel Țicleanu (67).

06.06.1981, Népstadion, Budapest; Attendance: 68,000
Referee: Paolo Casarin (Italy)
**HUNGARY - ENGLAND** **1-3(1-1)**
**HUN:** Béla Katzirz, Győző Martos, László Bálint, Imre Garaba, József Varga, Sándor Müller (55.András Komjáti), Tibor Nyilasi, József Mucha, László Fazekas (62.Béla Bodonyi), László Kiss, András Törőcsik. Trainer: Kálmán Mészöly.
**ENG:** Raymond Neal Clemence, Philip George Neal, Michael Dennis Mills, Philip Brian Thompson, David Victor Watson, Bryan Robson, Steven James Coppell, Terence McDermott, Paul Mariner, Trevor David Brooking (72.Raymond Colin Wilkins), Kevin Joseph Keegan (Cap). Manager: Ronald Greenwood.
**Goals**: 0-1 Trevor David Brooking (19), 1-1 Imre Garaba (45), 1-2 Trevor David Brooking (60), 1-3 Kevin Joseph Keegan (73 penalty).

17.06.1981, Ullevaal Stadion, Oslo; Attendance: 18,000
Referee: Eduard Shklovski (Soviet Union)
**NORWAY - SWITZERLAND** **1-1(0-0)**
**NOR:** Roy Amundsen, Tore Kordahl, Trond Pedersen, Einar Jan Aas, Svein Grøndalen, Åge Hareide (73.Svein Mathisen), Anders Giske, Jan Hansen (83.Vidar Davidsen), Pål Jacobsen, Arne Larsen Økland, Tom Lund. Trainer: Tor Røste Fossen.
**SUI:** Erich Burgener, Gian-Piero Zappa, Heinz Lüdi, André Egli, Herbert Hermann, Roger Wehrli, René Botteron, Umberto Barberis (86.Ernie Maissen), Alfred Scheiwiler, Claudio Sulser, Rudolf Elsener (61.Hanspeter Zwicker). Trainer: Paul Wolfisberg.
**Goals**: 0-1 Umberto Barberis (65), 1-1 Vidar Davidsen (88).

09.09.1981, Ullevaal Stadion, Oslo; Attendance: 28,500
Referee: Jerzy Kacprzak (Poland)
**NORWAY - ENGLAND** **2-1(2-1)**
**NOR:** Tore Antonsen, Bjarne Berntsen, Einar Jan Aas, Åge Hareide, Svein Grøndalen, Hallvar Thoresen, Roger Albertsen, Anders Giske, Tom Lund (75.Arne Dokken), Arne Larsen Økland (87.Trond Pedersen), Pål Jacobsen. Trainer: Tor Røste Fossen.
**ENG:** Raymond Neal Clemence, Philip George Neal, Michael Dennis Mills, Philip Brian Thompson, Russell Charles Osman, Bryan Robson, Kevin Joseph Keegan (Cap), Terence McDermott, Paul Mariner (75.Peter Withe), Trevor John Francis, Glenn Hoddle (65.Peter Simon Barnes). Manager: Ronald Greenwood.
**Goals**: 0-1 Bryan Robson (15), 1-1 Roger Albertsen (36), 2-1 Hallvar Thoresen (41).

**23.09.1981, Stadionul 23 August, București; Attendance: 70,000**
Referee: Erich Linemayr (Austria)
**ROMANIA - HUNGARY** **0-0**
**ROU**: Cristian Gheorghe, Nicolae Negrilă, Ștefan Sameș, Costică Ștefănescu (Cap), Ion Munteanu II, Aurel Beldeanu (75.Aurel Țicleanu), Tudorel Stoica, Anghel Iordănescu, Zoltan Crișan (63. Septimiu Virgil Cîmpeanu II), Rodion Gorun Cămătaru, Ilie Balaci. Trainer: Valentin Stănescu.
**HUN**: Ferenc Mészáros, Győző Martos, László Bálint, Imre Garaba, József Tóth, Sándor Sallai, Tibor Nyilasi, Tibor Rab, László Fazekas, András Törőcsik (61.Károly Csapó), László Kiss (51.Sándor Müller). Trainer: Kálmán Mészöly.

**10.10.1981, Stadionul 23 August, București; Attendance: 65,000**
Referee: Enzo Barbaresco (Italy)
**ROMANIA - SWITZERLAND** **1-2(0-0)**
**ROU**: Cristian Gheorghe, Nicolae Negrilă, Ștefan Sameș, Costică Ștefănescu (Cap), Ion Munteanu II, Aurel Țicleanu (53.Ionel Augustin), Tudorel Stoica, Anghel Iordănescu, Cornel Țălnar, Dudu Georgescu, Ilie Balaci. Trainer: Ștefan Kovács & Valentin Stănescu.
**SUI**: Erich Burgener, Gian-Piero Zappa, Heinz Lüdi, André Egli, Herbert Hermann, Roger Wehrli (64.Angelo Elia), Heinz Hermann, René Botteron, Umberto Barberis, Claudio Sulser, Rudolf Elsener (64.Robert Lüthi). Trainer: Paul Wolfisberg.
**Goals**: 1-0 Ilie Balaci (56), 1-1 Gian-Piero Zappa (68), 1-2 Robert Lüthi (75).

**14.10.1981, Népstadion, Budapest; Attendance: 65,000**
Referee: Tokat Talat (Turkey)
**HUNGARY - SWITZERLAND** **3-0(1-0)**
**HUN**: Ferenc Mészáros, Gábor Szántó, Attila Kerekes, Imre Garaba, József Tóth, Sándor Sallai, Tibor Nyilasi, Sándor Müller, László Fazekas, András Törőcsik, László Kiss (65.György Kerekes). Trainer: Kálmán Mészöly.
**SUI**: Erich Burgener, Gian-Piero Zappa, Heinz Lüdi, André Egli, Herbert Hermann, Roger Wehrli, René Botteron, Umberto Barberis (70.Robert Lüthi), Heinz Hermann, Claudio Sulser, Rudolf Elsener (33.Angelo Elia). Trainer: Paul Wolfisberg.
**Goals**: 1-0 Tibor Nyilasi (23), 2-0 Tibor Nyilasi (50), 3-0 László Fazekas (59).

**31.10.1981, Népstadion, Budapest; Attendance: 68,000**
Referee: Eduard Sostarić (Yugoslavia)
**HUNGARY - NORWAY** **4-1(1-1)**
**HUN**: Ferenc Mészáros, Győző Martos, László Bálint, Imre Garaba, József Tóth, Sándor Sallai, Tibor Nyilasi, Sándor Müller (69.Károly Csapó), László Fazekas, András Törőcsik, László Kiss. Trainer: Kálmán Mészöly.
**NOR**: Tore Antonsen, Trond Pedersen, Bjarne Berntsen, Frank Grønlund, Svein Grøndalen, Vidar Davidsen, Tom Jacobsen, Anders Giske (70.Svein Mathisen), Tom Lund, Pål Jacobsen, Isak Arne Refvik. Trainer: Tor Røste Fossen.
**Goals**: 1-0 László Bálint (12), 1-1 Tom Lund (35), 2-1 László Kiss (60), 3-1 László Fazekas (79), 4-1 László Kiss (85).

**11.11.1981, Wankdorf Stadion, Bern; Attendance: 27,000**
Referee: Cesar da Luz Diaz Correia (Portugal)
**SWITZERLAND - ROMANIA** **0-0**
**SUI**: Erich Burgener (46.Karl Engel), Gian-Piero Zappa, Heinz Lüdi, André Egli, Herbert Hermann (66.Angelo Elia), Roger Wehrli, René Botteron, Lucien Favre, Umberto Barberis, Claudio Sulser, Rudolf Elsener. Trainer: Paul Wolfisberg.
**ROU**: Dumitru Moraru, Mircea Rednic, Gino Iorgulescu, Costică Ștefănescu (Cap), Nelu Stănescu, Aurel Țicleanu (82.Ioan Andone), Ionel Augustin, Michael Klein, Ilie Balaci, Romulus Gabor, Mircea Sandu (90.Ladislau Bölöni). Trainer: Mircea Lucescu.

18.11.1981, Wembley Stadium, London; Attendance: 92,000
Referee: Georges Konrath (France)
**ENGLAND - HUNGARY** **1-0(1-0)**
**ENG:** Peter Leslie Shilton, Philip George Neal, Michael Dennis Mills, Philip Brian Thompson, Alvin Edward Martin, Bryan Robson, Kevin Joseph Keegan (Cap), Steven James Coppell (65.Anthony William Morley), Paul Mariner, Terence McDermott, Trevor David Brooking. Manager: Ronald Greenwood.
**HUN:** Ferenc Mészáros, Győző Martos, László Bálint, Imre Garaba, József Tóth, Sándor Müller, Károly Csapó (76.Gábor Szántó), Sándor Sallai, László Fazekas (46.György Kerekes), András Törőcsik, László Kiss. Trainer: Kálmán Mészöly.
Goal: 1-0 Paul Mariner (16).

## GROUP 5

| | | | |
|---|---|---|---|
| 10.09.1980 | Luxembourg | Luxembourg - Yugoslavia | 0-5(0-0) |
| 27.09.1980 | Ljubljana | Yugoslavia - Denmark | 2-1(2-1) |
| 11.10.1980 | Luxembourg | Luxembourg - Italy | 0-2(0-1) |
| 15.10.1980 | København | Denmark - Greece | 0-1(0-0) |
| 01.11.1980 | Roma | Italy - Denmark | 2-0(1-0) |
| 15.11.1980 | Torino | Italy - Yugoslavia | 2-0(1-0) |
| 19.11.1980 | København | Denmark - Luxembourg | 4-0(2-0) |
| 06.12.1980 | Athína | Greece - Italy | 0-2(0-1) |
| 28.01.1981 | Thessaloníki | Greece - Luxembourg | 2-0(2-0) |
| 11.03.1981 | Luxembourg | Luxembourg - Greece | 0-2(0-1) |
| 29.04.1981 | Split | Yugoslavia - Greece | 5-1(3-0) |
| 01.05.1981 | Luxembourg | Luxembourg - Denmark | 1-2(1-0) |
| 03.06.1981 | København | Denmark - Italy | 3-1(0-0) |
| 09.09.1981 | København | Denmark - Yugoslavia | 1-2(0-0) |
| 14.10.1981 | Thessaloníki | Greece - Denmark | 2-3(0-2) |
| 17.10.1981 | Beograd | Yugoslavia - Italy | 1-1(1-1) |
| 14.11.1981 | Torino | Italy - Greece | 1-1(0-0) |
| 21.11.1981 | Novi Sad | Yugoslavia - Luxembourg | 5-0(2-0) |
| 29.11.1981 | Athína | Greece - Yugoslavia | 1-2(1-2) |
| 05.12.1981 | Napoli | Italy - Luxembourg | 1-0(1-0) |

### FINAL STANDINGS

| | | | | | | | | | |
|---|---|---|---|---|---|---|---|---|---|
| 1. | **Yugoslavia** | 8 | 6 | 1 | 1 | 22 | - | 7 | 13 |
| 2. | **Italy** | 8 | 5 | 2 | 1 | 12 | - | 5 | 12 |
| 3. | Denmark | 8 | 4 | 0 | 4 | 14 | - | 11 | 8 |
| 4. | Greece | 8 | 3 | 1 | 4 | 10 | - | 13 | 7 |
| 5. | Luxembourg | 8 | 0 | 0 | 8 | 1 | - | 23 | 0 |

Yugoslavia and Italy qualified for the Final Tournament.

10.09.1980, Stade Municipal, Luxembourg; Attendance: 8,000
Referee: Franz Latzin (Austria)
**LUXEMBOURG - YUGOSLAVIA**      **0-5(0-0)**
**LUX:** Jeannot Moes, Jean-Paul Girres, Ernest Dax (72.Marcel Bossi), Jean Zuang (Cap), Hubert Meunier, Nico Wagner (83.Pierre Hoscheid), Carlo Weis, Gilbert Dresch, Marcel Di Domenico, Robert Langers, Jeannot Reiter. Trainer: Louis Pilot.
**YUG:** Dragan Pantelić, Zoran Vujović (85.Ivan Gudelj), Nikica Klinčarski, Nikola Jovanović, Ivan Buljan, Edhem Šljivo, Vladimir Petrović (Cap), Miloš Šestić (84.Ivan Šurjak), Zlatko Vujović, Safet Sušić, Džemal Šećerbegović. Trainer: Miljan Miljanić.
**Goals:** 0-1 Safet Sušić (50), 0-2 Zlatko Vujović (64), 0-3 Vladimir Petrović (70), 0-4 Zlatko Vujović (80), 0-5 Ivan Buljan (90).

27.09.1980, Gradski vrt Stadion, Ljubljana; Attendance: 20,000
Referee: Antonio José da Silva Garrido (Portugal)
**YUGOSLAVIA - DENMARK**      **2-1(2-1)**
**YUG:** Dragan Pantelić, Zoran Vujović, Miloš Hrstić, Nikola Jovanović, Boro Primorac, Ivan Buljan (72.Džemal Mustedanagić), Vladimir Petrović (Cap), Ive Jerolimov, Zlatko Vujović, Safet Sušić, Džemal Šećerbegović (88.Nikica Klinčarski). Trainer: Miljan Miljanić.
**DEN:** Ole Qvist, Ole Rasmussen, Sten Ziegler (Cap), Jens Steffensen, Søren Lerby, Jens Jørn Bertelsen, Frank Arnesen, Henning Jensen (73.Benny Nielsen), Per Røntved, Lars Bastrup, Preben Elkjær-Larsen. Trainer: Josef Piontek (West Germany).
**Goals:** 0-1 Frank Arnesen (6 penalty), 1-1 Dragan Pantelić (18 penalty), 2-1 Zoran Vujović (36).

11.10.1980, Stade Municipal, Luxembourg; Attendance: 10,000
Referee: Hendrik Weerink (Holland)
**LUXEMBOURG - ITALY**      **0-2(0-1)**
**LUX:** Jeannot Moes, Ernest Dax, Nicolas Rohmann, Marcel Bossi (39.Romain Schreiner), Hubert Meunier, Carlo Weis, Paul Philipp (Cap) (30.Nico Wagner), Gilbert Dresch, Marcel Di Domenico, Jeannot Reiter, Robert Langers. Trainer: Louis Pilot.
**ITA:** Dino Zoff, Claudio Gentile, Giuseppe Baresi I, Gabriele Oriali, Fulvio Collovatti, Gaetano Scirea, Marco Tardelli (46.Patrizio Sala), Alessandro Altobelli (66.Bruno Conti), Giancarlo Antognoni, Franco Causio, Roberto Bettega. Trainer: Enzo Bearzot.
**Goals:** 0-1 Fulvio Collovatti (33), 0-2 Roberto Bettega (77).
**Sent off:** Franco Causio (80), Giancarlo Antognoni (89).

15.10.1980, Idrætsparken, København; Attendance: 47,500
Referee: Eamonn Farrell (Republic of Ireland)
**DENMARK - GREECE**      **0-1(0-0)**
**DEN:** Ole Qvist, Jens Steffensen, Ole Rasmussen, Sten Ziegler (Cap), Morten Olsen, Frank Arnesen, Jens Jørn Bertelsen (58.Benny Nielsen), Søren Lerby, Allan Rodenkam Simonsen, Henning Jensen (75.Lars Bastrup), Preben Elkjær-Larsen. Trainer: Josef Piontek (West Germany).
**GRE:** Nikolaos Sarganis, Giánnis Kyrástas, Konstantinos Iosifidis, Anthimos Kapsís, Giórgos Firos, Giórgos Delikaris (Cap) (72.Giórgos Paráshos), Spyridon Livathinos, Hrístos Ardizoglou, Konstantinos Kouis, Giórgos Kostikos (87.Anastásios Mitropoulos), Thomás Mavros. Trainer: Alketas Panagoulias.
**Goal:** 0-1 Konstantinos Kouis (50).

01.11.1980, Stadio Olimpico, Roma; Attendance: 49,500
Referee: Belaïd Lacarne (Algeria)
**ITALY - DENMARK**  **2-0(1-0)**
**ITA:** Dino Zoff, Claudio Gentile, Giampiero Marini, Fulvio Collovatti, Antonio Cabrini, Gaetano Scirea, Bruno Conti, Marco Tardelli, Alessandro Altobelli, Francesco Graziani, Roberto Bettega. Trainer: Enzo Bearzot.
**DEN:** Ole Kjær, Ole Rasmussen, Morten Olsen, Per Røntved (Cap), Jens Steffensen, Jens Jørn Bertelsen, Frank Arnesen, Søren Lerby, Lars Bastrup, Henning Jensen, Preben Elkjær-Larsen. Trainer: Josef Piontek (West Germany).
**Goals**: 1-0 Francesco Graziani (5), 2-0 Francesco Graziani (50).

15.11.1980, Stadio Comunale, Torino; Attendance: 50,677
Referee: Abraham Klein (Israel)
**ITALY - YUGOSLAVIA**  **2-0(1-0)**
**ITA:** Dino Zoff, Claudio Gentile, Giampiero Marini, Fulvio Collovatti, Gaetano Scirea, Antonio Cabrini, Bruno Conti, Giancarlo Antognoni (79.Renato Zaccarelli), Marco Tardelli, Francesco Graziani, Roberto Bettega. Trainer: Enzo Bearzot.
**YUG:** Dragan Pantelić, Zoran Vujović, Zlatko Krmpotić, Ive Jerolimov (87.Mihajlo Petrović), Boro Primorac (Cap), Miroslav Simonović, Miloš Šestić (63.Vahid Halilhodžić), Edhem Šljivo, Zlatko Vujović, Nenad Šalov, Džemal Šećerbegović. Trainer: Miljan Miljanić.
**Goals**: 1-0 Antonio Cabrini (40 penalty), 2-0 Bruno Conti (75).

19.11.1980, Idrætsparken, København; Attendance: 10,500
Referee: Clive Bradley White (England)
**DENMARK - LUXEMBOURG**  **4-0(2-0)**
**DEN:** Ole Kjær, Ole Rasmussen, Ivan Nielsen, Per Røntved (Cap), Jens Steffensen, Frank Arnesen, Jens Jørn Bertelsen, Søren Lerby, Allan Rodenkam Simonsen, Lars Bastrup (82.Kenneth Brylle), Preben Elkjær-Larsen. Trainer: Josef Piontek (West Germany).
**LUX:** Jeannot Moes, Ernest Dax (80.Romain Michaux), Paul Philipp (Cap), Hubert Meunier, Marcel Bossi, Jean-Paul Girres, Gilbert Dresch, Marcel Di Domenico, Jeannot Reiter (65.William Bianchini), Carlo Weis, Robert Langers. Trainer: Louis Pilot.
**Goals**: 1-0 Frank Arnesen (19), 2-0 Frank Arnesen (39 penalty), 3-0 Preben Elkjær-Larsen (57), 4-0 Allan Rodenkam Simonsen (71).

06.12.1980, Panathínaïkos Stádio, Athína; Attendance: 25,000
Referee: Michel Vautrot (France)
**GREECE - ITALY**  **0-2(0-1)**
**GRE:** Nikolaos Sarganis, Giánnis Kyrástas, Giórgos Firos, Anthimos Kapsís, Konstantinos Iosifidis, Konstantinos Kouis, Spyridon Livathinos (46.Ilias Galakos), Giórgos Delikaris (Cap), Hrístos Ardizoglou, Giórgos Kostikos (66.Grigórios Haralambidis), Thomás Mavros. Trainer: Alketas Panagoulias.
**ITA:** Dino Zoff, Claudio Gentile, Fulvio Collovatti, Gaetano Scirea, Antonio Cabrini, Giampiero Marini, Bruno Conti, Marco Tardelli, Giancarlo Antognoni (86.Gabriele Oriali), Francesco Graziani, Alessandro Altobelli. Trainer: Enzo Bearzot.
**Goals**: 0-1 Giancarlo Antognoni (11), 0-2 Gaetano Scirea (81).

28.01.1981, Harilaou Stádio, Thessaloníki; Attendance: 10,000
Referee: Nikola Dudin (Bulgaria)
**GREECE - LUXEMBOURG** **2-0(2-0)**
**GRE:** Nikolaos Sarganis, Giánnis Kyrástas, Konstantinos Iosifidis, Pétros Ravousis, Anthimos Kapsís (Cap), Giánnis Damanakis, Konstantinos Kouis, Evangélios Kousoulakis (46.Giórgos Delikaris), Giórgos Kostikos, Nikolaos Anastopoulos (71.Grigóris Haralambidis), Ilías Galakos. Trainer: Alketas Panagoulias.
**LUX:** Jeannot Moes, Ernest Dax (68.Marcel Bossi), Paul Philipp (Cap), Nicolas Rohmann, Nico Wagner, Jean-Paul Girres, Gilbert Dresch, Jean Zuang, Marcel Di Domenico, Jeannot Reiter (57.Pierre Hoscheid), Robert Langers. Trainer: Louis Pilot.
**Goals:** 1-0 Konstantinos Kouis (8), 2-0 Giórgos Kostikos (38).

11.03.1981, Stade Municipal, Luxembourg; Attendance: 8,500
Referee: Peter Scherz (Switzerland)
**LUXEMBOURG - GREECE** **0-2(0-1)**
**LUX:** Jeannot Moes, Ernest Dax, Paul Philipp (Cap), Nicolas Rohmann, Nico Wagner (69.Hubert Meunier), Jean-Paul Girres, Carlo Weis, Gilbert Dresch, Jeannot Reiter, Robert Langers, Marcel Di Domenico. Trainer: Louis Pilot.
**GRE:** Nikolaos Sarganis, Giánnis Kyrástas, Konstantinos Iosifidis, Giórgos Firos, Anthimos Kapsís (Cap), Spyridon Livathinos, Evangélios Kousoulakis (68.Nikolaos Anastopoulos), Konstantinos Kouis, Giórgos Kostikos, Ilías Galakos (79.Nikolaos Vamvakoulas), Thomás Mavros. Trainer: Alketas Panagoulias.
**Goals:** 0-1 Konstantinos Kouis (31), 0-2 Thomás Mavros (54 penalty).

29.04.1981, Poljud Stadion, Split; Attendance: 45,000
Referee: Valeriy Butenko (Soviet Union)
**YUGOSLAVIA - GREECE** **5-1(3-0)**
**YUG:** Dragan Pantelić, Zlatko Krmpotić, Miloš Hrstić (46.Ive Jerolimov), Velimir Zajec (Cap), Nenad Stojković, Ivan Buljan, Zlatko Vujović, Blaž Slišković (46.Miloš Šestić), Vahid Halilhodžić, Edhem Šljivo, Predrag Pašić. Trainer: Miljan Miljanić.
**GRE:** Nikolaos Sarganis, Giánnis Gounaris, Anthimos Kapsís (Cap), Konstantinos Iosifidis, Giórgos Firos, Spyridon Livathinos (46.Giórgos Koudas), Konstantinos Ballis, Evangélios Kousoulakis, Hrístos Ardizoglou, Giórgos Kostikos, Konstantinos Kouis. Trainer: Alketas Panagoulias.
**Goals:** 1-0 Edhem Šljivo (7), 2-0 Vahid Halilhodžić (23), 3-0 Dragan Pantelić (42 penalty), 4-0 Zlatko Vujović (51), 5-0 Zlatko Vujović (57), 5-1 Giórgos Kostikos (76 penalty).

01.05.1981, Stade Municipal, Luxembourg; Attendance: 2,844
Referee: Louis Delsemme (Belgium)
**LUXEMBOURG - DENMARK** **1-2(1-0)**
**LUX:** Jeannot Moes, Hubert Meunier (88.Romain Schreiner), Nico Wagner, Ernest Dax, Paul Philipp (Cap), Alain Nurenberg, Jean-Paul Girres, Carlo Weis, Manou Scheitler (87.Guy Back), Robert Langers, Marcel Di Domenico. Trainer: Louis Pilot.
**DEN:** Ole Qvist, Ole Rasmussen, Søren Busk, Per Røntved (Cap), Henrik Eigenbrod (60.Allan Rodenkam Simonsen), Frank Arnesen, Morten Olsen, Jens Jørn Bertelsen, Søren Lerby, John Eriksen, Preben Elkjær-Larsen. Trainer: Josef Piontek (West Germany).
**Goals:** 1-0 Alain Nurenberg (37), 1-1 Preben Elkjær-Larsen (46), 1-2 Frank Arnesen (63).

03.06.1981, Idrætsparken, København; Attendance: 36,300
Referee: Franz Wöhrer (Austria)
**DENMARK - ITALY** **3-1(0-0)**
**DEN:** Ole Qvist, Ole Rasmussen, Søren Busk, Per Røntved (Cap), Søren Lerby, Frank Arnesen, Morten Olsen (75.Henrik Eigenbrod), Jens Jørn Bertelsen, Allan Rodenkam Simonsen, Lars Bastrup, Preben Elkjær-Larsen. Trainer: Josef Piontek (West Germany).
**ITA:** Dino Zoff, Claudio Gentile, Fulvio Collovatti, Gaetano Scirea, Antonio Cabrini, Giampiero Marini (67.Giuseppe Dossena), Bruno Conti, Marco Tardelli, Giancarlo Antognoni, Francesco Graziani, Roberto Bettega (67.Carlo Ancelotti). Trainer: Enzo Bearzot.
**Goals:** 1-0 Per Røntved (59), 2-0 Frank Arnesen (61), 2-1 Francesco Graziani (69), 3-1 Lars Bastrup (87).

09.09.1981, Idrætsparken, København; Attendance: 48,400
Referee: Siegfried Kirschen (East Germany)
**DENMARK - YUGOSLAVIA** **1-2(0-0)**
**DEN:** Ole Qvist, Ole Rasmussen, Sten Ziegler, Per Røntved (Cap), Ole Madsen II, Frank Arnesen, Jens Jørn Bertelsen, Søren Lerby, Allan Rodenkam Simonsen, Lars Bastrup, Preben Elkjær-Larsen. Trainer: Josef Piontek (West Germany).
**YUG:** Dragan Pantelić, Zlatko Krmpotič, Miloš Hrstić, Ivan Gudelj, Velimir Zajec, Nenad Stojković, Zlatko Vujović, Vladimir Petrović, Vahid Halilhodžić, Edhem Šljivo, Ivan Šurjak (Cap). Trainer: Miljan Miljanić.
**Goals:** 0-1 Zlatko Vujović (49), 1-1 Preben Elkjær-Larsen (61), 1-2 Vladimir Petrović (63).

14.10.1981, Harilaou Stádio, Thessaloníki; Attendance: 18,000
Referee: Josef Bucek (Austria)
**GREECE - DENMARK** **2-3(0-2)**
**GRE:** Vasílis Konstantinou, Giánnis Gounaris (46.Nikolaos Karoulias), Giórgos Firos, Athanásios Papazoglou, Konstantinos Iosifidis, Spyridon Livathinos, Giórgos Delikaris (23.Giórgos Kostikos), Konstantinos Kouis, Anastásios Mitropoulos, Nikolaos Anastopoulos, Giórgos Koudas (Cap). Trainer: Alketas Panagoulias.
**DEN:** Ole Qvist, Ole Rasmussen, Ivan Nielsen, Per Røntved (Cap), Søren Lerby, Frank Arnesen (85.Sten Ziegler), Jens Jørn Bertelsen, Morten Olsen, Allan Rodenkam Simonsen, Lars Bastrup, Preben Elkjær-Larsen. Trainer: Josef Piontek (West Germany).
**Goals:** 0-1 Søren Lerby (8), 0-2 Frank Arnesen (28), 1-2 Nikolaos Anastopoulos (60), 1-3 Preben Elkjær-Larsen (65), 2-3 Konstantinos Kouis (84).

17.10.1981, Crvena zvezda Stadion, Beograd; Attendance: 70,000
Referee: Walter Eschweiler (West Germany)
**YUGOSLAVIA - ITALY** **1-1(1-1)**
**YUG:** Dragan Pantelić, Ivan Buljan, Ivan Gudelj, Velimir Zajec, Nenad Stojković, Ivan Šurjak (Cap), Zlatko Vujović (78.Zoran Vujović), Vladimir Petrović, Vahid Halilhodžić, Edhem Šljivo, Predrag Pašić. Trainer: Miljan Miljanić.
**ITA:** Dino Zoff, Claudio Gentile, Fulvio Collovatti, Gaetano Scirea, Antonio Cabrini, Giuseppe Dossena, Bruno Conti, Marco Tardelli, Giancarlo Antognoni (62.Gabriele Oriali), Alessandro Altobelli, Roberto Bettega. Trainer: Enzo Bearzot.
**Goals:** 1-0 Zlatko Vujović (10), 1-1 Roberto Bettega (33).

14.11.1981, Stadio Comunale, Torino; Attendance: 39,670
Referee: Nicolae Rainea (Romania)
**ITALY - GREECE** **1-1(0-0)**
**ITA:** Dino Zoff, Claudio Gentile, Fulvio Collovatti, Gaetano Scirea, Antonio Cabrini, Giampiero Marini, Bruno Conti (85.Roberto Pruzzo), Giuseppe Dossena, Giancarlo Antognoni (66.Gabriele Oriali), Francesco Graziani, Franco Selvaggi. Trainer: Enzo Bearzot.
**GRE:** Panagiótis Pantelís, Nikolaos Karoulias, Anthimos Kapsís (Cap), Giórgos Firos, Konstantinos Iosifidis, Nikolaos Vamvakoulas, Giánnis Damanakis, Hrístos Ardizoglou (46.Giórgos Zindros), Konstantinos Kouis, Anastásios Mitropoulos (69.Giórgos Kostikos), Nikolaos Anastopoulos. Trainer: Alketas Panagoulias.
**Goals**: 1-0 Bruno Conti (61), 1-1 Konstantinos Kouis (87).

21.11.1981, Vojvodina Stadion, Novi Sad; Attendance: 20,000
Referee: Charles Scerri (Malta)
**YUGOSLAVIA - LUXEMBOURG** **5-0(2-0)**
**YUG:** Dragan Pantelić, Zlatko Krmpotić, Nenad Stojković, Ivan Gudelj, Velimir Zajec, Ivan Buljan, Zlatko Vujović, Vladimir Petrović, Vahid Halilhodžić (69.Predrag Pašić), Ivan Šurjak (Cap) (69.Ive Jerolimov), Safet Sušić. Trainer: Miljan Miljanić.
**LUX:** Jeannot Moes (Cap), Ernest Dax, Marcel Bossi (77.Alain Nurenberg), Nicolas Rohmann, John Clemens, Jean-Paul Girres, Carlo Weis, Gilbert Dresch, Marcel Di Domenico (69.Romain Schreiner), Robert Langers, Jeannot Reiter. Trainer: Louis Pilot
**Goals**: 1-0 Vahid Halilhodžić (1), 2-0 Vahid Halilhodžić (45), 3-0 Ivan Šurjak (68), 4-0 Predrag Pašić (72), 5-0 Zlatko Vujović (76).

29.11.1981, Karaïskáki Stádio, Peiraiás; Attendance: 22,000
Referee: George Courtney (England)
**GREECE - YUGOSLAVIA** **1-2(1-2)**
**GRE:** Panagiótis Pantelís (46.Giórgos Dafkos), Nikolaos Karoulias, Pétros Ravousis, Anthimos Kapsís (Cap), Konstantinos Iosifidis (46.Giórgos Kostikos), Nikolaos Vamvakoulas, Spyridon Livathinos, Konstantinos Kouis, Nikolaos Anastopoulos, Thomás Mavros, Anastásios Mitropoulos. Trainer: Alketas Panagoulias.
**YUG:** Dragan Pantelić, Zoran Vujović (84.Miloš Hrstić), Nenad Stojković, Ivan Gudelj, Velimir Zajec, Ivan Buljan, Zlatko Vujović (76.Predrag Pašić), Vladimir Petrović, Safet Sušić, Jure Jerković, Ivan Šurjak (Cap). Trainer: Miljan Miljanić.
**Goals**: 1-0 Thomás Mavros (8), 1-1 Ivan Šurjak (23), 1-2 Jure Jerković (39)

05.12.1981, Stadio „San Paolo", Napoli; Attendance: 49,247
Referee: Velichko Tsonchev (Bulgaria)
**ITALY - LUXEMBOURG** **1-0(1-0)**
**ITA:** Dino Zoff, Claudio Gentile, Fulvio Collovatti, Gaetano Scirea, Antonio Cabrini, Gabriele Oriali, Domenico Marocchino, Marco Tardelli, Giuseppe Dossena, Roberto Pruzzo, Francesco Graziani. Trainer: Enzo Bearzot.
**LUX:** Jeannot Moes (Cap), Hubert Meunier, Nicolas Rohmann, Marcel Bossi, John Clemens, Nico Wagner (88.Romain Schreiner), Carlo Weis, Gilbert Dresch, Marcel Di Domenico, Robert Langers, Jeannot Reiter (73.Jean-Paul Girres). Trainer: Louis Pilot.
**Goal**: 1-0 Fulvio Collovatti (6).

# GROUP 6

| | | | |
|---|---|---|---|
| 26.03.1980 | Tel Aviv | Israel - Northern Ireland | 0-0 |
| 18.06.1980 | Stockholm | Sweden - Israel | 1-1(1-0) |
| 10.09.1980 | Stockholm | Sweden - Scotland | 0-1(0-0) |
| 15.10.1980 | Belfast | Northern Ireland - Sweden | 3-0(3-0) |
| 15.10.1980 | Glasgow | Scotland - Portugal | 0-0 |
| 12.11.1980 | Tel Aviv | Israel - Sweden | 0-0 |
| 19.11.1980 | Lisboa | Portugal - Northern Ireland | 1-0(0-0) |
| 17.12.1980 | Lisboa | Portugal - Israel | 3-0(2-0) |
| 25.02.1981 | Tel Aviv | Israel - Scotland | 0-1(0-0) |
| 25.03.1981 | Glasgow | Scotland - Northern Ireland | 1-1(0-0) |
| 28.04.1981 | Glasgow | Scotland - Israel | 3-1(2-0) |
| 29.04.1981 | Belfast | Northern Ireland - Portugal | 1-0(0-0) |
| 03.06.1981 | Stockholm | Sweden - Northern Ireland | 1-0(0-0) |
| 24.06.1981 | Stockholm | Sweden - Portugal | 3-0(1-0) |
| 09.09.1981 | Glasgow | Scotland - Sweden | 2-0(1-0) |
| 14.10.1981 | Lisboa | Portugal – Sweden | 1-2(0-1) |
| 14.10.1981 | Belfast | Northern Ireland – Scotland | 0-0 |
| 28.10.1981 | Tel Aviv | Israel - Portugal | 4-1(4-1) |
| 18.11.1981 | Belfast | Northern Ireland - Israel | 1-0(1-0) |
| 18.11.1981 | Lisboa | Portugal - Scotland | 2-1(1-1) |

### FINAL STANDINGS

| | | | | | | | | | |
|---|---|---|---|---|---|---|---|---|---|
| 1. | **Scotland** | 8 | 4 | 3 | 1 | 9 | - | 4 | 11 |
| 2. | **Northern Ireland** | 8 | 3 | 3 | 2 | 6 | - | 3 | 9 |
| 3. | Sweden | 8 | 3 | 2 | 3 | 7 | - | 8 | 8 |
| 4. | Portugal | 8 | 3 | 1 | 4 | 8 | - | 11 | 7 |
| 5. | Israel | 8 | 1 | 3 | 4 | 6 | - | 10 | 5 |

Scotland and Northern Ireland qualified for the Final Tournament.

26.03.1980, National Stadium, Ramat-Gan, Tel Aviv; Attendance: 40,000
Referee: Stjepan Glavina (Yugoslavia)
**ISRAEL - NORTHERN IRELAND** **0-0**
**ISR:** Arie Haviv, Gadi Machnes, Haim Bar, Itzhak Shum, Yaacov Cohen, Rifat Turk, Giora Spiegel, Avi Cohen I, Gideon Damti, Viktor Peretz, Moshe Gariani (Oded Machnes). Trainer: Jack Mansell (England).
**NIR:** Patrick Anthony Jennings, James Michael Nicholl, Samuel Nelson, Christopher James Nicholl, John Patrick O'Neill, Martin Hugh Michael O'Neill, Samuel Baxter McIlroy, Thomas Cassidy, Gerard Joseph Armstrong, Thomas Finney (Derek William Spence), George Terence Cochrane. Manager: William Laurence Bingham.

18.06.1980, Råsunda Stadion, Stockholm; Attendance: 24,711
Referee: Martti Hirviniemi (Finland)
**SWEDEN - ISRAEL** **1-1(1-0)**
**SWE:** Jan Möller, Hans Borg, Leif Gustavsson, Håkan Arvidsson, Ingemar Erlandsson, Tord Holmgren, Sten-Ove Ramberg (65.Peter Nilsson), Thomas Sjöberg, Mats Nordgren, Rutger Backe, Ralf Edström. Trainer: Lars Arnesson.
**ISR:** Yossi Mizrahi, Gadi Machnes, Haim Bar, Itzhak Shum, Yaacov Cohen, Rifat Turk (32.Yaacov Ekhoiz), Giora Spiegel, Avi Cohen I, Moshe Gariani, Gideon Damti, Viktor Peretz (89.Israel Fogel). Trainer: Jack Mansell (England).
**Goals**: 1-0 Sten-Ove Ramberg (35), 1-1 Gideon Damti (80).

10.09.1980, Råsunda Stadion, Stockholm; Attendance: 39,831
Referee: Franz Wöhrer (Austria)
**SWEDEN - SCOTLAND** **0-1(0-0)**
**SWE:** Ronnie Carl Hellström, Johnny Gustafsson, Hans Borg, Per Olof Bild, Håkan Arvidsson, Ingemar Erlandsson (80.Peter Nilsson), Sten-Ove Ramberg, Mats Nordgren, Thomas Nilsson, Thomas Sjöberg, Billy Ohlsson. Trainer: Lars Arnesson.
**SCO:** Alan Roderick Rough, Daniel Fergus McGrain, Francis Tierney Gray, William Fergus Miller, Alexander McLeish, Alan David Hansen, Gordon David Strachan, Archibald Gemmill (Cap), John Neilson Robertson, Kenneth Mathieson Dalglish (80.Steven Archibald), Andrew Mullen Gray. Manager: John Stein.
**Goal**: 0-1 Gordon David Strachan (72).

15.10.1980, Windsor Park, Belfast; Attendance: 20,000
Referee: Alexis Ponnet (Belgium)
**NORTHERN IRELAND - SWEDEN** **3-0(3-0)**
**NIR:** James Archibald Platt, James Michael Nicholl, Malachy Martin Donaghy, Thomas Cassidy (76.David McCreery), Christopher James Nicholl, John McClelland, Noel Brotherston, Martin Hugh Michael O'Neill, William Robert Hamilton (76.George Terence Cochrane), Gerard Joseph Armstrong, Samuel Baxter McIlroy. Manager: William Laurence Bingham.
**SWE:** Jan Möller, Hans Borg, Håkan Arvidsson, Bo Börjesson, Tord Holmgren, Lennart Larsson, Sten-Ove Ramberg (46.Ingemar Erlandsson), Peter Nilsson, Thomas Nilsson, Ralf Edström, Billy Ohlsson (68.Thomas Sjöberg). Trainer: Lars Arnesson.
**Goals**: 1-0 Noel Brotherston (24), 2-0 Samuel Baxter McIlroy (28), 3-0 James Michael Nicholl (37).

15.10.1980, Hampden Park, Glasgow; Attendance: 60,765
Referee: Jan Redelfs (West Germany)
**SCOTLAND - PORTUGAL** **0-0**
**SCO:** Alan Roderick Rough, Daniel Fergus McGrain, Francis Tierney Gray, William Fergus Miller, Alan David Hansen, Gordon David Strachan, Graeme James Souness, Archibald Gemmill (Cap), John Neilson Robertson, Kenneth Mathieson Dalglish, Andrew Mullen Gray. Manager: John Stein.
**POR:** Manuel Galrinho Bento (Cap), Gabriel Azevedo Mendes, Carlos António Fonseca Simões, João Gonçalves Laranjeira, Minervino José Lopes Pietra, Carlos Manuel Correia dos Santos, Eurico Monteiro Gomes, José Alberto Costa, Fernando Albino de Sousa Chalana (59.Shéu Han), Manuel José Tavares Fernandes, Rui Manuel Trindade Jordão (63.Tamagnini Manuel Gomes Baptista „Nené"). Trainer: Júlio Cernadas Pereira „Juca".

12.11.1980, National Stadium, Ramat-Gan, Tel Aviv; Attendance: 46,000
Referee: George Courtney (England)
**ISRAEL - SWEDEN** **0-0**
**ISR:** Yossi Mizrahi, Avi Cohen I, Haim Bar, Itzhak Shum, Yaacov Cohen, Giora Spiegel, Rifat Turk (Nissim Cohen), Yaacov Ekhoiz, Moshe Gariani, Gideon Damti, Viktor Peretz (Oded Machnes). Trainer: Jack Mansell (England).
**SWE:** Thomas Wernersson, Stig Fredriksson, Håkan Arvidsson, Bo Börjesson, Ingemar Erlandsson, Lennart Larsson, Tord Holmgren, Robert Prytz (79.Peter Nilsson), Thomas Nilsson (84.Andreas Ravelli), Ralf Edström, Pär-Olof Ohlsson. Trainer: Lars Arnesson.

19.11.1980, Estádio da Luz, Lisboa; Attendance: 70,000
Referee: Georges Konrath (France)
**PORTUGAL - NORTHERN IRELAND** **1-0(0-0)**
**POR:** Manuel Galrinho Bento (Cap), Gabriel Azevedo Mendes, Carlos António Fonseca Simões, João Gonçalves Laranjeira, Minervino José Lopes Pietra, Shéu Han, Carlos Manuel Correia dos Santos (46.Tamagnini Manuel Gomes Baptista „Nené"), João António Ferreira Resende Alves (84.Adelino de Jesus Teixeira), José Alberto Costa, Fernando Albino de Sousa Chalana, Rui Manuel Trindade Jordão. Trainer: Júlio Cernadas Pereira „Juca".
**NIR:** James Archibald Platt, James Michael Nicholl, Malachy Martin Donaghy, Thomas Cassidy (78.David McCreery), Christopher James Nicholl, John Patrick O'Neill, Noel Brotherston, Martin Hugh Michael O'Neill (Cap), William Robert Hamilton (78.George Terence Cochrane), Gerard Joseph Armstrong, Samuel Baxter McIlroy. Manager: William Laurence Bingham.
**Goal**: 1-0 Rui Manuel Trindade Jordão (60).

17.12.1980, Estádio da Luz, Lisboa; Attendance: 55,000
Referee: Enzo Barbaresco (Italy)
**PORTUGAL - ISRAEL** **3-0(2-0)**
**POR:** Manuel Galrinho Bento, Gabriel Azevedo Mendes, Humberto Manuel de Jesus Coelho (Cap), João Gonçalves Laranjeira (54.Carlos António Fonseca Simões), Minervino José Lopes Pietra, Shéu Han, Carlos Manuel Correia dos Santos (85.Manuel José Tavares Fernandes), João António Ferreira Resende Alves, Fernando Albino de Sousa Chalana, Tamagnini Manuel Gomes Baptista „Nené", Rui Manuel Trindade Jordão. Trainer: Júlio Cernadas Pereira „Juca".
**ISR:** Yossi Mizrahi, Shlomo Kirat, Haim Bar, Noah Einstein, Yaacov Cohen, Rifat Turk, Yaacov Ekhoiz, Itzhak Shum, Moshe Gariani (72.Nissim Cohen), Gideon Damti, Viktor Peretz (72.Shalom Schwartz). Trainer: Jack Mansell (England).
**Goals**: 1-0 Humberto Manuel de Jesus Coelho (33), 2-0 Rui Manuel Trindade Jordão (37), 3-0 Humberto Manuel de Jesus Coelho (72).

25.02.1981, National Stadium, Ramat-Gan, Tel Aviv; Attendance: 35,000
Referee: Otto Anderco (Romania)
**ISRAEL - SCOTLAND** **0-1(0-0)**
**ISR:** Yossi Mizrahi, Gadi Machnes, Haim Bar, Avi Cohen I, Yaacov Cohen, Nissim Cohen, Yaacov Ekhoiz, Itzhak Shum, Moshe Sinai, Gideon Damti, Beni Tabak. Trainer: Jack Mansell (England).
**SCO:** Alan Roderick Rough, Daniel Fergus McGrain, Francis Tierney Gray, Kenneth Burns, Alexander McLeish, John Wark (46.William Fergus Miller), Graeme James Souness, Archibald Gemmill (Cap), John Neilson Robertson, Kenneth Mathieson Dalglish (69.Andrew Mullen Gray), Steven Archibald. Manager: John Stein.
**Goal**: 0-1 Kenneth Mathieson Dalglish (54).

25.03.1981, Hampden Park, Glasgow; Attendance: 78,444
Referee: Klaus Scheurell (East Germany)
**SCOTLAND - NORTHERN IRELAND** **1-1(0-0)**
**SCO:** Alan Roderick Rough (80.William Thomson), Daniel Fergus McGrain, Francis Tierney Gray, William Fergus Miller, Alexander McLeish, John Wark, Kenneth Burns (77.Richard Asa Hartford), Archibald Gemmill (Cap), John Neilson Robertson, Steven Archibald, Andrew Mullen Gray. Manager: John Stein.
**NIR:** Patrick Anthony Jennings, James Michael Nicholl, Samuel Nelson, John McClelland, Christopher James Nicholl, John Patrick O'Neill, George Terence Cochrane, David McCreery, William Robert Hamilton (78.Derek William Spence), Gerard Joseph Armstrong, Samuel Baxter McIlroy. Manager: William Laurence Bingham.
**Goals**: 0-1 William Robert Hamilton (70), 1-1 John Wark (75).

28.04.1981, Hampden Park, Glasgow; Attendance: 61,489
Referee: Guðmundur Haraldsson (Iceland)
**SCOTLAND - ISRAEL** 3-1(2-0)
**SCO:** Alan Roderick Rough, Daniel Fergus McGrain (Cap), Francis Tierney Gray, Alan David Hansen, Alexander McLeish, David Alexander Provan, Graeme James Souness, Richard Asa Hartford, John Neilson Robertson, Steven Archibald, Joseph Jordan. Manager: John Stein.
**ISR:** Yossi Mizrahi, Gadi Machnes, Haim Bar, Itzhak Shum, Yaacov Cohen, Cobi Zeituni, Yaacov Ekhoiz, Avi Cohen I, Moshe Sinai, Gideon Damti, Beni Tabak. Trainer: Jack Mansell (England).
**Goals**: 1-0 John Neilson Robertson (21 penalty), 2-0 John Neilson Robertson (30 penalty), 3-0 David Alexander Provan (53), 3-1 Moshe Sinai (57).

29.04.1981, Windsor Park, Belfast; Attendance: 18,000
Referee: Svein Inge Thime (Norway)
**NORTHERN IRELAND - PORTUGAL** 1-0(0-0)
**NIR:** Patrick Anthony Jennings, James Michael Nicholl, Samuel Nelson, David McCreery, Christopher James Nicholl, John Patrick O'Neill, George Terence Cochrane, Martin Hugh Michael O'Neill, William Robert Hamilton, Gerard Joseph Armstrong, Samuel Baxter McIlroy. Manager: William Laurence Bingham.
**POR:** Manuel Galrinho Bento, Gabriel Azevedo Mendes, Humberto Manuel de Jesus Coelho (Cap), Carlos António Fonseca Simões, Minervino José Lopes Pietra, Shéu Han, Carlos Manuel Correia dos Santos, João António Ferreira Resende Alves, José Alberto Costa, António Luís Alves Ribeiro Oliveira (61.Tamagnini Manuel Gomes Baptista „Nené"), Rui Manuel Trindade Jordão. Trainer: Júlio Cernadas Pereira „Juca".
**Goal**: Gerard Joseph Armstrong (71).

03.06.1981, Råsunda Stadion, Stockholm; Attendance: 21,431
Referee: Paolo Bergamo (Italy)
**SWEDEN - NORTHERN IRELAND** 1-0(0-0)
**SWE:** Thomas Ravelli, Stig Fredriksson, Glenn Ingvar Hysén, Bo Börjesson, Ingemar Erlandsson, Tony Persson, Hans Borg, Peter Nilsson, Thomas Nilsson (69.Torbjörn Nilsson), Thomas Sjöberg, Jan Svensson (83.Andreas Ravelli). Trainer: Lars Arnesson.
**NIR:** Patrick Anthony Jennings, James Michael Nicholl (62.John McClelland), Samuel Nelson, David McCreery, Christopher James Nicholl, John Patrick O'Neill, George Terence Cochrane, Martin Hugh Michael O'Neill, William Robert Hamilton (70.Derek William Spence), Gerard Joseph Armstrong, Samuel Baxter McIlroy. Manager: William Laurence Bingham.
**Goal**: 1-0 Hans Borg (49).

24.06.1981, Råsunda Stadion, Stockholm; Attendance: 34,531
Referee: Anatoly Milchenko (Soviet Union)
**SWEDEN - PORTUGAL** 3-0(1-0)
**SWE:** Thomas Ravelli, Stig Fredriksson, Glenn Ingvar Hysén, Bo Börjesson, Ingemar Erlandsson, Andreas Ravelli (78.Thomas Nilsson), Peter Nilsson, Karl-Gunnar Björklund, Tony Persson (81.Greger Hallén), Thomas Sjöberg, Jan Svensson. Trainer: Lars Arnesson.
**POR:** Manuel Galrinho Bento, Gabriel Azevedo Mendes, Carlos António Fonseca Simões, Eurico Monteiro Gomes, Minervino José Lopes Pietra, Shéu Han, Carlos Manuel Correia dos Santos, João António Ferreira Resende Alves (65.António Augusto Gomes de Silva „Sousa"), José Alberto Costa, Tamagnini Manuel Gomes Baptista „Nené" (Cap), Manuel José Tavares Fernandes (58.Fernando Albino de Sousa Chalana). Trainer: Júlio Cernadas Pereira „Juca".
**Goals**: 1-0 Bo Börjesson (39), 2-0 Glenn Ingvar Hysén (58), 3-0 Jan Svensson (73).

09.09.1981, Hampden Park, Glasgow; Attendance: 81,511
Referee: André Daina (Switzerland)
**SCOTLAND - SWEDEN** 2-0(1-0)
**SCO:** Alan Roderick Rough, Daniel Fergus McGrain (Cap), Francis Tierney Gray, Alan David Hansen, Alexander McLeish, David Alexander Provan, John Wark, Richard Asa Hartford, John Neilson Robertson, Kenneth Mathieson Dalglish (70.Andrew Mullen Gray), Joseph Jordan. Manager: John Stein.
**SWE:** Thomas Ravelli, Stig Fredriksson (46.Greger Hallén), Glenn Ingvar Hysén, Bo Börjesson, Andreas Ravelli, Ingemar Erlandsson, Hans Borg, Karl-Gunnar Björklund, Thomas Larsson, Jan Svensson(Tommy Holmgren), Thomas Sjöberg. Trainer: Lars Arnesson.
**Goals**: 1-0 Joseph Jordan (20), 2-0 John Neilson Robertson (83 penalty).

14.10.1981, Estádio da Luz, Lisboa; Attendance: 75,000
Referee: Ronald Bridges (Wales)
**PORTUGAL – SWEDEN** 1-2(0-1)
**POR:** Manuel Galrinho Bento (46.António Jorge Rodrigues Amaral), Gabriel Azevedo Mendes, Humberto Manuel de Jesus Coelho (Cap), Eurico Monteiro Gomes, Minervino José Lopes Pietra, Shéu Han, Carlos Manuel Correia dos Santos, Romeu Fernando Fernandes da Silva, Fernando Albino de Sousa Chalana (16.José Alberto Costa), Tamagnini Manuel Gomes Baptista „Nené", Rui Manuel Trindade Jordão. Trainer: Júlio Cernadas Pereira „Juca".
**SWE:** Thomas Ravelli, Greger Hallén, Glenn Ingvar Hysén, Andreas Ravelli (85.Tony Persson), Ingemar Erlandsson (Cap), Bo Börjesson, Hans Borg, Karl-Gunnar Björklund, Thomas Larsson, Sören Börjesson (76.Peter Nilsson), Tommy Holmgren. Trainer: Lars Arnesson.
**Goals**: 0-1 Thomas Larsson (39), 1-1 Minervino José Lopes Pietra (64), 1-2 Tony Persson (89).

14.10.1981, Windsor Park, Belfast; Attendance: 22,248
Referee: Valeriy Butenko (Soviet Union)
**NORTHERN IRELAND – SCOTLAND** 0-0
**NIR:** Patrick Anthony Jennings, James Michael Nicholl, Christopher James Nicholl, John Patrick O'Neill, Malachy Martin Donaghy, Martin Hugh Michael O'Neill, Samuel Baxter McIlroy, David McCreery, Gerard Joseph Armstrong, William Robert Hamilton, Noel Brotherston. Manager: William Laurence Bingham.
**SCO:** Alan Roderick Rough, Raymond Strean McDonald Stewart, Francis Tierney Gray, William Fergus Miller, Alan David Hansen, Gordon David Strachan, Graeme James Souness (76.Andrew Mullen Gray), Richard Asa Hartford (Cap), John Neilson Robertson, Kenneth Mathieson Dalglish, Steven Archibald. Manager: John Stein.

28.10.1981, National Stadium, Ramat-Gan, Tel Aviv; Attendance: 25,000
Referee: Sotos Afxentiou (Cyprus)
**ISRAEL - PORTUGAL** 4-1(4-1)
**ISR:** Yossi Mizrahi (30.Arie Haviv), Gadi Machnes, Haim Bar, Avi Cohen I, Yaacov Cohen, Uri Malmilian (Rifat Turk), Yaacov Ekhoiz, Itzhak Shum, Moshe Gariani, Gideon Damti, Beni Tabak. Trainer: Jack Mansell (England).
**POR:** António Jorge Rodrigues Amaral, Gabriel Azevedo Mendes, Humberto Manuel de Jesus Coelho (Cap) (46.Eduardo José Gomes Camassels Mendes „Dito"), Eurico Monteiro Gomes, Adelino de Jesus Teixeira, António Augusto Gomes de Silva „Sousa", Rodolfo dos Reis Ferreira, Romeu Fernando Fernandes da Silva, Manuel José Tavares Fernandes, Rui Manuel Trindade Jordão, Carlos Manuel da Silva Freire (46.Tamagnini Manuel Gomes Baptista „Nené"). Trainer: Júlio Cernadas Pereira „Juca".
**Goals**: 1-0 Beni Tabak (6), 1-1 Rui Manuel Trindade Jordão (8), 2-1 Gideon Damti (14), 3-1 Beni Tabak (18), 4-1 Beni Tabak (30).

18.11.1981, Windsor Park, Belfast; Attendance: 40,000
Referee: Emilio Carlos Guruceta Muro (Spain)
**NORTHERN IRELAND - ISRAEL** **1-0(1-0)**
**NIR:** Patrick Anthony Jennings, James Michael Nicholl, Christopher James Nicholl, John Patrick O'Neill, Malachy Martin Donaghy, David McCreery, Thomas Cassidy, Samuel Baxter McIlroy, Gerard Joseph Armstrong, William Robert Hamilton, Noel Brotherston. Manager: William Laurence Bingham.
**ISR:** Arie Haviv, Gadi Machnes, Haim Bar, Avi Cohen I, Yaacov Cohen, Uri Malmilian, Yaacov Ekhoiz, Itzhak Shum, Beni Lam (64.Moshe Sinai), Gideon Damti, Beni Tabak. Trainer: Jack Mansell (England).
**Goal**: 1-0 Gerard Joseph Armstrong (27).

18.11.1981, Estádio da Luz, Lisboa; Attendance: 25,000
Referee: Charles George Rainier Corver (Holland)
**PORTUGAL - SCOTLAND** **2-1(1-1)**
**POR:** Manuel Galrinho Bento (Cap), Carlos António Fonseca Simões, Gregório Francisco Penteado Freixo (50.António Augusto da Silva Veloso), Eurico Monteiro Gomes, Adelino de Jesus Teixeira, Eduardo José Gomes Camassels Mendes „Dito", Jaime Fernandes Magalhães (46.Diamantino Manuel Fernandes Miranda), Romeu Fernando Fernandes da Silva, António Luís Alves Ribeiro Oliveira, Manuel José Tavares Fernandes, José Alberto Costa. Trainer: Júlio Cernadas Pereira „Juca".
**SCO:** William Thomson, Raymond Strean McDonald Stewart, Francis Tierney Gray (42.Stuart Robert Kennedy), William Fergus Miller, Alan David Hansen, David Alexander Provan, Graeme James Souness, Richard Asa Hartford (Cap), Gordon David Strachan, Paul Whitehead Sturrock, Steven Archibald (65.Kenneth Mathieson Dalglish). Manager: John Stein.
**Goals**: 0-1 Paul Whitehead Sturrock (9), 1-1 Manuel José Tavares Fernandes (33), 2-1 Manuel José Tavares Fernandes (56).

# GROUP 7

| | | | | |
|---|---|---|---|---|
| 07.12.1980 | La Valletta | Malta - Poland | | 0-2(0-0) |
| 04.04.1981 | La Valletta | Malta - East Germany | | 1-2(1-2) |
| 02.05.1981 | Chorzów | Poland - East Germany | | 1-0(0-0) |
| 10.10.1981 | Leipzig | East Germany - Poland | | 2-3(0-2) |
| 11.11.1981 | Jena | East Germany - Malta | | 5-1(2-1) |
| 15.11.1981 | Wroclaw | Poland - Malta | | 6-0(1-0) |

## FINAL STANDINGS

| | | | | | | | | |
|---|---|---|---|---|---|---|---|---|
| 1. | Poland | 4 | 4 | 0 | 0 | 12 - 2 | | 8 |
| 2. | East Germany | 4 | 2 | 0 | 2 | 9 - 6 | | 4 |
| 3. | Malta | 4 | 0 | 0 | 4 | 2 - 15 | | 0 |

Poland qualified for the Final Tournament.

07.12.1980, Empire Stadium, Gzira; Attendance: 5,565
Referee: Dušan Maksimović (Yugoslavia)
**MALTA - POLAND** **0-2(0-0)***
**MLT:** John Bonello, John Holland (Cap), Edwin Farrugia, Emanuel Farrugia, Norman Buttigieg, Dennis Fenech, John Curmi (50.Leonard Farrugia), Emanuel Leli Fabri, Ernest Spiteri-Gonzi, Joseph Xuereb, George Xuereb. Trainer: Victor Scerri.
**POL:** Piotr Mowlik, Ryszard Milewski, Paweł Janas, Piotr Skrobowski, Wojciech Rudy, Leszek Lipka, Marek Dziuba (Cap), Włodzimierz Ciołek, Andrzej Pałasz, Andrzej Iwan, Włodzimierz Smolarek. Trainer: Ryszard Kulesza.
Goals: 0-1 Włodzimierz Smolarek (57), 0-2 Leszek Lipka (77).
*Match abandoned in the 78$^{th}$ minute. Degeorgio was about to enter the pitch at the time of the abandonment in place of Spiteri-Gonzi.*

04.04.1981, Empire Stadium, Gzira; Attendance: 3,873
Referee: Peter Geoffrey Reeves (England)
**MALTA - EAST GERMANY** **1-2(1-2)**
**MLT:** John Bonello, Edwin Farrugia, Albert Carter-Mizzi (46.Raymond Xuereb), John Holland (Cap), Norman Buttigieg, Emanuel Leli Fabri, Joseph Xuereb, Emanuel Farrugia, George Xuereb, Michael Degiorgio, Ernest Spiteri-Gonzi. Trainer: Victor Scerri.
**DDR:** Hans-Ulrich Grapenthin, Hans-Jürgen Dörner (Cap), Artur Ullrich (46.Dieter Strozniak), Rüdiger Schnuphase, Michael Noack, Reinhard Häfner, Wolfgang Steinbach, Matthias Liebers, Wolf-Rüdiger Netz, Joachim Streich, Martin Hoffmann. Trainer: Georg Buschner.
Goals: 1-0 Emanuel Leli Fabri (11), 1-1 Rüdiger Schnuphase (20 penalty), 1-2 Reinhard Häfner (44).

02.05.1981, Stadion Śląski, Chorzów; Attendance: 80,000
Referee: Vojtěch Christov (Czechoslovakia)
**POLAND - EAST GERMANY** **1-0(0-0)**
**POL:** Jan Tomaszewski, Paweł Janas, Władysław Żmuda, Marek Dziuba (Cap), Jan Jałocha, Janusz Kupcewicz, Andrzej Buncol, Grzegorz Lato, Andrzej Iwan (80.Piotr Skrobowski), Andrzej Szarmach, Włodzimierz Smolarek. Trainer: Antoni Piechniczek.
**DDR:** Hans-Ulrich Grapenthin, Hans-Jürgen Dörner (Cap), Dieter Strozniak, Udo Schmuck, Lothar Kurbjuweit, Reinhard Häfner, Rüdiger Schnuphase, Wolfgang Steinbach, Hans-Jürgen Riediger, Joachim Streich (70.Matthias Liebers), Martin Hoffmann (63.Andreas Bielau). Trainer: Georg Buschner.
Goal: 1-0 Andrzej Buncol (56).

10.10.1981, Zentralstadion, Leipzig; Attendance: 85,000
Referee: Augusto Lamo Castillo (Spain)
**EAST GERMANY - POLAND**                                          **2-3(0-2)**
**DDR:** Hans-Ulrich Grapenthin, Hans-Jürgen Dörner (Cap), Konrad Weise, Rüdiger Schnuphase, Jürgen Pommerenke (46.Wolfgang Steinbach), Lothar Kurbjuweit, Matthias Liebers, Frank Baum, Hans-Jürgen Riediger, Joachim Streich, Martin Trocha. Trainer: Georg Buschner.
**POL:** Józef Młynarczyk, Marek Dziuba (Cap) (65.Roman Wójcicki), Władysław Żmuda, Paweł Janas, Jan Jałocha, Stefan Majewski, Waldemar Matysik, Zbigniew Boniek, Grzegorz Lato, Andrzej Szarmach (9.Andrzej Iwan), Włodzimierz Smolarek. Trainer: Antoni Piechniczek.
**Goals:** 0-1 Andrzej Szarmach (2), 0-2 Włodzimierz Smolarek (5), 1-2 Rüdiger Schnuphase (57 penalty), 1-3 Włodzimierz Smolarek (62), 2-3 Joachim Streich (67).

11.11.1981, „Ernst Abbe" Stadion, Jena; Attendance: 2,000
Referee: Frederick McKnight (Northern Ireland)
**EAST GERMANY - MALTA**                                     **5-1(2-1)**
**DDR:** Bodo Rudwaleit, Rüdiger Schnuphase (Cap), Artur Ullrich, Rainer Troppa, Frank Baum, Matthias Liebers, Andreas Krause, Wolfgang Steinbach (79.Rainer Ernst), Andreas Bielau (59.Jürgen Heun), Joachim Streich, Martin Trocha. Trainer: Georg Buschner.
**MLT:** John Bonello, Constantino Consiglio (49.Mario Farrugia), Edwin Farrugia, John Holland (Cap), Norman Buttigieg, Emanuel Leli Fabri, Emanuel Farrugia, Joseph Xuereb, Ernest Spiteri-Gonzi, Raymond Xuereb, Dennis Fenech (83.Michael Degiorgio). Trainer: Victor Scerri
**Goals:** 1-0 Andreas Krause (11), 2-0 Joachim Streich (35), 2-1 Ernest Spiteri-Gonzi (41), 3-1 Joachim Streich (75), 4-1 Jürgen Heun (71), 5-1 John Holland (90 own goal).

15.11.1981, Stadion Olimpijski, Wrocław; Attendance: 25,000
Referee: Bo Helén (Sweden)
**POLAND - MALTA**                                                      **6-0(1-0)**
**POL:** Piotr Mowlik, Stefan Majewski, Władysław Żmuda (Cap), Jan Jałocha, Tadeusz Dolny, Waldemar Matysik (68.Andrzej Pałasz), Zbigniew Boniek, Andrzej Buncol, Włodzimierz Smolarek (68.Dariusz Dziekanowski), Andrzej Iwan, Mirosław Okoński. Trainer: Antoni Piechniczek.
**MLT:** Charles Sciberras, Emanuel Farrugia, Edwin Farrugia, John Holland (Cap), Norman Buttigieg, Emanuel Leli Fabri, Mario Farrugia, Joseph Xuereb, Ernest Spiteri-Gonzi, Raymond Xuereb, Dennis Fenech. Trainer: Victor Scerri.
**Goals:** 1-0 Andrzej Buncol (6), 2-0 Włodzimierz Smolarek (47), 3-0 Stefan Majewski (48), 4-0 Włodzimierz Smolarek (64), 5-0 Dariusz Dziekanowski (80), 6-0 Zbigniew Boniek (88).

# SOUTH AMERICA

## GROUP 1

| | | | | |
|---|---|---|---|---|
| 08.02.1981 | Caracas | Venezuela - Brazil | | 0-1(0-0) |
| 15.02.1981 | La Paz | Bolivia - Venezuela | | 3-0(1-0) |
| 22.02.1981 | La Paz | Bolivia - Brazil | | 1-2(1-1) |
| 15.03.1981 | Caracas | Venezuela - Bolivia | | 1-0(1-0) |
| 22.03.1981 | Rio de Janeiro | Brazil - Bolivia | | 3-1(1-0) |
| 29.03.1981 | Goiânia | Brazil - Venezuela | | 5-0(1-0) |

### FINAL STANDINGS

| | | | | | | | | |
|---|---|---|---|---|---|---|---|---|
| 1. **Brazil** | 4 | 4 | 0 | 0 | 11 | - | 2 | 8 |
| 2. Bolivia | 4 | 1 | 0 | 3 | 5 | - | 6 | 2 |
| 3. Venezuela | 4 | 1 | 0 | 3 | 1 | - | 9 | 2 |

Brazil qualified for the Final Tournament.

08.02.1981, Estadio Olímpico „Ciudad Universitaria", Caracas; Attendance: 35,000
Referee: Ramón Ivannoe Barreto Ruíz (Uruguay)
**VENEZUELA - BRAZIL**     **0-1(0-0)**
**VEN:** Vicente Emilio Vega, Omar Ochoa, Pedro Castro (Cap) (Nicolás Simonelli), Pedro Javier Acosta Sánchez, Emilio Campos Rodríguez, Carlos Enrique Marín, Ramón Echenáusi, Oscar Torres, Juan José Scarpeccio Sabattini, Iván García, Julio César Hernández (Ángel de Jesús Castillo). Trainer: José Walter Roque (Uruguay).
**BRA:** Valdir de Arruda Peres, Edevaldo de Freitas, José Oscar Bernardi, Luís Carlos Quintanilha "Luisinho", Leovegildo Lins Gama Júnior "Júnior I", João Batista da Silva, Antônio Carlos Cerezo "Toninho Cerezo", Arthur Antunes Coimbra "Zico", Paulo Isidoro de Jesus, Sérgio Bernardino "Serginho I", José Sérgio Presti "Zé Sérgio". Trainer: Telê Santana da Silva.
**Goal:** 0-1 Arthur Antunes Coimbra "Zico" (83 penalty).
**Sent off:** José Sérgio Presti "Zé Sérgio" (31), Paulo Isidoro de Jesus (83).

15.02.1981, Estadio „Hernándo Siles Zuazo", La Paz; Attendance: 40,000
Referee: Juan Francisco Escobar Váldez (Paraguay)
**BOLIVIA - VENEZUELA**     **3-0(1-0)**
**BOL:** Carlos Conrado Jiménez Hurtado, Juan Carlos Trigo, Edgar Vaca Barbosa, Erwin Espinoza, Windsor Del Llano Suárez, Carlos Fernando Borja, Eduardo Angulo Torme, Carlos Aragonés Espinosa, Erwin Romero Escudero, Gastón Taborga (32.Jesús Reynaldo Hurtado), Miguel Aguilar. Trainer: Ramiro Blacutt Rodríguez.
**VEN:** Vicente Emilio Vega, Omar Ochoa, Pedro Castro, Pedro Javier Acosta Sánchez, Emilio Campos Rodríguez, Juan José Scarpeccio Sabattini (69.Ordán Ramón Aguirre), Oscar Torres, Asdrúbal José Sánchez Urbina, Ángel de Jesús Castillo, Iván García, William Castillo (90.Vicente Flores). Trainer: José Walter Roque (Uruguay).
**Goals:** 1-0 Miguel Aguilar (38), 2-0 Carlos Aragonés Espinosa (67), 3-0 Jesús Reynaldo Hurtado (84).
**Sent off:** Eduardo Angulo Torme (83) / Ángel de Jesús Castillo (83).

22.02.1981, Estadio „Hernándo Siles Zuazo", La Paz; Attendance: 40,000
Referee: Enrique Lobo Revoredo (Peru)
**BOLIVIA - BRAZIL**                                                                                 **1-2(1-1)**
**BOL**: Carlos Conrado Jiménez Hurtado, Juan Carlos Trigo, Edgar Vaca Barbosa, Erwin Espinoza (67.Silvio Rojas), Windsor Del Llano Suárez, Carlos Fernando Borja, Johnny Villarroel Delgadillo (16.Aldo Fierro Banegas), Carlos Aragonés Espinosa, Erwin Romero Escudero, Jesús Reynaldo Hurtado, Miguel Aguilar. Trainer: Ramiro Blacutt Rodríguez.
**BRA**: Valdir de Arruda Peres, Edevaldo de Freitas, José Oscar Bernardi, Luís Carlos Quintanilha "Luisinho" (Édino Nazareth Filho "Edinho"), Leovegildo Lins Gama Júnior "Júnior I", Antônio Carlos Cerezo "Toninho Cerezo", Arthur Antunes Coimbra "Zico", Sócrates Brasileiro Sampaio Vieira de Oliveira, Mílton Queiroz da Paixão "Tita" (João Batista da Silva I), José Reinaldo da Lima "Reinaldo I", Éder Aleixo de Assis. Trainer: Telê Santana da Silva.
**Goals**: 0-1 Sócrates Brasileiro Sampaio Vieira de Oliveira (6), 1-1 Carlos Aragonés Espinosa (27), 1-2 José Reinaldo da Lima "Reinaldo I" (60).
**Sent off**: Antônio Carlos Cerezo "Toninho Cerezo" (63).

15.03.1981, Estadio Olímpico „Ciudad Universitaria", Caracas; Attendance: 25,000
Referee: Elías Victoriano Jácome Guerreiro (Ecuador)
**VENEZUELA - BOLIVIA**                                               **1-0(1-0)**
**VEN**: Vicente Emilio Vega, William Salas, Pedro Castro, Pedro Javier Acosta Sánchez, Emilio Campos Rodríguez, Carlos Enrique Marín (59.Ordán Ramón Aguirre), Víctor Filomeno, Pedro Juan Febles, Félix Gutiérrez, Iván García, Mario Luis Bosetti (51.William Castillo). Trainer: José Walter Roque (Uruguay).
**BOL**: Carlos Conrado Jiménez Hurtado, Juan Carlos Trigo, Edgar Vaca Barbosa, Erwin Espinoza, Windsor Del Llano Suárez, Carlos Fernando Borja, Johnny Villarroel Delgadillo, Carlos Aragonés Espinosa (75.José Milton Melgar), Erwin Romero Escudero (85.Jorge Camacho), Gastón Taborga, Miguel Aguilar. Trainer: José Saldanha.
**Goal**: 1-0 Pedro Javier Acosta Sánchez (24).

22.03.1981, Estádio „Jornalista Mário Filho" (Maracanã), Rio de Janeiro; Attendance: 121,750
Referee: Gastón Edmundo Castro Makuc (Chile)
**BRAZIL - BOLIVIA**                                                         **3-1(1-0)**
**BRA**: Valdir de Arruda Peres, Edevaldo de Freitas, José Oscar Bernardi, Luís Carlos Quintanilha "Luisinho", Leovegildo Lins Gama Júnior "Júnior I", João Batista da Silva, Sócrates Brasileiro Sampaio Vieira de Oliveira, Arthur Antunes Coimbra "Zico", Mílton Queiroz da Paixão "Tita" (70.José Sérgio Presti "Zé Sérgio"), José Reinaldo da Lima "Reinaldo I", Éder Aleixo de Assis. Trainer: Telê Santana da Silva.
**BOL**: Carlos Conrado Jiménez Hurtado, Juan Carlos Trigo, Edgar Vaca Barbosa, Erwin Espinoza, Windsor Del Llano Suárez, Luis González, Johnny Villarroel Delgadillo, Carlos Aragonés Espinosa, Erwin Romero Escudero, Gastón Taborga (46.Carlos Fernando Borja), Miguel Aguilar. Trainer: José Saldanha.
**Goals**: 1-0 Arthur Antunes Coimbra "Zico" (26 penalty), 2-0 Arthur Antunes Coimbra "Zico" (53), 2-1 Carlos Aragonés Espinosa (67), 3-1 Arthur Antunes Coimbra "Zico" (85).

29.03.1981, Estádio Serra Dourada, Goiânia; Attendance: 35,000
Referee: Jorge Eduardo Romero (Argentina)
**BRAZIL - VENEZUELA**     **5-0(1-0)**
**BRA:** Valdir de Arruda Peres, Getúlio Costa de Oliveira, José Oscar Bernardi, Luís Carlos Quintanilha "Luisinho", Leovegildo Lins Gama Júnior "Júnior I", João Batista da Silva, Sócrates Brasileiro Sampaio Vieira de Oliveira, Arthur Antunes Coimbra "Zico", Mílton Queiroz da Paixão "Tita", José Reinaldo da Lima "Reinaldo I" (60.Sérgio Bernardino "Serginho I"), Éder Aleixo de Assis (50.José Sérgio Presti "Zé Sérgio"). Trainer: Telê Santana da Silva.
**VEN:** Vicente Emilio Vega, Omar Ochoa, Pedro Castro, Pedro Javier Acosta Sánchez, William Salas, Nelson José Carrero Heras (60.Ordán Ramón Aguirre), Oscar Torres, Víctor Filomeno, Félix Gutiérrez (65.William Castillo), Iván García, Pedro Juan Febles. Trainer: José Walter Roque (Uruguay).
**Goals:** 1-0 Mílton Queiroz da Paixão "Tita" (35), 2-0 Sócrates Brasileiro Sampaio Vieira de Oliveira (55), 3-0 Mílton Queiroz da Paixão "Tita" (57), 4-0 Arthur Antunes Coimbra "Zico" (72), 5-0 Leovegildo Lins Gama Júnior "Júnior I" (84 penalty).

## GROUP 2

| | | | | |
|---|---|---|---|---|
| 26.07.1981 | Bogotá | Colombia - Peru | 1-1(0-0) |
| 09.08.1981 | Montevideo | Uruguay - Colombia | 3-2(1-1) |
| 16.08.1981 | Lima | Peru - Colombia | 2-0(1-0) |
| 23.08.1981 | Montevideo | Uruguay - Peru | 1-2(0-2) |
| 06.09.1981 | Lima | Peru - Uruguay | 0-0 |
| 13.09.1981 | Bogotá | Colombia - Uruguay | 1-1(1-1) |

### FINAL STANDINGS

| | | | | | | | | |
|---|---|---|---|---|---|---|---|---|
| 1. | **Peru** | 4 | 2 | 2 | 0 | 5 - 2 | 6 |
| 2. | Uruguay | 4 | 1 | 2 | 1 | 5 - 5 | 4 |
| 3. | Colombia | 4 | 0 | 2 | 2 | 4 - 7 | 2 |

Peru qualified for the Final Tournament.

26.07.1981, Estadio „Nemesio Camacho" 'El Campín', Bogotá; Attendance: 60,000
Referee: Arturo Andrés Ithurralde (Argentina)
**COLOMBIA - PERU**     **1-1(0-0)**
**COL:** Pedro Antonio Zape, Jorge Armando Porras, Francisco Maturana, Astolfo Romero, Fernando Castro, Rafael Otero (68.Angel María Torres Laso), César Frederico Arca Valverde (82.Rafael de Jesús Agudelo), Juan Edgardo Caicedo Vargas, Willington José Ortíz, Eduardo Emilio Vilarete, Hernán Darío Herrera. Trainer: Dr. Carlos Salvador Bilardo (Argentina).
**PER:** Ramón Quiroga Arancibia, Jaime Eduardo Duarte Huerta, Rubén Toribio Díaz Rivas, Héctor Eduardo Chumpitaz González, Roberto Rojas Tardío, José Manuel Velásquez Castillo (73.Jorge Andrés Olaechea Quijandría), César Augusto Cueto Villa, Julio César Uribe Flores (63.Guillermo La Rosa Laguna), Gerónimo Barbadillo González, Teófilo Juan Cubillas Arizaga, Juan Carlos Oblitas Saba. Trainer: Elba de Padua Lima "Tim" (Brazil).
**Goals**: 1-0 Hernán Darío Herrera (64), 1-1 Guillermo La Rosa Laguna (86).

09.08.1981, Estadio Centenario, Montevideo; Attendance: 71,000
Referee: Oscar Scolfaro (Brazil)
**URUGUAY - COLOMBIA**     **3-2(1-1)**
**URU:** Rodolfo Sergio Rodríguez, José Hermes Moreira, Juan Carlos Blanco, Hugo Eduardo De León, Daniel Martínez, Eduardo De la Peña (60.Jorge Wálter Barrios Balestrasse), Ariel José Krasouski, Rúben Walter Paz Márquez, Ernesto Vargas, Julio César Araújo Morales, Waldemar Barreto Victorino. Trainer: Roque Gastón Máspoli.
**COL:** Pedro Antonio Zape, Jorge Armando Porras, Francisco Maturana, Astolfo Romero, Fernando Castro, Rafael Otero (79.Juan Edgardo Caicedo Vargas), Angel María Torres Laso, César Frederico Arce Valverde, Pedro Enrique Sarmiento Solís, Willington José Ortíz (71.Diego Edison Umaña), Hernán Darío Herrera. Trainer: Dr. Carlos Salvador Bilardo (Argentina).
**Goals:** 1-0 Rúben Walter Paz Márquez (20), 1-1 Pedro Enrique Sarmiento Solís (41), 1-2 Hernán Darío Herrera (59), 2-2 Julio César Araújo Morales (78), 3-2 Julio César Araújo Morales (87 penalty).

16.08.1981, Estadio Nacional, Lima; Attendance: 43,942
Referee: Vicente Llobregat Vicedo (Venezuela)
**PERU - COLOMBIA**     **2-0(1-0)**
**PER:** Ramón Quiroga Arancibia, Jaime Eduardo Duarte Huerta, Rubén Toribio Díaz Rivas, Héctor Eduardo Chumpitaz González, Roberto Rojas Tardío, José Manuel Velásquez Castillo (69.Jorge Andrés Olaechea Quijandría), César Augusto Cueto Villa, Julio César Uribe Flores, Gerónimo Barbadillo González, Guillermo La Rosa Laguna, Juan Carlos Oblitas Saba. Trainer: Elba de Padua Lima "Tim" (Brazil).
**COL:** Pedro Antonio Zape, Jorge Armando Porras, Francisco Maturana, Luis Eduardo Reyes, Fernando Castro, Rafael Otero, Angel María Torres Laso, César Frederico Arce Valverde (55.Juan Edgardo Caicedo Vargas), Pedro Enrique Sarmiento Solís (46.Eduardo Emilio Vilarete), Willington José Ortíz, Hernán Darío Herrera. Trainer: Dr. Carlos Salvador Bilardo (Argentina).
**Goals:** 1-0 Gerónimo Barbadillo González (7), 2-0 Julio César Uribe Flores (71 penalty).
**Sent off:** Rafael Otero (72).

23.08.1981, Estadio Centenario, Montevideo; Attendance: 67,938
Referee: Juan Ambrosio Silvagno Cavanna (Chile)
**URUGUAY - PERU**     **1-2(0-2)**
**URU:** Rodolfo Sergio Rodríguez, José Hermes Moreira, Juan Carlos Blanco, Hugo Eduardo De León, Daniel Martínez, Jorge Wálter Barrios Balestrasse (50.Eduardo De la Peña), Ariel José Krasouski, Rúben Walter Paz Márquez, Ernesto Vargas (53.Heber Bueno), Waldemar Barreto Victorino, Julio Cesar Morales. Trainer: Roque Gastón Máspoli.
**PER:** Ramón Quiroga Arancibia, Jaime Eduardo Duarte Huerta, Rubén Toribio Díaz Rivas, Héctor Eduardo Chumpitaz González (Cap), Roberto Rojas Tardío, José Manuel Velásquez Castillo, César Augusto Cueto Villa, Julio César Uribe Flores, Gerónimo Barbadillo González, Guillermo La Rosa Laguna (60.Jorge Andrés Olaechea Quijandría), Juan Carlos Oblitas Saba. Trainer: Elba de Padua Lima "Tim" (Brazil).
**Goals:** 0-1 Guillermo La Rosa Laguna (40), 0-2 Julio César Uribe Flores (47), 1-2 Waldemar Barreto Victorino (64).

06.09.1981, Estadio Nacional, Lima; Attendance: 45,000
Referee: Arnaldo David César Coelho (Brazil)
**PERU - URUGUAY** **0-0**
**PER:** Ramón Quiroga Arancibia, Jaime Eduardo Duarte Huerta, Rubén Toribio Díaz Rivas, Héctor Eduardo Chumpitaz González (Cap), Roberto Rojas Tardío, José Manuel Velásquez Castillo, César Augusto Cueto Villa, Julio César Uribe Flores, Gerónimo Barbadillo González, Guillermo La Rosa Laguna, Juan Carlos Oblitas Saba (67.Jorge Andrés Olaechea Quijandría). Trainer: Elba de Padua Lima "Tim" (Brazil).
**URU:** Rodolfo Sergio Rodríguez, José Hermes Moreira, Juan Carlos Blanco, Hugo Eduardo De León, Daniel Martínez, Jorge Wálter Barrios Balestrasse (60.Julio César Araújo Morales), Eduardo De la Peña, Nelson Agresta (73.Ariel José Krasouski), Rúben Walter Paz Márquez, Heber Bueno, Waldemar Barreto Victorino. Trainer: Roque Gastón Máspoli.

13.09.1981, Estadio „Nemesio Camacho" 'El Campín', Bogotá; Attendance: 10,000
Referee: José Roberto Ramiz Wright (Brazil)
**COLOMBIA - URUGUAY** **1-1(1-1)**
**COL:** Carlos Valencia, Ever González, Luis Eduardo Reyes (64.Germán Morales), Miguel Augusto Prince, Fernando Castro, Angel María Torres Laso, César Frederico Arce Valverde, Felix Pedro Enrique Sarmiento Solís (72.Juan Edgardo Caicedo Vargas), Diego Edison Umaña, Rafael de Jesús Agudelo, Hernán Darío Herrera. Trainer: Dr. Carlos Salvador Bilardo (Argentina)..
**URU:** Rodolfo Sergio Rodríguez, José Hermes Moreira, Nelson Marcenaro, Juan Carlos Blanco, Daniel Martínez (58.Washington González), Jorge Wálter Barrios Balestrasse, Ariel José Krasouski (46.José Luis Russo), Rúben Walter Paz Márquez, Ernesto Vargas, Heber Bueno, Waldemar Barreto Victorino. Trainer: Roque Gastón Máspoli.
**Goals:** 0-1 Hernán Darío Herrera (12 penalty), 1-1 Waldemar Barreto Victorino (43).

## GROUP 3

| | | | | |
|---|---|---|---|---|
| 17.05.1981 | Guayaquil | Ecuador - Paraguay | 1-0(0-0) |
| 24.05.1981 | Guayaquil | Ecuador - Chile | 0-0 |
| 31.05.1981 | Asunción | Paraguay - Ecuador | 3-1(0-0) |
| 07.06.1981 | Asunción | Paraguay - Chile | 0-1(0-0) |
| 14.06.1981 | Santiago | Chile - Ecuador | 2-0(1-0) |
| 21.06.1981 | Santiago | Chile - Paraguay | 3-0(3-0) |

### FINAL STANDINGS

| | | | | | | | | |
|---|---|---|---|---|---|---|---|---|
| 1. | Chile | 4 | 3 | 1 | 0 | 6 - 0 | 7 |
| 2. | Ecuador | 4 | 1 | 1 | 2 | 2 - 5 | 3 |
| 3. | Paraguay | 4 | 1 | 0 | 3 | 3 - 6 | 2 |

Chile qualified for the Final Tournament.

17.05.1981, Estadio Modelo, Guayaquil; Attendance: 55,000
Referee: Luis Barrancos Alvarez (Bolivia)
**ECUADOR - PARAGUAY** **1-0(0-0)**
**ECU:** Carlos Omar Delgado, Flavio Perlaza, Ecuador Figueroa (46.Orly Klinger), José Francisco Paes, Digner Valencia, José Voltaire Villafuerte, Belford Parraga, Paúl Carrera (79.Fabian Vicente Burbano), Mario Tenorio, Lupo Senén Quiñónez, Wilson Nieves. Trainer: Juan Eduardo Hohberg (Uruguay).
**PAR:** Ever Hugo Almeida Almada, Alicio Ignacio Solalinde Miers, Roberto Rubén Paredes Vera, Flaminio Sosa Ovelar, Juan Bautista Torales, Aldo Andrés Florentín (46.Carlos Alberto Kiese), Adolfo Gustavo Benítez Bentos, Julio César Romero Insfrán, Evaristo Isasi Colmán, Carlos Diarte Martínez, Osvaldo Aquino (60.Julio Juan Díaz Rodríguez). Trainer: José Francisco Sasía (Uruguay).
**Goal:** 1-0 Orly Klinger (48).

24.05.1981, Estadio Modelo, Guayaquil; Attendance: 55,000
Referee: Juan Daniel Cardellino de San Vicente (Uruguay)
**ECUADOR - CHILE** **0-0**
**ECU:** Carlos Omar Delgado, Flavio Perlaza, Orly Klinger, José Francisco Paes, Digner Valencia, José Voltaire Villafuerte, Belford Parraga, Paúl Carrera (33.Gorky Eugenio Revelo), Mario Tenorio, Lupo Senén Quiñónez, Wilson Nieves (42.José Fabián Pazymiño). Trainer: Juan Eduardo Hohberg (Uruguay).
**CHI:** Mario Ignacio Osbén Méndez, Lizardo Antonio Garrido Bustamante (33.Enzo Sergio Escobar Olivares), Eduardo René Valenzuela Becker, Mario del Transito Soto Benavides, Vladimir David Bigorra López, Carlos Humberto Rivas Torres, Rodolfo del Rosario Dubó Segovia, Eduardo Guillermo Bonvallet Godoy, Manuel Antonio Rojas Zuniga (42.Miguel Angel Neira Pincheira), Carlos Humberto Caszely Garrido, Gustavo Segundo Moscoso Huencho. Trainer: Oscar Luis Santibáñez Díaz.

31.05.1981, Estadio Defensores del Chaco, Asunción; Attendance: 37,000
Referee: Roque Tito Cerullo Giuliano (Uruguay)
**PARAGUAY - ECUADOR** **3-1(0-0)**
**PAR:** Ever Hugo Almeida Almada, Juan Gualberto Espínola, Roberto Rubén Paredes Vera, Secundino Aifuch Osorio, Juan Bautista Torales, Aldo Andrés Florentín, Adolfo Gustavo Benítez Bentos, Julio César Romero Insfrán, Evaristo Isasi Colmán, Carlos Diarte Martínez (46.Miguel María Michelagnoli Ayala), Eugenio Félix Morel Bogado (Carlos de los Santos Jara Saguier). Trainer: José Francisco Sasía (Uruguay).
**ECU:** Carlos Omar Delgado, Flavio Perlaza, Ecuador Figueroa, José Francisco Paes, Orly Klinger, Digner Valencia, Belford Parraga, Paúl Carrera, Mario Tenorio (63.Fabian Vicente Burbano), Lupo Senén Quiñónez, Wilson Nieves. Trainer: Juan Eduardo Hohberg (Uruguay).
**Goals:** 1-0 Miguel María Michelagnoli Ayala (47), 2-0 Eugenio Félix Morel Bogado (63), 3-0 Julio

César Romero Insfrán (81), 3-1 Wilson Nieves (89).

07.06.1981, Estadio Defensores del Chaco, Asunción; Attendance: 46,178
Referee: Carlos Espósito (Argentina)
**PARAGUAY - CHILE**　　　　　　　　　　　　　　　　　　　　**0-1(0-0)**
**PAR:** Ever Hugo Almeida Almada, Juan Gualberto Espínola, Roberto Rubén Paredes Vera, Secundino Aifuch Osorio, Juan Bautista Torales, Aldo Andrés Florentín, Adolfo Gustavo Benítez Bentos, Julio César Romero Insfrán, Evaristo Isasi Colmán, Miguel María Michelagnoli Ayala (Carlos Diarte Martínez), Eugenio Félix Morel Bogado (Roberto Cabañas González). Trainer: José Francisco Sasía (Uruguay)..
**CHI:** Mario Ignacio Osbén Méndez, Lizardo Antonio Garrido Bustamante, Eduardo René Valenzuela Becker, Elías Ricardo Figueroa Brander, Mario del Transito Soto Benavides, Vladimir David Bigorra López, Eduardo Guillermo Bonvallet Godoy (Miguel Angel Neira Pincheira), Rodolfo del Rosario Dubó Segovia, Gustavo Segundo Moscoso Huencho, Patricio Nazario Yáñez Candia (Manuel Antonio Rojas Zuniga), Sandrino Castec Martínez. Trainer: Oscar Luis Santibáñez Díaz.
**Goal**: 0-1 Patricio Nazario Yáñez Candia (71).

14.06.1981, Estadio Nacional, Santiago; Attendance: 72,290
Referee: Gilberto Aristizábal Murcia (Colombia)
**CHILE - ECUADOR**　　　　　　　　　　　　　　　　　　　　**2-0(1-0)**
**CHI:** Mario Ignacio Osbén Méndez, Lizardo Antonio Garrido Bustamante, Eduardo René Valenzuela Becker, Elías Ricardo Figueroa Brander, Vladimir David Bigorra López, Carlos Humberto Rivas Torres, Sandrino Castec Martínez (75.Rodolfo del Rosario Dubó Segovia), Manuel Antonio Rojas Zuniga, Patricio Nazario Yáñez Candia (81.Oscar Herrera Hernández), Carlos Humberto Caszely Garrido, Gustavo Segundo Moscoso Huencho. Trainer: Oscar Luis Santibáñez Díaz.
**ECU:** Carlos Omar Delgado, Flavio Perlaza, Ecuador Figueroa, José Francisco Paes, Orly Klinger, Digner Valencia, Belford Parraga, José Voltaire Villafuerte, Mario Tenorio, Lupo Senén Quiñónez, Wilson Nieves. Trainer: Juan Eduardo Hohberg (Uruguay).
**Goals**: 1-0 Carlos Humberto Rivas Torres (10), 2-0 Carlos Humberto Caszely Garrido (85).
**Sent off**: Digner Valencia (86).

21.06.1981, Estadio Nacional, Santiago; Attendance: 75,075
Referee: Romualdo Arrpi Filho (Brazil)
**CHILE - PARAGUAY**　　　　　　　　　　　　　　　　　　　　**3-0(3-0)**
**CHI:** Mario Ignacio Osbén Méndez, Lizardo Antonio Garrido Bustamante, Eduardo René Valenzuela Becker, Mario del Transito Soto Benavides, Vladimir David Bigorra López, Miguel Angel Neira Pincheira, Manuel Antonio Rojas Zuniga, Rodolfo del Rosario Dubó Segovia, Patricio Nazario Yáñez Candia (25.Oscar Herrera Hernández), Carlos Humberto Caszely Garrido, Gustavo Segundo Moscoso Huencho. Trainer: Oscar Luis Santibáñez Díaz.
**PAR:** Ever Hugo Almeida Almada, Alicio Ignacio Solalinde Miers, Roberto Rubén Paredes Vera, Secundino Aifuch Osorio, Juan Bautista Torales, Aldo Andrés Florentín, Adolfo Gustavo Benítez Bentos (87.Vladimiro Schettina Chepini), Francisco Rivera Miltos (82.Osvaldo Aquino), Carlos Alberto Kiese, Evaristo Isasi Colmán, Miguel María Michelagnoli Ayala. Trainer: José Francisco Sasía (Uruguay).
**Goals**: 1-0 Carlos Humberto Caszely Garrido (10), 2-0 Patricio Nazario Yáñez Candia (11), 3-0 Miguel Angel Neira Pincheira (28).

# NORTH, CENTRAL AMERICA & CARIBBEAN

## NORTH AMERICAN ZONE

| | | | |
|---|---|---|---|
| 18.10.1980 | Toronto | Canada - Mexico | 1-1(1-0) |
| 25.10.1980 | Fort Lauderdale | United States - Canada | 0-0 |
| 01.11.1980 | Vancouver | Canada - United States | 2-1(2-0) |
| 09.11.1980 | Ciudad de México | Mexico - United States | 5-1(4-0) |
| 16.11.1980 | Ciudad de México | Mexico - Canada | 1-1(0-0) |
| 23.11.1980 | Fort Lauderdale | United States - Mexico | 2-1(1-1) |

### FINAL STANDINGS

| | | | | | | | | |
|---|---|---|---|---|---|---|---|---|
| 1. Canada | 4 | 1 | 3 | 0 | 4 | - | 3 | 5 |
| 2. Mexico | 4 | 1 | 2 | 1 | 8 | - | 5 | 4 |
| 3. United States | 4 | 1 | 1 | 2 | 4 | - | 8 | 3 |

Canada and Mexico qualified for the CONCACAF Zone Final.

18.10.1980, Exhibition Stadium, Toronto; Attendance: 10,000
Referee: Luis Paulino Siles Calderón (Costa Rica)
**CANADA - MEXICO**     **1-1(1-0)**
**CAN:** Martino Lettieri, Robert Iarusci, Robert Bolitho (19.Mike McLenaghen; 77.Mike Sweeney), John McGrane, Robert Lenarduzzi, Gerard Gray, Eugene Strenicer, Wesley McLeod, Branko Segota, Momcilo Stojanovic, Dale William Mitchell. Trainer: Barrie Clarke.
**MEX:** Ignacio Rodríguez Bahena, Vinicio Bravo Fentanes, Alfredo Tena Garduño, Arturo Vázquez Ayala, Mario Alberto Trejo Guzmán, Alejandro Ramírez Monroy (64.Adrián Camacho Solís), Pedro Munguía Munguía, Guillermo Mendizábal Sánchez (64.Juan Antonio Luna Castro), Leonardo Cuéllar Rivera, Ricardo Castro Valenzuela, Hugo Sánchez Márquez. Trainer: Raúl Cárdenas de la Vega.
**Goals:** 1-0 Momcilo Stojanovic (44), 1-1 Juan Antonio Luna Castro (89).

25.10.1980, Lockhart Stadium, Fort Lauderdale; Attendance: 7,864
Referee: Tomas Herrera García (El Salvador)
**UNITED STATES - CANADA**     **0-0**
**USA:** Arnold Mausser, Colin Fowles, Tyrone Keough, Steve Pecher (Cap), Gregory Makowski, Ringo Julio Cantillo, Boris Bandov, Angelo di Bernardo, Richard Dean Davis, Louis Nanchoff (64.Njego Pesa), Mark Liveric (77.Steve Moyers). Trainer: Walter Chyzowich.
**CAN:** Martino Lettieri, Robert Iarusci, Robert Lenarduzzi, Momcilo Stojanovic, Eugene Strenicer, Randolph Lee Ragan, Tibor Gemeri (46.Mike Sweeney), John McGrane, Gerard Gray, Wesley McLeod, Dale William Mitchell. Trainer: Barrie Clarke.

01.11.1980, Empire Stadium, Vancouver; Attendance: 13,598
Referee: Romulo Méndez Molina (Guatemala)
**CANADA - UNITED STATES**     **2-1(2-0)**
**CAN:** Martino Lettieri, Robert Lenarduzzi, Momcilo Stojanovic, Wesley McLeod, Gerard Gray, John McGrane, Robert Bolitho (46.Mike Sweeney), Eugene Strenicer (15.Carmine Marcantonio), Branko Segota, Robert Iarusci, Bruce Miller. Trainer: Barrie Clarke.
**USA:** Arnold Mausser, Antonio Crudo, Tyrone Keough, Steve Pecher (Cap), Gregory Makowski, Boris Bandov, Ringo Julio Cantillo, Angelo di Bernardo, Njego Pesa (66.Gregory Villa), Richard Dean Davis, Mark Liveric (76.Steve Moyers). Trainer: Walter Chyzowich.
**Goals:** 1-0 Robert Iarusci (21), 2-0 Branko Segota (42 penalty), 2-1 Gregory Villa (90).

09.11.1980, Estadio Azteca, Ciudad de México; Attendance: 80,000
Referee: José Luis Valverde Salazar (Costa Rica)
**MEXICO - UNITED STATES** **5-1(4-0)**
**MEX:** Ignacio Rodríguez Bahena, Mario Alberto Trejo Guzmán, Alfredo Tena Garduño, Arturo Vázquez Ayala, José Luis López Sánchez, Pedro Munguía Munguía, Guillermo Mendizábal Sánchez (62.Juan Antonio Luna Castro), José Luis González II Alcate, Cristóbal Ortega Martínez, Adrián Camacho Solís, Hugo Sánchez Márquez. Trainer: Raúl Cárdenas de la Vega.
**USA:** Winston DuBose, Colin Fowles, Tyrone Keough, Steve Pecher (Cap), Gregory Makowski, Ringo Julio Cantillo (30.Laurence Hulcer), Angelo di Bernardo, Percival Joseph van der Beck, Richard Dean Davis, Louis Nanchoff, Gregory Villa (61.Njego Pesa). Trainer: Walter Chyzowich.
**Goals**: 1-0 Hugo Sánchez Márquez (24), 2-0 Adrián Camacho Solís (31), 3-0 Guillermo Mendizábal Sánchez (37), 4-0 José Luis González II Alcate (40), 5-0 Adrián Camacho Solís (55), 5-1 Richard Dean Davis (76 penalty).
**Sent off**: Gregory Makowski (74).

16.11.1980, Estadio Azteca, Ciudad de México; Attendance: 108,000
Referee: Cecilio Midence Torres (Honduras)
**MEXICO - CANADA** **1-1(0-0)**
**MEX:** Ignacio Rodríguez Bahena, Mario Alberto Trejo Guzmán (69.Rodolfo Montoya Villegas), Alfredo Tena Garduño, Arturo Vázquez Ayala, José Luis López Sánchez, Pedro Munguía Munguía, Guillermo Mendizábal Sánchez (79.Juan Antonio Luna Castro), José Luis González II Alcate, Cristóbal Ortega Martínez, Adrián Camacho Solís, Hugo Sánchez Márquez. Trainer: Raúl Cárdenas de la Vega.
**CAN:** Martino Lettieri, Robert Iarusci, Robert Bolitho, John McGrane, Mike Sweeney (Randolph Lee Ragan), Mike McLenaghen, Gerard Gray, Robert Lenarduzzi, Wesley McLeod, Momcilo Stojanovic, Dale William Mitchell (Bruce Miller). Trainer: Barrie Clarke.
**Goals**: 1-0 Hugo Sánchez Márquez (74 penalty), 1-1 Gerard Gray (87).
**Sent off**: Wesley McLeod (77).

23.11.1980, Lockhart Stadium, Fort Lauderdale; Attendance: 2,126
Referee: Marco Antonio Gracía Regalado (Guatemala)
**UNITED STATES - MEXICO** **2-1(1-1)**
**USA:** Arnold Mausser, Boris Bandov (Cap), Colin Fowles, Richard Dean Davis, Laurence Hulcer, Percival Joseph van der Beck, Ringo Julio Cantillo, Angelo di Bernardo, Mark Liveric, Njego Pesa, Steve Moyers. Trainer: Walter Chyzowich.
**MEX:** Ignacio Rodríguez Bahena, Mario Alberto Trejo Guzmán, Alfredo Tena Garduño, Arturo Vázquez Ayala, José Luis López Sánchez, Gustavo Vargas (73.Ricardo Castro Valenzuela), Guillermo Mendizábal Sánchez, José Luis González II Alcate (67.Leonardo Cuéllar Rivera), Cristóbal Ortega Martínez, Adrián Camacho Solís, Hugo Sánchez Márquez. Trainer: Raúl Cárdenas de la Vega.
**Goals**: 1-0 Steve Moyers (31), 1-1 Hugo Sánchez Márquez (41), 2-1 Steve Moyers (65).
**Sent off**: Njego Pesa (68), Mario Alberto Trejo Guzmán (68).

# CENTRAL AMERICAN ZONE

| | | | |
|---|---|---|---|
| 02.07.1980 | Panama City | Panama - Guatemala | 0-2(0-1) |
| 30.07.1980 | Panama City | Panama - Honduras | 0-2(0-1) |
| 10.08.1980 | Panama City | Panama - Costa Rica | 1-1(1-0) |
| 24.08.1980 | Panama City | Panama - El Salvador | 1-3(0-1) |
| 01.10.1980 | San José | Costa Rica - Honduras | 2-3(0-2) |
| 05.10.1980 | San Salvador | El Salvador - Panama | 4-1(2-1) |
| 12.10.1980 | Cd. de Guatemala | Guatemala - Costa Rica | 0-0 |
| 26.10.1980 | Tegucigalpa | Honduras - Guatemala | 0-0 |
| 26.10.1980 | San Salvador | El Salvador - Costa Rica | 2-0* |
| 05.11.1980 | San José | Costa Rica - Panama | 2-0(1-0) |
| 09.11.1980 | Cd. de Guatemala | Guatemala - El Salvador | 0-0 |
| 16.11.1980 | Cd. de Guatemala | Guatemala - Panama | 5-0(2-0) |
| 16.11.1980 | Tegucigalpa | Honduras - Costa Rica | 1-1(0-1) |
| 23.11.1980 | San Salvador | El Salvador - Honduras | 2-1(1-0) |
| 26.11.1980 | San José | Costa Rica - Guatemala | 0-3(0-1) |
| 30.11.1980 | Tegucigalpa | Honduras - El Salvador | 2-0(1-0) |
| 07.12.1980 | Cd. de Guatemala | Guatemala - Honduras | 0-1(0-0) |
| 10.12.1980 | San José | Costa Rica - El Salvador | 0-0 |
| 14.12.1980 | Tegucigalpa | Honduras - Panama | 5-0(3-0) |
| 21.12.1980 | San Salvador | El Salvador - Guatemala | 1-0(0-0) |

### FINAL STANDINGS

| | | | | | | | | | |
|---|---|---|---|---|---|---|---|---|---|
| 1. | Honduras | 8 | 5 | 2 | 1 | 15 | - | 5 | 12 |
| 2. | El Salvador | 8 | 5 | 2 | 1 | 12 | - | 5 | 12 |
| 3. | Guatemala | 8 | 3 | 3 | 2 | 10 | - | 2 | 9 |
| 4. | Costa Rica | 8 | 1 | 4 | 3 | 6 | - | 10 | 6 |
| 5. | Panama | 8 | 0 | 1 | 7 | 3 | - | 24 | 1 |

Honduras and El Salvador qualified for the CONCACAF Zone Final.

02.07.1980, Estadio de la Revolución, Ciudad de la Revolución; Attendance: n/a
Referee: Robert Evans (United States)
**PANAMA - GUATEMALA**  **0-2(0-1)**
**PAN**: Edelberto Aguirre Tejera, Luis Aponte, Héctor Avila Bonilla, David Berroa Castrellón, Guillermo Blanford, Omar Campona Aguirre, Antonio Davis del Rosario, Jorge Méndez Daniels, Daniel Montillo Ruíz (54.Ricardo Paschal Chambers), Fernando Samaniego, Tomás Banard Conally (62.Virgilio Mendoza Vásquez). Trainer: Luis Borghini (Uruguay).
**GUA**: Edgar Ricardo Jérez Hidalgo, Juan José Pérez Monge, Allan Kenny Wellmann, Sergio Estuardio Rivera Hernández, Edgar René Bolaños Galdámez, Miguel Ángel Pérez, Julio Roberto Gómez Rendón, José Emilio Mitrovich, Selvin Manolo Galindo López (46.Miguel Ángel Cruz Martínez), Oscar Enrique Sánchez Rivas (75.Adan Onelio Paniagua Díaz), Marco Antonio Fion. Trainer: Rubén Amorín (Uruguay).
**Goals**: 0-1 Julio Roberto Gómez Rendón (27), 0-2 José Emilio Mitrovich (49).

30.07.1980, Estadío de la Revolución, Ciudad de Panamá; Attendance: n/a
Referee: Hubert Tromp (Netherlands Antilles)
**PANAMA - HONDURAS**  **0-2(0-1)**
**PAN**: Edelberto Aguirre Tejera, Luis Aponte, Eleuterio Arosemena Cruz, Héctor Avila Bonilla (48.Virgilio Mendoza Vásquez), David Berroa Castrellón, Selin González, Fernando Flores, Jorge Méndez Daniels, Daniel Montillo Ruíz, Ricardo Paschal Chambers (62.Sabino Valencia), Tomás Banard Conally. Trainer: Luis Borghini (Uruguay).

**HON**: Belarmino Rivera Jimminson, Domingo Drummond Cooper, Allan Anthony Costly Blyden, José Fernando Bulnes Zubiaga, Héctor Ramón Zelaya Rivera, Javier Francisco Toledo Rivera, Salvador Bernárdez Blanco (Roger Chavarria Reyes), Ramón Enrique Maradiaga Chávez, Prudencio Norales Martínez, Roberto James Bailey Sargent, Luis Alberto Reyes Núñez. Trainer: José de la Paz Herrera Ucles.
**Goals**: 0-1 Salvador Bernárdez Blanco (14), 0-2 Allan Anthony Costly Blyden (85).

10.08.1980, Estadío de la Revolución, Ciudad de Panamá; Attendance: n/a
Referee: Jacques Goede (Surinam)
**PANAMA - COSTA RICA**                                                      **1-1(1-0)**
**PAN**: Edelberto Aguirre Tejera, Luis Aponte, Eleuterio Arosemena Cruz, David Berroa Castrellón, Selin González (20.Guillermo Blanford), Antonio Davis del Rosario, Fernando Flores, Jorge Méndez Daniels, Daniel Montillo Ruíz, Ricardo Paschal Chambers, Tomás Banard Conally. Trainer: Luis Borghini (Uruguay).
**CRC**: Julio Morales Piedra, Mínor Alpízar Campos, Ricardo García Rodríguez Rodríguez, Carlos Toppings, Marvin Obando Obando, Dennis Marshall Herrón (58.Herberth Quesada), Francisco Hernández Ramírez (46.William Ávila), Tomás Velásquez Torres Áviles, Omar Arroyo Rodríguez, Róger Alvarez Sánchez, Jorge White Hocher. Trainer: Antonio Moyano Reyna (Spain).
**Goals**: 1-0 Daniel Montillo Ruíz (34), 1-1 Omar Arroyo Rodríguez (60).

24.08.1980, Estadio Nacional de Deportes, Ciudad de Panamá; Attendance: 3,547
Referee: Frederick Hoyte (Barbados)
**PANAMA - EL SALVADOR**                                                     **1-3(0-1)**
**PAN**: Edelberto Aguirre Tejera, Luis Aponte, Eleuterio Arosmena, David Borroa, Omar Campona Aguirre, Selin González, Omar Carles Morales (48.Ricardo Paschal Chambers), Jorge Méndez Daniels, Daniel Montillo Ruíz, Sergio González Montoto, Tomás Banard Conally. Trainer: Luis Borghini (Uruguay).
**SLV**: Julio Eduardo Hernández Fuentes, Mario Alfonso Castillo Díaz, Jaime Alberto Rodríguez Jiménez, Alfredo Rivera, Carlos Humberto Recinos Ortíz, Juan Gilberto Quinteros, José Norberto Huezo Montoya, José Antonio Infantozzi (Mauricio Alberto Alfaro Valladares), José María Rivas Martínez (Ever Francisco Hernández), Luis Baltazar Ramírez Zapata, Jorge Alberto González Barillas. Trainer: Mauricio Alonso Rodríguez Lindo.
**Goals**: 0-1 José María Rivas Martínez (17), 1-1 Ricardo Paschal Chambers (70), 1-2 José Norberto Huezo Montoya (74), 1-3 Jorge Alberto González Barillas (81).

01.10.1980, Estadío "Ricardo Saprissa", San José; Attendance: n/a
Referee: Constantinos Soupliotis (Canada)
**COSTA RICA - HONDURAS**                                                    **2-3(0-2)**
**CRC**: Bernardino Chaves, Nelson Bastos González, William Jiménez Mora, Frederico Méndez Rios, Mario Antonio Barrantes Quesada, Gerardo Ureña Picado, Rodolfo Leonardo Mills Palmer, Carlos Alberto Ugalde Asguedar, Carlos Torres Áviles, Javier Jiménez Báez, Carlos Camacho Carballo (82.Luis Fernández González). Trainer: Antonio Moyano Reyna (Spain).
**HON**: Belarmino Rivera Jimminson, Domingo Drummond Cooper, Jaime Enrique Villegas Roura, José Fernando Bulnes Zubiaga, Héctor Ramón Zelaya Rivera, Javier Francisco Toledo Rivera, Salvador Bernárdez Blanco, Ramón Enrique Maradiaga Chávez, Prudencio Norales Martínez (Luis Alberto Reyes Núñez), Roberto James Bailey Sargent, José Roberto Figueroa Padilla. Trainer: José de la Paz Herrera Ucles.
**Goals**: 0-1 José Fernando Bulnes Zubiaga (29), 0-2 Salvador Bernárdez Blanco (42), 0-3 Roberto James Bailey Sargent (67), 1-3 William Jiménez Mora (78 penalty), 2-3 Rodolfo Leonardo Mills Palmer (81).

05.10.1980, Estadio Cuscatlán, San Salvador; Attendance: 33,005
Referee: Werner Winsemann (Canada)
**EL SALVADOR - PANAMA** 4-1(2-1)
**SLV**: Julio Eduardo Hernández Fuentes, Mario Alfonso Castillo Díaz, Jaime Alberto Rodríguez Jiménez, Ramón Alfredo Fagoaga Romero, Carlos Humberto Recinos Ortíz, Juan Gilberto Quinteros, José Norberto Huezo Montoya (Mauricio Alberto Alfaro Valladares), Luis Baltazar Ramírez Zapata (José Luis Rugamas Portillo), José María Rivas Martínez, Ever Francisco Hernández, Jorge Alberto González Barillas. Trainer: Mauricio Alonso Rodríguez Lindo.
**PAN**: Edelberto Aguirre Tejera, David Berroa Castrellón, Edilberto Meléndez, Guillermo Blanford, Jorge Méndez Daniels, Antonio Davis del Rosario, Víctor René Mendieta, Daniel Montillo Ruíz, Héctor Ávila Bonilla, Selin González, Germán Salager. Trainer: Luis Borghini (Uruguay).
**Goals**: 0-1 Daniel Montillo Ruíz (27), 1-1 Jorge Alberto González Barillas (29), 2-1 José María Rivas Martínez (35), 3-1 Jorge Alberto González Barillas (61), 4-1 Jorge Alberto González Barillas (77).

12.10.1980, Estadio „Mateo Flores", Ciudad de Guatemala; Attendance: 40,000
Referee: Jorge Alberto Narváez Escobar (Mexico)
**GUATEMALA - COSTA RICA** 0-0
**GUA**: Edgar Ricardo Jérez Hidalgo, Juan José Pérez Monge, Allan Kenny Wellmann, Sergio Estuardio Rivera Hernández, Luis Guillermo Rodríguez Sandoval, Edgar René Bolaños Galdámez, Selvin Manolo Galindo López, Miguel Ángel Cruz Martínez, José Emilio Mitrovich, Julio Roberto Gómez Rendón, Oscar Enrique Sánchez Rivas (Adan Onelio Paniagua Díaz). Trainer: Rubén Amorín (Uruguay).
**CRC**: Víctor Eduardo Monge Rojas, Nelson Bastos González, William Jiménez Mora, Frederico Méndez Rios, Mario Antonio Barrantes Quesada (Manuel Quesada Chanto), Rodolfo Leonardo Mills Palmer, Luis Fernández González, Carlos Alberto Ugalde Asguedar, Carlos Torres Áviles, Carlos Camacho Carballo (Gerardo Ureña Picado), Jorge White Hocher. Trainer: Antonio Moyano Reyna (Spain).
**Sent off**: Carlos Alberto Ugalde Asguedar (84).

26.10.1980, Estadio Nacional, Tegucigalpa; Attendance: n/a
Referee: Marco Antonio Dorantes García (México)
**HONDURAS - GUATEMALA** 0-0
**HON**: Belarmino Rivera Jimminson, Domingo Drummond Cooper, Jaime Enrique Villegas Roura, José Fernando Bulnes Zubiaga, Héctor Ramón Zelaya Rivera, Roger Chavarria Reyes (39.Luis Alberto Reyes Núñez), Ramón Enrique Maradiaga Chávez, Salvador Bernárdez Blanco, Prudencio Norales Martínez (80.Jorge Bran Guevara), Roberto James Bailey Sargent, José Roberto Figueroa Padilla. Trainer: José de la Paz Herrera Ucles.
**GUA**: Edgar Ricardo Jérez Hidalgo, Juan José Pérez Monge, Allan Kenny Wellmann, Sergio Estuardio Rivera Hernández, Luis Guillermo Rodríguez Sandoval, Edgar René Bolaños Galdámez, Julio Rubén Paredes, Julio Roberto Gómez Rendón, Selvin Manolo Galindo López, Miguel Ángel Cruz Martínez, Miguel Ángel Pérez. Trainer: Rubén Amorín (Uruguay).

26.10.1980, Estadio Cuscatlán, San Salvador; Attendance: none
Referee: Domingo de la Mora García (Mexico)
**EL SALVADOR - COSTA RICA** 2-0*
*Due to the political situation in Costa Rica, no team was able to travel to El Salvador. The match was awarded by the FIFA 2-0 for El Salvador.*

05.11.1980, Estadío Nacional, San José; Attendance: n/a
Referee: Dante Maglio (Canada)
**COSTA RICA - PANAMA**  **2-0(1-0)**
**CRC**: Víctor Eduardo Monge Rojas, William Jiménez Mora, Frederico Méndez Rios (Manuel Quesada Chanto), Mario Antonio Barrantes Quesada, Nelson Bastos González, Luis Fernández González, Marvin Álvarez González, Jorge White Hocher, Carlos Torres Áviles, Omar Morera Barrantes (Rafael Ángel Hidalgo Venegas), Gerardo Ureña Picado. Trainer: Antonio Moyano Reyna (Spain).
**PAN**: Diogenes Cáceres, Antonio Davis del Rosario, Rogelio Sánchez Cáceres, Jorge Méndez Daniels, Edilberto Meléndez, Simeon Escobar (53.Delano Welch), Fernando Flores, Daniel Montillo Ruíz, Víctor René Mendieta, Germán Salager (61.Ricardo Buitrago), Eleuterio Arosemena Cruz. Trainer: Luis Borghini (Uruguay).
**Goals**: 1-0 Luis Fernández González (14), 2-0 William Jiménez Mora (48 penalty).
**Sent off**: Delano Welch (56).

09.11.1980, Estadio „Mateo Flores", Ciudad de Guatemala; Attendance: 42,453
Referee: David Socha (United States)
**GUATEMALA - EL SALVADOR**  **0-0**
**GUA**: Edgar Ricardo Jérez Hidalgo, Sergio Estuardio Rivera Hernández, Allan Kenny Wellmann, Juan José Pérez Monge, Luis Guillermo Rodríguez Sandoval, Edgar René Bolaños Galdámez, Julio Rubén Paredes Julio Rubén Paredes (Adan Onelio Paniagua Díaz), Julio Roberto Gómez Rendón, José Emilio Mitrovich, Miguel Ángel Pérez, Oscar Enrique Sánchez Rivas. Trainer: Rubén Amorín (Uruguay).
**SLV**: Julio Eduardo Hernández Fuentes, Mario Alfonso Castillo Díaz, Jaime Alberto Rodríguez Jiménez, Ramón Alfredo Fagoaga Romero, Carlos Humberto Recinos Ortíz, Juan Gilberto Quinteros, José Norberto Huezo Montoya, Joaquín Alonso Ventura (Mauricio Alberto Alfaro Valladares), José María Rivas Martínez, Luis Baltazar Ramírez Zapata, Jorge Alberto González Barillas. Trainer: Mauricio Alonso Rodríguez Lindo.

16.11.1980, Estadio „Mateo Flores", Ciudad de Guatemala; Attendance: n/a
Referee: Peter Johnson (Canada)
**GUATEMALA - PANAMA**  **5-0(2-0)**
**GUA**: Edgar Ricardo Jérez Hidalgo, Juan José Pérez Monge, Allan Kenny Wellmann, Sergio Estuardio Rivera Hernández, Luis Guillermo Rodríguez Sandoval, Miguel Ángel Cruz Martínez, Oscar Enrique Sánchez Rivas, Julio Roberto Gómez Rendón, Selvin Valentine Pennant Taylor, José Emilio Mitrovich (Miguel Ángel Pérez), Adan Onelio Paniagua Díaz (Selvin Manolo Galindo López). Trainer: Rubén Amorín (Uruguay).
**PAN**: Diogenes Cáceres, Rogelio Sánchez Cáceres, Guillermo Blanford, Edilberto Meléndez, Delano Welch, Simeon Escobar, Ricardo Buitrago, Fernando Flores, Daniel Montillo Ruíz, Lester Sabers, Germán Salager. Trainer: Luis Borghini (Uruguay).
**Goals**: 1-0 Oscar Enrique Sánchez Rivas (11), 2-0 Julio Roberto Gómez Rendón (26), 3-0 Mitrovich José Emilio (55), 4-0 Julio Roberto Gómez Rendón (69), 5-0 Allan Kenny Wellmann (85).
**Sent off**: Germán Salager (55).

16.11.1980, Estadío Nacional, Tegucigalpa; Attendance: n/a
Referee: David Stanley Socha (United States)
**HONDURAS - COSTA RICA**  **1-1(0-1)**
**HON**: Belarmino Rivera Jimminson, René Suazo Bernárdez, Jaime Enrique Villegas Roura, Héctor Ramón Zelaya Rivera, José Fernando Bulnes Zubiaga, Javier Francisco Toledo Rivera, Salvador Bernárdez Blanco (68.Walter Humberto Jimminson Warren), Ramón Enrique Maradiaga Chávez, Prudencio Norales Martínez, Matilde Lacayo (56.Moises Tomas Velásquez Torres), Luis Alberto Reyes Núñez. Trainer: José de la Paz Herrera Ucles.
**CRC**: Víctor Eduardo Monge Rojas, Nelson Bastos González, William Jiménez Mora, Frederico Méndez Rios, Mario Antonio Barrantes Quesada, Carlos Alberto Ugalde Asguedar (82.Gerardo Ureña Picado), Rodolfo Leonardo Mills Palmer, Julio Alfonso Fuller McKenzie, Carlos Torres Áviles, Jorge White Hocher, Omar Morera Barrantes (60.Rafael Ángel Hidalgo Venegas). Trainer: Antonio Moyano

Reyna (Spain).
**Goals**: 0-1 Omar Morera Barrantes (33), 1-1 Moises Tomas Velásquez Torres (73).

23.11.1980, Estadío Cuscatlán, San Salvador; Attendance: 40,851
Referee: Roland Beni Fusco (Canada)
**EL SALVADOR - HONDURAS**                                   **2-1(1-0)**
**SLV**: Julio Eduardo Hernández Fuentes, Mario Alfonso Castillo Díaz (Alfredo Rivera), Jaime Alberto Rodríguez Jiménez, Ramón Alfredo Fagoaga Romero, Carlos Humberto Recinos Ortíz, Juan Gilberto Quinteros, José Norberto Huezo Montoya, Joaquín Alonso Ventura, José María Rivas Martínez (Ever Francisco Hernández), Óscar Gustavo Guerrero Amaya, Jorge Alberto González Barillas. Trainer: Mauricio Alonso Rodríguez Lindo.
**HON**: Belarmino Rivera Jimminson, Domingo Drummond Cooper, Héctor Ramón Zelaya Rivera, José Fernando Bulnes Zubiaga, Allan Anthony Costly Blyden, Ramón Enrique Maradiaga Chávez, Prudencio Norales Martínez, José Roberto Figueroa Padilla, Salvador Bernárdez Blanco, Roger Chavarria Reyes, Jaime Enrique Villegas Roura. Trainer: José de la Paz Herrera Ucles.
**Goals**: 1-0 Jorge Alberto González Barillas (9), 2-0 Óscar Gustavo Guerrero Amaya (66), 2-1 José Roberto Figueroa Padilla (85).

26.11.1980, Estadío "Ricardo Saprissa", San José; Attendance: 17,042
Referee: Ilio Matos (Canada)
**COSTA RICA - GUATEMALA**                                   **0-3(0-1)**
**CRC**: Víctor Eduardo Monge Rojas, William Jiménez Mora, Carlos Alberto Ugalde Asguedar, Julio Alfonso Fuller McKenzie, Carlos Alberto Torres, Mario Antonio Barrantes Quesada, Omar Morera Barrantes (46.Luis Solano Chavarría), Frederico Méndez Rios, Nelson Bastos González, Luis Fernández González, Rodolfo Leonardo Mills Palmer. Trainer: Antonio Moyano Reyna (Spain).
**GUA**: Edgar Ricardo Jérez Hidalgo, Juan José Pérez Monge, Allan Kenny Wellmann, Sergio Estuardio Rivera Hernández, Luis Guillermo Rodríguez Sandoval, Miguel Ángel Cruz Martínez, Oscar Enrique Sánchez Rivas, Julio Roberto Gómez Rendón, Selvin Valentine Pennant Taylor, José Emilio Mitrovich (65.Miguel Ángel Pérez), Edgar René Bolaños Galdámez. Trainer: Rubén Amorín (Uruguay).
**Goals**: 0-1 Selvin Valentine Pennant Taylor (20), 0-2 Oscar Enrique Sánchez Rivas (62 penalty), 0-3 Oscar Enrique Sánchez Rivas (78).
**Sent off**: Edgar René Bolaños Galdámez.

30.11.1980, Estadio Nacional, Tegucigalpa; Attendance: 50,000
Referee: Antonio Evangelista (Canada)
**HONDURAS - EL SALVADOR**                                   **2-0(1-0)**
**HON**: Belarmino Rivera Jimminson, René Suazo Bernárdez, Jaime Enrique Villegas, Allan Anthony Costly Blyden, José Fernando Bulnes Zubiaga, Javier Francisco Toledo Rivera, Salvador Bernárdez Blanco, Luis Alberto Reyes Núñez (67.Jorge Alberto Bran Guevara), Ramón Enrique Maradiaga Chávez, Roberto James Bailey Sargent, José Roberto Figueroa Padilla. Trainer: José de la Paz Herrera Ucles.
**SLV**: Julio Eduardo Hernández Fuentes, Mario Alfonso Castillo Díaz, Jaime Alberto Rodríguez Jiménez, Ramón Alfredo Fagoaga Romero, Carlos Humberto Recinos Ortíz, Juan Gilberto Quinteros, José Norberto Huezo Montoya, Mauricio Alberto Alfaro Valladares, José María Rivas Martínez, Óscar Gustavo Guerrero Amaya, Jorge Alberto González Barillas. Trainer: Mauricio Alonso Rodríguez Lindo.
**Goals**: 1-0 Roberto James Bailey Sargent (23), 2-0 Roberto James Bailey Sargent (66).

07.12.1980, Estadio „Mateo Flores", Ciudad de Guatemala; Attendance: n/a
Referee: Toros Kibritjian (United States)
**GUATEMALA - HONDURAS**  **0-1(0-0)**
**GUA**: Edgar Ricardo Jérez Hidalgo, Juan José Pérez Monge, Allan Kenny Wellmann, Sergio Estuardio Rivera Hernández, Luis Guillermo Rodríguez Sandoval, Miguel Ángel Pérez, Oscar Enrique Sánchez Rivas, Julio Roberto Gómez Rendón, Selvin Valentine Pennant Taylor, José Emilio Mitrovich (Selvin Manolo Galindo López), Adan Onelio Paniagua Díaz (Julio Rubén Paredes). Trainer: Rubén Amorín (Uruguay).
**HON**: James Stewart Bodden, Domingo Drummond Cooper, Jaime Enrique Villegas, José Fernando Bulnes Zubiaga, Allan Anthony Costly Blyden, Javier Francisco Toledo Rivera, Salvador Bernárdez Blanco, Ramón Enrique Maradiaga Chávez, Luis Alberto Reyes Núñez, Roberto James Bailey Sargent (Héctor Ramón Zelaya Rivera), José Roberto Figueroa Padilla. Trainer: José de la Paz Herrera Ucles.
**Goal**: 0-1 Roberto James Bailey Sargent (71).

10.12.1980, Estadío "Ricardo Saprissa", San José; Attendance: 3,284
Referee: Mario Lamberto Rubio Vázquez (Mexico)
**COSTA RICA - EL SALVADOR**  **0-0**
**CRC**: Víctor Eduardo Monge Rojas, Julio Alfonso Fuller McKenzie, Manuel Quesada Chanto, Frederico Méndez Rios, Nelson Bastos González, Carlos Alberto Ugalde Asguedar, Gerardo Ureña Picado, Alfonso Álvaro Solano, Rafael Ángel Hidalgo Venegas, Jorge White Hocher, Omar Morera Barrantes. Trainer: Antonio Moyano Reyna (Spain).
**SLV**: Luis Ricardo Guevara Mora, Mario Alfonso Castillo Díaz, Jaime Alberto Rodríguez Jiménez, Ramón Alfredo Fagoaga Romero, Carlos Humberto Recinos Ortíz, Juan Gilberto Quinteros, José Norberto Huezo Montoya, José Luis Rugamas Portillo, José María Rivas Martínez (Ever Francisco Hernández), Luis Baltazar Ramírez Zapata (Óscar Gustavo Guerrero Amaya), Jorge Alberto González Barillas. Trainer: Mauricio Alonso Rodríguez Lindo.
**Sent off**: Jorge White Hocher.

14.12.1980, Estadio Nacional, Tegucigalpa; Attendance: 25,000
Referee: Enrique Mendoza Guillen (Mexico)
**HONDURAS - PANAMA**  **5-0(3-0)**
**HON**: Belarmino Rivera Jimminson, René Suazo Bernárdez (40.Moises Tomas Velásquez Torres), Jaime Enrique Villegas Roura, Héctor Ramón Zelaya Rivera, José Fernando Bulnes Zubiaga, Javier Francisco Toledo Rivera, Salvador Bernárdez Blanco, Ramón Enrique Maradiaga Chávez, Luis Alberto Reyes Núñez (57.Walter Humberto Jiminson Warren), Matilde Lacayo, José Roberto Figueroa Padilla. Trainer: José de la Paz Herrera Ucles.
**PAN**: César Hicks, Federico Bynce, Jesús González, Edgardo Ortega, Rogelio Sánchez Cáceres, Erick Luna, Delano Welch, Ricardo Paschal Chambers, Luis Alberto Menéndez, Lester Sabers, Víctor René Mendieta. Trainer: Luis Borghini (Uruguay).
**Goals**: 1-0 Salvador Bernárdez Blanco (6), 2-0 Salvador Bernárdez Blanco (21), 3-0 José Roberto Figueroa Padilla (32), 4-0 Salvador Bernárdez Blanco (69), 5-0 José Roberto Figueroa Padilla (77).

21.12.1980, Estadio Cuscatlán, San Salvador; Attendance: 22,813
Referee: Gino d'Ippolito (United States)
**EL SALVADOR - GUATEMALA**  **1-0(0-0)**
**SLV**: Luis Ricardo Guevara Mora, Mario Alfonso Castillo Díaz, Jaime Alberto Rodríguez Jiménez, Ramón Alfredo Fagoaga Romero, Carlos Humberto Recinos Ortíz, Juan Gilberto Quinteros (Alfredo Rivera), José Norberto Huezo Montoya, José Luis Rugamas Portillo, Joaquín Alonso Ventura, Silvio Romeo Aquino (José María Rivas Martínez), Jorge Alberto González Barillas. Trainer: Mauricio Alonso Rodríguez Lindo.
**GUA**: Edgar Ricardo Jérez Hidalgo, Juan José Pérez Monge, Allan Kenny Wellmann, Sergio Estuardio Rivera Hernández, Luis Guillermo Rodríguez Sandoval, Miguel Ángel Cruz Martínez, Miguel Ángel Pérez, Julio Roberto Gómez Rendón, Selvin Valentine Pennant Taylor, José Emilio Mitrovich, Oscar Enrique Sánchez Rivas (Julio Rubén Paredes). Trainer: Rubén Amorín (Uruguay).
**Goal**: 1-0 José Norberto Huezo Montoya (49).

# CARIBBEAN ZONE

## PRELIMINARY ROUND

| 30.03.1980 | Georgetown | Guyana - Grenada | 5-2(2-2) |
| 13.04.1980 | Saint George's | Grenada - Guyana | 2-3(0-2) |

### FINAL STANDINGS

| 1. Guyana | 2 | 2 | 0 | 0 | 8 - 4 | 4 |
| 2. Grenada | 2 | 0 | 0 | 2 | 4 - 8 | 0 |

Guyana qualified for the Subgroup A.

30.03.1980, Bourda Cricket Ground, Georgetown; Attendance: n/a
Referee: José Leonidas Rogel Rivera (El Salvador)
**GUYANA - GRENADA** **5-2(2-2)**
**GUY**: Denzil Thompson, Clive Fraser, Earl O'Neal, Clive Jordan, Clyde Forde, Aubrey Hutson, Gordon Braithwaite, Charles Ashford, Norton Anthony Smart, Ashton Canterbury, Clyde Watson. Trainer: Geralds Nurse.
**GRN**: Godfrey Williams, Jude Mitchell, Douglas Cherubin, Michael Nelson Bennion, Roderick Griffith, Brian Anthony Lewis, Jude Julien, Cyril Saint Louis, Carlton Belfon, Barry James, Hugh Commissong. Trainer: August Wooter.
**Goals**: 0-1 Jude Julien (15), 0-2 Carlton Belfon (17), 1-2 Gordon Braithwaite (33 penalty), 2-2 Clyde Ford (37), 3-2 Clyde Watson (50), 4-2 Ashton Canterbury (56), 5-2 Clyde Watson (87).

13.04.1980, Queen's Park, Saint George's; Attendance: 1,298
Referee: Juan Ramón Mollinero (Guatemala)
**GRENADA - GUYANA** **2-3(0-2)**
**GRN**: Tyrone Belfon, Michael Nelson Bennion, Douglas Cherubin, Jude Mitchell, Roderick Griffith, Brian Anthony Lewis, Jude Julien, Carlton Belfon, Patrick Baptiste (59.Norris Wilson), Barry James, David Edwards. Trainer: August Wooter.
**GUY**: Vibart Defreitas, Clive Fraser, Earl O'Neal, Ashton Canterbury, Neville Johnson, Aubrey Hutson, Gordon Braithwaite, Charles Ashford, Terrence Archer, Clyde Watson, Clyde Forde. Trainer: William Braithwaite.
**Goals**: 0-1 Clyde Watson (13), 0-2 Ashton Canterbury (16), 0-3 Clyde Watson (38), 1-3 Douglas Cherubin (56), 2-3 Jude Mitchell (87 penalty).

# SUBGROUP A

| | | | | |
|---|---|---|---|---|
| 17.08.1980 | Havana | Cuba - Suriname | 3-0(0-0) |
| 07.09.1980 | Paramaribo | Suriname - Cuba | 0-0 |
| 28.09.1980 | Georgetown | Guyana - Suriname | 0-1(0-1) |
| 12.10.1980 | Paramaribo | Suriname - Guyana | 4-0(2-0) |
| 09.11.1980 | Havana | Cuba - Guyana | 1-0(1-0) |
| 30.11.1980 | Linden | Guyana - Cuba | 0-3(0-3) |

## FINAL STANDINGS

| | | | | | | | | |
|---|---|---|---|---|---|---|---|---|
| 1. Cuba | 4 | 3 | 1 | 0 | 7 | - | 0 | 7 |
| 2. Suriname | 4 | 2 | 1 | 1 | 5 | - | 3 | 5 |
| 3. Guyana | 4 | 0 | 0 | 4 | 0 | - | 9 | 0 |

Cuba qualified for the CONCACAF Zone Final.

17.08.1980, Estadio „Pedro Marrero", La Habana; Attendance: 6,000
Referee: Antonio Márquez Ramírez (Mexico)
**CUBA - SURINAME**                                                            **3-0(0-0)**
**CUB:** Cálixto Martínez Quezada, Miguel López, Raimundo Roberto Frometa Carrión, Luis Manuel Sánchez Téllez (69.Reginoso Delgado Robau), René Bonora Puertas, Roberto Espinosa Cabriales, Andrés Roldán Cordero, Amado Lorenzo Povea Morillo, Dagoberto Lara Soriano, Ramón Núñez Armas, Roberto Pereira Hernández. Trainer: Tibor Ivanics (Hungary).
**SUR:** Carlo Monpellier, Aloysius Hankers, Adolf Hoen, Edgar Rust, Milton Lieveld, Roy Glenn George, Ortwien Pinas (69.Glenn Isselt), Johan Leisbergen, Rinaldo Stanley Entingh, Ronald Borgia (72.Kenneth Frank Borgia), Jacob Eduards. Trainer: Armand Sahadewsing.
**Goals**: 1-0 Reginoso Delgado Robau (69), 2-0 Roberto Pereira Hernández (71), 3-0 Roberto Pereira Hernández (78).

07.09.1980, Natsjonalstadion, Paramaribo; Attendance: 4,000
Referee: Hubert Tromp (Netherlands Antilles)
**SURINAME - CUBA**                                             **0-0**
**SUR:** Carlo Monpellier, Aloysius Hankers, Edgar Rust, Siegfried Rustenberg, Milton Lievald, Roy Glenn George, Kenneth Frank Borgia (Ortwien Pinas), Kenneth Stjeward, Jantje Voorn (Johann Leisbergen), Herman Nelom Fransman, Rinaldo Stanley Entingh,. Trainer: Armand Sahadewsing.
**CUB:** Fermín Hugo Madera Ramírez, Miguel López, Luis Roger Zenon Dreké (Amado Lorenzo Povea Morillo), Luis Manuel Sánchez Téllez, Andrés Roldán Cordero, Dagoberto Lara Soriano, Francisco Gutíerrez, Reginoso Delgado Robau, Jorge Rafael Masso Mustelier, Carlos Loredo Pérez, Roberto Pereira Hernández (Ramón Núñez Armas). Trainer: Tibor Ivanics (Hungary).
**Sent off**: Herman Nelom Fransman (32) / Carlos Loredo Pérez (32).

28.09.1980, Bourda Cricket Ground, Georgetown; Attendance: 6,000
Referee: Rudolph Reginald Wooding (Trinidad and Tobago)
**GUYANA - SURINAME**                                     **0-1(0-1)**
**GUY:** Denzil Thompson, Alfred Morrison, Earl O'Neal, Roger Alphonso, Eric Smith, Clyde Watson, Clyde Ford, Ashton Taylor (46.Terrence Archer), Norton Anthony Smart, Gordon Braithwaite, Aubrey Hutson. Trainer: Geralds Nurse.
**SUR:** Carlo Monpellier, Ortwien Pinas, Aloysius Hankers, Edgar Rust, Milton Lieveld, Roy Glenn George, Johan Leisbergen, Rinaldo Stanley Entingh, Jantje Voorn, Adolf Hoen, Kenneth Stjeward. Trainer: Armand Sahadewsing.
**Goal**: 0-1 Kenneth Stjeward (22).

12.10.1980, Natsjonalstadion, Paramaribo; Attendance: 10,000
Referee: Lionel de Boer (Netherlands Antilles)
**SURINAME - GUYANA** **4-0(2-0)**
**SUR:** Carlo Monpellier, Ortwien Pinas (Ricardo Calor), Jimmy Letnom, Aloysius Hankers, Edgar Rust, Roy Glenn George, Johan Leisbergen, Umberto Klinker, Jantje Voorn, Adolf Hoen, Kenneth Stjeward. Trainer: Armand Sahadewsing.
**GUY:** Denzil Thompson, Alfred Morrison, Earl O'Neal, Aubrey Hutson, Eric Smith, Clyde Watson, Clyde Ford, Terrence Archer, Gordon Braithwaite, Roger Alphonso, Neville Johnson. Trainer: Geralds Nurse.
**Goals:** 1-0 Johan Leisbergen (20), 2-0 Roy Glenn George (22), 3-0 Johan Leisbergen (40), 4-0 Ricardo Calor (80).

09.11.1980, Estadio „Pedro Marrero", La Habana; Attendance: 8,000
Referee: Wilson Davis Taylor (Jamaica)
**CUBA - GUYANA** **1-0(1-0)**
**CUB:** Fermín Hugo Madera Ramírez, Raimundo Roberto Frometa Carrión, Luis Manuel Sánchez Téllez, Roberto Espinosa Cabriales, Andrés Roldán Cordero, Amado Lorenzo Povea Morillo, Pedro Piedra (75.Jorge Luis Rodríguez Álcaraz), Luis Hernández Cobrera, Rolando Morales Amarilla, Jorge Rafael Masso Mustelier, Guillermo Díaz Mestre. Trainer: Tibor Ivanics (Hungary).
**GUY:** Vibart De Freitas, Clive Fraser, Marlon de Souza, Earl O'Neal, Aubrey Hutson (80.Monty Mentore), Norton Anthony Smart, Clyde Ford (85.David Kistoo), Terrence Archer, Selwin Vickery, Eric Smith, Neville Johnson. Trainer: Gerald Francisco.
**Goal:** 1-0 Luis Hernández Cobrera (14).

30.11.1980, „McKenzie Sports Club" Stadium, Lynden; Attendance: 7,664
Referee: Roel Jacques Goede (Suriname)
**GUYANA - CUBA** **0-3(0-3)**
**GUY:** Vibart De Freitas, Ovid Small, Marlon de Souza, Earl O'Neal, Monty Mentore, Clyde Ford, Gaston Bourne, Norton Anthony Smart, Selwin Vickery, Clive Fraser, Neville Johnson. Trainer: Gerald Francisco.
**CUB:** Fermín Hugo Madera Ramírez, Raimundo Roberto Frometa Carrión, Luis Manuel Sánchez Téllez, Luis Roger Zenon Dreké, Roberto Espinosa Cabriales, Andrés Roldán Cordero, Amado Lorenzo Povea Morillo, Dagoberto Lara Soriano, Francisco Farinas Gutiérrez, Luis Hernández Cobrera, Jorge Rafael Masso Mustelier. Trainer: Tibor Ivanics (Hungary).
**Goals:** 0-1 Luis Hernández Cobrera (8), 0-2 Roberto Espinosa Cabriales (17), 0-3 Andrés Roldán Cordero (18).
**Sent off:** Norton Anthony Smart (87).

# SUBGROUP B

| | | | | |
|---|---|---|---|---|
| 01.08.1980 | Port-au-Prince | Haiti - Trinidad and Tobago | | 2-0(0-0) |
| 17.08.1980 | San Fernando | Trinidad and Tobago - Haiti | | 1-0(0-0) |
| 12.09.1980 | Port-au-Prince | Haiti - Netherlands Antilles | | 1-0(0-0) |
| 09.11.1980 | Port of Spain | Trinidad and Tobago - Netherlands Antilles | | 0-0 |
| 29.11.1980 | Willemstad | Netherlands Antilles - Trinidad and Tobago | | 0-0 |
| 12.12.1980 | Willemstad | Netherlands Antilles - Haiti | | 1-1(0-1) |

### FINAL STANDINGS

| | | | | | | | | |
|---|---|---|---|---|---|---|---|---|
| 1. | Haiti | 4 | 2 | 1 | 1 | 4 - 2 | 5 |
| 2. | Trinidad and Tobago | 4 | 1 | 2 | 1 | 1 - 2 | 4 |
| 3. | Netherlands Antilles | 4 | 0 | 3 | 1 | 1 - 2 | 3 |

Haiti qualified for the CONCACAF Zone Final.

01.08.1980, Stade „Sylvio Cator", Port-au-Prince; Attendance: 15,000
Referee: Marcel Pérez Guevara (Mexico)
**HAITI - TRINIDAD AND TOBAGO**     **2-0(0-0)**
**HAI:** Wilner Piquant, Guy Allen, Goebbels Cadet, Ernest Jean-Joseph, Frantz Mathieu, Shiller Mondesir (Arthur Calixte), Carmin Velima (Serge Chrispin), Gérald Romulus, Fritz Bobo, Ernest Jean-Marie Baptiste, Jean-Joseph Mathelier. Trainer: Antoine Tassy.
**TRI:** Michael Maurice, Ralph Nelson, Derek Lewis, Garnet Craig, Reynold George, Michael Grayson, Leroy Spann, Michael Bain, Bertram Heptune, Keith Eddy, Anton Corneal. Trainer: Alvin Corneal.
**Goals:** 1-0 Serge Chrispin (84), 2-0 Fritz Bobo (89).

17.08.1980, San Fernando Stadium, San Fernando; Attendance: 5,535
Referee: Carlos Monge Solano (Costa Rica)
**TRINIDAD AND TOBAGO - HAITI**     **1-0(0-0)**
**TRI:** Michael Maurice, Ralph Nelson, Derek Lewis, Vernon Skinner, Reynold George, Stephen Pierre (55.Michael Bain), Leroy Spann, Trevor Fredericks, Richard Chinapoo, Andrew Highley, Bertram Heptune. Trainer: Alvin Corneal.
**HAI:** Wilner Piquant, Goebbels Cadet, Ernst Jean-Joseph, Guy Allen (80.Carlo Brevil), Reginald Vielot, Shiller Mondesir, Gérald Romulus, Arthur Calixte, Fritz Bobo, Serge Chrispin, Jean-Joseph Mathelier. Trainer: Antoine Tassy.
**Goal:** 1-0 Leroy Spann (55 penalty).

12.09.1980, Stade „Sylvio Cator", Port-au-Prince; Attendance: 8,606
Referee: Wilson Taylor (Jamaica)
**HAITI - NETHERLANDS ANTILLES**     **1-0(0-0)**
**HAI:** Wilner Piquant, Goebbels Cadet, Ernst Jean-Joseph, Jacques Louis, Frantz Mathieu, Reginald Vielot (Arthur Calixte), Carlo Brevil, Fritz Bobo, Gérald Romulus, Ernest Baptiste, Carmin Velima (Serge Chrispin). Trainer: Antoine Tassy.
**ANT:** Gregory S. D'Jaden, Nelson Martina, Oniel Leonora, Raymond Sophia, Rignald Alfonso Clemencia, Janin Andrade, Frensel Calmes, Rugelio Delfina (Humphrey Koots), Raymond Lucas, Erwin M. Godfriend, Ronald Braafhart. Trainer: Edmundo Confesor.
**Goal:** 1-0 Carlo Brevil (74).

09.11.1980, Public Serive Centre, Port of Spain; Attendance: 5,000
Referee: Frederick Hoyte (Barbados)
**TRINIDAD AND TOBAGO - NETHERLANDS ANTILLES        0-0**
**TRI:** Michael Maurice, Ralph Nelson, Brian Williams, Vernon Skinner, Reynold George, Leroy Spann, Brian John, Keith Eddy (Junior Phillips), Anton Corneal, Trevor Fredericks, Curtis Murrell. Trainer: Alvin Corneal.
**ANT:** Jozef Archangel Nivillac, Churney Hover, Oniel Leonora, Raymond Sophia, Rignald Alfonso Clemencia, Janin Andrade, Frensel Calmes, Humphrey Koots, Raymond Lucas, Erwin M. Godfriend (70.Sidney Bito), Eric Wever. Trainer: Edmundo Confesor.
**Sent off:** Raymond Lucas.

29.11.1980, Centro Deportivo Corson, Willemstad; Attendance: 7,991
Referee: Glenn Kranenburg (Suriname)
**NETHERLANDS ANTILLES - TRINIDAD AND TOBAGO        0-0**
**ANT:** Jozef Archangel Nivillac, Churney Hover, Oniel Leonora, Raymond Sophia, Rignald Alfonso Clemencia, Frensel Calmes, Glenn Kwidama, Eric Wever, Janin Andrade, Ronald Braafhart, Humphrey Koots (59.Sidney Bito; 77.Erwin M. Godfriend). Trainer: Edmundo Confesor.
**TRI:** Michael Maurice, Ralph Nelson, Brian Williams, Vernon Skinner (50.Vernon Charles), Reynold George, Steve Pierre, Leroy Spann, Noel John, Cleveland Mendes, Curtis Murrell, Nevick de Noon (71.Bertrand Haynes). Trainer: Kenneth Butcher.

12.12.1980, Centro Deportivo Corson, Willemstad; Attendance: 6,467
Referee: Domingo De la Mora García (Mexico)
**NETHERLANDS ANTILLES - HAITI        1-1(0-1)**
**ANT:** Gregory S. D'Jaden, Churney Hover, Oniel Leonora, Raymond Sophia, Rignald Alfonso Clemencia (46.Marelvo Felomina), Erwin Melfor (37.Eric Wever), Glenn Kwidama, Erwin M. Godfriend, Janin Andrade, Ronald Braafhart, Humphrey Koots. Trainer: Edmundo Confesor.
**HAI:** Wilner Piquant, Arsène Auguste, Goebbels Cadet, Ernst Jean-Joseph, Jacques Louis, Shiller Mondesir, Ernest Jean-Baptiste, Fritz Bobo, Arthur Calixte (63.Gérald Romulus), Serge Chrispin (73.Carmin Velima), Pierre Hugo. Trainer: Antoine Tassy.
**Goals:** 0-1 Serge Chrispin (3), 1-1 Glenn Kwidama (73).

# CONCACAF ZONE FINAL

| | | | |
|---|---|---|---|
| 01.11.1981 | Tegucigalpa | Mexico - Cuba | 4-0(2-0) |
| 02.11.1981 | Tegucigalpa | Canada – El Salvador | 1-0(0-0) |
| 03.11.1981 | Tegucigalpa | Honduras - Haiti | 4-0(2-0) |
| 06.11.1981 | Tegucigalpa | Canada - Haiti | 1-1(0-1) |
| 06.11.1981 | Tegucigalpa | El Salvador - Mexico | 1-0(0-0) |
| 08.11.1981 | Tegucigalpa | Honduras - Cuba | 2-0(1-0) |
| 11.11.1981 | Tegucigalpa | Cuba – El Salvador | 0-0 |
| 11.11.1981 | Tegucigalpa | Haiti - Mexico | 1-1(0-0) |
| 12.11.1981 | Tegucigalpa | Honduras - Canada | 2-1(1-1) |
| 15.11.1981 | Tegucigalpa | Cuba - Haiti | 2-0(0-0) |
| 15.11.1981 | Tegucigalpa | Mexico - Canada | 1-1(1-0) |
| 16.11.1981 | Tegucigalpa | Honduras – El Salvador | 0-0 |
| 19.11.1981 | Tegucigalpa | El Salvador - Haiti | 1-0(1-0) |
| 21.11.1981 | Tegucigalpa | Cuba - Canada | 2-2(1-0) |
| 22.11.1981 | Tegucigalpa | Honduras - Mexico | 0-0 |

## FINAL STANDINGS

| | | | | | | | | |
|---|---|---|---|---|---|---|---|---|
| 1. | **Honduras** | 5 | 3 | 2 | 0 | 8 - 1 | 8 |
| 2. | **El Salvador** | 5 | 2 | 2 | 1 | 2 - 1 | 6 |
| 3. | Mexico | 5 | 1 | 3 | 1 | 6 - 3 | 5 |
| 4. | Canada | 5 | 1 | 3 | 1 | 6 - 6 | 5 |
| 5. | Cuba | 5 | 1 | 2 | 2 | 4 - 8 | 4 |
| 6. | Haiti | 5 | 0 | 2 | 3 | 2 - 9 | 2 |

Honduras and El Salvador qualified for the Final Tournament.

01.11.1981, Estadio Nacional "Tiburcio Carías Andino", Tegucigalpa; Attendance: 40,720
Referee: Rómulo Méndez Molina (Guatemala)
**MEXICO - CUBA**     **4-0(2-0)**
**MEX**: Prudencio Cortés Sánchez, José Luis López Sánchez, Juan Manuel Álvarez Álvarez, Gustavo Vargas López, Rafael Toribio Arzáte, Pedro Munguía Munguía, Guillermo Mendizábal Sánchez, Manuel Manzo Ortega, Leonardo Cuéllar Rivera, Ricardo Castro Valenzuela, Hugo Sánchez Márquez. Trainer: Raúl Cárdenas de la Vega.
**CUB**: José Francisco Reinoso Zayas, Amado Lorenzo Povea Morillo, Luis Roger Zenon Dreké, Reginoso Delgado Robau, Luis Manuel Sánchez Téllez, Francisco Farinas Gutiérrez, Francisco Carranza Patrilge, Dagoberto Lara Soriano, Ramón Núñez Armas, Andrés Roldán Cordero, Roberto Pereira Hernández. Trainer: Tibor Ivánovics (Hungary).
**Goals**: 1-0 Ricardo Castro Valenzuela (18), 2-0 Hugo Sánchez Márquez (42), 3-0 Hugo Sánchez Márquez (51), 4-0 Manuel Manzo Ortega (53).

02.11.1981, Estadio Nacional "Tiburcio Carías Andino", Tegucigalpa; Attendance: 31,570
Referee: César Humberto Pagano Trucios (Peru)
**CANADA – EL SALVADOR**     **1-0(0-0)**
**CAN**: Martino Lettieri, Robert Iarusci, Robert Lenarduzzi, John McGrane, Bruce Alec Wilson, Gerard Gray, Brian Reginald Gant, Mike Sweeney, Dale William Mitchell (67.Gordon Sweetzer), Momcilo Stojanovic, Branko Segota. Trainer: Barrie Clarke.
**SLV**: Luis Ricardo Guevara Mora, Francisco Salvador Osorto Guardado, Jaime Alberto Rodríguez Jiménez, José Francisco Jovel Cruz, Carlos Humberto Recinos Ortíz, Juan Gilberto Quinteros (16.Miguel Guillermo González Barillas), José Norberto Huezo Montoya, José Luis Rugamas Portillo, Mauricio Quintanilla Villalobos (17.Mauricio Alberto Alfaro Valladares), Silvio Romeo Aquino, Jorge

Alberto González Barillas. Trainer: Mauricio Alonso Rodríguez Lindo.
**Goal**: 1-0 Momcilo Stojanovic (89).

03.11.1981, Estadio Nacional "Tiburcio Carías Andino", Tegucigalpa; Attendance: 45,386
Referee: José de Jesús Assis Aragão (Brazil)
**HONDURAS - HAITI**     **4-0(2-0)**
**HON:** Julio César Arzú, César Efraín Gutiérrez Álvarez, Jaime Enrique Villegas Roura, José Fernando Bulnes Zelaya, Allan Anthony Costly Blyden, Ramón Enrique Maradiaga Chávez, Eduardo Antonio Laing Carcamo, Javier Francisco Toledo Rivera, Jorge Elvir Urquía (49.Carlos Orlando Caballero Sánchez), José Roberto Figueroa Padilla (79.Salvador Bernárdez Blanco), David Buezo Guerrero. Trainer: José de la Paz Herrera Ucles.
**HAI:** Wilner Piquant, Daniel Cadet, Reginald Vielot, Guy Allen, Arsène Auguste, Shiller Mondesir, Frantz Mathieu, Gérald Romulus (Carmin Velima), Fritz Bobo, Emmanuel Sanon, Jean-Joseph Mathelier (Ernest Jean-Marie Baptiste). Trainer: Antoine Tassy.
**Goals:** 1-0 David Buezo Guerrero (35), 2-0 Jorge Elvir Urquía (40), 3-0 Eduardo Antonio Laing Carcamo (64), 4-0 José Roberto Figueroa Padilla (74).

06.11.1981, Estadio Nacional "Tiburcio Carías Andino", Tegucigalpa; Attendance: 33,358
Referee: Marco Antonio Regalado Méndez (Guatemala)
**CANADA - HAITI**     **1-1(0-1)**
**CAN:** Martino Lettieri, Robert Iarusci, Robert Lenarduzzi (46.Robert Bolitho), John McGrane, Bruce Alec Wilson, Gerard Gray, Brian Reginald Gant, Mike Sweeney, Gordon Sweetzer (68.Dale William Mitchell), Momcilo Stojanovic, Branko Segota. Trainer: Barrie Clarke.
**HAI:** Wilner Piquant, Daniel Cadet, Reginald Vielot, Frantz Mathieu, Guy Allen, Shiller Mondesir, Gérald Romulus, Ernest Jean-Marie Baptiste, Emmanuel Sanon, Carmin Velima, Maxime Auguste (57.Fritz Bobo). Trainer: Antoine Tassy.
**Goals**: 0-1 Gérald Romulus (34), 1-1 Momcilo Stojanovic (53).

06.11.1981, Estadio Nacional "Tiburcio Carías Andino", Tegucigalpa; Attendance: 33,237
Referee: José de Jesús Assis Aragão (Brazil)
**EL SALVADOR - MEXICO**     **1-0(0-0)**
**SLV:** Luis Ricardo Guevara Mora, Francisco Salvador Osorto Guardado (80.Miguel Ángel Díaz Arévalo), Ramón Alfredo Fagoaga Romero, José Francisco Jovel Cruz, Carlos Humberto Recinos Ortíz, Mauricio Alberto Alfaro Valladares (86.Joaquín Alonso Ventura), José Norberto Huezo Montoya, José Luis Rugamas Portillo, Ever Francisco Hernández, Silvio Romeo Aquino, Jorge Alberto González Barillas. Trainer: Mauricio Alonso Rodríguez Lindo.
**MEX:** Prudencio Cortés Sánchez, Mario Alberto Trejo Guzmán, Juan Manuel Álvarez Álvarez, Gustavo Vargas López, José Luis López Sánchez, Pedro Munguía Munguía (76.Jaime Cleofas Pajarito García), Guillermo Mendizábal Sánchez, Manuel Manzo Ortega (65.Tomás Juan Boy Espinosa), Leonardo Cuéllar Rivera, Ricardo Castro Valenzuela, Hugo Sánchez Márquez. Trainer: Raúl Cárdenas de la Vega.
**Goal**: 1-0 Ever Francisco Hernández (82).

08.11.1981, Estadio Nacional "Tiburcio Carías Andino", Tegucigalpa; Attendance: 33,876
Referee: Luis Paulino Siles Calderón (Costa Rica)
**HONDURAS - CUBA**     **2-0(1-0)**
**HON**: Julio César Arzú, César Efraín Gutiérrez Álvarez, Jaime Enrique Villegas Roura, Allan Anthony Costly Blyden, Hernán Santiago García Martínez, David Buezo Guerrero, Javier Francisco Toledo Rivera, Ramón Enrique Maradiaga Chávez, Eduardo Antonio Laing Carcamo (Carlos Orlando Caballero Sánchez), Jorge Elvir Urquía (Roberto James Bailey Sargent), José Roberto Figueroa Padilla. Trainer: José de la Paz Herrera Ucles.
**CUB**: José Francisco Reinoso Zayas, Carlos Loredo Pérez, Amado Lorenzo Povea Morillo, Francisco Carrazana Patrilge, Luis Manuel Sánchez Téllez, Dagoberto Lara Soriano, Reginoso Delgado Robau, Francisco Farinas Gutiérrez, Ramón Núñez Armas, Andrés Roldán Cordero (68.Carlos Gonzáles Acosta), Roberto Pereira Hernández. Trainer: Tibor Ivánovics (Hungary).
**Goals**: 1-0 David Buezo Guerrero (36), 2-0 Allan Anthony Costly Blyden (69).

11.11.1981, Estadio Nacional "Tiburcio Carías Andino", Tegucigalpa; Attendance: 22,774
Referee: David Stanley Socha (United States)
**CUBA – EL SALVADOR**     **0-0**
**CUB**: José Francisco Reinoso Zayas, Carlos Loredo Pérez, Amado Lorenzo Povea Morillo, Luis Manuel Sánchez Téllez, Reginoso Delgado Robau, Dagoberto Lara Soriano, Francisco Farinas Gutiérrez, Ramón Núñez Armas, Andrés Roldán Cordero, Francisco Carrazana Patrilge, Roberto Pereira Hernández. Trainer: Tibor Ivánovics (Hungary).
**SLV**: Luis Ricardo Guevara Mora, Francisco Salvador Osorto Guardado, Miguel Ángel Díaz Arévalo (Juan Gilberto Quinteros), José Francisco Jovel Cruz, Carlos Humberto Recinos Ortíz, Mauricio Alberto Alfaro Valladares, Joaquín Alonso Ventura (Mauricio Quintanilla Villalobos), José Norberto Huezo Montoya, Ever Francisco Hernández, Oscar Gustavo Guerrero Amaya, Jorge Alberto González Barillas. Trainer: Mauricio Alonso Rodríguez Lindo.

11.11.1981, Estadio Nacional "Tiburcio Carías Andino", Tegucigalpa; Attendance: 22,774
Referee: César Humberto Pagano Trucios (Peru)
**MEXICO - HAITI**     **1-1(0-0)**
**MEX**: Prudencio Cortés Sánchez, Mario Alberto Trejo Guzmán, Alfredo Tena Garduño (74.Tomás Juan Boy Espinosa), Juan Manuel Álvarez Álvarez, Rafael Toribio Arzáte, Gustavo Vargas López, Enrique López Zarza, Manuel Manzo Ortega, Leonardo Cuéllar Rivera, Ricardo Castro Valenzuela (68.Jaime Cleofas Pajarito García), Hugo Sánchez Márquez. Trainer: Raúl Cárdenas de la Vega.
**HAI**: Wilner Piquant, Daniel Cadet, Reginald Vielot (46.Guy Allen), Frantz Mathieu, Arsène Auguste, Shiller Mondesir, Gérald Romulus, Ernest Jean-Marie Baptiste, Carlo Brevil (27.Serge Chrispin), Emmanuel Sanon, Carmin Velima. Trainer: Antoine Tassy.
**Goals**: 0-1 Daniel Cadet (47), 1-1 Hugo Sánchez Márquez (87).

12.11.1981, Estadio Nacional "Tiburcio Carías Andino", Tegucigalpa; Attendance: 38,953
Referee: Marco Antonio Regalado Méndez (Guatemala)
**HONDURAS - CANADA**     **2-1(1-1)**
**HON**: Julio César Arzú, César Efraín Gutiérrez Álvarez, Jaime Enrique Villegas Roura, José Fernando Bulnes Zelaya, Allan Anthony Costly Blyden, Ramón Enrique Maradiaga Chávez, Héctor Ramón Zelaya Rivera, Carlos Orlando Caballero Sánchez, Jorge Elvir Urquía (83.Roberto James Bailey Sargent), José Roberto Figueroa Padilla, David Buezo Guerrero (74.Javier Francisco Toledo Rivera). Trainer: José de la Paz Herrera Ucles.
**CAN**: Martino Lettieri, Robert Iarusci, Robert Lenarduzzi, Ian Christopher Bridge, Bruce Alec Wilson, Gerard Gray (81.Dale William Mitchell), Wesley McLeod, Frank Ciaccia (46.Mike McLenaghen), Mike Sweeney, Momcilo Stojanovic, Branko Segota. Trainer: Barrie Clarke.
**Goals**: 1-0 Carlos Orlando Caballero Sánchez (12), 1-1 Ian Christopher Bridge (19), 2-1 José Roberto Figueroa Padilla (40).

15.11.1981, Estadio Nacional "Tiburcio Carías Andino", Tegucigalpa; Attendance: 22,396
Referee: Orlando Egbertus Biljout (Suriname)
**CUBA - HAITI** **2-0(0-0)**
CUB: José Francisco Reinoso Zayas, Carlos Loredo Pérez, Amado Lorenzo Povea Morillo, Luis Manuel Sánchez Téllez, Reginoso Delgado Robau (72.Carlos González Acosta), Dagoberto Lara Soriano, Francisco Farinas Gutiérrez, Ramón Núñez Armas, Andrés Roldán Cordero, Francisco Carrazana Patrilge, Roberto Pereira Hernández (35.Jorge Luis Rodríguez Álcaraz). Trainer: Tibor Ivánovics (Hungary).
HAI: Gérard Joseph, Daniel Cadet, Fritz Bobo, Frantz Mathieu, Jacques Louis (Jacques Jean-Louis), Ernest Jean-Marie Baptiste, Guy Allen, Shiller Mondesir, Carmin Velima (63.Maxime Auguste), Emmanuel Sanon, Gérald Romulus. Trainer: Antoine Tassy.
Goals: 1-0 Frantz Mathieu (55 own goal), 2-0 Ramón Núñez Armas (90).

15.11.1981, Estadio Nacional "Tiburcio Carías Andino", Tegucigalpa; Attendance: 22,395
Referee: David Stanley Socha (United States)
**MEXICO - CANADA** **1-1(1-0)**
MEX: Prudencio Cortés Sánchez, Mario Alberto Trejo Guzmán, Gustavo Vargas López, Fernando Quirarte Gutiérrez, Rafael Toribio Arzáte, Pedro Munguía Munguía (68.Manuel Negrete Arias), Enrique López Zarza, Tomás Juan Boy Espinosa, Leonardo Cuéllar Rivera, Ricardo Castro Valenzuela (46.Adrián Camacho Solís), Jaime Cleofas Pajarito García. Trainer: Raúl Cárdenas de la Vega.
CAN: Martino Lettieri, Robert Iarusci, Robert Lenarduzzi, Ian Christopher Bridge, Bruce Alec Wilson, Gerard Gray, Brian Reginald Gant (46.Mike Sweeney), Mike McLenaghen, Wesley McLeod, Momcilo Stojanovic (72.Gordon Sweetzer), Branko Segota. Trainer: Barrie Clarke.
Goals: 1-0 Ricardo Castro Valenzuela (29), 1-1 Ian Christopher Bridge (58).

16.11.1981, Estadio Nacional "Tiburcio Carías Andino", Tegucigalpa; Attendance: 39,882
Referee: Luis Paulino Siles Calderón (Costa Rica)
**HONDURAS – EL SALVADOR** **0-0**
HON: Julio César Arzú, César Efraín Gutiérrez Álvarez, Jaime Enrique Villegas Roura, José Fernando Bulnes Zelaya, Allan Anthony Costly Blyden, Ramón Enrique Maradiaga Chávez, Salvador Bernárdez Blanco, Javier Francisco Toledo Rivera, Carlos Orlando Caballero Sánchez, Junior Costly Rashford (Jorge Elvir Urquía 82), José Roberto Figueroa Padilla. Trainer: José de la Paz Herrera Ucles.
SLV: Luis Ricardo Guevara Mora, Francisco Salvador Osorto Guardado, Jaime Alberto Rodríguez Jiménez, José Francisco Jovel Cruz, Carlos Humberto Recinos Ortíz, Juan Gilberto Quinteros, José Luis Rugamas Portillo (83.Miguel Guillermo González Barillas), José Norberto Huezo Montoya, Ever Francisco Hernández, Silvio Romeo Aquino (62.Mauricio Quintanilla Villalobos), Jorge Alberto González Barillas. Trainer: Mauricio Alonso Rodríguez Lindo.

19.11.1981, Estadio Nacional "Tiburcio Carías Andino", Tegucigalpa; Attendance: 16,826
Referee: Osmond Downer (Trinidad and Tobago)
**EL SALVADOR - HAITI** **1-0(1-0)**
SLV: Luis Ricardo Guevara Mora, Francisco Salvador Osorto Guardado, Ramón Alfredo Fagoaga Romero, José Francisco Jovel Cruz (Miguel Ángel Díaz Arévalo), Carlos Humberto Recinos Ortíz, Mauricio Alberto Alfaro Valladares, José Norberto Huezo Montoya, José Luis Rugamas Portillo, Ever Francisco Hernández, Mauricio Quintanilla Villalobos, Miguel Guillermo González Barinas (Silvio Romeo Aquino). Trainer: Mauricio Alonso Rodríguez Lindo.
HAI: Gérard Joseph, Daniel Cadet, Guy Allen (Jean Louis), Frantz Mathieu, Shiller Mondesir, Gérald Romulus, Ernest Jean-Marie Baptiste, Jacques Louis (Fritz Bobo), Maxime Auguste, Emmanuel Sanon, Pierre Hugo. Trainer: Antoine Tassy.
Goal: 1-0 José Norberto Huezo Montoya (28 penalty).

21.11.1981, Estadio Nacional "Tiburcio Carías Andino", Tegucigalpa; Attendance: 16,458
Referee: César Humberto Pagano Trucios (Peru)
**CUBA - CANADA** **2-2(1-0)**
**CUB**: Cálixto Martínez Quezada, Carlos Loredo Pérez, Amado Lorenzo Povea Morillo, Luis Manuel Sánchez Téllez, Reginoso Delgado Robau, Dagoberto Lara Soriano, Francisco Farinas Gutiérrez (62.Carlos González Acosta), Ramón Núñez Armas, Andrés Roldán Cordero (83.Francisco López Rio), Francisco Carrazana Patrilge, Jorge Luis Rodríguez Álcaraz. Trainer: Tibor Ivánovics (Hungary).
**CAN:** Martino Lettieri, Robert Iarusci, Robert Lenarduzzi, Ian Christopher Bridge, Bruce Alec Wilson, Wesley McLeod, Gerard Gray, Mike Sweeney (68.Brian Reginald Gant), Dale William Mitchell (75.Robert Bolitho), Momcilo Stojanovic, Branko Segota. Trainer: Barrie Clarke.
**Goals**: 1-0 Jorge Luis Rodríguez (2), 1-1 Wesley McLeod (48), 2-1 Ramón Núñez Armas (74), 2-2 Robert Iarusci (84).

22.11.1981, Estadio Nacional "Tiburcio Carías Andino", Tegucigalpa; Attendance: 50,000
Referee: David Stanley Socha (United States)
**HONDURAS - MEXICO** **0-0**
**HON:** Julio César Arzú, César Efraín Gutiérrez Álvarez, Jaime Enrique Villegas Roura, José Fernando Bulnes Zelaya, Allan Anthony Costly Blyden, Ramón Enrique Maradiaga Chávez, Salvador Bernárdez Blanco, Héctor Ramón Zelaya Rivera, Carlos Orlando Caballero Sánchez (81.Juan Alberto Cruz Murillo), Jorge Elvir Urquía (69.Junior Costly Rashford), José Roberto Figueroa Padilla. Trainer: José de la Paz Herrera Ucles.
**MEX:** Francisco Castrejón Ramírez, Mario Alberto Trejo Guzmán, Juan Manuel Álvarez Álvarez, Fernando Quirarte Gutiérrez, José Luis López Sánchez, Gustavo Vargas López, Enrique López Zarza (69.Tomás Juan Boy Espinosa), Manuel Manzo Ortega, Guillermo Mendizábal Sánchez, Ricardo Castro Valenzuela, Hugo Sánchez Márquez. Trainer: Raúl Cárdenas de la Vega.

# AFRICA

## FIRST ROUND

Liberia, Sudan, Togo and Zimbabwe were directly qualified for the second round.

Egypt qualified for the second round (Ghana withdrew)

Madagascar qualified for the second round (Uganda withdrew)

| | | | | |
|---|---|---|---|---|
| 08.05.1980 | Tripoli | Libya – Gambia | 2-1(1-0) |
| 06.07.1980 | Banjul | Gambia - Libya | 0-0 |

### FINAL STANDINGS

| | | | | | | | | |
|---|---|---|---|---|---|---|---|---|
| 1. Libya | 2 | 1 | 1 | 0 | 2 | - | 1 | 3 |
| 2. Gambia | 2 | 0 | 1 | 1 | 1 | - | 2 | 1 |

Libya qualified for the second round.

08.05.1980, Stade 11 Juin, Tripoli; Attendance:
Referee: Gebre Jesús Tesfaye (Ethiopia)
**LIBYA – GAMBIA**     **2-1(1-0)**
LBY: Rajab El Fitouri, Tahir Saad Khair El Fezzani, Nagi Muftah El Gadi, Saleh Ali Sola, Abdulaziz Giuma El Shatani, Omar Mansour Mohammed, Salem Mohammed El Musmari, Garani Abdelrazik Salem, Abdul Nasir Mohammed Belhaj, Rashid Mohammed El Hashimi Rashid, Aboubakr Mohammed Bani.
GAM: Baboucarr Saho, Ibrahim Garba Touray, Francis Owen, Baboucar Bah, Momodou Sadi, Mustapha Badjié, Baboucar Sowe, Salihou Sarr, Alhagi N'Jié, Anthony Joiner, Assan Sarr. Trainer: Jallow Kabba.
**Goals**: *Goalscorers not known*!

06.07.1980, Box Bar Stadium, Banjul; Attendance: 1,240
Referee: Modibo N'Diaye (Mali)
**GAMBIA - LIBYA**     **0-0**
GAM: Baboucarr Saho, Ibrahim Garba Touray, Mustapha Badjié, Momodou Sibi, Baboucar Bah, Baboucar Sowe (60.Assan Sarr), Momodou Jah, Amat Joof, Anthony Joiner, Salihou Sarr, Sulayman Samba (60.Momadu Mousa). Trainer: Jallow Kabba.
LBY: Mohammed Ali Omar Lagha, Tahir Saad Khair El Fezzani, Salem Mohammed El Musmari, Saleh Ali Sola, Abdelrazik Salem Garana, Gumma Bashir Shushan, Nagi Muftah El Gadi, Abdul Nasir Mohammed Belhaj, El Sharif Abdul Salam El Marghani, Abubakr Mohammad Bani, Bashir Ali Salem.

| 18.05.1980 | Addis Abeba | Ethiopia - Zambia | 0-0 |
| 01.06.1980 | Ndola | Zambia - Ethiopia | 4-0(2-0) |

### FINAL STANDINGS

| | | | | | | | | |
|---|---|---|---|---|---|---|---|---|
| 1. Zambia | 2 | 1 | 1 | 0 | 4 | - | 0 | 3 |
| 2. Ethiopia | 2 | 0 | 1 | 1 | 0 | - | 4 | 1 |

Zambia qualified for the second round.

18.05.1980, National Stadium, Addis Abeba; Attendance: 20,000
Referee: Hussein Fahmi Bahig (Egypt)
**ETHIOPIA - ZAMBIA** **0-0**
**ETH:** Afework Tenagashaw, Asefa Solomon, Tereffe Degu, Gebre Neguse, Shewangezaw Tereffe, Adem Abdurahouman (35.Tesfa-Michael Dagnew), Olana Meseret, Mekonen Solomon, Takele Zewdu (68.Desalegn Bellete), Hailu Goshu, Asfaw Negusse. Trainer: Mengistu Worku.
**ZAM:** Kenneth Mwape, Milton Muke, Kaiser Kalambo, Michael Musonda, Kampela Katumba, Evans Katebe, Moses Simwala, Clement Banda, Alex Chola (68.Pele Kaimana), Godfrey Chitalu, Peter Kaumba. Trainer: Dick Chama.

01.06.1980, Dag Hammerskjoeld Stadium, Ndola; Attendance: 40,000
Referee: Zuberi Omari Bundallah (Tanzania)
**ZAMBIA - ETHIOPIA** **4-0(2-0)**
**ZAM:** Kenneth Mwape, Milton Muke, Kaiser Kalambo, Michael Musonda, Kampela Katumba, Evans Katebe, Moses Simwala, Clement Banda, Alex Chola, Godfrey Chitsula, Peter Kaumba (68.Pele Kaimana). Trainer: Dick Chama.
**ETH:** Afework Tenagashaw, Asefa Solomon, Tereffe Degu, Gebre Neguse, Shewangezaw Tereffe, Adem Abdurahouman, Mekonen Solomon (Desalegn Bellete), Tesfa-Michael Dagnew, Mamo Tamrate (Abedo Kedder), Hailu Goshu, Asfaw Negusse. Trainer: Mengistu Worku.
**Goals:** 1-0 Alex Chola (4), 2-0 Godfrey Chitalu (16), 3-0 Pele Kaimana (69), 4-0 Godfrey Chitalu (89).

| 31.05.1980 | Freetown | Sierra Leone - Algeria | 2-2(0-0) |
| 13.06.1980 | Oran | Algeria - Sierra Leone | 3-1(1-0) |

### FINAL STANDINGS

| | | | | | | | | |
|---|---|---|---|---|---|---|---|---|
| 1. Algeria | 2 | 1 | 1 | 0 | 5 | - | 3 | 3 |
| 2. Sierra Leone | 2 | 0 | 1 | 1 | 3 | - | 5 | 1 |

Algeria qualified for the second round.

31.05.1980, "Siaka Stevens" Stadium, Freetown; Attendance: 36,500
Referee: Tevi Lawson-Hetcheli (Togo)
**SIERRA LEONE - ALGERIA** **2-2(0-0)**
**SLE:** Thomas Okon Quinton, Amadu Kamara, Abdulai Jalloh, Kelfallah Kamara, Joseph Toby, George Floode, Alusine Sesay, Akie Noah, Sentu Johnson, Ismail Dyfan, Nabieu Bangura. Trainer: Kabba Kamara Wimen.
**ALG:** Lyacine Bentaala, Mahmoud Guendouz, Mustapha Kouici, Mohand Ouamar Grib, Chaabane Merzekane, Mohammed Kheddis, Mustapha Rabah Madjer (68.Djamel Menad), Ali Fergani, Tedj Bensaoula, Lakhdar Belloumi, Salah Assad. Trainer: Mahieddine Khalef.
**Goals:** 1-0 Akie Noah (58), 2-0 Ismael Dyfan (60), 2-1 Tedj Bensaoula (72), 2-2 Lakhdar Belloumi (85).

13.06.1980, Stade du 19 Juin, Oran; Attendance: 12,636
Referee: Youssef Mohammed El Ghoul (Libya)
**ALGERIA - SIERRA LEONE**                                             **3-1(1-0)**
**ALG:** Lyacine Bentaala, Mahmoud Guendouz (28.Salah Larbès), Mustapha Kouici, Abdelkader Horr, Chaabane Merzekane, Bouzid Mahyouz, Mustapha Rabah Madjer, Ali Fergani, Tedj Bensaoula, Lakhdar Belloumi, Salah Assad. Trainer: Mahieddine Khalef.
**SLE:** Thomas Okon Quinton, Amadu Kamara, Abdulai Jalloh, Kabba Kamara, Joseph Toby, George Floode, Alusine Sesay, Akie Noah, Sentu Johnson, Ismail Dyfan, Joseph Morsay. Trainer: Kabba Kamara Wimen.
**Goals:** 1-0 Ali Fergani (42), 2-0 Tedj Bensaoula (47), 3-0 Mustapha Rabah Madjer (78), 3-1 Sentu Johnson (79).

| | | | |
|---|---|---|---|
| 22.06.1980 | Dakar | Senegal - Morocco | 0-1(0-1) |
| 06.07.1980 | Casablanca | Morocco - Senegal | 0-0 |

### FINAL STANDINGS

| | | | | | | | | |
|---|---|---|---|---|---|---|---|---|
| 1. | Morocco | 2 | 1 | 1 | 0 | 1 | - 0 | 3 |
| 2. | Senegal | 2 | 0 | 1 | 1 | 0 | - 1 | 1 |

Morocco qualified for the second round.

22.06.1980, Stade "Demba Diop", Dakar; Attendance: 7,872
Referee: Aissaoui Boudabbous (Tunisia)
**SENEGAL - MOROCCO**                                        **0-1(0-1)**
**SEN:** Mansour El Hadji Wadé, Roger Mendy, Abdoulaye Ba, Momar Baye Diaw, Amadou Diakhou Gayé, Valera Jean-Dominique (Amadou Diop), Marie-Joseph Koto, Ba N'Diaye Ibrahim, Tassirou Diallo, Mamadou Lamine N'Diaye, Mohammed-Moustapha Ciss (El Hadj Salif Diagne). Trainer: Mady Kouyate.
**MAR:** Ezaki Badou, Houssin Bouchkhachekh, M'Barek El Filali, Ahmed Limane, Mohamed Mouhou, Fatmi Houmama, Said Sadiki, Abdelaziz Bouderbala (Mohamed Abdel Kebu), Jamal Jebrane, Abdelaziz Daidi, Mohamed Timoumi. Trainer: Yabram Hamidouch.
**Goal:** 0-1 Mohamed Timoumi (21).

06.07.1980, Stade d'Honneur, Casablanca; Attendance: 15,032
Referee: Théodore Koudou (Ivory Coast)
**MOROCCO - SENEGAL**                                        **0-0**
**MAR:** Ezaki Badou, Houcine Bouchkhachekh, M'Barek El Filali, Ahmed Limane, Mohamed Mouhou, Fatmi Houmama, Said Sadiki, Abdelaziz Bouderbala, Jamal Jebrane, Abdelaziz Daidi, Mohamed Timoumi (29.Ahmed Zebti). Trainer: Yabram Hamidouch.
**SEN:** Mansour El Hadji Wadé, Abdoulaye Ba, Oumar Touré, Amadou Diakhou Gayé, Jean-Dominique Valera, Roger Mendy, Thierno M'Boup, Macaty Camara, Marie-Joseph Koto, Jules François Bocandé, Mamadou Lamine N'Diaye. Trainer: Mady Kouyate.

| 22.06.1980 | Conakry | Guinea - Lesotho | 3-1(1-1) |
|---|---|---|---|
| 06.07.1980 | Maseru | Lesotho - Guinea | 1-1(0-1) |

### FINAL STANDINGS

| | | | | | | | | |
|---|---|---|---|---|---|---|---|---|
| 1. Guinea | 2 | 1 | 1 | 0 | 4 | - | 2 | 3 |
| 2. Lesotho | 2 | 0 | 1 | 1 | 2 | - | 4 | 1 |

Guinea qualified for the second round.

22.06.1980, Stade 28$^{ème}$ Septembre, Conakry; Attendance: 16,000
Referee: Doudou N'Jié (Gambia)
**GUINEA - LESOTHO**      **3-1(1-1)**
**GUI**: Mohammed Dioubaté, Moussa Camara, Salifou Sylla, Ibrahima Sory Touré, Alseny Diaby, Djibrill Diarra, Seydouba Bangoura, Aboubacar Touré (65.Kerfalla Bangoura), Naby Laye Camara (72.Mamady Cissé), Mory Koné, Camara Touré.
**LES**: Ronald Malefetse, Makhabane Mzili Mahkabane, Sele Leboela, Leboela Mohloli, Tseliso Khomari, Bahaleroe Leleka, Tsehla Mohloli, Seephephe Mochini Matete, Boniface N'Tsonyana, George M'Chunu, Dingaan Mefane. Trainer: Phumo Styles.
**Goals**: 1-0 Mory Koné (39), 1-1 Leboela Sele (44), 2-1 Naby Laye Camara (52 penalty), 3-1 Camara Touré (82).

06.07.1980, National Stadium, Maseru; Attendance: 4,325
Referee: Omari Bundalla Zuberi (Tanzania)
**LESOTHO - GUINEA**      **1-1(0-1)**
**LES**: Ronald Malefetse, Makhabane Mzili Makhabane (50.George M'Chunu), Sele Leboela, Leboela Mohloli, Mefane Dingaan, Leponesa Lulu Mefane, Tseliso Khomari, Seephephe Mochini Matete, Tsehla Mohloli, Sello Ramakau (80.Tsehla Lebone), Teboho Masia. Trainer: Phumo Styles.
**GUI**: Abdoulaye Keïta Sylla, Moussa Camara, Ibrahima Sory Touré, Alseny Diaby, Djibrill Diarra, Camara Touré, Seydouba Bangoura, Papa Camara, Mory Koné, Kerfalla Bangoura, Cheik Mohammed Keïta.
**Goals**: 0-1 Camara Touré (33), 1-1 Teboho Masia (65).


| 29.06.1980 | Yaoundé | Cameroon - Malawi | 3-0(1-0) |
|---|---|---|---|
| 20.07.1980 | Blantyre | Malawi - Cameroon | 1-1(0-0) |

### FINAL STANDINGS

| | | |
|---|---|---|
| 1. Cameroon | 2 | - |
| 2. Malawi | 2 | - |

Cameroon qualified for the second round.

29.06.1980, Stade "Ahmadu Ahdjo", Yaoundé; Attendance: 41,970
Referee: Festus Okubule (Nigeria)
**CAMEROON - MALAWI**      **3-0(1-0)**
**CMR:** Thomas N'Kono, Jacques Ename, Charles Epée (Dagoubert Moungram), Ibrahim Aoudou, Emmanuel Jerome Kundé, Grégoire M'Bida, Jacques N'Guea, René Emana, Théophile Abega, François N'Doumbé Lea, Roger Milla (Jean Manga Onguéné). Trainer: Branko Žutić (Yugoslavia).
**MWI:** Boniface Maganga, Harry Waya, Reuben Malola, Collins Thewe, Jack Chamangwana, Mosted Sichinga, Jonathan Billie, Maloya Siliya, Kinna Phiri, Stock Dandize, Barnet Gondwe. Trainer: Edward Powel.
**Goals**: 1-0 Roger Milla (35), 2-0 Emmanuel Jerome Kundé (54), 3-0 Théophile Abega (59).

20.07.1980, Kamazu Stadium, Blantyre; Attendance: 30,000
Referee: Nicholous Hoohlo (Lesotho)
**MALAWI - CAMEROON** **1-1(0-0)**
**MWI**: John Dzimbari, Harry Waya, Reuben Malola, Thomas Kazembe, Jack Chamangwana, Rodgers Yasini, Michael Kaimpa, Jonathan Billie, Kinna Phiri, Stock Dandize, Barnet Gondwe. Trainer: Edward Powell.
**CMR**: Thomas N'Kono, Charles Epée, Ibrahim Aoudou, François N'Doumbé Lea, Emmanuel Jerome Kundé, Grégoire M'Bida, Jacques Nolla, Jean Manga Onguéné, René Emana (Jean Daniel Eboué), Théophile Abega (Joseph Enanga), Jacques Ename. Trainer: Branko Žutić (Yugoslavia).
**Goals**: 0-1 Jean Manga Onguéné (70), 1-1 Stock Dandize (71).

| | | | |
|---|---|---|---|
| 29.06.1980 | Tunis | Tunisia - Nigeria | 2-0(1-0) |
| 12.07.1980 | Lagos | Nigeria - Tunisia | 2-0(1-0) |

### FINAL STANDINGS

| | | | | | | | |
|---|---|---|---|---|---|---|---|
| 1. Nigeria | 2 | 1 | 0 | 1 | 2 - 2 | | 2 |
| 2. Tunisia | 2 | 1 | 0 | 1 | 2 - 2 | | 2 |

Nigeria qualified for the second round.

29.06.1980, Stade Olympique d'El Menzah, Tunis; Attendance: 30,066
Referee: Ernst Dörflinger (Switzerland)
**TUNISIA - NIGERIA** **2-0(1-0)**
**TUN**: Mokhtar Naili, Mokhtar Dhouib, Ali Kaabi, Mohsen Jendoubi Labidi, Omar Jebaili, Samir Bakkaou (65.Khaled Ben Yahia), Témime Lahzami, Hedi Bayari (85.Mohammed Agrebi Ben Rehaiem), Mongi Ben Brahim, Tarak Dhiab, Mohammed Néjib Limam. Trainer: Ahmed Dhib.
**NGA**: Best Ogebegbe, David Adiele, Okey Isima, Muda Lawal, Frank Onwuachi, Tunde Bamidele, Segun Odegbami, Felix Owolabi, Ifeanyi Onyedika (Sylvanus Okpala), Alloysius Atuegbu, Adokiye Amiesimaka (Christian Chukwu). Trainer: Otto Martins Glória (Brazil).
**Goals**: 1-0 Mohammed Néjib Limam (31), 2-0 Témime Lahzami (52).

12.07.1980, National Stadium, Lagos; Attendance: 52,487
Referee: John Hunting (England)
**NIGERIA - TUNISIA** **2-0(1-0);**
**4-3 on penalties**
**NGA**: Best Ogebegbe, Sylvanus Okpala, Okey Isima, Ikhana Kadiri, Leotus Boateng, Tunde Bamidele, John Chiedozie (46.Felix Owolabi), Tunji Banjo, Segun Odegbami, Shefiu Mohammed (Emmanuel Osigwe), Adokie Amiesimaka. Trainer: Otto Martins Glória (Brazil).
**TUN**: Mokhtar Naili, Moktar Dhouib, Ali Kaabi, Mohsen Jendoubi Labidi, Omar Jebaili, Témime Lahzami, Samir Bakkaou, Mongi Ben Brahim, Tarak Dhiab (13.Hedi Bayari), Mohammed Néjib Limam, Khaled Ben Yahia. Trainer: Ahmed Dhib.
**Goals**: 1-0 Leotus Boateng (11), 2-0 Adokie Amiesimaka (74).

| 05.07.1980 | Nairobi | Kenya - Tanzania | 3-1(1-1) |
| 19.07.1980 | Dar es Salaam | Tanzania - Kenya | 5-0(1-0) |

**FINAL STANDINGS**

| | | | | | | | | |
|---|---|---|---|---|---|---|---|---|
| 1. | Tanzania | 2 | 1 | 0 | 1 | 6 | - 3 | 2 |
| 2. | Kenya | 2 | 1 | 0 | 1 | 3 | - 6 | 2 |

Tanzania qualified for the second round.

05.07.1980, City Stadium, Nairobi; Attendance: 8,650
Referee: Babiker Eise El Bedawi (Sudan)
**KENYA - TANZANIA**     **3-1(1-1)**
KEN: Mohammed Abbas, Joseph Chanzu, Peter Otieno, Hamisi Shamba, Josephat Murila, Jared Ingutia, Eric Omonge (46.Charles Ochieng), Jack Shikhul, Joe Masiga, Sammy Owino, Elly Adero. Trainer: Marshall Mulwa.
TAN: Juma Pondamali, Salim Amir, Leopold Tasso, Peter Tino, M'Temi Ramadhan, Mohammed Salim, Hussein N'gulungo (63.Juma N'Kambi), Ahmed Amasha, Omary Hussein (68.Charles Boniface), Thuwein Ally Wazir, Jella Matagwa. Trainer: Joel Bendera.
Goals: 1-0 Elly Adero (30), 1-1 Thuwein Ally Wazir (31), 2-1 Sammy Owino (57), 3-1 Sammy Owino (80 penalty).

19.07.1980, National Stadium, Dar es Salaam; Attendance: 5,940
Referee: Winston Gumboh (Zambia)
**TANZANIA - KENYA**     **5-0(1-0)**
TAN: Juma Pondamali, Mohammed Kajole, Leddegar Tenga, Leopold Tasso, Juma N'Kambi, Hussein N'gulungo, Tino Peter (46.Mohammed Salim), Mohammed Adolf Rishard, Thuwein Ally Wazir, Omary Hussein, Jella Matagwa. Trainer: Joel Bendera.
KEN: Mohammed Abbas, Joseph Chanzu, Charles Ochieng (46.Paul Ayongo), Hamisi Shamba, Josephat Murila, Jared Ingutia, James Ouma, Sammy Owino, Joe Masiga, Charles Otieno, Elly Adero. Trainer: Marshall Mulwa.
Goals: 1-0 Peter Tino (44), 2-0 Rashid Mohammed Adolf (52), 3-0 Peter Tino (70), 4-0 Thuwein Ally Wazir (72), 5-0 Thuwein Ally Wazir (80).


| 13.07.1980 | Kinshasa | Zaire - Mozambique | 5-2(1-1) |
| 27.07.1980 | Maputo | Mozambique - Zaire | 1-2(0-2) |

**FINAL STANDINGS**

| | | | | | | | | |
|---|---|---|---|---|---|---|---|---|
| 1. | Zaire | 2 | 2 | 0 | 0 | 7 | - 3 | 4 |
| 2. | Mozambique | 2 | 0 | 0 | 2 | 3 | - 7 | 0 |

Zaire qualified for the second round.

13.07.1980, Stade du 20$^{\text{ème}}$ Mai, Kinshasa; Attendance: 34,871
Referee: Stanislas Kamdem (Cameroon)
**ZAIRE - MOZAMBIQUE**     **5-2(1-1)**
ZAI: Robert Kazadi Mwamba, Suzeti M'Peti, Siluambanza Fila, Muzinga N'Goyi, Florian Lobilo Boba, Tshimini Mukandila (51.Mayanga Mutuale), Ayel Mayele, Tokodiafuansiuka Kiyika, Monga Lupeta (58.Muteba N'Daya), Ilunga Masengo, Mutubila N'Diela. Trainer: Mukendi Kalala.
MOZ: Jose Luis Da Silva, Federico Jane, Artur Meque, Joaquin João Fernandes, Armando Gaspar Mandito (46.Nito), Amade Chababe Amade, Francisco Rui Marcos, Eduardo Matsolo Dover, Gil Guiamba, Tomas Galton Banze, Miguel Júnior Xavier. Trainer: Cremildo Loforte.
Goals: 0-1 Gil Guiamba (23), 1-1 Tokodiafuansiuka Kiyika (30 penalty), 1-2 Gil Guiamba (50), 2-2 Muteba N'Daya (67), 3-2 Tokodiafuansiuka Kiyika (82 penalty), 4-2 Ilunga Masengo (85), 5-2 Muteba

N'Daya (87).

27.07.1980, Estadio Machava, Maputo; Attendance: 50,000
Referee: Raymond Ralibenia (Madagascar)
**MOZAMBIQUE - ZAIRE**  **1-2(0-2)**
**MOZ**: Luis Nuaila Sérgio, Federico Jane, Artur Meque, Joaquin João Fernandes, Armando Gaspar Mandito, Amade Chababe Amade, Francisco Rui Marcos, Eduardo Matsolo Dover, Gil Guiamba, Tomas Galton Banze (46.Alberto Siquice Ramos), Miguel Júnior Xavier. Trainer: Cremildo Loforte.
**ZAI**: Mukuaya N'Siampasi, Muzinga N'Goyi, Siluambanza Fila, Suzeti M'Peti, Imowa Malgbanga, Kamonga M'Welwa (14.Mayanga Mutuale), Ayel Mayele, Tokodiafuansiuka Kiyika, Muteba N'Daya, Kamonga M'Welwa, Ilunga Masengo. Trainer: Mukendi Kalala.
**Goals**: 0-1 Muteba N'Daya (15), 0-2 Ayel Mayele (17), 1-2 Francisco Rui Marcos (55 penalty).

| | | | |
|---|---|---|---|
| 16.07.1980 | Niamey | Niger - Somalia | 0-0 |
| 27.07.1980 | Mogadisho | Somalia - Niger | 1-1(0-1) |

### FINAL STANDINGS

| | | | | | | | | |
|---|---|---|---|---|---|---|---|---|
| 1. Niger | 2 | 0 | 2 | 0 | 1 | - | 1 | 2 |
| 2. Somalia | 2 | 0 | 2 | 0 | 1 | - | 1 | 2 |

Niger qualified for the second round.

16.07.1980, Stade "Général Seyni Kountché", Niamey; Attendance: 20,000
Referee: Lawson Tevi-Hetcheli (Togo)
**NIGER - SOMALIA**  **0-0**
**NIG**: Adamdogo Jacques Komlan, Daouda Tahirou, Hassane Adamou, Moussa Dari, D'Jibo Diamballa, Seydou Coulibaly, Amadou Diallo, Moussa Kamfideni, Garba Kamfideni, Mamane Ali, Bernard Akué Adjovi. Trainer: Adamou Bako.
**SOM**: Hassan Sheikh Awes, Salah Mohammed Omar, Mohidin Hagi Munye, Mohidin Ambar Khamis, Mohammed Ali Abdinoor, Ahmed Ibrahim Ali, Abdulatif Mohammed Bin Mohammed, Yusuf Mohammed Mahamud, Omar Abdullah Ali, Mohammed Ahmed Mukhtar, Islaw Yahia Mahadale. Trainer: Klaus Ebbighausen (West Germany).

27.07.1980, City Stadium, Mogadishu; Attendance: 13,000
Referee: Demeke Abate (Ethiopia)
**SOMALIA - NIGER**  **1-1(0-1)**
**SOM**: Hassan Sheikh Awes, Salah Mohammed Omar, Mohidin Hagi Muyne, Mohidin Ambar Khamis, Mohammed Haji, Ahmed Ibrahim Ali, Mohammed Noor Ibrahim, Omar Abdallah Ali, Islaw Yahia Mahadale, Abdulatif Mohammed Bin Mohammed (46.Mohammed Ahmed Mukhtar), Ismail Mohammed. Trainer: Klaus Ebbighausen (West Germany).
**NIG**: Jacques Adamdogo Komlan, Moussa Dari, Daouda Tahirou, Lawandidi Manzo, Hassane Adamou, Seyni D'Jibo, Garba Kanfideni, Mahaman Dodo, Bernard Akué Adjovi, Moussa Kanfideni, D'Jibo Diamballa. Trainer: Adamou Bako.
**Goals**: 0-1 Moussa Kanfideni (30), 1-1 Ismail Mohammed (90).

# SECOND ROUND

Egypt qualified for the third round (Libya withdrew)

| 12.10.1980 | Douala | Cameroon - Zimbabwe | 2-0(0-0) |
| 16.11.1980 | Harare | Zimbabwe - Cameroon | 1-0(1-0) |

### FINAL STANDINGS

| | | | | | | | | |
|---|---|---|---|---|---|---|---|---|
| 1. Cameroon | 2 | 1 | 0 | 1 | 2 | - | 1 | 2 |
| 2. Zimbabwe | 2 | 1 | 0 | 1 | 1 | - | 2 | 2 |

Cameroon qualified for the third round.

12.10.1980, Stade de la Reunification, Douala; Attendance: 47,840
Referee: Festus Okubule (Nigeria)
**CAMEROON - ZIMBABWE**     **2-0(0-0)**
**CMR:** Thomas N'Kono, Jacques Ename, Dagoubert Mougam, Ibrahim Aoudou, Emmanuel Jerome Kundé, René Emana, Eugene Ekeke, Jacques N'Guea (Jean Manga Onguéné), François N'Doumbé Lea, Jean Daniel Eboué (Grégoire M'Bida), Théophile Abega. Trainer: Branko Žutić (Yugoslavia).
**ZIM:** Bruce Grobbelaar, Oliver Kateya, Steven Chuma, Sunday Chidzamiga Marimo, George Rollo, David Isaac Mandigora, David Muchineripi, Charles Sibanda, Byron Manuel, Shackman Tauro, Majid Dhana. Trainer: John Rugg (Scotland).
**Goals**: 1-0 Grégoire M'Bida (50), 2-0 Jean Manga Onguéné (75).

00.00.1980, Rufaro Stadium, Salisbury; Attendance: 20,000
Referee: Lawrence Nyrenda Chayu (Zambia)
**ZIMBABWE - CAMEROON**     **1-0(1-0)**
**ZIM:** Bruce Grobbelaar, Oliver Kateya, Steven Chuma, Sunday Chidzamiga Marimo, Stanford Caitaunike, David Isaac Mandigora, David Muchineripi (60.George Rollo), Stanford MTizwa, Byron Manuel, Majid Dhana, Joseph Zulu. Trainer: John Rugg (Scotland).
**CMR:** Pierre Essers, Jacques Ename, Dagoubert Mougam, Ibrahim Aoudou, Emmanuel Jerome Kundé, Joseph Kamga (56.Jacques N'Guea), Grégoire M'Bida, Jean Manga Onguéné, René Emana, Jean Daniel Eboué, Théophile Abega. Trainer: Branko Žutić (Yugoslavia).
**Goal**: 1-0 David Muchineripi (29).


| 16.11.1980 | Fès | Morocco - Zambia | 2-0(2-0) |
| 30.11.1980 | Lusaka | Zambia - Morocco | 2-0(0-0) |

### FINAL STANDINGS

| | | | | | | | | |
|---|---|---|---|---|---|---|---|---|
| 1. Morocco | 2 | 1 | 0 | 1 | 2 | - | 2 | 2 |
| 2. Zambia | 2 | 1 | 0 | 1 | 2 | - | 2 | 2 |

Morocco qualified for the third round.

16.11.1980, Stade "Hassan II", Fés; Attendance: 6,375
Referee: Ali Ben Naceur (Tunisia)
**MOROCCO - ZAMBIA**     **2-0(2-0)**
**MAR:** Ezaki Badou, M'Barek El Filali, Abdelmajid Dolmy, Abbad Jawad El Andaloussi, Ahmed Limane, Fatmi Houmama, Mohamed Bousati, Mohamed Rabih, Jamal Jebrane, Abdelmajid Shaira (Abdelaziz Bouderbala), Ahmed Zebti (Mohamed Timoumi). Trainer: Yabram Hamidouch.

**ZAM:** Kenneth Mwape, Bernard Mutale, Kaiser Kalambo, Moffat Sinkala, Michael Musonda, Frederick Kashimoto, Alex Chola (Emmanuel Musonda), Pele Kaimana, Bizwell Phiri, Godfrey Chitalu, Willie Phiri. Trainer: Dick Chama & Theodore Dumitru.
**Goals:** 1-0 Mohamed Bousati (30), 2-0 Ahmed Limane (34).

30.11.1980, 7th April Stadium, Lusaka; Attendance: 6,334
Referee: Gebre Jesús Tesfaye (Ethiopia)
**ZAMBIA - MOROCCO**                        **2-0(0-0,2-0);**
                                                                             **4-5 on penalties**
**ZAM:** Kenneth Mwape, Emmanuel Musonda, Kaiser Kalambo, Moffat Sinkala, Michael Musonda, Frederick Kashimoto, Pele Kaimana (Harrison Bwalya), Willie Phiri, Alex Chola, Godfrey Chitalu, Bizwell Phiri. Trainer: Dick Chama & Theodore Dumitru.
**MAR:** Ezaki Badou, Driss Mouttaqui, M'Barek El Filali, Abbad Jawad El Andraloussi, Ahmed Limane, Fatmi Houmama, Mohamed Bousati, Jamal Jabrane, Mohamed Rabih, Abdelaziz Daidi, Abdelmajid Shaira (Khalid El Bied). Trainer: Yabram Hamidouch.
**Goals:** 1-0 Emmanuel Musonda (60), 2-0 Bizwell Phiri (78).

| 16.11.1980 | Antananarivo | Madagascar - Zaire | 1-1(1-0) |
| 21.12.1980 | Kinshasa | Zaire - Madagascar | 3-2(2-2) |

### FINAL STANDINGS

| | | | | | | | | |
|---|---|---|---|---|---|---|---|---|
| 1. | Zaire | 2 | 1 | 1 | 0 | 4 | - 3 | 3 |
| 2. | Madagascar | 2 | 0 | 1 | 1 | 3 | - 4 | 1 |

Zaire qualified for the third round.

16.11.1980, Stade Municipal de Mahamasina, Antananarivo; Attendance: 12,191
Referee: Jean Cyril Monty (Mauritius)
**MADAGASCAR - ZAIRE**                        **1-1(1-0)**
**MAD:** Ferdinand Rafalidianana, Jeremia Randriambololona, Raymond Realy, René Rabearisoa, Frédéric-Guy Rakotovao Daodisoa, Rodolphe Rakotoarisoa, Roland Rakotondrasoa, Jean-Jacques Razafimaharo, Augustus Marie Raonivelo, Michel Kira, Guy Rabemananjara. Trainer: Peter Schnittger (West Germany).
**ZAI:** Mukuaya N'Siampasi, Kuliwa Tshikalu, Siluambanza Fila, Suzeti M'Peti, Imowa Malgbanga, Kamonga M'Welwa, Ayel Mayele, Muyumba Nyenge, Muteba N'Daya, Mutubila N'Diela, Ilunga Masengo. Trainer: Mukendi Kalala.
**Goals:** 1-0 Michel Kira (26), 1-1 Malgbanga Imowa (74).

21.12.1980, Stade du 20[ème] Mai, Kinshasa; Attendance: 37,754
Referee: Angaud Joseph Blanchard (Congo)
**ZAIRE - MADAGASCAR**                        **3-2(2-2)**
**ZAI:** Robert Kazadi Mwamba, Kuliwa Tshikalu, Suzeti M'Peti, Siluambanza Fila, Imowa Malgbanga, Kamonga M'Welwa, Mayanga Mutuale, Ayel Mayele (Kongolo Wa Kongolo), Muyumba Nyenge, Ilunga Masengo, N'Tialukuna N'Zungu (Kasongo Museba). Trainer: Mukendi Kalala.
**MAD:** Ferdinand Rafalidianana, Harivony Andrianivosoa, Raymond Realy, René Rabearisoa, Frédéric-Guy Rakotovao Daodisoa, Rodolphe Rakotoarisoa, Roland Rakotondrasoa, Jean-Jacques Razafimaharo, Amidou Abdou Bin, Michel Kira, Guy Rabemananjara. Trainer: Peter Schnittger (West Germany).
**Goals:** 1-0 Suzeti M'Peti (1), 1-1 Kuliwa Tshikalu (19 own goal), 2-1 Ayel Mayele (26), 2-2 Amidou Abdou Bin (39), 3-2 Imowa Malbanga (75).

| 06.12.1980 | Lagos | Nigeria - Tanzania | 1-1(1-0) |
|---|---|---|---|
| 20.12.1980 | Dar es Salaam | Tanzania - Nigeria | 0-2(0-1) |

### FINAL STANDINGS

| | | | | | | | | |
|---|---|---|---|---|---|---|---|---|
| 1. Nigeria | 2 | 1 | 1 | 0 | 3 | - | 1 | 3 |
| 2. Tanzania | 2 | 0 | 1 | 1 | 1 | - | 3 | 1 |

Nigeria qualified for the third round.

06.12.1980, National Stadium, Lagos; Attendance: 70,000
Referee: Mohammed Larache (Morocco)
**NIGERIA - TANZANIA**     **1-1(1-0)**
**NGA**: Best Ogebegbe, Sylvanus Okpala, Okey Isima, Tunde Bamidele, Tunji Banjo, Franklin Howard, Alloysius Atuegbu (67.Henry Nwosu), Muda Lawal, Segun Odegbami, John Chiedozie, Felix Owolabi. Trainer: Otto Martins Glória (Brazil).
**TAN**: Juma Pondamali, Tair Yussuf Bana, Amasha Ahmed, Leddegar Tenga, Juma N'Kambi, Omary Hussein (46.Peter Tino), Charles Boniface, Mohammed Salim, Mohammed Adolf Rishard, Thuwein Ally Wazir (58.Mohammed Kajole), Jella Matagwa. Trainer: Joel Bendera.
**Goals**: 1-0 Muda Lawal (29), 1-1 Salim Mohammed (85).

20.12.1980, National Stadium, Dar-es-Salaam; Attendance: 30,000
Referee: Hussein Fahmi Bahig (Egypt)
**TANZANIA - NIGERIA**     **0-2(0-1)**
**TAN**: Juma Pondamali, Tair Yussuf Bana (54.Mohammed Adolf Rishard), Mohammed Kajole, Isihaka Hussein, Juma N'Kambi, Omary Hussein, Hussein N'gulungo (57.Charles Boniface), Peter Tino, Mohammed Salim, Thuwein Ally Wazir, Jella Matagwa. Trainer: Joel Bendera.
**NGA**: Best Ogebegbe, Sylvanus Okpala, Franklin Howard, Tunde Bamidele, Okey Isima, Alloysius Atuegbu, Muda Lawal, Tunji Banjo (46.Henry Nwosu), John Chiedozie, Christian N'Wokocha, Segun Odegbami. Trainer: Otto Martins Glória (Brazil).
**Goals**: 0-1 John Chiedozie (5), 0-2 Christian N'Wokocha (79).


| 07.12.1980 | Monrovia | Liberia - Guinea | 0-0 |
|---|---|---|---|
| 21.12.1980 | Conakry | Guinea - Liberia | 1-0(1-0) |

### FINAL STANDINGS

| | | | | | | | | |
|---|---|---|---|---|---|---|---|---|
| 1. Guinea | 2 | 1 | 1 | 0 | 1 | - | 0 | 3 |
| 2. Liberia | 2 | 0 | 1 | 1 | 0 | - | 1 | 1 |

Guinea qualified for the third round.

07.12.1980, Stade "Antoinette Tubman", Monrovia; Attendance: n/a
Referee: Tevi Lawson-Hetcheli (Togo)
**LIBERIA - GUINEA**     **0-0**
**LBR**: Boye Cooper, Charley Vinitius, Roland Browne, Nelson Sonpon, Joseph Nepay, Sarkpah N'vanseor, Klay Andrews, Walker Herron, Joseph Sion, Paul Broh, Frank Nagbae.
**GUI**: Mohammed Drenkali, Moussa Ekouasa, Djibrill Diarra, Ibrahima Sory Touré, Mamady Cissé, Sékou Sylla, Amara Touré, Cheik Mohammed Keïta, Mamadou Aliou Keïta, Jean Mara, Bengally Sylla.

21.12.1980, Stade 28ème Septembre, Conakry; Attendance: 15,524
Referee: Benjamin Kwabena Dwomoh (Ghana)
**GUINEA - LIBERIA** **1-0(1-0)**
**GUI**: Mohammed Dioubaté, Diaby Mamadi Cissé, Ibrahima Sory Touré, Siriman Kourouma, NFantsoumane Touré, Cheik Mohammed Keïta, Sékou Sylla, Mory Koné, Sylla Mohammed Lamine, Seydouba Bangoura (72.Jean Mara), Amara Touré.
**LBR**: Boye Cooper, Charley Vinitius, Roland Browne, Nelson Sonpon, Joseph Nepay, Sarkpah N'vanseor, Klay Andrews, Benedict Wisseh, Joseph Sion, Paul Broh, Morris Freeman.
**Goal**: 1-0 Seydouba Bangoura (55).

| | | | |
|---|---|---|---|
| 12.12.1980 | Constantine | Algeria - Sudan | 2-0(2-0) |
| 28.12.1980 | Khartoum | Sudan - Algeria | 1-1(0-0) |

### FINAL STANDINGS

| | | | | | | | | |
|---|---|---|---|---|---|---|---|---|
| 1. | Algeria | 2 | 1 | 1 | 0 | 3 | - 1 | 3 |
| 2. | Sudan | 2 | 0 | 1 | 1 | 1 | - 3 | 1 |

Algeria qualified for the third round.

12.12.1980, Stade du 17ème Juin, Constantine; Attendance: 50,000
Referee: Aissaoui Boudabbous (Tunisia)
**ALGERIA - SUDAN** **2-0(2-0)**
**ALG**: Mehdi Cerbah, Salah Larbès, Moustapha Kouici, Abdelkader Horr, Mahmoud Guendouz, Mohand Ouamar Grib, Ali Fergani, Tedj Bensaoula, Mohamed Kaci Saïd (75.Mustapha Rabah Madjer), Salah Assad (54.Nacereddine Abour), Djamel Menad. Trainer: Yevgeni Rogov (Soviet Union).
**SUD**: Ahmed Adam, Abdella Galal El Din, Sami Ezzeldin Hassan, Mohammed Faraq Fetah El Rahman, Said Defa Alla Hag, Moustapha Ahmed Ali Mohammed (Adam Abou Beida), Ammar Khalid, Mohammed El Rashied, Ibrahim Haroun Manzoul, Moustapha Ali Mohammed, Mohammed Mehi El Din (Abdel El Kheir El Gili). Trainer: Moreira.
**Goals**: 1-0 Tedj Bensaoula (10), 2-0 Ali Fergani (44).

28.12.1980, City Stadium, Khartoum; Attendance: 40,000
Referee: Youssef Mohammed El-Ghoul (Libya)
**SUDAN - ALGERIA** **1-1(0-0)**
**SUD**: Ahmed Adam, Abdella Galal El Din, Sami Ezzeldin Hassan, Abdella Salah El Din, Mohammed Faraq Fetah El Rahman, Said Defa Alla Hag, Ibrahim Haroun Manzoul (49.Mohammed Mehi El Din), Moustapha Ahmed Ali Mohammed, Ammar Khalid (72.Adam Abou Beida), Defaalla Abdelnour El Sayed, Monaim Abdel Monaim El Sheikh. Trainer: Amin Mohammed Zaki.
**ALG**: Mehdi Cerbah, Bouzid Mahyouz (88.Mahieddine Safsafi), Salah Larbès, Nourredine Abdallah Kourichi, Abdel Djadaoui, Mahmoud Guendouz, Ali Fergani, Mohand Ouamar Grib, Rabah Gamouh, Tedj Bensaoula, Salah Assad. Trainer: Yevgeni Rogov (Soviet Union).
**Goals**: 0-1 Rabah Gamouh (67), 1-1 Adam Aboa Beida (82).
**Sent off**: Monaim Abdel Monaim El Sheikh (87), Tedj Bensaoula (87).

| | | | | | | | | |
|---|---|---|---|---|---|---|---|---|
| 14.12.1980 | Niamey | | Niger - Togo | | | | | 0-1(0-0) |
| 28.12.1980 | Lomé | | Togo - Niger | | | | | 1-2(0-0) |

## FINAL STANDINGS

| | | | | | | | |
|---|---|---|---|---|---|---|---|
| 1. Niger | 2 | 1 | 0 | 1 | 2 | - | 2 | 2 |
| 2. Togo | 2 | 1 | 0 | 1 | 2 | - | 2 | 2 |

Niger qualified for the third round.

14.12.1980, Stade National, Niamey; Attendance: 10,000
Referee: Modibo N'Diaye (Mali)
**NIGER - TOGO** 0-1(0-0)
**NIG**: Jacques Komlan, Adamou D'Jibo, Daouda Tahirou, Djibril Djamala, Hassane Adamou, Diallo Adamou, Lawandidi Manzo (62.Seidou Samba), Mahmame Dodo, Bernard Akué Adjovi, Moussa Kanfideni, Garba Kanfideni (58.Abou Seydou). Trainer: Adamou Bako.
**TOG**: Ekpé Denagnon, Massaodou D'Jossé, Nassirou Alassani, Sakibou Issa, Kassi Denké, Mawuena Kodjovi, Ekué Montairou Rafiou, Akoulassi Djogou, Amouzougan (49.Ateha Yerima), Delali Agbetrobou, Adama Lobo. Trainer: Ibrahim Karim.
**Goal**: 0-1 Akoulassi Djogou (53).

28.12.1980, Stade "Général Eyadema", Lomé; Attendance: 10,000
Referee: Yardia Thiombiano (Upper Volta)
**TOGO - NIGER** 1-2(0-0)
**TOG**: Ekpé Denagnon, Massaodou D'Jossé, Nassirou Alassani, Sakibou Issa, Kassi Denké, Mawuena Kodjo, Delali Agbetrobou, Akoulassi Djogou, Ateha Yerima (37.Saibi Eklou Dodji), Ekué Montairou Rafiou, Kodjo Gnagnon (65.Abasse Ouré G'Belé). Trainer: Ibrahim Karim.
**NIG**: Jacques Komlan, D'Jibo Adamou, Daouda Tahirou, D'Jibo Diamballa, Hassane Adamou, Amadou Diallo, Lawandidi Manzo (46.Boukari Adamou), Abou Seydou, Garba Kanfideni (60.Bernard Akué Adjovi), Moussa Kanfideni, Mamane Ali. Trainer: Adamou Bako.
**Goals**: 0-1 Bernard Akué Adjovi (57), 1-1 Saibi Eklou Dodji (79), 1-2 Mamane Ali (82).

# THIRD ROUND

| 01.05.1981 | Constantine | Algeria - Niger | 4-0(1-0) |
|---|---|---|---|
| 31.05.1981 | Niamey | Niger - Algeria | 1-0(0-0) |

### FINAL STANDINGS

| | | | | | | | | |
|---|---|---|---|---|---|---|---|---|
| 1. | Algeria | 2 | 1 | 0 | 1 | 4 | - 1 | 2 |
| 2. | Niger | 2 | 1 | 0 | 1 | 1 | - 4 | 0 |

Algeria qualified for the fourth round.

01.05.1981, Stade du 17ème Juin, Constantine; Attendance: 60,000
Referee: Dodou N'Jie (Gambia)
**ALGERIA - NIGER**     **4-0(1-0)**
**ALG:** Lyacine Bentaala, Mahmoud Guendouz, Bouzid Mahyouz, Mustapha Kouici, Nourredine Abdallah Kourichi, Mustapha Dahleb, Mustapha Rabah Madjer, Ali Fergani, Lakhdar Belloumi, Tedj Bensaoula (78.Djamel Zidane), Salah Assad. Trainer: Yevgeni Rogov (Soviet Union).
**NIG**: Jacques Adangogo Komlan, D'Jibo Adamou, Daouda Tahirou, D'Jibo Diamballa, Hassane Adamou, Christova Adamou, Amadou Diallo (76.Boukari Adamou), D'Jibo Seyni, Lawandidi Manzo, Moussa Kanfideni, Mamane Ali. Trainer: Labo Chipraou.
**Goals**: 1-0 Mustapha Rabah Madjer (44), 2-0 Lakhdar Belloumi (46), 3-0 Nourredine Abdallah Kourichi (52), 4-0 Lakhdar Belloumi (78).

31.05.1981, Stade National, Niamey; Attendance: 7,000
Referee: Benjamin Kwabena Dwomoh (Ghana)
**NIGER - ALGERIA**     **1-0(0-0)**
**NIG**: Jacques Adangogo Komlan, Moussa Dari (21.Dan France), D'Jibo Adamou, Christova Adamou, Seyni D'Jibo, Lawandidi Manzo, Hassane Adamou, Moussa Kanfideni, Mamane Ali, Seydou Coulibaly, Bernard Akué Adjovi (75.Abou Seydou). Trainer: Labo Chipraou.
**ALG:** Lyacine Bentaala, Mahmoud Guendouz, Rabah Djenadi, Salah Larbès, Nourredine Abdallah Kourichi, Bouzid Mahyouz, Ali Fergani, Said Meghichi (83.Nasser Bouiche), Lakhdar Belloumi, Salah Assad, Mustapha Rabah Madjer (56.Mohamed Kaci Saïd). Trainer: Yevgeni Rogov (Soviet Union).
**Goal**: 1-0 Abou Seydou (89).

| 12.04.1981 | Conakry | Guinea - Nigeria | 1-1(0-1) |
|---|---|---|---|
| 25.04.1981 | Lagos | Nigeria - Guinea | 1-0(0-0) |

### FINAL STANDINGS

| | | | | | | | | |
|---|---|---|---|---|---|---|---|---|
| 1. | Nigeria | 2 | 1 | 1 | 0 | 2 | - 1 | 3 |
| 2. | Guinea | 2 | 0 | 1 | 1 | 1 | - 2 | 1 |

Nigeria qualified for the fourth round.

12.04.1981, Stade du 28ème Septembre, Conakry; Attendance: 30,000
Referee: Edward Bukenya (Uganda)
**GUINEA - NIGERIA**     **1-1(0-1)**
**GUI**: Abdoulaye Keïta Sylla, Mamadi Cissé, Djibrill Diarra, Ibrahima Sory Touré, Moussa Camara, Sékou Sylla, Cheik Mohammed Keïta, Naby Laye Camara (46.Aboubacar Ousmane Badara Bangoura), Mamadou Aliou Keïta (67.Kerfalla Bangoura), Seydouba Bangoura, Amara Touré.
**NGA**: Best Ogebegbe, Charles Yanchio, Leotis Boateng (Amos Edozegbe), Tunji Banjo, Tunde Bamidele, Okey Isima, Segun Odegbami (Anthony Orji), Christian N'Wokocha, Alloysius Atuegbu, John Chiedozie, Adokie Amiesimaka. Trainer: Gottlieb Göller (West Germany).

**Goals**: 0-1 John Chiedozie (21), 1-1 Ibrahim Touré (66 penalty).

25.04.1981, National Stadium, Lagos; Attendance: 70,000
Referee: Gebre Jesus Tesfaye (Ethiopia)
**NIGERIA - GUINEA**     **1-0(0-0)**
**NGA**: Best Ogebegbe, Sylvanus Okpala, Leotis Boateng, Tunde Bamidele, Tunji Banjo, Okey Isima, Segun Odegbami, Alloysius Atuegbo, Christian N'Wokocha, Henry Nwosu, Peter Egherevba (John Chiedozie). Trainer: Gottlieb Göller (West Germany).
**GUI**: Abdoulaye Keïta Sylla, Mamadi Cissé, Ibrahima Sory Touré, Moussa Camara, Djibrill Diarra, Sékou Sylla, Cheik Mohammed Keïta, Naby Laye Camara, Seydouba Bangoura, Amara Touré, Bengally Sylla.
**Goal**: 1-0 Henry Nwosu (90).

| 26.04.1981 | Casablanca | Morocco - Egypt | 1-0(1-0) |
| 08.05.1981 | Cairo | Egypt - Morocco | 0-0 |

### FINAL STANDINGS

| | | | | | | | | |
|---|---|---|---|---|---|---|---|---|
| 1. Morocco | 2 | 1 | 1 | 0 | 1 | - | 0 | 3 |
| 2. Egypt | 2 | 0 | 1 | 1 | 0 | - | 1 | 1 |

Morocco qualified for the fourth round.

26.04.1981, Stade d'Honneur, Casablanca; Attendance: 80,000
Referee: Nyrenda Lawrence Kabalamula Chayu (Zambia)
**MOROCCO - EGYPT**     **1-0(1-0)**
**MAR**: Abdelfattah BenM'Barek, Fatmi Houmama, Abdelmajid Dolmy, Abbad Jawad El Androussi, Mohamed Mouhou, Mohamed Rabih, Abdelaziz Daidi, Abdelaziz Bouderbala, Mohamed Bousati (75.Abdelmajid Shaira), Jamal Jebrane, Houssin Bouchkhachekh. Trainer: Yabram Hamidouch.
**EGY**: Ahmed Ikramy El Shahat, Hossam Mohammed El Badri, Ibrahim Youssef Awad Allah, Mohamed Maher Hammam Bedair Abu Kheir, Mohammed Omar El Zir, Hassan Ali Shehata (81.Ahmed Mohammed Hassan Mohammed), Shawki Ghareeb Bayoumi, Farouk Fouad Gaafar (75.Ramadan El Sayed Ali), Badawi Hammoudi Ibrahim, Moustafa Ahmed Abdou Ali, Mahmoud Ibrahim El Khateeb. Trainer: Karl-Heinz Heddergott (Germany).
**Goal**: 1-0 Abdelaziz Daidi (44).

08.05.1981, Nasser Stadium, Cairo; Attendance: 100,000
Referee: Cheikh D'Jibril M'Baye (Senegal)
**EGYPT - MOROCCO**     **0-0**
**EGY**: Ahmed Ikramy El Shahat, Hossam Mohammed El Badri, Ibrahim Youssef Awad Allah, Mohamed Maher Hammam Bedair Abu Kheir, Mohammed Omar El Zir, Ramadan El Sayed Ali, Shawki Ghareeb Bayoumi, Hassan Ali Shehata (Farouk Fouad Gaafar), Moustafa Ahmed Abdou Ali, Mahmoud Ibrahim El Khateeb, Mosaad Mustafa Mohammed Nour (Ahmed Mohammed Hassan Mohammed). Trainer: Karl-Heinz Heddergott (Germany).
**MAR**: Ezaki Badou, M'Barek El Filali, Abdelmajid Dolmy, Mohamed Mouhou, Abbad Jawad El Andaloussi, Fatmi Houmama, Abdelaziz Bouderbala, Mohamed Rabih, Jamal Jebrane, Abdelaziz Daidi, Mohamed Bousati. Trainer: Yabram Hamidouch.

| 12.04.1981 | Kinshasa | Zaire - Cameroon | 1-0(1-0) |
| 26.04.1981 | Yaoundé | Cameroon - Zaire | 6-1(3-0) |

## FINAL STANDINGS

| | | | | | | | | |
|---|---|---|---|---|---|---|---|---|
| 1. Cameroon | 2 | 1 | 0 | 1 | 6 | - | 2 | 2 |
| 2. Zaire | 2 | 1 | 0 | 1 | 2 | - | 6 | 2 |

Cameroon qualified for the fourth round.

12.04.1981, Stade du 20$^{ème}$ Mai, Kinshasa; Attendance: 80,000
Referee: Suleiman El Naim (Sudan)
**ZAIRE - CAMEROON** **1-0(1-0)**
**ZAI**: Mukuaya N'Siampasi, Suzeti M'Peti, Siluambanza Fila, Kanku Tshisambu, Imowa Malgbanga, Kamonga M'Welwa (72.Mayanga Mutuale), Ayel Mayele, Tshilumba Mukendi, Mondueni N'Kama, Kilengi Bumbu (46.Mobati N'Dalanco), Ilunga Masengo. Trainer: Mukendi Kalala.
**CMR:** Thomas N'Kono, René Brice N'Djeya, Ephrem M'Bom, François N'Doumbé Lea, Ibrahim Aoudou, Emmanuel Jerome Kundé, Grégoire M'Bida, Roger Milla, Paul Bahoken, Théophile Abega, Jacques N'Guea (Jean Manga Onguéné). Trainer: Branko Žutić (Yugoslavia).
**Goal**: 1-0 Mondueni N'Kama (23).

26.04.1981, Stade de le Reunification, Douala; Attendance: 55,197
Referee: Aissaoui Boudabbous (Tunisia)
**CAMEROON - ZAIRE** **6-1(3-0)**
**CMR:** Thomas N'Kono, René Brice N'Djeya, Ephrem M'Bom, François N'Doumbé Lea, Ibrahim Aoudou, Emmanuel Jerome Kundé, Théophile Abega (Joseph Kamga), Grégoire M'Bida, Roger Milla, Paul Bahoken (Jean Manga Onguéné), Jacques N'Guea. Trainer: Branko Žutić (Yugoslavia).
**ZAI**: Mukuaya N'Siampasi (48.Alima Monga), Suzeti M'Peti, Muzinga N'Goyi, Kanku Tshisambu, Imowa Malbanga, Kaniki Masengo, Ayel Mayele, Tshilumba Mukendi, Muteba N'Daya, Mondueni N'Kama (53.Mobati N'Dalanco), Ilunga Masengo. Trainer: Mukendi Kalala.
**Goals**: 1-0 Roger Milla (3), 2-0 Paul Bahoken (13), 3-0 Roger Milla (45), 4-0 Emmanuel Jerome Kundé (52), 4-1 Mondueni N'Kama (53), 5-1 Emmanuel Jerome Kundé (67 penalty), 6-1 Roger Milla (90).

# FOURTH ROUND

| 10.10.1981 | Lagos | Nigeria - Algeria | 0-2(0-2) |
| 30.10.1981 | Constantine | Algeria - Nigeria | 2-1(1-1) |

### FINAL STANDINGS

| | | | | | | | | |
|---|---|---|---|---|---|---|---|---|
| 1. | **Algeria** | 2 | 2 | 0 | 0 | 4 - 1 | 4 |
| 2. | Nigeria | 2 | 0 | 0 | 2 | 1 - 4 | 0 |

Algeria qualified for the Final Tournament.

10.10.1981, National Stadium, Lagos; Attendance: 80,000
Referee: Luigi Agnolin (Italy)
**NIGERIA - ALGERIA**      **0-2(0-2)**
**NGA:** Best Ogebegbe, Sylvanus Okpala, Okey Isima, Tunji Banjo, Christian Chukwu (46.Stephen Keshi), Tunde Bamidele, Segun Odegbami, Alloysius Atuegbu, Thompson Usiyan, Muda Lawal, Felix Owolabi (46.Christian N'Wokocha). Trainer: Gottlieb Göller (West Germany).
**ALG:** Mehdi Cerbah, Mahmoud Guendouz, Salah Larbès, Faouzi Mansouri, Nourredine Abdallah Kourichi, Mohamed Kaci Saïd, Fathi Chedel (Salah Assad), Ali Fergani, Djamel Zidane, Lakhdar Belloumi, Rabah Gamouh (Mustapha Kouici). Trainer: Yevgeni Rogov (Soviet Union).
**Goals:** 0-1 Lakhdar Belloumi (34), 0-2 Djamel Zidane (44).

30.10.1981, Stade de 17$^{ème}$ Juin, Constantine; Attendance: 60,000
Referee: André Daina (Switzerland)
**ALGERIA - NIGERIA**      **2-1(1-1)**
**ALG:** Mehdi Cerbah, Mahmoud Gendouz, Salah Larbès, Faouzi Mansouri, Nourredine Abdallah Kourichi, Mohamed Kaci Saïd, Mustapha Rabah Madjer, Bouzid Mahyouz, Djamel Zidane (31.Mustapha Dahleb), Lakhdar Belloumi, Rabah Gamouh. Trainer: Yevgeni Rogov (Soviet Union).
**NGA:** Best Ogedegbe, Sylvanus Okpala, Felix Owolabi, Augustine Fregene (64.Fatai Yekini), Leotis Boateng, John Chiedozie, Muda Lawal, Okey Isima, Henry Nwosu, Segun Odegbami, Tunde Bamidele. Trainer: Gottlieb Göller (West Germany).
**Goals:** 1-0 Lakhdar Belloumi (9), 1-1 Okey Isima (39), 2-1 Mustapha Rabah Madjer (84).


| 15.11.1981 | Kenitra | Morocco - Cameroon | 0-2(0-2) |
| 29.11.1981 | Yaoundé | Cameroon - Morocco | 2-1(1-1) |

### FINAL STANDINGS

| | | | | | | | | |
|---|---|---|---|---|---|---|---|---|
| 1. | **Cameroon** | 2 | 2 | 0 | 0 | 4 - 1 | 4 |
| 2. | Morocco | 2 | 0 | 0 | 2 | 1 - 4 | 0 |

Cameroon qualified for the Final Tournament.

15.11.1981, Stade Municipal, Kénitra; Attendance: 9,100
Referee: Cheikh D'Jibril M'Baye (Senegal)
**MOROCCO - CAMEROON**      **0-2(0-2)**
**MAR:** Raounaq El Jilali, Abdelmajid Dolmy, M'Barek El Filali, Mohamed Mouhou, Abbad Jawad El Andaloussi, Fatmi Houmama, Abdelaziz Bouderbala, Jamal Jebrane (65.Mohamed Abdelkebu Taissir), Mohamed Rabih, Azeddine Amanallah (46.Houssin Bouchkhachekh), Mohamed Bousati. Trainer: Yabram Hamidouch.
**CMR:** Thomas N'Kono, Michel Kaham, Ibrahim Aoudou, Emmanuel Jerome Kundé, Jean Daniel Eboué, Roger Milla, Jacques N'Guea, Jean-Pierre Tokoto, Paul Bahoken (80.Érnest-Lottin Ebongué), Théophile Abega, François N'Doumbé Lea. Trainer: Branko Žutić (Yugoslavia).

**Goals**: 0-1 Roger Milla (15 penalty), 0-2 Jean-Pierre Tokoto (40).

29.11.1981, Stade "Ahmadu Ahidjo", Yaoundé; Attendance: 100,000
Referee: Hussein Fahmi Bahig (Egypt)
**CAMEROON - MOROCCO** **2-1(1-1)**
**CMR:** Thomas N'Kono, Michel Kaham, Ibrahim Aoudou, Ephrem M'Bom, Grégoire M'Bida, Jean-Pierre Tokoto, Martin Maya, François N'Doumbé Lea, Roger Milla, Paul Bahoken, Théophile Abega.
Trainer: Branko Žutić (Yugoslavia).
**MAR:** Raounaq El Jilali, Houssin Bouchkhachekh, M'Barek El Filali, Abbad Jawad El Andaloussi, Noureddine Bouyahyaoui, Fatmi Houmama, Abdelaziz Bouderbala, Abdelkrim Merry, Azzeddine Amanallah (Mohamed Bousati), Mustapha Yaghcha, Mohamed Abdelkebu Taissir (Abdelaziz Daidi).
Trainer: Yabram Hamidouch.
**Goals**: 1-0 Ibrahim Aoudou (15 penalty), 1-1 Mustapha Yaghcha (25 penalty), 2-1 Roger Milla (47).

# ASIA / OCEANIA

## FIRST ROUND

### SUBGROUP A

| | | | | |
|---|---|---|---|---|
| 25.04.1981 | Auckland | New Zealand - Australia | 3-3(2-3) |
| 03.05.1981 | Suva | Fiji - New Zealand | 0-4(0-3) |
| 07.05.1981 | Taipei | Taiwan - New Zealand | 0-0 |
| 11.05.1981 | Jakarta | Indonesia - New Zealand | 0-2(0-1) |
| 16.05.1981 | Sydney | Australia - New Zealand | 0-2(0-1) |
| 20.05.1981 | Melbourne | Australia - Indonesia | 2-0(2-0) |
| 23.05.1981 | Auckland | New Zealand - Indonesia | 5-0(2-0) |
| 30.05.1981 | Auckland | New Zealand - Taiwan | 2-0(1-0) |
| 31.05.1981 | Suva | Fiji - Indonesia | 0-0 |
| 06.06.1981 | Suva | Fiji - Taiwan | 2-1(1-0) |
| 10.06.1981 | Adelaide | Australia - Taiwan | 3-2(1-0) |
| 15.06.1981 | Jakarta | Indonesia - Taiwan | 1-0(0-0) |
| 28.06.1981 | Taipei | Taiwan - Indonesia | 2-0(2-0) |
| 26.07.1981 | Suva | Fiji - Australia | 1-4(0-4) |
| 04.08.1981 | Taipei | Taiwan - Fiji | 0-0 |
| 10.08.1981 | Jakarta | Indonesia - Fiji | 3-3(3-1) |
| 14.08.1981 | Melbourne | Australia - Fiji | 10-0(3-0) |
| 16.08.1981 | Auckland | New Zealand - Fiji | 13-0(7-0) |
| 30.08.1981 | Jakarta | Indonesia - Australia | 1-0(0-0) |
| 06.09.1981 | Taipei | Taiwan - Australia | 0-0 |

### FINAL STANDINGS

| | | | | | | | | |
|---|---|---|---|---|---|---|---|---|
| 1. New Zealand | 8 | 6 | 2 | 0 | 31 | - | 3 | 14 |
| 2. Australia | 8 | 4 | 2 | 2 | 22 | - | 9 | 10 |
| 3. Indonesia | 8 | 2 | 2 | 4 | 5 | - | 14 | 6 |
| 4. Taiwan | 8 | 1 | 3 | 4 | 5 | - | 8 | 5 |
| 5. Fiji | 8 | 1 | 3 | 4 | 6 | - | 35 | 5 |

New Zealand qualified for the Asian Zone Final.

25.04.1981, Mount Smart Stadium, Auckland; Attendance: 10,000
Referee: Gianfranco Menegali (Italy)
**NEW ZEALAND - AUSTRALIA**     **3-3(2-3)**
**NZL**: Richard Hardie Wilson, John Bennett Hill, Richard Lloyd Herbert, Robert Ronald Almond, Glenn Laurence Dods, Duncan Edward Cole, Steven Paul Sumner, Keith Gordon MacKay (70.Adrian Coroon Elrick), Grant John Turner, Brian Alfred Turner (57.Clive Campbell), Stephen Wooddin. Trainer: John Adshead (England).
**AUS**: Allan Maher, Alan Davidson, Tony Henderson, Steve Blair, Steve Perry (84.John Yzendoorn), William Rogers, Murray Barnes, Kenneth Boden (69.Sebastian Giampaolo), John Kosmina, Edward Krncević, Peter Sharne. Trainer: Rudolf Gutendorf (West Germany).
**Goals**: 0-1 Edward Krncević (15), 1-1 Grant John Turner (24), 1-2 Kenneth Boden (31), 2-2 Stephen Wooddin (33), 2-3 Edward Krncević (42), 3-3 Steven Paul Sumner (80).

03.05.1981, Govind Stadium, Suva; Attendance: n/a
Referee: Othman Bin Omar (Malaysia)
**FIJI - NEW ZEALAND** **0-4(0-3)**
**FIJ**: Savenaca Waqa, Jone Nakosia, Choy Upendran, Abraham Watkins, Abdul Manaan, Vimlesh Singh (46.David Chung Leewai), Meli Vuilabasa, Feroz Khan, Inia Bola, Mohamed Saleem, Kalemedi Vosuga Cheeta (74.Gajendra Naidu). Trainer: Walter Cyril Joseph Hughes (New Zealand).
**NZL**: Richard Hardie Wilson, John Bennett Hill, Richard Lloyd Herbert, Robert Ronald Almond, Glenn Laurence Dods, Keith Gordon MacKay (Clive Campbell), Duncan Edward Cole, Steven Paul Sumner, Grant John Turner, Brian Alfred Turner, Stephen Wooddin (Samuel Alan Malcolmson). Trainer: John Adshead (England).
**Goals**: 0-1 Brian Alfred Turner (8), 0-2 Duncan Edward Cole (20), 0-3 Brian Alfred Turner (31), 0-4 Brian Alfred Turner (85).

07.05.1981, Municipal Stadium, Taipei; Attendance: 12,000
Referee: Toshio Asami (Japan)
**TAIWAN - NEW ZEALAND** **0-0**
**TPE**: Lin Chin-wang, Juang Jiunn-shiun, Hsu Chih-hsiang, Shiao Yung-fu, Chen Ing-ren (48.Tou Ten-sun), Chen Sing, Wu Jau-sin, Tsai Hong-yee, Jong Chien-wu, Lo Jin Fu-tson (75.Tou Ten-chen), Chang Kuo-chi. Trainer: Lew Pak.
**NZL**: Richard Hardie Wilson, John Bennett Hill, Richard Lloyd Herbert, Robert Ronald Almond, Glenn Laurence Dods, Clive Campbell (75.Allan Roderick Boath), Steven Paul Sumner, Duncan Edward Cole, Brian Alfred Turner (80.Adrian Coroon Elrick), Samuel Alan Malcolmson, Stephen Wooddin. Trainer: John Adshead (England).

11.05.1981, Senayan Stadium, Jakarta; Attendance: 47,000
Referee: Ausukont Nobnom (Thailand)
**INDONESIA - NEW ZEALAND** **0-2(0-1)**
**IDN**: Poerwono, Hamid Asnan, Didik Dharmadi, Suharno, Roland Hermanus Pattinasarany, Berty Tutuarima, Christian Wakano, Bambang Nurdiansyah, Zulham Effendy, Tanoto Wahyu (61.Bambang Sunarto), Rully Nere (77.Mettu Duaramuri). Trainer: Harry Tjong.
**NZL**: Richard Hardie Wilson, John Bennett Hill, Richard Lloyd Herbert, Robert Ronald Almond, Glenn Laurence Dods, Keith Gordon MacKay (75.Clive Campbell), Duncan Edward Cole, Steven Paul Sumner, Grant John Turner (79.Adrian Coroon Elrick), Brian Alfred Turner, Stephen Wooddin. Trainer: John Adshead (England).
**Goals**: 0-1 0-1 Brian Alfred Turner (14), 0-2 Grant John Turner (75).

16.05.1981, Cricket Ground, Sydney; Attendance: 12,000
Referee: George Roger Courtney (England)
**AUSTRALIA - NEW ZEALAND** **0-2(0-1)**
**AUS**: Gregory Woodhouse, Alan Davidson, John Yzendoorn, Steve Henderson, Steve Blair, Jim Tansey, William Rogers (46.Gary Cole), Murray Barnes, Edward Krncević (64.Kenneth Boden), Mark Jankovics, Peter Sharne. Trainer: Rudolf Gutendorf (West Germany).
**NZL**: Richard Hardie Wilson, John Bennett Hill, Richard Lloyd Herbert, Robert Ronald Almond, Glenn Laurence Dods, Duncan Edward Cole, Steven Paul Sumner, Keith Gordon MacKay (85.Samuel Alan Malcolmson), Grant John Turner, Brian Alfred Turner (85.Clive Campbell), Stephen Wooddin. Trainer: John Adshead (England).
**Goals**: 0-1 Stephen Wooddin (29), 0-2 Grant John Turner (84).

20.05.1981, Olympic Park, Melbourne; Attendance: 8,000
Referee: Viriato Graça Olivera (Portugal)
**AUSTRALIA - INDONESIA**     **2-0(2-0)**
**AUS**: Allan Maher, Steve Perry (76.Peter Katholos), Steve Blair, John Yzendoorn, Jim Tansey, Murray Barnes, Tony Henderson, Alan Davidson, Peter Sharne, Gary Cole, John Kosmina. Trainer: Ludwig Scheinflug.
**IDN:** Poerwono, Pasal Simson Rumah, Didik Dharmadi, Suharno, Roland Hermanus Pattinasarany, Subangkit, Waskito Kaihun, Bambang Nurdiansyah, Zulham Effendy, Rully Nere (71.Mettu Duaramuri), Berti Tutuarima (46.Tanoto Wahyu). Trainer: Harry Tjong.
**Goals**: 1-0 John Kosmina (29), 2-0 Alan Davidson (33).

23.05.1981, Mount Smart Stadium, Auckland; Attendance: n/a
Referee: Viriato Graça Oliva (Portugal)
**NEW ZEALAND - INDONESIA**     **5-0(2-0)**
**NZL**: Richard Hardie Wilson, John Bennett Hill, Richard Lloyd Herbert, Robert Ronald Almond, Glenn Laurence Dods (41.Adrian Coroon Elrick), Keith Gordon MacKay, Duncan Edward Cole, Steven Paul Sumner, Grant John Turner, Brian Alfred Turner (59.Clive Campbell), Stephen Wooddin. Trainer: John Adshead (England).
**IDN:** Poerwono, Simson Rumah Pasal, Didik Dharmadi, Roland Hermanus Pattinasarany, Subangkit, Tanoto Wahyu, Bambang Nurdiansyah, Suapri, Zulham Effendy, Rully Nere (72.Herry Kiswanto), Salasa Nasir. Trainer: Harry Tjong.
**Goals**: 1-0 Stephen Wooddin (9), 2-0 Brian Alfred Turner (34), 3-0 Grant John Turner (59), 4-0 Grant John Turner (65), 5-0 Adrian Coroon Elrick (81).
**Sent off**: Roland Hermanus Pattinasarany (59), Bambang Nurdiansyah (61).

30.05.1981, Mount Smart Stadium, Auckland; Attendance: 10,000
Referee: Anton Boskovic (Australia)
**NEW ZEALAND - TAIWAN**     **2-0(1-0)**
**NZL**: Richard Hardie Wilson, John Bennett Hill, Richard Lloyd Herbert, Robert Ronald Almond, Glenn Laurence Dods, Keith Gordon MacKay, Duncan Edward Cole, Steven Paul Sumner, Allan Roderick Boath (80.Clive Campbell), Grant John Turner, Stephen Wooddin. Trainer: John Adshead (England).
**TPE**: Lin Chin-wang, Hsu Chih-hsiang, Chen Sing, Tsai Hong-yee, Chow Tson-fu, Chang Kuo-chi, Lo Jin Fu-tson (62.Duh Deng-chyan), Wu Jau-sin, Duh Deng-sheng, Yu Jiann-cheng, Juang Jiunn-shiun. Trainer: Lew Pak.
**Goals**: 1-0 Stephen Wooddin (14), 2-0 Grant John Turner (75).

31.05.1981, National Stadium, Suva; Attendance: n/a
Referee: Lee Kok Leong (Singapore)
**FIJI - INDONESIA**     **0-0**
**FIJ**: Akuila Nataro Ravono, Jone Bulavinaka, Choy Upendran, Abraham Watkins, Inosi Tora, Abdul Manaan (46.Robert Kabakoro), Ananda Samy, Meli Vuilabasa, Feroz Khan, Mohamed Saleem, Ratu Jone. Trainer: Walter Cyril Joseph Hughes (New Zealand).
**IDN:** Poerwono, Hamid Asnan, Didik Dharmadi, Subangkit, Tanoto Wahyu, Zulham Effendy, Nasir Salasa, Herry Kiswanto, Christian Wakano (Mettu Duaramuri), Rully Nere, Badiaraja Manurung (Suharno). Trainer: Harry Tjong.

06.06.1981, National Stadium, Suva; Attendance: n/a
Referee: Harpajan Dhillon (Singapore)
**FIJI - TAIWAN** **2-1(1-0)**
**FIJ**: Akuila Nataro Ravono, Jone Bulavinaka, Abraham Watkins, Choy Upendran, Inosi Tora, Abdul Manaan, Ananda Samy, Meli Vuilabasa (52.Robert Tauni Kabakoro), Feroz Khan, Mohamed Saleem (72.Gajendra Naidu), Ratu Jone. Trainer: Walter Cyril Joseph Hughes (New Zealand).
**TPE**: Lin Chin-wang, Chang Kuo-chi, Chen Sing, Hsu Chih-hsiang, Chow Tson-fu, Tsai Hong-yee, Lo Jin Fu-tson (Duh Deng-chyan), Wu Jau-sin, Duh Deng-sheng, Yu Jiann-cheng, Juang Jiunn-shiun (Chang Huey-shiong). Trainer: Lew Pak.
**Goals**: 1-0 Ratu Jone (35), 1-1 Chang Kuo-chi (40), 2-1 Ratu Jone (55).

10.06.1981, Hindmarsh Stadium, Adelaide; Attendance: 1,800
Referee: Vichai Getkaew Charupont (Thailand)
**AUSTRALIA - TAIWAN** **3-2(1-0)**
**AUS**: Allan Maher, Robert Wheatley, Steve Blair, Tony Henderson, Alan Davidson, Gary Byrne, Peter Katholos, Murray Barnes, Edward Krncević, John Kosmina, David Mitchell. Trainer: Ludwig Scheinflug.
**TPE**: Lin Chin-wang (52.Chen Hung-chiang), Chang Kuo-chi, Chen Sing, Chen Ing-ren, Chie-Hsiang Hsu, Jong Chien-wu (63.Chang Huey-shiong), Chow Tson-fu, Lo Jin Fu-tson, Wu Jau-sin, Duh Deng-chyan, Duh Deng-sheng. Trainer: Lew Pak.
**Goals**: 1-0 Tony Henderson (18), 2-0 John Kosmina (56), 3-0 Gary Byrne (68 penalty), 3-1 Duh Deng-sheng (82), 3-2 Duh Deng-sheng (90).

15.06.1981, Gelora Bung Karno Stadium, Jakarta; Attendance: 14,000
Referee: Vichai Getkaew Charupont (Thailand)
**INDONESIA - TAIWAN** **1-0(0-0)**
**IDN**: Poerwono, Hamid Asnan (46.Pasal Simson Rumah), Didik Dharmadi, Berry Tutuarima, Herry Kiswanto, Nasir Salasa, Hadi Ismanto, Mettu Duararumi, Subangkit, Zulham Effendy (30.Christian Wakano), Rully Nere. Trainer: Harry Tjong.
**TPE**: Chen Hung-chiang, Chang Kuo-chi, Chen Ing-ren, Chen Sing, Chow Tson-fu, Lo Jin Fu-tson (57.Chang Huey-shiong), Lin Chiang-ming, Wu Jau-sin (46.Yu Jiann-cheng), Tsai Hong-yee, Duh Deng-sheng, Duh Deng-chyan. Trainer: Lew Pak.
**Goal**: 1-0 Hadi Ismanto (75).

28.06.1981, Municipal Stadium, Taipei; Attendance: 7,500
Referee: Nichi Junichi (Japan)
**TAIWAN - INDONESIA** **2-0(2-0)**
**TPE**: Lin Chin-wang, Chen Ing-ren, Hsu Chih-hsiang, Chen Sing, Chang Kuo-chi, Jong Chien-wu (46.Juang Jiunn-shiun), Chow Tson-fu, Lo Jin Fu-tson (74.Tsai Hong-yee), Wu Jau-sin, Duh Deng-chyan, Duh Deng-sheng. Trainer: Lew Pak.
**IDN**: Poerwono, Pasal Simson Rumah, Didik Dharmadi, Suharno (71.Hamid Asnan), Hadi Ismanto, Herry Riswanto, Zulham Effendy, Mettu Duararumi, Berry Tutuarima (31.Subangkit), Rully Nere, Nasir Salasa. Trainer: Eddang Witarsa.
**Goals**: 1-0 Duh Deng-chyan (32), 2-0 Lo Jin Fu-tson (37).

26.07.1981, National Stadium, Suva; Attendance: 11,000
Referee: Hardjowasito Sudarso (Indonesia)
**FIJI - AUSTRALIA** **1-4(0-4)**
**FIJ**: Akuila Nataro Ravono, Jone Bulavinaka, Abraham Watkins, Choy Upendran, Abdul Manaan, Ananda Samy (46.Feroz Kahn), Meli Vuilabasa, Mohamed Saleem, John Williams, Ratu Jone, Inosi Tora. Trainer: Walter Cyril Joseph Hughes (New Zealand).
**AUS**: Allan Maher, Alan Davidson (Robert Wheatley), Alan Niven, Tony Henderson, Steve Blair, Gary Byrne, Murray Barnes, Peter Katholos, Peter Sharne, Gary Cole, David Mitchell. Trainer: Ludwig Scheinflug.

**Goals**: 0-1 Gary Cole (4), 0-2 Murray Barnes (10), 0-3 Peter Sharne (28), 0-4 Gary Cole (31), 1-4 Abdul Manaan (83).

04.08.1981, Municipal Stadium, Taipei; Attendance: 5,600
Referee: César Brillantes (Philippines)
**TAIWAN - FIJI** **0-0**
TPE: Lin Chin-wang, Chen Ing-ren, Chang Kuo-chi, Hsu Chih-hsiang, Chen Sing, Shiao Yung-fu, Jong Chien-wu, Chow Tson-fu, Lo Jin Fu-tson, Duh Deng-sheng, Duh Deng-chyan. Trainer: Lew Pak.
FIJ: Akuila Nataro Ravono, Jone Nakosia, Abraham Watkins, Ram Vinod (30.John Morris Williams), Stanley Morrel, Inosi Tora, Mohamed Saleem, Meli Vuilabasa, Gajendra Naidu, Ratu Jone, Abdul Manaan. Trainer: Walter Cyril Joseph Hughes (New Zealand).

10.08.1981, Senayan Stadium, Jakarta; Attendance: 16,000
Referee: Tulu Gurkan (Philippines)
**INDONESIA - FIJI** **3-3(3-1)**
IDN: Poerwono, Simson Rumah Pasal, Didik Dharmadi, Nasir Salasa, Herry Kiswanto, Hadi Sofyan, Hadi Ismanto (77.Bambang Sunarto), Rully Nere, Herry Risdianto, Yohanes Budi, Stefanus Sirey (53.Dede Sulaiman). Trainer: Harry Tjong.
FIJ: Akuila Nataro Ravono, Choy Upendran, Abraham Watkins, Jone Bulavinaka, Inosi Tora, John Morris Williams, Meli Vuilabasa, Mohamed Saleem (31.Robert Tauni Kabakoro), Feroz Khan (46.Dewan Chand), Abdul Manaan, Ratu Jone. Trainer: Billy Singh.
**Goals**: 1-0 Nasir Salasa (9), 2-0 Herry Risdianto (18), 3-0 Herry Risdianto (39), 3-1 Williams John Morris (40), 3-2 Ratu Jone (47), 3-3 Bulavinaka Jone (85).

14.08.1981, Olympic Park, Melbourne; Attendance: 3,500
Referee: Ausujkont Nobnom (Thailand)
**AUSTRALIA - FIJI** **10-0(3-0)**
AUS: Martyn Crook, Alan Davidson, Steve Blair, Tony Henderson, Alan Niven, Murray Barnes, Gary Byrne, Peter Katholos, Peter Sharne, Gary Cole, David Mitchell. Trainer: Ludwig Scheinflug.
FIJ: Akuila Nataro Ravono, Jone Bulavinaka, Abraham Watkins, Choy Upendran, Stan Morrell (46.Mohamed Saleem), Abdul Manaan, Ananda Samy, Meli Vuilabasa, John Morris Williams, Ratu Jone, Inosi Tora. Trainer: Walter Cyril Joseph Hughes (New Zealand).
**Goals**: 1-0 David Mitchell (28), 2-0 Gary Cole (37), 3-0 David Mitchell (43), 4-0 Gary Cole (44), 5-0 Gary Cole (54), 6-0 Gary Cole (63), 7-0 Gary Cole (70), 8-0 Gary Cole (71), 9-0 Gary Cole (76), 10-0 David Mitchell (80).

16.08.1981, Mount Smart Stadium, Auckland; Attendance: 10,000
Referee: Vichai Getkaew Charupont (Thailand)
**NEW ZEALAND - FIJI** **13-0(7-0)**
NZL: Richard Hardie Wilson, John Bennett Hill (78.David John Bright), Richard Lloyd Herbert, Robert Ronald Almond, Adrian Coroon Elrick, Keith Gordon MacKay, Duncan Edward Cole, Steven Paul Sumner, Grant John Turner (48.Allan Roderick Boath), Brian Alfred Turner, Stephen Wooddin. Trainer: John Adshead (England).
FIJ: Eroni Kabulala (46.Akuila Nataro Ravono), Jone Bulavinaka, Abraham Watkins, Choy Upendran, Abdul Manaan, Meli Vuilabasa, Feroz Khan (24.John Morris Williams), Mohamed Saleem, Ratu Jone, Robert Tauni Kabakoro, Dewan Chand. Trainer: Manni Nikker.
**Goals**: 1-0 Stephen Wooddin (2), 2-0 Steven Paul Sumner (8), 3-0 Grant John Turner (9), 4-0 Grant John Turner (31), 5-0 Duncan Edward Cole (36), 6-0 Brian Alfred Turner (40), 7-0 Steven Paul Sumner (45), 8-0 Keith Gordon MacKay (48), 9-0 Steven Paul Sumner (55), 10-0 Steven Paul Sumner (60), 11-0 Steven Paul Sumner (72), 12-0 Brian Alfred Turner (85), 13-0 Steven Paul Sumner (86).

30.08.1981, "Gelora 10th November" Stadium, Suribaya; Attendance: 25,000
Referee: Reynaldo Reyes (Philippines)
**INDONESIA - AUSTRALIA**                                                1-0(0-0)
**IDN:** Poerwono, Pasal Simson Rumah, Didik Dharmadi, Hamid Asnan, Riono Asnan, Herry Kiswanto, Hadi Ismanto, Abdul Rachman Gurning, Herry Risdianto, Rully Nere, Stefanus Daniel Sirey (46.Dede Sulaiman). Trainer: Harry Tjong.
**AUS:** Glen Ahearn, Robert Wheatley (78.Howard Tredinnick), Oscar Crino, Steve Blair, Brett Woods, James Patikas (86.Dennis Colusso), Peter Raskopoulos, Paul Kay, Grant Lee, David Mitchell, Mark Koussas. Trainer: Ludwig Scheinflug.
**Goal:** 1-0 Herry Risdianto (88).

06.09.1981, Taipei Track & Field Stadium, Taipei; Attendance: 7,000
Referee: Tulu Gurkan (Philippines)
**TAIWAN - AUSTRALIA**                                                   0-0
**TPE:** Chen Hung-chiang, Hsu Chih-hsiang, Chen Ing-ren, Juang Jiunn-shiun, Chen Sing, Chow Tson-fu, Yu Jiann-cheng, Jong Chien-wu, Duh Deng-sheng, Chang Kuo-chi, Duh Deng-chyan. Trainer: Lew Pak.
**AUS:** Glen Ahearn, Robert Wheatley, Oscar Crino, Steve Blair, Howard Tredinnick, Peter Kay, Peter Raskopoulos, James Patikas, Grant Lee, David Mitchell, Mark Koussas. Trainer: Ludwig Scheinflug.

## SUBGROUP B

| Date | Venue | Match | Result |
|---|---|---|---|
| 18.03.1981 | Riyadh | Qatar - Iraq | 0-1(0-0) |
| 19.03.1981 | Riyadh | Syria - Bahrain | 0-1(0-0) |
| 21.03.1981 | Riyadh | Iraq - Saudi Arabia | 0-1(0-0) |
| 22.03.1981 | Riyadh | Qatar - Bahrain | 3-0(2-0) |
| 24.03.1981 | Riyadh | Syria - Saudi Arabia | 0-2(0-0) |
| 25.03.1981 | Riyadh | Iraq - Bahrain | 2-0(1-0) |
| 27.03.1981 | Riyadh | Qatar - Syria | 2-1(1-1) |
| 28.03.1981 | Riyadh | Bahrain - Saudi Arabia | 0-1(0-0) |
| 30.03.1981 | Riyadh | Iraq - Syria | 2-1(1-0) |
| 31.03.1981 | Riyadh | Qatar - Saudi Arabia | 0-1(0-0) |

### FINAL STANDINGS

| | | | | | | | | | |
|---|---|---|---|---|---|---|---|---|---|
| 1. | Saudi Arabia | 4 | 4 | 0 | 0 | 5 | - | 0 | 8 |
| 2. | Iraq | 4 | 3 | 0 | 1 | 5 | - | 2 | 6 |
| 3. | Qatar | 4 | 2 | 0 | 2 | 5 | - | 3 | 4 |
| 4. | Bahrain | 4 | 1 | 0 | 3 | 1 | - | 6 | 2 |
| 5. | Syria | 4 | 0 | 0 | 4 | 2 | - | 7 | 0 |

Saudi Arabia qualified for the Asian Zone Final.

18.03.1981, Malaz Stadium, Riyadh (Saudi Arabia); Attendance: 10,751
Referee: Anton Boskovic (Australia)
**QATAR - IRAQ**　　　　　　　　　　　　　　　　　　　　　　　**0-1(0-0)**
**QAT**: Mohammed Sami Wafah, Majid Bakhit Maayouf, Anbar Basheer Abubakr, Anbar Mubarak Al Ali, Samir Abbas Al Mas, Mohammed Saed Jaher Afifa, Hassan Matar Sayed Al Suwaidi, Hassan Abdul Rahman Abdullah Al Qadi, Ibrahim Khalfan Ahmed, Mansour Muftah Faraj Bekhit (89.Bader Bilal Salem), Khalid Mohammed Salman Al Muhannadi. Trainer: Evaristo de Macedo Filho (Brazil).
**IRQ**: Raad Hammoudi Salman, Ibrahim Ali Kadhim, Hassan Farhan Hassoon, Nadhim Shaker Salim, Adnan Darjal Matar, Natiq Hashim Abidoun, Hadi Ahmed Bashir (61.Jassem Mohammed Saad), Adel Khedeyer Hafidh, Salim Maliq Aziz (23.Nizar Ashraf Suleiman), Jasim Falah Hassan, Hussein Saeed Mohammed. Trainer: Vojo Gardašević (Yugoslavia).
**Goal**: 0-1 Hussein Saeed Mohammed (84).

19.03.1981, Malaz Stadium, Riyadh (Saudi Arabia); Attendance: 4,154
Referee: Toshikazu Sano (Japan)
**SYRIA - BAHRAIN**　　　　　　　　　　　　　　　　　　　　　**0-1(0-0)**
**SYR**: Ahmad Eid Maher Berakdar, Riad Mohammed Asfahany, Mohammed Shait Ahmed Jehad, Anwar Kasem (64.Dahbour Emad), Samir Zuhair Assassa, Hawash Ahmed (54.Watad Ahmed Mohammed), Haissam Mohammed Shehadeh, Mohammed Jazae'rly, Kivork Mardekian, Marwan Mohammed Medrati, Mohammed Ali Dahman. Trainer: Mohammed Azzam.
**BHR**: Hamoud Sultan Mazkoor, Mohammed Sultan Mazkoor, Rushdan Riyadh, Abdullah Bader, Abdul Karim Bekheit (33.Ali Abdul Aziz), Mohammed Al Zayyani, Ibrahim Zowayed (73.Jasem Al Khajam), Khalaf Mohammed Hamad, Ibrahim Al Farhan, Fouad Abou Shaqr, Shewaiaer Khalil. Trainer: Ali Farouk.
**Goal**: 0-1 Fouad Abou Shaqr (89 penalty).

21.03.1981, Malaz Stadium, Riyadh; Attendance: 18,738
Referee: Mario Rubio Vásquez (Mexico)
**IRAQ - SAUDI ARABIA**　　　　　　　　　　　　　　　　　　**0-1(0-0)**
**IRQ**: Raad Hammoudi Salman, Ibrahim Ali Kadhim, Nadhim Shaker Salim, Hassan Farhan Hassoon, Adnan Darjal Matar, Harres Mohammed Hassan (73.Natiq Hashim Abidoun), Hadi Ahmed Bashir, Adel Khedeyer Hafidh, Faisal Jabun, Hussein Saeed Mohammed (46.Nazar Ashraf Suleimann), Jasim Falah Hassan. Trainer: Vojo Gardašević (Yugoslavia).
**KSA**: Salim Abdul Rahman Aly Marwan, Abdullah Obeid Al Harbi, Saleh Mohammed Al Neaaimah, Mohammed Abdul Al Jawad, Othman Marzouq Al Fairoz Mubarak, Ahmed Yehya Al Nefawy, Amin Mohammed Dabo, Ahmed Abdullah Al Sagheer (60.Saleh Khalifah Hamid Al Dossary), Majed Ahmed Abdullah Al Mohammed (20.Saoud Mohammed Jassem Bo Saeed), Fahad Mohammed Saleh Al Mesaibeth, Yusuf Rashed Khamees Al Ola. Trainer: Rubens Francisco Minelli (Brazil).
**Goal**: 0-1 Amin Mohammed Dabo (82).
**Sent off**: Adel Khedeyer Hafidh (56).

22.03.1981, Malaz Stadium, Riyadh (Saudi Arabia); Attendance:
Referee: Lee Kok Leong (Singapore)
**QATAR - BAHRAIN**　　　　　　　　　　　　　　　　　　　　**3-0(2-0)**
**QAT**: Mohammed Sami Wafah, Majid Bakhit Maayouf, Anbar Basheer Abubakr, Anbar Mubarak Al Ali, Samir Abbas Al Mas, Hassan Abdul Rahman Abdullah Al Qadi, Mohammed Saed Jaber Afifa, Ibrahim Khalfah Ahmed, Hassan Matar Sayed Al Suwaidi, Mansour Muftah Faraj Bekhit (72.Bader Bilal Salem), Khalid Mohammed Salman Al Muhannadi. Trainer: Evaristo de Macedo Filho (Brazil).
**BHR**: Hamoud Sultan Mazkoor, Mohammed Sultan Mazkoor, Abdullah Bader, Ali Abdul Aziz, Rushdan Riyadh, Ibrahim Zowayed (47.Ibrahim Hassan), Mohammed Al Zayyani (70.Jasem Al Khajam), Khalaf Mohammed Hamad, Ibrahim Al Farhan, Fouad Abou Shaqr, Shewaiaer Khalil. Trainer: Ali Farouk.
**Goals**: 1-0 Mansour Muftah Faraj Bekhit (21), 2-0 Khalid Mohammed Salman Al Muhannadi (35), 3-0 Mansour Muftah Faraj Bekhit (64).

24.03.1981, Malaz Stadium, Riyadh; Attendance: 30,000
Referee: Nishi Junichi (Japan)
**SYRIA - SAUDI ARABIA**                                                                **0-2(0-0)**
**SYR**: Nafeh Abed El Kader Huwaij, Riad Mohammed Asfahany, Shalaby Hashem, Haissam Mohammed Shehadeh, Mohammed Ali Dahman, Anwar Kasem, Mohammed Horani Houssam (47.Mohammed Jazae'rly), Kivork Mardekian, Marwan Mohammed Medrati, Samir Zuhair Assassa (61.Watad Ahmed Mohammed), Hawash Ahmed. Trainer: Mohammed Azzam.
**KSA**: Salim Abdul Rahman Aly Marwan, Abdullah Obeid Al Harbi, Saleh Mohammed Al Neaaimah, Mohammed Abdul Al Jawad, Othman Marzouq Al Fairoz Mubarak, Ahmed Yehya Al Nefawy, Amin Mohammed Dabo (80.Saleh Khalifah Hamid Al Dossary), Ahmed Abdullah Al Sagheer (67.Kamal Ahmad Abdul Al Khatib), Saoud Mohammed Jassem Bo Saeed, Fahad Mohammed Saleh Al Mesaibeth, Yusuf Rashed Khamees Al Ola. Trainer: Rubens Francisco Minelli (Brazil).
**Goals**: 0-1 Saoud Mohammed Jassem Bo Saeed (47), 0-2 Saoud Mohammed Jassem Bo Saeed (62).

25.03.1981, Malaz Stadium, Riyadh (Saudi Arabia); Attendance: 30,000
Referee: Harpajan Singh Dhillon (Singapore)
**IRAQ - BAHRAIN**                                                                        **2-0(1-0)**
**IRQ**: Raad Hammoudi Salman, Ibrahim Ali Kadhim, Hassan Farhan Hassoon, Nadhim Shaker Salim, Adnan Darjal Matar, Natik Hashim Our, Hadi Ahmed Bashir, Jamal Ali Hamza (84.Jassem Mohammed Saad), Jasim Falah Hassan, Faisal Jabun, Nizar Ashraf Suleiman. Trainer: Vojo Gardašević (Yugoslavia).
**BHR**: Hamoud Sultan Mazkoor, Mohammed Sultan Mazkoor, Abdullah Bader, Rushdan Riyadh, Ali Abdul Aziz, Mohammed Al Zayyani, Jasem Al Khajam, Ibrahim Hassan (60.Shewaiaer Khalil), Fouad Abou Shaqr (80.Abdullah Abdul Hameed), Khalaf Mohammed Hamad, Ibrahim Farham. Trainer: Ali Farouk.
**Goals**: 1-0 Hadi Ahmed Bashir (71), 2-0 Adnan Darjal Matar (89).

27.03.1981, Malaz Stadium, Riyadh (Saudi Arabia); Attendance: 3,967
Referee: Peter Rampley (Australia)
**QATAR - SYRIA**                                                                      **2-1(1-1)**
**QAT**: Mohammed Sami Wafah, Majid Bakhit Maayouf, Anbar Mubarak Al Ali, Adel Ahmed Malulla, Samir Abbas Al Mas, Mohammed Saed Jaber Afifa (15.Bader Bilal Salem), Hassan Abdul Rahman Abdullah Al Qadi, Hassan Matar Sayed Al Suwaidi (72.Ali Mohammed Zied Al Sada), Ibrahim Khalfan Ahmed, Mansour Muftah Faraj Bekhit, Khalid Mohammed Salman Al Muhannadi. Trainer: Evaristo de Macedo Filho (Brazil).
**SYR**: Ahmad Eid Maher Berakdar, Haissam Mouaket, Mohammed Shait Ahmed Jehad, Anwar Kasem, Dahbour Emad, Samir Zuhair Assassa, Haissam Mohammed Shehadeh (65.Shalaby Hashem), Kivork Mardekian, Marwan Mohammed Medrati, Mohammed Ali Dahman, Mohammed Jazae'rly (83.Hawash Ahmed). Trainer: Mohammed Azzam.
**Goals**: 1-0 Ibrahim Khalfan Ahmed (8), 1-1 Mohammed Shait Ahmed Jehad (15), 2-1 Mansour Muftah Faraj Bekhit (53).

28.03.1981, Malaz Stadium, Riyadh; Attendance: 7,876
Referee: Sano Toshikazu (Japan)
**BAHRAIN - SAUDI ARABIA**                                          **0-1(0-0)**
**BHR**: Hamoud Sultan Mazkoor, Mohammed Sultan Mazkoor, Adel Bashir Al Maqhawy, Ali Abdul Aziz, Abdul Karim Bekheit, Rushdan Riyadh, Jasem Al Khajam, Ibrahim Hassan, Ibrahim Al Farhan, Farhan Ahmed (61.Shewaiaer Khalil), Khalaf Mohammed Hamad. Trainer: Ali Farouk.
**KSA**: Salim Abdul Rahman Aly Marwan, Abdullah Obeid Al Harbi, Saleh Mohammed Al Neaaimah, Mohammed Abdul Al Jawad, Othman Marzouq Al Fairoz Mubarak, Ahmed Yehya Al Nefawy, Salih Khalifa Hamid Al Dossary, Ahmed Abdullah Al Sagheer (77.Kamal Ahmad Abdul Al Khatib), Saoud Mohammed Jassem Bo Saeed, Fahad Mohammed Saleh Al Mesaibeth (62.Shaye Al Nafeesah), Yusuf Rashed Khamees Al Ola. Trainer: Rubens Francisco Minelli (Brazil).
**Goals**: 0-1 Saleh Khalifa Hamid Al Dossary (71).

30.03.1981, Malaz Stadium, Riyadh (Saudi Arabia); Attendance: 3,285
Referee: Peter Rampley (Australia)
**IRAQ - SYRIA**                                                                           **2-1(1-0)**
**IRQ**: Raad Hammoudi Salman, Ibrahim Ali Kadhim, Nadhim Shaker Salim, Hassan Farhan Hassoon, Adnan Darjal Matar, Hadi Ahmed Bashir, Natiq Hashim Abidoun (46.Jamal Ali Hamza), Adel Khedeyer Hafidh, Jasim Falah Hassan, Nizar Ashraf Suleiman, Hussein Saeed Mohammed. Trainer: Douglas Aziz Shamasha Eshaya.
**SYR**: Nafeh Abed El Kader Huwaij, Mohammed Shait Ahmed Jehad, Riad Mohammed Asfahany, Shalaby Hashem, Anwar Kasem, Kivork Mardekian, Dahbour Emad (87.Shafik Al Farra Faez), Watad Ahmed Mohammed (80.Samir Zuhair Assassa), Haissam Mohammed Shehadeh, Walid Selim Bitar, Marwan Mohammed Medrati. Trainer: Mohammed Azzam.
**Goals**: 1-0 Nizar Ashraf Suleiman (34), 1-1 Mohammed Shait Ahmed Jehad (47), 2-1 Adel Khedeyer Hafidh (63).

31.03.1981, Malaz Stadium, Riyadh; Attendance: 40,000
Referee: Anton Boskovic (Australia)
**QATAR - SAUDI ARABIA**                                   **0-1(0-0)**
**QAT**: Mohammed Sami Wafah, Majid Bakhit Maayouf, Anbar Basheer Abubakr, Anbar Mubarak Al Ali (51.Adel Ahmed Malulla), Samir Abbas Al Mas, Hassan Abdul Rahman Abdullah Al Qadi, Ibrahim Khalfah Ahmed, Mohammed Saed Jaber Afifa, Hassan Matar Sayed Al Suwaidi (68.Bader Bilal Salim), Mansour Muftah Faraj Bekhit, Khalid Mohammed Salman Al Muhannadi. Trainer: Evaristo de Macedo Filho (Brazil).
**KSA**: Salim Abdul Rahman Aly Marwan, Abdullah Obeid Al Harbi, Saleh Mohammed Al Neaaimah, Mohammed Abdul Al Jawad, Othman Marzouq Al Fairoz Mubarak, Ahmed Yehya Al Nefawy, Faraj Abdullah Abid Rabboh (60.Salih Khalifa Hamid Al Dossary), Ahmed Abdullah Al Sagheer (86.Kamal Ahmad Abdul Al Khatib), Majed Ahmed Abdullah Al Mohammed, Fahad Mohammed Saleh Al Mesaibeth, Yusuf Rashed Khamees Al Ola. Trainer: Rubens Francisco Minelli (Brazil).
**Goal**: 0-1 Yusuf Rashed Khamees Al Ola (85).

## SUBGROUP C

| Date | Venue | Match | Result |
|---|---|---|---|
| 21.04.1981 | Kuwait City | Malaysia - South Korea | 1-2(1-1) |
| 22.04.1981 | Kuwait City | Kuwait - Thailand | 6-0(4-0) |
| 24.04.1981 | Kuwait City | South Korea - Thailand | 5-1(2-1) |
| 25.04.1981 | Kuwait City | Kuwait - Malaysia | 4-0(2-0) |
| 27.04.1981 | Kuwait City | Malaysia - Thailand | 2-2(0-0) |
| 29.04.1981 | Kuwait City | Kuwait - South Korea | 2-0(0-0) |

### FINAL STANDINGS

| | | | | | | | | |
|---|---|---|---|---|---|---|---|---|
| 1. Kuwait | 3 | 3 | 0 | 0 | 12 | - | 0 | 6 |
| 2. South Korea | 3 | 2 | 0 | 1 | 7 | - | 4 | 4 |
| 3. Malaysia | 3 | 0 | 1 | 2 | 3 | - | 8 | 1 |
| 4. Thailand | 3 | 0 | 1 | 2 | 3 | - | 13 | 1 |

Kuwait qualified for the Asian Zone Final.

21.04.1981, Kazma Stadium, Kuwait City (Kuwait); Attendance: 10,000
Referee: Chan Tam Sun (Hong Kong)
**MALAYSIA - SOUTH KOREA**        **1-2(1-1)**
**MAS**: Ramasamy Arumugan (Keong Chow Chee), Mohammed Jamal Nasir Abdul Jalil, Soh Chin Aun, Yahaya Jusoh, Santokh Singh, Shukor Salleh, Muhidin Hussein, Khalid Ali (Huad Torairaju), James Wong Chye Fook, Hassan Sani, Mohammed Mokhtar Dahari. Trainer: Karl-Heinz Weigang (West Germany).
**KOR**: Cho Byung-Deouk, Cho Young-Jeung, Woe Jong-Jang, Park Sung-Hwa, Choi Jong-Deok, Hong Sung-Ho, Lee Kang-Jo, Lee Young-Moo (68.Lee Tae-Ho), Cho Kwang-Rae, Choi Soon-Ho (72.Oh Seok-Jae), Chung Hae-Won. Trainer: Kim Jung-Nam.
**Goals**: 1-0 James Wong Chye Fook (9), 1-1 Hong Sung-Ho (31), 1-2 Lee Kang-Jo (82).

22.04.1981, "Al Qadisiyah" Stadium, Kuwait City; Attendance: 5,000
Referee: Melwyn D'Souza (India)
**KUWAIT - THAILAND**        **6-0(4-0)**
**KUW**: Ahmed Khuder Al Tarabulsi, Naeem Saad Mubarak Fajah, Jamal Mohammed Yaqoub Al Qabandi, Mahboub Juma Mahboub Mubarak, Waleed Mohammed Al Jasem Al Mubarak, Saed Mohammed Abdul Aziz Al Houti, Nasser Abdullah Al Ghanem (67.Abdullah Mohammed Al Buloushi), Mohammed Ahmed Karam, Fatih Kamil Fayyaz Matar Marzouq (67.Faisal Ali Al Dakhil), Jassem Jamal Yaqoub Sultan, Abdul Aziz Saoud Al Anbari. Trainer: Carlos Alberto Gomes Parreira (Brazil).
**THA**: Yamsang Sirisak, Sittipultong Thaweepak, Vichai Vaitayangkol, Narong Arjarayut, Sompoch Noymak (78.Hongkajohn Chalor), Khan Thatat Songwuti, Somboon Suparapop, Daoyot Dara (78.Pakdee Choyasit), Jesdapon Na Phatalung, Piyapong Pue-On, Chirdsak Chaibutr. Trainer: Supakij Meelarpkij.
**Goals**: 1-0 Abdul Aziz Saoud Al Anbari (9), 2-0 Jassem Jamal Yaqoub Sultan (12), 3-0 Fatih Kamil Fayyaz Matar Marzouq (34), 4-0 Abdul Aziz Saoud Al Anbari (37), 5-0 Mohammed Ahmed Karam (62), 6-0 Faisal Ali Al Dakhil (80).

24.04.1981, Kazma Stadium, Kuwait City (Kuwait); Attendance: 1,000
Referee: Sudarso Hardjowasito (Indonesia)
**SOUTH KOREA - THAILAND** **5-1(2-1)**
**KOR:** Kim Hwang-Ho, Park Kyung-Joon, Cho Young-Jeung, Park Sung-Hwa, Choi Jong-Deok, Lee Tae-Ho, Lee Kang-Jo, Hong Sung-Ho (41.Oh Seok-Jae), Cho Kwang-Rae, Choi Soon-Ho, Chung Hae-Won. Trainer: Kim Jung-Nam.
**THA:** Yamsang Sirisak (79.Masapong Vasin), Sompit Suwanapluoh, Vichai Vaitayangkol, Wattana Sompong, Somboon Suparapop, Narong Arjarayult, Daoyot Dara (46.Piyapong Pue-On), Thong On-Tawee, Jesdapon Na Phatalung, Sangnapol Chalermvud, Chirdsak Chaibutr. Trainer: Supakij Meelarpkij.
**Goals:** 1-0 Choi Soon-Ho (23), 2-0 Choi Jong-Deok (33), 2-1 Vichai Vaitayangkol (35), 3-1 Oh Seok-Jae (69), 4-1 Lee Tae-Ho (71), 5-1 Choi Soon-Ho (80).

25.04.1981, "Al Qadisiyah" Stadium, Kuwait City; Attendance: 15,000
Referee: Cheung Kwok Kui (Hong Kong)
**KUWAIT - MALAYSIA** **4-0(2-0)**
**KUW:** Ahmed Khuder Al Tarabulsi, Naeem Saad Mubarak Fajah, Mahboub Juma Mahboub Mubarak, Waleed Mohammed Al Jasem Al Mubarak, Jamal Mohammed Yaqoub Al Qabandi, Saed Mohammed Abdul Aziz Al Houti, Nasser Abdullah Al Ghanem, Mohammed Ahmed Karam, Fatih Kamil Fayyaz Matar Marzouq, Jassem Jamal Yaqoub Sultan, Abdul Aziz Saoud Al Anbari (*Substitutes*: Hamoud Fulaiteh Al Shammari, Abdullah Mohammed Al Buloushi). Trainer: Carlos Alberto Gomes Parreira (Brazil).
**MAS:** Keong Choe Chee, Mohammed Jamal Nasir Abdul Jalil, Santokh Singh, Soh Chin Aun, Yahya Jusoh, Shukor Salleh, Khalid Ali, Keong Yip Chee (28.Huad Torairaju), Mohammed Mokhtar Dahari, James Wong Chye Fook, Hassan Sani (64.Zulkifli Hamza). Trainer: Karl-Heinz Weigang (West Germany).
**Goals:** 1-0 Jassem Jamal Yaqoub Sultan (1), 2-0 Mahboub Juma Mahboub Mubarak (23), 3-0 Mahboub Juma Mahboub Mubarak (46), 4-0 Nasser Abdullah Al Ghanem (59).

27.04.1981, Kazma Stadium, Kuwait City (Kuwait); Attendance: 2,000
Referee: Robert Bonar Valentine (Scotland)
**MALAYSIA - THAILAND** **2-2(0-0)**
**MAS:** Peter Rajah, Mohammed Jamal Nasir Abdul Jalil, Santokh Singh, S. Pushpanathan, Yahya Jusoh, Shukor Salleh, Huad Torairaju, Yusoff Ali Ahmed, James Wong Chye Fook, Mohammed Mokhtar Dahari, Sulkifli Hamzah (53.Ibrahim Din). Trainer: Karl-Heinz Weigang (West Germany).
**THA:** Masapong Vasin, Sompit Suwannapluoh, Wattana Sompong (77.Sittipultong Thaweepak), Narong Arjarayult, Somboon Suparapop, Saghapool Chalermvud, Pakdee Choyasit, Thong On Tawee (77.Daoyot Dara), Piyapong Pue-On, Khan Thatat Songwuti, Hongkajohn Chalor. Trainer: Supakij Meelarpkij.
**Goals**: 0-1 Sompit Suwannapluoh (49), 1-1 Ibrahim Din (54), 2-1 Ibrahim Din (70), 2-2 Khan Thatat Songwuti (74).

29.04.1981, "Al Qadisiyah" Stadium, Kuwait City; Attendance: 15,000
Referee: Gilberto Aristizábal Murcia (Colombia)
**KUWAIT - SOUTH KOREA** **2-0(0-0)**
**KUW:** Ahmed Khuder Al Tarabulsi, Naeem Saad Mubarak Fajah, Mahboub Juma Mahboub Mubarak, Jamal Mohammed Yaqoub Al Qabandi, Waleed Mohammed Al Jasem Al Mubarak, Saed Mohammed Abdul Aziz Al Houti, Nasser Abdullah Al Ghanem, Mohammed Ahmed Karam, Fathi Kamil Marzouq, Jassem Jamal Yaqoub Sultan (79.Abdullah Mohammed Al Buloushi), Abdul Aziz Saoud Al Anbari. Trainer: Carlos Alberto Gomes Parreira (Brazil).
**KOR:** Cho Byung-Deouk, Cho Young-Jeung, Park Sung-Hwa, Choi Jong-Deok (79.Park Kyung-Joon), Hong Sung-Ho, Lee Kang-Jo, Cho Kwang-Rae, Lee Tae-Ho, Hae-Won Chung, Oh Seok-Jae (36.Choi Soon-Ho), Lee Tae-Yeop. Trainer: Kim Jung-Nam.
**Goals**: 1-0 Abdul Aziz Saoud Al Anbari (50), 2-0 Nasser Abdullah Al Ghanem (82).

**Sent off**: Lee Tae-Ho (81).

## SUBGROUP D
## GROUP ALLOCATION MATCHES

| | | | |
|---|---|---|---|
| 21.12.1980 | Hong Kong | Hong Kong – China P.R. | 0-1(0-0) |
| 22.12.1980 | Hong Kong | North Korea - Macau | 3-0(2-0) |
| 22.12.1980 | Hong Kong | Singapore - Japan | 0-1(0-1) |

21.12.1980, National Government Stadium, Hong Kong; Attendance: 23,602
Referee: Abdul Rahman Ibrahim Al Marzan (Saudi Arabia)
**HONG KONG – CHINA P.R.** **0-1(0-0)**
**HKG**: Chan Wan Ngok, Leung Sui Wing, Lai Sun Cheung, Tsang Ting Fai, Choi York Yee, Chan Sai Kau, Fung Chi Ming, Hugh McCrory, Wu Kwok Hung, Sze Kin Hay, Cheung Ka Ping. Trainer: Georg Knobel (Holland).
**CHN**: Li Fu Sheng, Cai Jin Biao, Lin Lou Feng, Chi Shang Bin, Zuo Shu Sheng, Xu Yong Lai (46.Gang Jin Chen), Zang Cai Ling, Shen Xiangfu, Gu Guang Ming, Rong Zhi Hang, Chen Xi Rong (76.Wang Feng). Trainer: Yong Shun Su.
**Goal**: 0-1 Gang Jin Chen (89).

22.12.1980, National Government Stadium, Hong Kong (Hong Kong); Attendance: 3,730
Referee: Sarkis Demirdjian (Lebanon)
**NORTH KOREA - MACAU** **3-0(2-0)**
**PRK**: Kim Chang-Kun, Kang Myong-Sam, Li Song-Kun, Yun Yong-Hyon, Jon Byong-Ju, Kye Jin-Kyo, Li Jong-Man (76.Oh Yong-Su), Kim Jong-Man, Ri Chang-Ha, Ri Yong-Sob (69.Kim Yong-Nam), Kim Myong-Kun. Trainer: Han Bong-Jin.
**MAC**: Tou Veng Keong, Carlos Manuel da Conceição Ferreira, Fong Hung Man, Carlos Manuel Guerra Alves, Jaime Diamantino Madeira, Artur da Conceição Taborda, Chi Hong Wong, Yung Wai Kwok (86.Lam Iam Weng), Chiang I Seng, Carlos Prieto Marques Nunes, Eduardo Armando de Jesús Júnior. Trainer: Eduardo Dos Santos Atraca.
**Goals**: 1-0 Ri Yong-Sob (34), 2-0 Ri Chang-Ha (41), 3-0 Kim Jong-Man (87).

22.12.1980, National Government Stadium, Hong Kong (Hong Kong); Attendance: 3,730
Referee: Nobnom Ausukong (Thailand)
**SINGAPORE - JAPAN** **0-1(0-1)**
**SIN**: Edmund Wee, Samad Allapitchay, Syed Mutalib (81.Shafik Norhalis), Tambiayah Panthmanathan, Pak Kwan Au Yeong, Mohamed Hussein Noh, Suriamurthy Rajagopal (61.Malek Ayab), Nasir Jalil, Kim Song Quah, Manoharan Nair, Fandi Ahmad. Trainer: Jita Singh.
**JPN**: Yasuhito Suzuki, Hideki Maeda (Cap), Shigemitsu Sudo, Tetsuo Sugamata, Takeshi Koshida (85.Satoshi Tsunami), Nobutoshi Kaneda, Tetsuya Totsuka, Yahiro Kazama, Masafumi Yokoyama, Haruhisa Hasegawa, Kazushi Kimura. Trainer: Saburo Kawabuchi.
**Goal**: 0-1 Kazushi Kimura (19).

# GROUP 1

| | | | |
|---|---|---|---|
| 24.12.1980 | Hong Kong | China P.R. - Macau | 3-0(2-0) |
| 26.12.1980 | Hong Kong | China P.R. - Japan | 1-0(1-0) |
| 28.12.1980 | Hong Kong | Japan - Macau | 3-0(0-0) |

### FINAL STANDINGS

| | | | | | | | | |
|---|---|---|---|---|---|---|---|---|
| 1. | China P.R. | 2 | 2 | 0 | 0 | 4 - 0 | 4 |
| 2. | Japan | 2 | 1 | 0 | 1 | 3 - 1 | 2 |
| 3. | Macau | 2 | 0 | 0 | 2 | 0 - 6 | 0 |

China P.R. and Japan qualified for the Subgroup D Semi-Finals.

24.12.1980, National Government Stadium, Hong Kong (Hong Kong); Attendance: 16,000
Referee: Vijit Getkaew (Thailand)
**CHINA P.R. - MACAU**     **3-0(2-0)**
**CHN:** Li Fu Sheng, Cai Jin Biao, Lin Lou Feng, Chi Shang Bin, Zuo Shu Sheng, Zang Cai Ling, Shen Xiangfu (70.Yang Yu Ming), Gu Guang Ming, Wang Feng, Rong Zhi Hang (66.Huang Xiang Dong), Chen Xi Rong. Trainer: Yong Shun Su.
**MAC:** Pun Veng Keong, Kwok Wa Kit, Carlos Manuel Guerra Alves, Fong Hong Man, Chi Hong Vong, Carlos Manuel da Conceição Ferreira, Artur da Conceição Taborda (46.Chiang I Seng), Jaime Diamantino Madeira (84.Lam Iam Weng), Carlos Prieto Marques Nunes, Eduardo Armando de Jesús Júnior, Yung Wai Kwok. Trainer: Eduardo Dos Santos Atraca.
**Goals**: 1-0 Gu Guang Ming (17), 2-0 Zuo Shu Sheng (20), 3-0 Rong Zhi Hang (59).

26.12.1980, National Government Stadium, Hong Kong (Hong Kong); Attendance: 16,900
Referee: Abdulwahab Ali Al Bannai (Kuwait)
**CHINA P.R. - JAPAN**     **1-0(1-0)**
**CHN:** Li Fu Sheng, Cai Jin Biao, Lin Lou Feng, Chi Shang Bin, Zuo Shu Sheng, Zang Cai Ling, Shen Xiangfu, Gu Guang Ming (64.Chen Jin Gang), Wang Feng (46.Xu Yong Lai), Rong Zhi Hang, Chen Xi Rong. Trainer: Yong Shun Su.
**JPN:** Yasuhito Suzuki, Hideki Maeda (Cap), Shigemitsu Sudo, Tetsuo Sugamata, Satoshi Tsunami, Nobutoshi Kaneda, Tetsuya Totsuka, Yahiro Kazama, Masafumi Yokoyama, Haruhisa Hasegawa (63.Hiromi Hara), Kazushi Kimura (78.Masakuni Yamamoto). Trainer: Saburo Kawabuchi.
**Goal**: 1-0 Rong Zhi Hang (5).

28.12.1980, National Government Stadium, Hong Kong (Hong Kong); Attendance: 27,629
Referee: Marwan Arafat (Syria)
**JAPAN - MACAU**     **3-0(0-0)**
Yasuhito Suzuki, Hideki Maeda, Shigemitsu Sudo (Hiroyuki Sakashita), Tetsuo Sugamata, Satoshi Tsunami, Nobutoshi Kaneda (Cap), Tetsuya Totsuka (78.Shinji Tanaka), Yahiro Kazama, Masafumi Yokoyama, Haruhisa Hasegawa, Kazushi Kimura. Trainer: Saburo Kawabuchi.
**MAC:** Cheang I Wai (69.Tou Veng Keong), Kwok Wa Kit, Fong Hong Man, Carlos Manuel da Conceição Ferreira, Carlos Manuel Guerra Alves, Artur da Conceição Taborda, Jaime Diamantino Madeira, Yung Wai Kwok, Carlos Prieto Marques Nunes, Eduardo Armando de Jesús Júnior (69.Chiang I Seng), Chi Hong Wong. Trainer: Eduardo Dos Santos Atraca.
**Goals**: 1-0 Kazushi Kimura (68), 2-0 Hideki Maeda (81 penalty), 3-0 Haruhisa Hasegawa (88).
**Sent off**: Satoshi Tsunami (39), Jaime Diamantino Madeira (39).

# GROUP 2

| 24.12.1980 | Hong Kong | Hong Kong - Singapore | 1-1(0-0) |
| 26.12.1980 | Hong Kong | North Korea - Singapore | 1-0(1-0) |
| 28.12.1980 | Hong Kong | Hong Kong – North Korea | 2-2(1-2) |

### FINAL STANDINGS

| | | | | | | | | |
|---|---|---|---|---|---|---|---|---|
| 1. | North Korea | 2 | 1 | 1 | 0 | 3 | - 2 | 3 |
| 2. | Hong Kong | 2 | 0 | 2 | 0 | 3 | - 3 | 2 |
| 3. | Singapore | 2 | 0 | 1 | 1 | 1 | - 2 | 1 |

North Korea and Hong Kong qualified for the Subgroup D Semi-Finals.

24.12.1980, National Government Stadium, Hong Kong; Attendance: 16,562
Referee: Marwan Arafat (Syria)
**HONG KONG - SINGAPORE**      **1-1(0-0)**
**HKG**: Chan Wan Ngok (31.Liu Chun Fai), Leung Sui Wing, Lai Sun Cheung, Tsang Ting Fai, Choi York Yee, Chan Sai Kau, Fung Chi Ming, Hugh McCrory, Wan Chi Keung, Wu Kwok Hung, Lau Wing Yip. Trainer: Georg Knobel (Holland).
**SIN**: Edmund Wee, Lim Tang Boon (36.Hashim Hosni), Samad Allapitchay, Syed Mutalib, Mohamed Hussein Noh, Pak Kwan Au Yeong, Nasir Jalil, Fandi Ahmad (72.Manoharan Nair), Tambiayah Pathmanathan, Kim Song Quah, Suriamurthy Rajagopal. Trainer: Jita Singh.
**Goals**: 1-0 Choi York Yee (55), 1-1 Tambiayah Pathmanathan (87).

26.12.1980, National Government Stadium, Hong Kong (Hong Kong); Attendance: 16,900
Referee: Ebrahim Yousif Al Doy (Bahrain)
**NORTH KOREA - SINGAPORE**      **1-0(1-0)**
**PRK**: Kim Chang-Kun, Li Song-Kun, Yun Yong-Hyon, Oh Yong-Nam, Kye Jin-Kyo (29.Oh Yong-Su), Li Jong-Man, Kim Jong-Man, Ri Chang-Ha, Ri Yong-Sob, Kang Myong-Sam (69.La Bong-Ki), Kim Myong-Kun. Trainer: Han Bong-Jin.
**SIN**: Edmund Wee, Lim Tang Boon, Terry Panthmanathan, Samad Allapitchay, Syed Muthalib (40.Norhalis Shafik), Pak Kwan Au Yeong, Suriamurthy Rajagopal (81.Manoharan Nair), Nasir Jalil, Fandi Ahmad, Kim Song Quah, Mohamed Hussein Noh. Trainer: Jita Singh.
**Goal**: 1-0 Ri Yong-Sob (7).

28.12.1980, National Government Stadium, Hong Kong; Attendance: 27,629
Referee: Sarkis Demirdjian (Lebanon)
**HONG KONG – NORTH KOREA**      **2-2(1-2)**
**HKG**: Liu Chun Fai , Leung Sui Wing (30.Chee Yat Por), Lai Sun Cheung, Tsang Ting Fai, Choi York Yee, Fung Chi Ming, Hugh McCrory, Wu Kwok Hung, Sze Kin Hai, Lau Wing Yip (30.Wan Chi Keung), Chan Fat Chi. Trainer: Georg Knobel (Holland).
**PRK**: Kim Chang-Kun, Chon Byong-Ju, Yun Yong-Hyon, Li Song-Kun, Li Jong-Man, Li Chang Ha, Kye Jin-Kyo, Ri Yong-Sob (54.Kim Yong-Nam), Kim Myong-Kun, Oh Yong-Su, Kang Myong-Sam. Trainer: Han Bong-Jin.
**Goals**: 0-1 Li Jong-Man (3), 0-2 Ri Yong-Sob (25), 1-2 Wan Chi Keung (40), 2-2 Wu Kwok Hung (62).

## SUBGROUP D - SEMI-FINALS

| | | | |
|---|---|---|---|
| 30.12.1980 | Hong Kong | North Korea - Japan | 1-0(0-0,0-0) |
| 31.12.1980 | Hong Kong | China P.R. - Hong Kong | 5-4 pen |

North Korea and China P.R. qualified for the Subgroup D Final.

30.12.1980, National Government Stadium, Hong Kong (Hong Kong); Attendance: 8,266
Referee: Abdulwahab Ali Al Bannai (Kuwait)
**NORTH KOREA - JAPAN**     **1-0(0-0,0-0)**
**PRK:** Kim Chang-Kun, Chon Byong-Ju (1.Oh Yong-Nam), Li Song-Kun, Yun Yong-Hyon, Oh Yong-Su, Li Jong-Man, Kim Jong-Man (46.Kim Yong-Nam), Ri Chang-Ha, Ri Yong-Sob, Kang Myong-Sam. Trainer: Han Bong-Jin.
**JPN:** Yasuhito Suzuki, Hideki Maeda (Cap), Shigemitsu Sudo, Tetsuo Sugamata, Shinji Tanaka, Nobutoshi Kaneda (105.Masakuni Yamamoto), Tetsuya Totsuka, Yahiro Kazama, Masafumi Yokoyama (105.Hiromi Hara), Haruhisa Hasegawa, Kazushi Kimura. Trainer: Saburo Kawabuchi.
**Goal**: 1-0 Kim Yong-Nam (114).

31.12.1980, National Government Stadium, Hong Kong; Attendance: 27,629
Referee: Vijit Getkaew (Thailand)
**CHINA P.R. - HONG KONG**     **0-0; 5-4 on penalties**
**CHN:** Li Fu Sheng, Cai Jin Biao, Lin Lou Feng, Chi Shang Bin, Zuo Shu Sheng, Zang Cai Ling, Shen Xiangfu (60.Yang Yu Ming), Gu Guang Ming, Wang Feng, Rong Zhi Hang, Chen Xi Rong (99.Huang Xiang Dong). Trainer: Yong Shun Su.
**HKG:** Chan Wan Ngok, Lai Sun Cheung (80.Leung Sui Wing), Tsang Ting Fai, Choi York Yee, Chan Sai Kau (76.Hugh McCrory), Fung Chi Ming, Wan Chi Keung, Wu Kwok Hung, Sze Kin Hai, Chee Yat Por, Chan Fat Chi. Trainer: Georg Knobel (Holland).

## SUBGROUP D - FINAL

04.01.1981, National Government Stadium, Hong Kong (Hong Kong); Attendance: 15,974
Referee: Ebrahim Yousif Al Doy (Bahrain)
**CHINA P.R. – NORTH KOREA**     **4-2(1-1,2-2)**
**CHN:** Li Fu Sheng, Cai Jin Biao, Lin Lou Feng, Chi Shang Bin, Zang Cai Ling, Zuo Shu Sheng, Wang Feng (33.Huang Xiang Dong), Gu Guang Ming, Chen Xi Rong (96.Chen Jin Gang), Rong Zhi Hang, Yang Yu Ming. Trainer: Yong Shun Su.
**PRK:** Kim Chang-Kun, Oh Yong-Nam, Li Song-Kun, Yun Yong-Hyon, Li Jong-Man, Kim Jong-Man (46.Kye Jin-Kyo), Oh Yong-Su, Ri Chang-Ha, Ri Yong-Sob (60.Kim Yong-Nam), Kang Myong-Sam, Kim Myong-Kun. Trainer: Han Bong-Jin.
**Goals**: 0-1 Ri Chang-Ha (2), 1-1 Huang Xiang Dong (44), 2-1 Chen Xi Rong (55), 2-2 Oh Yong-Nam (57), 3-2 Huang Xiang Dong (110), 4-2 Gu Guang Ming (113).
China P.R. qualified for the Asian Zone Final.

# ASIAN ZONE FINAL

| | | | |
|---|---|---|---|
| 24.09.1981 | Beijing | China P.R. - New Zealand | 0-0 |
| 03.10.1981 | Auckland | New Zealand - China P.R. | 1-0(1-0) |
| 10.10.1981 | Auckland | New Zealand - Kuwait | 1-2(1-0) |
| 18.10.1981 | Beijing | China P.R. - Kuwait | 3-0(2-0) |
| 04.11.1981 | Riyadh | Saudi Arabia - Kuwait | 0-1(0-0) |
| 12.11.1981 | Kuala Lumpur | Saudi Arabia - China P.R. | 2-4(2-0) |
| 19.11.1981 | Kuala Lumpur | China P.R. - Saudi Arabia | 2-0(2-0) |
| 28.11.1981 | Auckland | New Zealand - Saudi Arabia | 2-2(1-1) |
| 30.11.1981 | Kuwait City | Kuwait - China P.R. | 1-0(1-0) |
| 07.12.1981 | Kuwait City | Kuwait - Saudi Arabia | 2-0(1-0) |
| 14.12.1981 | Kuwait City | Kuwait - New Zealand | 2-2(1-0) |
| 19.12.1981 | Riyadh | Saudi Arabia - New Zealand | 0-5(0-5) |

### FINAL STANDINGS

| | | | | | | | | |
|---|---|---|---|---|---|---|---|---|
| 1. | **Kuwait** | 6 | 4 | 1 | 1 | 8 - 6 | 9 |
| 2. | New Zealand | 6 | 2 | 3 | 1 | 11 - 6 | 7 |
| | China P.R. | 6 | 3 | 1 | 2 | 9 - 4 | 7 |
| 4. | Saudi Arabia | 6 | 0 | 1 | 5 | 4 - 16 | 1 |

Kuwait qualified for the Final Tournament.

24.09.1981, Workers Stadium, Beijing; Attendance: 80,000
Referee: Toshikazu Sano (Japan)
**CHINA P.R. - NEW ZEALAND** **0-0**
**CHN**: Li Fu Sheng, Cai Jin Biao, Lin Lou Feng, Chi Shang Bin, Zuo Shu Sheng, Gang Chen, Zang Cai Ling, Shen Xiangfu (70.Yang Yu Ming), Gu Guang Ming, Rong Zhi Hang (57.Huang Xiang Dong), Chen Xi Rong. Trainer: Yong Shun Su.
**NZL**: Richard Hardie Wilson, Glenn Laurence Dods (68.John Bennett Hill), Richard Lloyd Herbert, Robert Ronald Almond, Adrian Coroon Elrick, Keith Gordon MacKay, Duncan Edward Cole, Steven Paul Sumner, Grant John Turner, Brian Alfred Turner, Stephen Wooddin. Trainer: John Adshead (England).

03.10.1981, Mount Smart Stadium, Auckland; Attendance: 27,000
Referee: Vijit Getkaew (Thailand)
**NEW ZEALAND - CHINA P.R.** **1-0(1-0)**
**NZL**: Richard Hardie Wilson, Glenn Laurence Dods (46.John Bennett Hill), Richard Lloyd Herbert, Robert Ronald Almond, Adrian Coroon Elrick, Keith Gordon MacKay, Duncan Edward Cole, Steven Paul Sumner, William James Simon Mark McClure, Brian Alfred Turner, Grant John Turner (76.Allan Roderick Boath). Trainer: John Adshead (England).
**CHN**: Li Fu Sheng, Cai Jin Biao, Lin Lou Feng, Chi Shang Bin, Huang Xiang Dong, Yang Yu Ming (68.Shen Xiangfu), Gang Chen, Zang Cai Ling, Gu Guang Ming, Wang Feng (Zuo Shu Sheng), Chen Xi Rong. Trainer: Yong Shun Su.
**Goal**: 1-0 Richard Lloyd Herbert (45).

10.10.1981, Mount Smart Stadium, Auckland; Attendance: 27,000
Referee: Hardjowasito Sudarso (Indonesia)
**NEW ZEALAND - KUWAIT**  1-2(1-0)
NZL: Richard Hardie Wilson, John Bennett Hill, Richard Lloyd Herbert, Robert Ronald Almond, Adrian Coroon Elrick, Keith Gordon MacKay, Duncan Edward Cole, Steven Paul Sumner, Grant John Turner (74.William James Simon Mark McClure), Brian Alfred Turner, Stephen Wooddin. Trainer: John Adshead (England).
KUW: Ahmed Khuder Al Tarabulsi, Naeem Saad Mubarak Fajah, Abdullah Yousuf Ma'youf, Mahboub Juma Mahboub Mubarak, Waleed Mohammed Al Jasem Al Mubarak, Saed Mohammed Abdul Aziz Al Houti, Fatih Kamil Fayyaz Matar Marzouq, Abdullah Mohammed Al Buloushi, Mohammed Ahmed Karam (46.Abdul Aziz Saoud Al Anbari), Jassem Jamal Yaqoub Sultan, Faisal Ali Al Dakhil. Trainer: Carlos Alberto Gomes Parreira (Brazil).
Goals: 1-0 Stephen Wooddin (24), 1-1 Faisal Ali Al Dakhil (61 penalty), 1-2 Jassem Jamal Yaqoub Sultan (90).

18.10.1981, Workers Stadium, Beijing; Attendance: 63,000
Referee: Anton Boskovic (Australia)
**CHINA P.R. - KUWAIT**  3-0(2-0)
CHN: Li Fu Sheng, Cai Jin Biao, Shen Xiang Fu, Lin Lou Feng, Chi Shang Bin, Huang Xiang Dong, Zang Cai Ling, Gu Guang Ming, Liu Li Fu, Chen Xi Rong, Rong Zhi Hang (79.Chen Jin Gang). Trainer: Yong Shun Su.
KUW: Ahmed Khuder Al Tarabulsi, Naeem Saad Mubarak Fajah, Mahboub Juma Mahboub Mubarak, Jamal Mohammed Yaqoub Al Qabandi, Saed Mohammed Abdul Aziz Al Houti, Fatih Kamil Fayyaz Matar Marzouq, Abdullah Mohammed Al Buloushi (46.Nasser Abdullah Al Ghanem), Jassem Jamal Yaqoub Sultan, Abdul Aziz Saoud Al Anbari, Abdullah Yousuf Ma'youf, Faisal Ali Al Dakhil. Trainer: Carlos Alberto Gomes Parreira (Brazil).
Goals: 1-0 Rong Zhi Hang (25), 2-0 Gu Guang Ming (30), 3-0 Shen Xiang Fu (60).

04.11.1981, „Prince Faisal bin Fahd" Stadium, Riyadh; Attendance: 28,000
Referee: Alfred Grey (England)
**SAUDI ARABIA - KUWAIT**  0-1(0-0)
KSA: Salim Abdul Rahman Aly Marwan, Abdullah Obeid Al Harbi, Saleh Mohammed Al Neaaimah, Ahmed Yehya Al Newafy, Mohammed Abdul Jawad, Othman Marzouq Al Fairoz Mubarak (81.Abdullah Awad Foudah), Abdullah Abid Rabboh Faraj (65.Darwish Mohammed Saeed Awadh), Fahad Mohammed Saleh Al Mesaibeth, Salih Khalifa Hamid Al Dossary, Majed Ahmed Abdullah Al Mohammed, Yusuf Rashed Khamees Al Ola. Trainer: Rubens Francisco Minelli (Brazil).
KUW: Ahmed Khuder Al Tarabulsi, Naeem Saad Mubarak Fajah (53.Hamoud Fulaiteh Al Shammari), Waleed Mohammed Al Jasem Al Mubarak, Mahboub Juma Mahboub Mubarak, Saed Mohammed Abdul Aziz Al Houti, Abdullah Mohammed Al Buloushi, Abdul Aziz Saoud Al Anbari, Fatih Kamil Fayyaz Matar Marzouq (81.Mohammed Ahmed Karam), Abdullah Yousuf Ma'youf, Jassem Jamal Yaqoub Sultan, Faisal Ali Al Dakhil. Trainer: Carlos Alberto Gomes Parreira (Brazil).
Goal: 0-1 Abdul Aziz Saoud Al Anbari (53).

12.11.1981, Merdeka Stadium, Kuala Lumpur (Malaysia); Attendance: 40,000
Referee: Alexis Ponnet (Belgium)
**SAUDI ARABIA - CHINA P.R.**  2-4(2-0)
KSA: Salim Abdul Rahman Aly Marwan, Hussein Al Bishi, Ahmed Yehya Al Nefawy, Saleh Mohammed Al Neaaimah, Mohammed Abdul Jawad, Othman Marzouq Al Fairoz Mubarak, Salih Khalifah Hamid Al Dossary, Abdullah Abid Rabboh Faraj (55.Hashim Sroor Mubarak), Majed Ahmed Abdullah Al Mohammed, Fahad Mohammed Saleh Al Mesaibeth, Yusuf Rashed Khamees Al Ola (75.Saoud Mohammed Jassim Bo Saeed). Trainer: Rubens Francisco Minelli (Brazil).
CHN: Li Fu Sheng, Cai Jin Biao, Lin Lou Feng, Chi Shang Bin, Huang Xiang Dong, Shen Xiangfu (55.Chen Jin Gang), Zang Cai Ling, Gu Guang Ming, Rong Zhi Hang, Liu Li Fu (55.Zuo Shu Sheng), Chen Xi Rong. Trainer: Yong Shun Su.

**Goals**: 1-0 Ahmed Yehya Al Nefawy (10), 2-0 Majed Ahmed Abdullah Al Mohammed (17), 2-1 Zuo Shu Sheng (61), 2-2 Chen Jin Gang (62), 2-3 Gu Guang Ming (77), 2-4 Chin Shang Bin (89).

19.11.1981, Merdeka Stadium, Kuala Lumpur (Malaysia); Attendance: 80,000
Referee: José Roberto Ramiz Wright (Brazil)
**CHINA P.R. - SAUDI ARABIA**      **2-0(2-0)**
CHN: Li Fu Sheng, Cai Jin Biao, Lin Lou Feng, Chi Shang Bin, Huang Xiang Dong (30.Liu Li Fu), Zuo Shu Sheng, Zang Cai Ling, Shen Xiangfu (25.Chen Jin Gang), Gu Guang Ming, Rong Zhi Hang, Chen Xi Rong. Trainer: Yong Shun Su.
KSA: Salim Abdul Rahman Aly Marwan, Hussein Al Bishi, Salih Mohammed Al Neaaimah, Mohammed Abdul Jawad (Kamal Ahmad Abdul Al Khatib), Othman Marzouq Al Fairoz Mubarak, Ahmed Yeyha Al Nefawy, Salih Khalifah Hamid Al Dossary, Abdullah Abed Rabboh Faraj, Majed Ahmed Abdullah Al Mohammed, Fahad Mohammed Saleh Al Mesaibeth, Yusuf Rashed Khamees Al Ola (Shayea Al Nafeesah). Trainer: Rubens Francisco Minelli (Brazil).
**Goals**: 1-0 Huang Xiang Dong (23), 2-0 Cai Jin Biao (27).

28.11.1981, Mount Smart Stadium, Auckland; Attendance: 16,404
Referee: Arturo Andrés Ithurralde (Argentina)
**NEW ZEALAND - SAUDI ARABIA**      **2-2(1-2)**
NZL: Richard Hardie Wilson, Glenn Laurence Dods, Richard Lloyd Herbert, Robert Ronald Almond, Adrian Coroon Elrick, Keith Gordon MacKay, Duncan Edward Cole, Steven Paul Sumner, William James Simon Mark McClure (71.Samuel Alan Malcolmson), Stephen Wooddin, Grant John Turner (85.Allan Roderick Boath). Trainer: John Adshead (England).
KSA: Salim Abdul Rahman Aly Marwan, Hussein Al Bishi, Salih Mohammed Al Neaaimah, Mohammed Abdul Jawad, Othman Marzouq Al Fairoz Mubarak, Salih Khalifah Hamid Al Dossary, Abdullah Abed Rabboh Faraj, Majed Ahmed Abdullah Al Mohammed, Fahad Mohammed Saleh Al Mesaibeth, Yusuf Rashed Khamees Al Ola, Hamed Sobhi. Trainer: Rubens Francisco Minelli (Brazil).
**Goals**: 1-0 William James Simon Mark McClure (5), 1-1 Majed Ahmed Abdullah Al Mohammed (37), 1-2 Majed Ahmed Abdullah Al Mohammed (41), 2-2 Richard Lloyd Herbert (87).

30.11.1981, "Al Qadisiyah" Stadium, Kuwait City; Attendance: 15,000
Referee: Lee Kok Keong (Singapore)
**KUWAIT - CHINA P.R.**      **1-0(1-0)**
KUW: Ahmed Khuder Al Tarabulsi, Hamoud Fulaiteh Al Shammari (44.Naeem Saad Mubarak Fajah), Mahboub Juma Mahboub Mubarak, Abdullah Yousuf Ma'youf, Waleed Mohammed Al Jasem Al Mubarak, Saed Mohammed Abdul Aziz Al Houti, Abdullah Mohammed Al Buloushi, Mohammed Ahmed Karam, Jassem Jamal Yaqoub Sultan, Faisal Ali Al Dakhil, Abdul Aziz Saoud Al Anbari. Trainer: Carlos Alberto Gomes Parreira (Brazil).
CHN: Li Fu Sheng, Lin Lou Feng, Cai Jin Biao, Chi Shang Bin, Zang Cai Ling, Chen Xi Rong, Liu Li Fu (38.Chen Jin Gang), Zuo Shu Sheng, Gu Guang Ming, Rong Zhi Hang, Shen Xiang Fu (61.Xu Yong Lai). Trainer: Yong Shun Su.
**Goal**: 1-0 Abdul Aziz Saoud Al Anbari (7).

07.12.1981, "Al Qadisiyah" Stadium, Kuwait City; Attendance: 15,000
Referee: Jan Redelfs (West Germany)
**KUWAIT - SAUDI ARABIA**      **2-0(1-0)**
KUW: Ahmed Khuder Al Tarabulsi, Mahboub Juma Mahboub Mubarak, Waleed Mohammed Al Jasem Al Mubarak, Saed Mohammed Abdul Aziz Al Houti, Abdullah Mohammed Al Buloushi, Abdul Aziz Saoud Al Anbari, Sami Mohammed Al Hashash, Hamoud Fulaiteh Al Shammari, Mohammed Ahmed Karam, Jassem Jamal Yaqoub Sultan, Faisal Ali Al Dakhil. Trainer: Carlos Alberto Gomes Parreira (Brazil).
KSA: Salim Abdul Rahman Aly Marwan, Abdullah Obeid Al Harby, Salih Mohammed Al Neaaimah (84.Kamal Ahmad Abdul Al Khatib), Hussein Al Bishi, Fahad Mohammed Saleh Al Mesaibeth, Yusuf Rashed Khamees Al Ola, Majed Ahmed Abdullah Al Mohammed, Salih Khalifa Hamid Al Dossary, Saoud Mohammed Gasim Bo Saeed, Othman Marzouq Al Fairoz Mubarak, Ahmed Yehya Al Nefawy.

Trainer: Rubens Francisco Minelli (Brazil).
**Goals**: 1-0 Faisal Ali Al Dakhil (37), 2-0 Faisal Ali Al Dakhil (54).

14.12.1981, "Al Qadisiyah" Stadium, Kuwait City; Attendance: 20,000
Referee: Henning Lund-Sørensen (Denmark)
**KUWAIT - NEW ZEALAND**     **2-2(1-0)**
**KUW**: Ahmed Khuder Al Tarabulsi, Mahboub Juma Mahboub Mubarak, Waleed Mohammed Al Jasem Al Mubarak, Fatih Kamil Fayyaz Matar Marzouq, Abdullah Mohammed Al Buloushi, Abdul Aziz Saoud Al Anbari, Nasser Abdullah Al Ghanem, Sami Mohammed Al Hashash, Mohammed Ahmed Karam (73.Youssef Faraj Al Suwayed), Faisal Ali Al Dakhil. Trainer: Carlos Alberto Gomes Parreira (Brazil).
**NZL**: Richard Hardie Wilson, Glenn Laurence Dods, Richard Lloyd Herbert, Robert Ronald Almond, Adrian Coroon Elrick, Grant John Turner, Duncan Edward Cole, Steven Paul Sumner, Wynton Alan Whai Rufer (46.Kenneth Grant Cresswell), Brian Alfred Turner, Stephen Wooddin. Trainer: John Adshead (England).
**Goals**: 1-0 Fatih Kamil Fayyaz Matar Marzouq (41), 1-1 Steven Paul Sumner (65), 1-2 Wynton Alan Whai Rufer (66), 2-2 Sami Mohammed Al Hashash (89).

19.12.1981, „Prince Faisal bin Fahd" Stadium, Riyadh; Attendance: 5,000
Referee: Charles George Rainier Corver (Holland)
**SAUDI ARABIA - NEW ZEALAND**     **0-5(0-5)**
**KSA**: Salim Abdul Rahman Aly Marwan, Hussein Al Bishi, Mohammed Abdul Jawad, Abdullah Obeid Al Harbi, Othman Marzouq Al Fairoz Mubarak, Ahmed Yeyha Al Nefawy, Salih Khalifah Hamid Al Dossary, Majed Ahmed Abdullah Al Mohammed, Fahad Mohammed Saleh Al Mesaibeth, Yusuf Rashed Khamees Al Ola, Darwish Mohammed Saeed Awadh. Trainer: Rubens Francisco Minelli (Brazil).
**NZL**: Richard Hardie Wilson, Glenn Laurence Dods, Richard Lloyd Herbert, Robert Ronald Almond, Adrian Coroon Elrick, Allan Roderick Boath (74.Keith Gordon MacKay), Duncan Edward Cole, Steven Paul Sumner, Brian Alfred Turner (80.Samuel Alan Malcolmson), Wynton Alan Whai Rufer, Stephen Wooddin. Trainer: John Adshead (England).
**Goals**: 0-1 Wynton Alan Whai Rufer (16), 0-2 Brian Alfred Turner (17), 0-3 Stephen Wooddin (39), 0-4 Wynton Alan Whai Rufer (40), 0-5 Brian Alfred Turner (45).

## PLAY-OFF FOR THE SECOND PLACE

10.01.1982, National Stadium, Singapore (Singapore); Attendance: 60,000
Referee: Romualdo Arppi Filho (Brazil)
**NEW ZEALAND – CHINA P.R.**     **2-1(1-0)**
**NZL**: Richard Hardie Wilson, Glenn Laurence Dods, Richard Lloyd Herbert, Robert Ronald Almond, Adrian Coroon Elrick, Allan Roderick Boath (Peter Rex Simonsen), Duncan Edward Cole, Steven Paul Sumner, Grant John Turner, Wynton Alan Whai Rufer (Glen Neish Adam), Stephen Wooddin. Trainer: John Adshead (England).
**CHN**: Li Fu Sheng, Cai Jin Biao, Chi Shang Bin, Lin Lou Feng, Huang Xiang Dong, Zang Cai Ling, Zuo Shu Sheng (59.Yang Yu Ming), Gu Guang Ming (59.Liu Chen Der), Rong Zhi Hang, Chen Xi Rong, Wu Yu Hua. Trainer: Yong Shun Su.
**Goals**: 1-0 Stephen Wooddin (24), 2-0 Wynton Alan Whai Rufer (47), 2-1 Huang Xiang Dong (75).
New Zealand qualified for the Final Tournament.

# WORLD CUP 1982
# THE FINAL TOURNAMENT

The 12th edition of the FIFA World Cup, was held in Spain between 13th June and 11th July 1982, Spain having been chosen as the host nation by FIFA in London, England on 6th July 1966.

For the first time, the finals tournament was enlarged from 16 to 24 teams as more African and Asian countries were admitted and the First Round consisted of six groups of four teams, with a further four groups of three teams in the Second Round. Following the enlargement of the competition, no fewer than five countries (Algeria, Cameroon, Honduras, Kuwait, and New Zealand) participated in their first-ever finals series but, perhaps unsurprisingly, none progressed to the next round.

The 24 qualified teams were placed in 4 seeding pots:
Pot 1:
Spain (Hosts), Argentina (title holders), Brazil (3rd Place 1978), Italy (4th Place 1978), West Germany, England.
Pot 2:
Austria, Soviet Union, Hungary, Poland, Czechoslovakia, Yugoslavia.
Pot 3:
Belgium, Scotland, Northern Ireland, France, Chile, Peru.
Pot 4:
Algeria, Cameroon, Kuwait, El Salvador, Honduras, New Zealand.

The 24 teams were then drawn in following groups:

| GROUP 1 | GROUP 2 |
|---|---|
| Italy | West Germany |
| Poland | Algeria |
| Peru | Chile |
| Cameroon | Austria |

| GROUP 3 | GROUP 4 |
|---|---|
| Argentina | England |
| Belgium | France |
| Hungary | Czechoslovakia |
| El Salvador | Kuwait |

| GROUP 5 | GROUP 6 |
|---|---|
| Spain | Brazil |
| Honduras | Soviet Union |
| Yugoslavia | Scotland |
| Northern Ireland | New Zealand |

The teams finishing first and second in each group qualified for the second round.

The venues:
Alicante (Estadio "José Rico Pérez" – Capacity: 38,000)
Barcelona (Estadio Camp Nou – 120,000)
Barcelona (Estadio Sarrià – 44,000)
Bilbao (Estadio San Mamés – 47,000)
Elche (Estadio Nuevo – 40,000)
Gijón (Estadio El Molinón – 47,000)
La Coruña (Estadio Riazor – 34,600)
Madrid (Estadio „Santiago Bernabeu" - 76,000)
Madrid (Estadio „Vicente Calderón" - 66,000)
Málaga (Estadio La Rosaleda – 44,000)
Oviedo (Estadio "Carlos Tartiere" – 23,000)
Sevilla (Estadio "Benito Villamarín" – 47,500)
Sevilla (Estadio "Ramón Sánchez Pizjuán" – 70,500)
Valencia (Estadio "Luis Casanova" – 55,000)
Valladolid (Estadio "José Zorrilla" – 30,000)
Vigo (Estadio Balaídos – 31,800)
Zaragoza (Estadio La Romareda – 42,000)

 In the Second Round the reigning champions, Argentina, failed abysmally finishing bottom of their group and Brazil, too, failed to qualify for the semi-finals which were a completely European affair.
 Italy easily overcame an understrength Poland side in the first semi-final in a very one-sided game with Paolo Rossi scoring two goals but the real excitement came in the tie between France and West Germany. Undoubtedly the best game of the 1982 series and one of the best in World Cup history, this other semi-final was a real thriller. West Germany opened the score through Pierre Littbarski but France equalised just ten minutes later after Platini converted a penalty. In the $66^{th}$ minute a very unsavoury incident saw Battiston badly injured after the German goalkeeper Harald Schumacher rushed out of his goal and clattered into him as he attempted a shot. Battiston lost teeth and damaged a vertebra in the impact and was carried off the field unconscious. Incredibly, Schumacher avoided punishment for this dangerous challenge and the referee didn't even award a free-kick! Despite this setback, France took the advantage in the first period of extra-time with goals from Trésor and Giresse taking the scoreline to 3-1 and France looked set for the final. However, West Germany did not give up and goals from Rummenigge and Fischer meant that the score was 3-3 after extra-time. In the penalty shoot-out, Ulrich Stielike missed for the Germans, but France could not take advantage as both Maxime Bossis and Didier Six missed their penalties. Horst Hrubesch stepped up to score the decisive penalty, winning the shoot-out 5-4 and sending West Germany through to the final after a thrilling game.
 The Final, played in Madrid, remained goalless for almost an hour after Antonio Cabrini had missed a penalty for the Italians in the first half. In the $57^{th}$ minute, however, Paolo Rossi scored his sixth goal of the tournament to give Italy the lead and Marco Tardelli and Alessandro Altobelli added to these goals to create a commanding lead. Paul Breitner pulled one back for the Germans seven minutes from time, but it was to prove nothing more than a consolation. Italy (who had failed to win a match in the first group stage!) won their third World title, 44 years after previously lifting the World Cup. At 40 years of age, the Italian Captain, Dino Zoff, became the oldest player to win the World Cup.

# GROUP 1

| | | | | |
|---|---|---|---|---|
| 14.06.1982 | Vigo | Italy - Poland | | 0-0 |
| 15.06.1982 | La Coruña | Peru - Cameroon | | 0-0 |
| 18.06.1982 | Vigo | Italy - Peru | | 1-1(1-0) |
| 19.06.1982 | La Coruña | Poland - Cameroon | | 0-0 |
| 22.06.1982 | La Coruña | Poland - Peru | | 5-1(0-0) |
| 23.06.1982 | Vigo | Italy - Cameroon | | 1-1(0-0) |

## FINAL STANDINGS

| | | | | | | | | |
|---|---|---|---|---|---|---|---|---|
| 1. Poland | 3 | 1 | 2 | 0 | 5 | - | 1 | 4 |
| 2. Italy | 3 | 0 | 3 | 0 | 2 | - | 2 | 3 |
| 3. Cameroon | 3 | 0 | 3 | 0 | 1 | - | 1 | 3 |
| 4. Peru | 3 | 0 | 2 | 1 | 2 | - | 6 | 2 |

14.06.1982, Estadio Balaídos, Vigo; Attendance: 33,000
Referee: Michel Vautrot (France)
**ITALY - POLAND**      **0-0**
**ITA:** Dino Zoff, Claudio Gentile, Fulvio Collovatti, Gaetano Scirea, Antonio Cabrini, Giampiero Marini, Bruno Conti, Marco Tardelli, Giancarlo Antognoni, Paolo Rossi, Francesco Graziani. Trainer: Enzo Bearzot.
**POL:** Józef Młynarczyk, Paweł Janas, Jan Jałocha, Władysław Żmuda (Cap), Stefan Majewski, Waldemar Matysik, Andrzej Iwan (72.Marek Kusto), Andrzej Buncol, Grzegorz Lato, Włodzimierz Smolarek, Zbigniew Boniek. Trainer: Antoni Piechniczek.
**Cautions**: Giampiero Marini, Gaetano Scirea / Zbigniew Boniek.

15.06.1982, Estadio Riazor, La Coruña; Attendance: 11,000
Referee: Franz Wöhrer (Austria)
**PERU - CAMEROON**      **0-0**
**PER:** Ramón Quiroga Arancibia, Jaime Eduardo Duarte Huerta, Rubén Toribio Díaz Rivas (Cap), Rafael Salvador Salguero González, Jorge Andrés Olaechea Quijandría, José Manuel Velásquez Castillo, César Augusto Cueto Villa, Teófilo Juan Cubillas Arizaga (56.Guillermo La Rosa Laguna), Germán Carlos Leguía Dragó (66.Gerónimo Barbadillo González), Julio César Uribe Flores, Juan Carlos Oblitas Saba. Trainer: Elba de Padua Lima "Tim" (Brazil).
**CMR:** Thomas N'Kono (Cap), Michel Kaham, Ibrahim Aoudou, René Brice N'Djeya, Elie Onana Elondou, Emmanuel Jerome Kundé, Ephrem M'Bom, Grégoire M'Bida, Roger Milla (89.Jean-Pierre Tokoto), Théophile Abega, Jacques N'Guea (73.Paul Bahoken). Trainer: Jean Vincent (France).
**Cautions**: Thomas N'Kono.

18.06.1982, Estadio Balaídos, Vigo; Attendance: 25,000
Referee: Werner Eschweiler (West Germany)
**ITALY - PERU**      **1-1(1-0)**
**ITA:** Dino Zoff, Claudio Gentile, Fulvio Collovatti, Gaetano Scirea, Antonio Cabrini, Giampiero Marini, Bruno Conti, Marco Tardelli, Giancarlo Antognoni, Paolo Rossi (46.Franco Causio), Francesco Graziani. Trainer: Enzo Bearzot.
**PER:** Ramón Quiroga Arancibia, Jaime Eduardo Duarte Huerta, Rubén Toribio Díaz Rivas (Cap), Rafael Salvador Salguero González, Jorge Andrés Olaechea Quijandría, José Manuel Velásquez Castillo, César Augusto Cueto Villa, Teófilo Juan Cubillas Arizaga, Gerónimo Barbadillo González (65.Guillermo La Rosa Laguna), Julio César Uribe Flores (65.Germán Carlos Leguía Dragó), Juan Carlos Oblitas Saba. Trainer: Elba de Padua Lima "Tim" (Brazil).
**Goals**: 1-0 Bruno Conti (19), 1-1 Fulvio Collovati (84 own goal).
**Cautions**: Marco Tardelli / Jaime Eduardo Duarte Huerta.

19.06.1982, Estadio Riazor, La Coruña; Attendance: 19,000
Referee: Alexis Ponnet (Belgium)
**POLAND - CAMEROON** **0-0**
**POL:** Józef Młynarczyk, Paweł Janas, Jan Jałocha, Władysław Żmuda (Cap), Stefan Majewski, Zbigniew Boniek, Andrzej Buncol, Grzegorz Lato, Włodzimierz Smolarek, Andrzej Pałasz (67.Marek Kusto), Andrzej Iwan (27.Andrzej Szarmach). Trainer: Antoni Piechniczek.
**CMR:** Thomas N'Kono (Cap), Michel Kaham, René Brice N'Djeya, Elie Onana Elondou, Emmanuel Jerome Kundé, Ephrem M'Bom, Grégoire M'Bida, Roger Milla, Théophile Abega, Ibrahim Aoudou, Jacques N'Guea (46.Jean-Pierre Tokoto). Trainer: Jean Vincent (France).
**Cautions**: Andrzej Pałasz / Ibrahim Aoudou, Roger Milla.

22.06.1982, Estadio Riazor, La Coruña; Attendance: 25,000
Referee: Lamberto Mario Rubio Vásquez (Mexico)
**POLAND - PERU** **5-1(0-0)**
**POL:** Józef Młynarczyk, Paweł Janas, Jan Jałocha (26.Marek Dziuba), Władysław Żmuda (Cap), Stefan Majewski, Waldemar Matysik, Janusz Kupcewicz, Andrzej Buncol, Grzegorz Lato, Zbigniew Boniek, Włodzimierz Smolarek (74.Włodzimierz Ciołek). Trainer: Antoni Piechniczek.
**PER:** Ramón Quiroga Arancibia, Jaime Eduardo Duarte Huerta, Rubén Toribio Díaz Rivas (Cap), Rafael Salvador Salguero González, Jorge Andrés Olaechea Quijandría, César Augusto Cueto Villa, José Manuel Velásquez Castillo, Teófilo Juan Cubillas Arizaga (49.Julio César Uribe Flores), Germán Carlos Leguía Dragó, Guillermo La Rosa Laguna, Juan Carlos Oblitas Saba (49.Gerónimo Barbadillo González). Trainer: Elba de Padua Lima "Tim" (Brazil).
**Goals**: 1-0 Włodzimierz Smolarek (55), 2-0 Grzegorz Lato (58), 3-0 Zbigniew Boniek (61), 4-0 Andrzej Buncol (69), 5-0 Włodzimierz Ciołek (76), 5-1 Guillermo La Rosa Laguna (83).
**Cautions**: José Manuel Velásquez Castillo.

23.06.1982, Estadio Balaídos, Vigo; Attendance: 20,000
Referee: Bogdan Dochev (Bulgaria)
**ITALY - CAMEROON** **1-1(0-0)**
**ITA:** Dino Zoff, Claudio Gentile, Fulvio Collovatti, Gaetano Scirea, Antonio Cabrini, Gabriele Oriali, Bruno Conti, Marco Tardelli, Giancarlo Antognoni, Paolo Rossi, Francesco Graziani. Trainer: Enzo Bearzot.
**CMR:** Thomas N'Kono (Cap), Michel Kaham, René Brice N'Djeya, Elie Onana Elondou, Emmanuel Jerome Kundé, Ephrem M'Bom, Grégoire M'Bida, Roger Milla, Jean-Pierre Tokoto, Théophile Abega, Ibrahim Aoudou, Trainer: Jean Vincent (France).
**Goals**: 1-0 Francesco Graziani (61), 1-1 Grégoire M'Bida (61).
**Cautions**: Giancarlo Antognoni / René Brice N'Djeya.

# GROUP 2

| | | | | |
|---|---|---|---|---|
| 16.06.1982 | Gijón | West Germany - Algeria | 1-2(0-0) |
| 17.06.1982 | Oviedo | Chile - Austria | 0-1(0-1) |
| 20.06.1982 | Gijón | West Germany - Chile | 4-1(1-0) |
| 21.06.1982 | Oviedo | Algeria - Austria | 0-2(0-0) |
| 24.06.1982 | Oviedo | Algeria - Chile | 3-2(3-0) |
| 25.06.1982 | Gijón | West Germany - Austria | 1-0(1-0) |

## FINAL STANDINGS

| | | | | | | | | |
|---|---|---|---|---|---|---|---|---|
| 1. | West Germany | 3 | 2 | 0 | 1 | 6 | - | 3 | 4 |
| 2. | Austria | 3 | 2 | 0 | 1 | 3 | - | 1 | 4 |
| 3. | Algeria | 3 | 2 | 0 | 1 | 5 | - | 5 | 4 |
| 4. | Chile | 3 | 0 | 0 | 3 | 3 | - | 8 | 0 |

16.06.1982, Estadio El Molinón, Gijón; Attendance: 42,500
Referee: Enrique Labo Revoredo (Peru)
**WEST GERMANY - ALGERIA**     **1-2(0-0)**
**GER:** Harald Schumacher, Manfred Kaltz, Ulrich Stielike, Karlheinz Förster, Hans-Peter Briegel, Wolfgang Dremmler, Paul Breitner, Felix Magath (82.Klaus Fischer), Pierre Littbarski, Horst Hrubesch, Karl-Heinz Rummenigge (Cap). Trainer: Josef Derwall.
**ALG:** Mehdi Cerbah, Mahmoud Guendouz, Chaabane Merzekane, Nourredine Abdallah Kourichi, Mustapha Dahleb, Faouzi Mansouri, Ali Fergani (Cap), Lakhdar Belloumi, Mustapha Rabah Madjer (88.Salah Larbès), Djamel Zidane (64.Tedj Bensaoula), Salah Assad. Trainer: Rachid Mekhloufi.
**Goals:** 0-1 Mustapha Rabah Madjer (52), 1-1 Karl-Heinz Rummenigge (67), 1-2 Lakhdar Belloumi (68).
**Cautions:** Horst Hrubesch / Mustapha Rabah Madjer.

17.06.1982, Estadio „Carlos Tartiere", Oviedo; Attendance: 23,000
Referee: Juan Daniel Cardellino de San Vicente (Uruguay)
**CHILE - AUSTRIA**     **0-1(0-1)**
**CHI:** Mario Ignacio Osbén Méndez, Lizardo Antonio Garrido Bustamante, Eduardo René Valenzuela Becker, Elías Ricardo Figueroa Brander, Vladimir David Bigorra López, Miguel Angel Neira Pincheira (72.Manuel Antonio Rojas Zuniga), Rodolfo del Rosario Dubó Segovia, Eduardo Guillermo Bonvallet Godoy, Gustavo Segundo Moscoso Huencho (69.Miguel Angel Gamboa Pedemonte), Carlos Humberto Caszely Garrido, Patricio Nazario Yáñez Candia. Trainer: Oscar Luis Santibáñez Díaz.
**AUT:** Friedrich Koncilia, Bernd Krauss, Erich Obermayer, Bruno Pezzey, Josef Degeorgi (77.Ernst Baumeister), Herbert Prohaska, Roland Hattenberger, Heribert Weber (77.Gernot Jurtin), Reinhold Hintermaier, Walter Schachner, Johann Krankl. Trainers: Felix Latzke - Georg Schmidt.
**Goal:** 0-1 Walter Schachner (22).
**Cautions:** Lizardo Antonio Garrido Bustamante / Josef Degeorgi, Roland Hattenberger.

20.06.1982, Estadio El Molinón, Gijón; Attendance: 42,000
Referee: Bruno Galler (Switzerland)
**WEST GERMANY - CHILE**     **4-1(1-0)**
**GER:** Harald Schumacher, Manfred Kaltz, Ulrich Stielike, Karlheinz Förster, Hans-Peter Briegel, Wolfgang Dremmler, Paul Breitner (47.Lothar Herbert Matthäus), Felix Magath, Pierre Littbarski (79.Uwe Reinders), Horst Hrubesch, Karl-Heinz Rummenigge (Cap). Trainer: Josef Derwall.
**CHI:** Mario Ignacio Osbén Méndez, Lizardo Antonio Garrido Bustamante, Eduardo René Valenzuela Becker, Elías Ricardo Figueroa Brander, Vladimir David Bigorra López, Mario del Transito Soto Benavides (46.Juan Carlos Letelier Pizarro), Rodolfo del Rosario Dubó Segovia, Eduardo Guillermo Bonvallet Godoy, Gustavo Segundo Moscoso Huencho, Patricio Nazario Yáñez Candia, Miguel Angel Gamboa Pedemonte (66.Miguel Angel Neira Pincheira). Trainer: Oscar Luis Santibáñez Díaz.
**Goals:** 1-0 Karl-Heinz Rummenigge (9), 2-0 Karl-Heinz Rummenigge (57), 3-0 Karl-Heinz Rummenigge (66), 4-0 Uwe Reinders (81), 4-1 Gustavo Segundo Moscoso Huencho (90).
**Cautions:** Rodolfo del Rosario Dubó Segovia, Miguel Angel Gamboa Pedemonte.

21.06.1982, Estadio „Carlos Tartiere", Oviedo; Attendance: 36,000
Referee: Anton Boskovic (Australia)
**ALGERIA - AUSTRIA**     **0-2(0-0)**
**ALG:** Mehdi Cerbah, Mahmoud Guendouz, Chaabane Merzekane, Nourredine Abdallah Kourichi, Mustapha Dahleb (76.Djamel Tlemçani), Faouzi Mansouri, Ali Fergani (Cap), Lakhdar Belloumi (66.Tedj Bensaoula), Mustapha Rabah Madjer, Djamel Zidane, Salah Assad. Trainer: Rachid Mekhloufi.
**AUT:** Friedrich Koncilia, Bernd Krauss, Erich Obermayer, Bruno Pezzey, Josef Degeorgi, Roland Hattenberger, Herbert Prohaska (80.Heribert Weber), Reinhold Hintermaier, Ernst Baumeister (46.Kurt Welzl), Walter Schachner, Johann Krankl. Trainers: Felix Latzke - Georg Schmidt.
**Goals:** 0-1 Walter Schachner (56), 0-2 Johann Krankl (67).
**Cautions:** Faouzi Mansouri.

24.06.1982, Estadio „Carlos Tartiere", Oviedo; Attendance: 16,000
Referee: Romulo Méndez Molina (Guatemala)
**ALGERIA - CHILE**     **3-2(3-0)**
**ALG:** Mehdi Cerbah, Mahmoud Guendouz, Chaabane Merzekane, Nourredine Abdallah Kourichi, Salah Larbès, Abdelmadjid Bourrebou (31.Hocine Yahi), Faouzi Mansouri (73.Mustapha Dahleb), Ali Fergani (Cap), Mustapha Rabah Madjer, Tedj Bensaoula, Salah Assad. Trainer: Rachid Mekhloufi.
**CHI:** Mario Ignacio Osbén Méndez, Mario Enrique Galindo Calixto, Eduardo René Valenzuela Becker, Elías Ricardo Figueroa Brander, Vladimir David Bigorra López, Rodolfo del Rosario Dubó Segovia, Eduardo Guillermo Bonvallet Godoy (37.Mario del Transito Soto Benavides), Miguel Angel Neira Pincheira, Carlos Humberto Caszely Garrido (58.Juan Carlos Letelier Pizarro), Patricio Nazario Yáñez Candia, Gustavo Segundo Moscoso Huencho. Trainer: Oscar Luis Santibáñez Díaz.
**Goals:** 1-0 Assad Salah (7), 2-0 Assad Salah (31), 3-0 Tedj Bensaoula (35), 3-1 Miguel Angel Neira Pincheira (59 penalty), 3-2 Juan Carlos Letelier Pizarro (73).
**Cautions:** Juan Carlos Letelier Pizarro.

25.06.1982, Estadio El Molinon, Gijón; Attendance: 28,000
Referee: Robert Bonar Valentine (Scotland)
**WEST GERMANY - AUSTRIA**     **1-0(1-0)**
**GER:** Harald Schumacher, Manfred Kaltz, Ulrich Stielike, Karlheinz Förster, Hans-Peter Briegel, Wolfgang Dremmler, Paul Breitner, Felix Magath, Pierre Littbarski, Horst Hrubesch (68.Klaus Fischer), Karl-Heinz Rummenigge (Cap) (65.Lothar Herbert Matthäus). Trainer: Josef Derwall.
**AUT:** Friedrich Koncilia, Bernd Krauss, Erich Obermayer, Bruno Pezzey, Josef Degeorgi, Roland Hattenberger, Reinhold Hintermaier, Herbert Prohaska, Heribert Weber, Johann Krankl, Walter Schachner. Trainers: Felix Latzke - Georg Schmidt.
**Goal:** 1-0 Horst Hrubesch (10).
**Cautions:** Reinhold Hintermaier, Walter Schachner.

# GROUP 3

| | | | | |
|---|---|---|---|---|
| 13.06.1982 | Barcelona | Argentina - Belgium | 0-1(0-0) |
| 15.06.1982 | Elche | Hungary – El Salvador | 10-1(3-0) |
| 18.06.1982 | Alicante | Argentina - Hungary | 4-1(2-0) |
| 19.06.1982 | Elche | Belgium – El Salvador | 1-0(1-0) |
| 22.06.1982 | Elche | Belgium - Hungary | 1-1(0-1) |
| 23.06.1982 | Alicante | Argentina – El Salvador | 2-0(1-0) |

## FINAL STANDINGS

| | | | | | | | | |
|---|---|---|---|---|---|---|---|---|
| 1. Belgium | 3 | 2 | 1 | 0 | 3 | - | 1 | 5 |
| 2. Argentina | 3 | 2 | 0 | 1 | 6 | - | 2 | 4 |
| 3. Hungary | 3 | 1 | 1 | 1 | 12 | - | 6 | 3 |
| 4. El Salvador | 3 | 0 | 0 | 3 | 1 | - | 13 | 0 |

13.06.1982, Estadio Camp Nou, Barcelona; Attendance: 95,000
Referee: Vojtěch Christov (Czechoslovakia)
**ARGENTINA - BELGIUM**                           **0-1(0-0)**
**ARG:** Ubaldo Matildo Fillol, Jorge Mario Olguín, Luis Adolfo Galván, Daniel Alberto Passarella (Cap), Alberto César Tarantini, Osvaldo César Ardiles, Américo Rubén Gallego, Diego Armando Maradona, Ricardo Daniel Bertoni, Ramón Ángel Díaz (64.Jorge Alberto Francisco Valdano), Mario Alberto Kempes. Trainer: César Luis Menotti.
**BEL:** Jean-Marie Pfaff, Eric Gerets, Luc Millecamps, Maurits De Schrijver, Marc Baecke, Guy Vandersmissen, Ludo Coeck, Jan Ceulemans, Frank Vercauteren, Erwin Vandenbergh, Alexander Czerniatynski. Trainer: Guy Thys.
**Goal:** 0-1 Erwin Vandenbergh (63).
**Cautions:** Ricardo Daniel Bertoni / Luc Millecamps.

15.06.1982, Estadio Nuevo, Elche; Attendance: 20,000
Referee: Ebrahim Yousif Al Doy (Bahrain)
**HUNGARY – EL SALVADOR**                 **10-1(3-0)**
**HUN:** Ferenc Mészáros, Győző Martos, László Bálint, Imre Garaba, József Tóth, Sándor Müller (69.Lázár Szentes), Tibor Nyilasi, Sándor Sallai, László Fazekas, András Törőcsik (56.László Kiss), Gábor Pölöskei. Trainer: Kálmán Mészöly.
**SLV:** Luis Ricardo Guevara Mora, Mario Alfonso Castillo Díaz, Francisco José Jovel Cruz, Jaime Alberto Rodríguez Jiménez, Carlos Humberto Recinos Ortíz, Joaquín Alonso Ventura (77.Ramón Alfredo Fagoaga Romero), José Luis Rugamas Portillo (27.Luis Baltazar Ramírez Zapata), José Norberto Huezo Montoya, Jorge Alberto González Barillas, Ever Francisco Hernández, José María Rivas Martínez. Trainer: Mauricio Alonso Rodríguez Lindo.
**Goals:** 1-0 Tibor Nyilasi (4), 2-0 Gábor Pölöskei (11), 3-0 László Fazekas (24), 4-0 József Tóth (51), 5-0 László Fazekas (54), 5-1 Luis Baltazar Ramírez Zapata (64), 6-1 László Kiss (70), 7-1 Lázár Szentes (71), 8-1 László Kiss (73), 9-1 László Kiss (77), 10-1 Tibor Nyilasi (83).
**Cautions:** Tibor Nyilasi, László Fazekas.

18.06.1982, Estadio „José Rico Pérez", Alicante; Attendance: 32,000
Referee: Belaid Lacarne (Algeria)
**ARGENTINA - HUNGARY** **4-1(2-0)**
**ARG:** Ubaldo Matildo Fillol, Jorge Mario Olguín, Luis Adolfo Galván, Daniel Alberto Passarella (Cap), Alberto César Tarantini (51.Juan Alberto Barbas), Osvaldo César Ardiles, Américo Rubén Gallego, Diego Armando Maradona, Ricardo Daniel Bertoni, Jorge Alberto Francisco Valdano (24.Gabriel Humberto Calderón), Mario Alberto Kempes. Trainer: César Luis Menotti.
**HUN:** Ferenc Mészáros, Győző Martos (46.László Fazekas), László Bálint, Imre Garaba, József Tóth, Sándor Sallai, Tibor Nyilasi, Tibor Rab, József Varga, László Kiss (62.Lázár Szentes), Gábor Pölöskei. Trainer: Kálmán Mészöly.
**Goals**: 1-0 Ricardo Daniel Bertoni (26), 2-0 Diego Armando Maradona (28), 3-0 Diego Armando Maradona (57), 4-0 Osvaldo César Ardiles (60), 4-1 Gábor Pölöskei (76).

19.06.1982, Estadio Nuevo, Elche; Attendance: 38,749
Referee: Malcolm Moffatt (Northern Ireland)
**BELGIUM – EL SALVADOR** **1-0(1-0)**
**BEL:** Jean-Marie Pfaff, Eric Gerets, Luc Millecamps, Walter Meeuws, Marc Baecke, Guy Vandersmissen (45.François Vander Elst), Ludo Coeck, Frank Vercauteren, Jan Ceulemans (80.Wilfried Van Moer), Alexander Czerniatynski, Erwin Vandenbergh. Trainer: Guy Thys.
**SLV:** Luis Ricardo Guevara Mora, Francisco Salvador Osorto Guardado (46.Miguel Arevalo), Francisco José Jovel Cruz, Jaime Alberto Rodríguez Jiménez, Carlos Humberto Recinos Ortíz, Joaquín Alonso Ventura, Ramón Alfredo Fagoaga Romero, Luis Baltazar Ramírez Zapata, José Norberto Huezo Montoya, Jorge Alberto González Barillas, José María Rivas Martínez. Trainer: Mauricio Alonso Rodríguez Lindo.
**Goal**: 1-0 Ludo Coeck (18).
**Cautions**: Francisco Salvador Osorto Guardado, Ramón Alfredo Fagoaga Romero.

22.06.1982, Estadio Nuevo, Elche; Attendance: 37,000
Referee: Clive Bradley White (England)
**BELGIUM - HUNGARY** **1-1(0-1)**
**BEL:** Jean-Marie Pfaff, Eric Gerets (63.Gérard Plessers), Luc Millecamps, Walter Meeuws, Marc Baecke, Guy Vandersmissen (46.Wilfried Van Moer), Ludo Coeck, Frank Vercauteren, Jan Ceulemans, Alexander Czerniatynski, Erwin Vandenbergh. Trainer: Guy Thys.
**HUN:** Ferenc Mészáros, Győző Martos, Attila Kerekes, Imre Garaba, József Varga, Sándor Müller (68.Sándor Sallai), Tibor Nyilasi, Gábor Pölöskei, László Fazekas, András Törőcsik, László Kiss (70.Ferenc Csongrádi). Trainer: Kálmán Mészöly.
**Goals**: 0-1 József Varga (28), 1-1 Alexander Czerniatynski (76).
**Cautions**: Jean-Marie Pfaff, Walter Meeuws.

23.06.1982, Estadio „José Rico Pérez", Alicante; Attendance: 32,500
Referee: Luis Barrancos Alvarez (Bolivia)
**ARGENTINA – EL SALVADOR** **2-0(1-0)**
**ARG:** Ubaldo Matildo Fillol, Jorge Mario Olguín, Luis Adolfo Galván, Daniel Alberto Passarella (Cap), Alberto César Tarantini, Osvaldo César Ardiles, Américo Rubén Gallego, Diego Armando Maradona, Ricardo Daniel Bertoni (68.Ramón Ángel Díaz), Gabriel Humberto Calderón (78.Santiago Santamaría), Mario Alberto Kempes. Trainer: César Luis Menotti.
**SLV:** Luis Ricardo Guevara Mora, Francisco Salvador Osorto Guardado (34.Miguel Ángel Díaz Arévalo), Francisco José Jovel Cruz, Jaime Alberto Rodríguez Jiménez, Carlos Humberto Recinos Ortíz, Joaquín Alonso Ventura (79.Mauricio Alberto Alfaro Valladares), Luis Baltazar Ramírez Zapata, José Luis Rugamas Portillo, José Norberto Huezo Montoya, Jorge Alberto González Barillas, José María Rivas Martínez. Trainer: Mauricio Alonso Rodríguez Lindo.
**Goals**: 1-0 Daniel Alberto Passarella (22 penalty), 2-0 Ricardo Daniel Bertoni (52).
**Cautions**: Jorge Mario Olguín, Américo Rubén Gallego / Francisco Salvador Osorto Guardado, Luis Baltazar Ramírez Zapata, Carlos Humberto Recinos Ortíz.

## GROUP 4

| | | | | |
|---|---|---|---|---|
| 16.06.1982 | Bilbao | England - France | 3-1(1-1) |
| 17.06.1982 | Valladolid | Czechoslovakia - Kuwait | 1-1(1-0) |
| 20.06.1982 | Bilbao | England - Czechoslovakia | 2-0(0-0) |
| 21.06.1982 | Valladolid | France - Kuwait | 4-1(2-0) |
| 24.06.1982 | Valladolid | France - Czechoslovakia | 1-1(0-0) |
| 25.06.1982 | Bilbao | England - Kuwait | 1-0(1-0) |

### FINAL STANDINGS

| | | | | | | | | |
|---|---|---|---|---|---|---|---|---|
| 1. | England | 3 | 3 | 0 | 0 | 6 - 1 | 6 |
| 2. | France | 3 | 1 | 1 | 1 | 6 - 5 | 3 |
| 3. | Czechoslovakia | 3 | 0 | 2 | 1 | 2 - 4 | 2 |
| 4. | Kuwait | 3 | 0 | 1 | 2 | 2 - 6 | 1 |

16.06.1982, Estadio San Mames, Bilbao; Attendance: 44,172
Referee: Antonio José da Silva Garrido (Portugal)
**ENGLAND - FRANCE**  **3-1(1-1)**
**ENG**: Peter Leslie Shilton, Michael Dennis Mills (Cap), Kenneth Graham Sansom (90.Philip George Neal), Philip Brian Thompson, Terence Ian Butcher, Bryan Robson, Steven James Coppell, Raymond Colin Wilkins, Paul Mariner, Trevor John Francis, Graham Rix. Manager: Ronald Greenwood.
**FRA**: Jean-Luc Ettori, Patrick Battiston, Christian Lopez, Marius Trésor, Maxime Bossis, René Girard, Jean-François Larios (74.Jean Amadou Tigana), Michel Platini (Cap), Alain Giresse, Dominique Rocheteau (71.Didier Six), Gérard Soler. Trainer: Michel Hidalgo.
**Goals**: 1-0 Bryan Robson (1), 1-1 Gérard Soler (24), 2-1 Bryan Robson (67), 3-1 Paul Mariner (83).
**Cautions**: Terence Ian Butcher.

17.06.1982, Estadio „José Zorrilla", Valladolid; Attendance: 25,000
Referee: Benjamin Kwabana Dwomoh (Ghana)
**CZECHOSLOVAKIA - KUWAIT**  **1-1(1-0)**
**TCH**: Zdeněk Hruška, Jozef Barmoš, Jan Fiala, Ladislav Jurkemik, Jozef Kukučka, Antonín Panenka, Jan Berger, Tomáš Kříž (63.Přemysl Bičovský), Petr Janečka (69.Vlastimil Petržela), Zdeněk Nehoda (Cap), Ladislav Vízek. Trainer: Jozef Vengloš.
**KUW**: Ahmed Khuder Al Tarabulsi, Naeem Saad Mubarak Fajah, Abdullah Yousuf Ma'youf, Mahboub Juma Mahboub Mubarak, Waleed Mohammed Al Jasem Al Mubarak, Abdullah Mohammed Al Buloushi, Saed Mohammed Abdul Aziz Al Houti (Cap), Mohammed Ahmed Karam (57.Fatih Kamil Fayyaz Matar Marzouq), Abdul Aziz Saoud Al Anbari, Jassem Jamal Yaqoub Sultan, Faisal Ali Al Dakhil. Trainer: Carlos Alberto Gomes Parreira (Brazil).
**Goals**: 1-0 Antonín Panenka (20 penalty), 1-1 Faisal Ali Al Dakhil (57).

20.06.1982, Estadio „San Mamés", Bilbao; Attendance: 42,000
Referee: Charles George Rainier Corver (Holland)
**ENGLAND - CZECHOSLOVAKIA**  **2-0(0-0)**
**ENG**: Peter Leslie Shilton, Michael Dennis Mills (Cap), Philip Brian Thompson, Terence Ian Butcher, Kenneth Graham Sansom, Steven James Coppell, Bryan Robson (46.Glenn Hoddle), Raymond Colin Wilkins, Trevor John Francis, Paul Mariner, Graham Rix. Manager: Ronald Greenwood.
**TCH**: Stanislav Seman (75.Karel Stromšik), Jozef Barmoš, Rostislav Vojáček, Libor Radimec, Jan Fiala, Pavel Chaloupka, Ladislav Jurkemik, Jan Berger, Petr Janečka (77.Marián Masný), Zdeněk Nehoda (Cap), Ladislav Vízek. Trainer: Jozef Vengloš.
**Goals**: 1-0 Trevor John Francis (62), 2-0 Jozef Barmoš (66 own goal).
**Cautions**: Pavel Chaloupka.

21.06.1982, Estadio „José Zorilla", Valladolid; Attendance: 30,043
Referee: Miroslav Stupar (Soviet Union)
**FRANCE - KUWAIT** **4-1(2-0)**
**FRA:** Jean-Luc Ettori, Manuel Amoros, Gérard Janvion (60.Christian Lopez), Marius Trésor, Maxime Bossis, Alain Giresse, Michel Platini (Cap) (81.René Girard), Bernard Genghini, Gérard Soler, Bernard Lacombe, Didier Six. Trainer: Michel Hidalgo.
**KUW**: Ahmed Khuder Al Tarabulsi, Naeem Saad Mubarak Fajah, Abdullah Yousuf Ma'youf, Mahboub Juma Mahboub Mubarak, Waleed Mohammed Al Jasem Al Mubarak (78.Hamoud Fulaiteh Al Shammari), Abdullah Mohammed Al Buloushi, Saed Mohammed Abdul Aziz Al Houti (Cap), Mohammed Ahmed Karam (46.Fatih Kamil Fayyaz Matar Marzouq), Abdul Aziz Saoud Al Anbari, Jassem Jamal Yaqoub Sultan, Faisal Ali Al Dakhil. Trainer: Carlos Alberto Gomes Parreira (Brazil).
**Goals**: 1-0 Bernard Genghini (31), 2-0 Michel Platini (43), 3-0 Didier Six (48), 3-1 Abdullah Mohammed Al Buloushi (75), 4-1 Maxime Bossis (89).
**Cautions**: Manuel Amoros / Abdul Aziz Saoud Al Anbari, Fatih Kamil Fayyaz Matar Marzouq.

24.06.1982, Estadio „José Zorilla", Valladolid; Attendance: 28,000
Referee: Paolo Casarin (Italy)
**FRANCE - CZECHOSLOVAKIA** **1-1(0-0)**
**FRA:** Jean-Luc Ettori, Manuel Amoros, Gérard Janvion, Marius Trésor, Maxime Bossis, Alain Giresse, Michel Platini (Cap), Bernard Genghini, Gérard Soler (88.René Girard), Bernard Lacombe (70.Alain Couriol), Didier Six. Trainer: Michel Hidalgo.
**TCH:** Karel Stromšik, Jozef Barmoš, Libor Radimec, Rostislav Vojáček, Jan Fiala, Zdeněk Nehoda (Cap), František Štambachr, Přemsyl Bičovský, Tomáš Kříž (31.Marián Masný), Ladislav Vízek, Petr Janečka (70.Antonín Panenka). Trainer: Jozef Vengloš.
**Goals**: 1-0 Didier Six (66), 1-1 Antonín Panenka (84 penalty).
**Cautions:** Manuel Amoros / Antonín Panenka.
**Sent off**: Ladislav Vízek (88).

25.06.1982, Estadio San Mames, Bilbao; Attendance: 39,700
Referee: Gilberto Aristizábal Murcia (Colombia)
**ENGLAND - KUWAIT** **1-0(1-0)**
**ENG:** Peter Leslie Shilton, Philip George Neal, Philip Brian Thompson, Stephen Brian Foster, Michael Dennis Mills (Cap), Steven James Coppell, Glenn Hoddle, Raymond Colin Wilkins, Graham Rix, Paul Mariner, Trevor John Francis. Manager: Ronald Greenwood.
**KUW**: Ahmed Khuder Al Tarabulsi, Naeem Saad Mubarak Fajah, Abdullah Yousuf Ma'youf, Mahboub Juma Mahboub Mubarak, Waleed Mohammed Al Jasem Al Mubarak (76.Hamoud Fulaiteh Al Shammari), Abdullah Mohammed Al Buloushi, Saed Mohammed Abdul Aziz Al Houti (Cap), Fatih Kamil Fayyaz Matar Marzouq, Abdul Aziz Saoud Al Anbari, Yussef Faraj Al Suwayed, Faisal Ali Al Dakhil. Trainer: Carlos Alberto Gomes Parreira (Brazil).
**Goal**: 1-0 Trevor John Francis (27).
**Cautions**: Paul Mariner / Naeem Saad Mubarak Fajah.

# GROUP 5

| | | | | |
|---|---|---|---|---|
| 16.06.1982 | Valencia | Spain - Honduras | | 1-1(0-1) |
| 17.06.1982 | Zaragoza | Yugoslavia – Northern Ireland | | 0-0 |
| 20.06.1982 | Valencia | Spain - Yugoslavia | | 2-1(1-1) |
| 21.06.1982 | Zaragoza | Honduras – Northern Ireland | | 1-1(0-1) |
| 24.06.1982 | Zaragoza | Honduras - Yugoslavia | | 0-1(0-1) |
| 25.06.1982 | Valencia | Spain - Northern Ireland | | 0-1(0-0) |

### FINAL STANDINGS

| | | | | | | | |
|---|---|---|---|---|---|---|---|
| 1. | Northern Ireland | 3 | 1 | 2 | 0 | 2 - 1 | 4 |
| 2. | Spain | 3 | 1 | 1 | 1 | 3 - 3 | 3 |
| 3. | Yugoslavia | 3 | 1 | 1 | 1 | 2 - 2 | 3 |
| 4. | Honduras | 3 | 0 | 2 | 1 | 2 - 3 | 2 |

16.06.1982, Estadio „Luis Casanova", Valencia; Attendance: 47,000
Referee: Arturo Andrés Ithurralde (Argentina)
**SPAIN - HONDURAS**                                                                 **1-1(0-1)**
**ESP:** Luis Miguel Arkonada Echarre (Cap), José Antonio Camacho Alfaro, Miguel Tendillo Belenguer, José Ramón Alexanco Ventosa, Rafael Gordillo Vázquez, Miguel Ángel Alonso Oyarbide „Periko Alonso", Joaquín Alonso González (46.José Vicente Sánchez Felip), Jesús María Zamora Ansorena, Juan Enrique Gómez González „Juanito" (46.Enrique Saura Gil), Jesús María Satrústegui Azpiroz, Roberto López Ufarte. Trainer: José Emilio Santamaría Iglesias.
**HON:** Julio César Arzú, César Efrain Gutíerrez Álvarez, Allan Anthony Costly Blyden, Jaime Enrique Villegas Roura, José Fernando Bulnes Zubiaga, Ramón Enrique Maradiaga Chávez, Gilberto Geronimo Yearwood, Héctor Ramón Zelaya Rivera, Prudencio Norales Martínez (69.Carlos Orlando Caballero Sánchez), Porfirio Amando Betancourt Cortez, José Roberto Figueroa Padilla. Trainer: José de la Paz Herrera Ucles.
**Goals:** 0-1 Héctor Ramón Zelaya Rivera (7), 1-1 Roberto López Ufarte (65 penalty).

17.06.1982, Estadio La Romareda, Zaragoza; Attendance: 25,000
Referee: Erik Fredriksson (Sweden)
**YUGOSLAVIA – NORTHERN IRELAND**                                                **0-0**
**YUG:** Dragan Pantelić, Nikola Jovanović, Miloš Hrstić, Ivan Gudelj, Velimir Zajec, Nenad Stojnković, Vladimir Petrović, Edhem Šljivo, Ivan Šurjak (Cap), Safet Sušić, Zlatko Vujović. Trainer: Miljan Miljanić.
**NIR:** Patrick Anthony Jennings, James Michael Nicholl, Christopher James Nicholl, John McClelland, Malachy Martin Donaghy, Samuel Baxter McIlroy, Martin Hugh Michael O'Neill (Cap), David McCreery, Gerard Joseph Armstrong, William Robert Hamilton, Norman Whiteside. Manager: William Laurence Bingham.
**Cautions:** Norman Whiteside.

20.06.1982, Estadio „Luis Casanova", Valencia; Attendance: 50,000
Referee: Henning Lund Sørensen (Denmark)
**SPAIN - YUGOSLAVIA**                                                                **2-1(1-1)**
**ESP:** Luis Miguel Arkonada Echarre (Cap), José Antonio Camacho Alfaro, Miguel Tendillo Belenguer, José Ramón Alexanco Ventosa, Rafael Gordillo Vázquez, José Vicente Sánchez Felip (63.Enrique Saura Gil), Miguel Ángel Alonso Oyarbide „Periko Alonso", Jesús María Zamora Ansorena, Juan Enrique Gómez González „Juanito", Jesús María Satrústegui Azpiroz (63.Enrique Castro González „Quini"), Roberto López Ufarte. Trainer: José Emilio Santamaría Iglesias.
**YUG:** Dragan Pantelić, Nikola Jovanović (74.Vahid Halilhodžić), Nenad Stojnković, Ivan Gudelj, Velimir Zajec, Zlatko Krmpotić, Vladimir Petrović, Edhem Šljivo, Ivan Šurjak (Cap), Safet Sušić, Zlatko Vujović (81.Miloš Šestić). Trainer: Miljan Miljanić.

**Goals**: 0-1 Ivan Gudelj (10), 1-1 Juan Enrique Gómez González „Juanito" (14 penalty), 2-1 Enrique Saura Gil (66).
**Cautions**: Nenad Stojković, Edhem Šljivo / Jesús María Zamora Ansorena, Rafael Gordillo Vázquez.

21.06.1982, Estadio La Romareda, Zaragoza; Attendance: 15,000
Referee: Chan Tam Sung (Hong Kong)
**HONDURAS – NORTHERN IRELAND**     **1-1(0-1)**
**HON**: Julio César Arzú, César Efrain Gutíerrez Álvarez, Allan Anthony Costly Blyden, Jaime Enrique Villegas Roura, José Luis Cruz Figueroa, Ramón Enrique Maradiaga Chávez, Gilberto Geronimo Yearwood, Héctor Ramón Zelaya Rivera, Prudencio Norales Martínez (58.Eduardo Antonio Laing Carcamo), Porfirio Amando Betancourt Cortez, José Roberto Figueroa Padilla. Trainer: José de la Paz Herrera Ucles.
**NIR**: Patrick Anthony Jennings, James Michael Nicholl, Christopher James Nicholl, John McClelland, Malachy Martin Donaghy, Martin Hugh Michael O'Neill (Cap) (77.Patrick Joseph Healy), David McCreery, Samuel Baxter McIlroy, Gerard Joseph Armstrong, William Robert Hamilton, Norman Whiteside (65.Noel Brotherston). Manager: William Laurence Bingham.
**Goals**: 0-1 Gerard Joseph Armstrong (9), 1-1 Eduardo Antonio Laing Carcamo (60).

24.06.1982, Estadio La Romareda, Zaragoza; Attendance: 25,000
Referee: Gaston Edmundo Castro Makuc (Chile)
**HONDURAS - YUGOSLAVIA**     **0-1(0-1)**
**HON**: Julio César Arzú, Domingo Drummond Cooper, Allan Anthony Costly Blyden, Jaime Enrique Villegas Roura, José Fernando Bulnes Zubiaga, Ramón Enrique Maradiaga Chávez, Gilberto Geronimo Yearwood, Héctor Ramón Zelaya Rivera, Juan Alberto Cruz Murillo (65.Eduardo Antonio Laing Carcamo), Porfirio Amando Betancourt Cortez, José Roberto Figueroa Padilla. Trainer: José de la Paz Herrera Ucles.
**YUG**: Dragan Pantelić, Nikola Jovanović (46.Vahid Halilhodžić), Nenad Stojković, Ivan Gudelj, Velimir Zajec, Zlatko Krmpotić, Vladimir Petrović, Edhem Šljivo, Ivan Šurjak (Cap), Safet Sušić, Zlatko Vujović (62.Miloš Šestić). Trainer: Miljan Miljanić.
**Goal**: 0-1 Vladimir Petrović (87 penalty).
**Cautions**: Ramón Enrique Maradiaga Chávez / Zlatko Krmpotić.
**Sent off**: Gilberto Geronimo Yearwood (89).

25.06.1982, Estadio „Luis Casanova", Valencia; Attendance: 49,562
Referee: Héctor Froilan Ortíz Ramírez (Paraguay)
**SPAIN - NORTHERN IRELAND**     **0-1(0-0)**
**ESP**: Luis Miguel Arkonada Echarre (Cap), José Antonio Camacho Alfaro, Miguel Tendillo Belenguer, José Ramón Alexanco Ventosa, Rafael Gordillo Vázquez, Enrique Saura Gil, Miguel Ángel Alonso Oyarbide „Periko Alonso", José Vicente Sánchez Felip, Juan Enrique Gómez González „Juanito", Jesús María Satrústegui Azpiroz (46.Enrique Castro González „Quini"), Roberto López Ufarte (77.Ricardo Gallego Redondo). Trainer: José Emilio Santamaría Iglesias.
**NIR**: Patrick Anthony Jennings, James Michael Nicholl, Christopher James Nicholl, John McClelland, Malachy Martin Donaghy, David McCreery, Martin Hugh Michael O'Neill (Cap), Samuel Baxter McIlroy (50.Thomas Cassidy), Gerard Joseph Armstrong, William Robert Hamilton, Norman Whiteside (73.Samuel Nelson). Manager: William Laurence Bingham.
**Goal**: 0-1 Gerard Joseph Armstrong (48).
**Cautions**: Juan Enrique Gómez González „Juanito" / William Robert Hamilton, Samuel Baxter McIlroy.
**Sent off**: Malachy Martin Donaghy (62).

# GROUP 6

| | | | |
|---|---|---|---|
| 14.06.1982 | Sevilla | Brazil – Soviet Union | 2-1(0-1) |
| 15.06.1982 | Málaga | Scotland – New Zealand | 5-2(3-0) |
| 18.06.1982 | Sevilla | Brazil - Scotland | 4-1(1-1) |
| 19.06.1982 | Málaga | Soviet Union – New Zealand | 3-0(1-0) |
| 22.06.1982 | Málaga | Soviet Union - Scotland | 2-2(0-1) |
| 23.06.1982 | Sevilla | Brazil – New Zealand | 4-0(2-0) |

## FINAL STANDINGS

| | | | | | | | | |
|---|---|---|---|---|---|---|---|---|
| 1. | Brazil | 3 | 3 | 0 | 0 | 10 - 2 | 6 |
| 2. | Soviet Union | 3 | 1 | 1 | 1 | 6 - 4 | 3 |
| 3. | Scotland | 3 | 1 | 1 | 1 | 8 - 8 | 3 |
| 4. | New Zealand | 3 | 0 | 0 | 3 | 2 - 12 | 0 |

14.06.1982, Estadio „Ramón Sánchez Pizjuán", Sevilla; Attendance: 62,440
Referee: Augusto Lamo Castillo (Spain)
**BRAZIL – SOVIET UNION**      **2-1(0-1)**
**BRA:** Valdir de Arruda Peres, José Leandro de Souza Ferreira "Leandro I", José Oscar Bernardi, Luís Carlos Quintanilha "Luisinho", Leovegildo Lins Gama Júnior "Júnior I", Paulo Roberto Falcão, Sócrates Brasileiro Sampaio Vieira de Oliveira (Cap), Arthur Antunes Coimbra "Zico", Dirceu José Guimarães „Dirceu II" (46.Paulo Isidoro de Jesus), Sérgio Bernardino "Serginho I", Éder Aleixo de Assis. Trainer: Telê Santana da Silva.
**URS:** Rinat Dasaev, Tengiz Sulakvelidze, Sergey Baltacha, Aleksandr Chivadze (Cap), Anatoliy Demyanenko, Andrey Bal, Vitaliy Daraselia, Vladimir Bessonov, Ramaz Shengeliya (88.Sergey Andreev), Yuriy Gavrilov (73.Yuriy Susloparov), Oleg Blokhin. Trainer: Konstantin Beskov.
**Goals**: 0-1 Andrey Bal (34), 1-1 Sócrates Brasileiro Sampaio Vieira de Oliveira (75), 2-1 Éder Aleixo de Assis (88).

15.06.1982, Estadio La Rosaleda, Malaga; Attendance: 20,000
Referee: David Stanley Socha (United States)
**SCOTLAND – NEW ZEALAND**      **5-2(3-0)**
**SCO:** Alan Roderick Rough, Daniel Fergus McGrain (Cap), Francis Tierney Gray, Allan James Evans, Alan David Hansen, Gordon David Strachan (83.David Narey), Graeme James Souness, John Wark, John Neilson Robertson, Kenneth Mathieson Dalglish, Alan Bernard Brazil (53.Steven Archibald). Manager: John Stein.
**NZL:** Francesco Maria van Hattum, John Bennett Hill, Samuel Alan Malcolmson (77.Duncan Edward Cole), Robert Ronald Almond (65.Richard Lloyd Herbert), Adrian Coroon Elrick, Kenneth Grant Cresswell, Keith Gordon MacKay, Allan Roderick Boath, Steven Paul Sumner, Stephen Wooddin, Wynton Alan Whai Rufer. Trainer: John Adshead (England).
**Goals**: 1-0 Kenneth Mathieson Dalglish (18), 2-0 John Wark (29), 3-0 John Wark (32), 3-1 Steven Paul Sumner (54), 3-2 Stephen Wooddin (64), 4-2 John Neilson Robertson (73), 5-2 Steven Archibald (80).

18.06.1982, Estadio „Benito Villamarín", Sevilla; Attendance: 47,379
Referee: Luis Paulino Siles Calderón (Costa Rica)
**BRAZIL - SCOTLAND** **4-1(1-1)**
**BRA:** Valdir de Arruda Peres, José Leandro de Souza Ferreira "Leandro I", José Oscar Bernardi, Luís Carlos Quintanilha "Luisinho", Leovegildo Lins Gama Júnior "Júnior I", Paulo Roberto Falcão, Sócrates Brasileiro Sampaio Vieira de Oliveira (Cap), Arthur Antunes Coimbra "Zico", Antônio Carlos Cerezo "Toninho Cerezo", Sérgio Bernardino "Serginho I" (81.Paulo Isidoro de Jesus), Éder Aleixo de Assis. Trainer: Telê Santana da Silva.
**SCO:** Alan Roderick Rough, David Narey, Francis Tierney Gray, William Fergus Miller, Alan David Hansen, Gordon David Strachan (65.Kenneth Mathieson Dalglish), Graeme James Souness (Cap), Richard Asa Hartford (69.Alexander McLeish), John Neilson Robertson, John Wark, Steven Archibald. Manager: John Stein.
**Goals**: 0-1 David Narey (18), 1-1 Arthur Antunes Coimbra "Zico" (33), 2-1 José Oscar Bernardi (48), 3-1 Éder Aleixo de Assis (63), 4-1 Paulo Roberto Falcão (87).

19.06.1982, Estadio La Rosaleda, Malaga; Attendance: 34,905
Referee: Yousef Mohammed El Ghoul (Libya)
**SOVIET UNION – NEW ZEALAND** **3-0(1-0)**
**URS:** Rinat Dasaev, Tengiz Sulakvelidze, Sergey Baltacha, Aleksandr Chivadze (Cap), Anatoliy Demyanenko, Andrey Bal, Vitaliy Daraselia (45.Khoren Oganesyan), Vladimir Bessonov, Ramaz Shengeliya, Yuriy Gavrilov (78.Sergey Rodionov), Oleg Blokhin. Trainer: Konstantin Beskov.
**NZL:** Francesco Maria van Hattum, Glenn Laurence Dods, Richard Lloyd Herbert, Allan Roderick Boath, Adrian Coroon Elrick, Kenneth Grant Cresswell, Keith Gordon MacKay, Duncan Edward Cole, Steven Paul Sumner, Stephen Wooddin, Wynton Alan Whai Rufer. Trainer: John Adshead (England).
**Goals**: 1-0 Yuriy Gavrilov (24), 2-0 Oleg Blokhin (48), 3-0 Sergey Baltacha (68).

22.06.1982, Estadio La Rosaleda, Malaga; Attendance: 45,000
Referee: Nicolae Rainea (Romania)
**SOVIET UNION - SCOTLAND** **2-2(0-1)**
**URS:** Rinat Dasaev, Tengiz Sulakvelidze, Sergey Baltacha, Aleksandr Chivadze (Cap), Anatoliy Demyanenko, Andrey Bal, Sergey Borovskiy, Vladimir Bessonov, Ramaz Shengeliya (89.Sergey Andreev), Yuriy Gavrilov, Oleg Blokhin. Trainer: Konstantin Beskov.
**SCO:** Alan Roderick Rough, David Narey, Francis Tierney Gray, William Fergus Miller, Alan David Hansen, Gordon David Strachan (71.Daniel Fergus McGrain), Graeme James Souness (Cap), John Wark, John Neilson Robertson, Steven Archibald, Joseph Jordan (71.Alan Bernard Brazil). Manager: John Stein.
**Goals**: 0-1 Joseph Jordan (15), 1-1 Aleksandr Chivadze (59), 2-1 Ramaz Shengeliya (85), 2-2 Graeme James Souness (88).
**Cautions**: Graeme James Souness.

23.06.1982, Estadio „Benito Villamarín", Sevilla; Attendance: 43,000
Referee: Damir Matovinović (Yugoslavia)
**BRAZIL – NEW ZEALAND** **4-0(2-0)**
**BRA:** Valdir de Arruda Peres, José Leandro de Souza Ferreira "Leandro I", José Oscar Bernardi (73.Édino Nazareth Filho "Edinho"), Luís Carlos Quintanilha "Luisinho", Leovegildo Lins Gama Júnior "Júnior I", Antônio Carlos Cerezo "Toninho Cerezo", Paulo Roberto Falcão, Sócrates Brasileiro Sampaio Vieira de Oliveira (Cap), Arthur Antunes Coimbra "Zico", Sérgio Bernardino "Serginho I" (73.Paulo Isidoro de Jesus), Éder Aleixo de Assis. Trainer: Telê Santana da Silva.
**NZL:** Francesco Maria van Hattum, Glenn Laurence Dods, Richard Lloyd Herbert, Robert Ronald Almond, Adrian Coroon Elrick, Kenneth Grant Cresswell (78.Duncan Edward Cole), Keith Gordon MacKay, Allan Roderick Boath, Steven Paul Sumner, Stephen Wooddin, Wynton Alan Whai Rufer (78.Brian Alfred Turner). Trainer: John Adshead (England).
**Goals**: 1-0 Arthur Antunes Coimbra "Zico" (28), 2-0 Arthur Antunes Coimbra "Zico" (31), 3-0 Paulo Roberto Falcão (64), 4-0 Sérgio Bernardino "Serginho I" (71).

# SECOND ROUND

## GROUP A

| | | | |
|---|---|---|---|
| 28.06.1982 | Barcelona | Poland – Belgium | 3-0(2-0) |
| 01.07.1982 | Barcelona | Belgium – Soviet Union | 0-1(0-0) |
| 04.07.1982 | Barcelona | Poland – Soviet Union | 0-0 |

### FINAL STANDINGS

| | | | | | | | | |
|---|---|---|---|---|---|---|---|---|
| 1. | Poland | 2 | 1 | 1 | 0 | 3 - 0 | 3 |
| 2. | Soviet Union | 2 | 1 | 1 | 0 | 1 - 0 | 3 |
| 3. | Belgium | 2 | 0 | 0 | 2 | 0 - 4 | 0 |

28.06.1982, Estadio Camp Nou, Barcelona; Attendance: 65,000
Referee: Luis Paulino Siles Calderón (Costa Rica)
**POLAND - BELGIUM**     **3-0(2-0)**
**POL:** Józef Młynarczyk, Paweł Janas, Marek Dziuba, Władysław Żmuda (Cap), Stefan Majewski, Waldemar Matysik, Janusz Kupcewicz (82.Włodzimierz Ciołek), Andrzej Buncol, Grzegorz Lato, Zbigniew Boniek, Włodzimierz Smolarek. Trainer: Antoni Piechniczek
**BEL:** Theo Custers, Michel Renquin, Luc Millecamps, Walter Meeuws, Gérard Plessers (87.Marc Baecke), Wilfried Van Moer (46.François Vander Elst), Ludo Coeck, Jan Ceulemans, Frank Vercauteren, Alexander Czerniatynski, Erwin Vandenbergh. Trainer: Guy Thys.
**Goals:** 1-0 Zbigniew Boniek (3), 2-0 Zbigniew Boniek (25), 3-0 Zbigniew Boniek (54).
**Cautions:** Włodzimierz Smolarek.

01.07.1982, Estadio Camp Nou, Barcelona; Attendance: 45,000
Referee: Michel Vautrot (France)
**BELGIUM – SOVIET UNION**     **0-1(0-0)**
**BEL:** Jacques Munaron, Michel Renquin, Luc Millecamps, Walter Meeuws, Maurits De Schrijver (65.Marc Millecamps), Guy Vandersmissen (67.Alexander Czerniatynski), Ludo Coeck, René Verheyen, Frank Vercauteren, Erwin Vandenbergh. Jan Ceulemans. Trainer: Guy Thys.
**URS:** Rinat Dasaev, Sergey Borovskiy, Sergey Baltacha, Aleksandr Chivadze (Cap), Anatoliy Demyanenko, Andrey Bal (87.Vitaliy Daraselia), Vladimir Bessonov, Khoren Oganesyan, Ramaz Shengeliya (89.Sergey Rodionov), Yuriy Gavrilov, Oleg Blokhin. Trainer: Konstantin Beskov.
**Goal:** 0-1 Khoren Oganesyan (48).
**Cautions:** Vladimir Bessonov.

04.07.1982, Estadio Camp Nou, Barcelona; Attendance: 65,000
Referee: Robert Bonar Valentine (Scotland)
**POLAND – SOVIET UNION**     **0-0**
**POL:** Józef Młynarczyk, Marek Dziuba, Stefan Majewski, Władysław Żmuda (Cap), Paweł Janas, Grzegorz Lato, Andrzej Buncol, Waldemar Matysik, Janusz Kupcewicz (51.Włodzimierz Ciołek), Zbigniew Boniek, Włodzimierz Smolarek. Trainer: Antoni Piechniczek.
**URS:** Rinat Dasaev, Sergey Borovskiy, Sergey Baltacha, Aleksandr Chivadze (Cap), Anatoliy Demyanenko, Tengiz Sulakvelidze, Vladimir Bessonov, Khoren Oganesyan, Ramaz Shengeliya (57.Sergey Andreev), Yuriy Gavrilov (78.Vitaliy Daraselia), Oleg Blokhin. Trainer: Konstantin Beskov.
**Cautions:** Andrzej Buncol, Zbigniew Boniek / Aleksandr Chivadze, Sergey Borovskiy, Sergey Baltacha.

# GROUP B

| | | | |
|---|---|---|---|
| 29.06.1982 | Madrid | West Germany - England | 0-0 |
| 02.07.1982 | Madrid | West Germany - Spain | 2-1(0-0) |
| 05.07.1982 | Madrid | Spain - England | 0-0 |

## FINAL STANDINGS

| | | | | | | | | |
|---|---|---|---|---|---|---|---|---|
| 1. | West Germany | 2 | 1 | 1 | 0 | 2 - 1 | 3 |
| 2. | England | 2 | 0 | 2 | 0 | 0 - 0 | 2 |
| 3. | Spain | 2 | 0 | 1 | 1 | 1 - 2 | 1 |

29.06.1982, Estadio „Santiago Bernabéu", Madrid; Attendance: 75,000
Referee: Arnaldo David César Coelho (Brazil)
**WEST GERMANY - ENGLAND**                     **0-0**
**GER:** Harald Schumacher, Manfred Kaltz, Ulrich Stielike, Karlheinz Förster, Hans-Peter Briegel, Bernd Förster, Wolfgang Dremmler, Paul Breitner, Hans Müller (73.Klaus Fischer), Uwe Reinders (62.Pierre Littbarski), Karl-Heinz Rummenigge (Cap). Trainer: Josef Derwall.
**ENG:** Peter Leslie Shilton, Michael Dennis Mills (Cap), Philip Brian Thompson, Terence Ian Butcher, Kenneth Graham Sansom, Steven James Coppell, Raymond Colin Wilkins, Bryan Robson, Graham Rix, Trevor John Francis (77.Anthony Stewart Woodcock), Paul Mariner. Manager: Ronald Greenwood.
**Cautions**: Ulrich Stielike.

02.07.1982, Estadio „Santiago Bernabéu", Madrid; Attendance: 90,089
Referee: Paolo Casarin (Italy)
**WEST GERMANY - SPAIN**                     **2-1(0-0)**
**GER:** Harald Schumacher, Manfred Kaltz, Ulrich Stielike, Karlheinz Förster, Bernd Förster, Wolfgang Dremmler, Paul Breitner, Hans-Peter Briegel, Karl-Heinz Rummenigge (Cap) (46.Uwe Reinders), Klaus Fischer, Pierre Littbarski. Trainer: Josef Derwall.
**ESP:** Luis Miguel Arkonada Echarre (Cap), Santiago Urquiaga Pérez Lugar, Miguel Tendillo Belenguer, José Ramón Alexanco Ventosa, Rafael Gordillo Vázquez, Miguel Ángel Alonso Oyarbide „Periko Alonso", Jesús María Zamora Ansorena, José Antonio Camacho Alfaro, Juan Enrique Gómez González „Juanito" (46.Roberto López Ufarte), Carlos Alonso González „Santillana", Enrique Castro González „Quini" (65.José Vicente Sánchez Felip). Trainer: José Emilio Santamaría Iglesias.
**Goals**: 1-0 Pierre Littbarski (50), 2-0 Klaus Fischer (75), 2-1 Jesús María Zamora Ansorena (82).
**Cautions**: Klaus Fischer, Hans-Peter Briegel / José Ramón Alexanco Ventosa, José Antonio Camacho Alfaro, José Vicente Sánchez Felip.

05.07.1982, Estadio „Santiago Bernabéu", Madrid; Attendance: 60,000
Referee: Alexis Ponnet (Belgium)
**SPAIN - ENGLAND**                     **0-0**
**ESP:** Luis Miguel Arkonada Echarre (Cap), Santiago Urquiaga Pérez Lugar, Miguel Tendillo Belenguer (72.Antonio Maceda Francés), José Ramón Alexanco Ventosa, Rafael Gordillo Vázquez, Enrique Saura Gil (67.Pedro Jesús Uralde Hernáez), José Antonio Camacho Alfaro, Miguel Ángel Alonso Oyarbide „Periko Alonso", Jesús María Zamora Ansorena, Carlos Alonso González „Santillana", Jesús María Satrústegui Azpiroz. Trainer: José Emilio Santamaría Iglesias.
**ENG:** Peter Leslie Shilton, Michael Dennis Mills (Cap), Philip Brian Thompson, Terence Ian Butcher, Kenneth Graham Sansom, Raymond Colin Wilkins, Bryan Robson, Graham Rix (63.Trevor David Brooking), Trevor John Francis, Paul Mariner, Anthony Stewart Woodcock (63.Kevin Joseph Keegan). Manager: Ronald Greenwood.
**Cautions**: Raymond Colin Wilkins.

# GROUP C

| | | | |
|---|---|---|---|
| 29.06.1982 | Barcelona | Italy - Argentina | 2-1(0-0) |
| 02.07.1982 | Barcelona | Argentina - Brazil | 1-3(0-1) |
| 05.07.1982 | Barcelona | Brazil - Italy | 2-3(1-2) |

### FINAL STANDINGS

| | | | | | | | | |
|---|---|---|---|---|---|---|---|---|
| 1. | **Italy** | 2 | 2 | 0 | 0 | 5 - 3 | 4 |
| 2. | Brazil | 2 | 1 | 0 | 1 | 5 - 4 | 2 |
| 3. | Argentina | 2 | 0 | 0 | 2 | 2 - 5 | 0 |

29.06.1982, Estadio Sarría, Barcelona; Attendance: 43,000
Referee: Nicolae Rainea (Romania)
**ITALY - ARGENTINA**                                              **2-1(0-0)**
**ITA:** Dino Zoff, Claudio Gentile, Fulvio Collovatti, Gaetano Scirea, Antonio Cabrini, Gabriele Oriali (75.Giampiero Marini), Bruno Conti, Marco Tardelli, Giancarlo Antognoni, Paolo Rossi (80.Alessandro Altobelli), Francesco Graziani. Trainer: Enzo Bearzot.
**ARG:** Ubaldo Matildo Fillol, Jorge Mario Olguín, Luis Adolfo Galván, Daniel Alberto Passarella (Cap), Alberto César Tarantini, Osvaldo César Ardiles, Américo Rubén Gallego, Diego Armando Maradona, Ricardo Daniel Bertoni, Ramón Ángel Díaz (59.Gabriel Humberto Calderón), Mario Alberto Kempes (59.José Daniel Valencia). Trainer: César Luis Menotti.
**Goals**: 1-0 Marco Tardelli (57), 2-0 Antonio Cabrini (67), 2-1 Daniel Alberto Passarella (83).
**Cautions**: Claudio Gentile, Paolo Rossi / Mario Alberto Kempes, Diego Armando Maradona, Osvaldo César Ardiles.
**Sent off**: Américo Rubén Gallego (84).

02.07.1982, Estadio Sarría, Barcelona; Attendance: 44,000
Referee: Lamberto Mario Rúbio Vásquez (Mexico)
**ARGENTINA - BRAZIL**                                    **1-3(0-1)**
**ARG:** Ubaldo Matildo Fillol, Jorge Mario Olguín, Luis Adolfo Galván, Daniel Alberto Passarella (Cap), Alberto César Tarantini, Osvaldo César Ardiles, Juan Alberto Barbas, Diego Armando Maradona, Ricardo Daniel Bertoni (64.Santiago Santamaría), Gabriel Humberto Calderón, Mario Alberto Kempes (46. Ramón Ángel Díaz). Trainer: César Luis Menotti.
**BRA:** Valdir de Arruda Peres, José Leandro de Souza Ferreira "Leandro I" (82.Edevaldo de Freitas), José Oscar Bernardi, Luís Carlos Quintanilha "Luisinho", Leovegildo Lins Gama Júnior "Júnior I", Antônio Carlos Cerezo "Toninho Cerezo", Paulo Roberto Falcão, Sócrates Brasileiro Sampaio Vieira de Oliveira (Cap), Arthur Antunes Coimbra "Zico" (84.João Batista da Silva), Sérgio Bernardino "Serginho I", Éder Aleixo de Assis. Trainer: Telê Santana da Silva.
**Goals**: 1-0 Arthur Antunes Coimbra "Zico" (11), 2-0 Sérgio Bernardino "Serginho I" (66), 3-0 Leovegildo Lins Gama Júnior "Júnior I" (75), 3-1 Ramón Ángel Díaz (89).
**Cautions**: Daniel Alberto Passarella / Valdir de Arruda Peres, Paulo Roberto Falcão.
**Sent off**: Diego Armando Maradona (86).

05.07.1982, Estadio Sarría, Barcelona; Attendance: 44,000
Referee: Abraham Klein (Israel)
**BRAZIL - ITALY**  **2-3(1-2)**
**BRA:** Valdir de Arruda Peres, José Leandro de Souza Ferreira "Leandro I", José Oscar Bernardi, Luís Carlos Quintanilha "Luisinho", Leovegildo Lins Gama Júnior "Júnior I", Antônio Carlos Cerezo "Toninho Cerezo", Paulo Roberto Falcão, Sócrates Brasileiro Sampaio Vieira de Oliveira (Cap), Arthur Antunes Coimbra "Zico", Sérgio Bernardino "Serginho I" (71.Paulo Isidoro de Jesus), Éder Aleixo de Assis. Trainer: Telê Santana da Silva.
**ITA:** Dino Zoff, Claudio Gentile, Fulvio Collovatti (34.Giuseppe Bergomi), Gaetano Scirea, Antonio Cabrini, Gabriele Oriali, Bruno Conti, Marco Tardelli (75.Giampiero Marini), Giancarlo Antognoni, Paolo Rossi, Francesco Graziani. Trainer: Enzo Bearzot.
**Goals:** 0-1 Paolo Rossi (5), 1-1 Sócrates Brasileiro Sampaio Vieira de Oliveira (12), 1-2 Paolo Rossi (25), 2-2 Paulo Roberto Falcão (68), 2-3 Paolo Rossi (74).
**Cautions:** Claudio Gentile, Gabriele Oriali.

## GROUP D

| 28.06.1982 | Madrid | Austria - France | 0-1(0-1) |
| 01.07.1982 | Madrid | Austria – Northern Ireland | 2-2(0-1) |
| 04.07.1982 | Madrid | Northern Ireland - France | 1-4(0-1) |

### FINAL STANDINGS

| | | | | | | | | |
|---|---|---|---|---|---|---|---|---|
| 1. | **France** | 2 | 2 | 0 | 0 | 5 - 1 | 4 |
| 2. | Austria | 2 | 0 | 1 | 1 | 2 - 3 | 1 |
| 3. | Northern Ireland | 2 | 0 | 1 | 1 | 3 - 6 | 1 |

28.06.1982, Estadio „Vicente Calderón", Madrid; Attendance: 37,000
Referee: Károly Palotai (Hungary)
**AUSTRIA - FRANCE**  **0-1(0-1)**
**AUT:** Friedrich Koncilia, Bernd Krauss, Erich Obermayer, Bruno Pezzey, Josef Degeorgi (46.Ernst Baumeister), Roland Hattenberger, Reinhold Hintermaier, Herbert Prohaska, Kurt Jara (46.Kurt Welzl), Walter Schachner, Johann Krankl. Trainers: Felix Latzke - Georg Schmidt.
**FRA:** Jean-Luc Ettori, Patrick Battiston, Gérard Janvion, Marius Trésor (Cap), Maxime Bossis, Alain Giresse, Bernard Genghini (85.René Girard), Jean Amadou Tigana, Gérard Soler, Bernard Lacombe (15.Dominique Rocheteau), Didier Six. Trainer: Michel Hidalgo.
**Goal:** 0-1 Bernard Genghini (39).
**Cautions:** Erich Obermayer.

01.07.1982, Estadio „Vicente Calderón", Madrid; Attendance: 24,000
Referee: Adolf Prokop (East Germany)
**AUSTRIA – NORTHERN IRELAND**  **2-2(0-1)**
**AUT:** Friedrich Koncilia, Bernd Krauss, Bruno Pezzey, Erich Obermayer, Anton Pichler, Maximilian Hagmayr (46.Kurt Welzl), Josef Pregesbauer (46.Reinhold Hintermaier), Herbert Prohaska, Ernst Baumeister, Walter Schachner, Gernot Jurtin. Trainers: Felix Latzke - Georg Schmidt.
**NIR:** James Archibald Platt, James Michael Nicholl, Christopher James Nicholl, John McClelland, Samuel Nelson, David McCreery, Martin Hugh Michael O'Neill (Cap), Samuel Baxter McIlroy, Gerard Joseph Armstrong, William Robert Hamilton, Norman Whiteside (66.Noel Brotherston). Manager: William Laurence Bingham.
**Goals:** 0-1 William Robert Hamilton (27), 1-1 Bruno Pezzey (50), 2-1 Reinhold Hintermaier (68), 2-2 William Robert Hamilton (75).
**Cautions:** Anton Pichler.

04.07.1982, Estadio „Vicente Calderón", Madrid; Attendance: 37,000
Referee: Alojzy Jarguz (Poland)
**NORTHERN IRELAND - FRANCE** **1-4(0-1)**
**NIR:** Patrick Anthony Jennings, James Michael Nicholl, Christopher James Nicholl, Malachy Martin Donaghy, John McClelland, David McCreery (86.John Patrick O'Neill), Martin Hugh Michael O'Neill (Cap), Samuel Baxter McIlroy, Gerard Joseph Armstrong, Norman Whiteside, William Robert Hamilton. Manager: William Laurence Bingham.
**FRA:** Jean-Luc Ettori, Manuel Amoros, Gérard Janvion, Marius Trésor, Maxime Bossis, Jean Amadou Tigana, Alain Giresse, Bernard Genghini, Michel Platini (Cap), Gérard Soler (63.Didier Six), Dominique Rocheteau (83.Alain Couriol). Trainer: Michel Hidalgo.
**Goals:** 0-1 Alain Giresse (33), 0-2 Dominique Rocheteau (46), 0-3 Dominique Rocheteau (68), 1-3 Gerard Joseph Armstrong (75), 1-4 Alain Giresse (80).
**Cautions:** William Robert Hamilton / Jean Amadou Tigana.

## SEMI-FINALS

| 08.07.1982 | Barcelona | Poland - Italy | 0-2(0-1) |
| 08.07.1982 | Sevilla | West Germany - France | 5-4 pen |

08.07.1982, Estadio Camp Nou, Barcelona; Attendance: 50,000
Referee: Juan Daniel Cardellino de San Vicente (Uruguay)
**POLAND - ITALY** **0-2(0-1)**
**POL:** Józef Młynarczyk, Marek Dziuba, Stefan Majewski, Władysław Żmuda (Cap), Paweł Janas, Andrzej Buncol, Waldemar Matysik, Janusz Kupcewicz, Włodzimierz Ciołek (46.Andrzej Pałasz), Grzegorz Lato, Włodzimierz Smolarek (78.Marek Kusto). Trainer: Antoni Piechniczek.
**ITA:** Dino Zoff, Giuseppe Bergomi, Fulvio Collovatti, Gaetano Scirea, Antonio Cabrini, Gabriele Oriali, Bruno Conti, Marco Tardelli, Giancarlo Antognoni (28.Giampiero Marini), Paolo Rossi, Francesco Graziani (70.Alessandro Altobelli). Trainer: Enzo Bearzot.
**Goals:** 0-1 Paolo Rossi (22), 0-2 Paolo Rossi (73).
**Cautions:** Stefan Majewski, Władysław Żmuda, Włodzimierz Smolarek / Fulvio Collovatti.

08.07.1982, Estadio „Ramón Sánchez Pizjuán", Sevilla; Attendance: 70,000
Referee: Charles George Rainier Corver (Holland)
**WEST GERMANY - FRANCE** **3-3(1-1,1-1,3-3)**
**5-4 on penalties**
**GER:** Harald Schumacher, Manfred Kaltz (Cap), Ulrich Stielike, Karlheinz Förster, Bernd Förster, Wolfgang Dremmler, Paul Breitner, Hans-Peter Briegel (95.Karl-Heinz Rummenigge), Felix Magath (72.Horst Hrubesch), Pierre Littbarski, Klaus Fischer. Trainer: Josef Derwall.
**FRA:** Jean-Luc Ettori, Manuel Amoros, Gérard Janvion, Marius Trésor, Maxime Bossis, Jean Amadou Tigana, Alain Giresse, Bernard Genghini (50.Patrick Battiston; 60.Christian Lopez), Michel Platini (Cap), Dominique Rocheteau, Didier Six. Trainer: Michel Hidalgo.
**Goals:** 1-0 Pierre Littbarski (18), 1-1 Michel Platini (27 penalty), 1-2 Marius Trésor (93), 1-3 Alain Giresse (99), 2-3 Karl-Heinz Rummenigge (103), 3-3 Klaus Fischer (108).
**Penalties:** Alain Giresse 0-1; Manfred Kaltz 1-1; Manuel Amoros 1-2; Paul Breitner 2-2; Dominique Rocheteau 2-3; Ulrich Stielike (saved); Didier Six (missed); Pierre Littbarski 3-3; Michel Platini 3-4; Karl-Heinz Rummenigge 4-4; Maxime Bossis (saved); Horst Hrubesch 5-4.
**Cautions:** Bernd Förster / Alain Giresse, Bernard Genghini.

## 3rd PLACE PLAY-OFF

10.07.1982, Estadio „José Rico Pérez", Alicante; Attendance: 28,000
Referee: Antonio José da Silva Garrido (Portugal)
**POLAND - FRANCE**     **3-2(2-1)**
**POL:** Józef Młynarczyk, Marek Dziuba, Stefan Majewski, Władysław Żmuda (Cap), Paweł Janas, Grzegorz Lato, Waldemar Matysik (46.Roman Wójcicki), Janusz Kupcewicz, Andrzej Buncol, Zbigniew Boniek, Andrzej Szarmach. Trainer: Antoni Piechniczek.
**FRA:** Jean-Luc Castaneda, Manuel Amoros, Philippe Mahut, Marius Trésor (Cap), Gérard Janvion (66.Christian Lopez), Jean Amadou Tigana (83.Didier Six), René Girard, Jean-François Larios, Alain Couriol, Gérard Soler, Bruno Bellone. Trainer: Michel Hidalgo.
**Goals:** 0-1 René Girard (14), 1-1 Andrzej Szarmach (41), 2-1 Stefan Majewski (44), 3-1 Janusz Kupcewicz (46), 3-2 Alain Couriol (75).
**Cautions:** Andrzej Buncol, Roman Wójcicki / Gérard Soler.

## FINAL

11.07.1982, Estadio „Santiago Bernabéu", Madrid; Attendance: 90,089
Referee: Arnaldo David César Coelho (Brazil)
**ITALY – WEST GERMANY**     **3-1(0-0)**
**ITA:** Dino Zoff, Giuseppe Bergomi, Fulvio Collovatti, Gaetano Scirea, Antonio Cabrini, Claudio Gentile, Bruno Conti, Marco Tardelli, Gabriele Oriali, Paolo Rossi, Francesco Graziani (7.Alessandro Altobelli; 89.Franco Causio). Trainer: Enzo Bearzot.
**GER:** Harald Schumacher, Manfred Kaltz, Ulrich Stielike, Karlheinz Förster, Bernd Förster, Wolfgang Dremmler (62.Horst Hrubesch), Paul Breitner, Hans-Peter Briegel, Karl-Heinz Rummenigge (Cap) (70.Hans Müller), Pierre Littbarski, Klaus Fischer. Trainer: Josef Derwall.
**Goals:** 1-0 Paolo Rossi (56), 2-0 Marco Tardelli (69), 3-0 Alessandro Altobelli (80), 3-1 Paul Breitner (82).
**Cautions:** Bruno Conti, Gabriele Oriali / Wolfgang Dremmler, Ulrich Stielike, Pierre Littbarski.

# WORLD CUP 1982 FINAL RANKING

| # | Team | P | W | D | L | GF | - | GA | Pts |
|---|---|---|---|---|---|---|---|---|---|
| 1. | **Italy** | 7 | 4 | 3 | 0 | 12 | - | 6 | 11 |
| 2. | West Germany | 7 | 3 | 2 | 2 | 12 | - | 10 | 8 |
| 3. | Poland | 7 | 3 | 3 | 1 | 11 | - | 5 | 9 |
| 4. | France | 7 | 3 | 2 | 2 | 16 | - | 12 | 8 |
| 5. | Brazil | 5 | 4 | 0 | 1 | 15 | - | 6 | 8 |
| 6. | England | 5 | 3 | 2 | 0 | 6 | - | 1 | 8 |
| 7. | Soviet Union | 5 | 2 | 2 | 1 | 7 | - | 4 | 6 |
| 8. | Austria | 5 | 2 | 1 | 2 | 5 | - | 4 | 5 |
| 9. | Northern Ireland | 5 | 1 | 3 | 1 | 5 | - | 7 | 5 |
| 10. | Belgium | 5 | 2 | 1 | 2 | 3 | - | 5 | 5 |
| 11. | Argentina | 5 | 2 | 0 | 3 | 8 | - | 7 | 4 |
| 12. | Spain | 5 | 1 | 2 | 2 | 4 | - | 5 | 4 |
| 13. | Algeria | 3 | 2 | 0 | 1 | 5 | - | 5 | 4 |
| 14. | Hungary | 3 | 1 | 1 | 1 | 12 | - | 6 | 3 |
| 15. | Scotland | 3 | 1 | 1 | 1 | 8 | - | 8 | 3 |
| 16. | Yugoslavia | 3 | 1 | 1 | 1 | 2 | - | 2 | 3 |
| 17. | Cameroon | 3 | 0 | 3 | 0 | 1 | - | 1 | 3 |
| 18. | Honduras | 3 | 0 | 2 | 1 | 2 | - | 3 | 2 |
| 19. | Czechoslovakia | 3 | 0 | 2 | 1 | 2 | - | 4 | 2 |
| 20. | Peru | 3 | 0 | 2 | 1 | 2 | - | 6 | 2 |
| 21. | Kuwait | 3 | 0 | 1 | 2 | 2 | - | 6 | 1 |
| 22. | Chile | 3 | 0 | 0 | 3 | 3 | - | 8 | 0 |
| 23. | New Zealand | 3 | 0 | 0 | 3 | 2 | - | 12 | 0 |
| 24. | El Salvador | 3 | 0 | 0 | 3 | 1 | - | 13 | 0 |

# WORLD CUP 1982 AWARDS

**GOLDEN BALL (best player of the World Cup final tournament)**
Paolo Rossi (Italy)

**GOLDEN BOOT (best goalscorer)**
Paolo Rossi (Italy)

# GOALSCORERS

**6 goals:** Paolo Rossi (Italy)
**5 goals:** Karl-Heinz Rummenigge (West Germany)
**4 goals:** Arthur Antunes Coimbra "Zico" (Brazil)
Zbigniew Boniek (Poland)
**3 goals:** Paulo Roberto Falcão (Brazil)
Alain Giresse (France)
László Kiss (Hungary)
Gerard Joseph Armstrong (Northern Ireland)
**2 goals:** Assad Salah (Algeria), Ricardo Daniel Bertoni, Diego Armando Maradona, Daniel Alberto Passarella (Argentina), Walter Schachner (Austria), Éder Aleixo de Assis, Sérgio Bernardino "Serginho I", Sócrates Brasileiro Sampaio Vieira de Oliveira (Brazil), Antonín Panenka (Czechoslovakia), Trevor John Francis, Bryan Robson (England), Bernard Genghini, Michel Platini, Dominique Rocheteau, Didier Six (France), László Fazekas, Tibor Nyilasi, Gábor Pölöskei (Hungary), Marco Tardelli (Italy), William Robert Hamilton (Northern Ireland), John Wark (Scotland), Klaus Fischer, Pierre Littbarski (West Germany)
**1 goal:** Lakhdar Belloumi, Tedj Bensaoula, Mustapha Rabah Madjer (Algeria), Ramón Ángel Díaz, Osvaldo César Ardiles (Argentina), Reinhold Hintermaier, Johann Krankl, Bruno Pezzey (Austria), Ludo Coeck, Alexander Czerniatynski, Erwin Vandenbergh (Belgium), Leovegildo Lins Gama Júnior "Júnior I", José Oscar Bernardi (Brazil), Grégoire M'Bida (Cameroon), Juan Carlos Letelier Pizarro, Gustavo Segundo Moscoso Huencho, Miguel Angel Neira Pincheira (Chile), Luis Baltazar Ramírez Zapata (El Salvador), Paul Mariner (England), Maxime Bossis, Alain Couriol, René Girard, Gérard Soler, Marius Trésor (France), Eduardo Antonio Laing Carcamo, Héctor Ramón Zelaya Rivera (Honduras), Lázár Szentes, József Tóth, József Varga (Hungary), Alessandro Altobelli, Antonio Cabrini, Bruno Conti, Francesco Graziani (Italy), Abdullah Mohammed Al Buloushi, Faisal Ali Al Dakhil (Kuwait), Steven Paul Sumner, Stephen Wooddin (New Zealand), Guillermo La Rosa Laguna (Peru), Andrzej Buncol, Włodzimierz Ciołek, Janusz Kupcewicz, Grzegorz Lato, Stefan Majewski, Włodzimierz Smolarek, Andrzej Szarmach (Poland), Steven Archibald, Kenneth Mathieson Dalglish, Joseph Jordan, David Narey, John Neilson Robertson, Graeme James Souness (Scotland), Andrey Bal, Sergey Baltacha, Oleg Blokhin, Aleksandr Chivadze, Yuriy Gavrilov, Khoren Oganesyan, Ramaz Shengeliya (Soviet Union), Juan Enrique Gómez González „Juanito", Roberto López Ufarte, Enrique Saura Gil, Jesús María Zamora Ansorena (Spain), Paul Breitner, Horst Hrubesch, Uwe Reinders (West Germany), Ivan Gudelj, Vladimir Petrović (Yugoslavia)

Own goals:
2 Fulvio Collovati (Italy), against Peru
Jozef Barmoš (Czechoslovakia), against England

Total number of goals scored: **146**
Average goals per match: **2.80**

# LIST OF REFEREES

| Name | DOB | Country | M |
|---|---|---|---|
| Alexis Ponnet | 09.03.1939 | Belgium | 2 |
| Arnaldo David Cesar Coelho | 15.01.1943 | Brazil | 2 |
| Luis Paulino Siles Calderón | 13.12.1941 | Costa Rica | 2 |
| Michel Vautrot | 23.10.1945 | France | 2 |
| Charles George Reinier Corver | 16.01.1936 | Holland | 2 |
| Paolo Casarin | 12.05.1940 | Italy | 2 |
| Lamberto Mario Rúbio Vásquez | 28.11.1936 | Mexico | 2 |
| Antonio José Da Silva Garrido | 03.12.1932 | Portugal | 2 |
| Nicolae Rainea | 19.11.1933 | Romania | 2 |
| Robert Bonar Valentine | 10.05.1939 | Scotland | 2 |
| Juan Daniel Cardellino de San Vicente | 04.03.1942 | Uruguay | 2 |
| Belaid Lacarne | 26.10.1940 | Algeria | 1 |
| Arturo Andrés Ithurralde | 06.03.1934 | Argentina | 1 |
| Anton Boskovic | 27.01.1933 | Australia | 1 |
| Franz Wöhrer | 05.06.1939 | Austria | 1 |
| Ebrahim Yousif Al Doy | 22.01.1945 | Bahrain | 1 |
| Luis Barrancos Alvarez | 19.08.1946 | Bolivia | 1 |
| Bogdan Dochev | 26.06.1935 | Bulgaria | 1 |
| Gaston Edmundo Castro Makuc | 23.08.1948 | Chile | 1 |
| Gilberto Aristizábal Murcia | 08.09.1940 | Colombia | 1 |
| Vojtěch Christov | 16.03.1945 | Czechoslovakia | 1 |
| Henning Lund Sørensen | 20.03.1942 | Denmark | 1 |
| Adolf Prokop | 02.02.1939 | East Germany | 1 |
| Clive Bradley White | 02.05.1940 | England | 1 |
| Benjamin Kwabana Dwomoh | 01.07.1935 | Ghana | 1 |
| Romulo Méndez Molina | 21.12.1938 | Guatemala | 1 |
| Chan Tam Sung | 08.05.1941 | Hong Kong | 1 |
| Károly Palotai | 11.09.1935 | Hungary | 1 |
| Abraham Klein | 29.03.1934 | Israel | 1 |
| Yousef Mohammed El Ghoul | 01.06.1936 | Libya | 1 |
| Malcolm Moffatt | 02.02.1937 | Northern Ireland | 1 |
| Héctor Froilan Ortíz Ramírez | 05.04.1933 | Paraguay | 1 |
| Enrique Labo Revoredo | 02.03.1939 | Peru | 1 |
| Alojzy Jarguz | 19.03.1934 | Poland | 1 |
| Miroslav Stupar | 27.08.1941 | Soviet Union | 1 |
| Augusto Lamo Castillo | 25.09.1938 | Spain | 1 |
| Erik Fredriksson | 13.02.1943 | Sweden | 1 |
| Bruno Galler | 21.10.1946 | Switzerland | 1 |
| David Stanley Socha | 27.09.1938 | United States | 1 |
| Werner Eschweiler | 20.09.1935 | West Germany | 1 |
| Damir Matovinović | 06.04.1940 | Yugoslavia | 1 |

# WORLD CUP 1982 – THE SQUADS

## ALGERIA

| Nr | Name | DOB | Club |
|---|---|---|---|
| **Goalkeepers** | | | |
| 1 | Mehdi Cerbah | 03.01.1953 | Raed Chabab Kouba |
| 21 | Mourad Sadegh Amara | 19.02.1959 | JS de Kabylie Tizi-Ouzou |
| 22 | Yacine Bentalaa | 24.09.1955 | Nasr Athlétique de Hussein Dey |
| **Defenders** | | | |
| 2 | Mahmoud Guendouz | 24.02.1953 | Nasr Athlétique de Hussein Dey |
| 3 | Mustapha Kouici | 16.04.1954 | Nasr Athlétique de Hussein Dey |
| 4 | Nourredine Abdallah Kourichi | 12.04.1954 | Girondins de Bordeaux (FRA) |
| 5 | Chaabane Merzekane | 08.03.1959 | Nasr Athlétique de Hussein Dey |
| 12 | Salah Larbès | 16.09.1952 | JS de Kabylie Tizi-Ouzou |
| 16 | Faouzi Mansouri | 17.01.1956 | Montpellier SC (FRA) |
| 17 | Abdelkader Horr | 10.11.1953 | DNC Alger |
| **Midfielders** | | | |
| 6 | Ali Bencheikh | 09.01.1955 | Mouloudia Club dAlger |
| 8 | Ali Fergani | 21.09.1952 | JS de Kabylie Tizi-Ouzou |
| 10 | Lakhdar Belloumi | 29.12.1958 | Ghali Club de Mascara |
| 13 | Hocine Yahi | 25.04.1960 | Chabab Riadhi Belouizdad |
| 14 | Djamel Zidane | 28.04.1955 | KV Kortrijk (BEL) |
| 15 | Mustapha Dahleb | 08.02.1952 | Paris St. Germain FC (FRA) |
| 18 | Karim Maroc | 05.03.1958 | Tours FC (FRA) |
| 19 | Djamel Tlemçani | 16.04.1955 | Stade de Reims (FRA) |
| **Forwards** | | | |
| 7 | Salah Assad | 30.08.1958 | Raed Chabab Kouba |
| 9 | Tedj Bensaoula | 01.12.1954 | Mouloudia Club dOran |
| 11 | Mustapha Rabah Madjer | 15.02.1958 | Nasr Athlétique de Hussein Dey |
| 20 | Abdelmajid Bourebbou | 16.03.1951 | Stade Lavallois (FRA) |
| **Trainer:** | Rachid Mekhloufi | 12.08.1936 | |

## ARGENTINA

| Nr | Name | DOB | Club |
|---|---|---|---|
| **Goalkeepers** | | | |
| 2 | Héctor Rodolfo Baley | 16.11.1950 | CA Talleres de Córdoba |
| 7 | Ubaldo Matildo Fillol | 21.07.1950 | CA River Plate Buenos Aires |
| 16 | Nery Alberto Pumpido | 30.07.1957 | CA Vélez Sarsfield |
| **Defenders** | | | |
| 8 | Luis Adolfo Galván | 24.02.1948 | CA Talleres de Córdoba |
| 13 | Julio Jorge Olarticoechea | 18.10.1958 | CA River Plate Buenos Aires |
| 14 | Jorge Mario Olguín | 17.05.1952 | CA Independiente Avellaneda |
| 15 | Daniel Alberto Passarella | 25.05.1953 | CA River Plate Buenos Aires |
| 18 | Alberto César Tarantini | 03.12.1955 | CA River Plate Buenos Aires |
| 19 | Enzo Héctor Trossero | 23.05.1953 | CA Independiente Avellaneda |
| 22 | José Daniel Van Tuyne | 13.12.1954 | Racing Club de Avellaneda |
| **Midfielders** | | | |
| 1 | Osvaldo César Ardiles | 03.08.1952 | Tottenham Hotspur FC (ENG) |
| 3 | Juan Alberto Barbas | 23.08.1959 | Racing Club de Avellaneda |
| 5 | Gabriel Humberto Calderón | 07.02.1960 | CA Independiente Avellaneda |
| 9 | Américo Rubén Gallego | 25.04.1955 | CA River Plate Buenos Aires |
| 10 | Diego Armando Maradona | 30.10.1960 | CA Boca Juniors Buenos Aires |
| 12 | Patricio José Hernández | 16.08.1956 | Club Estudiantes de La Plata |
| 21 | José Daniel Valencia | 03.10.1955 | CA Talleres de Córdoba |
| **Forwards** | | | |
| 4 | Ricardo Daniel Bertoni | 14.03.1955 | AC Fiorentina (ITA) |
| 6 | Ramón Ángel Díaz | 29.08.1959 | CA River Plate Buenos Aires |
| 11 | Mario Alberto Kempes | 15.07.1954 | CA River Plate Buenos Aires |
| 17 | Santiago Santamaría | 22.08.1952 | CA Newell's Old Boys Rosario |
| 20 | Jorge Alberto Francisco Valdano | 04.10.1955 | CD Real Zaragoza (ESP) |
| **Trainer:** | César Luis Menotti | 05.11.1938 | |

## AUSTRIA

| Nr | Name | DOB | Club |
|---|---|---|---|
| | **Goalkeepers** | | |
| 1 | Friedrich Koncilia | 25.02.1948 | FK Austria Wien |
| 21 | Herbert Feurer | 14.01.1954 | SK Rapid Wien |
| 22 | Klaus Lindenberger | 28.05.1957 | Linzer ASK |
| | **Defenders** | | |
| 2 | Bernd Krauss | 08.05.1957 | SK Rapid Wien |
| 3 | Erich Obermayer | 23.01.1953 | Austria FK Austria Wien |
| 4 | Josef Degeorgi | 19.01.1960 | FC Admira/Wacker Wien |
| 5 | Bruno Pezzey | 03.02.1955 | SG Eintracht Frankfurt (GER) |
| 14 | Ernst Baumeister | 22.01.1957 | FK Austria Wien |
| 16 | Gerald Messlender | 01.10.1961 | FC Admira/Wacker Wien |
| 17 | Johann Pregesbauer | 08.06.1958 | SK Rapid Wien |
| 19 | Heribert Weber | 28.06.1955 | SK Rapid Wien |
| | **Midfielders** | | |
| 6 | Roland Hattenberger | 07.12.1948 | SSW Innsbruck |
| 8 | Herbert Prohaska | 08.08.1955 | Internazionale FC Milano (ITA) |
| 10 | Reinhold Hintermaier | 14.02.1956 | 1.FC Nürnberg (GER) |
| 12 | Anton Pichler | 04.10.1955 | Sturm Graz |
| 15 | Johann Dihanich | 24.10.1958 | FK Austria Wien |
| | **Forwards** | | |
| 7 | Walter Schachner | 01.02.1957 | AC Cesena (ITA) |
| 9 | Hans Krankl | 14.02.1953 | SK Rapid Wien |
| 11 | Kurt Jara | 14.10.1950 | Grasshopper-Club Zürich (SUI) |
| 13 | Max Hagmayr | 16.11.1956 | VÖEST Linz |
| 18 | Gernot Jurtin | 09.09.1955 | SK Sturm Graz |
| 20 | Kurt Welzl | 06.11.1954 | Valencia CF (ESP) |

**Trainer:** Felix Latzke – Georg Schmidt (01.02.1942 / 07.04.1927)

## BELGIUM

| Nr | Name | DOB | Club |
|---|---|---|---|
| | **Goalkeepers** | | |
| 1 | Jean-Marie Pfaff | 04.12.1953 | SK Beveren |
| 12 | Theo Custers | 10.08.1950 | RCD Español Barcelona (ESP) |
| 22 | Jacques Munaron | 08.09.1956 | RSC Anderlecht Bruxelles |
| | **Defenders** | | |
| 2 | Eric Gerets | 18.05.1954 | R Standard Liège |
| 3 | Luc Millecamps | 10.09.1951 | KSV Waregem |
| 4 | Walter Meeuws | 11.07.1951 | R Standard Liège |
| 5 | Michel Renquin | 03.11.1955 | RSC Anderlecht Bruxelles |
| 14 | Marc Baecke | 24.07.1956 | SK Beveren |
| 15 | Maurits De Schrijver | 26.06.1951 | KSC Lokeren |
| 16 | Gérard Plessers | 30.03.1959 | R Standard Liège |
| | **Midfielders** | | |
| 6 | Frank Vercauteren | 28.10.1956 | RSC Anderlecht Bruxelles |
| 7 | Joseph Daerden | 26.11.1954 | R Standard Liège |
| 8 | Wilfried Van Moer | 01.03.1945 | SK Beveren |
| 10 | Ludo Coeck | 25.09.1955 | RSC Anderlecht Bruxelles |
| 11 | Jan Ceulemans | 28.02.1957 | Club Brugge KV |
| 17 | René Verheyen | 20.03.1952 | KSC Lokeren |
| 18 | Raymond Mommens | 27.12.1958 | KSC Lokeren |
| 19 | Marc Millecamps | 09.10.1950 | KSV Waregem |
| 20 | Guy Vandersmissen | 25.12.1957 | R Standard Liège |
| | **Forwards** | | |
| 9 | Erwin Vandenbergh | 26.01.1959 | K Lierse SK |
| 13 | François Vander Elst | 01.12.1954 | West Ham United FC London (ENG) |
| 21 | Alexander Czerniatynski | 28.07.1960 | FC Antwerpen |

**Trainer:** Guy Thys  06.12.1922

## BRAZIL

| Nr | Name | DOB | Club |
|---|---|---|---|
| | **Goalkeepers** | | |
| 1 | Valdir de Arruda Peres | 02.01.1951 | São Paulo FC |
| 12 | Paulo Sérgio de Oliveira Lima | 24.07.1954 | Botafogo de FR Rio de Janeiro |
| 22 | Carlos Roberto Gallo | 04.03.1956 | AA Ponte Preta Campinas |
| | **Defenders** | | |
| 2 | José Leandro de Souza Ferreira "Leandro I" | 17.03.1959 | CR Flamengo Rio de Janeiro |
| 3 | José Oscar Bernardi | 20.06.1954 | São Paulo FC |
| 4 | Luiz Carlos Ferreira "Luisinho" | 22.10.1958 | Atlético Mineiro Belo Horizonte |
| 6 | Leovegildo Lins Gama Júnior "Júnior I" | 29.06.1954 | CR Flamengo Rio de Janeiro |
| 13 | Edevaldo de Freitas | 28.01.1958 | SC Internacional Porto Alegre |
| 14 | Alcides Fonseca Júnior "Juninho" | 29.08.1958 | AA Ponte Preta Campinas |
| 16 | Édino Nazareth Filho "Edinho" | 05.06.1955 | Fluminense FC Rio de Janeiro |
| 17 | Pedro Luís Vicençote "Pedrinho" | 22.10.1957 | CR Vasco da Gama Rio de Janeiro |
| | **Midfielders** | | |
| 5 | Antônio Carlos Cerezo "Toninho Cerezo" | 21.04.1955 | Atlético Mineiro Belo Horizonte |
| 7 | Paulo Isidoro de Jesus | 03.08.1953 | Grêmio Foot-ball Porto-Alegrense |
| 8 | Sócrates Brasileiro Sampaio Vieira de Oliveira | 19.02.1954 | SC Corinthians Paulista São Paulo |
| 10 | Arthur Antunes Coimbra "Zico" | 03.03.1953 | CR Flamengo Rio de Janeiro |
| 15 | Paulo Roberto Falcão | 16.10.1953 | AS Roma (ITA) |
| 18 | João Batista da Silva | 08.03.1955 | Grêmio Foot-ball Porto-Alegrense |
| 21 | Dirceu José Guimarães | 15.06.1952 | Club Atlético de Madrid (ESP) |
| | **Forwards** | | |
| 9 | Sérgio Bernardino "Serginho I" | 23.12.1953 | São Paulo FC |
| 11 | Éder Aleixo de Assis | 25.05.1957 | Atlético Mineiro Belo Horizonte |
| 19 | Carlos Renato Frederico | 21.02.1957 | São Paulo FC |
| 20 | Carlos Roberto de Oliveira "Roberto Dinamite" | 13.04.1954 | CR Vasco da Gama Rio de Janeiro |
| **Trainer:** | Telê Santana da Silva | 26.07.1931 | |

## CAMEROON

| Nr | Name | DOB | Club |
|---|---|---|---|
| | **Goalkeepers** | | |
| 1 | Thomas N'Kono | 20.07.1956 | Canon Sportif de Yaoundé |
| 12 | Joseph-Antoine Bell | 08.10.1954 | Africa Sports National Abidjan (CIV) |
| 22 | Simon Tchobang | 31.08.1951 | Dynamo Douala |
| | **Defenders** | | |
| 2 | Michel Kaham | 01.06.1952 | Stade Quimperois |
| 3 | Edmond Enoka | 17.12.1955 | Dragon Douala |
| 4 | René Brice N'Djeya | 09.10.1953 | Union Sportive de Douala |
| 5 | Elie Onana Elondou | 13.10.1958 | Federal Foumban |
| 15 | François N'Doumbé Lea | 30.01.1954 | Union Sportive de Douala |
| 16 | Ibrahim Aoudou | 23.08.1955 | AS Cannes (FRA) |
| | **Midfielders** | | |
| 6 | Emmanuel Jerome Kundé | 15.07.1956 | Canon Sportif de Yaoundé |
| 7 | Ephrem M'Bom | 19.10.1955 | Canon Sportif de Yaoundé |
| 8 | Grégoire M'Bida | 27.01.1955 | Canon Sportif de Yaoundé |
| 11 | Charles Toubé | 22.01.1958 | Tonnerre Club de Yaoundé |
| 14 | Théophile Abega | 09.07.1954 | Canon Sportif de Yaoundé |
| 17 | Joseph Kamga | 17.08.1953 | Union Sportive de Douala |
| 19 | Joseph Enanga | 18.11.1956 | Union Sportive de Douala |
| | **Forwards** | | |
| 9 | Roger Milla (Albert Roger Mooh Miller) | 20.05.1952 | SEC Bastia (FRA) |
| 10 | Jean-Pierre Tokoto | 26.01.1948 | Jacksonville Tea Men (United States) |
| 13 | Paul Bahoken | 07.07.1955 | AS Cannes (FRA) |
| 18 | Jacques N'Guea | 08.11.1955 | Canon Sportif de Yaoundé |
| 20 | Oscar Alain Eyobo Makongo | 23.10.1961 | Dynamo Douala |
| 21 | Érnest-Lottin Ebongué | 15.05.1962 | Tonnerre Club de Yaoundé |
| **Trainer:** | Jean Vincent (FRA) | 29.11.1930 | |

## CHILE

| Nr | Name | DOB | Club |
|---|---|---|---|
| **Goalkeepers** | | | |
| 1 | Oscar Raúl Wirth Lafuente | 05.11.1955 | CD Cobreloa Calama |
| 12 | Marco Antonio Cornez Bravo | 15.10.1957 | CD Palestino Santiago |
| 22 | Mario Ignacio Osbén Méndez | 14.07.1950 | CSD Colo Colo Santiago |
| **Defenders** | | | |
| 2 | Lizardo Antonio Garrido Bustamante | 25.08.1957 | CSD Colo Colo Santiago |
| 3 | Eduardo René Valenzuela Becker | 20.04.1955 | CD Universidad Católica Santiago |
| 4 | Vladimir David Bigorra López | 09.08.1954 | Club Universidad de Chile Santiago |
| 5 | Elías Ricardo Figueroa Brander | 25.10.1946 | CSD Colo Colo Santiago |
| 17 | Óscar Vladimir Rojas Giacomozzi | 15.11.1958 | CSD Colo Colo Santiago |
| 18 | Mario Enrique Galindo Calixto | 10.08.1951 | CSD Colo Colo Santiago |
| 19 | Enzo Sergio Escobar Olivares | 10.11.1951 | CD Cobreloa Calama |
| **Midfielders** | | | |
| 6 | Rodolfo del Rosario Dubó Segovia | 11.09.1953 | CD Palestino Santiago |
| 7 | Eduardo Guillermo Bonvallet Godoy | 13.01.1955 | CD Universidad Católica Santiago |
| 8 | Carlos Humberto Rivas Torres | 24.05.1953 | CSD Colo Colo Santiago |
| 10 | Mario del Transito Soto Benavides | 10.07.1950 | CD Cobreloa Calama |
| 11 | Gustavo Segundo Moscoso Huencho | 10.08.1955 | CD Universidad Católica Santiago |
| 14 | Raúl Elias Ormeño Pacheco | 21.06.1958 | CSD Colo Colo Santiago |
| 16 | Manuel Antonio Rojas Zuniga | 13.06.1954 | CD Universidad Católica Santiago |
| 20 | Miguel Angel Neira Pincheira | 09.10.1952 | CD Universidad Católica Santiago |
| **Forwards** | | | |
| 9 | Juan Carlos Letelier Pizarro | 20.05.1959 | CD Cobreloa Calama |
| 13 | Carlos Humberto Caszely Garrido | 05.07.1950 | CSD Colo Colo Santiago |
| 15 | Patricio Nazario Yáñez Candia | 20.01.1961 | CD San Luis de Quillota |
| 21 | Miguel Angel Gamboa Pedemonte | 21.06.1951 | Club Universidad de Chile Santiago |
| **Trainer:** | Oscar Luis Santibáñez Díaz | 07.02.1936 | |

## CZECHOSLOVAKIA

| Nr | Name | DOB | Club |
|---|---|---|---|
| **Goalkeepers** | | | |
| 1 | Stanislav Seman | 08.08.1952 | TJ Lokomotíva Košice |
| 21 | Zdeněk Hruška | 25.07.1954 | Bohemians ČKD Praha |
| 22 | Karel Stromšík | 12.04.1958 | ASVS Dukla Praha |
| **Defenders** | | | |
| 2 | František Jakubec | 12.04.1956 | Bohemians ČKD Praha |
| 3 | Jan Fiala | 19.05.1956 | ASVS Dukla Praha |
| 4 | Ladislav Jurkemik | 20.07.1953 | TJ Internacionál Slovnaft Bratislava |
| 5 | Jozef Barmoš | 28.08.1954 | TJ Internacionál Slovnaft Bratislava |
| 6 | Rostislav Vojáček | 23.02.1949 | TJ Baník Ostrava OKD |
| 14 | Libor Radimec | 22.05.1950 | TJ Baník Ostrava OKD |
| 15 | Jozef Kukučka | 13.03.1957 | TJ Plastika Nitra |
| **Midfielders** | | | |
| 7 | Ján Kozák | 17.04.1954 | ASVS Dukla Praha |
| 8 | Antonín Panenka | 02.12.1948 | SK Rapid Wien (AUT) |
| 12 | Přemysl Bičovský | 18.08.1950 | Bohemians ČKD Praha |
| 13 | Jan Berger | 27.11.1955 | AC Sparta Praha |
| 16 | Pavel Chaloupka | 04.05.1959 | Bohemians ČKD Praha |
| 17 | František Štambachr | 13.02.1953 | ASVS Dukla Praha |
| **Forwards** | | | |
| 9 | Ladislav Vízek | 22.01.1955 | ASVS Dukla Praha |
| 10 | Tomáš Kříž | 17.03.1959 | ASVS Dukla Praha |
| 11 | Zdeněk Nehoda | 09.05.1952 | ASVS Dukla Praha |
| 18 | Petr Janečka | 25.11.1957 | Zbrojovka Brno |
| 19 | Marián Masný | 13.08.1950 | Slovan CHZJD Bratislava |
| 20 | Vlastimil Petržela | 20.07.1953 | SK Slavia Praha |
| **Trainer:** | Dr. Jozef Vengloš | 18.02.1936 | |

## EL SALVADOR

| Nr | Name | DOB | Club |
|---|---|---|---|
| | **Goalkeepers** | | |
| 1 | Luis Ricardo Guevara Mora | 02.09.1961 | CD Platense Municipal Zacatecoluca |
| 19 | Julio Eduardo Hernández Fuentes | 31.01.1958 | CD Santiagueño |
| 20 | José Luis Munguía Linares | 28.10.1959 | CD FAS Santa Ana |
| | **Defenders** | | |
| 2 | Mario Alfonso Castillo Díaz | 30.10.1951 | CD Santiagueño |
| 3 | Francisco José Jovel Cruz | 26.05.1951 | CD Águila |
| 4 | Carlos Humberto Recinos Ortíz | 30.06.1950 | CD FAS Santa Ana |
| 5 | Ramón Alfredo Fagoaga Romero | 12.01.1952 | CD Atlético Marte San Salvador |
| 12 | Francisco Salvador Osorto Guardado | 20.03.1957 | CD Santiagueño |
| 15 | Jaime Alberto Rodríguez Jiménez | 17.01.1959 | FC Bayer 05 Uerdingen (GER) |
| 18 | Miguel Ángel Díaz Arévalo | 27.01.1957 | CD Atlético Marte San Salvador |
| | **Midfielders** | | |
| 6 | Joaquín Alonso Ventura | 27.10.1956 | CD Santiagueño |
| 7 | Silvio Romeo Aquino | 30.06.1949 | Alianza FC San Salvador |
| 8 | José Luis Rugamas Portillo | 05.06.1953 | CD Atlético Marte San Salvador |
| 10 | José Norberto Huezo Montoya | 06.06.1956 | CD Atlético Marte San Salvador |
| 16 | Mauricio Alberto Alfaro Valladares | 13.02.1956 | CD Platense Municipal Zacatecoluca |
| | **Forwards** | | |
| 9 | Ever Francisco Hernández | 11.12.1958 | CD Santiagueño |
| 11 | Jorge Alberto González Barillas | 13.03.1957 | CD FAS Santa Ana |
| 13 | José María Rivas Martínez | 12.05.1958 | Alianza FC San Salvador |
| 14 | Luis Baltazar Ramírez Zapata | 06.01.1954 | CD Atlético Marte San Salvador |
| 17 | Guillermo Lorenzana Ragazzone | 05.01.1956 | CD Atlético Marte San Salvador |
| **Trainer:** | Mauricio Alonso "Pipo" Rodríguez Lindo | 12.09.1945 | |

## ENGLAND

| Nr | Name | DOB | Club |
|---|---|---|---|
| | **Goalkeepers** | | |
| 1 | Raymond Neal Clemence | 05.08.1948 | Tottenham Hotspur FC London |
| 13 | Joseph Thomas Corrigan | 18.11.1948 | Manchester City FC |
| 22 | Peter Leslie Shilton | 18.09.1949 | Nottingham Forest FC |
| | **Defenders** | | |
| 2 | Vivian Alexander Anderson | 29.08.1956 | Nottingham Forest FC |
| 4 | Terence Ian Butcher | 28.12.1958 | Ipswich Town FC |
| 6 | Stephen Brian Foster | 24.09.1957 | Brighton and Hove Albion FC |
| 12 | Michael Dennis Mills | 04.01.1949 | Ipswich Town FC |
| 14 | Philip George Neal | 20.02.1951 | Liverpool FC |
| 17 | Kenneth Graham Sansom | 26.09.1958 | Arsenal FC London |
| 18 | Philip Brian Thompson | 21.01.1954 | Liverpool FC |
| | **Midfielders** | | |
| 3 | Trevor David Brooking | 02.10.1948 | West Ham United FC London |
| 5 | Steven James Coppell | 09.07.1955 | Blackburn Rovers FC |
| 9 | Glenn Hoddle | 27.10.1957 | Tottenham Hotspur FC London |
| 10 | Terence McDermott | 08.12.1951 | Liverpool FC |
| 15 | Graham Rix | 23.10.1957 | Arsenal FC London |
| 16 | Bryan Robson | 11.01.1957 | Blackburn Rovers FC |
| 19 | Raymond Colin Wilkins | 14.09.1956 | Blackburn Rovers FC |
| | **Forwards** | | |
| 7 | Kevin Joseph Keegan | 14.02.1951 | Southampton FC |
| 8 | Trevor John Francis | 19.04.1954 | Manchester City FC |
| 11 | Paul Mariner | 22.05.1953 | Ipswich Town FC |
| 20 | Peter Withe | 30.08.1951 | Aston Villa FC Birmingham |
| 21 | Anthony Stewart Woodcock | 06.12.1955 | 1.FC Köln (GER) |
| **Trainer:** | Ronald Greenwood | 11.11.1921 | |

## FRANCE

| Nr | Name | DOB | Club |
|---|---|---|---|
| | **Goalkeepers** | | |
| 1 | Dominique Baratelli | 26.12.1947 | Paris St. Germain FC |
| 21 | Jean-Luc Castaneda | 20.03.1957 | AS Saint-Étienne |
| 22 | Jean-Luc Ettori | 29.06.1955 | AS Monaco |
| | **Defenders** | | |
| 2 | Manuel AMoros | 01.02.1962 | AS Monaco |
| 3 | Patrick Battiston | 12.03.1957 | AS Saint-Étienne |
| 4 | Maxime Bossis | 26.06.1955 | FC Nantes |
| 5 | Gérard Janvion | 21.08.1953 | AS Saint-Étienne |
| 6 | Christian Lopez | 15.03.1953 | AS Saint-Étienne |
| 7 | Philippe Mahut | 04.03.1956 | FC Metz |
| 8 | Marius Trésor | 15.01.1950 | Girondins de Bordeaux |
| | **Midfielders** | | |
| 9 | Bernard Genghini | 18.01.1958 | FC Sochaux-Montbéliard |
| 10 | Michel Platini | 21.06.1955 | AS Saint-Étienne |
| 11 | René Girard | 04.04.1954 | Girondins de Bordeaux |
| 12 | Alain Giresse | 02.08.1952 | Girondins de Bordeaux |
| 13 | Jean-François Larios | 27.08.1956 | AS Saint-Étienne |
| 14 | Jean Amadou Tigana | 23.06.1955 | Girondins de Bordeaux |
| | **Forwards** | | |
| 15 | Bruno Bellone | 14.03.1962 | AS Monaco |
| 16 | Alain Couriol | 24.10.1958 | AS Monaco |
| 17 | Bernard Lacombe | 15.08.1952 | Girondins de Bordeaux |
| 18 | Dominique Rocheteau | 14.01.1955 | Paris St. Germain FC |
| 19 | Didier Six | 21.08.1954 | VfB Stuttgart (GER) |
| 20 | Gérard Soler | 29.03.1954 | Girondins de Bordeaux |
| **Trainer:** | Michel Hidalgo | 22.03.1933 | |

## HONDURAS

| Nr | Name | DOB | Club |
|---|---|---|---|
| | **Goalkeepers** | | |
| 1 | José Salomón Nazar Ordóñez | 07.09.1953 | Univ. Nacional Autonoma Hondureña |
| 21 | Julio César Arzú | 05.06.1954 | RCD España San Pedro Sula |
| 22 | James Steward Bodden | 09.12.1946 | RCD España San Pedro Sula |
| | **Defenders** | | |
| 2 | César Efraín Gutiérrez Álvarez | 07.05.1954 | Univ. Nacional Autonoma Hondureña |
| 3 | Jaime Enrique Villegas Roura | 05.07.1950 | RCD España San Pedro Sula |
| 4 | José Fernando Bulnes Zubiaga | 21.10.1946 | CD Olimpia Tegucigalpa |
| 5 | Allan Anthony Costly Blyden | 13.12.1954 | RCD España San Pedro Sula |
| 12 | Domingo Drummond Cooper | 14.04.1957 | CD Platense Puerto Cortés |
| 17 | José Luis Cruz Figueroa | 12.06.1949 | CD Motagua Tegucigalpa |
| | **Midfielders** | | |
| 6 | Ramón Enrique Maradiaga Chávez | 30.10.1954 | CD Motagua Tegucigalpa |
| 8 | Javier Francisco Toledo Rivera | 30.09.1959 | CD Marathón San Pedro Sula |
| 11 | David Buezo Guerrero | 05.05.1955 | Motagua |
| 13 | Prudencio Norales Martínez | 20.04.1956 | CD Olimpia Tegucigalpa |
| 14 | Juan Alberto Cruz Murillo | 27.02.1959 | Univ. Nacional Autonoma Hondureña |
| 15 | Héctor Ramón Zelaya Rivera | 12.07.1957 | CD Motagua Tegucigalpa |
| 18 | Carlos Orlando Caballero Sánchez | 05.12.1958 | RCD España San Pedro Sula |
| 20 | Gilberto Geronimo Yearwood | 15.03.1956 | Real Valladolid (ESP) |
| | **Forwards** | | |
| 7 | Eduardo Antonio Laing Carcamo | 27.12.1958 | CD Platense Puerto Cortés |
| 9 | Porfirio Amando Betancourt Cortez | 23.08.1956 | RC Strasbourg (FRA) |
| 10 | José Roberto Figueroa Padilla | 15.12.1959 | CSD Vida La Ceiba |
| 16 | Roberto James Bailey Sargent | 10.08.1952 | CD Marathón San Pedro Sula |
| 19 | Celso Fredy Güity Núñez | 07.08.1955 | CD Marathón San Pedro Sula |
| **Trainer:** | José de la Paz Herrera Ucles | 21.11.1940 | |

## HUNGARY

| Nr | Name | DOB | Club |
|---|---|---|---|
| | **Goalkeepers** | | |
| 1 | Ferenc Mészáros | 11.04.1950 | Sporting Clube de Portugal (POR) |
| 21 | Béla Katzirz | 27.07.1953 | Pécsi MSC |
| 22 | Imre Kiss | 10.08.1957 | Tatabányai Bányász SC |
| | **Defenders** | | |
| 2 | Győző Martos | 15.12.1949 | Thor Waterschei SV (BEL) |
| 3 | László Bálint | 01.02.1948 | Toulouse FC (FRA) |
| 4 | József Tóth | 2.12.1951 | Újpesti Dózsa SC |
| 6 | Imre Garaba | 29.07.1958 | Budapesti Honvéd SE |
| 13 | Tibor Rab | 02.10.1955 | Ferencvárosi TC |
| 14 | Sándor Sallai | 26.03.1960 | Debreceni VSC |
| 18 | Attila Kerekes | 04.04.1954 | Békéscsabai Előre Spartacus SC |
| 19 | József Varga | 09.10.1954 | Budapesti Honvéd SE |
| 20 | József Csuhay | 12.07.1957 | Videoton SC Székesfehérvár |
| | **Midfielders** | | |
| 5 | Sándor Müller | 21.09.1948 | Hércules CF Alicante (ESP) |
| 8 | Tibor Nyilasi | 18.01.1955 | Ferencvárosi TC |
| 16 | Ferenc Csongrádi | 29.03.1956 | Videoton SC Székesfehérvár |
| 17 | Károly Csapó | 23.02.1952 | Tatabányai Bányász SC |
| | **Forwards** | | |
| 7 | László Fazekas | 15.10.1947 | Royal Antwerp FC (BEL) |
| 9 | András Törőcsik | 01.05.1955 | Újpesti Dózsa SC |
| 10 | László Kiss | 12.03.1956 | Vasas SC Budapest |
| 11 | Gábor Pölöskei | 11.10.1961 | Ferencvárosi TC |
| 12 | Lázár Szentes | 12.12.1955 | Rába ETO Győr |
| 15 | Béla Bodonyi | 14.09.1956 | Budapesti Honvéd SE |
| **Trainer:** Kálmán Mészöly | | 16.07.1941 | |

## ITALY

| Nr | Name | DOB | Club |
|---|---|---|---|
| | **Goalkeepers** | | |
| 1 | Dino Zoff | 28.02.1942 | FC Juventus Torino |
| 12 | Ivano Bordon | 13.04.1951 | Internazionale FC Milano |
| 22 | Giovanni Galli | 29.04.1958 | AC Fiorentina Firenze |
| | **Defenders** | | |
| 2 | Franco Baresi | 08.05.1960 | Milan AC |
| 3 | Giuseppe Bergomi | 22.12.1963 | Internazionale FC Milano |
| 4 | Antonio Cabrini | 08.10.1957 | FC Juventus Torino |
| 5 | Fulvio Collovati | 09.05.1957 | Milan AC |
| 6 | Claudio Gentile | 27.09.1953 | FC Juventus Torino |
| 7 | Gaetano Scirea | 25.05.1953 | FC Juventus Torino |
| 8 | Pietro Vierchowod | 06.04.1959 | AC Fiorentina Firenze |
| | **Midfielders** | | |
| 9 | Giancarlo Antognoni | 01.04.1954 | AC Fiorentina Firenze |
| 10 | Giuseppe Dossena | 02.05.1958 | Torino Calcio |
| 11 | Giampiero Marini | 25.02.1951 | Internazionale FC Milano |
| 13 | Gabriele Oriali | 25.11.1952 | Nternazionale FC Milano |
| 14 | Marco Tardelli | 24.09.1954 | FC Juventus Torino |
| 15 | Franco Causio | 01.02.1949 | Udinese Calcio |
| 16 | Bruno Conti | 13.03.1955 | AS Roma |
| | **Forwards** | | |
| 17 | Daniele Massaro | 23.05.1961 | AC Fiorentina IFirenze |
| 18 | Alessandro Altobelli | 28.11.1955 | nternazionale FC Milano |
| 19 | Francesco Graziani | 12.12.1952 | AC Fiorentina Firenze |
| 20 | Paolo Rossi | 23.09.1956 | FC Juventus Torino |
| 21 | Franco Selvaggi | 15.05.1953 | US Cagliari |
| **Trainer:** Vincenzo „Enzo" Bearzot | | 26.09.1927 | |

## KUWAIT

| Nr | Name | DOB | Club |
|---|---|---|---|
| | **Goalkeepers** | | |
| 1 | Ahmed Khuder Al Tarabulsi | 22.03.1947 | Kuwait Sporting Club |
| 21 | Adam Marjan Ahmed | 23.09.1957 | Kazma Sporting Club |
| 22 | Jasem Mohammed Bahman | 15.02.1958 | Qadsia Sporting Club Kuwait City |
| | **Defenders** | | |
| 2 | Naeem Saad Mubarak Fajah | 01.10.1957 | Al Tadamun SC Al Farwaniya |
| 3 | Mahboub Juma Mahboub Mubarak | 17.09.1955 | Al Salmiya Sporting Club |
| 4 | Jamal Mohammed Yaqoub Al Qabandi | 07.04.1959 | Kazma Sporting Club |
| 5 | Waleed Mohammed Al Jasem Al Mubarak | 18.11.1959 | Kuwait Sporting Club |
| 13 | Mubarak Marzouq Hamed Al Issa | 01.01.1961 | Al Tadamun SC Al Farwaniya |
| 14 | Abdullah Yousuf Ma'youf | 03.12.1953 | Kazma Sporting Club |
| 15 | Sami Mohammed Al Hashash | 15.09.1959 | Al Arabi Sporting Club Kuwait City |
| 17 | Hamoud Fulaiteh Al Shammari | 26.09.1960 | Kazma Sporting Club |
| | **Midfielders** | | |
| 6 | Saed Mohammed Abdul Aziz Al Houti | 24.05.1954 | Kuwait Sporting Club |
| 8 | Abdullah Mohammed Al Buloushi | 16.02.1960 | Al Arabi Sporting Club Kuwait City |
| 11 | Nasser Abdullah Al Ghanem | 04.04.1961 | Kazma Sporting Club |
| 12 | Youssef Faraj Al Suwayed | 20.09.1958 | Kazma Sporting Club |
| 18 | Mohammed Ahmed Karam | 01.01.1955 | Al Arabi Sporting Club Kuwait City |
| | **Forwards** | | |
| 7 | Fatih Kamil Fayyaz Matar Marzouq | 23.05.1955 | Al Tadamun SC Al Farwaniya |
| 9 | Jassem Jamal Yaqoub Sultan | 25.10.1953 | Qadsia Sporting Club Kuwait City |
| 10 | Abdul Aziz Saoud Al Anbari | 03.01.1954 | Kuwait Sporting Club |
| 16 | Faisal Ali Al Dakhil | 13.08.1957 | Qadsia Sporting Club Kuwait City |
| 19 | Muayad Rehayyem Gamal Al Haddad | 01.01.1960 | Khaitan Sporting Club |
| 20 | Abdulaziz Hassan Mohammed Al Buloushi | 04.12.1962 | Al Arabi Sporting Club Kuwait City |
| **Trainer:** Carlos Alberto Gomes Parreira (BRA) | | 27.02.1943 | |

## NEW ZEALAND

| Nr | Name | DOB | Club |
|---|---|---|---|
| | **Goalkeepers** | | |
| 1 | Richard Hardie Wilson | 08.05.1956 | Preston Makedonia Soccer Club(AUS) |
| 21 | Barry Thomas Pickering | 12.12.1956 | Miramar Rangers AFC Wellington |
| 22 | Francesco Maria „Frank" van Hattum | 17.11.1958 | Manurewa AFC |
| | **Defenders** | | |
| 2 | Glenn Laurence Dods | 07.07.1957 | Adelaide City FC (AUS) |
| 3 | Richard Lloyd "Ricki" Herbert | 10.04.1961 | University-Mt. Wellington Auckland |
| 5 | David John Bright | 29.11.1949 | Manurewa AFC |
| 6 | Robert Ronald Almond | 16.04.1951 | Invercargill Thistle |
| 14 | Adrian Coroon Elrick | 29.09.1949 | Hanimex United North Shore |
| 15 | John Bennett Hill | 07.01.1950 | Gisborne City FC |
| 16 | Glen Neish Adam | 22.05.1959 | University-Mt. Wellington Auckland |
| | **Midfielders** | | |
| 4 | Brian Alfred Turner | 31.07.1949 | Gisborne City FC |
| 8 | Duncan Edward Cole | 12.07.1958 | Hanimex United North Shore |
| 10 | Steven Paul Sumner | 02.04.1955 | West Adelaide Hellas SC (AUS) |
| 11 | Samuel Alan Malcolmson | 02.04.1948 | East Coast Bays AFC Northcross |
| 12 | Keith Gordon Mackay | 08.12.1956 | Gisborne City FC |
| 13 | Kenneth Grant Cresswell | 04.06.1958 | Gisborne City FC |
| 17 | Allan Roderick Boath | 14.02.1958 | West Adelaide Hellas (AUS) |
| 18 | Peter Rex Simonsen | 17.04.1959 | Manurewa AFC |
| 19 | William James Simon Mark McClure | 04.01.1958 | University-Mt. Wellington Auckland |
| | **Forwards** | | |
| 7 | Wynton Alan Whai Rufer | 29.12.1962 | Miramar Rangers AFC Wellington |
| 9 | Stephen Wooddin | 16.01.1955 | South Melbourne FC (AUS) |
| 20 | Grant John Turner | 07.10.1958 | Gisborne City FC |
| **Trainer:** John Adshead (ENG) | | 27.03.1942 | |

## NORTHERN IRELAND

| Nr | Name | DOB | Club |
|---|---|---|---|
| **Goalkeepers** | | | |
| 1 | Patrick Anthony Jennings | 12.06.1945 | Arsenal FC London (ENG) |
| 17 | James Archibald Platt | 26.01.1952 | Middlesbrough FC (ENG) |
| 22 | George Dunlop | 16.01.1956 | Linfield FC Belfast |
| **Defenders** | | | |
| 2 | James Michael Nicholl | 28.02.1956 | Toronto Blizzard (CAN) |
| 3 | Malachy Martin Donaghy | 13.09.1957 | Luton Town FC (ENG) |
| 5 | Christopher James Nicholl | 12.10.1946 | Southampton FC (ENG) |
| 6 | John Patrick O'Neill | 11.03.1958 | Leicester City FC (ENG) |
| 12 | John McClelland | 07.12.1955 | Glasgow Rangers FC (SCO) |
| 13 | Samuel Nelson | 01.04.1949 | Brighton and Hove Albion FC (ENG) |
| **Midfielders** | | | |
| 4 | David McCreery | 16.09.1957 | Tulsa Roughnecks (USA) |
| 7 | Noel Brotherston | 18.11.1956 | Blackburn Rovers FC (ENG) |
| 8 | Martin Hugh Michael O'Neill | 01.03.1952 | Norwich City FC (ENG) |
| 10 | Samuel Baxter McIlroy | 02.08.1954 | Stoke City FC (ENG) |
| 14 | Thomas Cassidy | 18.11.1950 | Burnley FC (ENG) |
| 15 | Thomas Finney | 06.11.1952 | Cambridge United FC (ENG) |
| 16 | Norman Whiteside | 07.05.1965 | Manchester United FC (ENG) |
| 18 | John Charles Jameson | 11.03.1958 | Glentoran FC Belfast |
| 20 | James Cleary | 27.05.1956 | Glentoran FC Belfast |
| **Forwards** | | | |
| 9 | Gerard Joseph Armstrong | 23.05.1954 | Watford FC (ENG) |
| 11 | William Robert Hamilton | 09.05.1957 | Burnley FC (ENG) |
| 19 | Patrick Joseph Healy | 27.09.1955 | Coleraine FC |
| 21 | Robert McFaul Campbell | 13.09.1956 | Bradford City FC (ENG) |
| **Trainer:** William Laurence Bingham | | 05.08.1931 | |

## PERU

| Nr | Name | DOB | Club |
|---|---|---|---|
| **Goalkeepers** | | | |
| 1 | Eusebio Alfredo Acasuzo Colán | 08.04.1952 | Club Universitario de Deportes Lima |
| 12 | José Manuel Gonzáles Ganoza | 10.07.1954 | Club Alianza Lima |
| 21 | Ramón Quiroga Arancibia | 23.07.1950 | Club Sporting Cristal Lima |
| **Defenders** | | | |
| 2 | Jaime Eduardo Duarte Huerta | 27.02.1955 | Club Alianza Lima |
| 3 | Rafael Salvador Salguero González | 10.08.1951 | Club Alianza Lima |
| 4 | Alejandro Hugo Gastulo Ramírez | 09.01.1958 | Club Universitario de Deportes Lima |
| 15 | Rubén Toribio Díaz Rivas | 17.04.1952 | Club Sporting Cristal Lima |
| 16 | Jorge Andrés Olaechea Quijandría | 27.08.1956 | Club Alianza Lima |
| 17 | Franco Enrique Navarro Monteiro | 10.11.1961 | Club CD Municipal Lima |
| **Midfielders** | | | |
| 5 | Germán Carlos Leguía Dragó | 02.01.1954 | Club Universitario de Deportes Lima |
| 6 | José Manuel Velásquez Castillo | 04.06.1952 | CD Independiente Medellín (COL) |
| 8 | César Augusto Cueto Villa | 16.06.1952 | CD Atlético Nacional Medellín (COL) |
| 10 | Teófilo Juan Cubillas Arizaga | 08.03.1949 | Fort Lauderdale Strikers (USA) |
| 13 | Óscar Gilberto Arizaga | 20.08.1957 | Club Atlético Chalaco Callao |
| 14 | Miguel Ángel Gutiérrez | 19.11.1956 | Club Sporting Cristal Lima |
| 18 | Eduardo Hugo Malásquez Maldonado | 13.10.1957 | Club CD Municipal Lima |
| 22 | Luis Alberto Reyna Navarro | 16.05.1959 | Club Sporting Cristal Lima |
| **Forwards** | | | |
| 7 | Gerónimo Barbadillo González | 24.09.1952 | Tigres de la UA Nuevo León (MEX) |
| 9 | Julio César Uribe Flores | 09.05.1958 | Club Sporting Cristal Lima |
| 11 | Juan Carlos Oblitas Saba | 16.02.1951 | RFC Seraing (BEL) |
| 19 | Guillermo La Rosa Laguna | 06.06.1952 | CD Atlético Nacional Medellín (COL) |
| 20 | Percy Rojas Montero | 16.09.1949 | RFC Seraing (BEL) |
| **Trainer:** Elba de Pádua Lima „Tim" (BRA) | | 20.02.1915 | |

## POLAND

| Nr | Name | DOB | Club |
|----|------|-----|------|
| **Goalkeepers** | | | |
| 1 | Józef Młynarczyk | 20.09.1953 | RTS Widzew Łódź |
| 21 | Jacek Kazimierski | 17.08.1959 | KP Legia Warszawa |
| 22 | Piotr Mowlik | 21.04.1951 | Lech Poznań |
| **Defenders** | | | |
| 2 | Marek Dziuba | 19.12.1955 | ŁKS Łódź |
| 4 | Tadeusz Dolny | 07.05.1958 | KS Górnik Zabrze |
| 5 | Paweł Janas | 4.03.1953 | KP Legia Warszawa |
| 7 | Jan Jałocha | 18.07.1957 | Wisła Kraków |
| 9 | Władysław Żmuda | 06.06.1954 | RTS Widzew Łódź |
| 10 | Stefan Majewski | 31.01.1956 | KP Legia Warszawa |
| 12 | Roman Wójcicki | 08.01.1958 | KS Śląsk Wrocław |
| **Midfielders** | | | |
| 3 | Janusz Kupcewicz | 09.12.1955 | KS Arka Gdynia |
| 6 | Piotr Skrobowski | 16.10.1961 | Wisła Kraków |
| 8 | Waldemar Matysik | 27.09.1961 | KS Górnik Zabrze |
| 13 | Andrzej Buncol | 21.09.1959 | KP Legia Warszawa |
| 14 | Andrzej Pałasz | 22.07.1960 | KS Górnik Zabrze |
| 19 | Andrzej Iwan | 10.11.1959 | Wisła Kraków |
| **Forwards** | | | |
| 11 | Włodzimierz Smolarek | 16.07.1957 | RTS Widzew Łódź |
| 15 | Włodzimierz Ciołek | 24.03.1956 | FKS Stal Mielec |
| 16 | Grzegorz Lato | 08.04.1950 | KSC Lokeren (BEL) |
| 17 | Andrzej Szarmach | 03.10.1950 | AJ Auxerre (FRA) |
| 18 | Marek Kusto | 29.04.1954 | KP Legia Warszawa |
| 20 | Zbigniew Boniek | 03.03.1956 | RTS Widzew Łódź |
| **Trainer:** Antoni Piechniczek | | 03.05.1942 | |

## SCOTLAND

| Nr | Name | DOB | Club |
|----|------|-----|------|
| **Goalkeepers** | | | |
| 1 | Alan Roderick Rough | 25.11.1951 | Partick Thistle FC Glasgow |
| 12 | George Wood | 26.09.1952 | Arsenal FC London (ENG) |
| 22 | James Leighton | 24.07.1958 | Aberdeen FC |
| **Defenders** | | | |
| 2 | Daniel Fergus McGrain | 01.05.1950 | Celtic Glasgow FC |
| 3 | Francis Tierney Gray | 27.10.1954 | Leeds United FC (ENG) |
| 5 | Alan David Hansen | 13.06.1955 | Liverpool FC (ENG) |
| 6 | William Fergus Miller | 02.05.1955 | Aberdeen FC |
| 13 | Alexander McLeish | 21.01.1959 | Aberdeen FC |
| 14 | David Narey | 12.06.1956 | Dundee FC United |
| 17 | Allan James Evans | 12.10.1956 | Aston Villa FC Birmingham (ENG) |
| 21 | George Elder Burley | 03.06.1956 | Ipswich Town FC (ENG) |
| **Midfielders** | | | |
| 4 | Graeme James Souness | 06.05.1953 | Liverpool FC (ENG) |
| 7 | Gordon David Strachan | 09.02.1957 | Aberdeen FC |
| 10 | John Wark | 04.08.1957 | Ipswich Town FC (ENG) |
| 16 | Richard Asa Hartford | 24.10.1950 | Manchester City FC (ENG) |
| 20 | David Alexander Provan | 08.05.1956 | Celtic Glasgow FC |
| **Forwards** | | | |
| 8 | Kenneth Mathieson Dalglish | 04.03.1951 | Liverpool FC (ENG) |
| 9 | Alan Bernard Brazil | 15.06.1959 | Ipswich Town FC (ENG) |
| 11 | John Neilson Robertson | 20.01.1953 | Nottingham Forest FC (ENG) |
| 15 | Joseph Jordan | 15.12.1951 | Milan AC (ITA) |
| 18 | Steven Archibald | 27.09.1956 | Tottenham Hotspur FC (ENG) |
| 19 | Paul Whitehead Sturrock | 10.10.1956 | Dundee FC United |
| **Trainer:** John "Jock" Stein | | 05.10.1922 | |

## SOVIET UNION

| Nr | Name | DOB | Club |
|---|---|---|---|
| | **Goalkeepers** | | |
| 1 | Rinat Dasaev | 13.06.1957 | Spartak Moskva |
| 21 | Viktor Chanov | 21.07.1959 | Dinamo Kiev |
| 22 | Vyacheslav Chanov | 23.10.1951 | Torpedo Moskva |
| | **Defenders** | | |
| 2 | Tengiz Sulakvelidze | 23.07.1956 | Dinamo Tbilisi |
| 3 | Aleksandr Chivadze | 08.04.1955 | Dinamo Tbilisi |
| 4 | Vagiz Khidiyatullin | 03.03.1959 | CSKA Moskva |
| 5 | Sergei Baltacha | 17.02.1958 | Dinamo Kiev |
| 6 | Anatoliy Demyanenko | 19.02.1959 | Dinamo Kiev |
| 14 | Sergey Borovsky | 29.01.1956 | Dinamo Minsk |
| 18 | Yuriy Susloparov | 14.08.1958 | Torpedo Moskva |
| 20 | Oleg Romantzev | 04.01.1954 | Spartak Moskva |
| | **Midfielders** | | |
| 8 | Vladimir Bessonov | 05.03.1958 | Dinamo Kiev |
| 9 | Yuriy Gavrilov | 03.05.1953 | Spartak Moskva |
| 10 | Khoren Oganesyan | 10.01.1955 | Ararat Yerevan |
| 12 | Andrey Bal | 16.02.1958 | Dinamo Kiev |
| 13 | Vitaliy Daraselia | 09.10.1957 | Dinamo Tbilisi |
| 17 | Leonid Buryak | 10.07.1953 | Dinamo Kiev |
| 19 | Vadim Evtushenko | 01.01.1958 | Dinamo Kiev |
| | **Forwards** | | |
| 7 | Ramaz Shengeliya | 01.01.1957 | Dinamo Tbilisi |
| 11 | Oleg Blokhin | 05.11.1952 | Dinamo Kiev |
| 15 | Sergey Andreyev | 16.05.1956 | SKA Rostov/Don |
| 16 | Sergey Rodionov | 03.09.1962 | Spartak Moskva |
| **Trainer:** | Konstantin Beskov | 18.11.1920 | |

## SPAIN

| Nr | Name | DOB | Club |
|---|---|---|---|
| | **Goalkeepers** | | |
| 1 | Luis Miguel Arkonada Echarre | 26.06.1954 | Real Sociedad San Sebastián |
| 21 | Francisco Javier González „Urrutikoetxea" | 17.02.1952 | FC Barcelona |
| 22 | Miguel Ángel González Suárez | 24.12.1947 | Real Madrid CF |
| | **Defenders** | | |
| 2 | José Antonio Camacho Alfaro | 08.06.1955 | Real Madrid CF |
| 3 | Rafael Gordillo Vázquez | 24.02.1957 | Real Betis Balompié Sevilla |
| 5 | Miguel Tendillo Belenguer | 01.02.1961 | Valencia CF |
| 6 | José Ramón Alexanco Ventosa | 19.05.1956 | FC Barcelona |
| 12 | Santiago Urquiaga Pérez Lugar | 14.04.1958 | Athletic Club de Bilbao |
| 13 | Manuel Enrique Jiménez Abalo | 27.10.1956 | Real Sporting Gijón CF |
| 14 | Antonio Maceda Francés | 16.05.1957 | Real Sporting Gijón CF |
| | **Midfielders** | | |
| 4 | Miguel Ángel Alonso Oyarbide „Periko Alonso" | 01.02.1953 | Real Sociedad San Sebastián |
| 8 | Joaquín Alonso González | 09.06.1956 | Real Sporting Gijón CF |
| 10 | Jesús María Zamora Ansorena | 01.01.1955 | Real Sociedad San Sebastián |
| 15 | Enrique Saura Gil | 02.08.1954 | Valencia CF |
| 16 | José Vicente Sánchez Felip | 08.10.1956 | FC Barcelona |
| 17 | Ricardo Gallego Redondo | 08.02.1959 | Real Madrid CF |
| | **Forwards** | | |
| 7 | Juan Enrique Gómez González „Juanito" | 10.11.1954 | Real Madrid CF |
| 9 | Jesús María Satrústegui Azpiroz | 12.01.1954 | Real Sociedad San Sebastián |
| 11 | Roberto López Ufarte | 19.04.1958 | Real Sociedad San Sebastián |
| 18 | Pedro Jesús Uralde Hernáez | 02.03.1958 | Real Sociedad San Sebastián |
| 19 | Carlos Alonso González „Santillana" | 23.08.1952 | Real Madrid CF |
| 20 | Enrique Castro González „Quini" | 23.09.1949 | FC Barcelona |
| **Trainer:** | José Emilio Santamaría Iglesias | 31.07.1929 | |

## WEST GERMANY

| Nr | Name | DOB | Club |
|---|---|---|---|
| | **Goalkeepers** | | |
| 1 | Harald Schumacher | 06.03.1954 | 1.FC Köln |
| 21 | Bernd Franke | 12.02.1948 | TSV Eintracht Braunschweig |
| 22 | Eike Immel | 27.11.1960 | BV Borussia Dortmund |
| | **Defenders** | | |
| 4 | Karlheinz Förster | 25.07.1958 | VfB Stuttgart |
| 5 | Bernd Förster | 03.05.1956 | VfB Stuttgart |
| 12 | Wilfried Hannes | 17.05.1957 | Borussia VfL Mönchengladbach |
| 19 | Holger Hieronymus | 22.02.1959 | Hamburger SV |
| 20 | Manfred Kaltz | 06.01.1953 | Hamburger SV |
| | **Midfielders** | | |
| 2 | Hans-Peter Briegel | 11.10.1955 | 1.FC Kaiserslautern |
| 3 | Paul Breitner | 05.09.1951 | FC Bayern München |
| 6 | Wolfgang Dremmler | 12.07.1954 | FC Bayern München |
| 7 | Pierre Littbarski | 16.04.1960 | 1.FC Köln |
| 10 | Hans Müller | 27.07.1957 | VfB Stuttgart |
| 14 | Felix Magath | 26.07.1953 | Hamburger SV |
| 15 | Ulrich Stielike | 15.11.1954 | Real Madrid CF (ESP) |
| 17 | Stephan Engels | 06.09.1960 | 1.FC Köln |
| 18 | Lothar Herbert Matthäus | 21.03.1961 | Borussia VfL Mönchengladbach |
| | **Forwards** | | |
| 8 | Klaus Fischer | 27.12.1949 | 1.FC Köln |
| 9 | Horst Hrubesch | 17.04.1951 | Hamburger SV |
| 11 | Karl-Heinz Rummenigge | 25.09.1955 | FC Bayern München |
| 13 | Uwe Reinders | 19.01.1955 | SV Werder Bremen |
| 16 | Thomas Allofs | 17.11.1959 | TSV Fortuna Düsseldorf |
| **Trainer:** | Josef „Jupp" Derwall | 10.03.1927 | |

## YUGOSLAVIA

| Nr | Name | DOB | Club |
|---|---|---|---|
| | **Goalkeepers** | | |
| 1 | Dragan Pantelić | 09.12.1951 | Girondins de Bordeaux (FRA) |
| 12 | Ivan Pudar | 16.08.1961 | NK Hajduk Split |
| 22 | Ratko Svilar | 06.05.1950 | Royal Antwerp FC (BEL) |
| | **Defenders** | | |
| 4 | Velimir Zajec | 12.02.1956 | NK Dinamo Zagreb |
| 5 | Nenad Stojković | 26.05.1956 | FK Partizan Beograd |
| 6 | Zlatko Krmpotić | 07.08.1958 | FK Crvena zvezda Beograd |
| 9 | Zoran Vujović | 26.08.1958 | NK Hajduk Split |
| 14 | Nikola Jovanović | 18.09.1952 | FK Budučnost Titograd |
| 15 | Miloš Hrstić | 20.11.1955 | NK Rijeka |
| | **Midfielders** | | |
| 2 | Ive Jerolimov | 30.03.1958 | NK Rijeka |
| 3 | Ivan Gudelj | 21.09.1960 | NK Hajduk Split |
| 7 | Vladimir Petrović | 01.07.1955 | FK Crvena zvezda Beograd |
| 8 | Edhem Šljivo | 16.03.1950 | OGC Nice (FRA) |
| 10 | Zvonko Živković | 31.10.1959 | FK Partizan Beograd |
| 17 | Jure Jerković | 25.02.1950 | FC Zürich (SUI) |
| | **Forwards** | | |
| 11 | Zlatko Vujović | 26.08.1958 | NK Hajduk Split |
| 13 | Safet Sušić | 13.04.1955 | FK Sarajevo |
| 16 | Miloš Šestić | 08.08.1956 | FK Crvena zvezda Beograd |
| 18 | Stjepan Deverić | 20.08.1961 | NK Dinamo Zagreb |
| 19 | Vahid Halilhodžić | 15.10.1952 | FC Nantes (FRA) |
| 20 | Ivan Šurjak | 23.03.1953 | Paris St. Germain FC (FRA) |
| 21 | Predrag Pašić | 18.10.1958 | FK Sarajevo |
| **Trainer:** | Miljan Miljanić | 04.05.1930 | |

# 1986, MEXICO
(Copa Mundial de Fútbol México '86)

# WORLD CUP 1986 QUALIFIERS

A total of 121 teams entered the 1986 FIFA World Cup qualification rounds, competing for a total of 24 spots in the final tournament. Mexico, as the hosts, and Italy, as the defending champions, qualified automatically, leaving 22 spots open for competition. The 22 spots available were distributed among the continental zones as follows:

- Europe: 12.5 places, contested by 32 teams. The runners-up of both Group 1 and 5 played in a play-off for 1 place in the final tournament, while the runners-up of Group 7 advanced to the Intercontinental play-offs against the winner from Oceania;
- South America: 4, contested by 10 teams;
- North, Central America and Caribbean: 1 place, contested by 17 teams.
- Africa: 2 place, contested by 29 teams.
- Asia: 2 places, contested by 27 teams.
- Oceania: 0.5 places, contested by 4 teams (including Israel and Chinese Taipei).

A total of 110 teams played at least one in the qualifiers. Three teams qualified for the first time for the World Cup finals: Canada, Denmark and Iraq.

# EUROPE

## GROUP 1

| Date | Venue | Match | Result |
|---|---|---|---|
| 17.10.1984 | Bruxelles | Belgium - Albania | 3-1(0-0) |
| 17.10.1984 | Zabrze | Poland - Greece | 3-1(0-1) |
| 31.10.1984 | Mielec | Poland - Albania | 2-2(1-0) |
| 19.12.1984 | Athína | Greece - Belgium | 0-0 |
| 22.12.1984 | Tiranë | Albania - Belgium | 2-0(0-0) |
| 27.02.1985 | Athína | Greece - Albania | 2-0(2-0) |
| 27.03.1985 | Bruxelles | Belgium - Greece | 2-0(0-0) |
| 01.05.1985 | Bruxelles | Belgium - Poland | 2-0(1-0) |
| 19.05.1985 | Athína | Greece - Poland | 1-4(0-1) |
| 30.05.1985 | Tiranë | Albania - Poland | 0-1(0-1) |
| 11.09.1985 | Chorzów | Poland - Belgium | 0-0 |
| 30.10.1985 | Tiranë | Albania - Greece | 1-1(1-0) |

### FINAL STANDINGS

| | | | | | | | | | |
|---|---|---|---|---|---|---|---|---|---|
| 1. | **Poland** | 6 | 3 | 2 | 1 | 10 | - | 6 | 8 |
| 2. | *Belgium* | 6 | 3 | 2 | 1 | 7 | - | 3 | 8 |
| 3. | Albania | 6 | 1 | 2 | 3 | 6 | - | 9 | 4 |
| 4. | Greece | 6 | 1 | 2 | 3 | 5 | - | 10 | 4 |

Poland qualified for the Final Tournament.
Belgium qualified for the Play-offs against the runners-up from Group 5.

17.10.1984, Stade Heysel, Bruxelles; Attendance: 11,000
Referee: Arto Ravander (Finland)
**BELGIUM - ALBANIA** 3-1(0-0)
**BEL:** Jacques Munaron, Georges Grün, Dirk De Vriese, Michel Renquin, Michel De Wolf, Frank Vercauteren, René Vandereycken, Vincenzo Scifo, Léo Vander Elst (54.Marc Degryse), Nicolaas Pieter Claesen, Alexander Czerniatynski (79.Edouard Voordeckers). Trainer: Guy Thys.
**ALB:** Perlat Musta, Hysen Zmijani, Skënder Hodja, Muhedin Targaj (62.Kristaq Eksarko), Bedri Omuri, Haxhi Ballgjini, Sulejman Demollari, Shkëlqim Muça, Mirel Josa, Arben Minga, Agustin Kola (62.Ilir Lame). Trainer: Shyqyri Rreli.
**Goals:** 1-0 Nicolaas Pieter Claesen (59), 1-1 Bedri Omuri (72), 2-1 Vincenzo Scifo (84), 3-1 Edouard Voordeckers (88).

17.10.1984, Stadion Górnik, Zabrze; Attendance: 20,000
Referee: Svein Inge Thime (Norway)
**POLAND - GREECE** 3-1(0-1)
**POL:** Jacek Kazimierski, Dariusz Kubicki, Władysław Żmuda (Cap), Dariusz Wdowczyk, Roman Wójcicki, Andrzej Pałasz (83.Waldemar Matysik), Zbigniew Boniek, Jerzy Wijas, Andrzej Buncol (46.Jan Karaś), Dariusz Dziekanowski, Włodzimierz Smolarek. Trainer: Antoni Piechniczek.
**GRE:** Nikolaos Sarganis, Pétros Xanthopoulos, Nikolaos Karoulias, Pétros Mihos (87.Giánnis Dintsikos), Giórgos Mitsibonas, Giórgos Semertzidis, Nikolaos Vamvakoulas (75.Hrístos Ardizoglou), Polívios Hatzopoulos, Nikolaos Anastopoulos (Cap), Anastásios Mitropoulos, Sávvas Kofidis. Trainer: Miltos Papapostolou.
**Goals:** 0-1 Anastásios Mitropoulos (35), 1-1 Włodzimierz Smolarek (62), 2-1 Dariusz Dziekanowski (65), 3-1 Dariusz Dziekanowski (79).

31.10.1984, Stadion Stal, Mielec; Attendance: 25,000
Referee: Bruno Galler (Switzerland)
**POLAND - ALBANIA** 2-2(1-0)
**POL:** Jacek Kazimierski, Dariusz Kubicki, Władysław Żmuda (Cap), Roman Wójcicki (76.Marek Dziuba), Dariusz Wdowczyk, Kazimierz Buda (70.Ryszard Komornicki), Zbigniew Boniek, Waldemar Matysik, Andrzej Pałasz, Włodzimierz Smolarek, Dariusz Dziekanowski. Trainer: Antoni Piechniczek.
**ALB:** Perlat Musta, Ferit Rragami, Muhedin Targaj, Skënder Hodja, Bedri Omuri, Haxhi Ballgjini (60.Ilir Lame; 89.Kristaq Eksarko), Sulejman Demollari, Shkëlqim Muça, Mirel Josa, Arben Minga, Agustin Kola. Trainer: Shyqyri Rreli.
**Goals:** 1-0 Włodzimierz Smolarek (23), 1-1 Bedri Omuri (54), 1-2 Agustin Kola (76), 2-2 Andrzej Pałasz (80).

19.12.1984, Olympiako „Spiros Louis" Stádio, Athína; Attendance: 15,000
Referee: Heinz Fahnler (Austria)
**GREECE - BELGIUM** 0-0
**GRE:** Nikolaos Sarganis, Pétros Xanthopoulos, Nikolaos Karoulias, Stélios Manolas, Giánnis Kyrástas, Nikolaos Alavantas, Dimítris Saravakos, Nikolaos Vamvakoulas (80.Giórgos Kostikos), Nikolaos Anastopoulos (Cap), Anastásios Mitropoulos, Apóstolos Papaïoánnou. Trainer: Miltos Papapostolou.
**BEL:** Jean-Marie Pfaff, Georges Grün, Eddy Jaspers, Frank Richard Vander Elst, Michel Renquin, Michel De Groote, Vincenzo Scifo, Jan Ceulemans, Frank Vercauteren, Nicolaas Pieter Claesen, Alexander Czerniatynski (62.Edouard Voordeckers). Trainer: Guy Thys.

22.12.1984, Stadiumi „Qemal Stafa", Tiranë; Attendance: 20,000
Referee: Victoriano Arminio Sánchez (Spain)
**ALBANIA - BELGIUM** **2-0(0-0)**
**ALB:** Perlat Musta, Hysen Zmijani, Skënder Hodja, Muhedin Targaj, Adnan Ocelli, Ferit Rragami, Sulejman Demollari, Shkëlqim Muça (88.Arben Vila), Mirel Josa, Arben Minga, Agustin Kola. Trainer: Shyqyri Rreli.
**BEL:** Jean-Marie Pfaff, Georges Grün, Frank Richard Vander Elst, Michel De Groote, Eddy Jaspers, Michel Renquin, Vincenzo Scifo (46.Léo Albert Clijsters), Frank Vercauteren, Jan Ceulemans, Nicolaas Pieter Claesen, Alexander Czerniatynski (60.Edouard Voordeckers). Trainer: Guy Thys.
**Goals:** 1-0 Mirel Josa (69), 2-0 Arben Minga (86).

27.02.1985, Olympiako „Spiros Louis" Stádio, Athína; Attendance: 20,000
Referee: Ion Igna (Romania)
**GREECE - ALBANIA** **2-0(2-0)**
**GRE:** Nikolaos Sarganis, Nikolaos Alavantas, Nikolaos Karoulias, Giánnis Kyrástas, Stélios Manolas, Pétros Mihos, Dimítris Saravakos (85.Konstantinos Batsinilas), Konstantinos Antoniou, Nikolaos Anastopoulos (Cap), Apóstolos Papaïoánnou (89.Giórgos Semertzidis), Sávvas Kofidis. Trainer: Miltos Papapostolou.
**ALB:** Perlat Musta, Hysen Zmijani, Skënder Hodja (46.Arian Hametaj), Adnan Ocelli, Sulejman Demollari, Muhedin Targaj, Mirel Josa, Shkëlqim Muça, Haxhi Ballgjini (60.Ferit Rragami), Arben Minga, Agustin Kola. Trainer: Shyqyri Rreli.
**Goals:** 1-0 Dimítris Saravakos (9), 2-0 Konstantinos Antoniou (37).

27.03.1985, Stade Heysel, Bruxelles; Attendance: 41,500
Referee: Keith Stuart Hackett (England)
**BELGIUM - GREECE** **2-0(0-0)**
**BEL:** Jean-Marie Pfaff, Georges Grün, Michel Renquin, Gérard Plessers, Michel De Wolf, Vincenzo Scifo, René Vandereycken, Jan Ceulemans, Frank Vercauteren, Edouard Voordeckers, Erwin Vandenbergh. Trainer: Guy Thys.
**GRE:** Nikolaos Sarganis, Nikolaos Alavantas, Nikolaos Karoulias, Giánnis Kyrástas, Stélios Manolas, Pétros Mihos, Dimítris Saravakos (77.Athanásios Dimopoulos), Nikolaos Anastopoulos (Cap), Anastásios Mitropoulos, Apóstolos Papaïoánnou, Konstantinos Antoniou (29.Sávvas Kofidis). Trainer: Miltos Papapostolou.
**Goals:** 1-0 Frank Vercauteren (69), 2-0 Vincenzo Scifo (89).

01.05.1985, Stade Heysel, Bruxelles; Attendance: 48,310
Referee: Malcolm Moffatt (Northern Ireland)
**BELGIUM - POLAND** **2-0(1-0)**
**BEL:** Jacques Munaron, Georges Grün, Frank Richard Vander Elst, Michel Renquin, Gérard Plessers, Vincenzo Scifo (82.Léo Albert Clijsters), Jan Ceulemans, René Vandereycken, Frank Vercauteren (81.Raymond Mommens), Erwin Vandenbergh. Edouard Voordeckers. Trainer: Guy Thys.
**POL:** Józef Młynarczyk, Krzysztof Pawlak, Władysław Żmuda (Cap), Roman Wójcicki, Marek Ostrowski, Andrzej Buncol, Waldemar Matysik, Zbigniew Boniek, Jan Jałocha (46.Ryszard Komornicki), Dariusz Dziekanowski (65.Andrzej Pałasz), Włodzimierz Smolarek. Trainer: Antoni Piechniczek.
**Goals:** 1-0 Erwin Vandenbergh (30), 2-0 Frank Vercauteren (53).

19.05.1985, Olympiako „Spiros Louis" Stádio, Athína; Attendance: 45,000
Referee: Zoran Petrović (Yugoslavia)
**GREECE - POLAND** **1-4(0-1)**
**GRE:** Nikolaos Sarganis, Nikolaos Alavantas, Nikolaos Karoulias (67.Giórgos Skartados), Giánnis Kyrástas, Pétros Mihos, Giórgos Mitsibonas (46.Dimítris Saravakos), Konstantinos Antoniou, Hrístos Dimopoulos, Nikolaos Anastopoulos (Cap), Anastásios Mitropoulos, Apóstolos Papaïoánnou. Trainer: Miltos Papapostolou.
**POL:** Józef Młynarczyk, Krzysztof Pawlak, Roman Wójcicki, Kazimierz Przybyś, Marek Ostrowski, Andrzej Buncol, Waldemar Matysik, Jan Urban, Ryszard Tarasiewicz (15.Dariusz Dziekanowski), Zbigniew Boniek (Cap), Włodzimierz Smolarek. Trainer: Antoni Piechniczek.
**Goals:** 0-1 Włodzimierz Smolarek (25), 1-1 Nikolaos Anastopoulos (47), 1-2 Marek Ostrowski (58), 1-3 Zbigniew Boniek (78), 1-4 Dariusz Dziekanowski (90).

30.05.1985, Stadiumi „Qemal Stafa", Tiranë; Attendance: 20,000
Referee: Iordan Zhezhov (Bulgaria)
**ALBANIA - POLAND** **0-1(0-1)**
**ALB:** Perlat Musta, Hysen Zmijani, Skënder Hodja, Muhedin Targaj, Bedri Omuri, Fatbardh Jera (61.Kristaq Mile), Shkëlqim Muça, Sulejman Demollari (83.Andrea Marko), Mirel Josa, Arben Minga, Agustin Kola. Trainer: Shyqyri Rreli.
**POL:** Józef Młynarczyk, Krzysztof Pawlak, Roman Wójcicki, Kazimierz Przybyś, Marek Ostrowski, Andrzej Buncol, Waldemar Matysik, Jan Urban (88.Ryszard Tarasiewicz), Dariusz Dziekanowski, Zbigniew Boniek (Cap), Włodzimierz Smolarek. Trainer: Antoni Piechniczek.
**Goal:** 0-1 Zbigniew Boniek (24).

11.09.1985, Stadion Śląski, Chorzów; Attendance: 70,000
Referee: Robert Bonar Valentine (Scotland)
**POLAND - BELGIUM** **0-0**
**POL:** Józef Młynarczyk, Krzysztof Pawlak, Marek Ostrowski, Roman Wójcicki, Kazimierz Przybyś, Dariusz Dziekanowski, Waldemar Matysik, Ryszard Komornicki, Jan Urban, Zbigniew Boniek (Cap) (87.Andrzej Buncol), Włodzimierz Smolarek (64.Andrzej Pałasz). Trainer: Antoni Piechniczek.
**BEL:** Jean-Marie Pfaff, Eric Gerets, Frank Richard Vander Elst, Georges Grün (52.Marc Degryse), Michel Renquin, Vincenzo Scifo, Jan Ceulemans, René Vandereycken, Gérard Plessers, Erwin Vandenbergh (73.Léo Albert Clijsters), Edouard Voordeckers. Trainer: Guy Thys.

11.09.1985, Stadiumi „Qemal Stafa", Tiranë; Attendance: 17,000
Referee: Fernando Nazare (Portugal)
**ALBANIA - GREECE** **1-1(1-0)**
**ALB:** Perlat Musta, Hysen Zmijani, Muhedin Targaj, Skënder Hodja, Arian Bimo, Mirel Josa, Sulejman Demollari, Shkëlqim Muça, Bedri Omuri, Arben Minga, Edmond Abazi (46.Agustin Kola). Trainer: Agron Sulaj.
**GRE:** Nikolaos Sarganis, Nikolaos Alavantas, Giórgos Skartados, Stélios Manolas, Pétros Mihos, Konstantinos Mavridis, Pavlos Papaïoánnou (50.Konstantinos Antoniou), Nikolaos Anastopoulos (Cap), Sávvas Kofidis, Apóstolos Papaïoánnou (81.Giórgos Semertzidis), Anastásios Mitropoulos. Trainer: Miltos Papapostolou.
**Goals:** 1-0 Bedri Omuri (26), 1-1 Giórgos Skartados (54).

# GROUP 2

| Date | City | Match | Result |
|---|---|---|---|
| 23.05.1984 | Norrköping | Sweden - Malta | 4-0(2-0) |
| 12.09.1984 | Stockholm | Sweden Portugal | 0-1(0-0) |
| 14.10.1984 | Porto | Portugal - Czechoslovakia | 2-1(1-1) |
| 17.10.1984 | Köln | West Germany - Sweden | 2-0(0-0) |
| 31.10.1984 | Praha | Czechoslovakia - Malta | 4-0(2-0) |
| 14.11.1984 | Lisboa | Portugal - Sweden | 1-3(1-3) |
| 16.12.1984 | La Valletta | Malta - West Germany | 2-3(1-1) |
| 10.02.1985 | La Valletta | Malta - Portugal | 1-3(0-2) |
| 24.02.1985 | Lisboa | Portugal - West Germany | 1-2(0-2) |
| 27.03.1985 | Saarbrücken | West Germany - Malta | 6-0(5-0) |
| 21.04.1985 | La Valletta | Malta - Czechoslovakia | 0-0 |
| 30.04.1985 | Praha | Czechoslovakia - West Germany | 1-5(0-4) |
| 05.06.1985 | Stockholm | Sweden - Czechoslovakia | 2-0(0-0) |
| 25.09.1985 | Stockholm | Sweden - West Germany | 2-2(0-2) |
| 25.09.1985 | Praha | Czechoslovakia - Portugal | 1-0(1-0) |
| 12.10.1985 | Lisboa | Portugal - Malta | 3-2(1-0) |
| 16.10.1985 | Praha | Czechoslovakia - Sweden | 2-1(1-1) |
| 16.10.1985 | Stuttgart | West Germany - Portugal | 0-1(0-0) |
| 17.11.1985 | München | West Germany - Czechoslovakia | 2-2(1-0) |
| 17.11.1985 | La Valletta | Malta - Sweden | 1-2(0-1) |

## FINAL STANDINGS

| | | | | | | | | |
|---|---|---|---|---|---|---|---|---|
| 1. | **West Germany** | 8 | 5 | 2 | 1 | 22 - 9 | 12 |
| 2. | **Portugal** | 8 | 5 | 0 | 3 | 12 - 10 | 10 |
| 3. | Sweden | 8 | 4 | 1 | 3 | 14 - 9 | 9 |
| 4. | Czechoslovakia | 8 | 3 | 2 | 3 | 11 - 12 | 8 |
| 5. | Malta | 8 | 0 | 1 | 7 | 6 - 25 | 1 |

West Germany and Portugal qualified for the Final Tournament.

23.05.1984, Idrottspark Stadion, Norrköping; Attendance: 18,819
Referee: David F.T. Syme (Scotland)
**SWEDEN - MALTA** **4-0(2-0)**
**SWE:** Thomas Ravelli, Ingemar Erlandsson, Glenn Ingvar Hysén, Sven Dahlqvist, Stig Fredriksson, Robert Prytz (56.Sten-Ove Ramberg), Glenn Peter Strömberg, Ulf Eriksson, Tommy Holmgren (61.Hans Holmqvist), Dan Corneliusson, Thomas Sunesson. Trainer: Lars Arnesson.
**MLT:** Raymond Mifsud, John Joseph Aquilina, Alex Azzopardi, Joseph Borg, John Buttigieg, John Holland (Cap), Alfred Azzopardi (Stephen Theuma), Leonard Farrugia, Raymond Vella, Michael Degiorgio, Carmel Muscat (Joseph Gatt). Trainer: Guentcho Dobrev (Bulgaria).
**Goals:** 1-0 Thomas Sunesson (6), 2-0 Dan Corneliusson (39), 3-0 Ingemar Erlandsson (70), 4-0 Thomas Sunesson (76).

12.09.1984, Råsunda Stadion, Stockholm; Attendance: 30,136
Referee: Joël Quiniou (France)
**SWEDEN - PORTUGAL**     **0-1(0-0)**
**SWE:** Bernt Ljung, Ingemar Erlandsson, Glenn Ingvar Hysén, Sven Dahlqvist, Stig Fredriksson, Thomas Bergman (77.Hans Borg), Tord Holmgren, Ulf Eriksson, Tommy Holmgren, Håkan Sandberg, Hans Holmqvist. Trainer: Lars Arnesson.
**POR:** Manuel Galrinho Bento (Cap), João Domingos Silva Pinto, António José Lima Pereira, Eurico Monteiro Gomes, Augusto Soares Inácio, António Manuel Frasco Vieira, Carlos Manuel Correia dos Santos, Jaime Moreira Pacheco, António Augusto Gomes de Silva „Sousa", Fernando Mendes Soares Gomes (89.Paulo Jorge dos Santos Futre), Diamantino Manuel Fernandes Miranda (87.Carlos Manuel Oliveira Silva „Vermelhinho"). Trainer: José Augusto da Costa Séneca Torres.
**Goal**: 0-1 Fernando Mendes Soares Gomes (79).

14.10.1984, Estádio das Antas, Porto; Attendance: 32,500
Referee: George Courtney (England)
**PORTUGAL - CZECHOSLOVAKIA**     **2-1(1-1)**
**POR:** Manuel Galrinho Bento (Cap), João Domingos Silva Pinto, António José Lima Pereira, Eurico Monteiro Gomes, Augusto Soares Inácio, Jaime Fernandes Magalhães, António Manuel Frasco Vieira, Carlos Manuel Correia dos Santos (65.Virgílio Manuel Bagulho Lopes), Jaime Moreira Pacheco, Diamantino Manuel Fernandes Miranda (40.Paulo Jorge dos Santos Futre), Fernando Mendes Soares Gomes. Trainer: José Augusto da Costa Séneca Torres.
**TCH:** Luděk Mikloško, František Jakubec, Jan Fiala (Cap), Zdeněk Prokeš, Petr Rada, Peter Zelenský, Jan Berger, Karel Jarolím, Jiří Ondra (74.Stanislav Levý), Petr Janečka, Ivo Knoflíček (72.Tibor Mičinec). Trainer: Josef Masopust.
**Goals**: 1-0 Diamantino Manuel Fernandes Miranda (13), 1-1 Petr Janečka (39), 2-1 Carlos Manuel Correia dos Santos (48).

17.10.1984, Müngersdorfer Stadion, Köln; Attendance: 61,000
Referee: Robert Bonar Valentine (Scotland)
**WEST GERMANY - SWEDEN**     **2-0(0-0)**
**GER:** Harald Schumacher, Ditmar Jakobs, Matthias Herget, Karlheinz Förster, Hans-Peter Briegel, Andreas Brehme, Lothar Herbert Matthäus, Ralf Falkenmayer (59.Klaus Allofs), Felix Magath (75.Uwe Rahn), Karl-Heinz Rummenigge (Cap), Rudolf Völler. Trainer: Franz Beckenbauer.
**SWE:** Thomas Ravelli, Ingemar Erlandsson (33.Hans Borg), Glenn Ingvar Hysén, Sven Dahlqvist, Stig Fredriksson, Ulf Eriksson, Glenn Peter Strömberg, Tord Holmgren, Tommy Holmgren, Dan Corneliusson (68.Hans Holmqvist), Mats Gren. Trainer: Lars Arnesson.
**Goals**: 1-0 Uwe Rahn (75), 2-0 Karl-Heinz Rummenigge (88).

31.10.1984, Stadion Strahov, Praha; Attendance: 5,500
Referee: Gudmundur Haraldsson (Iceland)
**CZECHOSLOVAKIA - MALTA**     **4-0(2-0)**
**TCH:** Luděk Mikloško, František Straka, Jan Fiala (Cap), Jiří Ondra, Stanislav Levý (78.František Jakubec), Karel Jarolím, Jan Berger, Petr Zajaroš, Ladislav Vízek, Stanislav Griga (78.Tibor Mičinec), Petr Janečka. Trainer: Josef Masopust.
**MLT:** Raymond Mifsud, John Joseph Aquilina, Martin Scicluna, John Holland (Cap), John Buttigieg, Alfred Azzopardi (46.Alex Azzopardi), Leonard Farrugia, Raymond Vella, Carmel Muscat (80.Dennis Mizzi), Joseph Gatt, Michael Degiorgio. Trainer: Guentcho Dobrev (Bulgaria).
**Goals**: 1-0 Petr Janečka (4), 2-0 Karel Jarolím (35), 3-0 Petr Janečka (71), 4-0 Jan Berger (77 penalty).

14.11.1984, Estádio „José Alvalade", Lisboa; Attendance: 45,000
Referee: Roger Schoeters (Belgium)
**PORTUGAL - SWEDEN** **1-3(1-3)**
**POR:** Manuel Galrinho Bento (Cap), João Domingos Silva Pinto, António José Lima Pereira, Eurico Monteiro Gomes, Augusto Soares Inácio (78.António Augusto Gomes de Silva „Sousa"), Jaime Fernandes Magalhães, Carlos Manuel Correia dos Santos, António Manuel Frasco Vieira (46.Paulo Jorge dos Santos Futre), Diamantino Manuel Fernandes Miranda, Fernando Mendes Soares Gomes, Rui Manuel Trindade Jordão. Trainer: José Augusto da Costa Séneca Torres.
**SWE:** Thomas Ravelli, Ingemar Erlandsson (Cap), Glenn Ingvar Hysén, Sven Dahlqvist, Stig Fredriksson, Robert Prytz, Glenn Peter Strömberg, Peter Larsson (69.Tord Holmgren), Tommy Holmgren (88.Ulf Eriksson), Torbjörn Nilsson, Mats Gren. Trainer: Lars Arnesson.
**Goals:** 1-0 Rui Manuel Trindade Jordão (12), 1-1 Robert Prytz (25 penalty), 1-2 Robert Prytz (35), 1-3 Torbjörn Nilsson (37).

16.12.1984, National Stadium, Ta'Qali; Attendance: 30,202
Referee: Zoran Petrović (Yugoslavia)
**MALTA - WEST GERMANY** **2-3(1-1)**
**MLT:** Raymond Mifsud, John Joseph Aquilina, Martin Scicluna, George Xuereb, John Holland (Cap) (12.Alfred Azzopardi), Michael Woods, Carmel Busuttil, Raymond Vella, Carmel Muscat (61.Joseph Gatt), Raymond Xuereb, Michael Degiorgio. Trainer: Guentcho Dobrev (Bulgaria).
**GER:** Harald Schumacher, Karlheinz Förster, Matthias Herget, Ditmar Jakobs (46.Olaf Thon), Lothar Herbert Matthäus, Uwe Rahn, Andreas Brehme, Hans-Peter Briegel, Karl-Heinz Rummenigge (Cap), Rudolf Völler, Klaus Allofs. Trainer: Franz Beckenbauer.
**Goals:** 1-0 Carmel Busuttil (10), 1-1 Karlheinz Förster (43), 1-2 Klaus Allofs (69), 1-3 Klaus Allofs (85), 2-3 Raymond Xuereb (86).

10.02.1985, National Stadium, Ta'Qali; Attendance: 16,338
Referee: Miklós Nagy (Hungary)
**MALTA - PORTUGAL** **1-3(0-2)**
**MLT:** Raymond Mifsud, John Joseph Aquilina (29.Emanuel Farrugia), Martin Scicluna (33.Carmel Muscat), Alfred Azzopardi, Michael Woods, John Buttigieg, Carmel Busuttil, Raymond Vella (Cap), Raymond Xuereb, Leonard Farrugia, Michael Degiorgio. Trainer: Guentcho Dobrev (Bulgaria).
**POR:** Manuel Galrinho Bento (Cap), João Domingos Silva Pinto, António José Lima Pereira, Eurico Monteiro Gomes, Augusto Soares Inácio, António Manuel Frasco Vieira (82.Virgílio Manuel Bagulho Lopes), António dos Santos Ferreira André, Carlos Manuel Correia dos Santos, Jaime Fernandes Magalhães, Fernando Mendes Soares Gomes, Paulo Jorge dos Santos Futre (80.Diamantino Manuel Fernandes Miranda). Trainer: José Augusto da Costa Séneca Torres.
**Goals:** 0-1 Carlos Manuel Correia dos Santos (6), 0-2 Fernando Mendes Soares Gomes (13), 1-2 Leonard Farrugia (59), 1-3 Fernando Mendes Soares Gomes (73).

24.02.1985, Estádio Nacional, Lisboa; Attendance: 60,000
Referee: Paolo Casarin (Italy)
**PORTUGAL - WEST GERMANY** **1-2(0-2)**
**POR:** Manuel Galrinho Bento (Cap), João Domingos Silva Pinto, António José Lima Pereira (78.António Augusto Gomes de Silva „Sousa"), Eurico Monteiro Gomes, Augusto Soares Inácio, António dos Santos Ferreira André (46.Diamantino Manuel Fernandes Miranda), Jaime Fernandes Magalhães, Carlos Manuel Correia dos Santos, Jaime Moreira Pacheco, Fernando Mendes Soares Gomes, Paulo Jorge dos Santos Futre. Trainer: José Augusto da Costa Séneca Torres.
**GER:** Harald Schumacher (Cap), Thomas Berthold, Matthias Herget, Ditmar Jakobs, Michael Frontzeck, Lothar Herbert Matthäus, Felix Magath, Hans-Peter Briegel, Ralf Falkenmayer, Pierre Littbarski, Rudolf Völler. Trainer: Franz Beckenbauer.
**Goals:** 0-1 Pierre Littbarski (28), 0-2 Rudolf Völler (37), 1-2 Diamantino Manuel Fernandes Miranda (59).

27.03.1985, Ludwigspark Stadion, Saarbrücken; Attendance: 37,600
Referee: Talat Tokat (Turkey)
**WEST GERMANY - MALTA**             **6-0(5-0)**
**GER:** Harald Schumacher, Thomas Berthold, Matthias Herget, Karlheinz Förster, Michael Frontzeck, Uwe Rahn (67.Olaf Thon), Felix Magath, Hans-Peter Briegel (77.Andreas Brehme), Pierre Littbarski, Rudolf Völler, Karl-Heinz Rummenigge (Cap). Trainer: Franz Beckenbauer.
**MLT:** John Bonello, Alfred Azzopardi, Emanuel Farrugia (57.John Joseph Aquilina), Michael Woods, John Holland (Cap), John Buttigieg, Carmel Busuttil, Raymond Vella, Dennis Mizzi (Raymond Xuereb), Leonard Farrugia, Michael Degiorgio. Trainer: Guentcho Dobrev (Bulgaria).
**Goals**: 1-0 Uwe Rahn (10), 2-0 Felix Magath (13), 3-0 Uwe Rahn (17), 4-0 Pierre Littbarski (18), 5-0 Karl-Heinz Rummenigge (44), 6-0 Karl-Heinz Rummenigge (66).

21.04.1985, National Stadium, Ta'Qali; Attendance: 7,320
Referee: Victoriano Sánchez Arminio (Spain)
**MALTA - CZECHOSLOVAKIA**             **0-0**
**MLT:** John Bonello, John Joseph Aquilina, Alex Azzopardi, Michael Woods, John Holland (Cap), John Buttigieg, Carmel Busuttil (46.George Xuereb), Raymond Vella, Raymond Xuereb (Dennis Mizzi), Leonard Farrugia, Alfred Azzopardi. Trainer: Guentcho Dobrev (Bulgaria).
**TCH:** Vladimír Borovička, Ivan Hašek, Jan Fiala (Cap), Zdeněk Prokeš, Jozef Kukučka, Pavel Chaloupka (74.Peter Zelenský), Jan Berger, Jiří Sloup, Petr Janečka, Stanislav Griga, Ivo Knoflíček (74.Tibor Mičinec). Trainer: Josef Masopust.

30.04.1985, Stadion Strahov, Praha; Attendance: 35,000
Referee: Joël Quiniou (France)
**CZECHOSLOVAKIA - WEST GERMANY**             **1-5(0-4)**
**TCH:** Vladimír Borovička, Ivan Hašek, Zdeněk Prokeš, Jan Fiala (Cap), Jozef Kukučka, Pavel Chaloupka (64.Peter Zelenský), Jan Berger, Jiří Sloup (46.Jozef Chovanec), Ladislav Vízek, Stanislav Griga, Petr Janečka. Trainer: Josef Masopust.
**GER:** Harald Schumacher (Cap), Thomas Berthold, Ditmar Jakobs, Karlheinz Förster, Andreas Brehme, Matthias Herget, Lothar Herbert Matthäus (82.Olaf Thon), Felix Magath, Uwe Rahn (70.Klaus Allofs), Pierre Littbarski, Rudolf Völler. Trainer: Franz Beckenbauer.
**Goals**: 0-1 Thomas Berthold (8), 0-2 Pierre Littbarski (22), 0-3 Lothar Herbert Matthäus (37), 0-4 Matthias Herget (43), 0-5 Klaus Allofs (82), 1-5 Stanislav Griga (88).

05.06.1985, Råsunda Stadion, Stockholm; Attendance: 33,981
Referee: Eamonn A. Farrell (Republic of Ireland)
**SWEDEN - CZECHOSLOVAKIA**             **2-0(0-0)**
**SWE:** Thomas Ravelli, Andreas Ravelli, Sven Dahlqvist, Glenn Ingvar Hysén, Stig Fredriksson, Robert Prytz, Ingemar Erlandsson, Glenn Peter Strömberg, Jan Svensson, Peter Truedsson (70.Lars Larsson), Torbjörn Nilsson. Trainer: Lars Arnesson.
**TCH:** Luděk Mikloško, Aleš Bažant, Jan Berger, František Straka, Jan Fiala (Cap), Stanislav Pelc (74.Marián Brezina), Luboš Kubík, Jozef Chovanec, Karel Kula, Ladislav Vízek, Vladimír Hruška. Trainer: Josef Masopust.
**Goals**: 1-0 Robert Prytz (77 penalty), 2-0 Lars Larsson (85).

25.09.1985, Råsunda Stadion, Stockholm; Attendance: 39,157
Referee: Marcel Van Langenhove (Belgium)
**SWEDEN - WEST GERMANY**             **2-2(0-2)**
**SWE:** Thomas Ravelli, Ingemar Erlandsson, Glenn Ingvar Hysén, Sven Dahlqvist, Stig Fredriksson, Robert Prytz, Glenn Peter Strömberg, Jan Svensson (75.Hans Holmqvist), Andreas Ravelli (88.Mats Magnusson), Torbjörn Nilsson, Dan Corneliusson. Trainer: Lars Arnesson.
**GER:** Harald Schumacher, Thomas Berthold, Klaus Augenthaler, Karlheinz Förster, Andreas Brehme, Ditmar Jakobs, Matthias Herget, Hans-Peter Briegel, Pierre Littbarski, Rudolf Völler, Karl-Heinz Rummenigge (Cap). Trainer: Franz Beckenbauer.
**Goals**: 0-1 Rudolf Völler (23), 0-2 Matthias Herget (40), 1-2 Dan Corneliusson (63), 2-2 Mats

Magnusson (90).

25.09.1985, Stadion Strahov, Praha; Attendance: 9,000
Referee: Damir Matovinović (Yugoslavia)
**CZECHOSLOVAKIA - PORTUGAL** **1-0(1-0)**
**TCH:** Luděk Mikloško, Jozef Chovanec, Ivan Hašek, František Straka, Jiří Ondra, Pavel Chaloupka (58.Tibor Mičinec), Jan Berger, Karel Kula, Ladislav Vízek (Cap), Stanislav Griga (77.Vlastimil Lauda), Vladimír Hruška. Trainer: Josef Masopust.
**POR:** Manuel Galrinho Bento (Cap), João Domingos Silva Pinto, Frederico Nobre Rosa, Pedro Manuel Regateiro Venâncio, Augusto Soares Inácio, José Luís Lopes da Costa e Silva, Carlos Manuel Correia dos Santos, António dos Santos Ferreira André, António Augusto Gomes de Silva „Sousa" (46.José Joaquim Pimentel Ribeiro), Paulo Jorge dos Santos Futre (65.Pedro Alexandre Marques Caldas Xavier), Fernando Mendes Soares Gomes. Trainer: José Augusto da Costa Séneca Torres.
**Goal:** 1-0 Vladimír Hruška (21).

12.10.1985, Estádio da Luz, Lisboa; Attendance: 15,000
Referee: Alan Snoddy (Northern Ireland)
**PORTUGAL - MALTA** **3-2(1-0)**
**POR:** Manuel Galrinho Bento (Cap), João Domingos Silva Pinto, Frederico Nobre Rosa, Pedro Manuel Regateiro Venâncio, Álvaro Magalhães, Luís Filipe Vieira de Carvalho „Litos", Carlos Manuel Correia dos Santos, Jaime Moreira Pacheco, Rui Manuel Lima Correia Palhares (46.Jaime Jerónimo das Mercês), Rui Manuel Trindade Jordão (46.José António Silvestre Rafael), Fernando Mendes Soares Gomes. Trainer: José Augusto da Costa Séneca Torres.
**MLT:** John Bonello, John Buttigieg, John Joseph Aquilina, Michael Woods, John Holland (Cap), Alex Azzopardi, Raymond Vella (George Xuereb), Carmel Busuttil, Charles Scerri, Martin Gregory (51.Michael Degiorgio), Leonard Farrugia. Trainer: Guentcho Dobrev (Bulgaria).
**Goals:** 1-0 Fernando Mendes Soares Gomes (38), 1-1 Frederico Nobre Rosa (46 own goal), 2-1 José António Silvestre Rafael (53), 2-2 Michael Degiorgio (79), 3-2 Fernando Mendes Soares Gomes (82).

16.10.1985, Stadion Strahov, Praha; Attendance: 11,500
Referee: George Sandoz (Switzerland)
**CZECHOSLOVAKIA - SWEDEN** **2-1(1-1)**
**TCH:** Luděk Mikloško, Stanislav Levý, Jozef Chovanec, František Straka, Jiří Ondra, Ivan Hašek, Jan Berger, Karel Kula, Ladislav Vízek (Cap), Vlastimil Lauda (73.Milan Luhový), Tibor Mičinec (80.Josef Novák II). Trainer: Josef Masopust.
**SWE:** Thomas Ravelli, Ingemar Erlandsson, Glenn Ingvar Hysén, Sven Dahlqvist, Stig Fredriksson, Andreas Ravelli (65.Hans Holmqvist), Robert Prytz, Glenn Peter Strömberg, Jan Svensson (72.Mats Magnusson), Torbjörn Nilsson, Dan Corneliusson. Trainer: Lars Arnesson.
**Goals:** 0-1 Dan Corneliusson (7), 1-1 Andreas Ravelli (41 own goal), 2-1 Ladislav Vízek (69).

16.10.1985, Neckarstadion, Stuttgart; Attendance: 60,000
Referee: Keith Stuart Hackett (England)
**WEST GERMANY - PORTUGAL** **0-1(0-0)**
**GER:** Harald Schumacher, Thomas Berthold, Ditmar Jakobs (46.Heinz Gründel), Karlheinz Förster, Andreas Brehme, Karl Allgöwer, Matthias Herget, Norbert Meier, Hans-Peter Briegel, Pierre Littbarski (64.Thomas Allofs), Karl-Heinz Rummenigge (Cap). Trainer: Franz Beckenbauer.
**POR:** Manuel Galrinho Bento (Cap), João Domingos Silva Pinto, José António Prudêncio Conde Bargiela, Frederico Nobre Rosa, Pedro Manuel Regateiro Venâncio, Augusto Soares Inácio, António Augusto da Silva Veloso, Carlos Manuel Correia dos Santos (81.Luís Filipe Vieira de Carvalho „Litos"), Jaime Moreira Pacheco, Mário Jorge da Silva Pinho Fernandes, Fernando Mendes Soares Gomes (84.José António Silvestre Rafael). Trainer: José Augusto da Costa Séneca Torres.
**Goal:** 0-1 Carlos Manuel Correia dos Santos (53).

17.11.1985, Olympiastadion, München; Attendance: 18,000
Referee: Svein Inge Thime (Norway)
**WEST GERMANY - CZECHOSLOVAKIA** **2-2(1-0)**
**GER:** Harald Schumacher, Andreas Brehme, Klaus Augenthaler, Karlheinz Förster, Hans-Peter Briegel (46.Michael Frontzeck), Wolfgang Rolff, Karl Allgöwer, Olaf Thon, Pierre Littbarski (80.Uwe Rahn), Karl-Heinz Rummenigge (Cap), Ludwig Kögl. Trainer: Franz Beckenbauer.
**TCH:** Luděk Mikloško, Stanislav Levý, Jozef Chovanec, František Straka, Jiří Ondra, Ivan Hašek, Josef Novák II, Jan Berger, Karel Kula, Ladislav Vízek (Cap), Vlastimil Lauda (73.Milan Luhový). Trainer: Josef Masopust.
**Goals:** 1-0 Andreas Brehme (1), 1-1 Josef Novák II (52), 1-2 Vlastimil Lauda (61), 2-2 Karl-Heinz Rummenigge (86).

17.11.1985, National Stadium, Ta'Qali; Attendance: 6,849
Referee: Yusuf Namoglu (Turkey)
**MALTA - SWEDEN** **1-2(0-1)**
**MLT:** John Bonello, John Joseph Aquilina (60.Edwin Camilleri), Martin Scicluna, Michael Woods, John Holland (Cap), John Buttigieg, Carmel Busuttil, Raymond Vella, Martin Gregory (83.George Xuereb), Leonard Farrugia, Michael Degiorgio. Trainer: Guentcho Dobrev (Bulgaria).
**SWE:** Thomas Wernersson, Andreas Ravelli, Peter Larsson, Sven Dahlqvist, Stig Fredriksson, Ulf Eriksson, Robert Prytz (84.Tord Holmgren), Glenn Peter Strömberg, Håkan Sandberg (80.Lars Larsson), Hans Holmqvist, Tommy Holmgren. Trainer: Lars Arnesson.
**Goals:** 0-1 Robert Prytz (2), 1-1 Leonard Farrugia (65), 1-2 Glenn Peter Strömberg (75).

## GROUP 3

| Date | Venue | Match | Result |
|---|---|---|---|
| 27.05.1984 | Pori | Finland - Northern Ireland | 1-0(0-0) |
| 12.09.1984 | Belfast | Northern Ireland - Romania | 3-2(1-1) |
| 17.10.1984 | London | England - Finland | 5-0(2-0) |
| 31.10.1984 | Antalya | Turkey - Finland | 1-2(0-1) |
| 14.11.1984 | Belfast | Northern Ireland - Finland | 2-1(1-1) |
| 14.11.1984 | Istanbul | Turkey - England | 0-8(0-3) |
| 27.02.1985 | Belfast | Northern Ireland - England | 0-1(0-0) |
| 03.04.1985 | Craiova | Romania - Turkey | 3-0(3-0) |
| 01.05.1985 | Belfast | Northern Ireland - Turkey | 2-0(1-0) |
| 01.05.1985 | Bucureşti | Romania - England | 0-0 |
| 22.05.1985 | Helsinki | Finland - England | 1-1(1-0) |
| 06.06.1985 | Helsinki | Finland - Romania | 1-1(1-1) |
| 28.08.1985 | Timişoara | Romania - Finland | 2-0(1-0) |
| 11.09.1985 | Izmir | Turkey - Northern Ireland | 0-0 |
| 11.09.1985 | London | England - Romania | 1-1(1-0) |
| 25.09.1985 | Tampere | Finland - Turkey | 1-0(1-0) |
| 16.10.1985 | London | England - Turkey | 5-0(4-0) |
| 16.10.1985 | Bucureşti | Romania - Northern Ireland | 0-1(0-1) |
| 13.11.1985 | Izmir | Turkey - Romania | 1-3(0-2) |
| 13.11.1985 | London | England - Northern Ireland | 0-0 |

### FINAL STANDINGS

| | | | | | | | | | |
|---|---|---|---|---|---|---|---|---|---|
| 1. | **England** | 8 | 4 | 4 | 0 | 21 | - | 2 | 12 |
| 2. | **Northern Ireland** | 8 | 4 | 2 | 2 | 8 | - | 5 | 10 |
| 3. | Romania | 8 | 3 | 3 | 2 | 12 | - | 7 | 9 |
| 4. | Finland | 8 | 3 | 2 | 3 | 7 | - | 12 | 8 |
| 5. | Turkey | 8 | 0 | 1 | 7 | 2 | - | 24 | 1 |

England and Northern Ireland qualified for the Final Tournament.

27.05.1984, Porin Stadion, Pori; Attendance: 8,000
Referee: Karl-Heinz Tritschler (Germany)
**FINLAND - NORTHERN IRELAND**                     **1-0(0-0)**
**FIN:** Olavi Huttunen, Esa Pekonen, Pauno Kymäläinen, Jukka Ikäläinen (48.Jari Europaeus), Erkka Petäjä, Hannu Turunen, Leo Houtsonen, Kari Ukkonen, Jari Rantanen, Pasi Rautiainen, Ari Valvee. Trainer: Martti Kuusela.
**NIR:** Patrick Anthony Jennings, James Michael Nicholl, John McClelland, Gerard McElhinney, Malachy Martin Donaghy, Martin Hugh Michael O'Neill (Cap), Samuel Baxter McIlroy (78.Nigel Worthington), Gerard Joseph Armstrong (64.George Terence Cochrane), William Robert Hamilton, Norman Whiteside, Ian Edwin Stewart. Manager: William Laurence Bingham.
**Goal:** 1-0 Ari Valvee (55).

12.09.1984, Windsor Park, Belfast; Attendance: 26,000
Referee: Alexis Ponnet (Belgium)
**NORTHERN IRELAND - ROMANIA** 3-2(1-1)
**NIR:** Patrick Anthony Jennings, James Michael Nicholl, John McClelland, Gerard McElhinney, Malachy Martin Donaghy, Gerard Joseph Armstrong, Martin Hugh Michael O'Neill (Cap), David McCreery, Ian Edwin Stewart, William Robert Hamilton, Norman Whiteside. Trainer: William Laurence Bingham.
**ROU:** Silviu Lung, Mircea Rednic, Gino Iorgulescu, Costică Ştefănescu (Cap), Nicolae Ungureanu, Aurel Ţicleanu (81.Lică Movilă), Ioan Andone, Michael Klein, Mircea Irimescu (72.Ion Geolgău), Ionel Augustin, Gheorghe Hagi. Trainer: Mircea Lucescu.
**Goals:** 1-0 Gino Iorgulescu (34 own goal), 1-1 Gheorghe Hagi (36), 2-1 Norman Whiteside (66), 3-1 Martin Hugh Michael O'Neill (72), 3-2 Ion Geolgău (80).

17.10.1984, Wembley Stadium, London; Attendance: 47,234
Referee: Aleksander Suchanek (Poland)
**ENGLAND - FINLAND** 5-0(2-0)
**ENG:** Peter Leslie Shilton, Michael Duxburyy (46.Gary Andrew Stevens), Kenneth Graham Sansom, Steven Charles Williams, Mark Wright, Terence Ian Butcher, Bryan Robson (Cap) (75.Mark Valentine Chamberlain), Raymond Colin Wilkins, Mark Wayne Hateley, Anthony Stewart Woodcock, John Charles Bryan Barnes. Manager: Robert William Robson.
**FIN:** Olavi Huttunen, Esa Pekonen, Pauno Kymäläinen (Cap), Aki Lahtinen, Erkka Petäjä, Kai Haaskivi (46.Hannu Turunen), Leo Houtsonen, Kari Ukkonen, Jukka Ikäläinen, Pasi Rautiainen, Ari Valvee (70.Ari Hjelm). Trainer: Martti Kuusela.
**Goals:** 1-0 Mark Wayne Hateley (29), 2-0 Mark Wayne Hateley (49), 3-0 Anthony Stewart Woodcock (40), 4-0 Bryan Robson (70), 5-0 Kenneth Graham Sansom (85).

31.10.1984, "Kemal Atatürk" Stadı, Antalya; Attendance: 10,000
Referee: Velodi Miminoshvili (Soviet Union)
**TURKEY - FINLAND** 1-2(0-1)
**TUR:** Arif Peçenek, İsmail Kartal, Abdülkerim Durmaz, Muharrem Gürbüz, Cem Pamiroğlu, Riza Çalımbay (71.Müjdat Yetkiner), Raşit Çetiner, İlyas Tüfekçi, Aykut Yiğit (46.Rıdvan Dilmen), Hasan Şengün, Ali Erdal Keser. Trainer: Candan Tarhan.
**FIN:** Olavi Huttunen, Aki Lahtinen, Pauno Kymäläinen (Cap), Jukka Ikäläinen, Esa Pekonen, Hannu Turunen, Kari Virtanen, Kari Ukkonen, Leo Houtsonen, Mika Lipponen, Ari Hjelm (86.Ismo Lius). Trainer: Martti Kuusela.
**Goals:** 0-1 Ari Hjelm (10), 0-2 Mika Lipponen (65), 1-2 İlyas Tüfekçi (77 penalty).

14.11.1984, Windsor Park, Belfast; Attendance: 22,000
Referee: Alder Dante da Silva dos Santos (Portugal)
**NORTHERN IRELAND - FINLAND** 2-1(1-1)
**NIR:** Patrick Anthony Jennings, James Michael Nicholl, John Patrick O'Neill, John McClelland, Malachy Martin Donaghy, Martin Hugh Michael O'Neill (Cap), Samuel Baxter McIlroy, Gerard Joseph Armstrong, James Martin Quinn, Norman Whiteside, Ian Edwin Stewart. Manager: William Laurence Bingham.
**FIN:** Olavi Huttunen, Aki Lahtinen, Pauno Kymäläinen, Jari Europaeus, Esa Pekonen, Hannu Turunen, Leo Houtsonen, Kari Ukkonen, Jukka Ikäläinen, Mika Lipponen, Ari Hjelm. Trainer: Martti Kuusela.
**Goals:** 0-1 Mika Lipponen (20), 1-1 John Patrick O'Neill (42), 2-1 Gerard Joseph Armstrong (50 penalty).

14.11.1984, Ismet İnönü Stadı, Istanbul; Attendance: 40,000
Referee: Vojtěch Christov (Czechoslovakia)
**TURKEY - ENGLAND**                                                              **0-8(0-3)**
**TUR:** Yaşar Duran, İsmail Kartal, Yusuf Altıntaş, Kemal Serdar, Cem Pamiroğlu, Raşit Çetiner, Müjdat Yetkiner, Ahmet Keloğlu, İlyas Tüfekçi (46.Tuncay Soyak), Rıdvan Dilmen, Ali Erdal Keser. Trainer: Candan Tarhan.
**ENG:** Peter Leslie Shilton, Vivian Alexander Anderson, Kenneth Graham Sansom, Steven Charles Williams (69.Gary Andrew Stevens), Mark Wright, Terence Ian Butcher, Bryan Robson (Cap), Raymond Colin Wilkins, Peter Withe, Anthony Stewart Woodcock (69.Trevor John Francis), John Charles Bryan Barnes. Manager: Robert William Robson.
**Goals:** 0-1 Bryan Robson (13), 0-2 Anthony Stewart Woodcock (17), 0-3 Bryan Robson (44), 0-4 John Charles Bryan Barnes (48), 0-5 John Charles Bryan Barnes (53), 0-6 Bryan Robson (58), 0-7 Anthony Stewart Woodcock (61), 0-8 Vivian Alexander Anderson (87).

27.02.1985, Windsor Park, Belfast; Attendance: 28,500
Referee: Volker Roth (West Germany)
**NORTHERN IRELAND - ENGLAND**                              **0-1(0-0)**
**NIR:** Patrick Anthony Jennings, James Michael Nicholl, John McClelland, John Patrick O'Neill, Malachy Martin Donaghy, Samuel Baxter McIlroy (Cap), Paul Christopher Ramsey, Gerard Joseph Armstrong, Ian Edwin Stewart, James Martin Quinn, Norman Whiteside. Manager: William Laurence Bingham.
**ENG:** Peter Leslie Shilton, Vivian Alexander Anderson, Kenneth Graham Sansom, Alvin Edward Martin, Terence Ian Butcher, Trevor McGregor Steven, Raymond Colin Wilkins (Cap), Gary Andrew Stevens, Anthony Stewart Woodcock (78.Trevor John Francis), Mark Wayne Hateley, John Charles Bryan Barnes. Manager: Robert William Robson.
**Goal:** 0-1 Mark Wayne Hateley (77).

03.04.1985, Stadionul Central, Craiova; Attendance: 35,000
Referee: Itzhak Ben-Itzhak (Israel)
**ROMANIA - TURKEY**                                                         **3-0(3-0)**
**ROU:** Silviu Lung, Nicolae Negrilă, Gino Iorgulescu, Costică Ştefănescu (Cap), Nicolae Ungureanu, Mircea Rednic, Dorin Mateuţ, Mircea Irimescu (71.Ilie Balaci), Gheorghe Hagi, Marcel Coraş (75.Marius Lăcătuş), Rodion Gorun Cămătaru. Trainer: Mircea Lucescu.
**TUR:** Arif Peçenek, Müjdat Yetkiner, Semih Yuvakuran, Kemal Serdar, Abdülkerim Durmaz, Yusuf Altıntaş, Metin Tekin, Hüseyin Çakıroğlu, Rıdvan Dilmen, Selçuk Yula (75.İskender Gönen), Şenol Ustaömer (64.Hasan Şengün). Trainer: Yılmaz Gökdel.
**Goals:** 1-0 Gheorghe Hagi (21), 2-0 Rodion Gorun Cămătaru (28), 3-0 Rodion Gorun Cămătaru (42).

01.05.1985, Windsor Park, Belfast; Attendance: 16,000
Referee: Bruno Galler (Switzerland)
**NORTHERN IRELAND - TURKEY**                               **2-0(1-0)**
**NIR:** Patrick Anthony Jennings, James Michael Nicholl, John McClelland, John Patrick O'Neill, Malachy Martin Donaghy, Samuel Baxter McIlroy (Cap), Paul Christopher Ramsey, Noel Brotherston, Norman Whiteside, James Martin Quinn, Ian Edwin Stewart. Manager: William Laurence Bingham.
**TUR:** Erhan Arslan, İsmail Demiriz, Hasan Kemal Özdemir, Abdülkerim Durmaz, Semih Yuvakuran, İlyas Tüfekçi, Raşit Çetiner, Yusuf Altıntaş, Müjdat Yetkiner, Metin Tekin, Hasan Vezir. Trainer: Kálmán Mészöly (Hungary).
**Goals:** 1-0 Norman Whiteside (45), 2-0 Norman Whiteside (54).

01.05.1985, Stadionul 23 August, Bucureşti; Attendance: 60,000
Referee: Emilio Carlos Guruceta Muro (Spain)
**ROMANIA - ENGLAND** **0-0**
**ROU:** Silviu Lung, Nicolae Negrilă, Gino Iorgulescu (39.Ştefan Iovan), Costică Ştefănescu (Cap), Nicolae Ungureanu, Mircea Rednic, Ladislau Bölöni, Michael Klein, Gheorghe Hagi, Marcel Coraş (78.Marius Lăcătuş), Rodion Gorun Cămătaru. Trainer: Mircea Lucescu.
**ENG:** Peter Leslie Shilton, Vivian Alexander Anderson, Kenneth Graham Sansom, Terence Ian Butcher, Mark Wright, Raymond Colin Wilkins, Bryan Robson (Cap), Trevor McGregor Steven, John Charles Bryan Barnes (72.Christopher Roland Waddle), Paul Mariner (85.Gary Winston Lineker), Trevor John Francis. Manager: Robert William Robson.

22.05.1985, Olympiastadion, Helsinki; Attendance: 30,311
Referee: Siegfried Kirschen (East Germany)
**FINLAND - ENGLAND** **1-1(1-0)**
**FIN:** Olavi Huttunen, Aki Lahtinen (84.Erkka Petäjä), Pauno Kymäläinen (Cap), Jukka Ikäläinen, Jyrki Nieminen, Hannu Turunen, Leo Houtsonen, Kari Ukkonen (78.Ari Hjelm), Mika Lipponen, Pasi Rautiainen, Jari Rantanen. Trainer: Martti Kuusela.
**ENG:** Peter Leslie Shilton, Vivian Alexander Anderson, Kenneth Graham Sansom, Terence William Fenwick, Terence Ian Butcher, Trevor McGregor Steven (78.Christopher Roland Waddle), Raymond Colin Wilkins, Bryan Robson (Cap), Trevor John Francis, Mark Wayne Hateley, John Charles Bryan Barnes. Manager: Robert William Robson.
**Goals:** 1-0 Jari Rantanen (6), 1-1 Mark Wayne Hateley (50).

06.06.1985, Olympiastadion, Helsinki; Attendance: 24,863
Referee: Marcel Van Langenhove (Belgium)
**FINLAND - ROMANIA** **1-1(1-1)**
**FIN:** Olavi Huttunen, Aki Lahtinen, Pauno Kymäläinen (78.Esa Pekonen), Leo Houtsonen, Jyrki Nieminen (70.Erkka Petäjä), Hannu Turunen, Pasi Rautiainen (Cap), Kari Ukkonen, Jukka Ikäläinen, Mika Lipponen, Jari Rantanen. Trainer: Marti Kuusela.
**ROU:** Silviu Lung, Ştefan Iovan, Gino Iorgulescu, Costică Ştefănescu (Cap), Nicolae Ungureanu, Mircea Rednic, Ladislau Bölöni, Michael Klein, Gheorghe Hagi, Marcel Coraş (67.Marius Lăcătuş), Rodion Gorun Cămătaru. Trainer: Mircea Lucescu.
**Goals**: 0-1 Gheorghe Hagi (7), 1-1 Mika Lipponen (26).

28.08.1985, Stadionul 1 Mai, Timişoara; Attendance: 35,000
Referee: Zoran Petrović (Yugoslavia)
**ROMANIA - FINLAND** **2-0(1-0)**
**ROU:** Dumitru Moraru, Mircea Rednic, Gino Iorgulescu (65.Ştefan Iovan), Costică Ştefănescu (Cap), Nicolae Ungureanu, Dorin Mateuţ, Ladislau Bölöni, Michael Klein, Gheorghe Hagi, Marcel Coraş (46.Romulus Gabor), Rodion Gorun Cămătaru. Trainer: Mircea Lucescu.
**FIN:** Olavi Huttunen, Jari Europaeus, Hannu Turunen, Leo Houtsonen (Cap), Jyrki Nieminen, Kari Ukkonen (70.Erkka Petäjä), Jukka Ikäläinen, Pasi Rautiainen, Jari Rantanen, Ari Hjelm, Mika Lipponen. Trainer: Martti Kuusela.
**Goals**: 1-0 Gheorghe Hagi (6), 2-0 Dorin Mateuţ (56).

11.09.1985, "Kemal Atatürk" Stadı, Izmir; Attendance: 32,500
Referee: Michel Vautrot (France)
**TURKEY - NORTHERN IRELAND**  **0-0**
**TUR:** Yaşar Duran, İsmail Demiriz, Erdoğan Arica, Raşit Çetiner, Sedat III Özden, Müjdat Yetkiner, Hasan Vezir, Metin Tekin, Şenol Çorlu, İlyas Tüfekçi (74.Bahattin Güneş), Ali Erdal Keser (31.Tanju Çolak). Trainer: Coşkun Özarı.
**NIR:** Patrick Anthony Jennings, James Michael Nicholl, John McClelland, John Patrick O'Neill, Malachy Martin Donaghy, Paul Christopher Ramsey, James Martin Quinn, Samuel Baxter McIlroy (Cap) (74.David McCreery), Stephen Alexander Penney, Gerard Joseph Armstrong, Nigel Worthington. Manager: William Laurence Bingham.

11.09.1985, Wembley Stadium, London; Attendance: 59,500
Referee: Karl-Heinz Tritschler (West Germany)
**ENGLAND - ROMANIA**  **1-1(1-0)**
**ENG:** Peter Leslie Shilton, Gary Michael Stevens, Mark Wright,Terence William Fenwick, Kenneth Graham Sansom, Glenn Hoddle, Bryan Robson (Cap), Peter Reid, Mark Wayne Hateley, Gary Winston Lineker (80.Anthony Stewart Woodcock), Christopher Roland Waddle (69.John Charles Bryan Barnes). Manager: Robert William Robson.
**ROU:** Silviu Lung, Nicolae Negrilă, Ştefan Iovan, Costică Ştefănescu (Cap), Nicolae Ungureanu, Mircea Rednic, Ladislau Bölöni, Michael Klein (87.Dorin Mateuţ), Gheorghe Hagi, Marcel Coraş (82.Romulus Gabor), Rodion Gorun Cămătaru. Trainer: Mircea Lucescu.
**Goals**: 1-0 Glenn Hoddle (25), 1-1 Rodion Gorun Cămătaru (60).

25.09.1985, Ratina Stadion, Tampere; Attendance: 5,616
Referee: Rune Larsson (Sweden)
**FINLAND - TURKEY**  **1-0(1-0)**
**FIN:** Olavi Huttunen, Aki Lahtinen, Pauno Kymäläinen, Jari Rantanen, Jyrki Nieminen (79.Erkka Petäjä), Hannu Turunen, Leo Houtsonen, Kari Ukkonen (57.Mika Lipponen), Jukka Ikäläinen, Pasi Rautiainen, Ari Hjelm. Trainer: Martti Kuusela.
**TUR:** Yaşar Duran, İsmail Demiriz, Raşit Çetiner, Sedat III Özden, Erdoğan Arica, Yusuf Altintaş, Müjdat Yetkiner, Arif Kocabıyık (46.İlyas Tüfekçi), Hasan Vezir, Selçuk Yula, Şenol Çorlu. Trainer: Coşkun Özarı.
**Goal**: 1-0 Jari Rantanen (37).

16.10.1985, Wembley Stadium, London; Attendance: 52,500
Referee: Anatoli Milchenko (Soviet Union)
**ENGLAND - TURKEY**  **5-0(4-0)**
**ENG:** Peter Leslie Shilton, Gary Michael Stevens, Mark Wright, Terence William Fenwick, Kenneth Graham Sansom, Glenn Hoddle, Raymond Colin Wilkins, Bryan Robson (Cap) (66.Trevor McGregor Steven), Gary Winston Lineker, Mark Wayne Hateley (84.Anthony Stewart Woodcock), Christopher Roland Waddle. Manager: Robert William Robson.
**TUR:** Yaşar Duran, İsmail Demiriz, Yusuf Altintaş, Raşit Çetiner, Sedat III Özden, Abdülkerim Dürmaz, Müjdat Yetkiner, Şenol Çorlu (37.Hasan Şengün), Ünal Karaman, Hasan Vezir, Selçuk Yula. Trainer: Coşkun Özarı.
**Goals**: 1-0 Christopher Roland Waddle (14), 2-0 Gary Winston Lineker (18), 3-0 Bryan Robson (35), 4-0 Gary Winston Lineker (42), 5-0 Gary Winston Lineker (53).

16.10.1985, Stadionul 23 August, Bucureşti; Attendance: 45,000
Referee: Henning Lund Sørensen (Denmark)
**ROMANIA - NORTHERN IRELAND**     **0-1(0-1)**
**ROU:** Silviu Lung, Nicolae Negrilă (46.Ion Geolgău), Ştefan Iovan, Gino Iorgulescu, Nicolae Ungureanu, Dorin Mateuţ, Mircea Rednic, Ladislau Bölöni, Michael Klein, Gheorghe Hagi (Cap), Marcel Coraş (62.Victor Piţurcă). Trainer: Mircea Lucescu.
**NIR:** Patrick Anthony Jennings, James Michael Nicholl, Malachy Martin Donaghy, John Patrick O'Neill, Alan McDonald, David McCreery, Stephen Alexander Penney (72.Gerard Joseph Armstrong), Samuel Baxter McIlroy (Cap), James Martin Quinn, Norman Whiteside, Ian Edwin Stewart (46.Nigel Worthington). Manager: William Laurence Bingham.
**Goal**: 0-1 James Martin Quinn (29).

13.11.1985, "Kemal Atatürk" Stadı, Izmir; Attendance: 30,000
Referee: Volker Roth (West Germany)
**TURKEY - ROMANIA**     **1-3(0-2)**
**TUR:** Okan Gedikali, Müjdat Yetkiner, Erdoğan Arica, İsmail Demiriz, Yusuf Altıntaş, Riza Çalımbay, Ünal Karaman, Metin Tekin, Tanju Çolak, Şenol Çorlu (61.İsmail Kartal), Selçuk Yula. Trainer: Coşkun Özarı.
**ROU:** Silviu Lung, Ştefan Iovan, Gino Iorgulescu, Costică Ştefănescu (Cap), Ilie Bărbulescu, Mircea Rednic, Ladislau Bölöni, Michael Klein, Gheorghe Hagi, Marcel Coraş (83.Ion Geolgău), Victor Piţurcă (64.Rodion Gorun Cămătaru). Trainer: Mircea Lucescu.
**Goals**: 0-1 Gino Iorgulescu (15), 0-2 Marcel Coraş (28), 0-3 Ştefan Iovan (54), 1-3 Metin Tekin (78).

13.11.1985, Wembley Stadium, London; Attendance: 70,500
Referee: Erik Fredriksson (Sweden)
**ENGLAND - NORTHERN IRELAND**     **0-0**
**ENG:** Peter Leslie Shilton, Gary Michael Stevens, Kenneth Graham Sansom, Glenn Hoddle, Mark Wright, Terence William Fenwick, Paul William Bracewell, Raymond Colin Wilkins (Cap), Kerry Michael Dixon, Gary Winston Lineker, Christopher Roland Waddle. Manager: Robert William Robson.
**NIR:** Patrick Anthony Jennings, James Michael Nicholl, Malachy Martin Donaghy, John Patrick O'Neill, Alan McDonald, David McCreery, Stephen Alexander Penney (59.Gerard Joseph Armstrong), Samuel Baxter McIlroy (Cap), James Martin Quinn, Norman Whiteside, Ian Edwin Stewart (72.Nigel Worthington). Manager: William Laurence Bingham.

# GROUP 4

| | | | | |
|---|---|---|---|---|
| 29.09.1984 | Beograd | Yugoslavia - Bulgaria | | 0-0 |
| 13.10.1984 | Luxembourg | Luxembourg - France | | 0-4(0-4) |
| 20.10.1984 | Leipzig | East Germany - Yugoslavia | | 2-3(1-1) |
| 17.11.1984 | Esch-sur-Alzette | Luxembourg - East Germany | | 0-5(0-0) |
| 21.11.1984 | Paris | France - Bulgaria | | 1-0(0-0) |
| 05.12.1984 | Sofia | Bulgaria - Luxembourg | | 4-0(2-0) |
| 08.12.1984 | Paris | France - East Germany | | 2-0(1-0) |
| 27.03.1985 | Zenica | Yugoslavia - Luxembourg | | 1-0(1-0) |
| 03.04.1985 | Sarajevo | Yugoslavia - France | | 0-0 |
| 06.04.1985 | Sofia | Bulgaria - East Germany | | 1-0(0-0) |
| 01.05.1985 | Luxembourg | Luxembourg - Yugoslavia | | 0-1(0-0) |
| 02.05.1985 | Sofia | Bulgaria - France | | 2-0(1-0) |
| 18.05.1985 | Potsdam | East Germany - Luxembourg | | 3-1(3-0) |
| 01.06.1985 | Sofia | Bulgaria - Yugoslavia | | 2-1(1-1) |
| 11.09.1985 | Leipzig | East Germany - France | | 2-0(0-0) |
| 25.09.1985 | Luxembourg | Luxembourg - Bulgaria | | 1-3(0-3) |
| 28.09.1985 | Beograd | Yugoslavia - East Germany | | 1-2(0-0) |
| 30.10.1985 | Paris | France - Luxembourg | | 6-0(4-0) |
| 16.11.1985 | Paris | France - Yugoslavia | | 2-0(1-0) |
| 16.11.1985 | Karl-Marx-Stadt | East Germany - Bulgaria | | 2-1(2-1) |

### FINAL STANDINGS

| | | | | | | | | | |
|---|---|---|---|---|---|---|---|---|---|
| 1. | **France** | 8 | 5 | 1 | 2 | 15 | - | 4 | 11 |
| 2. | **Bulgaria** | 8 | 5 | 1 | 2 | 13 | - | 5 | 11 |
| 3. | East Germany | 8 | 5 | 0 | 3 | 16 | - | 9 | 10 |
| 4. | Yugoslavia | 8 | 3 | 2 | 3 | 7 | - | 8 | 8 |
| 5. | Luxembourg | 8 | 0 | 0 | 8 | 2 | - | 27 | 0 |

France and Bulgaria qualified for the Final Tournament.

29.09.1984, JNA Stadion, Beograd; Attendance: 20,000
Referee: László Pádár (Hungary)
**YUGOSLAVIA - BULGARIA**     **0-0**
**YUG:** Ranko Stojić, Zoran Vujović (37.Nenad Gračan), Mirsad Baljić, Ivan Gudelj, Faruk Hadžibegić, Ljubomir Radanović, Zlatko Vujović, Blaž Slišković, Fadilj Vokri (71.Darko Pančev), Mehmet Baždarević, Miloš Šestić (Cap). Trainer: Miloš Milutinović.
**BUL:** Borislav Mihailov, Petar Petrov, Nikolai Arabov, Aleksandar Markov, Georgi Dimitrov, Radoslav Zdravkov, Kostadin Yanchev (50.Lachezar Tanev), Anio Sadkov, Boicho Velichkov (66.Antim Pehlivanov), Jivko Gospodinov, Stoicho Mladenov. Trainer: Ivan Vutsov.

13.10.1984, Stade Municipal, Luxembourg; Attendance: 9,000
Referee: Henning Lund-Sørensen (Denmark)
**LUXEMBOURG - FRANCE**     **0-4(0-4)**
**LUX:** John van Rijswijck, Romain Michaux, René Scheuer, Pierre Petry, Hubert Meunier, Laurent Schonckert, Guy Hellers, Gilbert Dresch, Carlo Weis, Robert Langers, Jeannot Reiter. Trainer: Jozef Vliers (Belgium)
**FRA:** Joël Bats, Michel Bibard, Patrick Battiston, Maxime Bossis, Manuel Amoros, Luis Fernández, Alain Giresse, Michel Platini (Cap) (57.Jean-Marc Ferreri), Thierry Tusseau, Yannick Stopyra, François Brisson (72.Philippe Anziani). Trainer: Henri Michel.
**Goals**: 0-1 Patrick Battiston (2), 0-2 Michel Platini (12), 0-3 Yannick Stopyra (24), 0-4 Yannick Stopyra (32).

20.10.1984, Zentralstadion, Leipzig; Attendance: 63,000
Referee: Horst Brummeier (Austria)
**EAST GERMANY - YUGOSLAVIA**                                            **2-3(1-1)**
**DDR:** René Müller, Hans-Jürgen Dörner (Cap), Ronald Kreer, Dirk Stahmann, Uwe Zötzsche, Frank Rohde, Rainer Ernst (69.Joachim Streich), Rainer Troppa, Wolfgang Steinbach, Michael Glowatzky, Ralf Minge. Trainer: Bernd Stange.
**YUG:** Ranko Stojić, Miodrag Radović, Mirsad Baljić, Velimir Zajec (Cap), Faruk Hadžibegić, Ljubomir Radanović, Zlatko Vujović, Ivan Gudelj, Fadilj Vokri (89.Stjepan Deverić), Mehmet Baždarević, Miloš Šestić (84.Davor Jozić). Trainer: Miloš Milutinović.
**Goals:** 1-0 Michael Glowatzky (11), 1-1 Mehmet Baždarević (31), 1-2 Fadilj Vokri (48), 2-2 Rainer Ernst (50), 2-3 Miloš Šestić (80).

17.11.1984, Stade de la Frontière, Esch-sur-Alzette; Attendance: 1,179
Referee: Oliver Donnelly (Northern Ireland)
**LUXEMBOURG - EAST GERMANY**                              **0-5(0-0)**
**LUX:** John van Rijswijck, Jean-Paul Girres, Laurent Schonckert, Carlo Weis, René Scheuer, Hubert Meunier, Guy Hellers, Pierre Petry, Théo Malget (74.Gilbert Dresch), Robert Langers (71.Marcel Bossi), Jeannot Reiter. Trainer: Jozef Vliers (Belgium).
**DDR:** René Müller, Hans-Jürgen Dörner (Cap), Ronald Kreer, Dirk Stahmann (66.Jörg Stübner), Matthias Dörner, Andreas Thom, Rainer Troppa, Wolfgang Steinbach, Ralf Minge, Rainer Ernst, Michael Glowatzky (46.Matthias Liebers). Trainer: Bernd Stange.
**Goals:** 0-1 Rainer Ernst (60), 0-2 Ralf Minge (63), 0-3 Rainer Ernst (76), 0-4 Ralf Minge (78), 0-5 Rainer Ernst (81).

21.11.1984, Stade Parc des Princes, Paris; Attendance: 42,084
Referee: Karl-Heinz Tritschler (West Germany)
**FRANCE - BULGARIA**                                                         **1-0(0-0)**
**FRA:** Joël Bats, Michel Bibard, Didier Sénac, Maxime Bossis, Manuel Amoros, Luis Fernández, Bernard Genghini, Jean Amadou Tigana, Michel Platini (Cap), Yannick Stopyra (58.José Touré; 84.Thierry Tusseau), Bruno Bellone. Trainer: Henri Michel.
**BUL:** Borislav Mihailov, Plamen Nikolov, Nikolai Arabov, Aleksandar Markov, Georgi Dimitrov, Radoslav Zdravkov, Bojidar Iskrenov (46.Jivko Gospodinov), Anio Sadkov, Rusi Gochev, Nasko Sirakov, Stoicho Mladenov (75.Emil Spasov). Trainer: Ivan Vutsov.
**Goal:** 1-0 Michel Platini (62 penalty).

05.12.1984, „Vasil Levski" National Stadium, Sofia; Attendance: 15,000
Referee: Antonis Vassaras (Greece)
**BULGARIA - LUXEMBOURG**                                       **4-0(2-0)**
**BUL:** Borislav Mihailov, Plamen Nikolov, Nikolai Arabov, Aleksandar Markov (67.Plamen Getov), Georgi Dimitrov, Radoslav Zdravkov, Rusi Gochev (59.Stoicho Mladenov), Nasko Sirakov, Boicho Velichkov, Emil Spasov, Atanas Pashev. Trainer: Ivan Vutsov.
**LUX:** John van Rijswijck, Laurent Schonckert, René Scheuer, Carlo Weis, Pierre Petry, Hubert Meunier, Jean-Paul Girres, Guy Hellers, Jeannot Reiter (67.Marcel Bossi), Gilbert Dresch, Théo Malget (78.Pierre Hoscheid). Trainer: Jozef Vliers (Belgium).
**Goals:** 1-0 Nasko Sirakov (8), 2-0 Boicho Velichkov (29), 3-0 Stoicho Mladenov (66), 4-0 Georgi Dimitrov (70).
**Sent off:** Hubert Meunier (53).

08.12.1984, Stade Parc des Princes, Paris; Attendance: 43,174
Referee: Paolo Casarin (Italy)
**FRANCE - EAST GERMANY** **2-0(1-0)**
**FRA:** Joël Bats, Michel Bibard, Didier Sénac, Maxime Bossis, Manuel Amoros, Alain Giresse, Jean Amadou Tigana, Luis Fernández, Michel Platini (Cap), Yannick Stopyra (84.Philippe Anziani), Bruno Bellone. Trainer: Henri Michel.
**DDR:** René Müller, Hans-Jürgen Dörner (Cap), Andreas Trautmann, Dirk Stahmann, Matthias Dörner, Jörg Stübner, Rainer Troppa, Matthias Liebers, Wolfgang Steinbach (75.Hans Richter), Ralf Minge (79.Michael Glowatzky), Andreas Thom. Trainer: Bernd Stange.
**Goals**: 1-0 Yannick Stopyra (32), 2-0 Philippe Anziani (89).

27.03.1985, Bilino polje, Zenica; Attendance: 30,000
Referee: Aleksandr Mushkovets (Soviet Union)
**YUGOSLAVIA - LUXEMBOURG** **1-0(1-0)**
**YUG:** Ranko Stojić, Zoran Vujović, Mirsad Baljić, Ivan Gudelj, Faruk Hadžibegić, Ljubomir Radanović, Zlatko Vujović (Cap), Blaž Slišković, Milko Đurovski, Mehmet Baždarević, Predrag Pašić (79.Miloš Šestić). Trainer: Miloš Milutinović.
**LUX:** John van Rijswijck, Laurent Schonckert, Nico Wagner, Marcel Bossi, C. Rohmann, Jean-Pierre Barboni, Guy Hellers, Gilbert Dresch, Jeannot Reiter, Pierre Hoscheid (63.Théo Malget), Robert Langers. Trainer: Josy Kirchens.
**Goal**: Ivan Gudelj (36).

03.04.1985, Koševo Stadion, Sarajevo; Attendance: 53,500
Referee: Erik Fredriksson (Sweden)
**YUGOSLAVIA - FRANCE** **0-0**
**YUG:** Ranko Stojić, Vlado Čapljić, Mirsad Baljić, Ivan Gudelj, Faruk Hadžibegić, Ljubomir Radanović, Zlatko Vujović (63.Milko Đurovski), Velimir Zajec (Cap), Vahid Halilhodžić, Mehmet Baždarević, Miloš Šestić (68.Blaž Slišković). Trainer: Miloš Milutinović.
**FRA:** Joël Bats, William Ayache, Léonard Specht, Patrick Battiston, Manuel Amoros, Jean Amadou Tigana, Luis Fernández (82.Thierry Tusseau), Michel Platini (Cap), Alain Giresse, Yannick Stopyra (69.José Touré), Bruno Bellone. Trainer: Henri Michel.

06.04.1985, „Vasil Levski" National Stadium, Sofia; Attendance: 50,000
Referee: Franz Wöhrer (Austria)
**BULGARIA - EAST GERMANY** **1-0(0-0)**
**BUL:** Borislav Mihailov, Nikolai Iliev, Nikolai Arabov, Petar Petrov, Georgi Dimitrov, Radoslav Zdravkov, Rusi Gochev (26.Plamen Getov), Nasko Sirakov (58.Boicho Velichkov), Stoicho Mladenov, Anio Sadkov, Bojidar Iskrenov. Trainer: Ivan Vutsov.
**DDR:** René Müller, Hans-Jürgen Dörner (Cap), Ronald Kreer, Dirk Stahmann, Matthias Dörner, Jörg Stübner, Andreas Krause, Christian Backs (88.Bernd Schulz), Ralf Minge (88.Uwe Weidemann), Rainer Ernst, Andreas Thom. Trainer: Bernd Stange.
**Goal**: 1-0 Stoicho Mladenov (87).

01.05.1985, Stade Municipal, Luxembourg; Attendance: 7,000
Referee: Guðmundur Haraldsson (Iceland)
**LUXEMBOURG - YUGOSLAVIA** **0-1(0-0)**
**LUX:** John van Rijswijck, Laurent Schonckert, Nico Wagner, Marcel Bossi, C. Rohmann, Carlo Weis (72.Jean-Paul Girres), Jean-Pierre Barboni, Guy Hellers, Gilbert Dresch, Jeannot Reiter, Robert Langers. Trainer: Josy Kirchens.
**YUG:** Ranko Stojić, Branko Miljuš, Mirsad Baljić, Ivan Gudelj, Faruk Hadžibegić, Ljubomir Radanović (46.Milko Đurovski), Zlatko Vujović (62.Darko Pančev), Velimir Zajec (Cap), Fadilj Vokri, Mehmet Baždarević, Marko Mlinarić. Trainer: Miloš Milutinović.
**Goal**: 0-1 Fadilj Vokri (88).

02.05.1985, „Vasil Levski" National Stadium, Sofia; Attendance: 57,000
Referee: Brian McKinley (Scotland)
**BULGARIA - FRANCE** **2-0(1-0)**
**BUL:** Borislav Mihailov, Plamen Nikolov, Nikolai Arabov, Petar Petrov, Georgi Dimitrov, Radoslav Zdravkov, Plamen Getov (75.Atanas Pashev), Nasko Sirakov, Boicho Velichkov (56.Andrei Jeliazkov), Anio Sadkov, Stoicho Mladenov. Trainer: Ivan Vutsov.
**FRA:** Joël Bats, William Ayache, Léonard Specht, Maxime Bossis, Manuel Amoros, José Touré, Jean Amadou Tigana, Luis Fernández (69.Thierry Tusseau), Michel Platini (Cap), Yannick Stopyra, Bruno Bellone. Trainer: Henri Michel.
**Goals**: 1-0 Georgi Dimitrov (11), 2-0 Nasko Sirakov (63).

18.05.1985, „Karl Liebknecht" Stadion, Babelsberg; Attendance: 9,000
Referee: Charles Scerri (Malta)
**EAST GERMANY - LUXEMBOURG** **3-1(3-0)**
**DDR:** René Müller, Hans-Jürgen Dörner (Cap), Ronald Kreer, Frank Rohde (57.Matthias Dörner), Uwe Zötzsche, Hans-Uwe Pilz, Rainer Ernst, Matthias Liebers, Ulf Kirsten, Ralf Minge, Andreas Thom. Trainer: Bernd Stange.
**LUX:** John van Rijswijck, Laurent Schonckert (60.Hubert Meunier), Nico Wagner, Marcel Bossi, C.Rohmann, Carlo Weis, Jean-Pierre Barboni, Guy Hellers, Gilbert Dresch, Jeannot Reiter (81.Théo Malget), Robert Langers. Trainer: Josy Kirchens.
**Goals**: 1-0 Ralf Minge (19), 2-0 Ralf Minge (38), 3-0 Rainer Ernst (45 penalty), 3-1 Robert Langers (76).

01.06.1985, „Vasil Levski" National Stadium, Sofia; Attendance: 65,000
Referee: Vojtech Hristov (Czechoslovakia)
**BULGARIA - YUGOSLAVIA** **2-1(1-1)**
**BUL:** Borislav Mihailov, Plamen Nikolov, Nikolai Arabov, Petar Petrov, Georgi Dimitrov, Radoslav Zdravkov, Plamen Getov, Nasko Sirakov (53.Andrei Jeliazkov), Boicho Velichkov (46.Kostadin Kostadinov), Anio Sadkov, Stoicho Mladenov. Trainer: Ivan Vutsov
**YUG:** Ranko Stojić, Vlado Čapljić, Ljubomir Radanović, Ivan Gudelj, Velimir Zajec (Cap), Faruk Hadžibegić, Edin Bahtić (35.Mitar Mrkela), Marko Mlinarić, Fadilj Vokri, Mehmet Baždarević, Milko Đurovski. Trainer: Miloš Milutinović.
**Goals**: 1-0 Plamen Getov (27), 1-1 Milko Đurovski (29), 2-1 Plamen Getov (58).

11.09.1985, Zentralstadion, Leipzig; Attendance: 78,000
Referee: Pietro D'Elia (Italy)
**EAST GERMANY - FRANCE** **2-0(0-0)**
**DDR:** René Müller (Cap), Frank Rohde, Ronald Kreer, Carsten Sänger, Uwe Zötzsche, Jörg Stübner, Ralf Minge, Matthias Liebers, Andreas Thom, Ulf Kirsten, Rainer Ernst. Trainer: Bernd Stange.
**FRA:** Joël Bats, Michel Bibard, Yvon Le Roux, Maxime Bossis (Cap), William Ayache, Alain Giresse, Fabrice Poullain (75.Bruno Bellone), Luis Fernández, Michel Platini, Dominique Rocheteau, José Touré. Trainer: Henri Michel.
**Goals**: 1-0 Rainer Ernst (53), 2-0 Ronald Kreer (81).

25.09.1985, Stade Municipal, Luxembourg; Attendance: 3,500
Referee: David Findlay Taylor Syme (Scotland)
**LUXEMBOURG - BULGARIA** **1-3(0-3)**
**LUX:** John van Rijswijck, Laurent Schonckert, Gilbert Dresch, René Scheuer, Hubert Meunier, Gérard Jeitz, Carlo Weis (46.Jean-Paul Girres), Jean-Pierre Barboni (74.Théo Malget), Guy Hellers, Jeannot Reiter, Robert Langers. Trainer: Paul Philipp.
**BUL:** Ilia Valov, Radoslav Zdravkov, Nikolai Arabov, Petar Petrov, Georgi Dimitrov, Anio Sadkov, Plamen Getov (74.Hristo Kolev), Rusi Gochev, Kostadin Kostadinov, Jivko Gospodinov, Bojidar Iskrenov (80.Atanas Pashev). Trainer: Ivan Vutsov.
**Goals**: 0-1 Guy Hellers (3 own goal), 0-2 Kostadin Kostadinov (26), 0-3 Georgi Dimitrov (33), 1-3

Robert Langers (65 penalty).

28.09.1985, JNA Stadion, Beograd; Attendance: 35,000
Referee: Velodi Miminoshvili (Soviet Union))
**YUGOSLAVIA - EAST GERMANY**     **1-2(0-0)**
**YUG:** Živan Ljukovčan, Nenad Gračan, Mirza Kapetanović, Ivan Gudelj (60.Vlado Čapljić), Marko Elsner, Ljubomir Radanović, Jovica Nikolić (46.Milko Đurovski), Haris Škoro, Miloš Bursać, Mehmet Baždarević, Zlatko Vujović (Cap). Trainer: Miloš Milutinović.
**DDR:** René Müller (Cap), Frank Rohde, Ronald Kreer, Carsten Sänger, Uwe Zötzsche, Hans-Uwe Pilz, Ralf Minge, Matthias Liebers, Andreas Thom, Ulf Kirsten (89.Jürgen Heun), Rainer Ernst. Trainer: Bernd Stange.
**Goals:** 0-1 Andreas Thom (47), 0-2 Andreas Thom (59), 1-2 Haris Škoro (83)

30.10.1985, Stade Parc des Princes, Paris; Attendance: 28,597
Referee: Michal Listkiewicz (Poland)
**FRANCE - LUXEMBOURG**     **6-0(4-0)**
**FRA:** Joël Bats, William Ayache, Patrick Battiston, Maxime Bossis (28.Yvon Le Roux), Manuel Amoros, Jean Amadou Tigana, Alain Giresse, Michel Platini (Cap), Luis Fernández, Dominique Rocheteau (63.Bruno Bellone), José Touré. Trainer: Henri Michel.
**LUX:** John van Rijswijck, Hubert Meunier, Marcel Bossi, Gilbert Dresch, Laurent Schonckert, Carlo Weis, Gérard Jeitz (61.Nico Wagner), Guy Hellers, Pierre Hoscheid (82.Théo Scholten), Robert Langers, Jean-Paul Girres. Trainer: Paul Philipp.
**Goals:** 1-0 Dominique Rocheteau (4), 2-0 José Touré (24), 3-0 Dominique Rocheteau (29), 4-0 Alain Giresse (36), 5-0 Luis Fernández (49 penalty), 6-0 Dominique Rocheteau (51).

16.11.1985, Stade Parc des Princes, Paris; Attendance: 45,670
Referee: Alexis Ponnet (Belgium)
**FRANCE - YUGOSLAVIA**     **2-0(1-0)**
**FRA:** Joël Bats, William Ayache, Yvon Le Roux, Patrick Battiston, Manuel Amoros, Luis Fernández, Jean Amadou Tigana, Alain Giresse, Michel Platini (Cap), Dominique Rocheteau (77.Yannick Stopyra), José Touré. Trainer: Henri Michel.
**YUG:** Ranko Stojić, Branko Miljuš, Mirza Kapetanović, Ivan Gudelj, Vlada Vermezović, Ljubomir Radanović, Dragan Stojković (46.Haris Škoro), Blaž Slišković, Miloš Bursać, Mehmet Baždarević, Zlatko Vujović (Cap). Trainer: Miloš Milutinović.
**Goals:** 1-0 Michel Platini (3), 2-0 Michel Platini (71).
**Sent off:** Yvon Le Roux (84).

16.11.1985, „Ernst Thälmann" Stadion, Karl-Marx-Stadt; Attendance: 35,000
Referee: Johannes Nicolaas Ignatius „Jan" Keizer (Holland)
**EAST GERMANY - BULGARIA**     **2-1(2-1)**
**DDR:** René Müller (Cap), Frank Rohde, Ronald Kreer, Carsten Sänger, Uwe Zötzsche, Hans-Uwe Pilz, Matthias Liebers, Ralf Minge, Jörg Stübner (77.Jürgen Heun), Ulf Kirsten, Rainer Ernst (77.Michael Glowatzky). Trainer: Bernd Stange.
**BUL:** Ilia Valov, Emil Dimitrov, Krasimir Koev, Petar Petrov, Georgi Dimitrov, Radoslav Zdravkov (66.Hristo Kolev), Kostadin Kostadinov, Rusi Gochev, Andrei Jeliazkov, Jivko Gospodinov, Bojidar Iskrenov (80.Plamen Getov). Trainer: Ivan Vutsov.
**Goals:** 1-0 Uwe Zötzsche (4 penalty), 1-1 Rusi Gochev (39), 2-1 Matthias Liebers (40).

# GROUP 5

| | | | | |
|---|---|---|---|---|
| 02.05.1984 | Nicosia | Cyprus - Austria | | 1-2(0-1) |
| 26.09.1984 | Budapest | Hungary - Austria | | 3-1(0-1) |
| 17.10.1984 | Rotterdam | Holland - Hungary | | 1-2(1-1) |
| 14.11.1984 | Wien | Austria - Holland | | 1-0(1-0) |
| 17.11.1984 | Limassol | Cyprus - Hungary | | 1-2(1-0) |
| 23.12.1984 | Nicosia | Cyprus - Holland | | 0-1(0-0) |
| 27.02.1985 | Amsterdam | Holland - Cyprus | | 7-1(3-1) |
| 03.04.1985 | Budapest | Hungary - Cyprus | | 2-0(0-0) |
| 17.04.1985 | Wien | Austria - Hungary | | 0-3(0-2) |
| 01.05.1985 | Rotterdam | Holland - Austria | | 1-1(0-0) |
| 07.05.1985 | Graz | Austria - Cyprus | | 4-0(2-0) |
| 14.05.1985 | Budapest | Hungary - Holland | | 0-1(0-0) |

### FINAL STANDINGS

| | | | | | | | | | |
|---|---|---|---|---|---|---|---|---|---|
| 1. | **Hungary** | 6 | 5 | 0 | 1 | 12 | - | 4 | 10 |
| 2. | *Holland* | 6 | 3 | 1 | 2 | 11 | - | 5 | 7 |
| 3. | Austria | 6 | 3 | 1 | 2 | 9 | - | 8 | 7 |
| 4. | Cyprus | 6 | 0 | 0 | 6 | 3 | - | 18 | 0 |

Hungary qualified for the Final Tournament.
Holland qualified for the Play-offs against the runners-up from Group 1.

02.05.1984, Makareio Stádio, Nicosia; Attendance: 14,000
Referee: Moshe Ashkenazi (Israel)
**CYPRUS - AUSTRIA**     **1-2(0-1)**
**CYP:** Andreas Konstantinou II, Georgios Kezos, Costas Miamiliotis, Klitos Erotokritou, Nicos Pantziaras, Yiannakis Yiangoudakis, Pavlos Kounnas (69.Paschalis Christoforou), Filippos Dimitriou, Costas Foti, Lefteris Kouis (58.Marios Tsingis), Fanis Theofanous. Trainer: Bazil Spasov (Bulgaria).
**AUT:** Friedrich Koncilia, Bernd Krauss, Erich Obermayer, Josef Pregesbauer, Bruno Pezzey, Heribert Weber, Walter Schachner, Herbert Prohaska, Richard Niederbacher (88.Gerald Willfurth), Martin Gisinger, Walter Hörmann. Trainer: Erich Hof.
**Goals:** 0-1 Martin Gisinger (37), 1-1 Paschalis Christoforou (72), 1-2 Herbert Prohaska (75).

26.09.1984, Népstadion, Budapest; Attendance: 30,000
Referee: Michel Vautrot (France)
**HUNGARY - AUSTRIA**     **3-1(0-1)**
**HUN:** József Andrusch, József Csuhay (46.Sándor Sallai), Antal Róth, Imre Garaba, József Varga, József Kardos, Antal Nagy, Lajos Détári, József Kiprich, Tibor Nyilasi, Márton Esterházy. Trainer: György Mezey.
**AUT:** Friedrich Koncilia, Johann Dihanich, Bruno Pezzey, Gerald Messlender, Josef Pregesbauer, Herbert Prohaska, Heribert Weber, Felix Gasselich (65.Walter Hörmann), Martin Gisinger (75.Alfred Drabits), Walter Schachner, Anton Polster. Trainer: Erich Hof.
**Goals**: 0-1 Walter Schachner (23), 1-1 Antal Nagy (50), 2-1 Márton Esterházy (62), 3-1 József Kardos (78).

17.10.1984, Feyenoord Stadion, Rotterdam; Attendance: 55,000
Referee: André Daina (Switzerland)
**HOLLAND - HUNGARY**     **1-2(1-1)**
**NED:** Johannes Franciscus van Breukelen, Jan Jacobus Silooy, Ronald Spelbos, Hubertus Johannes Nicolaas Wijnstekers (Cap), Franklin Edmundo Rijkaard, Wilhelmus Antonius van de Kerkhof, Machiel Valke (67.Erwin Koeman), Ruud Gullit, Willem Cornelis Nicolaas Kieft, Marcelo van Basten (61.Petrus Johannes Houtman), René van der Gijp. Trainer: Marinus Henrikus Bernardus Michels.
**HUN:** József Andrusch, Sándor Sallai, Antal Róth, Imre Garaba (46.Ferenc Csongrádi), József Varga, József Kardos, Antal Nagy, Lajos Détári, József Kiprich (89.Béla Bodonyi), Tibor Nyilasi, Márton Esterházy. Trainer: György Mezey.
**Goals**: 1-0 Willem Cornelis Nicolaas Kieft (20), 1-1 Lajos Détári (26), 1-2 Márton Esterházy (55).

14.11.1984, Prater Stadion, Wien; Attendance: 15,000
Referee: Anatoli Milchenko (Soviet Union)
**AUSTRIA - HOLLAND**     **1-0(1-0)**
**AUT:** Friedrich Koncilia, Bruno Pezzey, Heribert Weber, Gerald Messlender (85.Leopold Lainer), Herbert Prohaska, Kurt Jara, Walter Hörmann, Karl Brauneder, Walter Schachner, Anton Polster, Gerhard Steinkogler. Trainer: Erich Hof.
**NED:** Johannes Franciscus van Breukelen, Ronald Spelbos (Cap), Ernestus Wilhelmus Johannes Brandts, Edo Ophof, Adrianus Andreas van Tiggelen, Peter Boeve (33.René van der Gijp), Wilhelmus Antonius van de Kerkhof, Ton Lokhoff (73.Mario Been), Machiel Valke, Ruud Gullit, Marcelo van Basten. Trainer: Marinus Henrikus Bernardus Michels.
**Goal**: 1-0 Machiel Valke (15 own goal).

17.11.1984, Tsirion Stádio, Limassol; Attendance: 12,000
Referee: Brian McGinlay (Scotland)
**CYPRUS - HUNGARY**     **1-2(1-0)**
**CYP:** Andreas Konstantinou II, Koulis Pantziaras, Nicos Pantziaras, Klitos Erotokritou, Costas Miamiliotis, Panayiotis Marangos, Georgios Savvides (88.Nicos Patikkis), Yiannakis Yiangoudakis, Christakis Mavris (85.Costas Konstantinou), Costas Foti, Sotiris Tsikkos. Trainer: Panikos Iacovou.
**HUN:** József Andrusch, Sándor Sallai, Antal Róth, Imre Garaba, József Varga, Ferenc Csongrádi (46.László Dajka), Antal Nagy, Lajos Détári, József Kiprich (66.Béla Bodonyi), Tibor Nyilasi, Márton Esterházy. Trainer: György Mezey.
**Goals**: 1-0 Costas Foti (28), 1-1 Antal Róth (49), 1-2 Tibor Nyilasi (89).

23.12.1984, Makareio Stádio, Nicosia; Attendance: 3,000
Referee: Pavel Dotchev (Bulgaria)
**CYPRUS - HOLLAND**     **0-1(0-0)**
**CYP:** Charis Konstantinou, Koulis Pantziaras, Costas Miamiliotis, Klitos Erotokritou, Nicos Pantziaras, Yiannakis Yiangoudakis, Christakis Mavris, Panayiotis Marangos, Sotiris Tsikkos, Costas Foti, Georgios Savvides. Trainer: Panikos Iacovou.
**NED:** Johannes Franciscus van Breukelen, Hubertus Johannes Nicolaas Wijnstekers, Ronald Spelbos (Cap), Peter Boeve, Wilhelmus Antonius van de Kerkhof, Machiel Valke, Ernestus Wilhelmus Johannes Brandts, René van der Gijp (77.Ronald Koeman), Petrus Johannes Houtman, Ruud Gullit, Marcelo van Basten. Trainer: Marinus Henrikus Bernardus Michels.
**Goal**: 0-1 Petrus Johannes Houtman (84).

27.02.1985, de Meer Stadion, Amsterdam; Attendance: 19,100
Referee: Dušan Krchnak (Czechoslovakia)
**HOLLAND - CYPRUS**     **7-1(3-1)**
**NED:** Johannes Franciscus van Breukelen, Hubertus Johannes Nicolaas Wijnstekers (Cap), Ernestus Wilhelmus Johannes Brandts, Peter Boeve, Wilhelmus Antonius van de Kerkhof, Dirk Hendrikus Schoenaker, Erwin Koeman, Ruud Gullit (77.René van der Gijp), Willem Cornelis Nicolaas Kieft, Marcelo van Basten, Simon Melkianus Tahamata. Trainer: Leo Beenhakker.
**CYP:** Charis Konstantinou, Koulis Pantziaras, Costas Miamiliotis, Klitos Erotokritou, Nicos Pantziaras, Costas Konstantinou, Panayiotis Marangos, Lefteris Kouis (67.Kypros Damianou), Georgios Savvides, Sotiris Tsikkos, Costas Foti. Trainer: Panikos Iacovou.
**Goals**: 0-1 Panayiotis Marangos (8), 1-1 Erwin Koeman (12), 2-1 Willem Cornelis Nicolaas Kieft (28), 3-1 Dirk Hendrikus Schoenaker (30), 4-1 Willem Cornelis Nicolaas Kieft (59), 5-1 Nikos Pantziaras (64 own goal), 6-1 Marcelo van Basten (65), 7-1 Dirk Hendrikus Schoenaker (79).

03.04.1985, Népstadion, Budapest; Attendance: 40,000
Referee: Einar Halle (Norway)
**HUNGARY - CYPRUS**     **2-0(0-0)**
**HUN:** Péter Disztl, Sándor Sallai, Antal Róth, Imre Garaba, József Varga, József Kardos, Antal Nagy, Lajos Détári, Béla Bodonyi (46.József Kiprich), Tibor Nyilasi, Márton Esterházy (72.László Szokolai). Trainer: György Mezey.
**CYP:** Andreas Konstantinou II, Costas Konstantinou, Costas Miamiliotis, Klitos Erotokritou, Nicos Pantziaras, Yiannakis Yiangoudakis, Marios Tsingis, Lakis Karseras (88.Floros Nicolaou), Panayiotis Marangos, Georgios Savvides (89.Loizos Mavroudis), Costas Foti. Trainer: Panikos Iacovou.
**Goals**: 1-0 Tibor Nyilasi (48), 2-0 László Szokolai (83).

17.04.1985, „Gerhard Hanappi" Stadion, Wien; Attendance: 21,000
Referee: Jakob Baumann (Switzerland)
**AUSTRIA - HUNGARY**     **0-3(0-2)**
**AUT:** Friedrich Koncilia, Leopold Lainer, Walter Hörmann, Josef Degeorgi (46.Ewald Türmer), Bruno Pezzey, Heribert Weber, Walter Schachner, Herbert Prohaska, Johann Krankl, Franz Oberacher (56.Anton Polster), Kurt Jara. Trainer: Branko Elsner (Yugoslavia).
**HUN:** Péter Disztl, Sándor Sallai, Antal Róth, Imre Garaba, Zoltán Péter, József Kardos, Antal Nagy, Lajos Détári, József Kiprich, Tibor Nyilasi, Márton Esterházy. Trainer: György Mezey.
**Goals**: 0-1 József Kiprich (21), 0-2 József Kiprich (34), 0-3 Lajos Détári (48).

01.05.1985, Feyenoord Stadion, Rotterdam; Attendance: 58,000
Referee: Luigi Agnolin (Italy)
**HOLLAND - AUSTRIA**     **1-1(0-0)**
**NED:** Johannes Franciscus van Breukelen, Michael Antonius Bernardus van de Korput, Hubertus Johannes Nicolaas Wijnstekers (Cap), Ernestus Wilhelmus Johannes Brandts, Wilhelmus Antonius van de Kerkhof, Dirk Hendrikus Schoenaker, Franklin Edmundo Rijkaard, Erwin Koeman, René van der Gijp (77.Robert Leonardus de Wit), Willem Cornelis Nicolaas Kieft, Simon Melkianus Tahamata. Trainer: Leo Beenhakker.
**AUT:** Friedrich Koncilia, Leopold Lainer, Bruno Pezzey, Ewald Türmer, Karl Brauneder, Walter Hörmann (46.Peter Hrstic), Herbert Prohaska, Gerald Willfurth, Reinhard Kienast, Walter Schachner, Anton Polster. Trainer: Branko Elsner (Yugoslavia).
**Goals**: 1-0 Willem Cornelis Nicolaas Kieft (55), 1-1 Walter Schachner (60).

07.05.1985, Liebenau Stadion, Graz; Attendance: 15,000
Referee: Alan Snoddy (Northern Ireland)
**AUSTRIA - CYPRUS** **4-0(2-0)**
**AUT:** Friedrich Koncilia, Leopold Lainer, Bruno Pezzey, Anton Pichler, Karl Brauneder, Walter Hörmann, Herbert Prohaska, Peter Hrstic, Gerald Willfurth, Walter Schachner, Anton Polster (67.Peter Pacult). Trainer: Branko Elsner (Yugoslavia).
**CYP:** Andreas Konstantinou II, Nicos Patikkis, Costas Konstantinou, Nicos Pantziaras (46.Koulis Pantziaras), Klitos Erotokritou, Panayiotis Marangos, Yiannakis Yiangoudakis, Floros Nicolaou, Marios Tsingis (87.Evagoras Christofi), Georgios Savvides, Costas Foti. Trainer: Panikos Iacovou.
**Goals**: 1-0 Peter Hrstic (2), 2-0 Anton Polster (36), 3-0 Walter Schachner (55), 4-0 Gerald Willfurth (74).

14.05.1985, Népstadion, Budapest; Attendance: 80,000
Referee: Karl-Josef Assenmacher (West Germany)
**HUNGARY - HOLLAND** **0-1(0-0)**
**HUN:** Péter Disztl, Sándor Sallai, Antal Róth, Imre Garaba, Zoltán Péter, József Kardos (57.József Varga), Antal Nagy, Lajos Détári, József Kiprich, Tibor Nyilasi, Márton Esterházy (71.Ferenc Mészáros). Trainer: György Mezey.
**NED:** Johannes Franciscus van Breukelen, Michael Antonius Bernardus van de Korput, Hubertus Johannes Nicolaas Wijnstekers (Cap), Adrianus Andreas van Tiggelen, Franklin Edmundo Rijkaard, Dirk Hendrikus Schoenaker, Ton Lokhoff (46.Robert Leonardus de Wit), Wilhelmus Antonius van de Kerkhof (62.Ronald Koeman), Marcelo van Basten, Willem Cornelis Nicolaas Kieft, Simon Melkianus Tahamata. Trainer: Leo Beenhakker.
**Goal**: 0-1 Robert Leonardus de Wit (68).

# GROUP 6

| | | | | |
|---|---|---|---|---|
| 12.09.1984 | Dublin | Republic of Ireland - Soviet Union | | 1-0(0-0) |
| 12.09.1984 | Oslo | Norway - Switzerland | | 0-1(0-1) |
| 26.09.1984 | København | Denmark - Norway | | 1-0(0-0) |
| 10.10.1984 | Oslo | Norway - Soviet Union | | 1-1(0-0) |
| 17.10.1984 | Bern | Switzerland - Denmark | | 1-0(1-0) |
| 17.10.1984 | Oslo | Norway - Republic of Ireland | | 1-0(1-0) |
| 14.11.1984 | København | Denmark - Republic of Ireland | | 3-0(1-0) |
| 17.04.1985 | Bern | Switzerland - Soviet Union | | 2-2(1-1) |
| 01.05.1985 | Dublin | Republic of Ireland - Norway | | 0-0 |
| 02.05.1985 | Moskva | Soviet Union - Switzerland | | 4-0(4-0) |
| 02.06.1985 | Dublin | Republic of Ireland - Switzerland | | 3-0(2-0) |
| 05.06.1985 | København | Denmark - Soviet Union | | 4-2(2-1) |
| 11.09.1985 | Bern | Switzerland - Republic of Ireland | | 0-0 |
| 25.09.1985 | Moskva | Soviet Union - Denmark | | 1-0(0-0) |
| 09.10.1985 | København | Denmark - Switzerland | | 0-0 |
| 16.10.1985 | Oslo | Norway - Denmark | | 1-5(1-0) |
| 16.10.1985 | Moskva | Soviet Union - Republic of Ireland | | 2-0(0-0) |
| 30.10.1985 | Moskva | Soviet Union - Norway | | 1-0(0-0) |
| 13.11.1985 | Dublin | Republic of Ireland - Denmark | | 1-4(1-2) |
| 13.11.1985 | Luzern | Switzerland - Norway | | 1-1(0-1) |

## FINAL STANDINGS

| | | | | | | | | | |
|---|---|---|---|---|---|---|---|---|---|
| 1. | **Denmark** | 8 | 5 | 1 | 2 | 17 | - | 6 | 11 |
| 2. | **Soviet Union** | 8 | 4 | 2 | 2 | 13 | - | 8 | 10 |
| 3. | Switzerland | 8 | 2 | 4 | 2 | 5 | - | 10 | 8 |
| 4. | Republic of Ireland | 8 | 2 | 2 | 4 | 5 | - | 10 | 6 |
| 5. | Norway | 8 | 1 | 3 | 4 | 4 | - | 10 | 5 |

Denmark and Soviet Union qualified for the Final Tournament.

12.09.1984, Lansdowne Road, Dublin; Attendance: 28,000
Referee: Johannes Nicolaas Ignatius „Jan" Keizer (Holland)
**REPUBLIC OF IRELAND - SOVIET UNION** **1-0(0-0)**
**IRL:** James Martin McDonagh, John Anthony Devine, David Anthony O'Leary, Mark Thomas Lawrenson, Christopher William Gerard Hughton, Ronald Andrew Whelan, Anthony Patrick Grealish (Cap), William Brady, Michael John Robinson, Michael Anthony Walsh (82.Eamonn Gerard O'Keefe), Anthony Galvin. Trainer: Eoin Hand.
**URS:** Rinat Dasaev, Tengiz Sulakvelidze, Aleksandr Chivadze (Cap), Sergey Baltacha, Anatoliy Demyanenko, Khoren Oganesyan (67.Sergey Gotzmanov), Gennadiy Litovchenko, Vladimir Bessonov (35.Andrey Zygmantovich), Sergey Aleynikov, Sergey Rodionov, Oleg Blokhin. Trainer: Eduard Malofeev.
**Goal**: 1-0 Michael Anthony Walsh (64).

12.09.1984, Ullevaal Stadion, Oslo; Attendance: 14,413
Referee: Eduard Sostarić (Yugoslavia)
**NORWAY - SWITZERLAND** **0-1(0-1)**
**NOR:** Erik Thorstvedt, Erik Solér, Åge Hareide, Terje Kojedal, Svein Grøndalen, Kai Erik Herlovsen, Per Egil Ahlsen, Vidar Davidsen, Anders Giske (62.Roger Albertsen), Arne Dokken, Sverre Brandhaug (42.Arve Seland). Trainer: Tor Røste Fossen.
**SUI:** Karl Engel, Roger Wehrli, Charles In-Albon, André Egli, Marco Schällibaum, Alain Geiger, Marcel Koller, Heinz Hermann, Umberto Barberis, Beat Sutter, Jean-Paul Brigger. Trainer: Paul Wolfisberg.
**Goal:** 0-1 André Egli (4 penalty).

26.09.1984, Idrætsparken, København; Attendance: 45,400
Referee: Ronald Bridges (Wales)
**DENMARK - NORWAY** **1-0(0-0)**
**DEN:** Ole Qvist, Søren Busk, Ivan Nielsen, Morten Olsen (Cap), Kim Christofte, Klaus Berggreen (55.Kenneth Brylle), Jens Jørn Bertelsen, Jan Mølby, Jesper Olsen (78.John Lauridsen), Michael Laudrup, Preben Elkjær-Larsen. Trainer: Josef Piontek (West Germany).
**NOR:** Erik Thorstvedt, Svein Fjælberg, Terje Kojedal, Åge Hareide, Svein Grøndalen, Erik Solér, Per Egil Ahlsen, Vidar Davidsen, Hallvar Thoresen, Pål Jacobsen (75.Svein Mathisen), Joar Vaadal (55.Ulf Moen). Trainer: Tor Røste Fossen.
**Goal:** 1-0 Preben Elkjær-Larsen (56).

10.10.1984, Ullevaal Stadion, Oslo; Attendance: 13,789
Referee: Volker Roth (West Germany)
**NORWAY - SOVIET UNION** **1-1(0-0)**
**NOR:** Erik Thorstvedt, Svein Fjælberg, Terje Kojedal, Åge Hareide, Per Edmund Mordt, Erik Solér, Per Egil Ahlsen, Vidar Davidsen (71.Egil Johansen), Hallvar Thoresen, Arne Larsen Økland, Pål Jacobsen. Trainer: Tor Røste Fossen.
**URS:** Rinat Dasaev (Cap), Tengiz Sulakvelidze, Aleksandr Bubnov, Sergey Baltacha, Boris Pozdnyakov, Gennadiy Litovchenko, Sergey Gotzmanov, Khoren Oganesyan (46.Andrey Zygmantovich), Sergey Aleynikov, Sergey Rodionov (67.Georgiy Kondratiev), Oleg Protasov. Trainer: Eduard Malofeev.
**Goals:** 1-0 Hallvar Thoresen (54 penalty), 1-1 Gennadiy Litovchenko (74).

17.10.1984, Wankdorf Stadion, Bern; Attendance: 37,000
Referee: Neil Midgley (England)
**SWITZERLAND - DENMARK** **1-0(1-0)**
**SUI:** Karl Engel, Roger Wehrli, Charles In-Albon, André Egli, Marco Schällibaum, Alain Geiger, Heinz Hermann, Georges Brégy, Umberto Barberis (84.Raimondo Ponte), Hanspeter Zwicker, Jean-Paul Brigger (75.Beat Sutter). Trainer: Paul Wolfisberg.
**DEN:** Ole Qvist, Morten Olsen (Cap), Søren Busk, Ivan Nielsen, Kim Christofte, Jan Mølby (56.Kenneth Brylle), Jens Jørn Bertelsen, Jesper Olsen, Klaus Berggreen (79.John Sivebæk), Preben Elkjær-Larsen, Michael Laudrup. Trainer: Josef Piontek (West Germany).
**Goal:** 1-0 Umberto Barberis (43).

17.10.1984, Ullevaal Stadion, Oslo; Attendance: 15,379
Referee: Klaus Scheurell (East Germany)
**NORWAY - REPUBLIC OF IRELAND** 1-0(1-0)
**NOR:** Erik Thorstvedt, Svein Fjælberg (33.Vidar Davidsen), Terje Kojedal, Åge Hareide, Per Edmund Mordt, Erik Solér, Kai Erik Herlovsen, Per Egil Ahlsen, Hallvar Thoresen, Arne Larsen Økland, Pål Jacobsen (89.Per Henriksen). Trainer: Tor Røste Fossen.
**IRL:** James Martin McDonagh, John Anthony Devine, David Anthony O'Leary, Mark Thomas Lawrenson, Christopher William Gerard Hughton, Anthony Patrick Grealish (Cap), Ronald Andrew Whelan (67.Kevin O'Callaghan), William Brady, Michael John Robinson (69.Michael Anthony Walsh), Francis Anthony Stapleton, Anthony Galvin. Trainer: Eoin Hand.
Goal: 1-0 Pål Jacobsen (42).

14.11.1984, Idrætsparken, København; Attendance: 45,300
Referee: Robert Würtz (France)
**DENMARK - REPUBLIC OF IRELAND** 3-0(1-0)
**DEN:** Ole Qvist, John Sivebæk, Ivan Nielsen, Morten Olsen (Cap), Søren Busk, Klaus Berggreen, Jens Jørn Bertelsen (58.Jan Mølby), Frank Arnesen, Søren Lerby, Michael Laudrup, Preben Elkjær-Larsen (64.Kenneth Brylle). Trainer: Josef Piontek (West Germany).
**IRL:** James Martin McDonagh, Mark Thomas Lawrenson, Michael Joseph McCarthy, David Anthony O'Leary, James Martin Beglin, Kevin Mark Sheedy, William Brady, Anthony Patrick Grealish, Anthony Galvin (46.Kevin O'Callaghan), Francis Anthony Stapleton (Cap), Michael Anthony Walsh. Trainer: Eoin Hand.
Goals: 1-0 Preben Elkjær-Larsen (30), 2-0 Preben Elkjær-Larsen (46), 3-0 Søren Lerby (55).

17.04.1985, Wankdorf Stadion, Bern; Attendance: 51,000
Referee: Robert Bonar Valentine (Scotland)
**SWITZERLAND - SOVIET UNION** 2-2(1-1)
**SUI:** Karl Engel, Roger Wehrli, Heinz Lüdi, Charles In-Albon, André Egli, Alain Geiger, Heinz Hermann, Umberto Barberis (78.Marco Schällibaum), Georges Brégy, Jean-Paul Brigger, Dominique Cina. Trainer: Paul Wolfisberg.
**URS:** Rinat Dasaev (Cap), Nikolay Larionov, Ivan Vishnevskiy, Sergey Baltacha, Anatoliy Demyanenko, Sergey Aleynikov, Sergey Gotzmanov, Gennadiy Litovchenko (71.Andrey Zygmantovich), Yuriy Gavrilov, Oleg Protasov, Georgiy Kondratiev. Trainer: Eduard Malofeev.
Goals: 0-1 Yuriy Gavrilov (36), 1-1 Georges Brégy (43 penalty), 1-2 Anatoliy Demyanenko (80), 2-2 André Egli (90).

01.05.1985, Lansdowne Road, Dublin; Attendance: 20,000
Referee: Lajos Németh (Hungary)
**REPUBLIC OF IRELAND - NORWAY** 0-0
**IRL:** Patrick Bonner, David Francis Langan (83.Paul McGrath), Mark Thomas Lawrenson, David Anthony O'Leary, James Martin Beglin, Gary Patrick Waddock, Gerard Anthony Daly, William Brady (67.Ronald Andrew Whelan), Anthony Galvin, Francis Anthony Stapleton (Cap), Michael John Robinson. Trainer: Eoin Hand.
**NOR:** Erik Thorstvedt, Svein Fjælberg, Terje Kojedal, Åge Hareide, Hans Hermann Henriksen, Kai Erik Herlovsen (57.Arne Erlandsen), Per Egil Ahlsen, Erik Solér, Arne Larsen Økland, Hallvar Thoresen, Ulf Moen (87.Pål Jacobsen). Trainer: Tor Røste Fossen.

02.05.1985 Lenin Stadium, Moskva; Attendance: 90,000
Referee: Roger Schoeters (Belgium)
**SOVIET UNION - SWITZERLAND**     **4-0(4-0)**
**URS:** Rinat Dasaev (Cap), Tengiz Sulakvelidze, Ivan Vishnevskiy, Nikolay Larionov, Anatoliy Demyanenko, Sergey Aleynikov, Sergey Gotzmanov, Gennadiy Litovchenko (79.Igor Belanov), Yuriy Gavrilov, Oleg Protasov, Georgiy Kondratiev. Trainer: Eduard Malofeev.
**SUI:** Karl Engel, Roger Wehrli, Charles In-Albon, Heinz Lüdi, André Egli, Alain Geiger, Marco Schällibaum, Heinz Hermann, Umberto Barberis (60.Christian Matthey), Georges Brégy (60.Manfred Braschler), Jean-Paul Brigger. Trainer: Paul Wolfisberg.
**Goals:** 1-0 Oleg Protasov (18), 2-0 Oleg Protasov (39), 3-0 Georgiy Kondratiev (44), 4-0 Georgiy Kondratiev (45).

02.06.1985, Lansdowne Road, Dublin; Attendance: 17,500
Referee: Paolo Bergamo (Italy)
**REPUBLIC OF IRELAND - SWITZERLAND**     **3-0(2-0)**
**IRL:** James Martin McDonagh, David Francis Langan, David Anthony O'Leary, Michael Joseph McCarthy, James Martin Beglin, Gerard Anthony Daly (46.Ronald Andrew Whelan), Anthony Patrick Grealish (63.Paul McGrath), William Brady, Kevin Mark Sheedy, Michael John Robinson, Francis Anthony Stapleton (Cap). Trainer: Eoin Hand.
**SUI:** Karl Engel (24.Erich Burgener), Roger Wehrli, Charles In-Albon, Heinz Lüdi, André Egli, Alain Geiger, Heinz Hermann, Umberto Barberis (59.Georges Brégy), Michel Decastel, Manfred Braschler, Christian Matthey. Trainer: Paul Wolfisberg.
**Goals:** 1-0 Francis Anthony Stapleton (7), 2-0 Anthony Patrick Grealish (33), 3-0 Kevin Mark Sheedy (57).

05.06.1985 Idrætsparken, København; Attendance: 45,700
Referee: Horst Brummeier (Austria)
**DENMARK - SOVIET UNION**     **4-2(2-1)**
**DEN:** Ole Qvist, Søren Busk, Morten Olsen (Cap), Ivan Nielsen, Klaus Berggreen, Frank Arnesen (78.Henrik Andersen), Jens Jørn Bertelsen, Søren Lerby, Jesper Olsen (46.Per Frimann), Preben Elkjær-Larsen, Michael Laudrup. Trainer: Josef Piontek (West Germany).
**URS:** Rinat Dasaev (Cap), Tengiz Sulakvelidze, Boris Pozdnyakov, Sergey Baltacha, Anatoliy Demyanenko, Sergey Aleynikov, Sergey Gotzmanov, Gennadiy Litovchenko (23.Andrey Zygmantovich), Yuriy Gavrilov, Oleg Protasov, Igor Belanov (70.Georgiy Kondratiev). Trainer: Eduard Malofeev.
**Goals:** 1-0 Preben Elkjær-Larsen (16), 2-0 Preben Elkjær-Larsen (19), 2-1 Oleg Protasov (25), 3-1 Michael Laudrup (61), 4-1 Michael Laudrup (64), 4-2 Sergey Gotzmanov (68).

11.09.1985, Wankdorf Stadion, Bern; Attendance: 24,000
Referee: Emilio Soriano Aladrén (Spain)
**SWITZERLAND - REPUBLIC OF IRELAND**     **0-0**
**SUI:** Karl Engel, André Egli, Charles In-Albon, Alain Geiger, Marco Schällibaum (75.Jean-Paul Brigger), Heinz Hermann, Georges Brégy, Philippe Perret, Marcel Koller, Robert Lüthi, Christian Matthey. Trainer: Paul Wolfisberg.
**IRL:** James Martin McDonagh, Christopher William Gerard Hughton, Michael Joseph McCarthy, David Anthony O'Leary, James Martin Beglin, William Brady, Gerard Anthony Daly (66.Paul McGrath), Mark Thomas Lawrenson, Anthony Guy Cascarino, Francis Anthony Stapleton (Cap), Kevin Mark Sheedy (71.Kevin O'Callaghan). Trainer: Eoin Hand.

25.09.1985, Lenin Stadium, Moskva; Attendance: 100,000
Referee: Antonis Vassaras (Greece)
**SOVIET UNION - DENMARK** **1-0(0-0)**
**URS:** Rinat Dasaev (Cap), Gennadiy Morozov, Aleksandr Chivadze, Aleksandr Bubnov, Anatoliy Demyanenko, Nikolay Larionov (26.Aleksandr Zavarov), Sergey Gotzmanov, Sergey Aleynikov, Fëdor Cherenkov, Oleg Protasov, Oleg Blokhin (79.Georgiy Kondratiev). Trainer: Eduard Malofeev.
**DEN:** Troels Rasmussen, John Sivebæk, Søren Busk, Morten Olsen (Cap), Ivan Nielsen (49.Jan Mølby), Klaus Berggreen, Jens Jørn Bertelsen, Søren Lerby, Frank Arnesen, Preben Elkjær-Larsen (14.Per Frimann), Michael Laudrup. Trainer: Josef Piontek (West Germany).
**Goal**: 1-0 Oleg Protasov (50).

09.10.1985, Idrætsparken, København; Attendance: 45,600
Referee: Joël Quiniou (France)
**DENMARK - SWITZERLAND** **0-0**
**DEN:** Troels Rasmussen, Søren Busk, Morten Olsen (Cap), Ivan Nielsen, Klaus Berggreen, Jens Jørn Bertelsen, Allan Rodenkam Simonsen (46.John Sivebæk), Søren Lerby, Frank Arnesen (81.Jan Mølby), Preben Elkjær-Larsen, Michael Laudrup. Trainer: Josef Piontek (West Germany).
**SUI:** Karl Engel, André Egli, Charles In-Albon, Alain Geiger, Heinz Lüdi, Marco Schällibaum, Georges Brégy, Heinz Hermann, Marcel Koller, Beat Sutter (64.Manfred Braschler), Christian Matthey. Trainer: Paul Wolfisberg.

16.10.1985, Ullevaal Stadion, Oslo; Attendance: 19,420
Referee: Ioan Igna (Romania)
**NORWAY - DENMARK** **1-5(1-0)**
**NOR:** Erik Thorstvedt, Svein Fjælberg (53.Terje Kojedal), Per Egil Ahlsen, Åge Hareide (72.Pål Jacobsen), Hans Hermann Henriksen, Vidar Davidsen, Kai Erik Herlovsen, Tom Sundby, Jørn Andersen, Arne Larsen Økland, Hallvar Thoresen. Trainer: Tor Røste Fossen.
**DEN:** Troels Rasmussen, John Sivebæk, Søren Busk, Morten Olsen (Cap), Ivan Nielsen, Klaus Berggreen, Jens Jørn Bertelsen (46.Jan Mølby), Frank Arnesen (70.Per Frimann), Søren Lerby, Michael Laudrup, Preben Elkjær-Larsen. Trainer: Josef Piontek (West Germany).
**Goals**: 1-0 Tom Sundby (43), 1-1 Michael Laudrup (56), 1-2 Søren Lerby (63 penalty), 1-3 Preben Elkjær-Larsen (65), 1-4 Klaus Berggreen (75), 1-5 Klaus Berggreen (78).

16.10.1985, Lenin Stadium, Moskva; Attendance: 100,000
Referee: Paolo Casarin (Italy)
**SOVIET UNION - REPUBLIC OF IRELAND** **2-0(0-0)**
**URS:** Rinat Dasaev (Cap), Gennadiy Morozov, Aleksandr Chivadze, Aleksandr Bubnov, Anatoliy Demyanenko, Aleksandr Zavarov (84.Vladimir Bessonov), Sergey Gotzmanov, Sergey Aleynikov, Fëdor Cherenkov, Oleg Protasov, Oleg Blokhin (55.Georgiy Kondratiev). Trainer: Eduard Malofeev.
**IRL:** James Martin McDonagh, Christopher William Gerard Hughton, Michael Joseph McCarthy, David Anthony O'Leary, James Martin Beglin (79.Kevin O'Callaghan), William Brady, Gary Patrick Waddock, Mark Thomas Lawrenson, Anthony Guy Cascarino, Francis Anthony Stapleton (Cap), Anthony Patrick Grealish (71.Ronald Andrew Whelan). Trainer: Eoin Hand.
**Goals**: 1-0 Fëdor Cherenkov (61), 2-0 Oleg Protasov (90).

30.10.1985, Lenin Stadium, Moskva; Attendance: 40,000
Referee: Brian McGinlay (Scotland)
**SOVIET UNION - NORWAY** **1-0(0-0)**
**URS:** Rinat Dasaev (Cap), Gennadiy Morozov, Aleksandr Chivadze, Aleksandr Bubnov, Anatoliy Demyanenko, Aleksandr Zavarov, Sergey Gotzmanov, Sergey Aleynikov (46.Vladimir Bessonov), Fëdor Cherenkov, Oleg Protasov (85.Yuriy Gavrilov), Georgiy Kondratiev. Trainer: Eduard Malofeev.
**NOR:** Erik Thorstvedt, Hans Hermann Henriksen, Terje Kojedal, Åge Hareide, Per Edmund Mordt, Vidar Davidsen, Kai Erik Herlovsen, Tom Sundby, Jørn Andersen (77.Sverre Brandhaug), Arne Larsen Økland, Hallvar Thoresen. Trainer: Tor Røste Fossen.

**Goal**: 1-0 Georgiy Kondratiev (58).

13.11.1985, Lansdowne Road, Dublin; Attendance: 12,000
Referee: Franz Wöhrer (Austria)
**REPUBLIC OF IRELAND - DENMARK**                      **1-4(1-2)**
**IRL**: James Martin McDonagh, Mark Thomas Lawrenson, James Martin Beglin, Kevin Bernard Moran, David Anthony O'Leary, William Brady, Paul McGrath, Anthony Patrick Grealish (30.Patrick Byrne II), Anthony Guy Cascarino, Francis Anthony Stapleton (Cap), Kevin Mark Sheedy (69.Michael John Robinson). Trainer: Eoin Hand.
**DEN**: Troels Rasmussen, John Sivebæk, Morten Olsen (Cap) (69.Frank Arnesen), Ivan Nielsen, Søren Busk, Klaus Berggreen, Jan Mølby, Søren Lerby (59.Jens Jørn Bertelsen), Jesper Olsen, Michael Laudrup, Preben Elkjær-Larsen. Trainer: Josef Piontek (West Germany).
**Goals**: 1-0 Francis Anthony Stapleton (6), 1-1 Preben Elkjær-Larsen (7), 1-2 Michael Laudrup (49), 1-3 John Sivebæk (57), 1-4 Preben Elkjær-Larsen (76).

13.11.1985, Allmend Stadion, Luzern; Attendance: 4,500
Referee: Ovadia Ben-Itzhak (Israel)
**SWITZERLAND - NORWAY**                                **1-1(0-1)**
**SUI**: Karl Engel, Marco Schällibaum, Heinz Lüdi, André Egli, Charles In-Albon, Alain Geiger, Georges Brégy (73.Marcel Koller), Heinz Hermann, Christian Matthey, Claudio Sulser (77.Dominique Cina), Jean-Paul Brigger. Trainer: Paul Wolfisberg.
**NOR**: Erik Thorstvedt, Hans Hermann Henriksen, Terje Kojedal, Åge Hareide, Per Edmund Mordt, Vidar Davidsen, Kai Erik Herlovsen, Per Egil Ahlsen (77.Sverre Brandhaug), Tom Sundby, Arne Larsen Økland (73.Jørn Andersen), Hallvar Thoresen. Trainer: Tor Røste Fossen.
**Goals**: 0-1 Tom Sundby (40), 1-1 Christian Matthey (54).

# GROUP 7

| | | | | |
|---|---|---|---|---|
| 12.09.1984 | Reykjavík | Iceland - Wales | | 1-0(0-0) |
| 17.10.1984 | Glasgow | Scotland - Iceland | | 3-0(2-0) |
| 17.10.1984 | Sevilla | Spain - Wales | | 3-0(1-0) |
| 14.11.1984 | Cardiff | Wales - Iceland | | 2-1(1-0) |
| 14.11.1984 | Glasgow | Scotland - Spain | | 3-1(2-0) |
| 27.02.1985 | Sevilla | Spain - Scotland | | 1-0(0-0) |
| 27.03.1985 | Glasgow | Scotland - Wales | | 0-1(0-1) |
| 30.04.1985 | Wrexham | Wales - Spain | | 3-0(1-0) |
| 28.05.1985 | Reykjavík | Iceland - Scotland | | 0-1(0-0) |
| 12.06.1985 | Reykjavík | Iceland - Spain | | 1-2(1-0) |
| 10.09.1985 | Cardiff | Wales - Scotland | | 1-1(1-0) |
| 25.09.1985 | Sevilla | Spain - Iceland | | 2-1(1-1) |

### FINAL STANDINGS

| | | | | | | | | |
|---|---|---|---|---|---|---|---|---|
| 1. | **Spain** | 6 | 4 | 0 | 2 | 9 - 8 | 8 |
| 2. | *Scotland* | 6 | 3 | 1 | 2 | 8 - 4 | 7 |
| 3. | Wales | 6 | 3 | 1 | 2 | 7 - 6 | 7 |
| 4. | Iceland | 6 | 1 | 0 | 5 | 4 - 10 | 2 |

Spain qualified for the Final Tournament.
Scotland qaulified for the Intercontinental Play-off against the Oceania Zone Winners.

12.09.1984, Laugardalsvöllur Stadium, Reykjavík; Attendance: 10,837
Referee: Erik Sten Jensen (Denmark)
**ICELAND - WALES** **1-0(0-0)**
**ISL:** Bjarni Sigurðsson, Þorgrímur Þráinsson, Árni Sveinsson, Magnús Bergs, Sævar Jónsson, Janus Guðlaugsson, Pétur Pétursson, Atli Eðvaldsson, Sigurður Grétarsson, Ásgeir Sigurvinsson (Cap), Guðmundur Þorbjörnsson. Trainer: Anthony Knapp (England).
**WAL:** Neville Southall, Neil John Slatter, Joseph Patrick Jones, Kevin Ratcliffe, Jeffrey Hopkins, Gordon John Davies (60.Jeremy Melvyn Charles), Kenneth Francis Jackett, Michael Reginald Thomas, Alan Davies, Robert Mark James, Leslie Mark Hughes. Manager: Harold Michael England.
**Goal**: 1-0 Magnús Bergs (52).

17.10.1984, Hampden Park, Glasgow; Attendance: 52,829
Referee: Egbert Mulder (Holland)
**SCOTLAND - ICELAND** **3-0(2-0)**
**SCO:** James Leighton, Stephen Nicol, Arthur Richard Albiston, William Fergus Miller, Alexander McLeish, David Cooper, Graeme James Souness (Cap), Paul Michael Lyons McStay, James Bett, Kenneth Mathieson Dalglish (68.Charles Nicholas), Maurice Johnston. Manager: John Stein.
**ISL:** Bjarni Sigurðsson, Þorgrímur Þráinsson, Árni Sveinsson, Magnús Bergs, Sævar Jónsson, Janus Guðlaugsson, Pétur Pétursson, Atli Eðvaldsson, Ragnar Margeirsson, Ásgeir Sigurvinsson (Cap), Arnór Guðjohnsen. Trainer: Anthony Knapp (England).
**Goals:** 1-0 Paul Michael Lyons McStay (22), 2-0 Paul Michael Lyons McStay (40), 3-0 Charles Nicholas (70).

17.10.1984, Estadio "Benito Villamarín", Sevilla; Attendance: 42,500
Referee: Erik Fredriksson (Sweden)
**SPAIN - WALES**     **3-0(1-0)**
**ESP:** Luis Miguel Arkonada Echarre (Cap), Juan Antonio Señor Gómez, Andoni Goikoetxea Olaskoaga, Antonio Maceda Francés, José Antonio Camacho Alfaro, Víctor Muñoz Manrique, Francisco Javier López Alfaro (33.Roberto Fernández Bonillo), Rafael Gordillo Vázquez, Francisco José Carrasco Hidalgo, Emilio Butragueño Santos, Hipólito Rincón Povedano (81.Julio Alberto Moreno Casas). Trainer: Miguel Muñoz Mozún.
**WAL:** Neville Southall, Neil John Slatter, David Owen Phillips, Kevin Ratcliffe, Jeremy Melvyn Charles, Kenneth Francis Jackett, Robert Mark James, Peter Nicholas, Michael Reginald Thomas (60.Nigel Mark Vaughan), Leslie Mark Hughes, Alan Thomas Curtis. Manager: Harold Michael England.
**Goals:** 1-0 Hipólito Rincón Povedano (7), 2-0 Francisco José Carrasco Hidalgo (83), 3-0 Emilio Butragueño Santos (89).

14.11.1984, Ninian Park, Cardiff; Attendance: 10,506
Referee: Eamonn Farrell (Republic of Ireland)
**WALES - ICELAND**     **2-1(1-0)**
**WAL:** Neville Southall, Neil John Slatter, David Owen Phillips, Kevin Ratcliffe, Jeremy Melvyn Charles (50.Jeffrey Hopkins), Kenneth Francis Jackett, Robert Mark James, Gordon John Davies, Michael Reginald Thomas, Ian James Rush, Leslie Mark Hughes. Manager: Harold Michael England.
**ISL:** Bjarni Sigurðsson, Þorgrímur Þráinsson, Árni Sveinsson, Magnús Bergs, Sævar Jónsson, Siðurdur Jónsson, Pétur Pétursson (Cap), Ragnar Margeirsson (82.Gunnar Gíslason), Sigurður Grétarsson (67.Njáll Eiðsson), Arnór Guðjohnsen, Guðmundur Þorbjörnsson. Trainer: Anthony Knapp (England).
**Goals:** 1-0 Michael Reginald Thomas (35), 1-1 Pétur Pétursson (55), 2-1 Leslie Mark Hughes (63).

14.11.1984, Hampden Park, Glasgow; Attendance: 74,299
Referee: Adolf Prokop (East Germany)
**SCOTLAND - SPAIN**     **3-1(2-0)**
**SCO:** James Leighton, Stephen Nicol, Arthur Richard Albiston, William Fergus Miller, Alexander McLeish, David Cooper, Graeme James Souness (Cap), Paul Michael Lyons McStay, James Bett, Kenneth Mathieson Dalglish, Maurice Johnston. Manager: John Stein.
**ESP:** Luis Miguel Arkonada Echarre (Cap), Santiago Urquiaga Pérez Lugar, Andoni Goikoetxea Olaskoaga, Antonio Maceda Francés, José Antonio Camacho Alfaro, Juan Antonio Señor Gómez, Víctor Muñoz Manrique, Rafael Gordillo Vázquez, Carlos Alonso González „Santillana", Ismael Urtubi Aróstegui (80.Francisco José Carrasco Hidalgo), Hipólito Rincón Povedano (46.Emilio Butragueño Santos). Trainer: Miguel Muñoz Mozún.
**Goals:** 1-0 Maurice Johston (33), 2-0 Maurice Johston (42), 2-1 Andoni Goikoetxea Olaskoaga (65), 3-1 Kenneth Mathieson Dalglish (75).

27.02.1985, Estadio „Ramón Sánchez Pizjuán", Sevilla; Attendance: 70,410
Referee: Michel Vautrot (France)
**SPAIN - SCOTLAND**     **1-0(0-0)**
**ESP:** Luis Miguel Arkonada Echarre (Cap), Gerardo Miranda Concepción, Andoni Goikoetxea Olaskoaga, Antonio Maceda Francés, José Antonio Camacho Alfaro, Juan Antonio Señor Gómez, Roberto Fernández Bonillo, Ricardo Gallego Redondo (80.Julio Alberto Moreno Casas), Rafael Gordillo Vázquez, Francisco Javier Clos Orozco, Emilio Butragueño Santos. Trainer: Miguel Muñoz Mozún.
**SCO:** James Leighton, Richard Charles Gough, Arthur Richard Albiston, William Fergus Miller, Alexander McLeish, David Cooper, Graeme James Souness (Cap), Paul Michael Lyons McStay (76.Gordon David Strachan), James Bett, Steven Archibald (84.Charles Nicholas), Maurice Johnston. Manager: John Stein.
**Goal:** 1-0 Francisco Javier Clos Orozco (48).

27.03.1985, Hampden Park, Glasgow; Attendance: 62,424
Referee: Alexis Ponnet (Belgium)
**SCOTLAND - WALES**                                                 **0-1(0-1)**
**SCO:** James Leighton, Stephen Nicol, Arthur Richard Albiston (57.Alan David Hansen), William Fergus Miller, Alexander McLeish, David Cooper, Graeme James Souness (Cap), Paul Michael Lyons McStay (75.Charles Nicholas), James Bett, Kenneth Mathieson Dalglish, Maurice Johnston. Manager: John Stein.
**WAL:** Neville Southall, Neil John Slatter, Joseph Patrick Jones, Kevin Ratcliffe, Kenneth Francis Jackett, David Owen Phillips, Robert Mark James, Peter Nicholas, Michael Reginald Thomas, Ian James Rush, Leslie Mark Hughes. Manager: Harold Michael England.
**Goal**: 0-1 Ian James Rush (37).

30.04.1985, The Racecourse Stadium, Wrexham; Attendance: 23,494
Referee: Johannes Nicolaas Ignatius „Jan" Keizer (Holland)
**WALES - SPAIN**                                                     **3-0(1-0)**
**WAL:** Neville Southall, Neil John Slatter, Patrick William Roger Van Den Hauwe, Kevin Ratcliffe, Kenneth Francis Jackett, David Owen Phillips, Robert Mark James, Peter Nicholas, Michael Reginald Thomas, Ian James Rush, Leslie Mark Hughes. Manager: Harold Michael England.
**ESP:** Luis Miguel Arkonada Echarre (Cap), Gerardo Miranda Concepción, Andoni Goikoetxea Olaskoaga, Antonio Maceda Francés, Julio Alberto Moreno Casas, Jesús Íñigo Liceranzu Ochoa, Víctor Muñoz Manrique, Ricardo Gallego Redondo (46.Ramón María Calderé Del Rey), Rafael Gordillo Vázquez, Juan Carlos Pérez Rojo, Hipólito Rincón Povedano (57.Francisco Javier Clos Orozco). Trainer: Miguel Muñoz Mozún.
**Goals**: 1-0 Ian James Rush (44), 2-0 Leslie Mark Hughes (53), 3-0 Ian James Rush (86).

28.05.1985, Laugardalsvöllur Stadium, Reykjavík; Attendance: 15,052
Referee: Anatoly Milchenko (Soviet Union)
**ICELAND - SCOTLAND**                                     **0-1(0-0)**
**ISL:** Eggert Guðmundsson, Þorgrímur Þráinsson, Árni Sveinsson, Magnús Bergs, Sævar Jónsson, Janus Guðlaugsson, Pétur Pétursson, Atli Eðvaldsson, Teitur Þórðarson (Cap) (57.Sigurður Grétarsson), Siðurdur Jónsson (25.Ómar Torfason), Guðmundur Þorbjörnsson. Trainer: Anthony Knapp (England).
**SCO:** James Leighton, Richard Charles Gough, Maurice Daniel Robert Malpas, William Fergus Miller, Alexander McLeish, Gordon David Strachan, Graeme James Souness (Cap), Robert Sime Aitken, James Bett, Andrew Mullen Gray (73.Steven Archibald), Graeme Marshall Sharp. Manager: John Stein.
**Goal**: 0-1 James Bett (86).

12.06.1985, Laugardalsvöllur Stadium, Reykjavík; Attendance: 10,400
Referee: André Daina (Switzerland)
**ICELAND - SPAIN**                                               **1-2(1-0)**
**ISL:** Bjarni Sigurðsson, Þorgrímur Þráinsson, Janus Guðlaugsson, Magnús Bergs, Sævar Jónsson, Ómar Torfason (68.Gunnar Gíslason), Ragnar Margeirsson, Atli Eðvaldsson, Teitur Þórðarson (Cap), Sigurður Grétarsson (77.Guðmundur Steinsson), Guðmundur Þorbjörnsson. Trainer: Anthony Knapp (England).
**ESP:** Andoni Zubizarreta Urreta, Gerardo Miranda Concepción, Andoni Goikoetxea Olaskoaga, Antonio Maceda Francés, José Antonio Camacho Alfaro (Cap), Víctor Muñoz Manrique, Ricardo Gallego Redondo (77.Ramón María Calderé Del Rey), Enrique Ramos González „Quique", Hipólito Rincón Povedano (46.Manuel Sarabia López), Carlos Alonso González „Santillana", Marcos Alonso Peña. Trainer: Miguel Muñoz Mozún.
**Goals**: 1-0 Teitur Þórðarson (33), 1-1 Manuel Sarabia López (50), 1-2 Marcos Alonso Peña (67).

10.09.1985, Ninian Park, Cardiff; Attendance: 39,500
Referee: Johannes Nicolaas Ignatius "Jan" Keizer (Holland)
**WALES - SCOTLAND** **1-1(1-0)**
**WAL:** Neville Southall, Joseph Patrick Jones, Patrick William Roger Van Den Hauwe, Kevin Ratcliffe, Kenneth Francis Jackett, Robert Mark James (80.Stephen John Lovell), David Owen Phillips, Peter Nicholas, Leslie Mark Hughes, Michael Reginald Thomas (83.Clayton Graham Blackmore), Ian James Rush. Manager: Harold Michael England.
**SCO:** James Leighton (46.Alan Roderick Rough), Richard Charles Gough, Maurice Daniel Robert Malpas, William Fergus Miller (Cap), Alexander McLeish, Gordon David Strachan (61.David Cooper), Stephen Nicol, Robert Sime Aitken, James Bett, David Robert Speedie, Graeme Marshall Sharp. Manager: John Stein.
**Goals**: 1-0 Leslie Mark Hughes (13), 1-1 David Cooper (81 penalty).

25.09.1985, Estadio "Benito Villamarín", Sevilla; Attendance: 45,000
Referee: Siegfried Kirschen (East Germany)
**SPAIN - ICELAND** **2-1(1-1)**
**ESP:** Andoni Zubizarreta Urreta, Gerardo Miranda Concepción, Andoni Goikoetxea Olaskoaga, Antonio Maceda Francés, José Antonio Camacho Alfaro (Cap), Rafael Gordillo Vázquez (88.Julio Alberto Moreno Casas), Víctor Muñoz Manrique, Ricardo Gallego Redondo, Hipólito Rincón Povedano (75.Marcos Alonso Peña), Emilio Butragueño Santos, Juan Carlos Pérez Rojo. Trainer: Miguel Muñoz Mozún.
**ISL:** Bjarni Sigurðsson, Þorgrímur Þráinsson, Atli Eðvaldsson, Janus Guðlaugsson, Sævar Jónsson, Arnór Guðjohnsen, Pétur Pétursson (74.Sigurður Grétarsson), Siðurdur Jónsson, Teitur Þórðarson (Cap), Ásgeir Sigurvinsson, Guðmundur Þorbjörnsson (65.Gunnar Gíslason). Trainer: Anthony Knapp (England).
**Goals**: 0-1 Guðmundur Þorbjörnsson (36), 1-1 Hipólito Rincón Povedano (44), 2-1 Rafael Gordillo Vázquez (51).

# EUROPEAN PLAY-OFF

| 16.10.1985 | Bruxelles | Belgium - Holland | 1-0(1-0) |
| 20.11.1985 | Rotterdam | Holland - Belgium | 2-1(0-0) |

### FINAL STANDINGS

| | | | | | | | |
|---|---|---|---|---|---|---|---|
| 1. **Belgium** | 2 | 1 | 0 | 1 | 2 - 2 | 2 |
| 2. Holland | 2 | 1 | 0 | 1 | 2 - 2 | 2 |

Belgium qualified for the Final Tournament.

16.10.1985, Parc Astrid, Bruxelles; Attendance: 36,500
Referee: Pietro d'Elia (Italy)
**BELGIUM - HOLLAND**                                                                              **1-0(1-0)**
**BEL:** Jean-Marie Pfaff, Eric Gerets, Georges Grün (69.Alexander Czerniatynski), Frank Richard Vander Elst, Michel Renquin, Léo Vander Elst, René Vandereycken, Jan Ceulemans, Frank Vercauteren, Nicolaas Pieter Claesen, Erwin Vandenbergh. **Trainer:** Guy Thys.
**NED:** Johannes Franciscus van Breukelen, Hubertus Johannes Nicolaas Wijnstekers (Cap), Michael Antonius Bernardus van de Korput, Ronald Spelbos, Adrianus Andreas van Tiggelen, Wilhelmus Antonius van de Kerkhof, Franklin Edmundo Rijkaard, Ruud Gullit (85.Edo Ophof), Marcelo van Basten, Willem Cornelis Nicolaas Kieft, Robert Leonardus de Wit (88.Simon Melkianus Tahamata). Trainer: Leo Beenhakker.
**Goal**: 1-0 Frank Vercauteren (20).
**Sent off**: Willem Cornelis Nicolaas Kieft (4).

20.11.1985, Feyenoord Stadion, Rotterdam; Attendance: 54,000
Referee: George Courtney (England)
**HOLLAND - BELGIUM**                                                         **2-1(0-0)**
**NED:** Johannes Franciscus van Breukelen, Hubertus Johannes Nicolaas Wijnstekers (Cap), Ronald Spelbos, Michael Antonius Bernardus van de Korput (46.Johannes Maria van Loen), Adrianus Andreas van Tiggelen, Machiel Valke, Franklin Edmundo Rijkaard, Ruud Gullit, Simon Melkianus Tahamata (80.Jan Jacobus Silooy), Petrus Johannes Houtman, Robert Leonardus de Wit. Trainer: Leo Beenhakker.
**BEL:** Jean-Marie Pfaff, Eric Gerets, Hugo Broos, Frank Richard Vander Elst (73.Daniel Veyt), Michel De Wolf, Frank Vercauteren, René Vandereycken, Léo Vander Elst (46.Georges Grün), Léo Albert Clijsters, Philippe De Smet, Jan Ceulemans. **Trainer:** Guy Thys.
**Goals**: 1-0 Petrus Johannes Houtman (66), 2-0 Robert Leonardus de Wit (74), 2-1 Georges Grün (84).

# SOUTH AMERICA

## GROUP 1

| | | | | |
|---|---|---|---|---|
| 26.05.1985 | Bogotá | Colombia - Peru | 1-0(1-0) |
| 26.05.1985 | San Cristóbal | Venezuela - Argentina | 2-3(1-2) |
| 02.06.1985 | Bogotá | Colombia - Argentina | 1-3(0-1) |
| 02.06.1985 | San Cristóbal | Venezuela - Peru | 0-1(0-0) |
| 09.06.1985 | Lima | Peru - Colombia | 0-0 |
| 09.06.1985 | Buenos Aires | Argentina - Venezuela | 3-0(1-0) |
| 16.06.1985 | Lima | Peru - Venezuela | 4-1(2-1) |
| 16.06.1985 | Buenos Aires | Argentina - Colombia | 1-0(1-0) |
| 23.06.1985 | San Cristóbal | Venezuela - Colombia | 2-2(1-1) |
| 23.06.1985 | Lima | Peru - Argentina | 1-0(1-0) |
| 30.06.1985 | Bogotá | Colombia - Venezuela | 2-0(2-0) |
| 30.06.1985 | Buenos Aires | Argentina - Peru | 2-2(1-2) |

### FINAL STANDINGS

| | | | | | | | | |
|---|---|---|---|---|---|---|---|---|
| 1. | **Argentina** | 6 | 4 | 1 | 1 | 12 | - 6 | 9 |
| 2. | *Peru* | 6 | 3 | 2 | 1 | 8 | - 4 | 8 |
| 3. | *Colombia* | 6 | 2 | 2 | 2 | 6 | - 6 | 6 |
| 4. | Venezuela | 6 | 0 | 1 | 5 | 5 | - 12 | 1 |

Argentina qualified for the Final Tournament.
Peru and Colombia qualified for the CONMEBOL Play-offs.

26.05.1985, Estadio „Nemesio Camacho" 'El Campín', Bogotá; Attendance: 53,000
Referee: Luis Barrancos Álvarez (Bolivia)
**COLOMBIA - PERU**     **1-0(1-0)**
**COL:** Pedro Antonio Zape, Víctor Emilio Luna, Nolberto Molina, Miguel Augusto Prince, Jorge Armando Porras, Willington José Ortíz, Pedro Enrique Sarmiento Solís, Germán Morales (78.Hernán Darío Herrera), Jesús Barrios (70.Wilson Américo Quiñónes), Arnoldo Alberto Iguarán, Víctor Lugo. Trainer: Gabriel Ochoa Uribe.
**PER:** Eusebio Alfredo Acasuzo Colán, Leonardo Rojas, Pedro Requena (16.Hugo Gástulo), Rubén Toribio Díaz Rivas, Jorge Andrés Olaechea Quijandría, César Augusto Cueto Villa, José Manuel Velásquez Castillo, Javier Chirinos, Gerónimo Barbadillo González, Franco Enrique Navarro Monteiro, Juan Carlos Oblitas Saba (69.Julio César Uribe Flores). Trainer: Moisés Barack.
**Goal**: 1-0 Miguel Augusto Prince (26 penalty).
**Sent off**: Rubén Toribio Díaz Rivas (50).

26.05.1985, Estadio Pueblo Nuevo, San Cristóbal; Attendance: 30,000
Referee: Juan Daniel Cardellino de San Vicente (Uruguay)
**VENEZUELA - ARGENTINA**     **2-3(1-2)**
**VEN:** César Renato Baéna, René Antonio Torres Lobo, Nicolás Simonelli, Pedro Javier Acosta Sánchez, Emilio Campos Rodríguez, Asdrúbal José Sánchez Urbina, William Méndez (46.Heberth Márquez), Nelson José Carrero Heras, Bernardo Añor, Pedro Juan Febles, Douglas Cedeño (76.Carlos Alberto Maldonado). Trainer: José Walter Roque (Uruguay).
**ARG:** Ubaldo Matildo Fillol, Néstor Rolando Clausen, Enzo Héctor Trossero, Daniel Alberto Passarella, Oscar Alfredo Garré, Miguel Ángel Russo, José Daniel Ponce, Diego Armando Maradona (Cap), Jorge Luis Burruchaga, Pedro Pablo Pasculli (82.Jorge Alberto Francisco Valdano), Ricardo Alberto Gareca (67.Alberto José Márcico). Trainer: Dr. Carlos Salvador Bilardo.

**Goals**: 0-1 Diego Armando Maradona (2), 1-1 René Antonio Torres Lobo (8), 1-2 Daniel Alberto Passarella (40), 1-3 Diego Armando Maradona (58), 2-3 Heberth Márquez (59).

02.06.1985, Estadio „Nemesio Camacho" 'El Campín', Bogotá; Attendance: 58,000
Referee: Arnaldo David César Coelho (Brazil)
**COLOMBIA - ARGENTINA**      **1-3(0-1)**
**COL**: Pedro Antonio Zape (3.Luis Octávio Gómez), Luis Norberto Gil, Nolberto Molina, Miguel Augusto Prince, Alfonso López, Willington José Ortíz, Pedro Enrique Sarmiento Solís, Germán Morales, Wilson Américo Quiñónes (46.Hernán Darío Herrera), Manuel Ascisclo Córdoba, Arnoldo Alberto Iguarán. Trainer: Gabriel Ochoa Uribe.
**ARG**: Ubaldo Matildo Fillol, Néstor Rolando Clausen, Enzo Héctor Trossero, Daniel Alberto Passarella, Oscar Alfredo Garré, Ricardo Omar Giusti, Miguel Ángel Russo, Marcelo Antonio Trobbiani (57.Juan Alberto Barbas), Diego Armando Maradona (Cap), Jorge Luis Burruchaga, Pedro Pablo Pasculli (86.Oscar Alberto Dertycia). Trainer: Dr. Carlos Salvador Bilardo.
**Goals**: 0-1 Pedro Pablo Pasculli (43), 1-1 Miguel Augusto Prince (60), 1-2 Pedro Pablo Pasculli (68), 1-3 Jorge Luis Burruchaga (85).

02.06.1985, Estadio Pueblo Nuevo, San Cristóbal; Attendance: 19,000
Referee: Jorge Orellana (Ecuador)
**VENEZUELA - PERU**      **0-1(0-0)**
**VEN**: César Renato Baéna, René Antonio Torres Lobo, Arnulfo Becerra, Pedro Javier Acosta Sánchez, Emilio Campos Rodríguez, Nelson José Carrero Heras (76.Douglas Cedeño), William Méndez, Asdrúbal José Sánchez Urbina, Bernardo Añor, Carlos Alberto Maldonado (65.Pedro Juan Febles), Heberth Márquez. Trainer: José Walter Roque (Uruguay).
**PER**: Eusebio Alfredo Acasuzo Colán, Leonardo Rojas, Javier Chirinos, Jorge Andrés Olaechea Quijandría, Alejandro Hugo Gastulo Ramírez, César Augusto Cueto Villa, José Manuel Velásquez Castillo, Julio César Uribe Flores, Gerónimo Barbadillo González, Franco Enrique Navarro Monteiro, Juan Carlos Oblitas Saba. Trainer: Moisés Barack.
**Goal**: 0-1 Julio César Uribe Flores (78).

09.06.1985, Estadio Nacional, Lima; Attendance: 45,000
Referee: Juan Daniel Cardellino (Uruguay)
**PERU - COLOMBIA**      **0-0**
**PER**: Eusebio Alfredo Acasuzo Colán, Leonardo Rojas, Jorge Andrés Olaechea Quijandría, Rubén Toribio Díaz Rivas, Alejandro Hugo Gastulo Ramírez, César Augusto Cueto Villa, Javier Chirinos, Julio César Uribe Flores, Gerónimo Barbadillo González (57.Eduardo Hugo Malásquez Maldonado), Franco Enrique Navarro Monteiro, Jorge Hirano (75.Guillermo La Rosa Laguna). Trainer: Moisés Barack
**COL**: Luis Octávio Gómez, Víctor Emilio Luna, Gonzalo Soto, Miguel Augusto Prince, Jorge Armando Porras, Willington José Ortíz, Pedro Enrique Sarmiento Solís, Germán Morales, Wilson Américo Quiñónes, Manuel Ascisclo Córdoba (66.Jesús Barrios), Arnoldo Alberto Iguarán (60.Víctor Lugo). Trainer: Gabriel Ochoa Uribe.

09.06.1985, Estadio Monumental „Antonio Vespucio Liberti", Buenos Aires; Attendance: 35,000
Referee: Gastón Edmundo Castro Makuc (Chile)
**ARGENTINA - VENEZUELA**      **3-0(1-0)**
**ARG**: Ubaldo Matildo Fillol, Néstor Rolando Clausen, Enzo Héctor Trossero, Daniel Alberto Passarella, Oscar Alfredo Garré, Ricardo Omar Giusti, Miguel Ángel Russo, Diego Armando Maradona (Cap), Jorge Luis Burruchaga, Pedro Pablo Pasculli, Jorge Alberto Francisco Valdano. Trainer: Dr. Carlos Salvador Bilardo.
**VEN**: César Renato Baéna, René Antonio Torres Lobo, Arnulfo Becerra, Pedro Javier Acosta Sánchez, Emilio Campos Rodríguez, Nelson José Carrero Heras, Robert Ellie (46.William Méndez; 66.Richard Nada), Asdrúbal José Sánchez Urbina, Bernardo Añor, Pedro Juan Febles, Douglas Cedeño. Trainer: José Walter Roque (Uruguay).
**Goals**: 1-0 Miguel Ángel Russo (28), 2-0 Néstor Rolando Clausen (87), 3-0 Diego Armando Maradona

(90).

16.06.1985, Estadio Nacional, Lima; Attendance: 10,327
Referee: Luis Carlos Ferreira (Brazil)
**PERU - VENEZUELA**      **4-1(2-1)**
**PER:** Eusebio Alfredo Acasuzo Colán, Leonardo Rojas, Jorge Andrés Olaechea Quijandría, Rubén Toribio Díaz Rivas, Alejandro Hugo Gastulo Ramírez, Eduardo Hugo Malásquez Maldonado (64.Jorge Hirano), José Manuel Velásquez Castillo, César Augusto Cueto Villa, Gerónimo Barbadillo González, Franco Enrique Navarro Monteiro (70.Guillermo La Rosa Laguna), Juan Carlos Oblitas. Trainer: Roberto Federico Chale Olarte.
**VEN:** César Renato Baéna, René Antonio Torres Lobo, Nicolás Simonelli, Pedro Javier Acosta Sánchez, Emilio Campos Rodríguez, Carlos Landaeta (74.Nelson José Carrero Heras), Asdrúbal José Sánchez Urbina, William Méndez, Bernardo Añor, Heberth Márquez (63.Carlos Alberto Maldonado), Pedro Juan Febles. Trainer: José Walter Roque (Uruguay).
**Goals**: 1-0 Franco Enrique Navarro Monteiro (15), 2-0 Gerónimo Barbadillo González (19), 2-1 Pedro Juan Febles (29), 3-1 Jorge Hirano (79), César Augusto Cueto Villa (81).

16.06.1985, Estadio Monumental „Antonio Vespucio Liberti", Buenos Aires; Attendance: 30,000
Referee: Gabriel González (Paraguay)
**ARGENTINA - COLOMBIA**      **1-0(1-0)**
**ARG:** Ubaldo Matildo Fillol, Néstor Rolando Clausen, Enzo Héctor Trossero, Daniel Alberto Passarella, Oscar Alfredo Garré, Ricardo Omar Giusti, Miguel Ángel Russo (46.Juan Alberto Barbas), Diego Armando Maradona (Cap), Jorge Luis Burruchaga, Pedro Pablo Pasculli, Jorge Alberto Francisco Valdano. Trainer: Dr. Carlos Salvador Bilardo.
**COL:** Luis Octávio Gómez, Víctor Emilio Luna, Gonzalo Soto, Miguel Augusto Prince, Jorge Armando Porras, Pedro Enrique Sarmiento Solís (46.Wilson Américo Quiñónes), Germán Morales, Willington José Ortíz, Manuel Ascisclo Córdoba, Arnoldo Alberto Iguarán, Víctor Lugo (57.Carlos Ricaurte). Trainer: Gabriel Ochoa Uribe.
**Goal**: 1-0 Jorge Alberto Francisco Valdano (26).

23.06.1985, Estadio Pueblo Nuevo, San Cristóbal; Attendance: 30,000
Referee: Ramón Ivannoe Barreto Ruíz (Uruguay)
**VENEZUELA - COLOMBIA**      **2-2(1-1)**
**VEN:** César Renato Baéna, René Antonio Torres Lobo, Nicolás Simonelli, Pedro Javier Acosta Sánchez, Emilio Campos Rodríguez, Carlos Landaeta (Carlos Alberto Maldonado), Asdrúbal José Sánchez Urbina, William Méndez, Bernardo Añor, Heberth Márquez, Douglas Cedeño (Nelson José Carrero Heras). Trainer: José Walter Roque (Uruguay).
**COL:** Luis Octávio Gómez, Víctor Emilio Luna, Gonzalo Soto, Miguel Augusto Prince, Jorge Armando Porras, Willington José Ortíz, Pedro Enrique Sarmiento Solís, Germán Morales, Wilson Américo Quiñónes (Hernán Darío Herrera), Jesús Barrios, Víctor Lugo (Luis Eduardo Reyes). Trainer: Gabriel Ochoa Uribe.
**Goals**: 1-0 Douglas Cedeño (6), 1-1 Willington José Ortíz (17), 1-2 Hernán Darío Herrera (60 penalty), 2-2 Bernardo Añor (69).

23.06.1985, Estadio Nacional, Lima; Attendance: 43,000
Referee: Hernán Silva Arce (Chile)
**PERU - ARGENTINA** **1-0(1-0)**
**PER:** Eusebio Alfredo Acasuzo Colán, Leonardo Rojas, Jorge Andrés Olaechea Quijandría, Rubén Toribio Díaz Rivas, Alejandro Hugo Gastulo Ramírez, Luis Alberto Reyna Navarro (76.Javier Chirinos), José Manuel Velásquez Castillo, César Augusto Cueto Villa, Gerónimo Barbadillo González (54.Julio César Uribe Flores), Franco Enrique Navarro Monteiro, Juan Carlos Oblitas Saba. Trainer: Roberto Federico Chale Olarte.
**ARG:** Ubaldo Matildo Fillol, Néstor Rolando Clausen (81.Oscar Alfredo Ruggeri), Enzo Héctor Trossero, Daniel Alberto Passarella, Oscar Alfredo Garré, Ricardo Omar Giusti, Miguel Ángel Russo (46.Pedro Pablo Pasculli), Juan Alberto Barbas, Diego Armando Maradona (Cap), Jorge Luis Burruchaga, Jorge Alberto Francisco Valdano. Trainer: Dr. Carlos Salvador Bilardo.
**Goal**: 1-0 Juan Carlos Oblitas Saba (7).

30.06.1985, Estadio „Nemesio Camacho" 'El Campín', Bogotá; Attendance: 10,000
Referee: Víctor Vásquez Sánchez (Chile)
**COLOMBIA - VENEZUELA** **2-0(2-0)**
**COL:** Carlos Fernández Navarro Montoya, Víctor Emilio Luna, Alvaro Escobar, Luis Eduardo Reyes, Jorge Armando Porras, Willington José Ortíz, Pedro Enrique Sarmiento Solís, Carlos Ricaurte (Eugenes Cuadrado), Hernán Darío Herrera (Jesús Barrios), Manuel Ascisclo Córdoba, Víctor Lugo. Trainer: Gabriel Ochoa Uribe.
**VEN:** Daniel Nikolac, René Antonio Torres Lobo, Cecilio González, Pedro Javier Acosta Sánchez, Carlos Betancourt, Nelson José Carrero Heras (Emilio Campos Rodríguez), Asdrúbal José Sánchez Urbina, Carlos Alberto Maldonado, Pedro Juan Febles, Heberth Márquez, Douglas Cedeño (William Méndez). Trainer: José Walter Roque (Uruguay).
**Goals**: 1-0 Manuel Ascisclo Córdoba (15), 2-0 Hernán Darío Herrera (27 penalty).

30.06.1985, Estadio Monumental „Antonio Vespucio Liberti", Buenos Aires; Attendance: 65,457
Referee: Romualdo Arppi Filho (Brazil)
**ARGENTINA - PERU** **2-2(1-2)**
**ARG:** Ubaldo Matildo Fillol, Julián José Camino (61.Ricardo Alberto Gareca), Enzo Héctor Trossero, Daniel Alberto Passarella, Oscar Alfredo Garré, Ricardo Omar Giusti, Juan Alberto Barbas (78.Marcelo Antonio Trobbiani), Diego Armando Maradona (Cap), Jorge Luis Burruchaga, Pedro Pablo Pasculli, Jorge Alberto Francisco Valdano. Trainer: Dr. Carlos Salvador Bilardo.
**PER:** Eusebio Alfredo Acasuzo Colán, Leonardo Rojas, Jorge Andrés Olaechea Quijandría, Rubén Toribio Díaz Rivas, Alejandro Hugo Gastulo Ramírez, Luis Alberto Reyna Navarro (68.Javier Chirinos), José Manuel Velásquez Castillo, César Augusto Cueto Villa, Gerónimo Barbadillo González, Franco Enrique Navarro Monteiro (5.Julio César Uribe Flores), Juan Carlos Oblitas Saba. Trainer: Roberto Federico Chale Olarte.
**Goals**: 1-0 Pedro Pablo Pasculli (12), 1-1 José Manuel Velásquez Castillo (24), 1-2 Gerónimo Barbadillo González (38), 2-2 Daniel Alberto Passarella (81)

# GROUP 2

| | | | | |
|---|---|---|---|---|
| 03.03.1985 | Quito | Ecuador - Chile | 1-1(1-1) |
| 10.03.1985 | Montevideo | Uruguay - Ecuador | 2-1(1-0) |
| 17.03.1985 | Santiago | Chile - Ecuador | 6-2(4-2) |
| 24.03.1985 | Santiago | Chile - Uruguay | 2-0(1-0) |
| 31.03.1985 | Quito | Ecuador - Uruguay | 0-2(0-0) |
| 07.04.1985 | Montevideo | Uruguay - Chile | 2-1(1-1) |

### FINAL STANDINGS

| | | | | | | | | |
|---|---|---|---|---|---|---|---|---|
| 1. | Uruguay | 4 | 3 | 0 | 1 | 6 - 4 | 6 |
| 2. | Chile | 4 | 2 | 1 | 1 | 10 - 5 | 5 |
| 3. | Ecuador | 4 | 0 | 1 | 3 | 4 - 11 | 1 |

Uruguay qualified for the Final Tournament.
Chile qualified for the CONMEBOL Play-offs.

03.03.1985, Estadio Olimpico „Atahualpa", Quito; Attendance: 40,000
Referee: José Roberto Ramiz Wright (Brazil)
**ECUADOR - CHILE**  1-1(1-1)
ECU: Israel Rodríguez, Flavio Perlaza, Holguer Abraham Quiñónez, Wilson Antonio Armas, Carlos Hans Maldonado, Marcelo Hurtado, José Elias De Negri, José Voltaire Villafuerte (Hamilton Emilio Cuvi Rivera), Jaime Fernando Baldeón, Hermen De Jesús Benítez, José Vicente Moreno (Lupo Senén Quiñónez). Trainer: Antônio Ferreira „Antoninho" (Brazil).
CHI: Roberto Antonio Rojas Saavedra, Lizardo Antonio Garrido Bustamante, Eduardo Gómez, Mario del Transito Soto Benavides, Luis Hormazábal, Miguel Angel Neira Pincheira, Patricio Mardones Díaz (Leonel Herrera), Alejandro Manuel Hisis Araya, Jorge Orlando Aravena Plaza, Patricio Nazario Yáñez Candia, Juan Carlos Letelier Pizarro. Trainer: Pedro Morales.
**Goals**: 0-1 Juan Carlos Letelier Pizarro (31), 1-1 Carlos Hans Maldonado (44 penalty).
**Sent off**: Holguer Abraham Quiñónez / Juan Carlos Letelier Pizarro.

10.03.1985, Estadio Centenario, Montevideo; Attendance: 65,000
Referee: Édison Pérez (Peru)
**URUGUAY - ECUADOR**  2-1(1-0)
URU: Rodolfó Sergio Rodríguez, Néstor Mario Montelongo, Nelson Daniel Gutiérrez Luongo, Eduardo Mario Acevedo Cardozo, Daniel Martínez, Jorge Wálter Barrios Balestrasse (65.Venancio Ariel Ramos Villanueva), Miguel Angel Bossio Bastianini, Enzo Francéscoli Uriarte, Carlos Alberto Aguilera Nova, Carlos Amaro Nadal, Jorge Orosmán da Silva Echeverrito (59.Wilmar Rubens Cabrera Sappa). Trainer: Omar Borrás.
ECU: Israel Rodríguez, Flavio Perlaza, Orly Klinger, Wilson Antonio Armas, Carlos Hans Maldonado, Marcelo Hurtado, José Elias De Negri, José Voltaire Villafuerte, Hamilton Emilio Cuvi Rivera, Jaime Fernando Baldeón (80.Hermen De Jesús Benítez), Lupo Senén Quiñónez (86.Galo Fidean Vásquez). Trainer: Antônio Ferreira „Antoninho" (Brazil).
**Goals**: 1-0 Carlos Alberto Aguilera Nova (34), 1-1 Hamilton Emilio Cuvi Rivera (54), 2-1 Venancio Ariel Ramos Villanueva (90).

17.03.1985, Estadio Nacional, Santiago; Attendance: 60,892
Referee: Orázio Di Rosa (Venezuela)
**CHILE - ECUADOR**     **6-2(4-2)**
**CHI:** Roberto Antonio Rojas Saavedra, Lizardo Antonio Garrido Bustamante, Eduardo Gómez, Mario del Transito Soto Benavides, Luis Hormazábal, Miguel Angel Neira Pincheira, Alejandro Manuel Hisis Araya, Jorge Orlando Aravena Plaza, Hugo Eduardo Rubio Montecinos (Oscar Herrera Hernández), Carlos Humberto Caszely Garrido (Patricio Mardones Díaz), Héctor Eduardo Puebla. Trainer: Pedro Morales.
**ECU:** Israel Rodríguez, Flavio Perlaza, Orly Klinger, Wilson Antonio Armas, Carlos Hans Maldonado (Eddie José Valencia), Marcelo Hurtado, José Elias De Negri, José Voltaire Villafuerte, Hamilton Emilio Cuvi Rivera, Jaime Fernando Baldeón, Hermen De Jesús Benítez. Trainer: Antônio Ferreira „Antoninho" (Brazil).
**Goals:** 1-0 Héctor Eduardo Puebla (21), 1-1 Jaime Fernando Baldeón (23), 2-1 Carlos Humberto Caszely Garrido (29), 3-1 Alejandro Manuel Hisis Araya (34), 3-2 Jaime Fernando Baldeón (37), 4-2 Carlos Humberto Caszely Garrido (40), 5-2 Jorge Orlando Aravena Plaza (51), 6-2 Jorge Orlando Aravena Plaza (89).

24.03.1985, Estadio Nacional, Santiago; Attendance: 79,911
Referee: Jesús Díaz Palacios (Colombia)
**CHILE - URUGUAY**     **2-0(1-0)**
**CHI:** Roberto Antonio Rojas Saavedra, Eduardo Gómez, Mario del Transito Soto Benavides, Lizardo Antonio Garrido Bustamante, Luis Hormazábal, Alejandro Manuel Hisis Araya, Miguel Angel Neira Pincheira, Jorge Orlando Aravena Plaza, Hugo Eduardo Rubio Montecinos, Carlos Humberto Caszely Garrido, Héctor Eduardo Puebla. Trainer: Pedro Morales.
**URU:** Rodolfó Sergio Rodríguez, Néstor Mario Montelongo, Nelson Daniel Gutiérrez Luongo, Eduardo Mario Acevedo Cardozo, Víctor Hugo Diogo Silva, Jorge Wálter Barrios Balestrasse (58.Venancio Ariel Ramos Villanueva), Miguel Angel Bossio Bastianini, Sergio Rodolfo Santín, Enzo Francéscoli Uriarte, Carlos Alberto Aguilera Nova (58.Carlos Amaro Nadal), Wilmar Rubens Cabrera Sappa. Trainer: Omar Borrás.
**Goals:** 1-0 Hugo Eduardo Rubio Montecinos (28), 2-0 Jorge Orlando Aravena Plaza (54).

31.03.1985, Estadio Olimpico „Atahualpa", Quito; Attendance: 30,000
Referee: Juan Francisco Escobar Váldez (Paraguay)
**ECUADOR - URUGUAY**     **0-2(0-0)**
**ECU:** Israel Rodríguez (69.Pedro Carlos Latino), Luis Enrique Capurro Bautista, Orly Klinger, Wilson Antonio Armas, Carlos Hans Maldonado, Marcelo Hurtado (46.Eddie José Valencia), José Voltaire Villafuerte, José Elias De Negri, Hamilton Emilio Cuvi Rivera, Jaime Fernando Baldeón, Lupo Senén Quiñónez. Trainer: Antônio Ferreira „Antoninho" (Brazil).
**URU:** Rodolfó Sergio Rodríguez, Víctor Hugo Diogo Silva, Nelson Daniel Gutiérrez Luongo, Alfonso Darío Pereyra Bueno, José Alberto Batista González, Mario Daniel Saralegui, Miguel Angel Bossio Bastianini, Sergio Rodolfo Santín, Enzo Francéscoli Uriarte, Venancio Ariel Ramos Villanueva (72.Wilmar Rubens Cabrera Sappa), Carlos Amaro Nadal (55.Jorge Orosmán da Silva Echeverrito). Trainer: Omar Borrás.
**Goals**: 0-1 Mario Daniel Saralegui (71), 0-2 Enzo Francéscoli Uriarte (87).

07.04.1985, Estadio Centenario, Montevideo; Attendance: 66,500
Referee: Carlos Alfonso Espósito (Argentina)
**URUGUAY - CHILE**                                              **2-1(1-1)**
**URU:** Rodolfó Sergio Rodríguez, Néstor Mario Montelongo, Nelson Daniel Gutiérrez Luongo, Alfonso Darío Pereyra Bueno, José Alberto Batista González, Mario Daniel Saralegui, Miguel Angel Bossio Bastianini, Sergio Rodolfo Santín, Enzo Francéscoli Uriarte, Venancio Ariel Ramos Villanueva (89.Wilmar Rubens Cabrera Sappa), Carlos Amaro Nadal (70.Jorge Orosmán da Silva Echeverrito). Trainer: Omar Borrás.
**CHI:** Roberto Antonio Rojas Saavedra, Hugo Tabilo, Eduardo René Valenzuela Becker, Eduardo Gómez (62.Juan Carlos Letelier Pizarro), Mario del Transito Soto Benavides, Alejandro Manuel Hisis Araya, Luis Hormazábal, Miguel Angel Neira Pincheira, Hugo Eduardo Rubio Montecinos, Carlos Humberto Caszely Garrido, Jorge Orlando Aravena Plaza. Trainer: Pedro Morales.
**Goals**: 1-0 José Alberto Batista González (10), 1-1 Jorge Orlando Aravena Plaza (28 penalty), 2-1 Venancio Ariel Ramos Villanueva (57 penalty).

# GROUP 3

| | | | | |
|---|---|---|---|---|
| 26.05.1985 | Santa Cruz | Bolivia - Paraguay | | 1-1(1-0) |
| 02.06.1985 | Santa Cruz | Bolivia - Brazil | | 0-2(0-0) |
| 09.06.1985 | Asunción | Paraguay - Bolivia | | 3-0(2-0) |
| 16.06.1985 | Asunción | Paraguay - Brazil | | 0-2(0-1) |
| 23.06.1985 | Rio de Janeiro | Brazil - Paraguay | | 1-1(1-1) |
| 30.06.1985 | São Paulo | Brazil - Bolivia | | 1-1(1-0) |

### FINAL STANDINGS

| | | | | | | | | |
|---|---|---|---|---|---|---|---|---|
| 1. | Brazil | 4 | 2 | 2 | 0 | 6 - 2 | | 6 |
| 2. | *Paraguay* | 4 | 1 | 2 | 1 | 5 - 4 | | 4 |
| 3. | Bolivia | 4 | 0 | 2 | 2 | 2 - 7 | | 2 |

Brazil qualified for the Final Tournament.
Paraguay qualified for the CONMEBOL Play-offs.

26.05.1985, Estadio „Ramón 'Tahuichi' Aguilera", Santa Cruz de la Sierra; Attendance: 20,000
Referee: Elías Victoriano Jácome Guerreiro (Ecuador)
**BOLIVIA - PARAGUAY**     **1-1(1-0)**
**BOL:** Luis Galarza Mayereger, Johnny Herrera, Edgar Vaca Barbosa, Rolando Coimbra, Marciano Saldías, José Milton Melgar, Edgar Castillo, Erwin Romero Escudero (Carlos Fernando Borja), Rolando Paniagua (David Paniagua Yepez), Juan Carlos Sánchez, Silvio Rojas. Trainer: Carlos Rodríguez.
**PAR:** Ever Hugo Almeida Almada, Virginio Cáceres Villalba, César Zabala Fernández, Rogelio Wilfrido Delgado Casco, Juan Bautista Torales, Marciano Rolando Chilavert González, Adolfo Gustavo Benítez Bentos, Jorge Amado Núñez Infrán, Buenaventura Ferreira Gómez, Javier Villalba, Alfredo Damián Mendoza Sulewski (Eulalio Alberto Mora Barreto). Trainer: Cayetano Ré Ramírez.
**Goals**: 1-0 Silvio Rojas (9), 1-1 Jorge Amado Núñez Infrán (82).

02.06.1985, Estadio „Ramón 'Tahuichi' Aguilera", Santa Cruz de la Sierra; Attendance: 25,000
Referee: Jorge Eduardo Romero (Argentina)
**BOLIVIA - BRAZIL**     **0-2(0-0)**
**BOL:** Luis Galarza Mayereger, Johnny Herrera, Edgar Vaca Barbosa (51.Miguel Ángel Noro), Rolando Coimbra, Roberto Pérez, José Milton Melgar, Edgar Castillo, Erwin Romero Escudero, Rolando Paniagua, Juan Carlos Sánchez, Silvio Rojas. Trainer: Carlos Rodríguez.
**BRA:** Carlos Roberto Gallo, José Leandro de Souza Ferreira "Leandro I", José Oscar Bernardi, Édino Nazareth Filho "Edinho", Leovegildo Lins Gama Júnior "Júnior I", Antônio Carlos Cerezo "Toninho Cerezo", Sócrates Brasileiro Sampaio Vieira de Oliveira, Arthur Antunes Coimbra "Zico", Renato Portaluppi "Renato Gaúcho", Wálter Casagrande Júnior (65.Antônio de Oliveira Filho "Careca I"), Éder Aleixo de Assis. Trainer: Telê Santana da Silva.
**Goals**: 0-1 Wálter Casagrande Júnior (57), 0-2 Miguel Ángel Noro (60 own goal).

09.06.1985, Estadio Defensores del Chaco, Asunción; Attendance: 40,000
Referee: Gilberto Aristizábal Murcia (Colombia)
**PARAGUAY - BOLIVIA** **3-0(2-0)**
**PAR:** Ever Hugo Almeida Almada, Virginio Cáceres Villalba (Juan Bautista Torales), César Zabala Fernández, Rogelio Wilfrido Delgado Casco, Justo Pastor Jacquet Muñoz, Adolfo Gustavo Benítez Bentos, Jorge Amado Núñez Infrán, Julio César Romero Insfrán, Buenaventura Ferreira Gómez, Javier Villalba, Alfredo Damián Mendoza Sulewski (Enrique Atanasio Villalba). Trainer: Cayetano Ré Ramírez.
**BOL:** Luis Galarza Mayereger, José Wilson Avila, Miguel Ángel Noro, Rolando Coimbra, Roberto Pérez, José Milton Melgar, Edgar Castillo, Erwin Romero Escudero, Rolando Paniagua, Erwin Cespedes (Carlos Fernando Borja), Silvio Rojas (Juan Carlos Sánchez). Trainer: Carlos Rodríguez.
**Goals**: 1-0 Alfredo Damián Mendoza Sulewski (17), 2-0 Justo Pastor Jacquet Muñoz (34), 3-0 Julio César Romero Insfrán (49).

16.06.1985, Estadio Defensores del Chaco, Asunción; Attendance: 55,000
Referee: Gastón Edmundo Castro Makuc (Chile)
**PARAGUAY - BRAZIL** **0-2(0-1)**
**PAR:** Ever Hugo Almeida Almada, Virginio Cáceres Villalba, César Zabala Fernández, Rogelio Wilfrido Delgado Casco, Justo Pastor Jacquet Muñoz, Adolfo Gustavo Benítez Bentos (46.Enrique Atanasio Villalba), Jorge Amado Núñez Infrán, Julio César Romero Insfrán, Javier Villalba, Buenaventura Ferreira Gómez, Alfredo Damián Mendoza Sulewski. Trainer: Cayetano Ré Ramírez.
**BRA:** Carlos Roberto Gallo, José Leandro de Souza Ferreira "Leandro I", José Oscar Bernardi, Édino Nazareth Filho "Edinho", Leovegildo Lins Gama Júnior "Júnior I", Antônio Carlos Cerezo "Toninho Cerezo", Sócrates Brasileiro Sampaio Vieira de Oliveira, Arthur Antunes Coimbra "Zico", Renato Portaluppi "Renato Gaúcho" (78.Ricardo Rogério de Brito "Alemão"), Wálter Casagrande Júnior, Éder Aleixo de Assis. Trainer: Telê Santana da Silva.
**Goals**: 0-1 Wálter Casagrande Júnior (28), 0-2 Arthur Antunes Coimbra "Zico" (70).

23.06.1985, Estádio „Jornalista Mário Filho" (Maracanã), Rio de Janeiro; Attendance: 139,923
Referee: José Luis Martínez Bazán (Uruguay)
**BRAZIL - PARAGUAY** **1-1(1-1)**
**BRA:** Carlos Roberto Gallo, José Leandro de Souza Ferreira "Leandro I", José Oscar Bernardi, Édino Nazareth Filho "Edinho", Leovegildo Lins Gama Júnior "Júnior I", Antônio Carlos Cerezo "Toninho Cerezo", Sócrates Brasileiro Sampaio Vieira de Oliveira, Arthur Antunes Coimbra "Zico", Renato Portaluppi "Renato Gaúcho", Wálter Casagrande Júnior, Éder Aleixo de Assis (75.Ricardo Rogério de Brito "Alemão"). Trainer: Telê Santana da Silva.
**PAR:** Ever Hugo Almeida Almada, Virginio Cáceres Villalba, César Zabala Fernández, Rogelio Wilfrido Delgado Casco, Justo Pastor Jacquet Muñoz (55.Juan Bautista Torales), Adolfo Gustavo Benítez Bentos, Jorge Amado Núñez Infrán, Isidro Sandoval, Julio César Romero Insfrán, Buenaventura Ferreira Gómez, Alfredo Damián Mendoza Sulewski. Trainer: Cayetano Ré Ramírez.
**Goals**: 1-0 Sócrates Brasileiro Sampaio Vieira de Oliveira (25), 1-1 Julio César Romero Insfrán (41).

30.06.1985, Estádio „Cicero Pompeu de Toledo" Morumbi, São Paulo; Attendance: 90,709
Referee: Enrique Labó Revoredo (Peru)
**BRAZIL - BOLIVIA** **1-1(1-0)**
**BRA:** Carlos Roberto Gallo, Édson Boaro, José Oscar Bernardi, Édino Nazareth Filho "Edinho", Leovegildo Lins Gama Júnior "Júnior I", Antônio Carlos Cerezo "Toninho Cerezo", Sócrates Brasileiro Sampaio Vieira de Oliveira, Arthur Antunes Coimbra "Zico", Renato Portaluppi "Renato Gaúcho", Antônio de Oliveira Filho "Careca I", Éder Aleixo de Assis. Trainer: Telê Santana da Silva.
**BOL:** Luis Galarza Mayereger, José Wilson Avila, Erwin Espinoza, Rolando Coimbra, Marciano Saldías, José Milton Melgar, Edgar Castillo, Erwin Romero Escudero, Rolando Paniagua (David Paniagua Yepez), Juan Carlos Sánchez, Silvio Rojas (Carlos Fernando Borja). Trainer: Carlos Rodríguez.
**Goals**: 1-0 Antônio de Oliveira Filho "Careca I" (19), 1-1 Juan Carlos Sánchez (75).

# CONMEBOL PLAY-OFFS
## SEMI-FINALS

| | | | | |
|---|---|---|---|---|
| 27.10.1985 | Asunción | Paraguay - Colombia | | 3-0(1-0) |
| 03.11.1985 | Cali | Colombia - Paraguay | | 2-1(0-0) |

### FINAL STANDINGS

| | | | | | | | | |
|---|---|---|---|---|---|---|---|---|
| 1. Paraguay | | 2 | 1 | 0 | 1 | 4 - 2 | | 2 |
| 2. Colombia | | 2 | 1 | 0 | 1 | 2 - 4 | | 2 |

Paraguay qualified for the Final.

27.10.1985, Estadio Defensores del Chaco, Asunción; Attendance: 40,000
Referee: Carlos Espósito (Argentina)
**PARAGUAY - COLOMBIA**     **3-0(1-0)**
**PAR:** Roberto Eladio Fernández Roa, Juan Bautista Torales, Rogelio Wilfrido Delgado Casco, César Zabala Fernández, Vladimiro Schettina Chepini (Virginio Cáceres Villalba), Julio César Romero Insfrán, Jorge Amado Núñez Infrán, Adolfino Cañete Azcurra, Buenaventura Ferreira Gómez, Ramón Angel Hicks Cáceres, Roberto Cabañas González (Jorge Alberto Guasch Bazán). Trainer: Cayetano Ré Ramírez.
**COL:** Carlos Fernández Navarro Montoya, Félix Polo, Alvaro Escobar, Miguel Augusto Prince (Jorge Ambuila), Carlos Mario Hoyos, Gabriel Jaime Gómez, Luis Aldemar Murillo, Germán Morales, José Hernández (Carlos Alberto Valderrama Palacio), Willington José Ortíz, John Castaño. Trainer: Gabriel Ochoa Uribe.
**Goals:** 1-0 Ramón Angel Hicks Cáceres (15), 2-0 Julio César Romero Insfrán (70 penalty), 3-0 Roberto Cabañas González (79).

03.11.1985, Estadio „Pascual Guerrero", Cali; Attendance: 8,000
Referee: José Roberto Ramiz Wright (Brazil)
**COLOMBIA - PARAGUAY**     **2-1(0-0)**
**COL:** Carlos Fernández Navarro Montoya, Víctor Emilio Luna, Alvaro Escobar, Miguel Augusto Prince, Jorge Ambuila, Willington José Ortíz, Alexander Escobar, Luis Aldemar Murillo, Carlos Alberto Valderrama Palacio, Anthony William de Ávila Charris (Sergio Angulo Bolaños), John Castaño (Víctor Lugo). Trainer: Gabriel Ochoa Uribe.
**PAR:** Roberto Eladio Fernández Roa, Juan Bautista Torales, Rogelio Wilfrido Delgado Casco, César Zabala Fernández, Vladimiro Schettina Chepini, Julio César Romero Insfrán, Jorge Amado Núñez Infrán, Adolfino Cañete Azcurra, Buenaventura Ferreira Gómez, Ramón Angel Hicks Cáceres (Alfredo Damián Mendoza Sulewski), Roberto Cabañas González (Jorge Alberto Guasch Bazán). Trainer: Cayetano Ré Ramírez.
**Goals:** 0-1 Buenaventura Ferreira Gómez (57), 1-1 Sergio Angulo Bolaños (66), 2-1 Willington José Ortíz (88).

| | | | | | | | |
|---|---|---|---|---|---|---|---|
| 27.10.1985 | Santiago | Chile - Peru | | | | 4-2(1-1) | |
| 03.11.1985 | Lima | Peru - Chile | | | | 0-1(0-0) | |

### FINAL STANDINGS

| | | | | | | | |
|---|---|---|---|---|---|---|---|
| 1. Chile | 2 | 2 | 0 | 0 | 5 - 2 | 4 |
| 2. Peru  | 2 | 0 | 0 | 2 | 2 - 5 | 0 |

Chile qualified for the Final.

27.10.1985, Estadio Nacional, Santiago; Attendance: 40,340
Referee: José Luis Martínez Bazán (Uruguay)
**CHILE - PERU**        **4-2(3-1)**
**CHI:** Roberto Antonio Rojas Saavedra, Lizardo Antonio Garrido Bustamante (80.Rubén Alberto Espinoza), Eduardo Gómez, Mario del Transito Soto Benavides, Luis Hormazábal, Miguel Angel Neira Pincheira (67.Mario Lepe), Alejandro Manuel Hisis Araya, Jorge Orlando Aravena Plaza, Patricio Nazario Yáñez Candia, Hugo Eduardo Rubio Montecinos, Héctor Eduardo Puebla. Trainer: Pedro Morales.
**PER:** Eusebio Alfredo Acasuzo Colán (18.Ramón Quiroga Arancibia), Leonardo Rojas, Pedro Requena, Rubén Toribio Díaz Rivas, Alejandro Hugo Gastulo Ramírez, César Augusto Cueto Villa (67.Eugenio La Rosa), José Manuel Velásquez Castillo, Jorge Andrés Olaechea Quijandría, Gerónimo Barbadillo González, Franco Enrique Navarro Monteiro, Juan Carlos Oblitas Saba. Trainer: Roberto Federico Chale Olarte.
**Goals:** 1-0 Jorge Orlando Aravena Plaza (7), 2-0 Hugo Eduardo Rubio Montecinos (9), 3-0 Alejandro Manuel Hisis Araya (15), 3-1 Franco Enrique Navarro Monteiro (45), 4-1 Jorge Orlando Aravena Plaza (65 penalty), 4-2 Franco Enrique Navarro Monteiro (76).
**Sent off:** Rubén Toribio Díaz Rivas (68).

03.11.1985, Estadio Nacional, Lima; Attendance: 45,244
Referee: Arnaldo David César Coelho (Brazil)
**PERU - CHILE**        **0-1(0-0)**
**PER:** Ramón Quiroga Arancibia, Leonardo Rojas, Pedro Requena, Jaime Eduardo Duarte Huerta, Alejandro Hugo Gastulo Ramírez, César Augusto Cueto Villa (65.Eduardo Hugo Malásquez Maldonado), José Manuel Velásquez Castillo, Julio César Uribe Flores, Gerónimo Barbadillo González, Franco Enrique Navarro Monteiro, Juan Carlos Oblitas Saba (62.Jorge Hirano). Trainer: Roberto Federico Chale Olarte.
**CHI:** Roberto Antonio Rojas Saavedra, Lizardo Antonio Garrido Bustamante, Eduardo Gómez, Mario del Transito Soto Benavides, Luis Hormazábal, Alejandro Manuel Hisis Araya, Mario Lepe, Jorge Orlando Aravena Plaza, Patricio Nazario Yáñez Candia (65.Rubén Alberto Espinoza), Hugo Eduardo Rubio Montecinos, Héctor Eduardo Puebla. Trainer: Pedro Morales.
**Goal:** 0-1 Jorge Orlando Aravena Plaza (64).

# CONMEBOL PLAY-OFFS
## FINAL

| | | | | |
|---|---|---|---|---|
| 10.11.1985 | Asunción | Paraguay - Chile | | 3-0(1-0) |
| 17.11.1985 | Santiago | Chile - Paraguay | | 2-2(1-2) |

### FINAL STANDINGS

| | | | | | | | | |
|---|---|---|---|---|---|---|---|---|
| 1. | **Paraguay** | 2 | 1 | 1 | 0 | 5 - 2 | 3 |
| 2. | Chile | 2 | 0 | 1 | 1 | 2 - 5 | 1 |

Paraguay qualified for the Final Tournament.

10.11.1985, Estadio Defensores del Chaco, Asunción; Attendance: 45,000
Referee: Arnaldo David César Coelho (Brazil)
**PARAGUAY - CHILE**     **3-0(1-0)**
**PAR:** Roberto Eladio Fernández Roa, Juan Bautista Torales, Rogelio Wilfrido Delgado Casco (Virginio Cáceres Villalba), César Zabala Fernández, Vladimiro Schettina Chepini, Julio César Romero Insfrán, Marciano Rolando Chilavert González, Adolfino Cañete Azcurra, Buenaventura Ferreira Gómez, Ramón Angel Hicks Cáceres (Adriano Samaniego Giménez), Roberto Cabañas González. Trainer: Cayetano Ré Ramírez.
**CHI:** Roberto Antonio Rojas Saavedra, Lizardo Antonio Garrido Bustamante, Eduardo Gómez, Mario del Transito Soto Benavides, Luis Hormazábal, Alejandro Manuel Hisis Araya, Mario Lepe (Miguel Angel Neira Pincheira), Jorge Orlando Aravena Plaza, Hugo Eduardo Rubio Montecinos, Juan Carlos Letelier Pizarro, Héctor Eduardo Puebla. Trainer: Pedro Morales.
**Goals**: 1-0 Roberto Cabañas González (9), 2-0 Rogelio Wilfrido Delgado Casco (46), 3-0 Lizardo Antonio Garrido Bustamante (84 own goal).

17.11.1985, Estadio Nacional, Santiago; Attendance: 62,592
Referee: Juan Daniel Cardellino de San Vicente (Uruguay)
**CHILE - PARAGUAY**     **2-2(1-2)**
**CHI:** Roberto Antonio Rojas Saavedra, Rubén Alberto Espinoza, Leonel Herrera (Juan Carlos Letelier Pizarro), Mario del Transito Soto Benavides, Luis Hormazábal, Miguel Angel Neira Pincheira, Alejandro Manuel Hisis Araya, Jorge Orlando Aravena Plaza, Patricio Nazario Yáñez Candia, Hugo Eduardo Rubio Montecinos (Jorge Muñoz), Héctor Eduardo Puebla. Trainer: Pedro Morales.
**PAR:** Roberto Eladio Fernández Roa, Juan Bautista Torales, Rogelio Wilfrido Delgado Casco (Virginio Cáceres Villalba), César Zabala Fernández, Vladimiro Schettina Chepini, Julio César Romero Insfrán (Jorge Alberto Guasch Bazán), Eufemio Raúl Fernández Cabral, Marciano Rolando Chilavert González, Adolfino Cañete Azcurra, Buenaventura Ferreira Gómez, Roberto Cabañas González. Trainer: Cayetano Ré Ramírez.
**Goals**: 1-0 Hugo Eduardo Rubio Montecinos (21), 1-1 Vladimiro Schettina Chepini (22), 1-2 Julio César Romero Insfrán (39), 2-2 Jorge Muñoz (77).
**Sent off**: Alejandro Manuel Hisis Araya (78).

# NORTH, CENTRAL AMERICA & CARIBBEAN

## FIRST ROUND

### GROUP 1

| | | | |
|---|---|---|---|
| 29.07.1984 | San Salvador | El Salvador - Puerto Rico | 5-0(4-0) |
| 05.08.1984 | San Juan | Puerto Rico - El Salvador | 0-3(0-2) |

**FINAL STANDINGS**

| | | | | | | | |
|---|---|---|---|---|---|---|---|
| 1. El Salvador | 2 | 2 | 0 | 0 | 8 - 0 | | 4 |
| 2. Puerto Rico | 2 | 0 | 0 | 2 | 0 - 8 | | 0 |

El Salvador qualified for the Second Round.

29.07.1984, Estadio Cuscatlán, San Salvador; Attendance: 23,333
Referee: Romulo Méndez Molina (Guatemala)
**EL SALVADOR - PUERTO RICO**     **5-0(4-0)**
**SLV**: Luis Ricardo Guevara Mora, William Rosales, Francisco José Jovel Cruz, Jorge Martínez, Ramón Alfredo Fagoaga Romero, José Luis Rugamas Portillo, Patricio Mancia (46.Dagoberto López), Mauricio Alberto Alfaro Valladares (60.Campos), Ever Francisco Hernández, Luis Baltazar Ramírez Zapata, José María Rivas Martínez. Trainer: Juan Quarterone Carbone (Argentina).
**PUR**: Antonio Natal Léon, Roberto Santana, Edwin Cáceres, Figueroa Valles, Manuel López Colón, Raúl Pérez Rivera, Daniel Ramos Soto, Jorge González, Luis Caroballo Rosa (58.Rivera), Francisco Alberto Abreu (75.Cotto), Leonel Rey Reyfebus.
**Goals**: 1-0 Ever Francisco Hernández (7), 2-0 Ever Francisco Hernández (18), 3-0 José María Rivas Martínez (29), 4-0 Mauricio Alberto Alfaro Valladares (44), 5-0 Dagoberto López (84).

05.08.1984, Estadio "Sixto Escobar", San Juan; Attendance: n/a
Referee: Rex Osborne (Bermuda)
**PUERTO RICO - EL SALVADOR**     **0-3(0-2)**
**PUR**: Oscar Rosa, Roberto Santana, Edwin Cáceres, Figueroa Valles, Manuel Colón López, Raúl Pérez Rivera, José Reyfebus, Daniel Ramos Soto (46.Santiga), Jorge González (71.Luis Caroballo Rosa), Wilfredo Vinas, Leonel Rey Reyfebus.
**SLV**: José Luis Munguía Linares, William Rosales, Francisco José Jovel Cruz, Ramón Alfredo Fagoaga Romero, José Luis Rugamas Portillo, José Antonio Velasco (52.Dagoberto López), Luis Baltazar Ramírez Zapata (75.Campos), José María Rivas Martínez, Mauricio Alberto Alfaro Valladares, Thomas Eduardo Lucero Mendoza, Ever Francisco Hernández. Trainer: Juan Quarterone Carbone (Argentina).
**Goals**: 0-1 Mauricio Alberto Alfaro Valladares, 0-2 Luis Baltazar Ramírez Zapata, 0-3 José María Rivas Martínez.
**Sent off**: Leonel Rey Reyfebus (58).

| 15.06.1984 | Colón | Panama - Honduras | 0-3(0-1) |
| 24.06.1984 | Tegucigalpa | Honduras - Panama | 1-0(0-0) |

### FINAL STANDINGS

| | | | | | | | | |
|---|---|---|---|---|---|---|---|---|
| 1. | Honduras | 2 | 2 | 0 | 0 | 4 | - 0 | 4 |
| 2. | Panama | 2 | 0 | 0 | 2 | 0 | - 4 | 0 |

Honduras qualified for the Second Round.

15.06.1984, Estadio "Roberto Mariano Bula", Colón; Attendance: n/a
Referee: José Ortíz Cardoza (El Salvador)
**PANAMA - HONDURAS**                                   **0-3(0-1)**
**PAN**: Diogenes Cáceres, Eleuterio Arosemena Cruz, Jesús González, Luis Abrego, Sergio González Montoto, Germán Salager, Armando Javier Dely Valdés, Víctor René Mendieta, Ricardo Buitrago, Carlos Dely, Rubén Guevara. Trainer: Carlos Albert Cavagnaro (Argentina).
**HON**: Julio César Arzú, Domingo Drummond Cooper, Jaime Enrique Villegas Roura, Allan Anthony Costly Blyden, Javier Francisco Toledo Rivera, José Enrique Mendoza Duarté, Ramón Enrique Maradiaga Chávez, Eduardo Antonio Laing Carcamo, José Roberto Figueroa Padilla, Gamboa, Carlos Orlando Caballero Sánchez (72.Chavarría). Trainer: José de la Paz Herrera Ucles.
**Goals**: 0-1 Eduardo Antonio Laing Carcamo (16), 0-2 José Roberto Figueroa Padilla (54), 0-3 José Roberto Figueroa Padilla (62).

24.06.1984, Estadio Nacional, Tegucigalpa; Attendance: 38,000
Referee: Mike Constantine (United States)
**HONDURAS - PANAMA**                                   **1-0(0-0)**
**HON**: José Belarmino Rivera Rosales, Allan Anthony Costly Blyden, César Efrain Gutíerrez Álvarez, Jaime Enrique Villegas Roura, Antonio Daniel Zapata Martínez, Carlos Orlando Caballero Sánchez (80.Raúl Matthews), Javier Francisco Toledo Rivera, Roberto James Bailey Sargent (46.Eduardo Antonio Laing Carcamo), José Roberto Figueroa Padilla, Ramón Enrique Maradiaga Chávez, Juan Alberto Cruz Murillo. Trainer: José de la Paz Herrera Ucles.
**PAN**: Diogenes Cáceres, Eleuterio Arosemena Cruz, Sergio González Montoto, Ricardo Buitrago (84.Rubén Guevara), Víctor René Mendieta, Enrique Herrera (46.Armando Javier Dely Valdés), Lester Sabers, Jesús González, Germán Salager, Jorge Méndez Daniels, Luis Abrego. Trainer: Carlos Albert Cavagnaro (Argentina).
**Goal**: 1-0 José Roberto Figueroa Padilla (73).


| 15.08.1984 | Paramaribo | Suriname - Guyana | 1-0(0-0) |
| 29.08.1984 | Georgetown | Guyana - Suriname | 1-1(1-0) |

### FINAL STANDINGS

| | | | | | | | | |
|---|---|---|---|---|---|---|---|---|
| 1. | Suriname | 2 | 1 | 1 | 0 | 2 | - 1 | 3 |
| 2. | Guyana | 2 | 0 | 1 | 1 | 1 | - 2 | 1 |

Suriname qualified for the Second Round.

15.08.1984, "André Kamperveen" Stadion, Paramaribo; Attendance: n/a
Referee: Lee Tai Kong (Netherlands Antilles)
**SURINAME - GUYANA**                                                                          **1-0(0-0)**
**SUR**: Guno Vyent, Harold Hart, Allen Rampach, Siegfried Rustenberg (85.Frank Westenburg), Floyd Griffith, Kenneth Francis, Kenneth Frank Borgia (87.Jacob Eduards), Rinaldo Stanley Entingh, Delando Righters, Kenneth Stjeward, Umberto Klinker. Trainer: Walter Braithwaite.
**GUY**: Gerald Austin, Marlon de Souza, Gordon Braithwaite, Aubrey Hutson, Rupert Gordon, Terence Gordon, Leonard Williams, Nigel Cummings, Trevor Maxwell (60.Norton Anthony Smart), Julian Moe, Roger Alphonso. Trainer: Arthur Lennox.
**Goal**: 1-0 Jacob Edwards (89).

29.08.1984, Bourda Cricket Ground, Georgetown; Attendance: n/a
Referee: Sirjuesingh Lennox (Trinidad and Tobago)
**GUYANA - SURINAME**                                                                       **1-1(1-0)**
**GUY**: Gerald Austin, Aubrey Hutson, Marlon de Souza, Roger Alphonso, Gordon Braithwaite, Terrence Archer, Leonard Williams, Nigel Cummings, Trevor Maxwell (50.Barron), Julian Moe, Rupert Gordon. Trainer: Arthur Lennox.
**SUR**: Carlo Monpellier, Siegfried Rustenberg, Allen Rampach, Ronald Borgia (59.Jacob Eduards), Kenneth Stjeward, Kenneth Frank Borgia, Floyd Griffith, Kenneth Francis, Rinaldo Stanley Entingh, Delando Righters, Umberto Klinker. Trainer: Walter Braithwaite.
**Goals**: 1-0 : Terrence Archer (17), 1-1 Umberto Klinker (67).

# GROUP 2

| 04.08.1984 | Port-au-Prince | Antigua and Barbuda - Haiti | 0-4(0-2) |
| 07.08.1984 | Port-au-Prince | Haiti - Antigua and Barbuda | 1-2(1-1) |

### FINAL STANDINGS

| | | | | | | | | |
|---|---|---|---|---|---|---|---|---|
| 1. | Haiti | 2 | 1 | 0 | 1 | 5 - 2 | | 2 |
| 2. | Antigua and Barbuda | 2 | 1 | 0 | 1 | 2 - 5 | | 2 |

Haiti qualified for the Second Round.

04.08.1984, Stade „Sylvio Cator", Port-au-Prince; Attendance: 2,766
Referee: W. Taylor (Jamaica)
**ANTIGUA AND BARBUDA - HAITI**                                             **0-4(0-2)**
**ATG**: Andy Christian, Dave Richards (Martin), Fernando Abrahim, Everton Richardson, Alen Ferrance, Cedric Joseph (D. Richards), Andy Nesbitt, David Warner, Everton Gonsalves, Mervin Richards, Elvis Roberts.
**HAI**: Louis-Thelmy Demeuranty, Goebbels Cadet, Desilus Donet, Gérald Jean-Pierre, Jean-Robert Civil, Edward Vorbe, Françen Alexandre, Jean-Joseph Mathelier, Antoine Eleazard, Keslin Thomas, Maxime Auguste. Trainer: Claude Barthélemy.
**Goals**: 0-1 Maxime Auguste (14), 0-2 Maxime Auguste (36), 0-3 Keslin Thomas (63), 0-4 Maxime Auguste (77).

07.08.1984, Stade „Sylvio Cator", Port-au-Prince; Attendance: 1,576
Referee: Campbell (Jamaica)
**HAITI - ANTIGUA AND BARBUDA**                                     **1-2(1-1)**
**HAI**: Louis-Thelmy Demeuranty, Goebbels Cadet, Donet Desilus, Gérald Jean-Pierre, Antoine Eleazard, Jean-Joseph Mathelier (Henry Claude Charmant), Maxime Auguste, Edward Vorbe, Keslin Thomas, Jean-Robert Civil, Eric Auguste. Trainer: Claude Barthélemy.
**ATG**: Andy Christian, Fernando Abrahim, Barry Gordon, Alen Ferrance, Cedric Joseph, Beverly Deterville (70.Andy Nesbitt), Everton Gonsalves, Mervin Richards, Elvis Roberts, Trevor Richards, Everton Richardson.
**Goals**: 0-1 Everton Gonsalves (16), 1-1 Edward Vorbe (38), 1-2 Elvis Roberts (87).

Canada qualified for the Second Round (Jamaica withdrew)

Guatemala qualified for the Second Round

# GROUP 3

| 29.09.1984 | Willemstad | Netherlands Antilles - United States | 0-0 |
| 06.10.1984 | Saint Louis | United States - Netherlands Antilles | 4-0(0-0) |

**FINAL STANDINGS**

| | | | | | | | |
|---|---|---|---|---|---|---|---|
| 1. United States | 2 | 1 | 1 | 0 | 4 - 0 | 3 |
| 2. Netherlands Antilles | 2 | 0 | 1 | 1 | 0 - 4 | 1 |

United States qualified for the Second Round.

29.09.1984, Willemstad; Attendance: 6,109
Referee: Goede (Surinam)
**NETHERLANDS ANTILLES - UNITED STATES**                **0-0**
**ANT**: Jozef Archangel Nivillac, John Bacuna, Erick Oleana, Edsel Neuman, Sherman Fonseca, Sixto Rovina, Rudsel St. Jago, Raymond Lucas (78.Wensly Martina), Erwin Bernardina, Erroll Maximino St. Jago, Stanley Grigorie (62.Julia).
**USA**: Winston DuBose, Bruce Savage, Gregg Thompson, Jeffery Durgan, Dan Canter, Angelo di Bernardo (75.Kevin Troy Crow), Hernán Antonio Borja, Richard Dean Davis (Cap), Ade Coker, Hugo Pérez, Andrew Parkinson. Trainer: Alketas Panagoulias (Greece).

06.10.1984, Big Arch Stadium, St Louis; Attendance: 10,718
Referee: Rolando Fusco (Canada)
**UNITED STATES - NETHERLANDS ANTILLES**             **4-0(0-0)**
**USA**: David Joseph Brcic, Erhardt Kapp, Jeffery Durgan, Dan Canter, Kevin Troy Crow, Hernán Antonio Borja, Richard Dean Davis (Cap), Angelo di Bernardo, Charles Fajkus (70.Percival Joseph van der Beck), Chance Fry (24.Ade Coker), Hugo Pérez. Trainer: Alketas Panagoulias (Greece).
**ANT**: Jozef Archangel Nivillac, John Bacuna, Erick Oleana, Edsel Neuman, Sherman Fonseca, Erwin Bernardina, Sixto Rovina, Erroll Maximino St. Jago, Glenn Kwidama (59.Alexander Craane; 88.Wensly Martina), Rudsel St. Jago, Stanley Grigorie.
**Goals**: 1-0 Angelo di Bernardo (50), 2-0 Ade Coker (58), 3-0 Ade Coker (67), 4-0 Erhardt Kapp (85).
**Sent off**: Rudsel St. Jago (42), Edsel Neuman (55).

Costa Rica qualified for the Second Round (Barbados withdrew)
Trinidad and Tobago qualified for the Second Round (Grenada withdrew)

# SECOND ROUND

## GROUP 1

| | | | | |
|---|---|---|---|---|
| 24.02.1985 | San Salvador | Suriname – El Salvador | | 0-3(0-1) |
| 27.02.1985 | San Salvador | El Salvador - Suriname | | 3-0(0-0) |
| 03.03.1985 | Tegucigalpa | Suriname - Honduras | | 1-1(1-1) |
| 06.03.1985 | Tegucigalpa | Honduras - Suriname | | 2-1(1-0) |
| 10.03.1985 | San Salvador | El Salvador – Honduras | | 1-2(0-1) |
| 14.03.1985 | Tegucigalpa | Honduras – El Salvador | | 0-0 |

### FINAL STANDINGS

| | | | | | | | | |
|---|---|---|---|---|---|---|---|---|
| 1. | Honduras | 4 | 2 | 2 | 0 | 5 - 3 | 6 |
| 2. | El Salvador | 4 | 2 | 1 | 1 | 7 - 2 | 5 |
| 3. | Suriname | 4 | 0 | 1 | 3 | 2 - 9 | 1 |

Honduras qualified for the CONCACAF Zone Final.

24.02.1985, Estadio Cuscatlán, San Salvador; Attendance: 35,652
Referee: Berny Morera Ulloa (Costa Rica)
**SURINAME – EL SALVADOR**     **0-3(0-1)**
**SUR**: Carlo Monpellier, Siegmar Nora, Siegfried Rustenberg, Floyd Griffith, Regillo Doest (70.Umberto Klinker), Kenneth Frank Borgia, Rinaldo Stanley Entingh, Delando Righters, Frank Westenburg, Kenneth Stjeward, Dennis Wyks (57.Jacob Eduards). Trainer: Walter Braithwaite.
**SLV**: José Luis Munguía, Thomas Lucero, José Francisco Jovel Cruz, Ramón Alfredo Fagoaga Romero, José Luis Rugamas Portillo, Mauricio Alberto Alfaro Valladares, Luis Baltazar Ramírez Zapata, José María Rivas Martínez (77.Dagoberto López), Wilfredo Huezo, Marcial Turcios (46.Luis Mauricio Perla Alfaro), Ever Francisco Hernández. Trainer: Juan Quartarone Carbone (Argentina).
**Goals**: 0-1 Mauricio Alberto Alfaro Valladares (25), 0-2 Wilfredo Huezo (52), 0-3 Ever Francisco Hernández (79).

27.02.1985, Estadio Cuscatlán, San Salvador; Attendance: 18,918
Referee: Mario Efraín Escobar López (Guatemala)
**EL SALVADOR - SURINAME**     **3-0(0-0)**
**SLV**: José Luis Munguía, Thomas Lucero, José Francisco Jovel Cruz, Ramón Alfredo Fagoaga Romero, José Luis Rugamas Portillo, Mauricio Alberto Alfaro Valladares, Ever Francisco Hernández, Luis Baltazar Ramírez Zapata (48.Dagoberto López), José María Rivas Martínez, Wilfredo Huezo (80.Luis Mauricio Perla Alfaro), Carlos Vargas. Trainer: Juan Quartarone Carbone (Argentina).
**SUR**: Carlo Monpellier, Siegmar Nora, Dennis Wyks (80.Kenneth Francis), Siegfried Rustenberg, Floyd Griffith, Regillo Doest, Kenneth Frank Borgia, Rinaldo Stanley Entingh (65.Leisberg), Delando Righters, Frank Westenburg, Kenneth Stjeward. Trainer: Walter Braithwaite.
**Goals**: 1-0 José María Rivas Martínez (68), 2-0 Luis Baltazar Ramírez Zapata (76), 3-0 José María Rivas Martínez (80).

03.03.1985, Estadio Nacional "Tiburcio Carías Andino", Tegucigalpa; Attendance: 35,000
Referee: Mamerto Negreros Castellanos (Guatemala)
**SURINAME - HONDURAS**     **1-1(1-1)**
**SUR**: Carlo Monpellier (46.Roy Belfor), Siegmar Nora, Siegfried Rustenberg, Floyd Griffith, Regillo Doest, Kenneth Frank Borgia, Rinaldo Stanley Entingh, Kenneth Francis, Umberto Klinker, Frank Westenburg, Kenneth Stjeward. Trainer: Walter Braithwaite.
**HON**: Julio César Arzú, Jaime Enrique Villegas Roura, Allan Anthony Costly Blyden, Carlos Orlando Caballero Sánchez, Javier Francisco Toledo Rivera, Roberto James Bailey Sargent (67.Lacayo), Juan Espinoza (46.José Enrique Mendoza Duarte), Ramón Enrique Maradiaga Chávez, Domingo Cooper Droumond, Eduardo Antonio Laing Carcamo, Antonio Zapata. Trainer: José de la Paz Herrera Ucles.

**Goals**: Rinaldo Entingh / Eduardo Antonio Laing Carcamo.

07.03.1985, Estadio Nacional "Tiburcio Carías Andino", Tegucigalpa; Attendance: 27,453
Referee: Carlos Luis Alfaro Venegas (Costa Rica)
**HONDURAS - SURINAME**                                              **2-1(1-0)**
**HON**: Julio César Arzú, Gilberto Gerónimo Yearwood, Jaime Enrique Villegas Roura, Allan Anthony Costly Blyden, Ramón Enrique Maradiaga Chávez, Carlos Orlando Caballero Sánchez, Javier Francisco Toledo Rivera, José Roberto Figueroa Padilla, Domingo Cooper Droumond, Eduardo Antonio Laing Carcamo (68.Roberto James Bailey Sargent), Antonio Zapata (82.Celso Fredy Güity Núñez). Trainer: José de la Paz Herrera Ucles.
**SUR**: Roy Belfor, Siegmar Nora, Ruben Nijhs, Siegfried Rustenberg, Floyd Griffith, Regillo Doest, Kenneth Frank Borgia, Rinaldo Stanley Entingh, Kenneth Francis (79.Delando Righters), Frank Westenburg, Kenneth Stjeward. Trainer: Walter Braithwaite.
**Goals**: José Roberto Figueroa Padilla 2 / Kenneth Stjeward.

10.03.1985, Estadio Cuscatlán, San Salvador; Attendance: 51,555
Referee: David Stanley Socha (United States)
**EL SALVADOR – HONDURAS**                                           **1-2(0-1)**
**SLV**: José Luis Munguía, Thomas Lucero, José Francisco Jovel Cruz, Ramón Alfredo Fagoaga Romero, Mauricio Alberto Alfaro Valladares, Carlos Vargas, Norberto Huezo, Jorge Alberto González Barillas, José Luis Rugamas Portillo, Luis Baltazar Ramírez Zapata (46.José María Rivas Martínez), Ever Francisco Hernández. Trainer: Juan Quartarone Carbone (Argentina).
**HON**: Julio César Arzú, Domingo Cooper Droumond, Jaime Enrique Villegas Roura, Allan Anthony Costly Blyden, César Efraín Gutiérrez Álvarez, Javier Francisco Toledo Rivera, Gilberto Gerónimo Yearwood, Ramón Enrique Maradiaga Chávez, José Roberto Figueroa Padilla, Roberto James Bailey Sargent, Celso Fredy Güity Núñez (8.Eduardo Antonio Laing Carcamo). Trainer: José de la Paz Herrera Ucles.
**Goals**: 0-1 Roberto James Bailey Sargent (1), 1-1 José María Rivas Martínez (63), 1-2 Eduardo Antonio Laing Carcamo (77).

14.03.1985, Estadio Nacional "Tiburcio Carías Andino", Tegucigalpa; Attendance: 38,175
Referee: Antonio Evangelista (Canada)
**HONDURAS – EL SALVADOR**                                           **0-0**
**HON**: Julio César Arzú, Gilberto Gerónimo Yearwood, César Efraín Gutiérrez Álvarez, Ramón Enrique Maradiaga Chávez (84.Celso Fredy Güity Núñez), Carlos Orlando Caballero Sánchez, Javier Francisco Toledo Rivera, Roberto James Bailey Sargent (71.Eduardo Antonio Laing Carcamo), José Roberto Figueroa Padilla, Domingo Cooper Droumond, José Enrique Mendoza Duarte, Richardson Smith. Trainer: José de la Paz Herrera Ucles.
**SLV**: José Luis Munguía, José Francisco Jovel Cruz, Jorge Martínez Abrego (76.Carlos Vargas), Ramón Alfredo Fagoaga Romero, José Luis Rugamas Portillo, Jaime Alberto Rodríguez Jiménez, Norberto Huezo, Ever Francisco Hernández, Luis Baltazar Ramírez Zapata, José María Rivas Martínez, Jorge Alberto González Barillas. Trainer: Juan Quartarone Carbone (Argentina).

# GROUP 2

| | | | | |
|---|---|---|---|---|
| 13.04.1985 | Vancouver | Canada - Haiti | 2-0 | (2-0) |
| 20.04.1985 | Vancouver | Canada - Guatemala | 2-1 | (2-0) |
| 26.04.1985 | Port-au-Prince | Haiti - Guatemala | 0-1 | (0-0) |
| 05.05.1985 | Cd. de Guatemala | Guatemala - Canada | 1-1 | (1-1) |
| 08.05.1985 | Port-au-Prince | Haiti – Canada | 0-2 | (0-1) |
| 15.05.1985 | Cd. de Guatemala | Guatemala - Haiti | 4-0 | (1-0) |

### FINAL STANDINGS

| | | | | | | | | |
|---|---|---|---|---|---|---|---|---|
| 1. | Canada | 4 | 3 | 1 | 0 | 7 - 2 | 7 |
| 2. | Guatemala | 4 | 2 | 1 | 1 | 7 - 3 | 5 |
| 3. | Haiti | 4 | 0 | 0 | 4 | 0 - 9 | 0 |

Canada qualified for the CONCACAF Zone Final.

13.04.1985, Royal Athletic Ground, Victoria; Attendance: 5,000
Referee: Angelo Bratsis (United States)
**CANADA - HAITI**     **2-0(2-0)**
CAN: Kenneth Paul Dolan, Robert Lenarduzzi, Shaun Lowther, Randolph Fitzgerald Samuel, Bruce Alec Wilson, David McDonald Norman, George Pakos, Randolph Lee Ragan, Mike Sweeney, Igor Vrablic, Kenneth Garraway. Trainer: Anthony Keith Waiters.
HAI: Louis-Thelmy Demeuranty, Jean-Robert Cadet, André François, Desilus Donet, Françen Alexandre (57.Eric Auguste), Eddy Nizieuk (84.James Boule), Jean-Joseph Mathelier, Maxime Auguste, Antoine Eleazard, Henry Claude Charmant, Daniel Cadet. Trainer: Claude Barthélemy.
**Goals**: 1-0 Igor Vrablic (29), 2-0 Mike Sweeney (41).

20.04.1985, Royal Athletic Ground, Victoria; Attendance: 5,000
Referee: Edgardo Codesal Méndez (Mexico)
**CANADA - GUATEMALA**     **2-1(2-0)**
CAN: Kenneth Paul Dolan, Robert Lenarduzzi, Ian Christopher Bridge, Randolph Fitzgerald Samuel, Bruce Alec Wilson, Paul John James, Randolph Lee Ragan, George Pakos, David McDonald Norman, Dale William Mitchell, Igor Vrablic (70.Kenneth Garraway). Trainer: Anthony Keith Waiters.
GUA: Hermenegildo Pepp Castro, Juan Pérez, Víctor Hugo Monzón Pérez, Rendón, Carlos Estrada, Raúl Chacón Estrada, Alfredo Solorzano (73.Selvin Galindo), Luis Guillermo Rodríguez Sandoval (33.Julio Gómez Rendón), Sergio Rivera, Allan Kenny Wellmann, Erwin Rafael Donis Duran. Trainer: Dragoslav Šekularac (Yugoslavia).
**Goals**: 1-0 Dale William Mitchell (22), 2-0 Dale William Mitchell (43), 2-1 Julio Gómez Rendón (65).

26.04.1985, Stade „Sylvio Cator", Port-au-Prince; Attendance: n/a
Referee: Edward Bellion (United States)
**HAITI - GUATEMALA**     **0-1(0-0)**
HAI: Louis-Thelmy Demeuranty, Jean-Robert Cadet, André François, Desilus Donet, Eric Auguste, Jean-Paul Pierre Louis, Jean-Joseph Mathelier (64.Keslin Thomas), James Boule, Antoine Eleazard, Fritz Bobo (64.Maxime Auguste), Daniel Cadet. Trainer: Claude Barthélemy.
GUA: Hermenegildo Pepp Castro, Juan Pérez, Víctor Hugo Monzón Pérez, Julio Gómez Rendón (38.Carlos Estrada), Raúl Chacón Estrada, Byron Romeo Pérez Solórzano(77.Carías Hernández), Sergio Rivera, Allan Kenny Wellmann, Juan Manuel Funés Fernández, Erwin Rafael Donis Duran. Trainer: Dragoslav Šekularac (Yugoslavia).
**Goal**: 0-1 Carlos Estrada (63).

05.05.1985, Estadio „Mateo Flores", Ciudad de Guatemala; Attendance: 60,000
Referee: Luis Paulino Siles Calderón (Costa Rica)
**GUATEMALA - CANADA**     **1-1(1-1)**
**GUA:** Hermenegildo Pepp Castro, Juan Pérez, Víctor Hugo Monzón Pérez, Carlos Estrada, Raúl Chacón Estrada, Byron Romeo Pérez Solórzano, Luis Guillermo Rodríguez Sandoval (46.Alfredo Solorzano), Sergio Rivera, Allan Kenny Wellmann, Juan Manuel Funés Fernández (42.Morales), Erwin Rafael Donis Duran. Trainer: Dragoslav Šekularac (Yugoslavia).
**CAN:** Kenneth Paul Dolan, Robert Lenarduzzi, Ian Christopher Bridge, Randolph Fitzgerald Samuel, Bruce Alec Wilson, Paul John James, Randolph Lee Ragan, George Pakos (23.Pasquale DeLuca), David McDonald Norman, Dale William Mitchell, Igor Vrablic. Trainer: Anthony Keith Waiters.
**Goals**: 0-1 Dale William Mitchell (39), 1-1 Byron Romeo Pérez Solórzano (42).

08.05.1985, Stade „Sylvio Cator", Port-au-Prince; Attendance: 7,000
Referee: Rex Osbourne (Bermuda)
**HAITI – CANADA**     **0-2(0-1)**
**HAI**: Louis-Thelmy Demeuranty (60.Elias Sejour), Jean-Robert Cadet, Jean-Claude Moise, Donet Desilus, Eric Auguste, Jean-Paul Pierre Louis, Maxime Auguste, Antoine Eleazard (68.Henry Claude Charmant), Keslin Thomas, James Boule, Daniel Cadet. Trainer: Claude Barthélemy.
**CAN:** Kenneth Paul Dolan, Robert Lenarduzzi, Ian Christopher Bridge, Randolph Fitzgerald Samuel, Bruce Alec Wilson, Paul John James, Randolph Lee Ragan, Pasquale DeLuca (71.Shaun Lowther), David McDonald Norman, Dale William Mitchell, Igor Vrablic. Trainer: Anthony Keith Waiters.
**Goals**: 0-1 Dale William Mitchell (14), 0-2 Igor Vrablic (56).

15.05.1985, Estadio „Mateo Flores", Ciudad de Guatemala; Attendance: n/a
Referee: Rodolfo Martínez Mejía (Honduras)
**GUATEMALA - HAITI**     **4-0(1-0)**
**GUA:** Edgar Ricardo Jérez Hidalgo, Víctor Hugo Monzón Pérez, Alejandro Ortíz Obregón, Eddy Suárez, Carlos Estrada (26.Alfredo Solorzano), Raúl Chacón Estrada, Kevin Shannon, Selvin Galindo (50.Byron Romeo Pérez Solórzano), Sergio Rivera, Juan Manuel Funés Fernández, Erwin Rafael Donis Duran. Trainer: Dragoslav Šekularac (Yugoslavia).
**HAI**: Elias Sejour, Selin Sainsou, Desilus Donet, Eric Auguste, Jean-Paul Pierre Louis, Jean-Joseph Mathelier, Maxime Auguste, Antoine Eleazard (30.Jean-Paul Pierre Louis), Jean-Claude Moise, Fritz Bobo (55.Henry Claude Charmant), Daniel Cadet. Trainer: Claude Barthélemy.
**Goals**: 1-0 Raúl Chacón Estrada (44), 2-0 Selvin Galindo (48), 3-0 Juan Manuel Funés Fernández (62), 4-0 Alfredo Solorzano (71).

## GROUP 3

| | | | |
|---|---|---|---|
| 24.04.1985 | San José | Trinidad and Tobago - Costa Rica | 0-3(0-1) |
| 28.04.1985 | San José | Costa Rica - Trinidad and Tobago | 1-1(0-1) |
| 15.05.1985 | St. Louis | United States - Trinidad and Tobago | 2-1(1-1) |
| 19.05.1985 | Los Angeles | Trinidad and Tobago – United States | 0-1(0-1) |
| 26.05.1985 | Alajuela | Costa Rica - United States | 1-1(1-1) |
| 31.05.1985 | Los Angeles | United States – Costa Rica | 0-1(0-1) |

### FINAL STANDINGS

| | | | | | | | | |
|---|---|---|---|---|---|---|---|---|
| 1. | Costa Rica | 4 | 2 | 2 | 0 | 6 - 2 | 6 |
| 2. | United States | 4 | 2 | 1 | 1 | 4 - 3 | 5 |
| 3. | Trinidad and Tobago | 4 | 0 | 1 | 3 | 2 - 7 | 1 |

Costa Rica qualfied for the CONCACAF Zone Final.

24.04.1985, Estadio Nacional, San José; Attendance: 9,689
Referee: Rodolfo Martínez Mejía (Honduras)
**TRINIDAD AND TOBAGO - COSTA RICA**   **0-3(0-1)**
**TRI:** Michael Maurice, Julien García, Francis Furlonge, Clayton Morris, Anthony Pope (24.Larry Joseph), Nevick de Noon (18.Steve Pompey), Winston Phillips, Adrian Funrose, Wendell Moore, Kelvin Jones, Miguel Hakett. Trainer: Roderick Warner.
**CRC:** Román González, Freddy Méndez, Marvin Obando Obando, Nilton Nóbrega, Franklin Williams (21.Evaristo Coronado Salas), Álvaro Solano, Mínor Alpízar, Enrique Alberto Díaz Harvey, Miguel Lacey, Tomás Velásquez (2.Óscar Ramírez Hernández), Jorge Ulate. Trainer: Odir Jacques Ferreira (Brazil).
**Goals:** 0-1 Franklin Williams (15), 0-2 Miguel Lacey (65), 0-3 Nilton Nóbrega (79).

28.04.1985, Estadio Nacional, San José; Attendance: 10,839
Referee: Rómulo Méndez Molina (Guatemala)
**COSTA RICA - TRINIDAD AND TOBAGO**   **1-1(0-1)**
**CRC:** Román González, Óscar Ramírez Hernández, Freddy Méndez, Marvin Obando Obando, Nilton Nóbrega (52.Tomás Velasquez), Franklin Williams, Álvaro Solano, Mínor Alpízar (65.Evaristo Coronado Salas), Enrique Alberto Díaz Harvey, Miguel Lacey, Jorge Ulate. Trainer: Odir Jacques Ferreira (Brazil).
**TRI:** Michael Maurice, Julien García, Bertram O'Brien, Clayton Morris, Anthony Pope, Nevick de Noon, Larry Joseph, Winston Phillips (75.Francis Furlonge), Adrian Funrose, Kelvin Jones, Miguel Hakett. Trainer: Roderick Warner.
**Goals:** 0-1 Nevick de Noon (20), 1-1 Jorge Ulate (65).

15.05.1985, Big Arch Stadium, St. Louis; Attendance: 15,823
Referee: Robert Allen (Canada)
**UNITED STATES - TRINIDAD AND TOBAGO**   **2-1(1-1)**
**USA:** David Joseph Brcic, Percival Joseph van der Beck, Dan Canter, Jeffery Durgan (46.Paul David Caligiuri), Erhardt Kapp, Charles Fajkus (66.Michael Anthony Fox), Angelo di Bernardo, Richard Dean Davis, Hernán Antonio Borja, Mark Peterson, Hugo Ernesto Pérez Granados. Trainer: Alketas Panagoulias (Greece).
**TRI:** Michael Maurice, Garnet Craig, Julien García, Francis Furlonge, Bertram O'Brien, Clayton Morris, Winston Phillips, Adrian Funrose, Wendell Moore, Kelvin Jones (89.Anthony Pope), Nevick de Noon (61.Curtis Murrell). Trainer: Roderick Warner.
**Goals:** 0-1 Adrian Funrose (18), 1-1 Hernán Antonio Borja (29), 2-1 Mark Peterson (88).

19.05.1985, Torrance; Attendance: 6,115
Referee: Jorge Alberto Leanza (Mexico)
**TRINIDAD AND TOBAGO – UNITED STATES** **0-1(0-1)**
**TRI**: Michael Maurice, Bertram O'Brien (54.Kelvin Jones), Perec Lewis, Garnet Craig, Julien García, Wendell Moore, Clayton Morris, Allan Anderson (77.Nevick de Noon), Winston Phillips, Adrian Funrose, Philibert Jones. Trainer: Roderick Warner.
**USA**: Arnold Mausser, Dan Canter, Paul David Caligiuri, Gregg Thompson, Michael Windischmann, Percival Joseph van der Beck, Angelo di Bernardo, Richard Dean Davis, Hernán Antonio Borja (77.Michael Anthony Fox), Hugo Ernesto Pérez Granados, Mark Peterson (46.John Kerr). Trainer: Alketas Panagoulias (Greece).
**Goal**: 0-1 Paul David Caligiuri (15).

26.05.1985, Estadio „Alejandro Morera Soto", Alajuela; Attendance: 20,173
Referee: Jorge Urrera Reyes (Mexico)
**COSTA RICA - UNITED STATES** **1-1(1-1)**
**CRC**: Alejandro González, Óscar Ramírez Hernández, Róger Flores Solano, Tomás Segura, Rodolfo Mills Palmer, Álvaro Solano (69.Leonidas Flores Reyes), Omar Arroyo Rodríguez, Jorge Chévez, Jorge Contreras, Raquel Ledezma, Jorge Ulate (70.Evaristo Coronado Salas). Trainer: Odir Jacques Ferreira (Brazil).
**USA**: Arnold Mausser, Gregg Thompson, Paul David Caligiuri, Dan Canter, Michael Windischmann, Percival Joseph van der Beck, Richard Dean Davis, Michael Anthony Fox, Edward Radwanski (46.Angelo di Bernardo), Jeffrey Scott Hooker (46.Mark Peterson), John Kerr. Trainer: Alketas Panagoulias (Greece).
**Goals**: 1-0 Óscar Ramírez Hernández (42), 1-1 John Kerr (45).

31.05.1985, Torrance; Attendance: 11,800
Referee: John Meachin (Canada)
**UNITED STATES – COSTA RICA** **0-1(0-1)**
**USA**: Arnold Mausser, Gregg Thompson, Paul David Caligiuri, Dan Canter, Michael Windischmann, Kevin Troy Crow, Percival Joseph van der Beck (64.Angelo di Bernardo), Richard Dean Davis, Michael Anthony Fox, John Kerr, Hugo Ernesto Pérez Granados. Trainer: Alketas Panagoulias (Greece).
**CRC**: Alejandro González, Óscar Ramírez Hernández, Róger Flores Solano, Edwin Salazar, Rodolfo Mills Palmer, Evaristo Coronado Salas (65.Jorge Ulate), Omar Arroyo Rodríguez, Jorge Chévez, Luis Enrique Galagarza, Juan Arnoldo Cayasso Reid, Jorge Contreras. Trainer: Odir Jacques Ferreira (Brazil).
**Goal**: 0-1 Evaristo Coronado Salas (34).
**Sent off**: Jorge Ulate (89).

# CONCACAF ZONE FINAL

| | | | | |
|---|---|---|---|---|
| 11.08.1985 | San José | Costa Rica - Honduras | 2-2(1-2) |
| 17.08.1985 | Toronto | Canada – Costa Rica | 1-1(0-1) |
| 25.08.1985 | Tegucigalpa | Honduras - Canada | 0-1(0-0) |
| 01.09.1985 | San José | Costa Rica - Canada | 0-0 |
| 08.09.1985 | Tegucigalpa | Honduras – Costa Rica | 3-1(1-1) |
| 14.09.1985 | Saint John's | Canada - Honduras | 2-1(1-0) |

## FINAL STANDINGS

| | | | | | | | | |
|---|---|---|---|---|---|---|---|---|
| 1. | Canada | 4 | 2 | 2 | 0 | 4 - 2 | 6 |
| 2. | Honduras | 4 | 1 | 1 | 2 | 6 - 6 | 3 |
| 3. | Costa Rica | 4 | 0 | 3 | 1 | 4 - 6 | 3 |

Canada qualified for the Final Tournament.

11.08.1985, Estadio Nacional, San José; Attendance: 20,043
Referee: Edward Bellion (United States)
**COSTA RICA - HONDURAS**      **2-2(1-2)**
CRC: Alejandro González, Róger Flores Solano, Edwin Salazar, Rodolfo Mills Palmer, Álvaro Solano, Omar Arroyo Rodríguez, Jorge Chévez (63.Evaristo Coronado Salas), Germán José Chavarría Jiménez, Johnny Williams, Luis Enrique Galagarza (28.Leonidas Flores Reyes). Trainer: Álvaro Grant MacDonald.
HON: Julio César Arzú, César Efraín Gutiérrez Álvarez, Jaime Enrique Villegas Roura, Allan Anthony Costly Blyden, Ramón Enrique Maradiaga Chávez, Javier Francisco Toledo Rivera, Gilberto Gerónimo Yearwood, Porfirio Armando Betancourt, José Roberto Figueroa Padilla, Domingo Cooper Droumond, Celso Fredy Güity Núñez (66.Eduardo Antonio Laing Carcamo). Trainer: José de la Paz Herrera Ucles.
**Goals**: 0-1 José Roberto Figueroa Padilla (8 penalty), 1-1 Álvaro Solano (19), 1-2 Porfirio Armando Bentancourt (23), 2-2 Johnny Williams (86).

17.08.1985, Varsity Stadium, Toronto; Attendance: 13,486
Referee: Enrique Mendoza Guillén (Mexico)
**CANADA – COSTA RICA**      **1-1(0-1)**
CAN: Martino Lettieri, Robert Lenarduzzi, Terence Moore, Ian Christopher Bridge, Bruce Alec Wilson, Paul John James, Randolph Lee Ragan, Mike Sweeney, David McDonald Norman, John Catliff (82.Kenneth Garraway), Igor Vrablic. Trainer: Anthony Keith Waiters.
CRC: Alejandro González, Róger Flores Solano, Edwin Salazar, Rodolfo Mills Palmer, Álvaro Solano, Omar Arroyo Rodríguez, Jorge Chévez (82.Jorge Contreras), Evaristo Coronado Salas (78.Jorge Ulate), Juan Arnoldo Cayasso Reid, Germán José Chavarría Jiménez, Johnny Williams. Trainer: Álvaro Grant MacDonald.
**Goals**: 0-1 Johnny Williams (12), 1-1 Paul John James (58).
**Sent off**: Kenneth Garraway (89), Rodolfo Mills Palmer (89).

25.08.1985, Estadio Nacional "Tiburcio Carías Andino", Tegucigalpa; Attendance: 55,000
Referee: Charles Marshall (Bermuda)
**HONDURAS - CANADA**      **0-1(0-0)**
HON: Julio César Arzú, Gilberto Gerónimo Yearwood, César Efraín Gutiérrez Álvarez, Domingo Cooper Droumond, Jaime Enrique Villegas Roura, Allan Anthony Costly Blyden, Ramón Enrique Maradiaga Chávez, Carlos Orlando Caballero Sánchez (65.Eduardo Antonio Laing Carcamo), Javier Francisco Toledo Rivera (65.Juan Alberto Cruz Murillo), Porfirio Armando Betancourt, José Roberto Figueroa Padilla. Trainer: José de la Paz Herrera Ucles.
CAN: Martino Lettieri, Robert Lenarduzzi, Terence Moore, Ian Christopher Bridge, Bruce Alec Wilson, Paul John James, Randolph Lee Ragan, Mike Sweeney, David McDonald Norman, John

Catliff (21.George Pakos), Igor Vrablic (20.Randolph Fitzgerald Samuel). Trainer: Anthony Keith Waiters.
**Goal**: 0-1 George Pakos (58).

01.09.1985, Estadio Nacional, San José; Attendance: 23,398
Referee: Jorge Ortíz Cardoza (El Salvador)
**COSTA RICA - CANADA**     **0-0**
**CRC:** Marcos Antonio Rojas Porras, Róger Flores Solano, Edwin Salazar (55.Óscar Ramírez Hernández), Alexandre Borges Guimarães, Álvaro Solano (67.Jorge Contreras), Omar Arroyo Rodríguez, Thomás Segura, Juan Arnoldo Cayasso Reid, César Hines Céspedes, Leonidas Flores Reyes, Johnny Williams. Trainer: Álvaro Grant MacDonald.
**CAN:** Martino Lettieri, Robert Lenarduzzi, Terence Moore, Ian Christopher Bridge, Bruce Alec Wilson, Paul John James (80.Pasquale DeLuca), Randolph Lee Ragan, Mike Sweeney, David McDonald Norman, George Pakos, Igor Vrablic (77.Randolph Fitzgerald Samuel). Trainer: Anthony Keith Waiters.
**Sent off**: Mike Sweeney (60).

08.09.1985, Estadio Nacional "Tiburcio Carías Andino", Tegucigalpa; Attendance: n/a
Referee: Richard Ramcharan (Trinidad and Tobago)
**HONDURAS – COSTA RICA**     **3-1(1-1)**
**HON**: Julio César Arzú, Jaime Enrique Villegas Roura, Allan Anthony Costly Blyden, Ramón Enrique Maradiaga Chávez, Carlos Orlando Caballero Sánchez (46.Salvador Bernárdez Blanco), Gilberto Gerónimo Yearwood, Porfirio Armando Betancourt, José Roberto Figueroa Padilla, Domingo Cooper Droumond, Juan Alberto Cruz (68.Richardson Smith), Antonio Zapata. Trainer: José de la Paz Herrera Ucles.
**CRC**: Alejandro González, Óscar Ramírez Hernández, Thomás Segura, Rodolfo Mills Palmer, Alexandre Borges Guimarães, Omar Arroyo Rodríguez, Jorge Chévez (46.Evaristo Coronado Salas), Jorge Contreras, Juan Arnoldo Cayasso Reid, César Hines Céspedes (70.Guillén), Germán José Chavarría Jiménez. Trainer: Álvaro Grant MacDonald.
**Goals**: 0-1 Alexandre Borges Guimarães (7), 1-1 Porfirio Armando Betancourt (40), 2-1 José Roberto Figueroa Padilla (51), 3-1 José Roberto Figueroa Padilla (66 penalty).

14.09.1985, St. John's; Attendance: 7,500
Referee: Rómulo Méndez Molina (Guatemala)
**CANADA - HONDURAS**     **2-1(1-0)**
**CAN:** Martino Lettieri, Robert Lenarduzzi, Ian Christopher Bridge (46.Kenneth Garraway), Randolph Fitzgerald Samuel, Bruce Alec Wilson, Paul John James, Randolph Lee Ragan, George Pakos, David McDonald Norman, Carl Howard Valentine (87.Pasquale DeLuca), Igor Vrablic. Trainer: Anthony Keith Waiters.
**HON**: Julio César Arzú, César Efraín Gutiérrez Álvarez, Jaime Enrique Villegas Roura, Danilo Galindo, Ramón Enrique Maradiaga Chávez, Javier Francisco Toledo Rivera (75.Richardon Smith), Gilberto Gerónimo Yearwood, Porfirio Armando Betancourt, José Roberto Figueroa Padilla, Domingo Cooper Droumond, Celso Fredy Güity Núñez (46.Carlos Orlando Caballero Sánchez). Trainer: José de la Paz Herrera Ucles.
**Goals**: 1-0 George Pakos (15), 1-1 Porfirio Armando Betancourt (49), 2-1 Igor Vrablic (61).

# AFRICA

3 teams (Algeria, Cameroon, Ghana) received byes and advanced to the Second Round directly.

## FIRST ROUND

| | | | |
|---|---|---|---|
| 30.06.1984 | Freetown | Sierra Leone - Morocco | 0-1(0-0) |
| 15.07.1984 | Rabat | Morocco - Sierra Leone | 4-0(1-0) |

### FINAL STANDINGS

| | | | | | | | | |
|---|---|---|---|---|---|---|---|---|
| 1. Morocco | 2 | 2 | 0 | 0 | 5 | - | 0 | 4 |
| 2. Sierra Leone | 2 | 0 | 0 | 2 | 0 | - | 5 | 0 |

Morocco qualified for the Second Round.

30.06.1984, National Stadium, Freetown; Attendance: n/a
Referee: Watekou Agbala (Togo)
**SIERRA LEONE - MOROCCO**  **0-1(0-0)**
SLE: Brima Kamara, Abu Sesay (85.A. Kamara), Joseph Toby, Faday Sesay, Terry Alusine, Abu Sankoh, Amadu Kamara, Michael Effiong, John Johnson, Saidu Kanu, Idrissa Kamara. Trainer: Kamara Ao.
MAR: Ezaki Badou, Saad Dahhan, Abdelmajid Lamris, Mustapha El Biyaz, Noureddine Bouyahyaoui, Abdelmajid Dolmy, Mustapha El Haddaoui, Driss Mouttaqui, Abdelsalam Laghrissi, Hassan Hanini (85.Mustapha Merry), Hazam Larbi (35.Khalid El Bied). Trainer: José Faria (Brazil).
**Goal**: 0-1 Mustapha Merry (87).

15.07.1984, Stade "Prince Moulay Abdellah", Rabat; Attendance: n/a
Referee: Badara Sené (Senegal)
**MOROCCO - SIERRA LEONE**  **4-0(1-0)**
MAR: Ezaki Badou, Saad Dahhan, Abdelmajid Lamris, Mustapha El Biyaz, Noureddine Bouyahyaoui, Abdelmajid Dolmy, Mustapha El Haddaoui (46.Hassan Hanini), Driss Mouttaqui, Mustapha Merry (75.Safri), Mohamed Timoumi, Khalid El Bied. Trainer: José Faria (Brazil).
SLE: Brima Kamara (70.Suma), Momoh Kanu, Joseph Toby, Faday Sesay, Terry Alusine, Abu Sesay, Amadu Kamara (73.Dumbuya), Abdul Cole, John Johnson, Saidu Kanu, Idrissa Kamara. Trainer: Kamara Ao.
**Goals**: 1-0 Mustapha Merry (34), 2-0 Saad Dahhan (51), 3-0 Mustapha Merry (77), 4-0 Khalid El Bied (81).

| | | | |
|---|---|---|---|
| 01.07.1984 | Luanda | Angola - Senegal | 1-0(0-0) |
| 15.07.1984 | Dakar | Senegal - Angola | 3-4 pen |

### FINAL STANDINGS

| | | | | | | | | |
|---|---|---|---|---|---|---|---|---|
| 1. Angola | 2 | 1 | 0 | 1 | 1 | - | 1 | 2 |
| 2. Senegal | 2 | 1 | 0 | 1 | 1 | - | 1 | 2 |

Angola qualified for the Second Round.

01.07.1984, Estádio Coqueiros, Luanda; Attendance: n/a
Referee: Simon Bantsimba (Congo)
**ANGOLA - SENEGAL**     **1-0(0-0)**
**ANG**: Napoleão Brandão, André Nzuzi, Tandum Mendes, Lourenço Caquinta, Pedro Torres Garcia, Fusa N'Kosi, Daniel Ndunguidi, Ivo Raimundo Traça, José Diers Carmo (46.Joseph Maluka), Seke Sarmento, Nsuka Melo (75.Osvaldo F.S. Oliveira).
**SEN**: Cagar Koné, Mustapha Nmaye, Abdoulaye Ba, Amadou Racine Kané, Sidi Hamed N'Diaye, Abdoulaye N'Diaye, Lamine Sylla Karanté (65.J. Dermeville), Ignace Coly, Abdoukarim Seyé, Thierno Youm, El Hadj Salif Diagne. Trainer: Kouyate Mady.
**Goal**: 1-0 Ivo Raimundo Traça (57).

15.07.1984, Stade "Demba Diop", Dakar; Attendance: n/a
Referee: Paul-Alain Hioba-Hioba (Cameroon)
**SENEGAL - ANGOLA**     **1-0(1-0,1-0,1-0)**
    **3-4 on penalties**
**SEN**: Cheikh Ahmet Seck, Seye Abdoukarim, Abdoulaye Ba, Amadou Racine Kané, Abdouranmane Fall Papa, Sidi Hamed N'Diaye, Diagne El Hadj Salif, Mamadou Tew, Roger Mendy, Amadou Diop, Thierno Youm. Trainer: Kouyate Mady.
**ANG**: Napoleão Brandão, André Nzuzi, Francisco Dinis, Lourenço Caquinta, Pedro Torres Garcia, Fusa N'Kosi, Ivo Raimundo Traça, Osvaldo F.S. Oliveira, Joseph Maluka, Seke Sarmento, Antonio Vicy.
**Goal**: 1-0 Seye Abdoukarim (24).

| | | | | |
|---|---|---|---|---|
| 15.07.1984 | Curepipe | Mauritius - Malawi | 0-1(0-1) |
| 28.07.1984 | Lilongwe | Malawi - Mauritius | 4-0(1-0) |

**FINAL STANDINGS**

| | | | | | | | | |
|---|---|---|---|---|---|---|---|---|
| 1. | Malawi | 2 | 2 | 0 | 0 | 5 - 0 | 4 |
| 2. | Mauritius | 2 | 0 | 0 | 2 | 0 - 5 | 0 |

Malawi qualified for the Second Round.

15.07.1984, "King George V" Stadium, Curepipe; Attendance: 10,892
Referee: Said Ali Khamis (Kenya)
**MAURITIUS - MALAWI**     **0-1(0-1)**
**MRI**: Sharma Kanhye, Sarjoo Gowreesunkur, Bernard Leclezio, Gilbert Herbu (74.Lallmahomed), Rid Typhis, Hedley Jacquotte, Gérard A.Tombe, Benjamin Theodore, Jacques Jackson (75.Serge Bardottier), Saleem Moussa, Patrice Perdrau, Trainer: Mohammad Anwar Elahee.
**MWI**: John Dzimbiri, Harry Waya, Reuben Malola, Peterkins Kayira (76.Patson Nyengo), Jack Chamangwana, Young Chimodzi, Jonathan Billie, Frank Sinalo, Ricky Phuka, Msiya, Lawrence Waya. Trainer: Henry Moyo.
**Goal**: 0-1 Ricky Phuka (44).

28.07.1984, Silver Stadium, Lilongwe; Attendance: n/a
Referee: Jean Fidèle Diramba (Gabon)
**MALAWI - MAURITIUS**     **4-0(1-0)**
**MWI**: John Dzimbiri, Harry Waya, Reuben Malola, Peterkins Kayira, Jack Chamangwana, Young Chimodzi, Jonathan Billie, Frank Sinalo, Ricky Phuka (81.James Makoloni), Clifton Msiya, Lawrence Waya. Trainer: Henry Moyo.
**MRI**: Sharma Kanhye, Sarjoo Gowreesunkur, Paul Elie Songor (46.Bernard Leclezio), Gérard A.Tombe, Rid Typhis, Benjamin Theodore, Decotter John, Saleem Moussa, Hedley Jacquotte, Serge Bardottier (57.Patrice Perdrau), Palmyre Chanda. Trainer: Mohammad Anwar Elahee.
**Goals**: 1-0 Frank Sinalo (2), 2-0 Bernard Leclezio (48 own goal), 3-0 Harry Waya (84), 4-0 Frank

Sinalo (89).

| 29.07.1984 | Ndola | Zambia - Uganda | 3-0(1-0) |
|---|---|---|---|
| 25.08.1984 | Kampala | Uganda - Zambia | 1-0(0-0) |

### FINAL STANDINGS

| | | | | | | | | |
|---|---|---|---|---|---|---|---|---|
| 1. Zambia | 2 | 1 | 0 | 1 | 3 | - | 1 | 2 |
| 2. Uganda | 2 | 1 | 0 | 1 | 1 | - | 3 | 2 |

Zambia qualified for the Second Round.

29.07.1984, Dag Hammerskjoeld Stadium, Ndola; Attendance: n/a
Referee: Hafidh Ali Tahir (Tanzania)
**ZAMBIA - UGANDA** **3-0(1-0)**
**ZAM:** David Chabala, John Kalusa, Kapambwe Mulenga, Fighton Simuhonda, Jones Chilengi, Frederick Kashimoto, Golden Kazika, Mutale Dominic, Fanny Hangunyu, Wisdom Chansa (46.Lucky Msiska), Kalusha Bwalya. Trainer: Butler.
**UGA:** Paul Ssali, Fred Migisha (Nsubuga), Geofrey Hisenyi, Isa Sekatawa, John Latigo, Ronald Vubya, Paul Hasule, Fred Mukasa (Sundayin Moriri), Charles Katumba, Tom Lwanga, Sam Muzambe. Trainer: George Mukasa.
**Goals:** 1-0 Fanny Hangunyu (44), 2-0 Lucky Msiska (51), 3-0 Kalusha Bwalya (89).

25.08.1984, Nakivubo Stadium, Kampala; Attendance: n/a
Referee: Salahudeen Alhati (Niger)
**UGANDA - ZAMBIA** **1-0(0-0)**
**UGA:** Paul Ssali, Isa Sekatawa, John Latigo, Moses Ndaula, Charles Masiko, Peter Mazinga (Frederic Musaka), Paul Hasule, Godfrey Kateregga, Godfrey Kisitu, Charles Katumba, Shaban Mulindwa (Obwoya). Trainer: George Mukasa.
**ZAM:** David Chabala, John Kalusa, Kapambwe Mulenga, Fighton Simuhonda, Jones Chilengi, Frederick Kashimoto, Lucky Msiska, Dominic Mutale, Fanny Hangunyu, Wisdom Chansa (Banda), Golden Kazika. Trainer: Butler.
**Goal:** 1-0 Godfrey Kateregga (73).

| 28.08.1984 | Cairo | Egypt - Zimbabwe | 1-0(1-0) |
|---|---|---|---|
| 30.09.1984 | Harare | Zimbabwe - Egypt | 1-1(1-1) |

### FINAL STANDINGS

| | | | | | | | | |
|---|---|---|---|---|---|---|---|---|
| 1. Egypt | 2 | 1 | 1 | 0 | 2 | - | 1 | 3 |
| 2. Zimbabwe | 2 | 0 | 1 | 1 | 1 | - | 2 | 1 |

Egypt qualified for the Second Round.

28.08.1984, Nasser Stadium, Cairo; Attendance: n/a
Referee: Tesfaye Gebreyesus (Ethiopia)
**EGYPT - ZIMBABWE** **1-0(1-0)**
**EGY:** Hussain Adel El Maamour, Ali Shehata, Ibrahim Youssef Awad Allah, Mohammed Hamada Sedki, Mohamed Rabie Yassin, Alaa Mohamed Mayhoub, Magdi Abdelghani Sayed Ahmed, Mohammed Helmi, Emad Soliman, Tarek Mohammed Yehia (46.Moustafa Ahmed Abdou Ali), Mahmoud Ibrahim El Khateeb (46.Rabei El Sayed). Trainer: John Michael Smith (Wales).
**ZIM:** Bruce Grobbelaar, James Taraoaoa, Ephraim Chena-Kumba, Ephert Lungu, Misheck Chiozambura, David Mwanza, Stanley Ndunduma (Chiruna), Joel Shambo, Shacky Tauro, Stanford Mtizua, Moses Chunga (Ndhloun).
**Goal:** 1-0 Mayhoub Alaa Mohamed.

30.09.1984, National Stadium, Harare; Attendance: n/a
Referee: William J. Phambala (Malawi)
**ZIMBABWE - EGYPT**                                                                 **1-1(1-1)**
**ZIM:** Mparitisa Japhet, James Taraoaoa, Ephraim Chena-Kumba, Ephert Lungu, Misheck Chiozambura, David Mwanza, Stanley Ndunduma, Joel Shambo, Shacky Tauro, Stanford Mtizua, Moses Chunga.
**EGY:** Hussain Adel El Maamour, Ali Shehata, Mohammed Omar El Zir, Ibrahim Youssef Awad Allah, Mohammed Hamada Sedki, Shawki Ghareeb Bayoumi, Nabil Alaa El Din Morsy, Mahmoud Ibrahim El Khateeb, Emad Soliman, Alaa Mohamed Mayhoub, Magdi Abdelghani Sayed Ahmed. Trainer: John Michael Smith (Wales).
**Goals**: 1-0 Mohammed Hamada Sedki (9 own goal), 1-1 Emad Soliman (34).

| 13.10.1984 | Nairobi | Kenya - Ethiopia | 2-1(1-1) |
| 28.10.1984 | Addis Abeba | Ethiopia - Kenya | 3-3(2-0) |

### FINAL STANDINGS

| | | | | | | | | | |
|---|---|---|---|---|---|---|---|---|---|
| 1. | Kenya | 2 | 1 | 1 | 0 | 5 | - | 4 | 3 |
| 2. | Ethiopia | 2 | 0 | 1 | 1 | 4 | - | 5 | 1 |

Kenya qualified for the Second Round.

13.10.1984, Nyayo National Stadium, Nairobi; Attendance: n/a
Referee: Mohamed Jama Bashir (Somalia)
**KENYA - ETHIOPIA**                                                                 **2-1(1-1)**
**KEN**: Mohammed Abbas, John Okelo, John Ogolla, Hussein Kheri, Josephat Murila, Samuel Tabu, Wilberforce Mulamba, Joe Masiga, Elly Adero (Sammy Onyango), Ambrose Ayoyi (Mahila), George Otieno. Trainer: Bernhard Zgoll.
**ETH**: Zewag Tekabe, Demissie Dagnachew, Tafesse Tamrat, Tesfaye Dagne, Argaoi Zenete, Mamo Sisaye, Dedass Godefam, Abre Bne, Kebede Mulugeta, Haile Medihiy, Asfaw Negusse. Trainer: Tilaun Tesfaye.
**Goals**: 0-1 Kebede Mulugeta (15), 1-1 Joe Masiga (16), 2-1 Samuel Tabu (62).

28.10.1984, "Haile Selassie" Stadium, Addis Abeba; Attendance: n/a
Referee: John Nkathazo (Zimbabwe)
**ETHIOPIA - KENYA**                                                                 **3-3(2-0)**
**ETH**: Zewag Tekabe, Demissie Dagnachew, Tafesse Tamrat, Mamo Sisaye, Argaoi Zenete, Tesfaye Dagne, Abre Bne, Kebede Mulugeta, Dedass Godefam, Haile Medihiy, Asfaw Negusse. Trainer: Tilaun Tesfaye.
**KEN**: Mohammed Abbas, John Ogolla, Samuel Tabu, Ambrose Ayoyi, Wilberforce Mulamba, Douglas Masiga, Kheri Hussein, Douglas Mutua, Sammy Onyango, George Otieno. Trainer: Bernhard Zgoll.
**Goals**: 1-0 Haile Medihiy (9), 2-0 Tesfaye Dagne (37), 2-1 Ambrose Ayoyi (48), 2-2 Joe Masiga (56), 3-2 Kebede Mulugeta (80), 3-3 Sammy Onyango (88).

| 13.10.1984 | Mwanza | Tanzania - Sudan | 1-1(1-0) |
| 27.10.1984 | Khartoum | Sudan - Tanzania | 0-0 |

### FINAL STANDINGS

| | | | | | | | | | |
|---|---|---|---|---|---|---|---|---|---|
| 1. | Sudan | 2 | 0 | 2 | 0 | 1 | - | 1 | 2 |
| 2. | Tanzania | 2 | 0 | 2 | 0 | 1 | - | 1 | 2 |

Sudan qualified for the Second Round.

13.10.1984, CCM Kirumba Stadium, Mwanza; Attendance: n/a
Referee: George Wamala Katumba (Uganda)
**TANZANIA - SUDAN** **1-1(1-0)**
**TAN**: Iddi Pazzi, William Lenard, Mohammed Adolf Rishard (Lenny Ramadhani), Lila Shomari, Khamis Abdallah Athumani, Ahmed Amasha, Charles Boniface, Mrope Ortovan, Peter Tino, Celestine Mbunga, Mugella Ramoyoni.
**SUD:** Hamid Eisa Biraima, Ahmed Hassan Fouda, Sami Ezzeldin Hassan, Adam Ahmed, Sharaf Siddig Mohammed El Din, Gamal Ibrahim, Adeel Ghasem El Seed, Tawfiq Fadeel El Seed, Gabir Gafar Rodel, Mohamed Abdallah Ahmed. Trainer: Sayed Mohamed Saleem.
**Goals**: 1-0 Peter Tino (28), 1-1 Mohamed Abdallah Ahmed (68).

27.10.1984, Al Hilal Stadium, Khartoum; Attendance: n/a
Referee: Zakaria Amin Salem (Egypt)
**SUDAN - TANZANIA** **0-0**
**SUD:** Hamid El Ansa, Ahmed Hassan Fouda, Sami Ezzeldin Hassan, Adam Ahmed, Tawfiq Fadeel El Seed, Sharaf Siddig Mohammed El Din, Adeel Ghasem El Seed, Ibrahim Gamal, Gabir Gafar Rodel, Ahmed Mohamed Bireish. Trainer: Sayed Mohamed Saleem.
**TAN**: Iddi Pazzi, Kiwelm Nusa, Khamis Abdallah Athumani, Lila Shomari, Ahmed Amasha, Mohammed Adolf Rishard, Lenny Ramadhani, Mrope Ortovan, Peter Tino, Mugella Ramoyoni, Celestine Mbunga.

| 20.10.1984 | Lagos | Nigeria - Liberia | 3-0(2-0) |
| 04.11.1984 | Monrovia | Liberia - Nigeria | 0-1(0-1) |

### FINAL STANDINGS

| 1. Nigeria | 2 | 2 | 0 | 0 | 4 - 0 | 4 |
| 2. Liberia | 2 | 0 | 0 | 2 | 0 - 4 | 0 |

Nigeria qualified for the Second Round.

20.10.1984, National Stadium, Lagos; Attendance: 50,000
Referee: Joseph-Marie Ouédrago (Burkina Faso)
**NIGERIA - LIBERIA** **3-0(2-0)**
**NGA:** Peter Rufai, Yisa Shofowre, Bright Omokaro, Stephen Keshi, Wahab Adesina, Sunday Eboigbe, John Chiedozie, Ademola Adesina (22.Fatai Amoo), Samson Ozoqula (46.Richard Owubokiri), Henry Nwosu, Humphrey Edobor. Trainer: Christopher Udemezue.
**LBR**: Lucretius Togba, Washington Blay, Vinitius, Browne Mathew, Nelson Sonpon, Theophilus Swaucy, Jerry Johnson (61.Sam Surno), Isaiah Lincoln (46.Simpson), Francis Jallah, Joseph Sion, Edwin Morgan. Trainer Charley: Jostah Johnson.
**Goals**: 1-0 Humphrey Edobor (8), 2-0 Humphrey Edobor (15), 3-0 Ademola Adesina (66).

04.11.1984, "Samuel Doe" Sports Complex, Monrovia; Attendance: 10,000
Referee: Amadou Mamoudou (Niger)
**LIBERIA - NIGERIA** **0-1(0-1)**
**LBR**: Boye Cooper, Gray William, Washington Blay, Charley Vinitius, Nelson Sonpon, Theophilus Swaucy, Francis Jallah, Joseph Bion (27.Weeks), Sam Surno, Ezekiel Doe, Jerry Johnson (22.Simpson). Trainer: Jostah Johnson.
**NGA:** Peter Rufai, Yisa Shofowre, Bright Omokaro, Stephen Keshi, Wahab Adesina (32.Benjamin Nzeakor), Sunday Eboigbe, Clemente Temile, Disu Tajudeen (22.Samson Siasia), Samson Ozoqula, Henry Nwosu, Humphrey Edobor. Trainer: Christopher Udemezue.
**Goal**: 0-1 Clemente Temile (42).

21.10.1984  Abidjan        Ivory Coast - Gambia        4-0(0-0)
04.11.1984  Banjul         Gambia - Ivory Coast        3-2(1-1)

### FINAL STANDINGS

1. Ivory Coast    2  1  0  1   6 - 3    2
2. Gambia         2  1  0  1   3 - 6    2

Ivory Coast qualified for the Second Round.

21.10.1984, Stade "Félix Houphouet Boigny", Abidjan, Attendance: n/a
Referee: Karim Camara (Guinea)
**IVORY COAST - GAMBIA**                                  **4-0(0-0)**
**CIV**: Jean-Paul Billy-Groyou, Gaston Adjoukoua, Leopold Sacré Abialy, Abdoulaye Traoré, Oumar Ben-Salah, François Monguéhi, Gadji Celi Saint-Joseph, Grabroyou Aurelient Behiri, Aimé Tchéchté (46.Pascal Kouassi-N'Dri), Jean-Michel Guéde Akenon, Lucien Kassy Kouadio. Trainer: Victor Amoah.
**GAM**: Sang Ndong, Ibrahim Garba Touray, Francis Owen, Baboucar Sowe, Paul Ogoo, Alagi Sarr, Essa Fayé, Amadou Adams, James Gomez, Sulayman Samba, Malleh Wadda.
**Goals**: 1-0 Abdoulaye Traoré (47), 2-0 Abdoulaye Traoré (62), 3-0 Pascal Kouassi-N'Dri (66), 4-0 Oumar Ben-Salah (84).

04.11.1984, Independence Stadium, Banjul; Attendance: n/a
Referee: Idrissa Marcel Traoré (Mali)
**GAMBIA - IVORY COAST**                                  **3-2(1-1)**
**GAM**: Sang Ndong, Ibrahim Garba Touray, Baboucar Sowe, Paul Ogoo, Alagi Sarr, Abdou Sarr, James Gomez, John Loum, Sheikh Ndure, Malleh Wadda, Monodon Touray.
**CIV**: Jean-Paul Billy-Groyou, Gaston Adjoukoua, Leopold Sacré Abialy, Abdoulaye Traoré, Oumar Ben-Salah, François Monguéhi, Gadji Celi Saint-Joseph, Pascal Kouassi-N'Dri, Djibril Cissé (46.Johan Joël Tiehi), Jean-Michel Guéde Akenon, Lucien Kassy Kouadio. Trainer: Victor Amoah.
**Goals**: 1-0 Baboucar Sowe (22), 1-1 Abdoulaye Traoré (40), 1-2 Johan Joël Tiehi (54), 2-2 Sheikh Ndure (66), 3-2 Malleh Wadda (81).


28.10.1984  Cotonou        Benin - Tunisia             0-2(0-0)
13.11.1984  Tunis          Tunisia - Benin             4-0(2-0)

### FINAL STANDINGS

1. Tunisia        2  2  0  0   6 - 0    4
2. Benin          2  0  0  2   0 - 6    0

Tunisia qualified for the Second Round.

28.10.1984, Stade de lAmitié, Cotonou; Attendance: 7,723
Referee: Ouattara Katinan (Ivory Coast)
**BENIN - TUNISIA**                                       **0-2(0-0)**
**BEN**: Jean Louis Noumakagnan, Theodore Aboussou, Gilbert Edjekpoto, Sylvain Zevounov, Victor Zevounov, Ludovic Alikparah, Rudolph Campbell (46.Souleiman Seidou), Amadou Bagri, Mohamed Sidi-Ali, Georges Ogoumissy, Henri Assouramon (62.Aboudou Madjidou Bryme). Trainer: Barnaba Liebhaber.
**TUN**: Mondher Ben Jaballah, Mohamed Kasni, Latfi Jebara, Hamda Ben Doulet, Faisal Jelassi, Abdelhamid Hergal, Hosni Zouaoui, Nabil Maâloul (88.Ben Messaoud), Abderrazak Rakbaori, Abdelrazak Chahat (64.H. Soudani), Bassam Jeridi. Trainer: Youssef Zouaoui.
**Goals**: 0-1 Bassam Jeridi, 0-2 Mohamed Kasni.

13.11.1984, Stade Olympique d'El Menzah, Tunis; Attendance: 12,000
Referee: Baba Laouissi (Morocco)
**TUNISIA - BENIN** **4-0(2-0)**
**TUN:** Mondher Ben Jaballah, Mohamed Gasri, Hamda Ben Doulet, Zouaoui Hosni, Faisal Jelassi, Nabil Maâloul, Abdelhamid Hergal, Ben Yahia Khaled, Abderrazak Rakbaori, Abdelrazak Chahat (60.H. Soudani), Bassam Jeridi: Trainer: Youssef Zouaoui.
**BEN:** Jean Louis Noumakagnan, Theodore Aboussou, Gilbert Edjekpoto, Sylvain Zevounov, Victor Zevounov, Ludovic Alikparah, Rudolph Campbell, Amadou Bagri (60.Aboudou Madjidou Bryme), Douhanadou Boukari, Georges Ogoumissy, Henri Assouramon (70.Djibril Karim). Trainer: Barnaba Liebhaber.
**Goals:** 1-0 Bassam Jeridi (5), 2-0 Bassam Jeridi (17), 3-0 Abderrazak Rakbaori (58), 4-0 Gasri Mohamed (74).

Madagascar qualified for the Second Round (Lesotho withdrew)
Libya qualified for the Second Round (Niger withdrew)
Guinea qualified for the Second Round (Togo withdrew)

Algeria, Cameroon and Ghana qualified automatically for the Second Round.

## SECOND ROUND

| 10.02.1985 | Conakry | Guinea - Tunisia | 1-0(1-0) |
| 24.02.1985 | Tunis | Tunisia - Guinea | 2-0(1-0) |

### FINAL STANDINGS

| | | | | | | | | |
|---|---|---|---|---|---|---|---|---|
| 1. | Tunisia | 2 | 1 | 0 | 1 | 2 | - 1 | 2 |
| 2. | Guinea | 2 | 1 | 0 | 1 | 1 | - 2 | 2 |

Tunisia qualified for the Third Round.

10.02.1985, Stade 28ème Septembre, Conakry; Attendance: 20,000
Referee: Adonis Pascal Eboulé (Ivory Coast)
**GUINEA - TUNISIA** **1-0(1-0)**
**GUI:** Mohammed Dioubaté, Seydouba Camara, Karifa Kourouma, Aboubacar Keïta, Soryba Edenté Soumah, Mamady Cissé (20.Mohammed Lamine), Naby Laye Camara, Camara Touré, Fofana Bafodé, Alseny Diaby, Ibrahima Barry (82.Lucien Guilao). Trainer: Habib Majeri.
**TUN:** Mondher Ben Jaballah, Mohamed Gasri, Hamda Ben Doulet (25.Lotfi Hsoumi), Mohamed Cheriti, Faisal Jelassi, Hosni Zouaoui, Khaled Ben Yahia, Hafedh Houarbi, Hakim Braham (32.Lassaad Abdelli), Adel Latrache, Bassam Jeridi. Trainer: Youssef Zouaoui.
**Goal:** 1-0 Alseny Diaby (20).

24.02.1985, Stade Olympique d'El Menzah, Tunis; Attendance: 12,000
Referee: Sherif Salem Bashir (Libya)
**TUNISIA - GUINEA** **2-0(1-0)**
**TUN:** Mondher Ben Jaballah, Mohamed Gasri, Mohamed Jelassi, Khaled Ben Yahia, Hosni Zouaoui, Faisal Jelassi, Abdelhamid Hergal, Lotfi Hsoumi, Hakim Braham, Nabil Maâloul, Bassam Jeridi (43.Adel Latrache; 70.Lassaad Abdelli). Trainer: Youssef Zouaoui.
**GUI:** Sylla Fodé, Seydouba Camara, Fofana Bafodé, Aboubacar Keïta, Camara Touré, Soryba Edenté Soumah, Lucien Guilao (20.Karifa Kourouma), Mamady Cissé, Ibrahima Barry, Alseny Diaby, Naby Laye Camara (28.Soumah II). Trainer: Habib Majeri.
**Goals:** 1-0 Hakim Braham (24), 2-0 Hsoumi Lotfi (78).

| 22.02.1985 | Khartoum | Sudan - Libya | 0-0 |
| 08.03.1985 | Tripoli | Libya - Sudan | 4-0(0-0) |

### FINAL STANDINGS

| | | | | | | | | | |
|---|---|---|---|---|---|---|---|---|---|
| 1. | Libya | 2 | 1 | 1 | 0 | 4 | - | 0 | 3 |
| 2. | Sudan | 2 | 0 | 1 | 1 | 0 | - | 4 | 1 |

Libya qualified for the Third Round.

22.02.1985, Khartoum; Attendance: n/a
Referee: Ali Khamis Said (Kenya)
**SUDAN - LIBYA**    **0-0**
**SUD:** Hamid Eisa Biraima, Adam Ahmed, Kamal Abdel Ghani, Gibril Abbas El Fadil, Eisa Sabah El Kheir, Isam Abdel Ghani (65.Mohamed Abdallah Ahmed), Tawfiq Fadeel El Seed, Adeel Ghasem El Seed, Ahmed Mohamed Bireish (80.Bakheit Badr El Din), Amosa Matia Kumba, Zakaria Abdel Aziz. Trainer: Sayed Mohamed Saleem.
**LBY:** Musbah Younen Shangab, Sasi Ageli Omar, Aboubaker Bani, Salem Ali Sola, Suleiman Omar Attia, Ayad El Ghadi, Ibrahim Ben Abubaker, Fawzi El Aisawi, Ibrahim Salem Maadi, Ali Musa El Beshari, Omar Ali Gzeri (46.Jamal Abounuara). Trainer: El Hashim El Bahalol.

08.03.1985, Stade 11 Juin, Tripoli; Attendance: n/a
Referee: Hama Djibo (Niger)
**LIBYA - SUDAN**    **4-0(0-0)**
**LBY:** Musbah Younen Shangab (78.El Jemani), Sasi El Ageli, Aboubaker Bani, Salem Ali Sola, Suleiman Omar Attia (60.Omar Ali Gzeri), Attia Reda, Ayad El Ghadi, Fawzi El Aisawi, Ibrahim Ben Abubaker, Ali Musa El Beshari, Ibrahim El Madani. Trainer: El Hashim El Bahalol.
**SUD:** Hamid Eisa Biraima, Gibril Abbas El Fadil, Nadir Mansour, Kamal Abdel Ghani, Tawfiq Fadeel El Seed (46.Nuwar), Bakheit Badr El Din (80.Zakaria Abdel Aziz), Mohamed Ibrahim Ibrahim, Ahmed Mohamed Bireish, Adeel Ghasem El Seed, Amosa Matia Kumba, Eisa Sabah El Kheir. Trainer: Sayed Mohamed Saleem.
**Goals:** 1-0 Ibrahim Abubaker (51), 2-0 Ali Musa El Beshari (53), 3-0 Musbah Younen Shangab (59 penalty), 4-0 Aboubaker Bani (70).


| 31.03.1985 | Luanda | Angola - Algeria | 0-0 |
| 19.04.1985 | Alger | Algeria - Angola | 3-2(2-0) |

### FINAL STANDINGS

| | | | | | | | | | |
|---|---|---|---|---|---|---|---|---|---|
| 1. | Algeria | 2 | 1 | 1 | 0 | 3 | - | 2 | 3 |
| 2. | Angola | 2 | 0 | 1 | 1 | 2 | - | 3 | 1 |

Algeria qualified for the Third Round.

31.03.1985, Estádio Coqueiros, Luanda; Attendance: 6,000
Referee: Karim Camara (Guinea)
**ANGOLA - ALGERIA**    **0-0**
**ANG**: Napoleão Brandão, Carlos Manuel Ribeiro (46.Campos), André Nzuzi, Diogo Domingos, Francisco Alonso, Fusa N'Kosi, Almeida Macueria, Osvaldo F.S. Oliveira, Eduardo Machado (75.Daniel Ndunguidi), Seke Sarmento, Nsuka Melo.
**ALG:** Nacerdine Drid, Mahmoud Guendouz, Said Meghichi, Nourredine Abdallah Kourichi, Chaabane Merzekane, Mohamed Kaci Saïd, Nasser Bouiche (80.Mustapha Rabah Madjer), Djamel Jafjaf, Menad Djamel, Salah Assad, Hocine Yahi (60.Ali Bencheik). Trainer: Mady Kou Yate.

19.04.1985, Stade du 5ème Juillet, Alger; Attendance: n/a
Referee: Idrissa Marcel Traoré (Mali)
**ALGERIA - ANGOLA** 3-2(2-0)
**ALG**: Nacerdine Drid, Mahmoud Guendouz, Faouzi Mansouri (Ali Bencheik), Fodil Megharia, Chaabane Merzekane, Said Meghichi, Nasser Bouiche, Djamel Jafjaf (Tedj Bensaoula), Menad Djamel, Mustapha Rabah Madjer, Hocine Yahi. Trainer: Mady Kou Yate.
**ANG**: Napoleão Brandão, Carlos Manuel Ribeiro, André Nzuzi, Diogo Domingos, Francisco Alonso, Seke Sarmento (Daniel Ndunguidi), Fusa N'Kosi, Almeida Macueria, Osvaldo F.S. Oliveira, Eduardo Machado, Nsuka Melo.
**Goals**: 1-0 Faouzi Mansouri (14), 2-0 Djamel Menad (44), 3-0 Nasser Bouiche (66), 3-1 Osvaldo F.S. Oliveira (70), 3-2 Eduardo Machado (79).

| 05.04.1985 | Cairo | Egypt - Madagascar | 1-0(0-0) |
| 21.04.1985 | Tananarive | Madagascar - Egypt | 1-0; 2-4pen |

### FINAL STANDINGS

| | | | | | | | | |
|---|---|---|---|---|---|---|---|---|
| 1. | Egypt | 2 | 1 | 0 | 1 | 1 | - 1 | 2 |
| 2. | Madagascar | 2 | 1 | 0 | 1 | 1 | - 1 | 2 |

Egypt qualified for the Third Round.

05.04.1985, Nasser Stadium, Cairo; Attendance: n/a
Referee: Belaïd Lacarne (Algeria)
**EGYPT - MADAGASCAR** 1-0(0-0)
**EGY**: Ahmed Ikramy El Shahat, Mohamed Rabie Yassin, Mohamed Salah El Din, Ibrahim Youssef Awad Allah, Amer Taher Abouzeid El Sayed, Hussain Ayman Younis, Alaa Mohamed Mayhoub, Magdi Abdelghani Sayed Ahmed, Mohammed Hamada Sedki, Emad Soliman, Moustafa Gamal Abdelhamid. Trainer: Mohammed Abdou Saleh El Wahsh.
**MAD**: Ferdinand Rafalidianana, Claude Aimé Jean-Marie, Clément, René Rabearisoa, Frédéric-Guy Rakotovao Daodisoa, Rodolphe Rakotoarisoa, Roland Rakotondrasoa, Hervé Arsène, Herilia Rafanodina, Frédéric Remi, Ardriananifal Raharimanana. Trainer: Vincent De Paul Randriamirado.
**Goal**: 1-0 Emad Soliman (63).

21.04.1985, Stade Municipal de Mahamasina, Antananarivo; Attendance: n/a
Referee: Sydney Picon-Ackong (Mauritius)
**MADAGASCAR - EGYPT** 1-0(0-0,1-0,1-0)
2-4 on penalties
**MAD**: Ferdinand Rafalidiana, Jeremie Randriambololona, Raymond Realy, René Rabearisoa, Frédéric-Guy Rakotovao Daodisoa, Rodolphe Rakotoarisoa, Roland Rakotondrasoa (83.Andrianasolo), Robin Andriamiaingo (95.Guy Rabemananjara), Hervé Arsène, Frédéric Remi, Herilia Rafanodina. Trainer: Vincent De Paul Randriamirado.
**EGY**: Ahmed Ikramy El Shahat, Ali Shehata, Mohamed Rabie Yassin, Mohammed Hamada Sedki, Ibrahim Youssef Awad Allah (46.Mahmoud Saleh), Nabil Alaa El Din Morsy (106.Mohammed Ramadan), Shawki Ghareeb Bayoumi, Magdi Abdelghani Sayed Ahmed, Mahmoud Ibrahim El Khateeb, Emad Soliman, Alaa Mohamed Mayhoub. Trainer: Mohammed Abdou Saleh El Wahsh.
**Goal**: 1-0 Herilia Rafanodina (57).

| 06.04.1985 | Nairobi | Kenya - Nigeria | 0-3(0-2) |
| 20.04.1985 | Lagos | Nigeria - Kenya | 3-1(2-1) |

### FINAL STANDINGS

| | | | | | | | | |
|---|---|---|---|---|---|---|---|---|
| 1. | Nigeria | 2 | 2 | 0 | 0 | 6 - 1 | 4 |
| 2. | Kenya | 2 | 0 | 0 | 2 | 1 - 6 | 0 |

Nigeria qualified for the Third Round.

06.04.1985, Moi International Sports Centre, Nairobi; Attendance: 50,000
Referee: Bester Kalombo (Malawi)
**KENYA - NIGERIA** 0-3(0-2)
KEN: Tirus Omondi, Francis Iveche, Hussein Kheri, John Ogolla, John Arieno, Samuel Tabu, Dan Musuku, Issa Suleiman, Ambrose Ayoyi, George Adembo, Mike Amiday. Trainer: Bernhard Zgoll.
NGA: Patrick Okalla, Yisa Shofowre, Augustine Eke, Muda Lawal, Fawole Ogboin, Michael Emenalo, Dahiru Sadi, Richard Owubokiri (Rashidi Yekini), Fatai Amoo, Humphrey Edobor, Charles Okorigwe (Benjamin Nzeakor). Trainer: Patrick Ekeji.
Goals: 0-1 Humphrey Edobor (12), 0-2 Dahiru Sadi (45), 0-3 Rashidi Yekini (47).

20.04.1985, National Stadium, Lagos; Attendance: 35,000
Referee: Dodou N'Jie (Gambia)
**NIGERIA - KENYA** 3-1(2-1)
NGA: Peter Rufai, Yisa Shofowre, Augustine Eke, Fawole Ogboin, Michael Emanalo, Charles Okorigwe, Dahiru Sadi (Wahab Adesina), Fatai Amoo, Muda Lawal, Rashidi Yekini (Benjamin Nzeakor), Humphrey Edobor. Trainer: Patrick Ekeji.
KEN: Mohammed Abbas, Francis Makuku, Hussein Kheri, John Ogolla, Josephat Murila, Samuel Tabu, Ambrose Ayoyi, Douglas Mutua, Joe Masiga, George Odhiambo, Sammy Onyango. Trainer: Bernhard Zgoll.
Goals: 1-0 Dahiru Sadi (18), 2-0 Rashidi Yekini (20), 2-1 Joe Masiga (36), 3-1 Yisa Shofowre (89).


| 07.04.1985 | Lusaka | Zambia - Cameroon | 4-1(4-0) |
| 21.04.1985 | Yaoundé | Cameroon - Zambia | 1-1(1-1) |

### FINAL STANDINGS

| | | | | | | | | |
|---|---|---|---|---|---|---|---|---|
| 1. | Zambia | 2 | 1 | 1 | 0 | 5 - 2 | 3 |
| 2. | Cameroon | 2 | 0 | 1 | 1 | 2 - 5 | 1 |

Zambia qualified for the Third Round.

07.04.1985, Independence Stadium, Lusaka; Attendance: n/a
Referee: Frank Valdemarca (Zimbabwe)
**ZAMBIA - CAMEROON** 4-1(4-0)
ZAM: David Chabala, Fighton Simuhonda, Kapambwe Mulenga, John Mwanza, Jones Chilengi, Jerry Shinde, Lucky Msiska (81.Mulala), Aaron Njoyu (77.Derby Makinka), Michael Chabala, Jack Chanda, Kalusha Bwalya.
CMR: Joseph-Antoine Bell, Isaac Sinkot, Michel N'Galamo, Ibrahim Aoudou (81.Paul Bahoken), Emmanuel Jerome Kundé, André Kana-Biyik (58.Oscar Alain Eyobo Makongo), François Oman-Biyik, Dagobert Dang, Charles Toubé, Bonaventure Djonkep, François N'Doumbé Lea. Trainer: Claude Marie François Le Roy (France).
Goals: 1-0 Michael Chabala (22), 2-0 Aaron Njoyu (25), 3-0 Michael Chabala (28), 4-0 Michael Chabala (33), 4-1 André Kana-Biyik (75).

21.04.1985, Stade "Ahmadu Adhijo", Yaoundé; Attendance: n/a
Referee: Jean Fidèle Diramba (Gabon)
**CAMEROON - ZAMBIA**  **1-1(1-1)**
**CMR:** Thomas N'Kono, Isaac Sinkot, Michel N'Galamo, Ibrahim Aoudou, Louis M'Fedé, Eugène Ekeke (55.Dagobert Dang), Roger Milla, Charles Toubé, François Oman-Biyik, Bonaventure Djonkep (70.Paul Bahoken), François N'Doumbé Lea. Trainer: Claude Marie François Le Roy (France).
**ZAM:** David Chabala, Laban Chishala, Edwin Kampanta, John Mwanza, Jones Chilengi, Jerry Shinde, Michael Chabala, Aaron Njoyu (75.Derby Makinka), Fanny Hangunyu (54.Mulala), Jack Ghanda, Kalusha Bwalya. Trainer: Baldwin Banda.
**Goals:** 0-1 Jones Chilengi (5), 1-1 Louis M'Fedé (31).

| | | | |
|---|---|---|---|
| 07.04.1985 | Rabat | Morocco - Malawi | 2-0(1-0) |
| 21.04.1985 | Lilongwe | Malawi - Morocco | 0-0 |

### FINAL STANDINGS

| | | | | | | | |
|---|---|---|---|---|---|---|---|
| 1. Morocco | 2 | 1 | 1 | 0 | 2 - 0 | 3 |
| 2. Malawi | 2 | 0 | 1 | 1 | 0 - 2 | 1 |

Morocco qualified for the Third Round.

07.04.1985, Stade "Prince Moulay Abdellah", Rabat; Attendance: 20,862
Referee: Ali Bennaceur (Tunisia)
**MOROCCO - MALAWI**  **2-0(1-0)**
**MAR:** Ezaki Badou, Saad Dahhan, Abdelmajid Lamris, Mustapha El Biyaz, Noureddine Bouyahyaoui, Abdelfattah El Alaoui Mehamdi, Mustapha El Haddaoui, Abdellah Haidamou, Khalid El Bied, Mohamed Timoumi, Abdelaziz Souleimani. Trainer: José Faria (Brazil).
**MWI:** John Dzimbiri, Harry Waya, Reuben Malola, Collins Thewe, Jack Chamangwana, Peterkins Kayira, Young Chimodzi, Jonathan Billie, Frank Sinalo, Clifton Msiya, Lawrence Waya. Trainer: Henry Moyo.
**Goals:** 1-0 Mustapha El Haddaoui (10), 2-0 Saad Dahhan (73).

21.04.1985, Chichiri Stadium, Blantyre; Attendance: n/a
Referee: Kamabula Nyrenda Chayu (Zambia)
**MALAWI - MOROCCO**  **0-0**
**MWI:** John Dzimbiri, Harry Waya, Collins Thewe (51.Kennedy Malunga), Gilbert Chirwa, Peterkins Kayira, Young Chimodzi, Jonathan Billie, Frank Sinalo (65.Holman Malunga), Clifton Msiya, Dixon Mbetewa, Lawrence Waya. Trainer: Henry Moyo.
**MAR:** Ezaki Badou, Saad Dahhan, Abdelmajid Lamris, Mustapha El Biyaz, Noureddine Bouyahyaoui, Abdelmajid Dolmy, Mustapha El Haddaoui (70.Abdellah Haidamou), Mustapha Bidane, Khalid El Bied (55.Abdelfettah Rhiati), Mohamed Timoumi, Abdelaziz Souleimani. Trainer: José Faria (Brazil).

| | | | | | | | | | |
|---|---|---|---|---|---|---|---|---|---|
| 07.04.1985 | Abidjan | Ivory Coast - Ghana | | | | | 0-0 | | |
| 21.04.1985 | Accra | Ghana - Ivory Coast | | | | | 2-0(0-0) | | |

### FINAL STANDINGS

| | | | | | | | | |
|---|---|---|---|---|---|---|---|---|
| 1. Ghana | 2 | 1 | 1 | 0 | 2 | - | 0 | 3 |
| 2. Ivory Coast | 2 | 0 | 1 | 1 | 0 | - | 2 | 1 |

Ghana qualified for the Third Round.

07.04.1985, Stade "Félix Houphouet-Boigny" Abidjan; Attendance: 40,000
Referee: Baba Laouissi (Morocco)
**IVORY COAST - GHANA** **0-0**
**CIV**: Zagouli Gbolié, Emile Gnahoré Depié, Leopold Sacré Abialy, Patrice Lago, Jean-Denise Sihaly, François Monguéhi, Gadji Celi Saint-Joseph, Akénou Jille Sueili, Abdoulaye Traoré, Lucien Kassy Kouadio (78.Pascal Kouassi-N'Dri), Pascal Miézan Aka. Trainer: Victor Amoah.
**GHA**: Owusu Mensah, Joseph Odoi, Ofei Ansah, Sampson Lamptey, Addae Khenkyeheme, Abedi Ayew, John Bannerman, Yaaya Kassimu, Afriye Opoku, Mohammed Ahmed, George Alhassan. Trainer: César Augusto Gonzáles.

21.04.1985, National Sports Council Stadium, Kumasi; Attendance: 78,000
Referee: Simon Bantsimba (Congo)
**GHANA - IVORY COAST** **2-0(0-0)**
**GHA:** Owusu Mensah, Joseph Odoi, Sampson Lamptey, Addae Kyenkyehene, Abedi Ayew, Ofei Ansah, Afriye Opoku (79.John Bannerman), George Lamptey (60.Yaaya Kassimu), George Alhassan, Samuel Opoku Nti, Mohammed Ahmed, Trainer: César Augusto Gonzáles.
Zagouli Gbolié, Emile Gnahoré Depié, Leopold Sacré Abialy, Patrice Lago, Jean-Denise Sihaly (76.Lucien Kassy Kouadio), François Monguéhi, Gadji Celi Saint-Joseph, Youssouf Fofana, Abdoulaye Traoré, Aman Miézan, Pascal Miézan Aka (78.Pascal Kouassi-N'Dri). Trainer: Victor Amoah.
**Goals**: 1-0 Samuel Opoku Nti (50), 2-0 George Alhassan (79).

# THIRD ROUND

| 06.07.1985 | Lagos | Nigeria - Tunisia | 1-0(0-0) |
| 20.07.1985 | Tunis | Tunisia - Nigeria | 2-0(2-0) |

### FINAL STANDINGS

| | | | | | | | | |
|---|---|---|---|---|---|---|---|---|
| 1. Tunisia | 2 | 1 | 0 | 1 | 2 | - | 1 | 2 |
| 2. Nigeria | 2 | 1 | 0 | 1 | 1 | - | 2 | 2 |

Tunisia qualified for the Fourth Round.

06.07.1985, Surulere Stadium, Lagos; Attendance: 60,000
Referee: Jean-Fidèle Diramba (Gabon)
**NIGERIA - TUNISIA**     **1-0(0-0)**
**NGA:** Peter Rufai, Bright Omokaro, Yisa Shofowre, Sunday Eboigbe, Michael Emenalo, Sadi Dahiry, Sylvanus Okdala, Richard Owoboior, Nwajoibi Emeka (31.Sunday Daniel), Rashidi Yekini, Humphrey Edobor (69.Okey Isima). Trainer: Patrick Ekeji.
**TUN:** Mondher Ben Jaballah, Mohamed Gasri, Mohamed Cheriti, Moncef Chergui, Nabil Maâloul, Hosni Zouaoui (74.Faisal Jelassi), Abdelhamid Hergal, Khaled Ben Yahia, Abdelkader Bakbaoui, Lotfi Hsoumi (78.Hakim Braham), Bassam Jeridi. Trainer: Youssef Zouaoui.
**Goal**: 1-0 Okey Isima (79).

20.07.1985, Stade Olympique d'El Menzah, Tunis; Attendance: 33,000
Referee: Mohamed Hansal (Algeria)
**TUNISIA - NIGERIA**     **2-0(2-0)**
**TUN:** Mondher Ben Jaballah, Mohamed Gasri, Mohamed Cheriti, Moncef Chergui, Nabil Maâloul, Hosni Zouaoui, Abdelhamid Hergal, Abderrazak Rakbaori (86.Hakim Braham), Lotfi Hsoumi (75.Lassaad Abdelli), Jeridi Bassam, Khaled Ben Yahia. Trainer: Youssef Zouaoui.
**NGA:** Peter Rufai, Augustine Eke, Yisa Shofowre, Muda Lawal, Sunday Eboigbe, Michael Emenalo, John Chiedozie, Sylvanus Okdala, Richard Owubokiri, Okey Isima (78.Dahiru Sadi), Humphrey Edobor (78.Rashidi Yekini). Trainer: Patrick Ekeji.
**Goals**: 1-0 Jeridi Bassam (8), 2-0 Jeridi Bassam (28).

| 12.07.1985 | Cairo | Egypt - Morocco | 0-0 |
| 28.07.1985 | Casablanca | Morocco - Egypt | 2-0(1-0) |

### FINAL STANDINGS

| | | | | | | | | |
|---|---|---|---|---|---|---|---|---|
| 1. Morocco | 2 | 1 | 1 | 0 | 2 | - | 0 | 3 |
| 2. Egypt | 2 | 0 | 1 | 1 | 0 | - | 2 | 1 |

Morocco qualified for the Fourth Round.

12.07.1985, National Stadium, Cairo; Attendance: n/a
Referee: Frank Valdemarca (Zimbabwe)
**EGYPT - MOROCCO**     **0-0**
**EGY**: Ahmed Ikramy El Shahat, Ali Shehata, Mohammed Hamada Sedki, Mohammed Omar El Zir (Mahmoud Saleh), Ahmed Barelden, Shawki Ghareeb Bayoumi, Magdi Abdelghani Sayed Ahmed, Emad Soliman, Tarek Mohammed Yehia, Alaa Mohamed Mayhoub (Mahmoud Ibrahim El Khateeb), Mohammed Ramadan. Trainer: Mohammed Abdou Saleh El Wahsh.
**MAR:** Ezaki Badou, Mustapha Bidane, Abdelmajid Lamris, Mustapha El Biyaz, Noureddine Bouyahyaoui, Abdelmajid Dolmy, Mustapha El Haddaoui, Hamou Fadili, Khalid El Bied, Mohamed Timoumi, Abdellah Haidamou. Trainer: José Faria (Brazil).

28.07.1985, Stade "Mohamed V", Casablanca; Attendance: n/a
Referee: Badara Sené (Senegal)
**MOROCCO - EGYPT**  **2-0(1-0)**
**MAR:** Ezaki Badou, Mustapha Bidane, Abdelmajid Lamris (88.Hamou Fadili), Lahcen Ouadani, Noureddine Bouyahyaoui, Abdelmajid Dolmy, Mustapha El Haddaoui, Abdelaziz Bouderbala, Mustapha Merry, Mohamed Timoumi, Khalid El Bied (83. Abdelfettah Rhiati). Trainer: José Faria (Brazil).
**EGY:** Ahmed Ikramy El Shahat, Ali Shehata, Ibrahim Youssef Awad Allah (62.Mahmoud Saleh), Mohammed Hamada Sedki, Mohamed Rabie Yassin, Shawki Ghareeb Bayoumi (81.Nabil Alaa El Din Morsy), Magdi Abdelghani Sayed Ahmed, Hussain Ayman Younis, Amer Taher Abouzeid El Sayed, Emad Soliman, Moustafa Gamal Abdelhamid. Trainer: Mohammed Abdou Saleh El Wahsh.
**Goals:** 1-0 Mohamed Timoumi (37), 2-0 Abdel Aziz Bouderbala (85).


| 13.07.1985 | Alger | Algeria - Zambia | 2-0(1-0) |
| 28.07.1985 | Lusaka | Zambia - Algeria | 0-1(0-0) |

### FINAL STANDINGS

| | | | | | | | | |
|---|---|---|---|---|---|---|---|---|
| 1. | Algeria | 2 | 2 | 0 | 0 | 3 | - 0 | 4 |
| 2. | Zambia  | 2 | 0 | 0 | 2 | 0 | - 3 | 0 |

Algeria qualified for the Fourth Round.

13.07.1985, Stade du 5$^{ème}$ Juillet, Alger; Attendance: n/a
Referee: Mohamed Hussam El Din (Egypt)
**ALGERIA - ZAMBIA**  **2-0(1-0)**
**ALG:** Nacerdine Drid, Mahmoud Guendouz, Faouzi Mansouri, Nourredine Abdallah Kourichi, Bouabdallah Medjadi (71.Abdelhamid Sadmi), Mohamed Kaci Saïd, Karim Maroc, Djamel Menad, Mustapha Rabah Madjer, Salah Assad (60.Hocine Yahi), Tedj Bensaoula. Trainer: Rabah Saadane.
**ZAM:** David Chabala, Laban Chishala, Edwin Kampanta, John Mwanza, Jones Chilengi, Jerry Shinde, Lucky Msiska (80.Mubanza), Willie Chibwika (55.Derby Makinka), Michael Chabala, Jack Chanda, Kalusha Bwalya. Trainer: Baldwin Banda.
**Goals:** 1-0 Tedj Bensaoula (16), 2-0 Mustapha Rabah Madjer (85).

28.07.1985, Independence Stadium, Lusaka; Attendance: 30,000
Referee: Sydney Picon-Ackong (Mauritius)
**ZAMBIA - ALGERIA**  **0-1(0-0)**
**ZAM:** David Chabala, Laban Chishala, Edwin Kampanta, John Mwanza, Jones Chilengi, Jerry Shinde, Leckson Mwinuna, Derby Makinka, Michael Chabala, Jack Chanda, Kalusha Bwalya. Trainer: Baldwin Banda.
**ALG:** Nacerdine Drid, Mahmoud Guendouz, Faouzi Mansouri, Fadil Megharia, Abdelhamid Sadmi, Mohamed Kaci Saïd, Karim Maroc, Djamel Menad, Mustapha Rabah Madjer, Salah Assad, Tedj Bensaoula. Trainer: Rabah Saadane.
**Goal:** 0-1 Tedj Bensaoula (76).

| 14.07.1985 | Accra | Ghana - Libya | 0-0 |
| 26.07.1985 | Benghazi | Libya - Ghana | 2-0(1-0) |

**FINAL STANDINGS**

| | | | | | | | | |
|---|---|---|---|---|---|---|---|---|
| 1. Libya | 2 | 1 | 1 | 0 | 2 | - | 0 | 3 |
| 2. Ghana | 2 | 0 | 1 | 1 | 0 | - | 2 | 1 |

Libya qualified for the Fourth Round.

14.07.1985, National Sports Council Stadium, Accra; Attendance: n/a
Referee: Alhagi Fayé (Gambia)
**GHANA - LIBYA** **0-0**
GHA: Andrews Quamsan, Joseph Odoi, Sampson Lamptey, Addae Kyenkyehene, Abedi Ayew, Ofei Ansah, John Bannerman (70.Afriye Opoku), George Lamptey, George Alhassan, Emmanuel Quarshie (78.Karim Abdul Razak Tanko), Francis Kumi. Trainer: César Augusto Gonzáles.
LBY: Musbah Younen Shangab, Abdusalam Maghrabi, Aboubaker Bani, Salem Ali Sola, Ayad El Ghadi, Jamal Abounuara, Reda Attia, Abdureda Poabaria, Suleiman Omar Attia, Abdurrazagh Firgani, Ali Musa El Beshari. Trainer: El Hashim El Bahalol.

26.07.1985, Stade 28 Mars, Benghazi; Attendance: n/a
Referee: Baba Laouissi (Morocco)
**LIBYA - GHANA** **2-0(1-0)**
LBY: Musbah Younen Shangab, Sasi El Fazani, Aboubaker Bani, Salem Ali Sola, Ayad El Ghadi, Jamal Abounuara, Abdureda Poabaria, Fawzi El Aisawi, Abdurrazagh Firgani, Ali Musa El Beshari, Reda Attia. Trainer: El Hashim El Bahalol.
GHA: Andrews Quamsan, Joseph Odoi, Sampson Lamptey, Addae Kyenkyehene, Abedi Ayew, Ofei Ansah, John Bannerman, George Lamptey, George Alhassan (75.Emmanuel Quarshie), Mohammed Ahmed, Samuel Opoku Nti (82.Francis Kumi). Trainer: César Augusto Gonzáles.
**Goals**: 1-0 Abdureda Poabaria (33), 2-0 Ayad El Ghadi (70).
**Sent off**: Joseph Odoi (8), Abedi Ayew (76), Mohammed Ahmed (76).

# FOURTH ROUND

06.10.1985 Tunis     Tunisia - Algeria     1-4(1-2)
18.10.1985 Alger     Algeria - Tunisia     3-0(2-0)

## FINAL STANDINGS

| | | | | | | | | |
|---|---|---|---|---|---|---|---|---|
| 1. Algeria | 2 | 2 | 0 | 0 | 7 | - | 1 | 4 |
| 2. Tunisia | 2 | 0 | 0 | 2 | 1 | - | 7 | 0 |

Algeria qualified for the Final Tournament.

06.10.1985, Stade Olympique d'El Menzah, Tunis; Attendance: 33,000
Referee: Roger Schoeters (Belgium)
**TUNISIA - ALGERIA**     **1-4(1-2)**
**TUN:** Sahbi Jsebai, Salem Jaziri (Hakim Braham), Moncef Chergui, Nabil Maâloul, Mohamed Cheriti, Hosni Zouaoui, Abdelhamid Hergal, Abderrazak Rakbaori, Montacer Ammar (Hafedh Houarbi), Bassam Jeridi, Khaled Ben Yahia. Trainer: Youssef Zouaoui.
**ALG:** Nacerdine Drid, Mahmoud Guendouz, Faouzi Mansouri, Nourredine Abdallah Kourichi, Abdelhamid Sadmi, Mohamed Kaci Saïd, Karim Maroc, Djamel Menad, Lakhdar Belloumi (82.Mohammed Chaib), Salah Assad, Mustapha Rabah Madjer (74.Hocine Yahi). Trainer: Rabah Saadane.
**Goals**: 1-0 Abderrazak Rakbaori (16), 1-1 Mustapha Rabah Madjer (24), 1-2 Djamel Menad (43), 1-3 Mohamed Kaci Saïd (67), 1-4 Djamel Menad (87).

18.10.1985, Stade 5 Juillet 1962, Alger; Attendance:
Referee: Bruno Galler (Switzerland)
**ALGERIA - TUNISIA**     **3-0(2-0)**
**ALG:** Nacerdine Drid, Mahmoud Guendouz, Faouzi Mansouri, Fodil Megharia, Abdelhamid Sadmi, Mohamed Kaci Saïd, Karim Maroc, Djamel Menad, Lakhdar Belloumi (74.Hocine Yahi), Salah Assad (79.Tedj Bensaoula), Mustapha Rabah Madjer. Trainer: Rabah Saadane.
**TUN:** Sahbi Jsebai, Mohamed Gasri, Mohamed Cheriti, Nabil Maâloul, Samir Khemiri (Hafedh Houarbi), Hosni Zouaoui, Abdelhamid Hergal, Khaled Ben Yahia, Abderrazak Rakbaori, Hakim Braham, Bassam Jeridi (Henchiri). Trainer: Youssef Zouaoui.
**Goals**: 1-0 Mustapha Rabah Madjer (8), 2-0 Djamel Menad (34), 3-0 Hocine Yahi (78).

| | | | | | | | |
|---|---|---|---|---|---|---|---|
| 06.10.1985 | Rabat | Morocco - Libya | | | | | 3-0(1-0) |
| 18.10.1985 | Benghazi | Libya - Morocco | | | | | 1-0(1-0) |

### FINAL STANDINGS

| | | | | | | | |
|---|---|---|---|---|---|---|---|
| 1. **Morocco** | 2 | 1 | 0 | 1 | 3 - 1 | 2 |
| 2. Libya | 2 | 1 | 0 | 1 | 1 - 3 | 2 |

Morocco qualified for the Final Tournament.

06.10.1985, Stade "Prince Moulay Abdellah", Rabat; Attendance: n/a
Referee: Kamabula Chayu (Zambia)
**MOROCCO - LIBYA** **3-0(1-0)**
**MAR:** Ezaki Badou, Hamou Fadili (73.Abdelfettah Rhiati), Abdelmajid Lamris, Mustapha El Biyaz, Noureddine Bouyahyaoui, Abdelmajid Dolmy, Mustapha El Haddaoui, Abdelaziz Bouderbala, Mustapha Merry (46.Abderrazak Khairi), Mohamed Timoumi, Khalid El Bied. Trainer: José Faria (Brazil).
**LBY:** Musbah Younen Shangab, Sasi El Fazani, Ali Musa El Beshari, Aboubaker Bani, Abdusalam Maghrabi, Ayad El Ghadi, Jalal Damgee (65.Faraj El Brnawi), Reda Attia, Aboureda Boabaria, Fawzi El Aisawi, Muftah Weddawi. Trainer: El Hashim El Bahalol.
**Goals:** 1-0 Mustapha Merry (44), 2-0 Mohamed Timoumi (85), 3-0 Abdel Aziz Bouderbala (90).

18.10.1985, Bin Ghashir Stadium, Bin Ghashir; Attendance: n/a
Referee: Luigi Agnolin (Italy)
**LIBYA - MOROCCO** **1-0(1-0)**
**LBY:** Musbah Younen Shangab, Sasi El Fazani, Ali Musa El Beshari, Aboubaker Bani, Abdusalam Maghrabi, Ayad El Ghadi, Sharif El Marghani, Abdureda Poabaria, Ibrahim Ben Abubaker, Fawzi El Aisawi, Abdurrazagh Firgani. Trainer: El Hashim El Bahalol.
**MAR:** Ezaki Badou, Hamou Fadili, Abdelmajid Lamris, Mustapha El Biyaz, Noureddine Bouyahyaoui, Abdelmajid Dolmy, Abderrazak Khairi, Mustapha Merry, Mohamed Timoumi, Abdelaziz Souleimani, Lahcen Ouadani. Trainer: José Faria (Brazil).
**Goal:** 1-0 Abdurrazagh Firgani (43).

# ASIA

## ZONE A – FIRST ROUND

## GROUP 1A

Oman withdrew.
| | | | |
|---|---|---|---|
| 12.04.1985 | Riyadh | Saudi Arabia - United Arab Emirates | 0-0 |
| 19.04.1985 | Dubai | United Arab Emirates - Saudi Arabia | 1-0(1-0) |

### FINAL STANDINGS

| | | | | | | | |
|---|---|---|---|---|---|---|---|
| 1. United Arab Emirates | 2 | 1 | 1 | 0 | 1 - 0 | 3 |
| 2. Saudi Arabia | 2 | 0 | 1 | 1 | 0 - 1 | 1 |

United Arab Emirates qualified for the Zone A - Second Round.

12.04.1985, „King Fahd" Stadium, Riyadh; Attendance: 30,973
Referee: Mohamad Al Sakran (Jordan)
**SAUDI ARABIA - UNITED ARAB EMIRATES**                  **0-0**
**KSA**: Mohamed Abdullaziz Al Deayea, Nasser Al Miawid, Hussein Al Bishi, Mohammed Abdul Jawad, Salih Mohammed Al Neaaimah, Abdullah Rashod, Musaed Ibrahim (35.Bandar Al Nakhli), Yusuf Rashed Khamees Al Ola (28.Fahad Al Bishi), Majed Ahmed Abdullah Al Mohammed, Fahad Mohammed Saleh Al Mesaibeth, Mohsin Mubarak Al Dosary. Trainer: Khalil Ibrahim Rashid Al Zayani.
**UAE**: Mohamed Hassan Abdulqader, Fahad Abdullah Abdulrahman, Khalil Ghanim Mubarak, Hassan Darwish, Mubarak Ghanim Mubarak, Abdullah Ali Sultan Ahmed, Fahad Khamees Mohamed Mubarak, Abdulrazaq Al Booshi (32.Khalid Khameed Mubarak), Abdullah Farouq, Mushin Musabah Faraj, Adnan Khamees Al Taliyani. Trainer: Carlos Alberto Gomes Parreira (Brazil).

19.04.1985, Al Wasl Stadium, Dubai; Attendance: 15,000
Referee: Robert Bonar Valentine (Scotland)
**UNITED ARAB EMIRATES - SAUDI ARABIA**               **1-0(1-0)**
**UAE**: Mohamed Hassan Abdulqader, Fahad Abdullah Abdulrahman, Khalil Ghanim Mubarak, Hassan Ali Mohamed, Mubarak Ghanim Mubarak, Abdullah Ali Sultan Ahmed (76.Ali Thani Juma), Farouk Abdul Rahman, Fahad Khamees Mohamed Mubarak, Abdul Razaq Ibrahim (59.Khalid Khameed Mubarak), Mohamed Mubarak Salim, Adnan Khamees Al Taliyani. Trainer: Carlos Alberto Gomes Parreira (Brazil).
**KSA**: Mohamed Abdullaziz Al Deayea, Nasser Al Miawid, Hussein Al Bishi, Mohammed Abdul Jawad, Salih Mohammed Al Neaaimah, Yahya Amer, Modalla Al Rashid (46.Fahad Al Bishi), Hathal Al Dosary, Majed Ahmed Abdullah Al Mohammed, Fahad Mohammed Saleh Al Mesaibeth, Mohsin Mubarak Al Dosary (65.Musaed Ibrahim). Trainer: Khalil Ibrahim Rashid Al Zayani.
**Goal**: 1-0 Fahad Khamees Mohamed Mubarak (5).

# GROUP 1B

| | | | |
|---|---|---|---|
| 15.03.1985 | Kuwait City | Iraq - Lebanon | 6-0* |
| 15.03.1985 | Amman | Jordan - Qatar | 1-0(0-0) |
| 18.03.1985 | Kuwait City | Iraq - Lebanon | 6-0* |
| 22.03.1985 | Doha | Qatar - Lebanon | 7-0* |
| 27.03.1985 | Doha | Qatar - Lebanon | 8-0* |

*Lebanon withdrew, their matches were annulled.

| | | | |
|---|---|---|---|
| 29.03.1985 | Amman | Jordan - Iraq | 2-3(0-1) |
| 05.04.1985 | Doha | Qatar - Iraq | 3-0(1-0) |
| 12.04.1985 | Doha | Qatar - Jordan | 2-0(0-0) |
| 19.04.1985 | Kuwait City | Iraq - Jordan | 2-0(0-0) |
| 05.05.1985 | Calcutta | Iraq - Qatar | 2-1(1-1) |

### FINAL STANDINGS

| | | | | | | | |
|---|---|---|---|---|---|---|---|
| 1. Iraq | 4 | 3 | 0 | 1 | 7 - 6 | 6 |
| 2. Qatar | 4 | 2 | 0 | 2 | 6 - 3 | 4 |
| 3. Jordan | 4 | 1 | 0 | 3 | 3 - 7 | 2 |

Iraq qualified for the Zone A – Second Round.

15.03.1985, "King Abdullah" Stadium, Amman; Attendance: n/a
Referee: Abuwahid Shambe Al Baluchi (Oman)
**JORDAN - QATAR**     **1-0(0-0)**
**JOR**: Tayim Bassem, Naser Mohammed Al Odali, Zied Al Shara, Husam Azmi Sinnokrat, Khaled Abdel Atef, Issam Said Saleh, Tawfeeq Al Saheb (75.Abdel Hadi), Ghassan Obeid, Jamal Abu Abed, Jamal Sabah (46.Rateb Al Dawoud), Khaled Khalil Awad.
**QAT**: Younis Lari, Mohammed Al Suwaidi, Adel Ahmed Malulla, Anbar Mubarak Al Ali, Ibrahim Khalfah Ahmed, Mansour Muftah Faraj Bekhit, Khalid Mohammed Salman Al Muhannadi (84.Mohammed Khalifa Al Ammari), Abdel Mubarak Khamis (65.Ali Mohamed Zaid Al Sadah), Ahmed Issa Al Mohannadi, Mubarak Salem Al Khater, Ibrahim Saeed Al Rumaihi. Trainer: Evaristo de Macedo Filho (Brazil).
**Goal**: 1-0 Issam Said Saleh (83).

29.03.1985, "King Abdullah" Stadium, Amman; Attendance: n/a
Referee: Abdul-Aziz Saleh Al Salmi (Kuwait)
**JORDAN - IRAQ**     **2-3(0-1)**
**JOR**: Tayim Bassem, Naser Mohammed Al Odali, Husam Azmi Sonnokrat, Zied Al Shara, Issam Said Saleh, Rateb Al Dawoud, Jamal Sabah, Tawfeeq Al Saheb (64.Ibrahim Khalih Saddieh), Jamal Abu Abed, Khaled Khalil Awad (52.Ghassan Obeid), Khaled Said.
**IRQ**: Jassim Abdul-Fatah Nasif, Khalil Mohammed Allawi, Jamal Ali Hamza, Abdul Khadim Mutashar, Mahmoud Hamza Shaker, Ali Hussein Shihab, Basil Gorgis Hanna, Natiq Hashim Abidoun, Wadim Mounir (70.Karim Mohammed Allawi), Ahmad Radhi Amaiesh Al Salehi, Hussein Saeed Mohammed. Trainer: Akram Salman Ahmed.
**Goals**: Rateb Al Dawoud, Jamal Abu Abed / Hussein Saeed Mohammed, Munier Wamaidh, Ahmad Radhi Amaiesh Al Salehi.

05.04.1985, Al Ahli Stadium, Doha; Attendance: n/a
Referee: George Courtney (England)
**QATAR - IRAQ**     **3-0(1-0)**
**QAT**: Younis Ahmed Lari, Mohammed Al Suwaidi, Anbar Mubarak Al Ali, Ali Mohamed Zaid Al Sadah, Adel Ahmed Malulla, Ibrahim Khalfah Ahmed, Mansour Muftah Faraj Bekhit, Ibrahim Saeed Al Rumaihi, Ahmed Issa Al Mohannadi, Mohammed Khalifa Al Ammari, Mubarak Salem Al Khater. Trainer: Evaristo de Macedo Filho (Brazil).
**IRQ**: Jassim Abdul-Fatah Nasif, Jamal Ali Hamza, Khalil Mohammed Allawi, Abdul Khadim Mutashar, Mahmoud Hamza Shaker, Ali Hussein Shihab, Basil Gorgis Hanna, Natiq Hashim Abidoun, Wadim Mounir, Ahmad Radhi Amaiesh Al Salehi, Hussein Saeed Mohammed. Trainer: Akram Salman Ahmed.
**Goals**: 1-0 Mansour Muftah Faraj Bekhit (42), 2-0 Ahmed Issa Al Mohannadi (52 penalty), 3-0 Mohammed Khalifa Al Ammari (71).

12.04.1985, Al Ahli Stadium, Doha; Attendance: n/a
Referee: Lee Kok Leong (Singapore)
**QATAR - JORDAN**     **2-0(0-0)**
**QAT**: Younis Ahmed Lari, Mohammed Al Suwaidi, Adel Ahmed Malulla, Ibrahim Khalfah Ahmed, Mansour Muftah Faraj Bekhit, Anbar Mubarak Al Ali, Ibrahim Saeed Al Rumaihi, Adel Mubarak Khamis, Ahmed Issa Al Mohannadi, Mubarak Salem Al Khater, Ali Mohammed Al Saadah. Trainer: Evaristo de Macedo Filho (Brazil).
**JOR**: Tayim Bassem, Naser Mohammed Al Odali, Husam Azmi Sinnokrat, Zied Al Shara, Tawfeeq Al Saheb, Ahmed Al Shboul Haitham, Abu Abed Ahmed Jamal, Khaled Khalil Awad, Khaled Abdel Atef, Jamal Sabah, Ibrahim Khalih Saddieh.
**Goals**: 1-0 Ali Mohammed Al Saadah, 2-0 Adel Ahmed Malulla.

19.04.1985, National Stadium, Kuwait City (Kuwait); Attendance: n/a
Referee: Jamal Al Sharif (Syria)
**IRAQ - JORDAN**     **2-0(0-0)**
**IRQ**: Raad Hammoudi Salman, Jamal Ali Hamza, Khalil Mohammed Allawi, Abdul Kharim Idi, Mahmoud Hamza Shaker, Ali Hussein Shihab, Ahmad Radhi Amaiesh Al Salehi, Karim Mohammed Allawi, Basil Gorgis Hanna, Karim Saddam Minshid, Hamid Abid Noor. Trainer: Akram Salman Ahmed.
**JOR**: Hashim Jaber Izzal, Naser Mohammed Al Odali, Husam Azmi Sinnokrat, Zied Al Shara, Tawfeeq Al Saheb, Jamal Abu Abed, Rateb Al Dawoud, Issam Said Saleh, Khaled Abdel Atef, Jamal Sabah, Ibrahim Khalih Saddieh.
**Goals**: 1-0 Ahmad Radhi Amaiesh Al Salehi (46), 2-0 Khalil Mohammed Allawi (50).

05.05.1985, Salt Lake City Stadium, Calcutta (India); Attendance: n/a
Referee: George Courtney (England)
**IRAQ - QATAR**     **2-1(1-1)**
**IRQ**: Raad Hammoudi Salman, Jamal Ali Hamza, Khalil Mohammed Allawi, Abdul Khadi Humaidi, Mahmoud Hamza Shaker, Ali Hussein Shihab, Basil Gorgis Hanna, Natiq Hashim Abidoun, Ahmad Radhi Amaiesh Al Salehi (89.Sabah Hadi), Karim Saddam Minshid (78.Mamid Yaakoob), Karim Mohammed Allawi. Trainer: Akram Salman Ahmed.
**QAT**: Younis Ahmed Lari, Mohammed Al Suwaidi, Adel Ahmed Malulla, Ali Mohamed Zaid Al Sadah (73.Adel Mubarak Khamis), Ibrahim Khalfah Ahmed (46.Hassan Matar Sayed Al Suwaidi), Anbar Mubarak Al Ali, Ibrahim Saeed Al Rumaihi, Mohammed Khalifa Al Ammari, Ahmed Issa Al Mohannadi, Mubarak Salem Al Khater, Mansour Muftah Faraj Bekhit. Trainer: Evaristo de Macedo Filho (Brazil).
**Goals**: 1-0 Ahmad Radhi Amaiesh Al Salehi (21), 1-1 Mansour Muftah Faraj Bekhit (44), 2-1 Karim Mohammed Allawe (76).

# GROUP 2A

| | | | |
|---|---|---|---|
| 22.03.1985 | Damascus | Syria - Kuwait | 1-0(0-0) |
| 29.03.1985 | Sana'a | North Yemen - Syria | 0-1(0-0) |
| 05.04.1985 | Kuwait City | Kuwait - North Yemen | 5-0(2-0) |
| 12.04.1985 | Kuwait City | Kuwait - Syria | 0-0 |
| 19.04.1985 | Damascus | Syria - North Yemen | 3-0(2-0) |
| 26.04.1985 | Sana'a | North Yemen - Kuwait | 1-3(0-2) |

## FINAL STANDINGS

| | | | | | | | | |
|---|---|---|---|---|---|---|---|---|
| 1. | Syria | 4 | 3 | 1 | 0 | 5 - 0 | 7 |
| 2. | Kuwait | 4 | 2 | 1 | 1 | 8 - 2 | 5 |
| 3. | North Yemen | 4 | 0 | 0 | 4 | 1 - 12 | 0 |

Syria qualified for the Zone A – Second Round.

22.03.1985, Assyrian Stadium, Damascus; Attendance: 21,000
Referee: Ahmad Bash (Jordan)
**SYRIA - KUWAIT** **1-0(0-0)**
**SYR**: Ahmad Eid Maher Berakdar, Rashid Khalid, Mohammed Ali Dahman, Jihad Ashrafi, I. Mahrous, Radwan Al Shaikh, Walid Abou El Sel, Abdul Kader Kurdghli, Fouad Aziz, Marwan Mohammed Medrati, Nizar Mahrous. Trainer: Avedis Kavlakian.
**KUW**: Khalid Al Shammari, Hamoud Fulaiteh Al Shammari, Jamal Mohammed Yaqoub Al Qabandi, Waleed Mohammed Al Jasem Al Mubarak, Abdulaziz Hassan Mohammed Al Buloushi, Sami Mohammed Al Hashash, Majed Sultan Salmin (80.Nasser Abdullah Al Ghanem), Abdullah Mohammed Al Buloushi, Muayad Rehayyem Gamal Al Haddad, Faisal Ali Al Dakhil, Abdul Aziz Saoud Al Anbari. Trainer: Antônio Lopes dos Santos (Brazil).
**Goal**: 1-0 Marwan Mohammed Medrati (78).

29.03.1985, Revolution 1962 Stadium, Sana'a; Attendance: 15,000
Referee: Abuwahid Shambe Al Baluchi (Oman)
**NORTH YEMEN - SYRIA** **0-1(0-0)**
**NYE**: Amin Al Sanini, Faisal Asad, Abdul Rahman Al Yarimy, Khalid Al Arashi, Anwar Hodeini (88.Khalid Drawan), Jamal Hamdi, Shanar Hamadi, Ahmad Ghaleb, Abdullah Al Sanaani, Tareq Al Sayyed (80.Abdulnaser Abbas), Abdulmalek Thabet. Trainer: Miroslav Vitsičić (Yugoslavia).
**SYR**: Ahmad Eid Maher Berakdar (34.Malek Shakkouhi), Rashid Khalid, Mohammed Ali Dahman, Jihad Ashrafi, I. Mahrous, Nizar Mahrous, Walid Abou El Sel, Abdul Kader Kurdghli, Fouad Aziz, Marwan Mohammed Medrati (78.Mahmoud Al Sayed), Radwan Al Shaikh. Trainer: Avedis Kavlakian.
**Goal**: 0-1 Walid Abou El Sel (70).

05.04.1985, National Stadium, Kuwait City; Attendance: n/a
Referee: Hussein Suleiman Awil (Jordan)
**KUWAIT - NORTH YEMEN** **5-0(2-0)**
**KUW**: Khalid Al Shammari, Hamoud Fulaiteh Al Shammari, Sami Mohammed Al Hashash, Jamal Mohammed Yaqoub Al Qabandi, Waleed Mohammed Al Jasem Al Mubarak, Abdulaziz Hassan Mohammed Al Buloushi, Abdullah Mohammed Al Buloushi, Salah Al Hasawi, Nasser Abdullah Al Ghanem (58.Khaled Al Shareeda), Faisal Ali Al Dakhil, Abdul Aziz Saoud Al Anbari (75.Muayad Rehayyem Gamal Al Haddad). Trainer: Malcolm Alexander Allison (England).
**NYE**: Amin Al Sanini, Faisal Asad, Mohammad Al Hareemi (65.Asadi), Jamal Hamdi, Khalid Al Arashi, Khalid Al Naderi (83.Shanar Hammadi), Abdulnaser Abbas, Ahmad Ghaleb, Abdullah Al Sanaani, Tareg Al Sayyed, Abdulmalek Thabet. Trainer: Miroslav Vitsičić (Yugoslavia).
**Goals**: 1-0 Abdul Aziz Saoud Al Anbari (39), 2-0 Abdul Aziz Saoud Al Anbari (44), 3-0 Salah Al Hasawi (58), 4-0 Faisal Ali Al Dakhil (80), 5-0 Jamal Yaqoub (88).

12.04.1985, National Stadium, Kuwait City; Attendance: n/a
Referee: Jassim Mandi Abdul-Rahman (Bahrain)
**KUWAIT - SYRIA** **0-0**
**KUW**: Khalid Al Shammari, Adel Hussain Abbas, Hamoud Fulaiteh Al Shammari, Jamal Mohammed Yaqoub Al Qabandi, Waleed Mohammed Al Jasem Al Mubarak, Abdulaziz Hassan Mohammed Al Buloushi (60.Amer Al Amer), Khaled Al Shareeda, Abdullah Mohammed Al Buloushi, Salah Al Hasawi, Faisal Ali Al Dakhil, Abdul Aziz Saoud Al Anbari (60.Muayad Rehayyem Gamal Al Haddad). Trainer: Malcolm Alexander Allison (England).
**SYR**: Malek Shakkouhi, Rashid Khalid, Mohammed Ali Dahman, Jihad Ashrafi, I. Mahrous, Mahmoud Al Sayed, Walid Abou El Sel (88.Mohamed Mahrous), Abdul Kader Jardaghly (78.Nizar Mahrous), Marwan Mohammed Medrati, Georges Khouri, Radwan Al Shaikh. Trainer: Avedis Kavlakian.

19.04.1985, Assyrian Stadium, Damascus; Attendance: 28,000
Referee: Ahmed Jassim Mohamed (Bahrain)
**SYRIA - NORTH YEMEN** **3-0(2-0)**
**SYR**: Malek Shakkouhi, Rashid Khalid, Mohammed Ali Dahman, Jihad Ashrafi, I. Mahrous, Mahmoud Al Sayed, Walid Abou El Sel, Abdul Kader Kurdghli, Marwan Mohammed Medrati, Georges Khouri, Radwan Al Shaikh. Trainer: Avedis Kavlakian.
**NYE**: Amin Al Sanini, Fuad Al Fagih, Faisal Asad, Khalid Al Arashi, Khalid Drawan, Jamal Hamdi, Khalid Al Naderi, Ahmad Ghaleb, Abdullah Al Sanaani, Tareq Al Sayyed, Abdulmalek Thabet. Trainer: Miroslav Vitsičić (Yugoslavia).
**Goals**: 1-0 Mahmoud Al Sayed (31), 2-0 Radwan Al Shaikh (40), 3-0 Mahmoud Al Sayed (75).

26.04.1985, Revolution 1962 Stadium, Sana'a; Attendance: 10,000
Referee: Mohamed Saleh Alawi Al Farisi (Oman)
**NORTH YEMEN - KUWAIT** **1-3(0-2)**
**NYE**: Amin Al Sanini, Faisal Asad, Khalid Drawan, Khalid Al Arashi, Anwar Hodeini (46.Khalid Al Naderi), Jamal Hamdi, Fuad Al Fagih, Ahmad Ghaleb, Abdullah Al Sanaani, Abdulmalek Thabet, Abdulnaser Abbas. Trainer: Miroslav Vitsičić (Yugoslavia).
**KUW**: Khalid Al Shammari, Adel Hussain Abbas, Hamoud Fulaiteh Al Shammari, Jamal Mohammed Yaqoub Al Qabandi, Waleed Mohammed Al Jasem Al Mubarak, Abdulaziz Hassan Mohammed Al Buloushi, Majed Sultan Salmin, Abdullah Mohammed Al Buloushi, Salah Al Hasawi, Faisal Ali Al Dakhil (46.Muayad Rehayyem Gamal Al Haddad), Abdul Aziz Saoud Al Anbari. Trainer: Malcolm Alexander Allison (England).
**Goals**: 0-1 Salah Al Hasawi (13), 0-2 Faisal Ali Al Dakhil (25), 0-3 Salah Al Hasawi (57), 1-3 Abdulnaser Abbas (88).

# GROUP 2B

Iran refused to play its home matches on neutral grounds and was suspended by FIFA.
29.03.1985  Aden        South Yemen - Bahrain           1-4(0-2)
12.04.1985  Manama      Bahrain - South Yemen           3-3(0-1)

## FINAL STANDINGS

| | | | | | | | | |
|---|---|---|---|---|---|---|---|---|
| 1. Bahrain     | 2 | 1 | 1 | 0 | 7 | - | 4 | 3 |
| 2. South Yemen | 2 | 0 | 1 | 1 | 4 | - | 7 | 1 |

Bahrain qualified for the Zone A – Second Round.

29.03.1985, Mortayer Yard Stadium, Aden; Attendance: 19,082
Referee: Fallaj Khuzam Al Shanar (Saudi Arabia)
**SOUTH YEMEN - BAHRAIN**                                    **1-4(0-2)**
**SYE**: Abdulrahman Ibrahim, Jamil Sharaf, Abdulla Yassin Mahmoud, Taher Haj Ba Saad, Ahmed Al Ahmady, Adnan Ahmed Al Sabou, Abdulla Moukaish, Ihab Haidar, Kassim Tariq Abdullah, Abdo Saidi Showkri, Abobaker Ibrahim Al Mass. Trainer: Azzam Khalifa.
**BHR**: Khalil Nema, Marjan Eid (Hassan Radi), Salman Al Harbi, Adnan Ali Daif, Ibrahim Al Hardan, Karim Bukheet Saif, Yousif Al Sobaei, Ali Jaffar Husain, Ibrahim Al Farhan, Jasem Al Khajam, Khalaf Mohammed Hamad. Trainer: Harry Keith Burkinshaw (England).
**Goals**: 0-1 Ibrahim Al Farhan (9), 0-2 Ibrahim Al Hardan (17), 0-3 Ibrahim Al Farhan (50), 0-4 Yousif Al Sobaei (60), 1-4 Abobaker Ibrahim Al Mass (74).

12.04.1985, Bahrain National Stadium, Manama; Attendance: 3,216
Referee: Abdullah Ghareeb Shehab (Kuwait)
**BAHRAIN - SOUTH YEMEN**                                    **3-3(0-1)**
**BHR**: Mohamed Saleh, Karim Bukheet Saif, Salman Al Harbi, Ali Jaffar Husain, Adnan Ali Daif, Ibrahim Al Hardan, Abdullah Rahman Hisham, Ibrahim Al Farhan, Jasem Al Khajam (59.Waleed Showaiter), Khalaf Mohammed Hamad (79.Mohammed Khalaf Abdullah), Yousif Al Sobaei. Trainer: Harry Keith Burkinshaw (England).
**SYE**: Abdulrahman Ibrahim, Abdo Saidi Showkri (72.Al Barek), Abdulla Yassin Mahmoud, Ahmed Ahmed Saeed, Taher Haj Ba Saad, Bin Saleh Husain Mahmoud, Wagdan Mahmoud Shadli, Kassim Tariq Abdullah, Adnan Ahmed Al Sabou, Abobaker Ibrahim Al Mass, Ali Mohamed Salim (54.Abdulla Moukaish). Trainer: Abdullali Saleh Khobani.
**Goals**: 0-1 Wagdan Mahmoud Shadli (18), 1-1 Ibrahim Al Hardan (48), 2-1 Abdullah Rahman Hisham (66), 3-1 Adnan Ali Daif (69), 3-2 Kassim Tariq Abdullah (75), 3-3 Adnan Ahmed Al Sabou (88).

# ZONE A – SECOND ROUND

| 20.09.1985 | Dubai | United Arab Emirates - Iraq | 2-3(1-1) |
| 27.09.1985 | Taif  | Iraq - United Arab Emirates | 1-2(0-1) |

### FINAL STANDINGS

| | | | | | | | | |
|---|---|---|---|---|---|---|---|---|
| 1. | Iraq | 2 | 1 | 0 | 1 | 4 | - 4 | 2 |
| 2. | United Arab Emirates | 2 | 1 | 0 | 1 | 4 | - 4 | 2 |

Iraq qualified on away goals rule for the Zone A - Final Round.

20.09.1985, Zabeel Stadium, Dubai; Attendance: n/a
Referee: Abdul-Aziz Saleh Al Salmi (Kuwait)
**UNITED ARAB EMIRATES - IRAQ**          **2-3(1-1)**
**IRQ**: Raad Hammoudi Salman, Adnan Darjal Matar, Khalil Mohammed Allawi, Abdul Khadi Humaidi, Jassim Ghanim Oraibi Al Roubai, Haris Mohammed Hassan, Ali Hussein Shihab, Anad Abid Tweresh, Ahmad Radhi Amaiesh Al Salehi, Hussein Saeed Mohammed, Karim Mohammed Allawi. Trainer: Jorge Silva Vieira (Brazil).
**UAE**: Mohamed Hassan Abdulqader, Fahad Abdullah Abdulrahman, Hassan Ali Mohamed, Bader Ahmed Saleh, Abdullah Ali Sultan Ahmed, Adel Hadeed Gharib, Fahad Khamees Mohamed Mubarak, Saeed Abdullah Ibrahim, Khalid Mubarak Ismail, Adnan Khamees Al Taliyani, Khalid Khameed Mubarak. Trainer: Carlos Alberto Gomes Parreira (Brazil).
**Goals**: 0-1 Hussein Saeed Mohammed (15), 1-1 Adnan Khamees Al Taliyani (42), 1-2 Haris Mohammed Hassan (60), 1-3 Hussein Saeed Mohammed (79), 2-3 Adnan Khamees Al Taliyani (81).

27.09.1985, "King Fahd" Sports City Stadium, Ta'if; Attendance: 4,175
Referee: André Daina (Switzerland)
**IRAQ - UNITED ARAB EMIRATES**          **1-2(0-1)**
**IRQ**: Raad Hammoudi Salman, Adnan Darjal Matar, Khalil Mohammed Allawi, Abdul Khadi Humaidi, Basim Qasim Hamdan, Ali Hussein Shihab, Natiq Hashim Abidoun, Mahmoud Hamza Shaker, Ahmad Radhi Amaiesh Al Salehi (49.Karim Saddam Minshid), Hussein Saeed Mohammed, Karim Mohammed Allawi. Trainer: Jorge Silva Vieira (Brazil).
**UAE**: Mohamed Hassan Abdulqader, Fahad Abdullah Abdulrahman, Khalil Ghanim Mubarak, Hussain Ghuloum Abbas, Abdullah Ali Sultan Ahmed, Khalid Abdul Aziz, Bader Ahmed Saleh, Fahad Khamees Mohamed Mubarak, Khalid Mubarak Ismail, Abdul Razaq Ibrahim, Adnan Khamees Al Taliyani. Trainer: Carlos Alberto Gomes Parreira (Brazil).
**Goals**: 0-1 Khamees Mubarak Fahad (2), 0-2 Adnan Khamees Al Taliyani (60), 1-2 Khalil Mohammed Allawi (90).


| 06.09.1985 | Manama   | Bahrain - Syria | 1-1(1-0) |
| 20.09.1985 | Damascus | Syria - Bahrain | 1-0(1-0) |

### FINAL STANDINGS

| | | | | | | | | |
|---|---|---|---|---|---|---|---|---|
| 1. | Syria   | 2 | 1 | 1 | 0 | 2 | - 1 | 3 |
| 2. | Bahrain | 2 | 0 | 1 | 1 | 1 | - 2 | 1 |

Syria qualified for the Zone A - Final Round.

06.09.1985, Bahrain National Stadium, Manama; Attendance: 8,224
Referee: Ahmad Bash (Jordan)
**BAHRAIN - SYRIA** **1-1(1-0)**
**BHR**: Hamoud Sultan Mazkoor, Marjan Eid (Hassan Radi), Salman Al Harbi, Adnan Ali Daif, Karim Bukheet Saif, Hisham Baloushi, Ali Al Ansari, Ibrahim Al Farhan (Ahmed Rashdan), Ebrahim Isa Ahmed Al Isa, Ibrahim Al Hardan, Khalaf Mohammed Hamad. Trainer: Harry Keith Burkinshaw (England).
**SYR**: Malek Shakkouhi, Rashid Khalid, Mohamed Ali Dahman, Jihad Ashrafi, Mohamed Mahrous, Georges Khouri, Radwan Al Shaikh, Nizar Mahrous, Abdul Kader Kurdghli, Fouad Aziz, Marwan Mohammed Medrati. Trainer: Avedis Kavlakian.
**Goals**: 1-0 Ebrahim Isa Ahmed Al Isa (42), 1-1 Nizar Mahrous (61).

20.09.1985, Abbassyin Stadium, Damascus; Attendance: 25,000
Referee: Abuwahid Shambe Al Baluchi (Oman)
**SYRIA - BAHRAIN** **1-0(1-0)**
**SYR**: Malek Shakkouhi, Rashid Khalid (82.Darwish), Mohammed Ali Dahman, Jihad Ashrafi, I. Mahrous, Georges Khouri, Radwan Al Shaikh, Nizar Mahrous, Abdul Kader Kurdghli, Fouad Aziz (11.Mahmoud Al Sayed), Marwan Mohammed Medrati. Trainer: Avedis Kavlakian.
**BHR**: Hamoud Sultan Mazkoor, Yousef Sharida, Salman Al Harbi, Adnan Ali Daif, Ali Al Ansari, Marjan Eid, Karim Bukheet Saif, Waleed Showaiter (85.Yacoub Hassan), Ibrahim Al Farhan, Ibrahim Al Hardan, Khalaf Mohammed Hamad. Trainer: Harry Keith Burkinshaw (England).
**Goal**: 1-0 Abdul Kader Kurdghli (4).

## ZONE A – FINAL ROUND

| 15.11.1985 | Damascus | Syria - Iraq | 0-0 |
| 29.11.1985 | Taif | Iraq - Syria | 3-1(1-0) |

### FINAL STANDINGS

| | | | | | | | | |
|---|---|---|---|---|---|---|---|---|
| 1. | Iraq | 2 | 1 | 1 | 0 | 3 - 1 | 3 |
| 2. | Syria | 2 | 0 | 1 | 1 | 1 - 3 | 1 |

Iraq qualified for the Final Tournament.

15.11.1985, Abbassyin Stadium, Damascus; Attendance: 25,000
Referee: Michel Vautrot (France)
**SYRIA - IRAQ** **0-0**
**SYR**: Malek Shakkouhhi, Rashid Khalid, Mohammed Ali Dahman, Radwan Al Shaikh, I. Mahrous, Jihad Ashrafi, Walid Abou El-Sel, Abdul Kader Kurdghli, Georges Khouri, Nizar Mahrous, Marwan Mohammed Medrati. Trainer: Avedis Kavlakian.
**IRQ**: Raad Hammoudi Salman, Adnan Darjal Matar, Khalil Mohammed Allawi, Abdul Khadim Mutashar, Jassim Ghanim Oraibi Al Roubai, Natiq Hashim Abidoun, Basil Gorgis Hanna, Ali Hussein Shihab, Haris Mohammed Hassan, Ahmad Radhi Amaiesh Al Salehi, Hussein Saeed Mohammed. Trainer: Jorge Silva Vieira (Brazil).

29.11.1985, "King Fahd" Sports City Stadium, Ta'if; Attendance: 4,500
Referee: Erik Fredriksson (Sweden)
**IRAQ - SYRIA**     **3-1(1-0)**
**IRQ**: Raad Hammoudi Salman, Adnan Darjal Matar, Khalil Mohammed Allawi, Abdul Khadi Humaidi, Jassim Ghanim Oraibi Al Roubai, Ali Hussein Shihab, Haris Mohammed Hassan, Basil Gorgis Hanna, Mahmoud Hamza Shaker (80.Natiq Hashim Abidoun), Ahmad Radhi Amaiesh Al Salehi, Hussein Saeed Mohammed. Trainer: Jorge Silva Vieira (Brazil).
**SYR**: Malek Shakkouhi, Rashid Khalid, Mohammed Ali Dahman, Jihad Ashrafi (51.Haissam Mohammed Shehadeh), I. Mahrous, Georges Khouri, Nizar Mahrous, Mohamad Jaflan (80.Mahmoud Al Sayed), Walid Abou El Sel, Abdul Kader Kurdghli, Marwan Mohammed Medrati. Trainer: Avedis Kavlakian.
**Goals**: 1-0 Hussein Saeed Mohammed (28), 2-0 Mahmoud Hamza Shaker (49), 2-1 Walid Abou El Sel (54), 3-1 Khalil Mohammed Allawi (72).

## ZONE B – FIRST ROUND

## GROUP 3A

| 02.03.1985 | Katmandu | Nepal - South Korea | 0-2(0-1) |
| 10.03.1985 | Kuala Lumpur | Malaysia - South Korea | 1-0(0-0) |
| 16.03.1985 | Katmandu | Nepal - Malaysia | 0-0 |
| 31.03.1985 | Kuala Lumpur | Malaysia - Nepal | 5-0(5-0) |
| 06.04.1985 | Seoul | South Korea - Nepal | 4-0(3-0) |
| 19.05.1985 | Seoul | South Korea - Malaysia | 2-0(2-0) |

**FINAL STANDINGS**

| | | | | | | | | | |
|---|---|---|---|---|---|---|---|---|---|
| 1. | South Korea | 4 | 3 | 0 | 1 | 8 | - | 1 | 6 |
| 2. | Malaysia | 4 | 2 | 1 | 1 | 6 | - | 2 | 5 |
| 3. | Nepal | 4 | 0 | 1 | 3 | 0 | - | 11 | 1 |

South Korea qualified for the Zone B – Second Round.

02.03.1985, Dasharath Rangasala Stadium, Kathmandu; Attendance: 40,000
Referee: Zhang Daqiao (China P.R.)
**NEPAL - SOUTH KOREA**     **0-2(0-1)**
**NEP**: Shahi Lok Bahadur, Drirendra Kuma Pradhan, Rajkarnikar B., Ganesh Pandey, Ranjitkar Ram Shriram, Suresh Panthi, Man Bahadur Malla, Krishna Thapa (66.Gyanu Shresth), Raju Kaji Shakya, Rupak Ray Sharma, Ganesh Thapa. Trainer: Thapa Bhim.
**KOR:** Choi In-Young, Park Kyung-Hoon, Chung Jong-Soo, Chung Yong-Hwan, Yoo Byung-Ok, Huh Jung-Moo, Kim Seok-Won, Choi Gwang-Ji (65.Choi Jin-Han), Choi Soon-Ho, Byun Byung-Joo, Lee Tae-Ho. Trainer: Moon Jung-Sik.
**Goals**: 0-1 Rupak Ray Sharma (35 own goal), 0-2 Lee Tae-Ho (63 penalty).

10.03.1985, Merdeka Stadium, Kuala Lumpur; Attendance: 36,738
Referee: Samuel Chan Yam-Ming (Hong Kong)
**MALAYSIA - SOUTH KOREA**     **1-0(0-0)**
**MAS**: Ramasamy Arumugan, Ibrahim Saad, Serbegeth Singh, Mohamed Noor Yassin, Yusoff Abdul Nasir, Ismail Fadzil (39.Ahmed Alid), Ali Ahmed Yusuf, Wong Hung Nung, Abidin Hassan Zainal, Dollah Salleh, Kim Lim Teong. Trainer: Frank Lord (England).
**KOR:** Oh Yeon-Kyo, Park Kyung-Hoon, Chung Jong-Soo, Chung Yong-Hwan, Lee Tae-Ho, Byun Byung-Joo, Huh Jung-Moo (Cap), Choi Soon-Ho (68.Kim Seok-Won), Kwak Sung-Ho (37.Choi Gwang-Ji), Yoo Byung-Ok, Choi Jin-Han. Trainer: Moon Jung-Sik.

**Goal**: 1-0 Dollah Salleh (49).

16.03.1985, Dasharath Rangasala Stadium, Kathmandu; Attendance: 8,000
Referee: Nadasen Chandra (Singapore)
**NEPAL - MALAYSIA**     **0-0**
**NEP**: Shahi Lok Bahadur, Drirendra Kuma Pradhan, Karnikar Bhakta Raj, Gyanu Shrestha, Ranjitkar Ram Shriram, Suresh Panthi, Umesh Pradhan, Man Bahadur Malla, Rupak Ray Sharma, Raju Kaji Shakya, Ganesh Thapa. Trainer: Thapa Bhim.
**MAS**: Ramasamy Arumugan, Ibrahim Saad, Serbegeth Singh, Mohamed Noor Yusuf, Abidin Hassan Zainal, Ismail Fadzil, Ali Ahmed Yusuf, Dollah Salleh, Kim Lim Teong, Yusoff Abdul Nasir, Wong Hung Nung. Trainer: Frank Lord (England).

31.03.1985, Merdeka Stadium, Kuala Lumpur; Attendance: 33,000
Referee: Lourenço Reinaldo (Macau)
**MALAYSIA - NEPAL**     **5-0(5-0)**
**MAS**: Ramasamy Arumugan, Ibrahim Saad, Serbegeth Singh, Mohamed Noor Yassin, Yusoff Abdul Nasir, Abidin Hassan Zainal (82.Marman), Dollah Salleh, Kim Lim Teong, Aljif Yunus, Wong Hung Nung, Khan Hung Meng (75.A. Rukumaran). Trainer: Frank Lord (England).
**NEP**: Shahi Lok Bahadur, Drirendra Kuma Pradhan, Karnikar Bhakta Raj, Ganesh Pandey, Ranjitkar Ram Shriram, Suresh Panthi, Umesh Pradhan, Gyanu Shrestha (46.Krishna Thapa), Raju Kaji Shakya (87.Kedar Rajesh Mamandhar), Yb Ghale, Ganesh Thapa. Trainer: Thapa Bhim.
**Goals**: 1-0 Abidin Hassan Zainal (4), 2-0 Abidin Hassan Zainal (26), 3-0 Dollah Salleh (29), 4-0 Abidin Hassan Zainal 833), 5-0 Aljif Yunus (40).

06.04.1985, Dongdaemun Stadium, Seoul; Attendance: n/a
Referee: Kwok Kui Cheung (Hong Kong)
**SOUTH KOREA - NEPAL**     **4-0(3-0)**
**KOR**: Oh Yeon-Kyo, Park Kyung-Hoon, Chung Jong-Soo, Cho Kwang-Rae, Chung Yong-Hwan, Kim Seok-Won (Lee Tae-Ho), Cho Young-Jeung (Paek Jong-Cheol), Choi Soon-Ho, Park Chang-Sun (Cap), Yoo Byung-Ok, Huh Jung-Moo. Trainer: Kim Jung-Nam.
**NEP**: Shahi Lok Bahadur, Drirendra Kuma Pradhan (71.Umesh Pradan), Karnikar Bhakta Raj (38.Kedar Rajesh Mamandhar), Ganesh Pandey, Suresh Panthi, Ganesh Thapa, Man Bahadur Malla, Krishna Thapa, Raju Kaji Shakya, Gayle Yb, Bigyan Ray Sharma. Trainer: Thapa Bhim.
**Goals**: 1-0 Huh Jung-Moo (18), 2-0 Kim Seok-Won (36), 3-0 Chung Jong-Soo (41), 4-0 Huh Jung-Moo (57).

19.05.1985, Olympic Stadium, Seoul; Attendance: 80,000
Referee: Shizuo Takada (Japan)
**SOUTH KOREA - MALAYSIA**     **2-0(2-0)**
**KOR**: Choi In-Young, Park Kyung-Hoon, Chung Jong-Soo, Cho Kwang-Rae, Chung Yong-Hwan, Kim Seok-Won, Choi Soon-Ho (76.Cho Young-Jeung), Park Chang-Sun (Cap), Cho Min-Kook, Yoo Byung-Ok, Huh Jung-Moo (76.Byun Byung-Joo). Trainer: Kim Jung-Nam.
**MAS**: Ong Yu Tiang, Ibrahim Saad, Kamarul Jahman, Jaidee Mokthar, Shukor Salleh, Kim Lim Teong, Mohamed Mohktar Dahari, Dharmalingam P. (39.Khan Hung Eng), Yusoff Abdul Nasir, Ali Ahmed Yusuf, Amid Hassan. Trainer: Mohammed Bakar.
**Goals**: 1-0 Park Chang-Sun (12 penalty), 2-0 Cho Min-Kook (18).

# GROUP 3B

| | | | | |
|---|---|---|---|---|
| 15.03.1985 | Jakarta | Indonesia - Thailand | | 1-0(0-0) |
| 18.03.1985 | Jakarta | Indonesia - Bangladesh | | 2-0(0-0) |
| 21.03.1985 | Jakarta | Indonesia - India | | 2-1(1-1) |
| 23.03.1985 | Bangkok | Thailand - Bangladesh | | 3-0(1-0) |
| 26.03.1985 | Bangkok | Thailand - India | | 0-0 |
| 29.03.1985 | Bangkok | Thailand - Indonesia | | 0-1(0-1) |
| 30.03.1985 | Dhaka | Bangladesh - India | | 1-2(1-1) |
| 02.04.1985 | Dhaka | Bangladesh - Indonesia | | 2-1(0-1) |
| 05.04.1985 | Dhaka | Bangladesh - Thailand | | 1-0(0-0) |
| 06.04.1985 | Calcutta | India - Indonesia | | 1-1(0-1) |
| 09.04.1985 | Calcutta | India - Thailand | | 1-1(0-0) |
| 12.04.1985 | Calcutta | India - Bangladesh | | 2-1(1-1) |

## FINAL STANDINGS

| | | | | | | | | | |
|---|---|---|---|---|---|---|---|---|---|
| 1. | Indonesia | 6 | 4 | 1 | 1 | 8 | - | 4 | 9 |
| 2. | India | 6 | 2 | 3 | 1 | 7 | - | 6 | 7 |
| 3. | Thailand | 6 | 1 | 2 | 3 | 4 | - | 4 | 4 |
| 4. | Bangladesh | 6 | 2 | 0 | 4 | 5 | - | 10 | 4 |

Indonesia qualified for the Zone B – Second Round.

15.03.1985, Senayan Stadium, Jakarta; Attendance: 60,000
Referee: Tulu Gurkan (Philippines)
**INDONESIA - THAILAND**                                                    **1-0(0-0)**
**IDN:** Hermansyah, Ristomoyo, Marzuki, Warta Kusuma, Aun Harhara, Herry Kiswanto, Elly Idris, Lubis Hamdani Zulkanain, Bambang Nurdiansyah (65.Sain), Rully Nere, Tanoto Wahyu (30.Dede Sulaiman). Trainer: Sinyo Aliandu.
**THA:** Surak Chaikitti, Narasak Boonkleang, Sittipultong Thaweepak, Sangnapol Chalermvud, Narong Arjarayult, Sutin Chaikitti, Pairat Rattalerngsuk, Vidthaya Laohakul, Sunthara Klamarong, Boonnum Sukswat (Uthaikul), Hongkajohn Chalor. Trainer: Sainer Chaiyong.
**Goal:** 1-0 Dede Sulaiman (84).

18.03.1985, Senayan Stadium, Jakarta; Attendance: 40,000
Referee: Cesar Brillantes (Philippines)
**INDONESIA - BANGLADESH**                                  **2-0(0-0)**
**IDN:** Hermansyah, Ristomoyo, Tonggo Tambunan (81.Aun Harhara), Nyakmad Marzuki, Herry Kiswanto, Warta Kusuma, Dede Sulaiman, Elly Idris, Lubis Hamdani Zulkanain, Bambang Nurdiansyah (66.Imris), Rully Nere. Trainer: Sinyo Aliandu.
**BAN:** Mohammed Moshin, Nazir Ahmed Alok, Jony Sultan Imtiaz, Abdul Baten, Ali Azmat, Ashrafuddin Ahmed Chunnu (57.Kazi Jashimuddin), Wasim Iqbal Kandokar, Elias Hossain (80.Abdus Mursedi Salam), Ashis Bhadra, Khurshudalam Babul, Hamid Kaiser. Trainer: Abdul Rahim.
**Goals:** 1-0 Bambang Nurdiansyah (48), 2-0 Dede Sulaiman (57).

21.03.1985, Senayan Stadium, Jakarta; Attendance: 70,000
Referee: Reynaldo Reyes (Philippines)
**INDONESIA - INDIA** 2-1(1-1)
**IDN**: Hermansyah, Ristomoyo, Dede Sulaiman, Aun Harhara, Warta Kusuma, Fabanyo Syafudin, Herry Kiswanto, Elly Idris, Lubis Hamdani Zulkanain, Bambang Nurdiansyah (35.Tanoto Wahyu; 78.Ferrel), Rully Nere. Trainer: Sinyo Aliandu.
**IND**: Atanu Bhattachearjee, Ahmed Musher, Tarun Dey, Sudip Chattaerjee, Aloke Mukenjee, Panji Bikash, Bishwaich Bhattachearjee, Mauricio Afanso, Shishir Ghosh, Camillo Gonsalves (55.Narendar Thapa), Krishann Dey (46.Babu Mani). Trainer: Arun Gosh.
**Goals**: 0-1 Krishann Dey (34), 1-1 Bambang Nurdiansyah (41), 2-1 Bambang Nurdiansyah (49).

23.03.1985, Suphachalasai Stadium, Bangkok; Attendance: n/a
Referee: Nakanishi Shunsaku (Japan)
**THAILAND - BANGLADESH** 3-0(1-0)
**THA**: Surak Chaikitti, Sangnapol Chalermvud, Narong Arjarayult, Sutin Chaikitti, Wattana Sompong, Pairuj Ruttalerng (57.Tongmee Sakdarin), Vidthaya Laohakul, Boonnum Sukswat (48.Vitoon Kijmongkol), Hongkajohn Chalor, Thanis Areesngarkul, Nantapraparsil Sompong. Trainer: Sainer Chaiyong.
**BAN**: Mohammed Moshin, Nazir Ahmed Alok, Jony Sultan Imtiaz, Abdul Baten (46.Kumar Das Swapan), Ali Azmat, Kazi Jashimuddin, Wasim Iqbal, Elias Hossain, Ashis Bhadra, Abdus Mursedi Salam (46.Hamid Kaiser), Khurshudalam Babul. Trainer: Abdul Rahim.
**Goals**: 1-0 Thanis Areesngarkul, 2-0 Vitoon Kijmongkol, 3-0 Tongmee Sakdarin.

26.03.1985, Suphachalasai Stadium, Bangkok; Attendance: n/a
Referee: Nakanishi Shunsaku (Japan)
**THAILAND - INDIA** 0-0
**THA**: Surak Chaikitti, Narasak Boonkleang, Voravudh Daengsamer, Sangnapol Chalermvud, Narong Arjarayult, Sutin Chaikitti, Chalit Suttabin, Thanis Areesngarkul, Hongkajohn Chalor, Vidthaya Laohakul, Vitoon Kijmongkol. Trainer: Sainer Chaiyong.
**IND**: Atanu Bhattachearjee, Abdul Mazid, Tarun Dey, Sudip Chattaerjee, Aloke Mukenjee, Panji Bikash, Mauricio Afanso, Camilio Gonsalves, Narendar Thapa, Bishwaich Bhattachearjee, Krishann Dey. Trainer: Arun Gosh.

29.03.1985, Suphachalasai Stadium, Bangkok; Attendance: n/a
Referee: Toshikazu Sano (Japan)
**THAILAND - INDONESIA** 0-1(0-1)
**THA**: Surak Chaikitti, Chalit Suttabin, Voravudh Daengsamer, Wattana Sompong, Sangnapol Chalermvud, Sutin Chaikitti, Hongkajohn Chalor, Thanis Areesngarkul, Nantapraparsil Sompong, Vidthaya Laohakul, Vitoon Kijmongkol. Trainer: Sainer Chaiyong.
**IDN**: Hermansyah, Ristomoyo, Aun Harhara, Warta Kusuma, Nyakmad Marzuki, Herry Kiswanto, Elly Idris, Lubis Hamdani Zulkanain, Bambang Nurdiansyah, Rully Nere, Tanoto Wahyu. Trainer: Sinyo Aliandu.
**Goal**: 0-1 Herry Kiswanto (30).

30.03.1985, Bangabandhu Stadium, Dhaka; Attendance: 8,000
Referee: Liu Jing Li (China P.R.)
**BANGLADESH - INDIA** 1-2(1-1)
**BAN**: Mohammed Moshin, Nazir Ahmed Alok, Jony Sultan Imtiaz, Abdul Baten, Ali Azmat, Ashrafuddin Ahmed Chunnu, Wasim Iqbal, Elias Hossain, Mohamed Aslam (67.Kazi Jashimuddin), Ashis Bhadra, Khurshudalam Babul. Trainer: Abdul Rahim.
**IND**: Atanu Bhattachearjee, Abdul Mazid, Tarun Dey, Sudip Chattaerjee, Aloke Mukenjee, Panji Bikash, Mauricio Afanso, Narendar Thapa, Shishir Ghosh (88.Babu Mani), Bishwaich Bhattachearjee, Krishann Dey. Trainer: Arun Gosh.
**Goals**: 0-1 Shishir Ghosh (34), 1-1 Ashrafuddin Ahmed Chunnu (42), 1-2 Panji Bikash (84).

02.04.1985, Bangabandhu Stadium, Dhaka; Attendance: 5,000
Referee: Xia Changfa (China P.R.)
**BANGLADESH - INDONESIA**     **2-1(0-1)**
**BAN**: Mohammed Moshin, Nazir Ahmed Alok, Jon Sultan Intiaz, Ali Azmat, Ashrafuddin Ahmed Chunnu, Kumar Das Swapan, Wasim Iqbal, Elias Hossain, Ashis Bhadra, Abdus Mursedi Salam (62.Kazi Jashimuddin; 84.Khurshudalam Babul), Hamid Kaiser. Trainer: Abdul Rahim.
**IDN**: Hermansyah, Ristomoyo, Nyakmad Marzuki, Herry Kiswanto, Dede Sulaiman, Warta Kusuma, Aun Harhara, Elly Idris, Lubis Hamdani Zulkanain (23.Ferrel), Bambang Nurdiansyah (76.Imris), Tanoto Wahyu. Trainer: Sinyo Aliandoe.
**Goals**: 0-1 Bambang Nurdiansyah (11), 1-1 Hamid Kaiser (75), 2-1 Ashrafuddin Ahmed Chunnu (81).

05.04.1985, Bangabandhu Stadium, Dhaka; Attendance: 7,000
Referee: Shengcai Chen (China P.R.)
**BANGLADESH - THAILAND**     **1-0(0-0)**
**BAN**: Mohammed Mohsin, Nazir Ahmed Alok, Jony Sultan Imtiaz, Dadal Kumar Roy, Ali Azmat, Kumar Das Swapan, Wasim Iqbal, Elias Hossain, Ashis Bhadra, Ashrafuddin Ahmed Chunnu, Hamid Kaiser. Trainer: Abdul Rahim.
**THA**: Surak Chaikitti, Narasak Boonkleang, Sittipultong Thaweepak, Sunthara Klamarong, Tongmee Sakdarin, Hongkajohn Chalor, Somphol Chomcuen, Voravudh Daengsamer, Numcoke Chaijaleon, Vidthaya Laohakul, Vitoon Kijmongkol. Trainer: Sainer Chaiyong.
**Goal**: 1-0 Elias Hossain (76).
**Sent off**: Vitoon Kijmongkol (77).

06.04.1985, Salt Lake Stadium, Calcutta; Attendance: 10,000
Referee: Mustafa Farouk Towfiq (Iraq)
**INDIA - INDONESIA**     **1-1(0-1)**
**IND**: Atanu Bhattachearjee, Abdul Mazid, Tarun Dey, Sudip Chattaerjee, Aloke Mukenjee, Panji Bikash, Mauricio Afanso, Shishir Ghosh (75.Camillo Gonsalves), Narendar Thapa, Bishwaich Battachearjee (46.Babu Mani), Krishann Dey. Trainer: Arun Gosh.
**IDN**: Hermansyah, Ristomoyo, Aun Harhara, Fabanyo Syafudin, Nyakmad Marzuki, Warta Kusuma, Elly Edris, Lubis Hamdani Zulkanain, Bambang Nurdiansyah (62.Bakhtiyar), Herry Kiswanto, Dede Sulaiman (62.Tonggo Tambunan). Trainer: Sinyo Aliandu.
**Goals**: 0-1 Dede Sulaiman (20), 1-1 Narendar Thapa (89).

09.04.1985, Salt Lake Stadium, Calcutta; Attendance: 6,000
Referee: Abdulkader Abdul Latif Shokor (Iraq)
**INDIA - THAILAND**     **1-1(0-0)**
**IND**: Pratap Ghosh, Mushir Ahmed, Tarun Dey, Sudip Chattaerjee, Perera Derek, Shishir Ghosh, Babu Mani (60.Camillo Gonsalves), KC Murmu, Mauricio Afanso, Bhatiachrsze Bismjit (46.Lal Charanzit), Krishann Dey. Trainer: Arun Gosh.
**THA**: Surak Chaikitti, Pongsamadi Vachari (59.Narasak Boonkleang), Numcoke Chaijaleon, Voravudh Daengsamer, Sittipultong Thaweepak, Sutin Chaikitti, Sunthara Klamarong, Tongmee Sakdarin, Hongkajohn Chalor, Nantapraparsil Sompong, Vidthaya Laohakul. Trainer: Sainer Chaiyong.
**Goals**: 0-1 Narasak Boonkleang (76), 1-1 Tarun Dey (85).

12.04.1985, Salt Lake Stadium, Calcutta; Attendance: 8,000
Referee: Abdul Karim Saadi Salih (Iraq)
**INDIA - BANGLADESH**     **2-1(1-1)**
**IND**: Atanu Bhattachearjee, Pradip Talukdar (40.Camillo Gonsalves), Tarun Dey, Sudip Chattaerjee (64.Ahmed Musher), Aloke Mukenjee, Panji Bikash, Mauricio Afanso, Shishir Ghosh, K.C. Murmu, Abdul Mazid, Krishann Dey. Trainer: Khan Amjad.
**BAN**: Mohammed Moshin, Nazir Ahmed Alok (62.Abdus Mursedi Salam), Jony Sultan Imtiaz, Das Badlal, Ali Azmat, Kumar Das Swapan, Wasim Iqbal, Elias Hossain (46.Dilip), Ashis Bhadra, Ashrafuddin Ahmed Chunnu, Hamid Kaiser. Trainer: Abdul Rahim.

**Goals**: 0-1 Ashis Bhadra (15), 1-1 Panji Bikash (36), 2-1 Camillo Gonsalves (54).

## GROUP 4A

| | | | |
|---|---|---|---|
| 17.02.1985 | Macau | Macau - Brunei | 2-0(0-0) |
| 17.02.1985 | Hong Kong | Hong Kong - China P.R. | 0-0 |
| 20.02.1985 | Macau | Macau - China P.R. | 0-4(0-1) |
| 23.02.1985 | Hong Kong | Hong Kong - Brunei | 8-0(3-0) |
| 26.02.1985 | Macau | China P.R.- Brunei | 8-0(4-0) |
| 01.03.1985 | Hong Kong | Brunei - China P.R. | 0-4(0-2) |
| 06.04.1985 | Bandar Seri Begawan | Brunei - Hong Kong | 1-5(0-3) |
| 13.04.1985 | Bandar Seri Begawan | Brunei - Macau | 1-2(0-0) |
| 28.04.1985 | Macau | Macau - Hong Kong | 0-2(0-0) |
| 04.05.1985 | Hong Kong | Hong Kong - Macau | 2-0(2-0) |
| 12.05.1985 | Beijing | China P.R.- Macau | 6-0(3-0) |
| 19.05.1985 | Beijing | China P.R.- Hong Kong | 1-2(1-1) |

### FINAL STANDINGS

| | | | | | | | | | |
|---|---|---|---|---|---|---|---|---|---|
| 1. | Hong Kong | 6 | 5 | 1 | 0 | 19 | - | 2 | 11 |
| 2. | China P.R. | 6 | 4 | 1 | 1 | 23 | - | 2 | 9 |
| 3. | Macau | 6 | 2 | 0 | 4 | 4 | - | 15 | 4 |
| 4. | Brunei | 6 | 0 | 0 | 6 | 2 | - | 29 | 0 |

Hong Kong qualified for the Zone B – Second Round.

17.02.1985, National Stadium, Macao; Attendance: 495
Referee: Reynaldo Reyes (Philippines)
**MACAU - BRUNEI**     **2-0(0-0)**
**MAC**: Simões Massad, José Babaroca, Lei Peng Kong, Lou Pui Kong (46.Meng Kam Jong), Chi Kit Ng, Cham Sea Con, Fernando Coelho (46.Pun Veng Keong), Lai Keng Wa, Ja Kok Tam, Daniel Pinto, Alberto Carvalhal. Trainer: Chang Meng Hoi.
**BRU**: Ahmad Rahim, George Malek, Ahmad Mohin, Ahmad Salleh, Jaafar Idris, Kasim Ampuan, Rahman Metali, Alinudin Gillen (75.Yakob Abu Bakar), Jaafar Hamid (75.Rahman Badar), Jamhari Lani, Salam Marjuki. Trainer: Ahmad Metarsad.
**Goals**: 1-0 Meng Kam Jong (76), 2-0 Alberto Carvalhal (82).

17.02.1985, Government Stadium, Hong Kong; Attendance: 20,935
Referee: Maidin Bin Singah (Singapore)
**HONG KONG - CHINA P.R.**     **0-0**
**HKG**: Liu Chun Fai, Leung Sui Wing, Yu Kwok Sum, Cheung Chi Tak, Tam Yiu Wah, Cheung Ka Ping (48.Lai Law Kau), Ku Kam Fai, Yue Kin Tak, Wong Kwok On, Lau Wing Yip, Wu Kwok Hung. Trainer: Kwok Ka Ming.
**CHN**: Lu Jan Ren, Zhu Bo, Lin Lou Feng, Lu Hong Xiang, Jia Xiu Quan, Lin Qang, Gu Guang Ming, Zhao Da Yu (83.Li Hua Jun), Zuo Shu Sheng, Li Hui, Yang Zhao Hui (46.Liu Hai Guang). Trainer: Zeng Xue Lin.

20.02.1985, National Stadium, Macau; Attendance: 1,048
Referee: Suppiah Balasundram (Malaysia)
**MACAU - CHINA P.R.** **0-4(0-1)**
**MAC**: Simões Massad, José Babaroca, Chi Kit Ng (85.Pun Veng Keong), Lei Peng Kong, Lai Keng Wa, Chi Vai Moc (83.Tam Kouc Wa), Daniel Pinto, Chi Hong Vong, Wai Hon Wong, Meng Kam Jong, Alberto Carvalhal. Trainer: Chang Meng Hoi.
**CHN**: Lu Jan Ren, Zhu Bo, Lin Lou Feng, Lu Hong Xiang, Jia Xiu Quan, Lin Qang, Gu Guang Ming, Liu Hai Guang, Qin Quo Rong, Zuo Shu Sheng, Li Hui (60.Li Hua Jun). Trainer: Zeng Xue Lin.
**Goals**: 0-1 Li Hui (44), 0-2 Lin Qang (51), 0-3 Zuo Shu Sheng (52), 0-4 Lin Lou Feng (62).

23.02.1985, Government Stadium, Hong Kong; Attendance: 12,401
Referee: Stephen Ovinis (Malaysia)
**HONG KONG - BRUNEI** **8-0(3-0)**
**HKG**: Liu Chun Fai, Leung Sui Wing, Yu Kwok Sum, See Wai Shan (76.Wong Kwok On), Cheung Chi Tak, Ku Kam Fai, Mak King Fun, Lai Wing Cheong, Yue Kin Tak (86.Xong Yiu Shun), Wu Kwok Hung, Lau Wing Yip. Trainer: Kwok Ka Ming.
**BRU**: Ahmad Rahim, Rahman Metali, Ahmad Mohin, Ahmad Salleh, Jaafar Idris, Rahman Badar (32.Jaafar Hamid), Yakob Abu Bakar, Alinudin Gillen, Jamhari Lani, George Malek, Jaafar Sulong. Trainer: Oscar da Silva.
**Goals**: 1-0 Mak King Fun (2), 2-0 Lai Wing Cheong (4), 3-0 See Wai Shan (30), 4-0 Mak King Fun (51), 5-0 Lau Wing Yip (74), 6-0 Mak King Fun (79), 7-0 Mak King Fun (85), 8-0 Lau Wing Yip (87).

26.02.1985, Macau Stadium, Macau; Attendance: 960
Referee: Pamon Saismutr (Thailand)
**CHINA P.R.- BRUNEI** **8-0(4-0)**
**CHN:** Lu Jan Ren, Zhu Bo, Lin Lou Feng, Lu Hong Xiang, Jia Xiu Quan (66.Yang Zhao Hui), Lin Qang (21.Li Hua Jun), Gu Guang Ming, Zhao Du Yu, Zuo Shu Sheng, Li Hui, Liu Hai Guang. Trainer: Zeng Xue Lin.
**BRU**: Ahmad Rahim, George Malek, Ahmad Mohin, Ahmad Salleh, Jaafar Idris, Rahman Metali, Yakob Abu Bakar (71.Ahmad Kassim), Alinudin Gillen, Jamhari Lani (62.Jaafar Hamid), Salam Sulong, Jaafar Sulong. Trainer: Oscar da Silva.
**Goals**: 1-0 Zhao Da Yu (26), 2-0 Jia Xiu Quan (38), 3-0 Li Hui (40), 4-0 Liu Hai Guang (44), 5-0 Liu Hai Guang (47), 6-0 Zuo Shu Sheng (65), 7-0 Zhao Da Yu (85), 8-0 Zhao Da Yu (90).

01.03.1985, Siu Sai Wan Sports Ground, Hong Kong; Attendance: 2,019
Referee: Mohammed Jahirul Haq (Bangladesh)
**BRUNEI - CHINA P.R.** **0-4(0-2)**
**BRU**: Ahmad Rahim, George Malek, Ahmad Mohin, Ahmad Salleh, Jaafar Idris, Ahmad Kassim, Alinudin Gillen, Jaafar Hamid (Jamhari Lani), Rahman Metali, Jaafar Sulong, Salam Marjuki. Trainer: Oscar da Silva.
**CHN**: Lu Jan Ren, Zhu Bo, Lin Lou Feng, Jia Xiu Quan, Lin Qang, Qu Quang Ming, Zhao Da Yu, Zuo Shu Sheng, Li Hui (Yang Zhao Hui), Li Hua Jun (Chi Ming Hua), Liu Hai Guang. Trainer: Zeng Xue Lin.
**Goals**: 0-1 Zhao Da Yu (8), 0-2 Liu Hai Guang (15), 0-3 Zhao Da Yu (74), 0-4 Liu Hai Guang (80).

06.04.1985, "Sultan Hassal Bolkiah" Stadium, Bandar Seri Begawan; Attendance: n/a
Referee: Sudarso Hardjowasito (Indonesia)
**BRUNEI - HONG KONG** **1-5(0-3)**
**BRU**: Jusof Yunus, Ahmad Salleh, Zahrin Zunaidi, George Malek, Ali Rashad, Kassim Zainudin, Faisal Mohamed Eusoff, Alinudin Gillen, Jaafar Sulong, Sahari Timbang, Salam Marjuki. Trainer: Oscar da Silva.
**HKG**: Chan Wan Ngok, Leung Sui Wing, Yu Kwok Sum, Lai Law Kau, Wan Chi Keung, Cheung Chi Tak, Chan Fat Chi, Lai Wing Cheong (Wong Yiu Shun), Ku Kam Fai, Wu Kwok Hung, Lau Wing Yip. Trainer: Kwok Ka Ming.

**Goals**: 0-1 Wan Chi Keung (4), 0-2 Lai Wing Cheung (7), 0-3 Lau Wing Yip (38), 1-3 Kassim Zainudin (49), 1-4 Wan Chi Keung (82), 1-5 Lau Wing Yip (83).

13.04.1985, "Sultan Hassal Bolkiah" Stadium, Bandar Seri Begawan; Attendance: n/a
Referee: Djadja Mudjahidin (Indonesia)
**BRUNEI - MACAU**      **1-2(0-0)**
**BRU**: Jusof Yunus, Ahmad Salleh, George Malek, Kassim Zainudin, Ahmad Mohin, Jaafar Idris, Yakob Abu Baka (Ahmed Rahim), Jaafar Sulong, Sahari Timbang, Jamhari Lani, Rahman Metali. Trainer: Oscar da Silva.
**MAC**: Simões Massad, Cham Sea Con, Chi Kit Ng, Lei Peng Kong, Lai Keng Wa, Lou Pui Kong, Daniel Pinto, Wai Hon Wong, Alberto Carvalhal, Meng Kam Jong, Tam Kouc Wa. Trainer: Chang Meng Hoi.
**Goals**: Ahmed Rahim / Alberto Carvalhal, Daniel Pinto.

28.04.1985, Estadio Campo Desportivo, Macau; Attendance: n/a
Referee: Patcharamukdakorn Somporn (Thailand)
**MACAU - HONG KONG**      **0-2(0-0)**
**MAC**: Simões Massad, José Babaroca (63.Victor Hugo), Lei Peng Kong, Cham Sea Con, Lai Keng Wa, Chi Kit Ng, Daniel Pinto, Wai Hon Wong, Alberto Carvalhal, Meng Kam Jong, Tam Kouc Wa. Trainer: Oscar da Silva.
**HKG**: Chan Wan Ngok (60.Liu Chun Fai), Leung Sui Wing, Yu Kwok Sum, Lai Law Kau, See Wai Shan (60.Cheung Ka Ping), Cheung Chi Tak, Ku Kam Fai, Wan Chi Cheung, Wong Kwok On, Wu Kwok Hung, Lau Wing Yip. Trainer: Kwok Ka Ming.
**Goals**: 0-1 Lau Wing Yip (80), 0-2 Cheung Ka Ping (88).

04.05.1985, Government Stadium, Hong Kong; Attendance: n/a
Referee: Kil Ki-Chul (South Korea)
**HONG KONG - MACAU**      **2-0(2-0)**
**HKG**: Chan Wan Ngok, Cheung Chi Tak, Leung Sui Wing, Ku Kam Fai, Yu Kwok Sum, Chan Fat Chi, Wu Kwok Hung (See Wai Shan), Lai Wing Cheong, Cheung Ka Ping (Wong Kwok On), Wan Chi Keung, Lau Wing Yip. Trainer: Kwok Ka Ming.
**MAC**: Simões Massad, José Babaroca, Wai Hon Wong, Lei Peng Kong, Chi Kit Ng, Lai Keng Wa, Cham Sea Con, Daniel Pinto, Meng Kam Jong (Victor Hugo), Alberto Carvalhal, Ja Kok Tam. Trainer: Oscar da Silva.
**Goals**: 1-0 Lau Wing Yip (8), 2-0 Lau Wing Yip (30).

12.05.1985, Workers Stadium, Beijing; Attendance: 30,000
Referee: Shetty Sheena (India)
**CHINA P.R.- MACAU**      **6-0(3-0)**
**CHN**: Lu Jan Ren, Zhu Bo, Lin Lou Feng, Lu Hong Xiang, Jia Xiu Quan, Lin Qang, Gu Guang Ming (65.Zhao Da Yu), Zuo Shu Sheng (46.Li Hua Jun), Li Hui, Wang Hui Liang, Yang Zhao Hui. Trainer: Zeng Xue Lin.
**MAC**: Simões Massad, José Babaroca (85.Chi Hong Vong), Chi Kit Ng, Lei Peng Kong, Lai Keng Wa, Cham Sea Con, Victor Hugo, Fernando Coelho (70.Pun Veng Keong), Alberto Carvalhal, Meng Kam Jong, Kok Va Tar. Trainer: Oscar da Silva.
**Goals**: 1-0 Jia Xiu Quan (10), 2-0 Li Hui (12), 3-0 Yang Zhao Hui (27), 4-0 Yang Zhao Hui (50), 5-0 Wang Hui Liang (60), 6-0 Zhao Da Yu (67).

19.05.1985, Workers Stadium, Beijing; Attendance: 60,000
Referee: Referee: Melvyn J. Victor D'Souza (India)
**CHINA P.R.- HONG KONG** **1-2(1-1)**
**CHN:** Lu Jan Ren, Zhu Bo, Lin Lou Feng, Lu Hong Xiang, Jia Xiu Quan, Lin Qang, Gu Guang Ming, Zuo Shu Sheng (40.Li Hua Jun), Li Hui, Wang Hui Liang (65.Zhao Da Yu), Yang Zhao Hui. Trainer: Zeng Xue Lin.
**HKG**: Chan Wan Ngok, Leung Sui Wing, Yu Kwok Sum, Lai Law Kau, Chan Fat Chi (81.Tam Yiu Wa), Wan Chi Keung, Ku Kam Fai, Cheung Chi Tak, Wong Kwok On, Lau Wing Yip, Wu Kwok Hung. Trainer: Kwok Ka Ming.
**Goals**: 0-1 Lau Wing Yip (26), 1-1 Li Hui (32), 1-2 Wong Kwok On (60).

## GROUP 4B

| Date | Venue | Match | Score |
|---|---|---|---|
| 19.01.1985 | Singapore | Singapore - North Korea | 1-1(1-0) |
| 23.02.1985 | Singapore | Singapore - Japan | 1-3(1-1) |
| 21.03.1985 | Tokyo | Japan - North Korea | 1-0(1-0) |
| 30.04.1985 | P'yŏngyang | North Korea - Japan | 0-0 |
| 18.05.1985 | Tokyo | Japan - Singapore | 5-0(0-0) |
| 25.05.1985 | P'yŏngyang | North Korea - Singapore | 2-0(1-0) |

### FINAL STANDINGS

| | | | | | | | | |
|---|---|---|---|---|---|---|---|---|
| 1. | Japan | 4 | 3 | 1 | 0 | 9 - 1 | 7 |
| 2. | North Korea | 4 | 1 | 2 | 1 | 3 - 2 | 4 |
| 3. | Singapore | 4 | 0 | 1 | 3 | 2 - 11 | 1 |

Japan qualified for the Zone B - Second Round.

19.01.1985, National Stadium, Singapore; Attendance: n/a
Referee: Hardjowasito Sudarso (Indonesia)
**SINGAPORE - NORTH KOREA** **1-1(1-0)**
**SIN**: David Lee Chye Soon, Malek Awab, Arj Mani, Rahman Latif (Yahya Madon), Shafik Norhalis, Hashim Hosni, Tokijan Darimosuvito, Dali Sudiat, Saad Razali, Pak Kwan Au Yeong, Tay Peng Kee. Trainer: Hussein Al Junied.
**PRK**: Kim Gang-Il, Kim Gwang-Sung, Oh Yong-Nam, Kim Gwang-Min, Kim Jong-Hun, Kim Hun, Kim Jong-Su, Li Jong-Man, Han Hyong-Il (Tao Un-Choi), Song Chol-Yu, Tak Yong Bin. Trainer: Jong Yong-Song.
**Goals**: 1-0 Pak Kwan Au Yeong, 1-1 Song Chol-Yu (penalty).

23.02.1985, National Stadium, Singapore; Attendance: 16,146
Referee: Soetoyo Hartasardjono (Indonesia)
**SINGAPORE - JAPAN** **1-3(1-1)**
**SIN**: David Lee Chye Soon, Malek Awab, Arj Mani, Dali Sudiat, Saad Razali, Shafik Norhalis, Hashim Hosni (67.Ramu S.), Tokijan Darimosuvito, Yahya Madon, Pak Kwan Au Yeong, Tay Peng Kee. Trainer: Hussein Al Junied.
**JPN**: Kiyotaka Matsui, Yasutaro Matsuki, Akira Ishikami, Hisashi Kato, Satoshi Tsunami, Akihiro Nishimura, Satoshi Miyauchi, Atsushi Uchiyama, Kazushi Kimura, Koichi Hashiratani, Hiromi Hara. Trainer: Takaji Mori.
**Goals**: 0-1 Kazushi Kimura (20), 1-1 Yahya Madon (39), 1-2 Koichi Hashiratani (47), 1-3 Hisashi Kato (84 penalty).

21.03.1985, Yoyoki National Stadium, Tokyo; Attendance: 25,000
Referee: Timothy Joseph (Malaysia)
**JAPAN - NORTH KOREA** **1-0(1-0)**
**JPN:** Kiyotaka Matsui, Hisashi Kato, Akira Ishikami, Yasutaro Matsuki, Satoshi Tsunami, Akihiro Nishimura, Kazushi Kimura (75.Hiroshi Hirakawa), Satoshi Miyauchi, Takafumi Mizunuma, Hiromi Hara, Koichi Hashiratani. Trainer: Takaji Mori.
**PRK:** Kim Gang-Il, Kim Gwang-Sung, Oh Yong-Nam, Mun Gwang-Ok, Kim Jong-Hun, Kim Yong-Nam (58.Oh Dong-Kun), Han Hyong-Il, Yun Jong-Su, Kim Jong-Man, Kim Gwang-Ho, Li Jong-Man. Trainer: Jong Yong-Song
**Goal:** 1-0 Hiromi Hara (20).

30.04.1985, "Kim Il-Song" Stadium, P'yŏngyang; Attendance: 80,000
Referee: Samuel Chan Yam-Ming (Hong Kong)
**NORTH KOREA - JAPAN** **0-0**
**PRK:** Kim Gang-Il, Kim Gwang-Sung, Oh Yong-Nam, Kim Jong-Man, Li Bong-Nam, Li Jong-Man, Yun Jong-Su, Kim Gwang-Ho, Kim Yong-Nam, Tak Yong-Bin, Han Hyong-Il. Trainer: Jong Yong-Song.
**JPN:** Kiyotaka Matsui, Yutaka Ikeuchi, Akira Ishikami, Hisashi Kato, Satoshi Tsunami, Akihiro Nishimura, Satoshi Miyauchi, Kazushi Kimura (59.Hiroshi Hirakawa), Takafumi Mizunuma, Koichi Hashiratani, Hiromi Hara. Trainer: Takaji Mori.

18.05.1985, Yoyoki National Stadium, Tokyo; Attendance: 28,000
Referee: Cha Kyung-Bok (South Korea)
**JAPAN - SINGAPORE** **5-0(0-0)**
**JPN:** Kiyotaka Matsui, Yasutaro Matsuki, Akira Ishikami (70.Shinji Tanaka), Hisashi Kato, Satoshi Tsunami, Akihiro Nishimura, Kazuaki Nagasawa, Kazushi Kimura, Takafumi Mizunuma, Hiromi Hara, Koichi Hashiratani. Trainer: Takaji Mori.
**SIN:** David Lee Chye Soon, Malek Awab, Rahman Latif, Shafik Norhalis, Ramu S., Dali Sudiat, Saad Razali, Arj Mani, Tay Peng Kee, Pak Kwan Au Yeong, Tokijan. Trainer: Hussein Al Junied.
**Goals:** 1-0 Takafumi Mizunuma (48), 2-0 Akihiro Nishimura (57), 3-0 Akihiro Nishimura (59), 4-0 Hiromi Hara (79), 5-0 Kazumi Kimura (86).
**Sent off:** Ramu S. (9)

25.05.1985, Nampo Stadium, Nampo; Attendance: 25,000
Referee: Sukho Vuddhijoti (Thailand)
**NORTH KOREA - SINGAPORE** **2-0(1-0)**
**PRK:** Kim Gang-Il, Kim Gwang-Min, Oh Yong-Nam, Kim Jong-Hun, Jong Chol-Ho, Li Jong-Man, Yun Jong-Su, Kim Jong-Su, Han Hyong-Il, Kim Jong-Man, Tak Yong-Bin. Trainer: Jong Yong-Song.
**SIN:** David Lee Chye Soon, Dali Sudiat, Rahman Latif, Shafik Norhalis, Malek Awab, Saad Razali, Arj Mani, Tay Peng Kee, Yahya Madon, Tokijan Darimosuvito, Rashid Razali. Trainer: Hussein Al Junied.
**Goals:** 1-0 Yun Jong-Su (25), 2-0 Han Hyong-Il (55).

# ZONE B – SECOND ROUND

| 21.07.1985 | Seoul | South Korea - Indonesia | 2-0(0-0) |
|---|---|---|---|
| 30.07.1985 | Jakarta | Indonesia - South Korea | 1-4(0-3) |

### FINAL STANDINGS

| | | | | | | | | |
|---|---|---|---|---|---|---|---|---|
| 1. | South Korea | 2 | 2 | 0 | 0 | 6 - 1 | 4 |
| 2. | Indonesia | 2 | 0 | 0 | 2 | 1 - 6 | 0 |

South Korea qualified for the Zone A - Final Round.

21.07.1985, Olympic Stadium, Seoul; Attendance: 80,000
Referee: Booncherd Pratumthong (Thailand)
**SOUTH KOREA - INDONESIA**     **2-0(0-0)**
**KOR:** Oh Yeon-Kyo, Chung Jong-Soo, Cho Kwang-Rae, Chung Yong-Hwan, Kim Seok-Won (61.Kim Joo-Sung), Choi Soon-Ho, Park Chang-Sun (Cap), Kim Pyung-Seok, Cho Min-Kook, Yoo Byung-Ok, Huh Jung-Moo (39.Byun Byung-Joo). Trainer: Kim Jung-Nam.
**IDN:** Hermansyah, Ristomoyo, Didik Dharmadi (31.Aun Harhara), Warta Kusuma, Elly Idris, Zulkarnain Lubis, Bambang Nurdiansyah, Rully Nere, Nyakmad Marzuki, Herry Kiswanto, Dede Sulaiman. Trainer: Sinyo Aliandu.
**Goals**: 1-0 Byun Byung-Joo (74), 2-0 Kim Joo-Sung (82).

30.07.1985, Senayan Stadium, Jakarta; Attendance: 80,000
Referee: Timothy Joseph (Malaysia)
**INDONESIA - SOUTH KOREA**     **1-4(0-3)**
**IDN:** Hermansyah (22.Toni Ratiperisa), Ristomoyo, Didik Dharmadi, Warta Kusuma, Elly Idris, Bambang Nurdiansyah, Rully Nere, Nyakmad Marzuki, Noah Meriem (71.Lubis Hamdani Zulkanain), Herry Kiswanto, Dede Sulaiman. Trainer: Sinyo Aliandu.
**KOR:** Choi In-Young, Chung Jong-Soo, Cho Kwang-Rae, Chung Yong-Hwan, Choi Soon-Ho (61.Lee Tae-Ho), Park Chang-Sun (Cap), Byun Byung-Joo, Kim Pyung-Seok, Yoo Byung-Ok, Kim Joo-Sung, Huh Jung-Moo (56.Cho Young-Jeung). Trainer: Kim Jung-Nam.
**Goals**: 0-1 Byun Byung-Joo (7), 0-2 Choi Soon-Ho (9), 0-3 Jung-Moo Huh (32), 0-4 Kim Joo-Sung (47), 1-4 Dede Sulaiman (87).

| 11.08.1985 | Kobe | Japan - Hong Kong | 3-0(2-0) |
|---|---|---|---|
| 22.09.1985 | Hong Kong | Hong Kong - Japan | 1-2(0-1) |

### FINAL STANDINGS

| | | | | | | | | |
|---|---|---|---|---|---|---|---|---|
| 1. | Japan | 2 | 2 | 0 | 0 | 5 - 1 | 4 |
| 2. | Hong Kong | 2 | 0 | 0 | 2 | 1 - 5 | 0 |

Japan qualified for the Zone A - Final Round.

11.08.1985, Kobe Sports Complex Athletics Stadium Kobe; Attendance: 19,000
Referee: Tulu Gurkan (Philippines)
**JAPAN - HONG KONG**     **3-0(2-0)**
**JPN:** Kiyotaka Matsui, Antaro Matsuka, Hisashi Kato (Cap), Yutaka Ikeuchi, Satoshi Tsunami, Akihiro Nishimura, Satoshi Miyauchi, Kazumi Kimura (68.Takeshi Okada), Takafumi Mizunuma, Koichi Hashiratani (78.Satoshi Tetsuka), Hiromi Hara. Trainer: Takaji Mori.
**HKG:** Liu Chun Fai, Leung Sui Wing, Lai Law Kau, Cheung Chi Tak, Wong Yiu Shun, Ku Kam Fai, Wan Chi Cheung, Yue Kin Tak, Wong Kwok On, Wu Kwok Hung, Lau Wing Yip. Trainer: Kwok Ka Ming.

**Goals**: 1-0 Kazumi Kimura (9 penalty), 2-0 Hiromi Hara (21), 3-0 Takafumi Mizunuma (53).

22.09.1985, Government Stadium, Hong Kong; Attendance: 28,000
Referee: Lee Kok Leong (Singapore)
**HONG KONG - JAPAN**                                **1-2(0-1)**
**HKG**: Liu Chun Fai, Leung Sui Wong, Yu Kwok Sum, Cheung Chi Tak, Wan Chi Keung, Mak King Fun (66.Wong Yiu Shun), Lai Wing Cheong (41.Lau Wing Yip), Yue Kin Tak, Wong Kwok On, Wu Kwok Hung, Ku Kam Fai. Trainer: Kwok Ka Ming.
**JPN**: Shinichi Morishita, Antaro Matsuka, Hisashi Kato (Cap), Akira Ishikami, Toshinobu Katsuya, Akihiro Nishimura, Satoshi Miyauchi, Kazumi Kimura (63.Satoshi Tetsuka), Takafumi Mizunuma, Koichi Hashiratani, Hiromi Hara. Trainer: Takaji Mori.
**Goals**: 0-1 Kazumi Kimura (45), 1-1 Chi Keung Wang (79 penalty), 1-2 Hiromi Hara (90).

## ZONE B – FINAL ROUND

| 26.10.1985 | Tokyo | Japan - South Korea | 1-2(1-2) |
| 03.11.1985 | Seoul | South Korea - Japan | 1-0(0-0) |

### FINAL STANDINGS

| | | | | | | | | |
|---|---|---|---|---|---|---|---|---|
| 1. | **South Korea** | 2 | 2 | 0 | 0 | 3 | - 1 | 4 |
| 2. | Japan | 2 | 0 | 0 | 2 | 1 | - 3 | 0 |

South Korea qualified for the Final Tournament.

26.10.1985, Yoyoki National Stadium, Tokyo; Attendance: 62,000
Referee: Maidin Bin Singh (Singapore)
**JAPAN - SOUTH KOREA**                           **1-2(1-2)**
**JPN**: Kiyotaka Matsui, Hisashi Kato (Cap), Akira Ishikami, Yasutaro Matsuki, Satoshi Tsunami, Akihiro Nishimura, Kazushi Kimura (82.George Yonashiro), Tetsuya Totsuka (77.Hiroshi Hirakawa), Takafumi Mizunuma, Satoshi Miyauchi, Hiromi Hara. Trainer: Takaji Mori.
**KOR**: Cho Byung-Deouk, Park Kyung-Hoon, Cho Kwang-Rae, Chung Yong-Hwan, Lee Tae-Ho (78.Cho Young-Jeung), Choi Soon-Ho, Park Chang-Sun (Cap), Byun Byung-Joo, Kim Pyung-Seok, Cho Min-Kook, Kim Joo-Sung (46.Kim Jong-Boo). Trainer: Kim Jung-Nam.
**Goals**: 0-1 Chung Yong-Hwan (30), 0-2 Lee Tae-Ho (42), 1-2 Kazushi Kimura (43).

03.11.1985, Olympic Stadium, Seoul; Attendance: 70,000
Referee: Othman Bin Omar (Malaysia)
**SOUTH KOREA - JAPAN**                           **1-0(0-0)**
**KOR**: Cho Byung-Deouk, Park Kyung-Hoon, Cho Kwang-Rae, Chung Yong-Hwan, Lee Tae-Ho (46.Huh Jung-Moo), Kim Jong-Boo, Choi Soon-Ho, Park Chang-Sun (Cap), Kim Pyung-Seok, Cho Min-Kook, Kim Joo-Sung. Trainer: Kim Jung-Nam.
**JPN**: Kiyotaka Matsui, Hisashi Kato (Cap), Akira Ishikami (46.Takeshi Koshida), Toshinobu Katsuya, Satoshi Tsunami, George Yonashiro, Kazushi Kimura, Tetsuya Totsuka (80.Hiroshi Hirakawa), Satoshi Miyauchi, Hiromi Hara, Koichi Hashiratani. Trainer: Takaji Mori.
**Goal**: 1-0 Huh Jung-Moo (61).

# OCEANIA

| | | | | |
|---|---|---|---|---|
| 03.09.1985 | Tel Aviv | Israel - Taiwan | | 6-0(3-0) |
| 08.09.1985 | Tel Aviv | Taiwan - Israel | | 0-5(0-2) |
| 21.09.1985 | Auckland | New Zealand - Australia | | 0-0 |
| 05.10.1985 | Auckland | New Zealand - Taiwan | | 5-1(3-1) |
| 08.10.1985 | Tel Aviv | Israel - Australia | | 1-2(0-0) |
| 12.10.1985 | Christchurch | Taiwan - New Zealand | | 0-5(0-2) |
| 20.10.1985 | Melbourne | Australia - Israel | | 1-1(1-0) |
| 23.10.1985 | Adelaide | Australia - Taiwan | | 7-0(2-0) |
| 26.10.1985 | Auckland | New Zealand - Israel | | 3-1(2-1) |
| 27.10.1985 | Sydney | Taiwan - Australia | | 0-8(0-1) |
| 03.11.1985 | Sydney | Australia - New Zealand | | 2-0(1-0) |
| 10.11.1985 | Tel Aviv | Israel - New Zealand | | 3-0(0-0) |

### FINAL STANDINGS

| | | | | | | | | | |
|---|---|---|---|---|---|---|---|---|---|
| 1. | Australia | 6 | 4 | 2 | 0 | 20 | - | 2 | 10 |
| 2. | Israel | 6 | 3 | 1 | 2 | 17 | - | 6 | 7 |
| 3. | New Zealand | 6 | 3 | 1 | 2 | 13 | - | 7 | 7 |
| 4. | Taiwan | 6 | 0 | 0 | 6 | 1 | - | 36 | 0 |

Australia qualified for the Intercontinental Play-offs.

03.09.1985, National Stadium, Ramat-Gan, Tel Aviv; Attendance: 30,000
Referee: Mircea Salomir (Romania)
**ISRAEL - TAIWAN**     **6-0(3-0)**
**ISR:** Arie Haviv, Gadi Machnes (21.Gabriel Lasri), Shlomo Kirat, Avi Cohen I, David Pizanti, Uri Malmilian, Rifat Turk, Yaacov Ekhoiz (76.Roni Rosenthal), Moshe Sinai, Zahi Armeli, Eli Ohana. Trainer: Yosef Mirmovich.
**TPE**: Lien Jim-hen, Chen Sing, Shiao Yung-fu, Chang Yao-chuan (32.Huang Sung-shun), Chang Huey-shiong, Wu Shui-chi, Chen In-jen, Tsai Hong-yee (76.Yu Ming-jen), Duh Deng-sheng, Duh Deng-chyan, Wang Yi-wen. Trainer: Chiang Chia.
**Goals**: 1-0 Rifat Turk (30), 2-0 Rifat Turk (33), 3-0 Zahi Armeli (39), 4-0 Uri Malmilian (54), 5-0 Rifat Turk (74), 6-0 Uri Malmilian (89).

08.09.1985, National Stadium, Ramat-Gan, Tel Aviv; Attendance: 10,000
Referee: Ioan Igna (Romania)
**TAIWAN - ISRAEL**     **0-5(0-2)**
**TPE**: Lien Jim-hen, Chen Sing (63.Yu Ming-jen), Shiao Yung-fu, Chang Huey-shiong, Chang Yao-chuan, Tsai Hong-yee, Chen In-jen, Chen Jing-an (79.Wang Yi-wen), Huang Sung-shun, Duh Deng-sheng, Duh Deng-chyan. Trainer: Chiang Chia.
**ISR:** Arie Haviv, Gabriel Lasri (26.Roni Rosenthal), Shlomo Kirat, Avi Cohen I, David Pizanti, Uri Malmilian, Rifat Turk, Yaacov Ekhoiz, Moshe Sinai, Zahi Armeli, Eli Ohana. Trainer: Yosef Mirmovich.
**Goals**: 0-1 Avi Cohen I (7), 0-2 Zahi Armeli (18), 0-3 Eli Ohana (56), 0-4 Eli Ohana (72), 0-5 Eli Ohana (79).

21.09.1985, Mount Smart Stadium, Auckland; Attendance: 14,826
Referee: Keith Hackett (England)
**NEW ZEALAND - AUSTRALIA**                                          **0-0**
**NZL**: Francesco Maria van Hattum, Shane Rufer, Allan Roderick Boath, Ceri Evans, Malcolm Dunford, Kenneth Grant Cresswell, Declan John Edge (89.Peter Henry), Steven Paul Sumner, Grant John Turner, Wynton Alan Whai Rufer, Colin Walker. Trainer: Kevin Fallon.
**AUS**: Terry Greedy, Charles Yankos, Zarko Odzakov, David Ratcliffe, Steve O'Connor (60.Robert Dunn), Graham Jennings, Joseph Watson, Ken Murphy, Oscar Crino, John Kosmina, David Mitchell. Trainer: Frank Arok.

05.10.1985, Mount Smart Stadium, Auckland; Attendance: 5,152
Referee: Christopher Francis Bambridge (Australia)
**NEW ZEALAND - TAIWAN**                                             **5-1(3-1)**
**NZL**: Francesco Maria van Hattum, Allan Roderick Boath (29.Sean Patrick Byrne), Richard Mulligan, Ceri Evans, Malcolm Dunford, Kenneth Grant Cresswell, Duncan Edward Cole, Steven Paul Sumner, Grant John Turner, Colin Walker, Declan John Edge. Trainer: Kevin Fallon.
**TPE**: Chiou Jeng-tsair, Chen In-jen, Shiao Yung-fu, Tsai Hong-yee, Wang Duen-jeng, Chen Jing-an, Liu Jung-tsung, Chang Chun-kuei, Chang Yao-chuan, Duh Deng-chyan, Deng Sheng Duh, Trainer: Chiang Chia.
**Goals**: 1-0 Declan John Edge (13), 2-0 Colin Walker (25), 3-0 Steven Paul Sumner (31 penalty), 3-1 Chen Jing-an (42), 4-1 Steven Paul Sumner (51), 5-1 Steven Paul Sumner (89).

08.10.1985, National Stadium, Ramat-Gan, Tel Aviv; Attendance: 45,000
Referee: Luigi Agnolin (Italy)
**ISRAEL - AUSTRALIA**                                               **1-2(0-0)**
**ISR**: Arie Haviv, Gadi Machnes (50.Roni Rosenthal), Shlomo Kirat (61.Moshe Selecter), Avi Cohen I, David Pizanti, Uri Malmilian, Rifat Turk, Yaacov Ekhoiz, Moshe Sinai, Zahi Armeli, Eli Ohana. Trainer: Yosef Mirmovich.
**AUS**: Terry Greedy (37.Jeff Olver), Charles Yankos, Alan Davidson, David Ratcliffe, Steve O'Connor, Graham Jennings, Joseph Watson (82.Robert Dunn), Oscar Crino, Ken Murphy, John Kosmina, David Mitchell. Trainer: Frank Arok.
**Goals**: 0-1 David Mitchell (46), 0-2 John Kosmina (49), 1-2 Zahi Armeli (65).
**Sent off**: Ken Murphy (85).

12.10.1985, "Queen Elizabeth II" Stadium, Christchurch (New Zealand); Attendance: 5,200
Referee: Don Campbell (Australia)
**TAIWAN - NEW ZEALAND**                                             **0-5(0-2)**
**TPE**: Chiou Jeng-tsair, Chen In-jen, Shiao Yung-fu (77.Chang Huey-shiong), Liu Jung-tsung, Wang Duen-jeng, Chang Yao-chuan, Chang Chun-kuei (71.Yu Ming-jen), Tsai Hong-yee, Duh Deng-chyan, Deng Sheng Duh, Chen Jing-an, Trainer: Chiang Chia.
**NZL**: Francesco Maria van Hattum, Richard Mulligan, Ceri Evans, Allan Roderick Boath, Malcolm Dunford, Kenneth Grant Cresswell, Duncan Edward Cole, Steven Paul Sumner (46.Kevin Hagan), Declan John Edge, Grant John Turner, Colin Walker. Trainer: Kevin Fallon.
**Goals**: 0-1 Allan Roderick Boath 19, 0-2 Grant John Turner (32), 0-3 Colin Walker (57), 0-4 Colin Walker (65 penalty), 0-5 Grant John Turner (76).

20.10.1985, Olympic Park, Melbourne; Attendance: 27,000
Referee: José Rosa Dos Santos (Portugal)
**AUSTRALIA - ISRAEL**      **1-1(1-0)**
**AUS**: Terry Greedy, Charles Yankos, Alan Davidson, David Ratcliffe, Steve O'Connor, Graham Jennings, Joseph Watson (82.James Patikas), Zarko Odzakov, Oscar Crino, John Kosmina, David Mitchell. Trainer: Frank Arok.
**ISR**: Arie Haviv, Zion Marili, Shlomo Kirat, Avi Cohen I, David Pizanti, Uri Malmilian (79.Moshe Selecter), Rifat Turk (68.Roni Rosenthal), Yaacov Ekhoiz, Moshe Sinai, Zahi Armeli, Eli Ohana. Trainer: Yosef Mirmovich
**Goals**: 1-0 David Ratcliffe (32), 1-1 Avi Cohen I (47).
**Sent off**: Eli Ohana (65).

23.10.1985, Hindmarsh Stadium, Adelaide; Attendance: 2,000
Referee: John Cameron (New Zealand)
**AUSTRALIA - TAIWAN**      **7-0(2-0)**
**AUS**: Jeff Olver, Zarko Odzakov, Steve O'Connor, David Ratcliffe, Graham Jennings, James Patikas, Ken Murphy (46.Frank Farina), Robert Dunn, Oscar Crino (78.Ian Gray), David Mitchell, Graham Arnold. Trainer: Frank Arok.
**TPE**: Chiou Jeng-tsair (78.Yang Ji-hsiung), Shiao Yung-fu, Chang Chun-kuei (65.Liu Jung-tsung), Chen In-jen, Chang Yao-chuan, Chien I-shiu, Chen Jing-an, Tsai Hong-yee, Wang Duen-jeng, Duh Deng-sheng, Duh Deng-chyan. Trainer: Chiang Chia.
**Goals**: 1-0 Robert Dunn (2), 2-0 Chang Chun-kuei (13 own goal), 3-0 David Mitchell (57), 4-0 David Mitchell (59), 5-0 Graham Arnold (68), 6-0 David Mitchell (87), 7-0 Robert Dunn (89 penalty).

26.10.1985, Mount Smart Stadium, Auckland; Attendance: 10,600
Referee: Egbert Mulder (Holland)
**NEW ZEALAND - ISRAEL**      **3-1(2-1)**
**NZL**: Francesco Maria van Hattum, Shane Rufer, Ceri Evans, Allan Roderick Boath, Malcolm Dunford, Kenneth Grant Cresswell, Grant John Turner, Duncan Edward Cole (4.Steven Paul Sumner), Declan John Edge (74.Kevin Hagan), Colin Walker, Wynton Alan Whai Rufer. Trainer: Kevin Fallon.
**ISR**: Boni Ginzburg, Zion Marili, Nissim Barda (42.Moshe Selecter), Avi Cohen I, David Pizanti, Uri Malmilian (83.Nissim Cohen), Shlomo Kirat, Yaacov Ekhoiz, Moshe Sinai, Zahi Armeli, Roni Rosenthal. Trainer: Yosef Mirmovich.
**Goals**: 1-0 Wynton Alan Whai Rufer (3), 1-1 Zahi Armeli (23), 2-1 Malcolm Dunford (29), 3-1 Colin Walker (68).

27.10.1985, "St. George" Stadium, Sydney; Attendance: 2,694
Referee: William Munro (New Zealand)
**TAIWAN - AUSTRALIA**      **0-8(0-1)**
**TPE**: Yang Ji-hsiung, Shiao Yung-fu (46.Liu Jung-tsung), Chang Chun-kuei, Chen In-jen, Chang Yao-chuan, Yu Ming-jen, Tsai Hong-yee, Chen Jing-an, Chien I-shiu, Duh Deng-sheng, Duh Deng-chyan. Trainer: Chiang Chia.
**AUS**: Terry Greedy, Zarko Odzakov, Charles Yankos, David Ratcliffe, Graham Jennings (60.Tom McCulloch), Joseph Watson, Robert Dunn, Oscar Crino, Frank Farina, John Kosmina, Graeme Arnold (73.Ian Gray). Trainer: Frank Arok.
**Goals**: 0-1 Zarko Odzakov (41), 0-2 Oscar Crino (52), 0-3 Zarko Odzakov (56), 0-4 John Kosmina (65 penalty), 0-5 Zarko Odzakov (69), 0-6 John Kosmina (72), 0-7 John Kosmina (88), 0-8 Ian Gray (89).

03.11.1985, Sports Ground, Sydney; Attendance: 21,910
Referee: Gerard Geurds (Holland)
**AUSTRALIA - NEW ZEALAND** **2-0(1-0)**
**AUS:** Terry Greedy, Charles Yankos, Alan Davidson, David Ratcliffe, Steve O'Connor, Graham Jennings, Joseph Watson (74.Zarko Odazkov), Oscar Crino, Ken Murphy, John Kosmina, David Mitchell. Trainer: Frank Arok.
**NZL:** Francesco Maria van Hattum, Shane Rufer (65.Richard Mulligan), Malcolm Dunford, Ceri Evans, Kenneth Grant Cresswell, Allan Roderick Boath, Steven Paul Sumner (56.Declan John Edge), Richard Lloyd Herbert, Grant John Turner, Wynton Alan Whai Rufer, Colin Walker. Trainer: Kevin Fallon.
**Goals:** 1-0 John Kosmina (12), 2-0 David Mitchell (48).

10.11.1985, National Stadium, Ramat-Gan, Tel Aviv; Attendance: 4,500
Referee: Dieter Pauly (West Germany)
**ISRAEL - NEW ZEALAND** **3-0(0-0)**
**ISR:** Arie Haviv, Gabriel Lasri, Shlomo Kirat, Nissim Barda, Zion Marili, Uri Malmilian, Nissim Cohen, Yaacov Ekhoiz, Moshe Sinai (Efraim Davidi), Zahi Armeli, Moshe Selecter. Trainer: Yosef Mirmovich.
**NZL:** Francesco Maria van Hattum, Richard Mulligan, Sean Patrick Byrne, Malcolm Dunford, Ceri Evans, Kenneth Grant Cresswell, William McClure, Allan Roderick Boath (46.Steven Paul Sumner), Declan John Edge, Kevin Hagan, Colin Walker. Trainer: Kevin Fallon.
**Goals:** 1-0 Nissim Cohen (67), 2-0 Uri Malmilian (75), 3-0 Zahi Armeli (85).

# INTERCONTINENTAL PLAY-OFFS

## GROUP 1

| | | | | |
|---|---|---|---|---|
| 20.11.1985 | Glasgow | Scotland - Australia | 2-0(0-0) |
| 04.12.1985 | Melbourne | Australia - Scotland | 0-0 |

### FINAL STANDINGS

| | | | | | | | | |
|---|---|---|---|---|---|---|---|---|
| 1. | **Scotland** | 2 | 1 | 1 | 0 | 2 - 0 | 3 |
| 2. | Australia | 2 | 0 | 1 | 1 | 0 - 2 | 1 |

Scotland qualified for the Final Tournament.

20.11.1985, Hampden Park, Glasgow; Attendance: 61,920
Referee: Vojtěch Christov (Czechoslovakia)
**SCOTLAND - AUSTRALIA**      **2-0(0-0)**
**SCO:** James Leighton, Stephen Nicol, Maurice Daniel Robert Malpas, William Fergus Miller, Alexander McLeish, Gordon David Strachan (84.James Bett), Graeme James Souness (Cap), Robert Sime Aitken, David Cooper, Kenneth Mathieson Dalglish (72.Graeme Marshall Sharp), Francis McAvennie. Manager: Alexander Chapman Ferguson.
**AUS:** Terry Greedy, Charles Yankos, Alan Davidson, David Ratcliffe, Steve O'Connor (82.Robert Dunn), Graham Jennings, Joseph Watson (65.James Patikas), Ken Murphy, Oscar Crino, David Mitchell, John Kosmina. Trainer: Frank Arok.
**Goals:** 1-0 David Cooper (58), 2-0 Francis McAvennie (60).

04.12.1985, Olympic Park, Melbourne; Attendance: 32,000
Referee: José Roberto Ramiz Wright (Brazil)
**AUSTRALIA - SCOTLAND**      **0-0**
**AUS:** Terry Greedy, Charles Yankos, Alan Davidson, David Ratcliffe, Robert Dunn (75.Frank Farina), Graham Jennings, James Patikas, Oscar Crino (68.Zarko Odzakov), Ken Murphy, John Kosmina, David Mitchell. Trainer: Frank Arok.
**SCO:** James Leighton, Richard Charles Gough, Maurice Daniel Robert Malpas, William Fergus Miller, Alexander McLeish, Robert Sime Aitken, Graeme James Souness (Cap), Paul Michael Lyons McStay, David Cooper, David Robert Speedie (76.Graeme Marshall Sharp), Francis McAvennie. Manager: Alexander Chapman Ferguson.

# WORLD CUP 1986
# THE FINAL TOURNAMENT

The 13th edition of the FIFA World Cup, was held in Mexico between 31st May and 29th June 1986 although Colombia had, originally, been chosen as hosts. The Colombians, however, were unable to fulfil their economic obligations and therefore surrendered their right to be hosts during 1982. Mexico was then selected as the new host in May 1983 and became the first country to host the FIFA World Cup on two occasions.

The format of the competition remained the same for the first round with six groups of four teams but the second round reverted to a straight knockout competition. The top two teams from each group and the four best third-placed teams qualified for the second round.

The 24 qualified teams were placed in 4 seeding pots:
Pot 1:
Mexico (hosts), Italy (title holders), West Germany (1982 runners-up), Poland (1982 third place), France (1982 fourth place), Brazil.
Pot 2:
England, Soviet Union, Argentina, Spain, Paraguay, Uruguay.
Pot 3:
Algeria, Canada, Denmark, Iraq, Morocco, South Korea.
Pot 4:
Belgium, Bulgaria, Hungary, Northern Ireland, Portugal, Scotland.

The 24 teams were then drawn in following groups:

| GROUP A | GROUP B |
|---|---|
| Italy | Mexico |
| Bulgaria | Belgium |
| Argentina | Paraguay |
| South Korea | Iraq |

| GROUP C | GROUP D |
|---|---|
| France | Brazil |
| Canada | Spain |
| Soviet Union | Algeria |
| Hungary | Northern Ireland |

| GROUP E | GROUP F |
|---|---|
| West Germany | Poland |
| Uruguay | Morocco |
| Scotland | Portugal |
| Denmark | England |

The venues:

Ciudad de México (Estadio Azteca – Capacity: 114,600);
Ciudad de México (Estadio Olímpico Universitario – 72,000);
Guadalajara (Estadio Monumental Jalisco –66,000);
Irapuato (Estadio „Sergio León Chávez" – 32,000);
León (Estadio Campo Nuevo – 35,000);
Monterrey (Estadio Tecnológico – 38,000);
Nezahualcoyotl (Estadio Neza 86 – 35,000);
Puebla (Estadio Cuauhtémoc – 46,000);
Querétaro (Estadio La Corregidora – 40,785);
San Nicolás de los Garza (Estadio Universitário – 42,000);
Toluca (Estadio "Nemesio Díez" – 30,000);
Zapopan (Estadio Tres de Marzo – 30,000);

The round of 16 brought a few unexpected surprises. Belgium defeated the Soviet Union after extra-time as a hat-trick of goals from Belanov was not enough to beat the Belgians, the game finishing with a 4-3 scoreline! The title-holders Italy were eliminated by the European champions, Michel Platini's talented French team, and although Denmark opened the scoring against Spain, then were then hammered 5-1! Brazil crushed Poland 4-0 while West Germany squeaked through 1-0 against the unfancied Moroccans.

Three of the quarter-finals were decided on penalties after extra-time, with Belgium, France and West Germany progressing to the semi-finals. The other quarter-final between Argentina and England was dominated by controversy as Diego Maradona showed both sides of his character, clearly punching the ball into the English net for the opening goal, before scoring a second after a brilliant solo run. Lineker got a goal back in the 80$^{th}$ minute (earning him the 'Golden Boot' award as top scorer for the tournament), but this was to prove nothing more than a consolation. Maradona earned much criticism for his lack of embarrassment over his gamesmanship, shamelessly claiming after the match that the first goal was scored by the "Hand of God".

As in 1982, France met West Germany in the semi-finals and, once again, the Germans progressed to the Final where they faced an Argentinian side who had comfortably beaten the Belgians. The Final itself saw West Germany recover from a poor start to the game, which left them trailing by two goals after 55 minutes, to level the game at 2-2 with goals from Rummenigge and Völler. However, the Germans were not able to complete the comeback as Maradona quickly set up a goal for Burruchaga and the Germans were unable to respond. This was the second World title won by Argentina and there was little doubt that this one was well-deserved.

# GROUP A

| | | | | |
|---|---|---|---|---|
| 31.05.1986 | Ciudad de México | Italy - Bulgaria | 1-1(1-0) |
| 02.06.1986 | Ciudad de México | Argentina – South Korea | 3-1(2-0) |
| 05.06.1986 | Puebla | Italy - Argentina | 1-1(1-1) |
| 05.06.1986 | Ciudad de México | South Korea - Bulgaria | 1-1(0-1) |
| 10.06.1986 | Puebla | South Korea - Italy | 2-3(0-1) |
| 10.06.1986 | Ciudad de México | Argentina - Bulgaria | 2-0(1-0) |

## FINAL STANDINGS

| | | | | | | | | |
|---|---|---|---|---|---|---|---|---|
| 1. | Argentina | 3 | 2 | 1 | 0 | 6 - 2 | 5 |
| 2. | Italy | 3 | 1 | 2 | 0 | 5 - 4 | 4 |
| 3. | Bulgaria | 3 | 0 | 2 | 1 | 2 - 4 | 2 |
| 4. | South Korea | 3 | 0 | 1 | 2 | 4 - 7 | 1 |

31.05.1986, Estadio Azteca, Ciudad de México; Attendance: 95,000
Referee: Erik Fredriksson (Sweden)
**ITALY - BULGARIA** 1-1(1-0)
**ITA:** Giovanni Galli, Giuseppe Bergomi, Pietro Vierchowod, Gaetano Scirea, Antonio Cabrini, Bruno Conti (65.Gianluca Vialli), Fernando De Napoli, Salvatore Bagni, Giuseppe Galderisi, Antonio Di Gennaro, Alessandro Altobelli. Trainer: Enzo Bearzot.
**BUL:** Borislav Mihailov, Radoslav Zdravkov, Georgi Dimitrov (Cap), Nikolai Arabov, Aleksandar Markov, Anio Sadkov, Nasko Sirakov, Plamen Getov, Jivko Gospodinov (74.Andrei Jeliazkov), Bojidar Iskrenov (66.Kostadin Kostadinov), Stoicho Mladenov. Trainer: Ivan Vutsov.
**Goals**: 1-0 Alessandro Altobelli (43), 1-1 Nasko Sirakov (85).
**Cautions**: Giuseppe Bergomi, Antonio Cabrini / Aleksandar Markov.

02.06.1986, Estadio Olímpico Universitario, Ciudad de México; Attendance: 60,000
Referee: Victoriano Sánchez Arminio (Spain)
**ARGENTINA – SOUTH KOREA** 3-1(2-0)
**ARG:** Nery Alberto Pumpido, Néstor Rolando Clausen, José Luis Brown, Oscar Alfredo Ruggeri, Oscar Alfredo Garré, Ricardo Omar Giusti, Sergio Daniel Batista (75.Julio Jorge Olarticoechea), Jorge Luis Burruchaga, Diego Armando Maradona (Cap), Pedro Pablo Pasculli (74.Carlos Daniel Tapia), Jorge Alberto Francisco Valdano. Trainer: Dr. Carlos Salvador Bilardo.
**KOR:** Oh Yeon-Kyo, Park Kyung-Hoon, Cho Min-Kook, Chung Yong-Hwan, Kim Pyung-Seok (23.Cho Kwang-Rae), Huh Jung-Moo, Park Chang-Sun (Cap), Kim Joo-Sung, Kim Yong-Se (46.Yoo Byung-Ok), Cha Bum-Kun, Choi Soon-Ho. Trainer: Kim Jung-Nam.
**Goals**: 1-0 Jorge Alberto Francisco Valdano (5), 2-0 Oscar Alfredo Ruggeri (14), 3-0 Jorge Alberto Francisco Valdano (47), 3-1 Park Chang-Sun (73).
**Cautions**: Huh Jung-Moo, Park Chang-Sun.

05.06.1986, Estadio Cuauhtémoc, Puebla; Attendance: 32,000
Referee: Johannes Nicolaas Ignatius „Jan" Keizer (Holland)
**ITALY - ARGENTINA** 1-1(1-1)
**ITA:** Giovanni Galli, Giuseppe Bergomi, Pietro Vierchowod, Gaetano Scirea, Antonio Cabrini, Fernando De Napoli (87.Giuseppe Baresi I), Bruno Conti (64.Gianluca Vialli), Salvatore Bagni, Giuseppe Galderisi, Antonio Di Gennaro, Alessandro Altobelli. Trainer: Enzo Bearzot.
**ARG:** Nery Alberto Pumpido, José Luis Cuciuffo, José Luis Brown, Oscar Alfredo Ruggeri, Oscar Alfredo Garré, Ricardo Omar Giusti, Sergio Daniel Batista (50.Julio Jorge Olarticoechea), Jorge Luis Burruchaga, Diego Armando Maradona (Cap), Claudio Daniel Borghi (75.Héctor Adolfo Enrique), Jorge Alberto Francisco Valdano. Trainer: Dr. Carlos Salvador Bilardo.
**Goals**: 1-0 Alessandro Altobelli (6 penalty), 1-1 Diego Armando Maradona (34).

**Cautions**: Giuseppe Bergomi / Ricardo Omar Giusti, Oscar Alfredo Garré.

05.06.1986, Estadio Olímpico Universitario, Ciudad de México; Attendance: 45,000
Referee: Fallaj Khuzam Al Shanar (Saudi Arabia)
**SOUTH KOREA - BULGARIA**                                              **1-1(0-1)**
**KOR:** Oh Yeon-Kyo, Park Kyung-Hoon, Cho Young-Jeung, Chung Yong-Hwan, Huh Jung-Moo, Cho Kwang-Rae (72.Cho Min-Kook), Park Chang-Sun (Cap), Noh Soo-Jin (46.Kim Jong-Boo), Kim Joo-Sung, Cha Bum-Kun, Byun Byung-Joo. Trainer: Kim Jung-Nam.
**BUL:** Borislav Mihailov, Radoslav Zdravkov, Georgi Dimitrov (Cap), Nikolai Arabov, Petar Petrov, Anio Sadkov, Nasko Sirakov, Plamen Getov (58.Andrei Jeliazkov), Jivko Gospodinov, Bojidar Iskrenov (46.Kostadin Kostadinov), Stoicho Mladenov. Trainer: Ivan Vutsov.
**Goals:** 0-1 Plamen Getov (10), 1-1 Kim Jong-Boo (70).
**Cautions**: Kim Jong-Boo, Cho Young-Jeung / Jivko Gospodinov.

10.06.1986, Estadio Cuauhtémoc, Puebla; Attendance: 20,000
Referee: David Stanley Socha (United States)
**SOUTH KOREA - ITALY**                                                **2-3(0-1)**
**KOR:** Oh Yeon-Kyo, Park Kyung-Hoon, Cho Young-Jeung, Chung Yong-Hwan, Huh Jung-Moo, Cho Kwang-Rae, Park Chang-Sun (Cap), Kim Joo-Sung (46.Chung Jong-Soo), Byun Byung-Joo (70. Kim Jong-Boo), Choi Soon-Ho, Cha Bum-Kun. Trainer: Kim Jung-Nam.
**ITA:** Giovanni Galli, Pietro Vierchowod, Fulvio Collovatti, Gaetano Scirea, Antonio Cabrini, Fernando De Napoli, Bruno Conti, Salvatore Bagni (68.Giuseppe Baresi I), Giuseppe Galderisi (88.Gianluca Vialli), Antonio Di Gennaro, Alessandro Altobelli. Trainer: Enzo Bearzot.
**Goals:** 0-1 Alessandro Altobelli (18), 1-1 Choi Soon-Ho (62), 1-2 Alessandro Altobelli (73), 1-3 Cho Kwang Rae (82 own goal), 2-3 Huh Jung-Moo (89).
**Cautions**: Kim Joo-Sung, Park Kyung-Hoon, Cho Young-Jeung / Salvatore Bagni, Gaetano Scirea, Pietro Vierchowod.

10.06.1986, Estadio Olímpico Universitario, Ciudad de México; Attendance: 40,000
Referee: Berny Ulloa Morera (Costa Rica)
**ARGENTINA - BULGARIA**                                               **2-0(1-0)**
**ARG:** Nery Alberto Pumpido, José Luis Cuciuffo, José Luis Brown, Oscar Alfredo Ruggeri, Oscar Alfredo Garré, Ricardo Omar Giusti, Sergio Daniel Batista (46.Julio Jorge Olarticoechea), Jorge Luis Burruchaga, Diego Armando Maradona (Cap), Claudio Daniel Borghi (46.Héctor Adolfo Enrique), Jorge Alberto Francisco Valdano. Trainer: Dr. Carlos Salvador Bilardo.
**BUL:** Borislav Mihailov, Aleksandar Markov, Georgi Dimitrov (Cap), Petar Petrov, Anio Sadkov, Nasko Sirakov (72.Radoslav Zdravkov), Plamen Getov, Andrei Jeliazkov, Georgi Iordanov, Plamen Markov, Stoicho Mladenov (53.Boicho Velichkov). Trainer: Ivan Vutsov.
**Goals:** 1-0 Jorge Alberto Francisco Valdano (3), 2-0 Jorge Luis Burruchaga (76).
**Cautions**: José Luis Cuciuffo.

# GROUP B

| Date | Venue | Match | Result |
|---|---|---|---|
| 03.06.1986 | Ciudad de México | Mexico - Belgium | 2-1(2-1) |
| 04.06.1986 | Toluca | Paraguay - Iraq | 1-0(1-0) |
| 07.06.1986 | Ciudad de México | Mexico - Paraguay | 1-1(1-1) |
| 08.06.1986 | Toluca | Iraq - Belgium | 1-2(0-2) |
| 11.06.1986 | Ciudad de México | Mexico - Iraq | 1-0(0-0) |
| 11.06.1986 | Toluca | Belgium - Paraguay | 2-2(1-0) |

### FINAL STANDINGS

| | | | | | | | | |
|---|---|---|---|---|---|---|---|---|
| 1. | Mexico | 3 | 2 | 1 | 0 | 4 - 2 | 5 |
| 2. | Paraguay | 3 | 1 | 2 | 0 | 4 - 3 | 4 |
| 3. | Belgium | 3 | 1 | 1 | 1 | 5 - 5 | 3 |
| 4. | Iraq | 3 | 0 | 0 | 3 | 1 - 4 | 0 |

03.06.1986, Estadio Azteca, Ciudad de México; Attendance: 110,000
Referee: Carlos Alfonso Espósito (Argentina)
**MEXICO - BELGIUM**      **2-1(2-1)**
**MEX:** Pablo Larios Iwasaki, Mario Alberto Trejo Guzmán, Félix Cruz Barbosa Ríos, Fernando Quirarte Gutiérrez, Raúl Servín Monetti, Carlos Eduardo Muñoz Remolina, Javier Aguirre Onaindía, Manuel Negrete Arias, Tomás Juan Boy Espinoza (Cap) (67.Miguel España Garcés), Hugo Sánchez Márquez, Luis Enrique Flores Ocaranza (79.Francisco Javier Cruz Jiménez). Trainer: Velibor Milutinović (Yugoslavia).
**BEL:** Jean-Marie Pfaff, Eric Gerets, Hugo Broos, Frank Richard Vander Elst, Michel De Wolf, Vincenzo Scifo, René Vandereycken, Frank Vercauteren, Jan Ceulemans, Philippe De Smet (58.Nicolaas Pieter Claesen), Erwin Vandenbergh (63.Stéphane Demol). Trainer: Guy Thys.
**Goals**: 1-0 Fernando Quirarte Gutiérrez (22), 2-0 Hugo Sánchez Márquez (39), 2-1 Erwin Vandenbergh (45).
**Cautions**: Hugo Sánchez Márquez, Carlos Eduardo Muñoz Remolina / Frank Richard Vander Elst.

04.06.1986, Estadio „Nemesio Díez", Toluca; Attendance: 24,000
Referee: Edwin Sydney Picon-Ackong (Mauritius)
**PARAGUAY - IRAQ**      **1-0(1-0)**
**PAR:** Roberto Eladio Fernández Roa, Juan Bautista Torales, Rogelio Wilfrido Delgado Casco (Cap), César Zabala Fernández, Vladimiro Schettina Chepini, Jorge Amado Núñez Infrán, Buenaventura Ferreira Gómez, Julio César Romero Insfrán, Adolfino Cañete Azcurra, Roberto Cabañas González, Alfredo Damián Mendoza Sulewski (88.Jorge Alberto Guasch Bazán). Trainer: Cayetano Ré Ramírez.
**IRQ**: Raad Hammoudi Salman, Khalil Mohammed Allawi, Jassim Ghanim Oraibi Al Roubai, Ali Hussein Shihab, Nadhim Shaker Salim, Samir Shaker Mahmoud, Haris Mohammed Hassan (67.Abdul-Rahim Hamed Aufi), Basil Gorgis Hanna (81.Basim Qasim Hamdan), Hussein Saeed Mohammed, Ahmad Radhi Amaiesh Al Salehi, Natiq Hashim Abidoun. Trainer: Evaristo de Macedo Filho (Brazil).
**Goal**: 1-0 Julio César Romero Insfrán (36).
**Cautions**: Vladimiro Schettina Chepini / Samir Shaker Mahmoud.

07.06.1986, Estadio Azteca, Ciudad de México; Attendance: 110.000
Referee: George Courtney (England)
**MEXICO - PARAGUAY**      **1-1(1-1)**
**MEX:** Pablo Larios Iwasaki, Mario Alberto Trejo Guzmán, Félix Cruz Barbosa Ríos, Fernando Quirarte Gutiérrez, Raúl Servín Monetti, Carlos Eduardo Muñoz Remolina, Javier Aguirre Onaindía, Manuel Negrete Arias, Tomás Juan Boy Espinoza (Cap) (54.Miguel España Garcés), Hugo Sánchez Márquez, Luis Enrique Flores Ocaranza (72.Francisco Javier Cruz Jiménez). Trainer: Velibor Milutinović (Yugoslavia).

**PAR:** Roberto Eladio Fernández Roa, Juan Bautista Torales (81.Ramón Angel Hicks Cáceres), César Zabala Fernández, Rogelio Wilfrido Delgado Casco (Cap), Vladimiro Schettina Chepini, Jorge Amado Núñez Infrán, Buenaventura Ferreira Gómez, Julio César Romero Insfrán, Roberto Cabañas González, Adolfino Cañete Azcurra, Alfredo Damián Mendoza Sulewski (63.Jorge Alberto Guasch Bazán). Trainer: Cayetano Ré Ramírez.
**Goals**: 1-0 Luis Enrique Flores Ocaranza (2), 1-1 Julio César Romero Insfrán (85).
**Cautions**: Manuel Negrete Arias, Hugo Sánchez Márquez, Mario Alberto Trejo Guzmán / Alfredo Damián Mendoza Sulewski, Vladimiro Schettina Chepini.

08.06.1986, Estadio „Nemesio Díez", Toluca; Attendance: 20,000
Referee: Jesús Díaz Palacio (Colombia)
**IRAQ - BELGIUM** 1-2(0-2)
**IRQ**: Raad Hammoudi Salman, Khalil Mohammed Allawi, Jassim Ghanim Oraibi Al Roubai, Ali Hussein Shihab, Nadhim Shaker Salim, Samir Shaker Mahmoud, Haris Mohammed Hassan, Basil Gorgis Hanna, Natiq Hashim Abidoun, Karim Saddam Minshid (81.Abdul-Rahim Hamed Aufi), Ahmad Radhi Amaiesh Al Salehi. Trainer: Evaristo de Macedo Filho (Brazil).
**BEL:** Jean-Marie Pfaff, Eric Gerets, Frank Richard Vander Elst, Stéphane Demol (66.Léo Albert Clijsters), Michel De Wolf, Vincenzo Scifo (68.Georges Grün), René Vandereycken, Jan Ceulemans, Frank Vercauteren, Philippe De Smet, Nicolaas Pieter Claesen. Trainer: Guy Thys.
**Goals**: 0-1 Vincenzo Scifo (16), 0-2 Nicolaas Pieter Claesen (22 penalty), 1-2 Ahmad Radhi Amaiesh Al Salehi (59).
**Cautions**: Basil Gorgis Hanna, Raad Hammoudi Salman, Nadhim Shaker Salim, Haris Mohammed Hassan, Samir Shaker Mahmoud, Natiq Hashim Abidoun / Nicolaas Pieter Claesen.
**Sent off**: Basil Gorgis Hanna (51).

11.06.1986, Estadio Azteca, Ciudad de México; Attendance: 108,673
Referee: Zoran Petrović (Yugoslavia)
**MEXICO - IRAQ** 1-0(0-0)
**MEX:** Pablo Larios Iwasaki, Rafael Amador Flores (62.Alejandro Domínguez Escoto), Félix Cruz Barbosa Ríos, Fernando Quirarte Gutiérrez, Raúl Servín Monetti, Carlos de los Cobos Martínez (78.Francisco Javier Cruz Jiménez), Miguel España Garcés, Manuel Negrete Arias, Tomás Juan Boy Espinoza, Javier Aguirre Onaindía, Luis Enrique Flores Ocaranza. Trainer: Velibor Milutinović (Yugoslavia).
**IRQ**: Jassim Abdul-Fatah Nasif, Ali Hussein Shihab, Khalil Mohammed Allawi, Anad Abid Tweresh (68.Mahmoud Hamza Shaker), Nadhim Shaker Salim, Maad Ibrahim Majid, Karim Saddam Minshid, Basim Qasim Hamdan, Natiq Hashim Abidoun (60.Abdul-Rahim Hamed Aufi), Jassim Ghanim Oraibi Al Roubai, Ahmad Radhi Amaiesh Al Salehi. Trainer: Evaristo de Macedo Filho (Brazil).
**Goal**: 1-0 Fernando Quirarte Gutiérrez (53).

11.06.1986, Estadio „Nemesio Díez", Toluca; Attendance: 16,000
Referee: Bogdan Dotchev (Bulgaria)
**BELGIUM - PARAGUAY** 2-2(1-0)
**BEL:** Jean-Marie Pfaff, Georges Grün (89.Léo Vander Elst), Hugo Broos, Michel Renquin, Patrick Vervoort, Vincenzo Scifo, Stéphane Demol, Jan Ceulemans, Frank Vercauteren, Daniel Veyt, Nicolaas Pieter Claesen. Trainer: Guy Thys.
**PAR:** Roberto Eladio Fernández Roa, Juan Bautista Torales, César Zabala Fernández, Rogelio Wilfrido Delgado Casco (Cap), Jorge Alberto Guasch Bazán, Jorge Amado Núñez Infrán, Buenaventura Ferreira Gómez, Julio César Romero Insfrán, Roberto Cabañas González, Adolfino Cañete Azcurra, Alfredo Damián Mendoza Sulewski (81.Ramón Angel Hicks Cáceres). Trainer: Cayetano Ré Ramírez.
**Goals**: 1-0 Frank Vercauteren (32), 1-1 Roberto Cabañas González (50), 2-1 Daniel Veyt (60), 2-2 Roberto Cabañas González (75).
**Cautions**: Jan Ceulemans / Julio César Romero Insfrán.

# GROUP C

| | | | |
|---|---|---|---|
| 01.06.1986 | León | France - Canada | 1-0(0-0) |
| 02.06.1986 | Irapuato | Soviet Union - Hungary | 6-0(3-0) |
| 05.06.1986 | León | France – Soviet Union | 1-1(0-0) |
| 06.06.1986 | Irapuato | Hungary - Canada | 2-0(1-0) |
| 09.06.1986 | León | France - Hungary | 3-0(1-0) |
| 09.06.1986 | Irapuato | Soviet Union - Canada | 2-0(0-0) |

## FINAL STANDINGS

| | | | | | | | | |
|---|---|---|---|---|---|---|---|---|
| 1. Soviet Union | 3 | 2 | 1 | 0 | 9 | - | 1 | 5 |
| 2. France | 3 | 2 | 1 | 0 | 5 | - | 1 | 5 |
| 3. Hungary | 3 | 1 | 0 | 2 | 2 | - | 9 | 2 |
| 4. Canada | 3 | 0 | 0 | 3 | 0 | - | 5 | 0 |

01.06.1986, Estadio Campo Nuevo, León; Attendance: 35,748
Referee: Hernán Silva Arce (Chile)
**FRANCE - CANADA** **1-0(0-0)**
**FRA:** Joël Bats, Manuel Amoros, Patrick Battiston, Maxime Bossis, Thierry Tusseau, Alain Giresse, Jean Amadou Tigana, Luis Fernández, Michel Platini (Cap), Jean-Pierre Papin, Dominique Rocheteau (70.Yannick Stopyra). Trainer: Henri Michel.
**CAN:** Kenneth Paul Dolan, Robert Lenarduzzi, Ian Christopher Bridge, Randolph Fitzgerald Samuel, Bruce Alec Wilson, Paul John James (83.Branko Segota), Randolph Lee Ragan, Mike Sweeney (54.Jamie Lowery), David McDonald Norman, Carl Howard Valentine, Igor Vrablic. Trainer: Anthony Keith Waiters.
**Goal:** 1-0 Jean-Pierre Papin (79).

02.06.1986, Estadio „Sergio León Chávez", Irapuato; Attendance: 15,000
Referee: Luigi Agnolin (Italy)
**SOVIET UNION - HUNGARY** **6-0(3-0)**
**URS:** Rinat Dasaev, Vladimir Bessonov, Nikolay Larionov, Oleg Kuznetzov, Anatoliy Demyanenko (Cap), Pavel Yakovenko (72.Vadim Evtushenko), Ivan Yaremchuk, Vasiliy Ratz, Sergey Aleynikov, Aleksandr Zavarov, Igor Belanov (70.Sergey Rodionov). Trainer: Valeriy Lobanovskiy.
**HUN:** Péter Disztl, Sándor Sallai, Antal Róth (12.Győző Burcsa), Imre Garaba, Zoltán Péter (62.László Dajka), József Kardos, Antal Nagy, Lajos Détári, György Bognár, József Kiprich, Márton Esterházy. Trainer: György Mezey.
**Goals:** 1-0 Pavel Yakovenko (2), 2-0 Sergey Aleynikov (4), 3-0 Igor Belanov (24 penalty), 4-0 Ivan Yaremchuk (66), 5-0 László Dajka (75 own goal), 6-0 Sergey Rodionov (83).

05.06.1986, Estadio Campo Nuevo, León; Attendance: 36,540
Referee: Romualdo Arppi Filho (Brazil)
**FRANCE – SOVIET UNION** **1-1(0-0)**
**FRA:** Joël Bats, William Ayache, Patrick Battiston, Maxime Bossis, Manuel Amoros, Alain Giresse (83.Philippe Vercruysse), Luis Fernández, Michel Platini (Cap), Jean Amadou Tigana, Jean-Pierre Papin (76.Bruno Bellone), Yannick Stopyra. Trainer: Henri Michel.
**URS:** Rinat Dasaev, Vladimir Bessonov, Nikolay Larionov, Oleg Kuznetzov, Anatoliy Demyanenko (Cap), Pavel Yakovenko (70.Sergey Rodionov), Ivan Yaremchuk, Vasiliy Ratz, Sergey Aleynikov, Aleksandr Zavarov (59.Oleg Blokhin), Igor Belanov. Trainer: Valeriy Lobanovskiy.
**Goals:** 0-1 Vasiliy Ratz (53), 1-1 Luis Fernández (62).
**Cautions:** Vasiliy Ratz, Igor Belanov / Luis Fernández, Manuel Amoros.

06.06.1986, Estadio „Sergio León Chávez", Irapuato; Attendance: 10,000
Referee: Jamal Al Sharif (Syria)
**HUNGARY - CANADA** **2-0(1-0)**
**HUN:** József Szendrei, Sándor Sallai, József Kardos, Imre Garaba, József Varga, Győző Burcsa (27.Antal Róth), Antal Nagy (62.László Dajka), Lajos Détári, György Bognár, József Kiprich, Márton Esterházy. Trainer: György Mezey.
**CAN:** Martino Lettieri, Robert Lenarduzzi, Ian Christopher Bridge, Randolph Fitzgerald Samuel, Bruce Alec Wilson (40.Mike Sweeney), Paul John James (60.Branko Segota), Randolph Lee Ragan, Gerard Gray, David McDonald Norman, Carl Howard Valentine, Igor Vrablic. Trainer: Anthony Keith Waiters.
**Goals:** 1-0 Márton Esterházy (2), 2-0 Lajos Détári (76).
**Cautions:** Mike Sweeney, Robert Lenarduzzi.
**Sent off:** Mike Sweeney (85).

09.06.1986, Estadio Campo Nuevo, León; Attendance: 31,420
Referee: Carlos Alberto Da Silva Valente (Portugal)
**FRANCE - HUNGARY** **3-0(1-0)**
**FRA:** Joël Bats, William Ayache, Maxime Bossis, Patrick Battiston, Manuel Amoros, Alain Giresse, Luis Fernández, Jean Amadou Tigana, Michel Platini (Cap), Yannick Stopyra (71.Jean-Marc Ferreri), Jean-Pierre Papin (61.Dominique Rocheteau). Trainer: Henri Michel.
**HUN:** Péter Disztl, Sándor Sallai, József Kardos, Antal Róth, Imre Garaba, József Varga, László Dajka, Péter Hannich (46.Antal Nagy), Lajos Détári, Kálmán Kovács (65.György Bognár), Márton Esterházy. Trainer: György Mezey.
**Goals:** 1-0 Yannick Stopyra (30), 2-0 Jean Amadou Tigana (63), 3-0 Dominique Rocheteau (84).
**Cautions:** William Ayache, Dominique Rocheteau.

09.06.1986, Estadio „Sergio León Chávez", Irapuato; Attendance: 14,200
Referee: Idrissa Marcel Traoré (Mali)
**SOVIET UNION - CANADA** **2-0(0-0)**
**URS:** Viktor Chanov, Gennadiy Morozov, Aleksandr Bubnov, Oleg Kuznetsov, Andrey Bal, Sergey Aleynikov, Gennadiy Litovchenko, Vadim Evtushenko, Oleg Blokhin (Cap) (62.Aleksandr Zavarov), Oleg Protasov (57.Igor Belanov), Sergey Rodionov. Trainer: Valeriy Lobanovskiy.
**CAN:** Martino Lettieri, Robert Lenarduzzi, Ian Christopher Bridge, Randolph Fitzgerald Samuel, Bruce Alec Wilson, Paul John James (4.Branko Segota), Randolph Lee Ragan, Gerard Gray (69.George Pakos), David McDonald Norman, Carl Howard Valentine, Dale William Mitchell. Trainer: Anthony Keith Waiters.
**Goais:** 1-0 Oleg Blokhin (58), 2-0 Aleksandr Zavarov (74).

# GROUP D

| | | | | |
|---|---|---|---|---|
| 01.06.1986 | Guadalajara | Brazil - Spain | 1-0(0-0) |
| 03.06.1986 | Zapopan | Algeria – Northern Ireland | 1-1(0-1) |
| 06.06.1986 | Guadalajara | Brazil - Algeria | 1-0(0-0) |
| 07.06.1986 | Zapopan | Spain - Northern Ireland | 2-1(2-0) |
| 12.06.1986 | Guadalajara | Brazil - Northern Ireland | 3-0(2-0) |
| 12.06.1986 | Monterrey | Spain - Algeria | 3-0(1-0) |

## FINAL STANDINGS

| | | | | | | | | |
|---|---|---|---|---|---|---|---|---|
| 1. | **Brazil** | 3 | 3 | 0 | 0 | 5 - 0 | 6 |
| 2. | **Spain** | 3 | 2 | 0 | 1 | 5 - 2 | 4 |
| 3. | Northern Ireland | 3 | 0 | 1 | 2 | 2 - 6 | 1 |
| 4. | Algeria | 3 | 0 | 1 | 2 | 1 - 5 | 1 |

01.06.1986, Estadio Monumental Jalisco, Guadalajara; Attendance: 65,500
Referee: Christopher Francis Bambridge (Australia)
**BRAZIL - SPAIN**                                                              **1-0(0-0)**
**BRA**: Carlos Roberto Gallo, Édson Boaro, Júlio César da Silva, Édino Nazareth Filho "Edinho", Cláudio Ibrahim Vaz Leal "Branco", Elzo Aloísio Coelho, Ricardo Rogério de Brito "Alemão", Leovegildo Lins Gama Júnior "Júnior I" (78.Paulo Roberto Falcão), Sócrates Brasileiro Sampaio Vieira de Oliveira, Wálter Casagrande Júnior (66.Luís Antônio Corrêa da Costa "Müller"), Antônio de Oliveira Filho "Careca I". Trainer: Telê Santana da Silva.
**ESP**: Andoni Zubizarreta Urreta, Pedro Tomás Reñones Grego, Andoni Goikoetxea Olaskoaga, Antonio Maceda Francés, José Antonio Camacho Alfaro (Cap), José Miguel González Martín del Campo „Míchel", Víctor Muñoz Manrique, Francisco Javier López Alfaro (81.Juan Antonio Señor Gómez), Julio Alberto Moreno Casas, Julio Salinas Fernández, Emilio Butragueño Santos. Trainer: Miguel Muñoz Mozún.
**Goal**: 1-0 Sócrates Brasileiro Sampaio Vieira de Oliveira (62).
**Cautions**: Cláudio Ibrahim Vaz Leal "Branco" / Julio Alberto Moreno Casas.

03.06.1986, Estadio Tres de Marzo, Zapopan; Attendance: 22,000
Referee: Valeri Butenko (Soviet Union)
**ALGERIA – NORTHERN IRELAND**                            **1-1(0-1)**
**ALG**: Larbi El Hadi, Abdellah Medjadi Liegeon, Nourredine Abdallah Kourichi, Mahmoud Guendouz (Cap), Faouzi Mansouri, Mohamed Kaci Saïd, Halim Ben Mabrouk, Karim Maroc, Mustapha Rabah Madjer (33.Rachid Harkouk), Djamel Zidane (71.Lakhdar Belloumi), Salah Assad. Trainer: Rabah Saadane.
**NIR**: Patrick Anthony Jennings, James Michael Nicholl, Malachy Martin Donaghy, John Patrick O'Neill, Alan McDonald, Nigel Worthington, Stephen Alexander Penney (67.Ian Edwin Stewart), Samuel Baxter McIlroy (Cap), David McCreery, William Robert Hamilton, Norman Whiteside (Colin John Clarke). Manager: William Laurence Bingham.
**Goals**: 0-1 Norman Whiteside (6), 1-1 Djamel Zidane (59).
**Cautions**: Faouzi Mansouri / Nigel Worthington, Samuel Baxter McIlroy, Norman Whiteside.

06.06.1986, Estadio Monumental Jalisco, Guadalajara; Attendance: 40,000
Referee: Romulo Méndez Molina (Guatemala)
**BRAZIL - ALGERIA**                                                   **1-0(0-0)**
**BRA**: Carlos Roberto Gallo, Édson Boaro (10.Paulo Roberto Falcão), Júlio César da Silva, Édino Nazareth Filho "Edinho", Cláudio Ibrahim Vaz Leal "Branco", Elzo Aloísio Coelho, Ricardo Rogério de Brito "Alemão", Sócrates Brasileiro Sampaio Vieira de Oliveira, Leovegildo Lins Gama Júnior "Júnior I", Wálter Casagrande Júnior (59.Luís Antônio Corrêa da Costa "Müller"), Antônio de Oliveira

Filho "Careca I". Trainer: Telê Santana da Silva.
**ALG**: Nacerdine Drid, Abdellah Medjadi Liegeon, Fodil Megharia, Mahmoud Guendouz (Cap), Faouzi Mansouri, Mohamed Kaci Saïd, Halim Ben Mabrouk, Mustapha Rabah Madjer, Djamel Menad, Lakhdar Belloumi (79.Djamel Zidane), Salah Assad (79.Tedj Bensaoula). Trainer: Rabah Saadane.
**Goal**: 1-0 Antônio de Oliveira Filho "Careca I" (66).

07.06.1986, Estadio Tres de Marzo, Zapopan; Attendance: 28,000
Referee: Horst Brummeier (Austria)
**SPAIN - NORTHERN IRELAND**  **2-1(2-0)**
**ESP**: Andoni Zubizarreta Urreta, Pedro Tomás Reñones Grego, Andoni Goikoetxea Olaskoaga, Ricardo Gallego Redondo, José Antonio Camacho Alfaro (Cap), José Miguel González Martín del Campo „Míchel", Víctor Muñoz Manrique, Francisco Javier López Alfaro, Rafael Gordillo Vázquez (53.Ramón María Calderé Del Rey), Julio Salinas Fernández (79.Juan Antonio Señor Gómez), Emilio Butragueño Santos. Trainer: Miguel Muñoz Mozún.
**NIR**: Patrick Anthony Jennings, James Michael Nicholl, Malachy Martin Donaghy, John Patrick O'Neill, Alan McDonald, Nigel Worthington (70.William Robert Hamilton), Stephen Alexander Penney (54.Ian Edwin Stewart), Samuel Baxter McIlroy (Cap), David McCreery, Colin John Clarke, Norman Whiteside. Manager: William Laurence Bingham.
**Goals**: 1-0 Emilio Butragueño Santos (2), 2-0 Julio Salinas Fernández (18), 2-1 Colin John Clarke (48).
**Cautions**: Víctor Muñoz Manrique / William Robert Hamilton.

12.06.1986, Estadio Monumental Jalisco, Guadalajara; Attendance: 40,000
Referee: Siegfried Kirschen (East Germany)
**BRAZIL - NORTHERN IRELAND**  **3-0(2-0)**
**BRA**: Carlos Roberto Gallo, Josimar Higino Pereira, Júlio César da Silva, Édino Nazareth Filho "Edinho", Cláudio Ibrahim Vaz Leal "Branco", Elzo Aloísio Coelho, Ricardo Rogério de Brito "Alemão", Sócrates Brasileiro Sampaio Vieira de Oliveira (68.Arthur Antunes Coimbra "Zico"), Leovegildo Lins Gama Júnior "Júnior I", Luís Antônio Corrêa da Costa "Müller" (26.Wálter Casagrande Júnior), Antônio de Oliveira Filho "Careca I". Trainer: Telê Santana da Silva.
**NIR**: Patrick Anthony Jennings, James Michael Nicholl, Malachy Martin Donaghy, John Patrick O'Neill, Alan McDonald, David McCreery, Samuel Baxter McIlroy (Cap), Ian Edwin Stewart, Colin John Clarke, Norman Whiteside (67.William Robert Hamilton), David Anthony Campbell (71.Gerard Joseph Armstrong). Manager: William Laurence Bingham.
**Goals**: 1-0 Antônio de Oliveira Filho "Careca I" (15), 2-0 Josimar Higino Pereira (42), 3-0 Antônio de Oliveira Filho "Careca I" (88).
**Cautions**: Malachy Martin Donaghy.

12.06.1986, Estadio Tecnológico, Monterrey; Attendance: 23,980
Referee: Shizuo Takada (Japan)
**SPAIN - ALGERIA**  **3-0(1-0)**
**ESP**: Andoni Zubizarreta Urreta, Pedro Tomás Reñones Grego, Andoni Goikoetxea Olaskoaga, Ricardo Gallego Redondo, José Antonio Camacho Alfaro (Cap), José Miguel González Martín del Campo „Míchel" (67.Juan Antonio Señor Gómez), Víctor Muñoz Manrique, Francisco Javier López Alfaro, Ramón María Calderé Del Rey, Julio Salinas Fernández, Emilio Butragueño Santos (46.Eloy José Olaya Prendes). Trainer: Miguel Muñoz Mozún.
**ALG**: Nacerdine Drid (20.Larbi El Hadi), Nourredine Abdallah Kourichi, Fodil Megharia, Mahmoud Guendouz (Cap), Faouzi Mansouri, Mohamed Kaci Saïd, Djamel Zidane (59.Djamel Menad), Karim Maroc, Mustapha Rabah Madjer, Rachid Harkouk, Lakhdar Belloumi. Trainer: Rabah Saadane.
**Goals**: 1-0 Ramón María Calderé Del Rey (15), 2-0 Ramón María Calderé Del Rey (68), 3-0 Eloy José Olaya Prendes (70).
**Cautions**: Andoni Goikoetxea Olaskoaga / Mustapha Rabah Madjer.

# GROUP E

| | | | |
|---|---|---|---|
| 04.06.1986 | Querétaro | West Germany - Uruguay | 1-1(0-1) |
| 04.06.1986 | Nezahualcoyotl | Denmark - Scotland | 1-0(0-0) |
| 08.06.1986 | Querétaro | West Germany - Scotland | 2-1(1-1) |
| 08.06.1986 | Nezahualcoyotl | Denmark - Uruguay | 6-1(2-1) |
| 13.06.1986 | Querétaro | Denmark – West Germany | 2-0(1-0) |
| 13.06.1986 | Nezahualcoyotl | Scotland - Uruguay | 0-0 |

## FINAL STANDINGS

| | | | | | | | | |
|---|---|---|---|---|---|---|---|---|
| 1. Denmark | 3 | 3 | 0 | 0 | 9 | - | 1 | 6 |
| 2. West Germany | 3 | 1 | 1 | 1 | 3 | - | 4 | 3 |
| 3. Uruguay | 3 | 0 | 2 | 1 | 2 | - | 7 | 2 |
| 4. Scotland | 3 | 0 | 1 | 2 | 1 | - | 3 | 1 |

04.06.1986, Estadio La Corregidora, Querétaro; Attendance: 30,500
Referee: Vojtěch Christov (Czechoslovakia)
**WEST GERMANY - URUGUAY**     **1-1(0-1)**
**GER:** Harald Schumacher (Cap), Thomas Berthold, Klaus Augenthaler, Karlheinz Förster, Hans-Peter Briegel, Norbert Eder, Lothar Herbert Matthäus (73.Karl-Heinz Rummenigge), Felix Magath, Andreas Brehme (46.Pierre Littbarski), Rudolf Völler, Klaus Allofs. Trainer: Franz Beckenbauer.
**URU:** Fernando Harry Álvez Mosquera, Víctor Hugo Diogo Silva, Eduardo Mario Acevedo Cardozo, Nelson Daniel Gutiérrez Luongo, José Alberto Batista González, Miguel Angel Bossio Bastianini, Jorge Wálter Barrios Balestrasse (56.Mario Daniel Saralegui), Sérgio Rodolfo Santín Spinelli, Enzo Francéscoli Uriarte, Antonio Alzamendi Casas (82.Venancio Ariel Ramos Villanueva), Jorge Orosmán da Silva Echeverrito. Trainer: Omar Borrás.
**Goals**: 0-1 Antonio Alzamendi Casas (5), 1-1 Klaus Allofs (85).
**Cautions**: Víctor Hugo Diogo Silva, Mario Daniel Saralegui.

04.06.1986, Estadio Neza 86, Nezahualcoyotl; Attendance: 18,000
Referee: Lajos Németh (Hungary)
**DENMARK - SCOTLAND**     **1-0(0-0)**
**DEN:** Troels Rasmussen, Søren Busk, Morten Olsen (Cap), Ivan Nielsen, Klaus Berggreen, Frank Arnesen (75.John Sivebæk), Jens Jørn Bertelsen, Søren Lerby, Jesper Olsen (83.Jan Mølby), Michael Laudrup, Preben Elkjær-Larsen. Trainer: Josef Piontek (West Germany).
**SCO:** James Leighton, Richard Charles Gough, Maurice Daniel Robert Malpas, William Fergus Miller, Alexander McLeish, Gordon David Strachan (74.Eamonn John Peter Bannon), Robert Sime Aitken, Graeme James Souness (Cap), Stephen Nicol, Paul Whitehead Sturrock (61.Francis McAvennie), Charles Nicholas. Manager: Alexander Chapman Ferguson.
**Goal**: 1-0 Preben Elkjær-Larsen (57).
**Cautions**: Klaus Berggreen.

08.06.1986, Estadio La Corregidora, Querétaro; Attendance: 30,000
Referee: Ioan Igna (Romania)
**WEST GERMANY - SCOTLAND**     **2-1(1-1)**
**GER:** Harald Schumacher (Cap), Thomas Berthold, Klaus Augenthaler, Karlheinz Förster, Hans-Peter Briegel (61.Ditmar Jakobs), Norbert Eder, Lothar Herbert Matthäus, Felix Magath, Pierre Littbarski (75.Karl-Heinz Rummenigge), Rudolf Völler, Klaus Allofs. Trainer: Franz Beckenbauer.
**SCO:** James Leighton, Richard Charles Gough, Maurice Daniel Robert Malpas, David Narey, William Fergus Miller, Gordon David Strachan, Robert Sime Aitken, Graeme James Souness (Cap), Stephen Nicol (59.Francis McAvennie), Eamonn John Peter Bannon (74.David Cooper), Steven Archibald. Manager: Alexander Chapman Ferguson.

**Goals**: 0-1 Gordon David Strachan (18), 1-1 Rudolf Völler (22), 2-1 Klaus Allofs (50).
**Cautions**: Steven Archibald, Eamonn John Peter Bannon, Maurice Daniel Robert Malpas.

08.06.1986, Estadio Neza 86, Nezahualcoyotl; Attendance: 26,500
Referee: Antonio Márquez Ramírez (Mexico)
**DENMARK - URUGUAY** **6-1(2-1)**
**DEN**: Troels Rasmussen, Søren Busk, Morten Olsen (Cap), Ivan Nielsen, Henrik Andersen, Frank Arnesen, Klaus Berggreen, Jens Jørn Bertelsen (56.Jan Mølby), Søren Lerby, Michael Laudrup (81.Jesper Olsen), Preben Elkjær-Larsen. Trainer: Josef Piontek (West Germany).
**URU**: Fernando Harry Álvez Mosquera, Víctor Hugo Diogo Silva, Eduardo Mario Acevedo Cardozo, Nelson Daniel Gutiérrez Luongo, José Alberto Batista González, Miguel Angel Bossio Bastianini, Mario Daniel Saralegui, Sérgio Rodolfo Santín Spinelli (57.José Luis Zalazar Rodríguez), Enzo Francéscoli Uriarte, Antonio Alzamendi Casas (57.Venancio Ariel Ramos Villanueva), Jorge Orosmán da Silva Echeverrito. Trainer: Omar Borrás.
**Goals**: 1-0 Preben Elkjær-Larsen (11), 2-0 Søren Lerby (41), 2-1 Enzo Francéscoli Uriarte (45 penalty), 3-1 Michael Laudrup (52), 4-1 Preben Elkjær-Larsen (68), 5-1 Preben Elkjær-Larsen (79), 6-1 Jesper Olsen (89).
**Cautions**: Ivan Nielsen / Miguel Angel Bossio Bastianini, Jorge Orosmán da Silva Echeverrito.
**Sent off**: Miguel Angel Bossio Bastianini (19).

13.06.1986, Estadio La Corregidora, Querétaro; Attendance: 36,000
Referee: Alexis Ponnet (Belgium)
**DENMARK – WEST GERMANY** **2-0(1-0)**
**DEN**: Lars Høgh, John Sivebæk, Søren Busk, Morten Olsen (Cap), Henrik Andersen, Frank Arnesen, Jan Mølby, Søren Lerby, Jesper Olsen (70.Allan Rodenkam Simonsen), Michael Laudrup, Preben Elkjær-Larsen (46.John Eriksen). Trainer: Josef Piontek (West Germany).
**GER**: Harald Schumacher (Cap), Thomas Berthold, Ditmar Jakobs, Karlheinz Förster (70.Karl-Heinz Rummenigge), Andreas Brehme, Norbert Eder, Matthias Herget, Wolfgang Rolff (46.Pierre Littbarski), Lothar Herbert Matthäus, Rudolf Völler, Klaus Allofs. Trainer: Franz Beckenbauer.
**Goals**: 1-0 Jesper Olsen (44 penalty), 2-0 John Eriksen (63).
**Cautions**: Frank Arnesen / Norbert Eder, Ditmar Jakobs.
**Sent off**: Frank Arnesen (88).

13.06.1986, Estadio Neza 86, Nezahualcoyotl; Attendance: 20,000
Referee: Joël Quiniou (France)
**SCOTLAND - URUGUAY** **0-0**
**SCO**: James Leighton, Richard Charles Gough, Arthur Richard Albiston, David Narey, William Fergus Miller (Cap), Gordon David Strachan, Robert Sime Aitken, Paul Michael Lyons McStay, Stephen Nicol (70.David Cooper), Paul Whitehead Sturrock (70.Charles Nicholas), Graeme Marshall Sharp. Manager: Alexander Chapman Ferguson.
**URU**: Fernando Harry Álvez Mosquera, Víctor Hugo Diogo Silva, Eduardo Mario Acevedo Cardozo, Nelson Daniel Gutiérrez Luongo, José Alberto Batista González, Alfonso Darío Pereyra Bueno, Jorge Wálter Barrios Balestrasse, Sérgio Rodolfo Santín Spinelli, Enzo Francéscoli Uriarte (84 Antonio Alzamendi Casas), Venancio Ariel Ramos Villanueva (71.Mario Daniel Saralegui), Wilmar Rubens Cabrera Sappa. Trainer: Omar Borrás.
**Cautions**: David Narey, Stephen Nicol / Wilmar Rubens Cabrera Sappa, Víctor Hugo Diogo Silva, Fernando Harry Álvez Mosquera.
**Sent off**: José Alberto Batista González (1).

# GROUP F

| | | | |
|---|---|---|---|
| 02.06.1986 | San Nicolás | Morocco - Poland | 0-0 |
| 03.06.1986 | Monterrey | Portugal - England | 1-0(0-0) |
| 06.06.1986 | Monterrey | England - Morocco | 0-0 |
| 07.06.1986 | San Nicolás | Poland - Portugal | 1-0(0-0) |
| 11.06.1986 | Monterrey | England - Poland | 3-0(3-0) |
| 11.06.1986 | Guadalajara | Morocco - Portugal | 3-1(2-0) |

## FINAL STANDINGS

| | | | | | | | | |
|---|---|---|---|---|---|---|---|---|
| 1. | Morocco | 3 | 1 | 2 | 0 | 3 | - 1 | 4 |
| 2. | England | 3 | 1 | 1 | 1 | 3 | - 1 | 3 |
| 3. | Poland | 3 | 1 | 1 | 1 | 1 | - 3 | 3 |
| 4. | Portugal | 3 | 1 | 0 | 2 | 2 | - 4 | 2 |

02.06.1986, Estadio Universitario, San Nicolás de los Garza; Attendance: 12,000
Referee: José Luis Martínez Bazán (Uruguay)
**MOROCCO - POLAND** **0-0**
**MAR:** Ezaki Badou, Khaled Khalifa, Abdelmajid Lamris, Mustapha El Biyaz, Noureddine Bouyahyaoui, Abdelmajid Dolmy, Mustapha El Haddaoui (90.Abderrazak Khairi), Abdelaziz Bouderbala, Abdelkrim Merry, Mohamed Timoumi (90.Abdelaziz Souleimani), Mustapha Merry. Trainer: José Faria (Brazil).
**POL:** Józef Młynarczyk, Dariusz Kubicki (46.Kazimierz Przybyś), Roman Wójcicki, Stefan Majewski, Marek Ostrowski, Andrzej Buncol, Waldemar Matysik, Zbigniew Boniek (Cap), Ryszard Komornicki, Dariusz Dziekanowski (56.Jan Urban), Włodzimierz Smolarek. Trainer: Antoni Piechniczek.
**Cautions**: Mohamed Timoumi.

03.06.1986, Estadio Tecnológico, Monterrey; Attendance: 19,998
Referee: Volker Roth (West Germany)
**PORTUGAL - ENGLAND** **1-0(0-0)**
**POR:** Manuel Galrinho Bento (Cap), Álvaro Monteiro de Magalhães, Frederico Nobre Rosa, António Henriques Fonseca de Jesus Oliveira, Augusto Soares Inácio, António dos Santos Ferreira André, Diamantino Manuel Fernandes Miranda (83.José António Prudêncio Conde Bargiela), Carlos Manuel Correia dos Santos, Jaime Moreira Pacheco, António Augusto Gomes de Silva „Sousa", Fernando Mendes Soares Gomes (71.Paulo Jorge dos Santos Futre). Trainer: José Augusto da Costa Séneca Torres.
**ENG:** Peter Leslie Shilton, Gary Michael Stevens, Kenneth Graham Sansom, Glenn Hoddle, Terence William Fenwick, Terence Ian Butcher, Bryan Robson (Cap) (80.Stephen Brian Hodge), Raymond Colin Wilkins, Mark Wayne Hateley, Gary Winston Lineker, Christopher Roland Waddle (80.Peter Andrew Beardsley). Manager: Robert William Robson.
**Goal**: 1-0 Carlos Manuel Correia dos Santos (74).
**Cautions**: Jaime Moreira Pacheco / Terence William Fenwick, Terence Ian Butcher.

06.06.1986, Estadio Tecnológico, Monterrey; Attendance: 22,200
Referee: Efrain Gabriel González Roa (Paraguay)
**ENGLAND - MOROCCO** **0-0**
**ENG:** Peter Leslie Shilton, Gary Michael Stevens, Kenneth Graham Sansom, Glenn Hoddle, Terence William Fenwick, Terence Ian Butcher, Bryan Robson (Cap) (41.Stephen Brian Hodge), Raymond Colin Wilkins, Mark Wayne Hateley (75.Gary Andrew Stevens), Gary Winston Lineker, Christopher Roland Waddle. Manager: Robert William Robson.
**MAR:** Ezaki Badou, Khaled Khalifa, Abdelmajid Lamris (73.Lahcen Ouadani), Mustapha El Biyaz, Noureddine Bouyahyaoui, Abdelmajid Dolmy, Abdelaziz Bouderbala, Abdelkrim Merry, Mohamed

Timoumi, Mustapha Merry (86.Abdelaziz Souaimain), Abderrazak Khairi. Trainer: José Faria (Brazil).
**Cautions**: Raymond Colin Wilkins, Mark Wayne Hateley / Khaled Khalifa, Abderrazak Khairi.
**Sent off**: Raymond Colin Wilkins (42).

07.06.1986, Estadio Universitario, San Nicolás de los Garza; Attendance: 19,915
Referee: Ali Bennaceur (Tunisia)
**POLAND - PORTUGAL**                                                  **1-0(0-0)**
**POL:** Józef Młynarczyk, Krzysztof Pawlak, Roman Wójcicki, Stefan Majewski, Marek Ostrowski, Waldemar Matysik, Ryszard Komornicki (57.Jan Karaś), Jan Urban, Zbigniew Boniek (Cap), Dariusz Dziekanowski, Włodzimierz Smolarek (75.Andrzej Zgutczyński). Trainer: Antoni Piechniczek.
**POR:** Vítor Manuel Alfonso Damas de Oliveira, Álvaro Monteiro de Magalhães, Frederico Nobre Rosa, António Henriques Fonseca de Jesus Oliveira, Augusto Soares Inácio, António dos Santos Ferreira André (73.Jaime Fernandes Magalhães), Diamantino Manuel Fernandes Miranda, Carlos Manuel Correia dos Santos, Jaime Moreira Pacheco, António Augusto Gomes de Silva „Sousa", Fernando Mendes Soares Gomes (Cap) (46.Paulo Jorge dos Santos Futre). Trainer: José Augusto da Costa Séneca Torres.
**Goal**: 1-0 Włodzimierz Smolarek (68).
**Cautions**: Roman Wójcicki, Dariusz Dziekanowski.

11.06.1986, Estadio Universitario, San Nicolás de los Garza; Attendance: 22,700
Referee: André Daina (Switzerland)
**ENGLAND - POLAND**                                                  **3-0(3-0)**
**ENG:** Peter Leslie Shilton (Cap), Gary Michael Stevens, Kenneth Graham Sansom, Glenn Hoddle, Terence William Fenwick, Terence Ian Butcher, Trevor McGregor Steven, Peter Reid, Gary Winston Lineker (80.Kerry Michael Dixon), Peter Andrew Beardsley (75.Christopher Roland Waddle), Stephen Brian Hodge. Manager: Robert William Robson.
**POL:** : Józef Młynarczyk, Krzysztof Pawlak, Roman Wójcicki, Stefan Majewski, Marek Ostrowski, Dariusz Dziekanowski, Waldemar Matysik (46.Andrzej Buncol), Ryszard Komornicki (24.Jan Karaś), Jan Urban, Zbigniew Boniek (Cap), Włodzimierz Smolarek. Trainer: Antoni Piechniczek.
**Goals**: 1-0 Gary Winston Lineker (8), 2-0 Gary Winston Lineker (14), 3-0 Gary Winston Lineker (36).
**Cautions**: Terence William Fenwick.

11.06.1986, Estadio Tres de Marzo, Guadalajara; Attendance: 28,000
Referee: Alan Snoddy (Northern Ireland)
**MOROCCO - PORTUGAL**                                          **3-1(2-0)**
**MAR:** Ezaki Badou, Khaled Khalifa, Abdelmajid Lamris, Mustapha El Biyaz, Noureddine Bouyahyaoui, Abdelmajid Dolmy, Mustapha El Haddaoui (71.Abdelaziz Souleimani), Abdelaziz Bouderbala, Abdelkrim Merry, Mohamed Timoumi, Abderrazak Khairi. Trainer: José Faria (Brazil).
**POR:** Vítor Manuel Alfonso Damas de Oliveira, Álvaro Monteiro de Magalhães (53.José Rui Lopes Águas), Frederico Nobre Rosa, António Henriques Fonseca de Jesus Oliveira, Augusto Soares Inácio, Jaime Fernandes Magalhães, Carlos Manuel Correia dos Santos, Jaime Moreira Pacheco, António Augusto Gomes de Silva „Sousa" (68.Diamantino Manuel Fernandes Miranda), Fernando Mendes Soares Gomes (Cap), Paulo Jorge dos Santos Futre. Trainer: José Augusto da Costa Séneca Torres.
**Goals**: 1-0 Abderrazak Khairi (19), 2-0 Abderrazak Khairi (26), 3-0 Abdelkrim Merry (62), 3-1 Diamantino Manuel Fernandes Miranda (79).
**Cautions**: Fernando Mendes Soares Gomes.

# SECOND ROUND

| 15.06.1986 | Ciudad de México | Mexico - Bulgaria | 2-0(1-0) |
|---|---|---|---|
| 15.06.1986 | León | Soviet Union - Belgium | 3-4 aet |
| 16.06.1986 | Guadalajara | Brazil - Poland | 4-0(1-0) |
| 16.06.1986 | Puebla | Argentina - Uruguay | 1-0(0-0) |
| 17.06.1986 | Ciudad de México | France - Italy | 2-0(1-0) |
| 17.06.1986 | San Nicolás | West Germany – Morocco | 1-0(0-0) |
| 18.06.1986 | Ciudad de México | England - Paraguay | 3-0(1-0) |
| 18.06.1986 | Querétaro | Denmark - Spain | 1-5(1-1) |

15.06.1986, Estadio Azteca, Ciudad de México; Attendance: 114,550
Referee: Romualdo Arppi Filho (Brazil)
**MEXICO - BULGARIA**  **2-0(1-0)**
**MEX:** Pablo Larios Iwasaki, Rafael Amador Flores, Félix Cruz Barbosa Ríos, Fernando Quirarte Gutiérrez, Raúl Servín Monetti, Carlos Eduardo Muñoz Remolina, Miguel España Garcés, Manuel Negrete Arias, Tomás Juan Boy Espinoza (Cap) (79.Carlos de los Cobos Martínez), Javier Aguirre Onaindía, Hugo Sánchez Márquez. Trainer: Velibor Milutinović (Yugoslavia).
**BUL:** Borislav Mihailov, Radoslav Zdravkov, Nikolai Arabov, Petar Petrov, Georgi Dimitrov (Cap), Anio Sadkov, Georgi Iordanov, Kostadin Kostadinov, Jivko Gospodinov, Atanas Pashev (71.Bojidar Iskrenov), Plamen Getov (60.Nasko Sirakov. Trainer: Ivan Vutsov.
**Goals:** 1-0 Manuel Negrete Arias (34), 2-0 Raúl Servín Monetti (61).
**Cautions:** Nikolai Arabov.

15.06.1986, Estadio Nou Camp, León; Attendance: 32,277
Referee: Erik Fredriksson (Sweden)
**SOVIET UNION - BELGIUM**  **3-4(1-0,2-2)**
**URS:** Rinat Dasaev, Vladimir Bessonov, Andrey Bal, Oleg Kuznetzov, Anatoliy Demyanenko (Cap), Pavel Yakovenko (79.Vadim Evtushenko), Ivan Yaremchuk, Vasiliy Ratz, Sergey Aleynikov, Aleksandr Zavarov (72.Sergey Rodionov), Igor Belanov. Trainer: Valeriy Lobanovskiy.
**BEL:** Jean-Marie Pfaff, Georges Grün (99.Léo Albert Clijsters), Stéphane Demol, Eric Gerets (112.Léo Vander Elst), Michel Renquin, Patrick Vervoort, Vincenzo Scifo, Daniel Veyt, Jan Ceulemans, Frank Vercauteren, Nicolaas Pieter Claesen. Trainer: Guy Thys.
**Goals:** 1-0 Igor Belanov (27), 1-1 Vincenzo Scifo (56), 2-1 Igor Belanov (69), 2-2 Jan Ceulemans (78), 2-3 Stéphane Demol (102), 2-4 Nicolaas Pieter Claesen (109), 3-4 Igor Belanov (110 penalty).
**Cautions:** Michel Renquin.

16.06.1986, Estadio Monumental Jalisco, Guadalajara; Attendance: 40,000
Referee: Volker Roth (West Germany)
**BRAZIL - POLAND**  **4-0(1-0)**
**BRA:** Carlos Roberto Gallo, Josimar Higino Pereira, Júlio César da Silva, Édino Nazareth Filho "Edinho", Cláudio Ibrahim Vaz Leal "Branco", Elzo Aloísio Coelho, Ricardo Rogério de Brito "Alemão", Sócrates Brasileiro Sampaio Vieira de Oliveira (70.Arthur Antunes Coimbra "Zico"), Leovegildo Lins Gama Júnior "Júnior I", Luís Antônio Corrêa da Costa "Müller" (73.Paulo Silas do Prado Pereira), Antônio de Oliveira Filho "Careca I". Trainer: Telê Santana da Silva.
**POL:** Józef Młynarczyk, Kazimierz Przybyś (60.Jan Furtok), Roman Wójcicki, Stefan Majewski, Marek Ostrowski, Jan Karaś, Ryszard Tarasiewicz, Dariusz Dziekanowski, Jan Urban (84.Władysław Żmuda), Zbigniew Boniek (Cap), Włodzimierz Smolarek. Trainer: Antoni Piechniczek.
**Goals:** 1-0 Sócrates Brasileiro Sampaio Vieira de Oliveira (29 penalty), 2-0 Josimar Higino Pereira (53), 3-0 Édino Nazareth Filho "Edinho" (77), 4-0 Antônio de Oliveira Filho "Careca I" (83 penalty).
**Cautions:** Antônio de Oliveira Filho "Careca I", Édino Nazareth Filho "Edinho".

16.06.1986, Estadio Cuauhtémoc, Puebla; Attendance: 26,000
Referee: Luigi Agnolin (Italy)
**ARGENTINA - URUGUAY**　　　　　　　　　　　　　　　　　**1-0(0-0)**
**ARG:** Nery Alberto Pumpido, José Luis Cuciuffo, José Luis Brown, Oscar Alfredo Ruggeri, Oscar Alfredo Garré, Ricardo Omar Giusti, Sergio Daniel Batista (87.Julio Jorge Olarticoechea), Jorge Luis Burruchaga, Diego Armando Maradona (Cap), Pedro Pablo Pasculli, Jorge Alberto Francisco Valdano. Trainer: Dr. Carlos Salvador Bilardo.
**URU:** Fernando Harry Álvez Mosquera, Nelson Daniel Gutiérrez Luongo, Eduardo Mario Acevedo Cardozo (61.Rúben Walter Paz Márquez), Eliseo Roque Rivero Pérez, Sérgio Rodolfo Santín Spinelli, Venancio Ariel Ramos Villanueva, Miguel Angel Bossio Bastianini, Jorge Wálter Barrios Balestrasse, Alfonso Darío Pereyra Bueno, Wilmar Rubens Cabrera Sappa (46.Jorge Orosmán da Silva Echeverrito), Enzo Francéscoli Uriarte. Trainer: Omar Borrás.
**Goal**: 1-0 Pedro Pablo Pasculli (42).
**Cautions**: Oscar Alfredo Garré, José Luis Brown, Nery Alberto Pumpido / Enzo Francéscoli Uriarte, Eduardo Mario Acevedo Cardozo, Sérgio Rodolfo Santín Spinelli, Jorge Orosmán da Silva Echeverrito.

17.06.1986, Estadio Olímpico Universitario, Ciudad de México; Attendance: 71,449
Referee: Carlos Alfonso Espósito (Argentina)
**FRANCE - ITALY**　　　　　　　　　　　　　　　　　　　　**2-0(1-0)**
**FRA:** Joël Bats, William Ayache, Maxime Bossis, Patrick Battiston, Manuel Amoros, Alain Giresse, Luis Fernández (73.Thierry Tusseau), Jean Amadou Tigana, Michel Platini (Cap) (71.Jean-Marc Ferreri), Dominique Rocheteau, Yannick Stopyra. Trainer: Henri Michel.
**ITA:** Giovanni Galli, Giuseppe Bergomi, Pietro Vierchowod, Gaetano Scirea, Antonio Cabrini, Giuseppe Baresi I (46.Antonio Di Gennaro), Fernando De Napoli, Giuseppe Galderisi (57.Gianluca Vialli), Salvatore Bagni, Bruno Conti, Alessandro Altobelli. Trainer: Enzo Bearzot.
**Goals**: 1-0 Michel Platini (15), 2-0 Yannick Stopyra (57).
**Cautions**: William Ayache / Fernando De Napoli, Antonio Di Gennaro.

17.06.1986, Estadio Universitário, San Nicolás de los Garza; Attendance: 19,800
Referee: Zoran Petrović (Yugoslavia)
**WEST GERMANY – MOROCCO**　　　　　　　　　　　　　**1-0(0-0)**
**GER:** Harald Schumacher, Thomas Berthold, Ditmar Jakobs, Karlheinz Förster, Hans-Peter Briegel, Norbert Eder, Lothar Herbert Matthäus, Felix Magath, Karl-Heinz Rummenigge (Cap), Rudolf Völler (46.Pierre Littbarski), Klaus Allofs. Trainer: Franz Beckenbauer.
**MAR:** Ezaki Badou, Khaled Khalifa, Abdelmajid Lamris, Noureddine Bouyahyaoui, Abdelmajid Dolmy, Mustapha El Haddaoui, Abdelaziz Bouderbala, Abdelkrim Merry, Mohamed Timoumi, Lahcen Ouadani, Abderrazak Khairi. Trainer: José Faria (Brazil).
**Goal**: 1-0 Lothar Herbert Matthäus (88).
**Cautions**: Abdelmajid Lamris, Khaled Khalifa.

18.06.1986, Estadio Azteca, Ciudad de México; Attendance: 98,728
Referee: Jamal Al Sharif (Syria)
**ENGLAND - PARAGUAY**　　　　　　　　　　　　　　　　**3-0(1-0)**
**ENG:** Peter Leslie Shilton (Cap), Gary Michael Stevens, Kenneth Graham Sansom, Glenn Hoddle, Alvin Edward Martin, Terence Ian Butcher, Trevor McGregor Steven, Peter Reid (57.Gary Andrew Stevens), Gary Winston Lineker, Peter Andrew Beardsley (80.Mark Wayne Hateley), Stephen Brian Hodge. Manager: Robert William Robson.
**PAR:** Roberto Eladio Fernández Roa, Juan Bautista Torales (63.Jorge Alberto Guasch Bazán), César Zabala Fernández, Rogelio Wilfrido Delgado Casco (Cap), Vladimiro Schettina Chepini, Jorge Amado Núñez Infrán, Buenaventura Ferreira Gómez, Julio César Romero Insfrán, Roberto Cabañas González, Adolfino Cañete Azcurra, Alfredo Damián Mendoza Sulewski. Trainer: Cayetano Ré Ramírez.
**Goals**: 1-0 Gary Winston Lineker (32), 2-0 Gary Winston Lineker (72), 3-0 Peter Andrew Beardsley (56).
**Cautions**: Alvin Edward Martin, Stephen Brian Hodge / Jorge Amado Núñez Infrán.

18.06.1986, Estadio La Corregidora, Querétaro; Attendance: 38,500
Referee: Johannes Nicolaas Ignatius „Jan" Keizer (Holland)
**DENMARK - SPAIN**     **1-5(1-1)**
**DEN:** Lars Høgh, Søren Busk, Morten Olsen (Cap), Ivan Nielsen, Henrik Andersen (60.John Eriksen), Klaus Berggreen, Jens Jørn Bertelsen, Søren Lerby, Jesper Olsen (72.Jan Mølby), Michael Laudrup, Preben Elkjær-Larsen. Trainer: Josef Piontek (West Germany).
**ESP:** Andoni Zubizarreta Urreta, Pedro Tomás Reñones Grego, Andoni Goikoetxea Olaskoaga, Ricardo Gallego Redondo, José Antonio Camacho Alfaro (Cap), Ramón María Calderé Del Rey, Víctor Muñoz Manrique, José Miguel González Martín del Campo „Míchel" (82.Francisco Javier López Alfaro), Julio Alberto Moreno Casas, Julio Salinas Fernández (46.Eloy José Olaya Prendes), Emilio Butragueño Santos. Trainer: Miguel Muñoz Mozún.
**Goals:** 1-0 Jesper Olsen (33 penalty), 1-1 Emilio Butragueño Santos (43), 1-2 Emilio Butragueño Santos (51), 1-3 Andoni Goikoetxea Olaskoaga (68 penalty), 1-4 Emilio Butragueño Santos (80), 1-5 Emilio Butragueño Santos (88 penalty).
**Cautions:** Henrik Andersen / Andoni Goikoetxea Olaskoaga, José Antonio Camacho Alfaro, José Miguel González Martín del Campo „Míchel".

## QUARTER-FINALS

| | | | |
|---|---|---|---|
| 21.06.1986 | Guadalajara | Brazil – France | 3-4 pen |
| 21.06.1986 | San Nicolás | West Germany - Mexico | 4-1 pen |
| 22.06.1986 | Ciudad de México | Argentina - England | 2-1(0-0) |
| 22.06.1986 | Puebla | Belgium - Spain | 5-4 pen |

21.06.1986, Estadio Jalisco, Guadalajara; Attendance: 65,777
Referee: Ioan Igna (Romania)
**BRAZIL – FRANCE**     **1-1(1-1,1-1,1-1);**
    **3-4 on penalties**
**BRA:** Carlos Roberto Gallo, Josimar Higino Pereira, Júlio César da Silva, Édino Nazareth Filho "Edinho", Cláudio Ibrahim Vaz Leal "Branco", Elzo Aloísio Coelho, Ricardo Rogério de Brito "Alemão", Sócrates Brasileiro Sampaio Vieira de Oliveira, Leovegildo Lins Gama Júnior "Júnior I" (91.Paulo Silas do Prado Pereira), Luís Antônio Corrêa da Costa "Müller" (72.Arthur Antunes Coimbra "Zico"), Antônio de Oliveira Filho "Careca I". Trainer: Telê Santana da Silva.
**FRA:** Joël Bats, Manuel Amoros, Maxime Bossis, Patrick Battiston, Thierry Tusseau, Luis Fernández, Alain Giresse (84.Jean-Marc Ferreri), Michel Platini (Cap), Jean Amadou Tigana, Dominique Rocheteau (99.Bruno Bellone), Yannick Stopyra. Trainer: Henri Michel.
**Goals:** 1-0 Antônio de Oliveira Filho "Careca I" (17), 1-1 Michel Platini (41).
**Penalties:** Sócrates Brasileiro Sampaio Vieira de Oliveira (saved); Yannick Stopyra 0-1; Ricardo Rogério de Brito "Alemão" 1-1; Manuel Amoros 1-2; Arthur Antunes Coimbra "Zico" 2-2; Bruno Bellone 2-3; Cláudio Ibrahim Vaz Leal "Branco" 3-3; Michel Platini (missed); Júlio César da Silva (missed); Luis Fernández 3-4.

21.06.1986, Estadio Universitário, San Nicolás de los Garza; Attendance: 41,700
Referee: Jesús Díaz Palacio (Colombia)
**WEST GERMANY - MEXICO**  0-0; 4-1 on penalties
**GER:** Harald Schumacher, Thomas Berthold, Ditmar Jakobs, Karlheinz Förster, Hans-Peter Briegel, Norbert Eder (115.Pierre Littbarski), Andreas Brehme, Lothar Herbert Matthäus, Felix Magath, Karl-Heinz Rummenigge (Cap) (58.Dieter Hoeneß), Klaus Allofs. Trainer: Franz Beckenbauer
**MEX:** Pablo Larios Iwasaki, Rafael Amador Flores (70.Francisco Javier Cruz Jiménez), Félix Cruz Barbosa Ríos, Fernando Quirarte Gutiérrez, Raúl Servín Monetti, Carlos Eduardo Muñoz Remolina, Miguel España Garcés, Manuel Negrete Arias, Tomás Juan Boy Espinoza (Cap) (32.Carlos de los Cobos Martínez), Javier Aguirre Onaindía, Hugo Sánchez Márquez. Trainer: Velibor Milutinović (Yugoslavia).
**Penalties**: Klaus Allofs 1-0; Manuel Negrete Arias 1-1; Andreas Brehme 2-1; Raúl Servín Monetti (missed); Lothar Herbert Matthäus 3-1; Fernando Quirarte Gutiérrez (missed); Pierre Littbarski 4-1.
**Cautions**: Klaus Allofs, Karlheinz Förster, Lothar Herbert Matthäus / Javier Aguirre Onaindía, Fernando Quirarte Gutiérrez, Carlos de los Cobos Martínez, Raúl Servín Monetti, Hugo Sánchez Márquez
**Sent off**: Thomas Berthold (66), Javier Aguirre Onaindía (100).

22.06.1986, Estadio Azteca, Ciudad de México; Attendance: 114,500
Referee: Ali Bennaceur (Tunisia)
**ARGENTINA - ENGLAND**  2-1(0-0)
**ARG:** Nery Alberto Pumpido, José Luis Cuciuffo, José Luis Brown, Oscar Alfredo Ruggeri, Julio Jorge Olarticoechea, Ricardo Omar Giusti, Sergio Daniel Batista, Jorge Luis Burruchaga (76.Carlos Daniel Tapia), Héctor Adolfo Enrique, Diego Armando Maradona (Cap), Jorge Alberto Francisco Valdano. Trainer: Dr. Carlos Salvador Bilardo.
**ENG:** Peter Leslie Shilton (Cap), Gary Michael Stevens, Kenneth Graham Sansom, Glenn Hoddle, Terence Ian Butcher, Terence William Fenwick, Trevor McGregor Steven (73.John Charles Bryan Barnes), Peter Reid (63.Christopher Roland Waddle), Gary Winston Lineker, Peter Andrew Beardsley, Stephen Brian Hodge. Manager: Robert William Robson.
**Goals**: 1-0 Diego Armando Maradona (52), 2-0 Diego Armando Maradona (56), 2-1 Gary Winston Lineker (81).
**Cautions**: Sergio Daniel Batista / Terence William Fenwick.

22.06.1986, Estadio Cuauhtémoc, Puebla; Attendance: 44,962
Referee: Siegfried Kirschen (East Germany)
**BELGIUM - SPAIN**  1-1(1-0,1-1,1-1);
 5-4 on penalties
**BEL:** Jean-Marie Pfaff, Eric Gerets, Georges Grün, Michel Renquin, Stéphane Demol, Patrick Vervoort, Vincenzo Scifo, Jan Ceulemans, Daniel Veyt (83.Hugo Broos), Nicolaas Pieter Claesen, Frank Vercauteren (105.Léo Vander Elst). Trainer: Guy Thys.
**ESP:** Andoni Zubizarreta Urreta, Pedro Tomás Reñones Grego (46.Juan Antonio Señor Gómez), Miguel Porlán Noguera „Chendo", Ricardo Gallego Redondo, José Antonio Camacho Alfaro (Cap), Ramón María Calderé Del Rey, Víctor Muñoz Manrique, José Miguel González Martín del Campo „Míchel", Julio Alberto Moreno Casas, Julio Salinas Fernández (63.Eloy José Olaya Prendes), Emilio Butragueño Santos. Trainer: Miguel Muñoz Mozún.
**Goals**: 1-0 Jan Ceulemans (35), 1-1 Juan Antonio Señor Gómez (85).
**Penalties**: Juan Antonio Señor Gómez 0-1; Nicolaas Pieter Claesen 1-1; Eloy José Olaya Prendes (saved); Vincenzo Scifo 2-1; Miguel Porlán Noguera „Chendo" 2-2; Hugo Broos 3-2; Emilio Butragueño Santos 3-3; Patrick Vervoort 4-3; Víctor Muñoz Manrique 4-4; Léo Vander Elst 5-4.
**Cautions**: Stéphane Demol, Georges Grün / Pedro Tomás Reñones Grego, Ramón María Calderé Del Rey.

# SEMI-FINALS

| | | | |
|---|---|---|---|
| 25.06.1986 | Guadalajara | France – West Germany | 0-2(0-1) |
| 25.06.1986 | Ciudad de México | Argentina - Belgium | 2-0(1-0) |

25.06.1986, Estadio Jalisco, Guadalajara; Attendance: 47,500
Referee: Luigi Agnolin (Italy)
**FRANCE – WEST GERMANY**                                                    **0-2(0-1)**
**FRA:** Joël Bats, William Ayache, Maxime Bossis, Patrick Battiston, Manuel Amoros, Luis Fernández, Jean Amadou Tigana, Alain Giresse (71.Philippe Vercruysse), Michel Platini (Cap), Yannick Stopyra, Bruno Bellone (66.Daniel Xuereb). Trainer: Henri Michel.
**GER:** Harald Schumacher, Andreas Brehme, Ditmar Jakobs, Karlheinz Förster, Hans-Peter Briegel, Norbert Eder, Lothar Herbert Matthäus, Wolfgang Rolff, Felix Magath, Karl-Heinz Rummenigge (Cap) (56.Rudolf Völler), Klaus Allofs. Trainer: Franz Beckenbauer.
**Goals:** 0-1 Andreas Brehme (9), 0-2 Rudolf Völler (90).
**Cautions:** Luis Fernández / Felix Magath.

25.06.1986, Estadio Azteca, Ciudad de México; Attendance: 110,820
Referee: Antonio Márquez Ramírez (Mexico)
**ARGENTINA - BELGIUM**                                                 **2-0(1-0)**
**ARG:** Nery Alberto Pumpido, José Luis Cuciuffo, José Luis Brown, Oscar Alfredo Ruggeri, Julio Jorge Olarticoechea, Ricardo Omar Giusti, Sergio Daniel Batista, Jorge Luis Burruchaga (86.Ricardo Enrique Bochini), Héctor Adolfo Enrique, Diego Armando Maradona (Cap), Jorge Alberto Francisco Valdano. Trainer: Dr. Carlos Salvador Bilardo.
**BEL:** Jean-Marie Pfaff, Eric Gerets, Georges Grün, Michel Renquin (66.Philippe De Smet), Stéphane Demol, Patrick Vervoort, Vincenzo Scifo, Jan Ceulemans, Frank Vercauteren, Daniel Veyt, Nicolaas Pieter Claesen. Trainer: Guy Thys.
**Goals:** 1-0 Diego Armando Maradona (52), 2-0 Diego Armando Maradona (63).
**Cautions:** Jorge Alberto Francisco Valdano / Daniel Veyt.

## 3rd PLACE PLAY-OFF

28.06.1986, Estadio Cuauhtémoc, Puebla; Attendance: 21,500
Referee: George Courtney (England)
**FRANCE - BELGIUM** 4-2(2-1,2-2)
**FRA:** Albert Rust, Michel Bibard, Yvon Le Roux (56.Maxime Bossis), Patrick Battiston (Cap), Manuel Amoros, Jean Amadou Tigana (84.Thierry Tusseau), Bernard Genghini, Jean-Marc Ferreri, Philippe Vercruysse, Jean-Pierre Papin, Bruno Bellone. Trainer: Henri Michel.
**BEL:** Jean-Marie Pfaff, Eric Gerets, Stéphane Demol, Michel Renquin (46.Frank Richard Vander Elst), Georges Grün, Patrick Vervoort, Vincenzo Scifo (64.Léo Vander Elst), Raymond Mommens, Jan Ceulemans, Daniel Veyt, Nicolaas Pieter Claesen. Trainer: Guy Thys.
**Goals:** 0-1 Jan Ceulemans (11), 1-1 Jean-Marc Ferreri (27), 2-1 Jean-Pierre Papin (43), 2-2 Nicolaas Pieter Claesen (73), 3-2 Bernard Genghini (104), 4-2 Manuel Amoros (111 penalty).
**Cautions:** Jean-Marie Pfaff.

## FINAL

29.06.1986, Estadio Azteca, Ciudad de México; Attendance: 114,600
Referee: Romualdo Arppi Filho (Brazil)
**ARGENTINA – WEST GERMANY** 3-2(1-0)
**ARG:** Nery Alberto Pumpido, José Luis Cuciuffo, José Luis Brown, Oscar Alfredo Ruggeri, Julio Jorge Olarticoechea, Ricardo Omar Giusti, Sergio Daniel Batista, Diego Armando Maradona (Cap), Héctor Adolfo Enrique, Jorge Luis Burruchaga (89.Marcelo Antonio Trobbiani), Jorge Alberto Francisco Valdano. Trainer: Dr. Carlos Salvador Bilardo.
**GER:** Harald Schumacher, Thomas Berthold, Ditmar Jakobs, Karlheinz Förster, Hans-Peter Briegel, Norbert Eder, Andreas Brehme, Lothar Herbert Matthäus, Felix Magath (61.Dieter Hoeneß), Karl-Heinz Rummenigge (Cap), Klaus Allofs (46.Rudolf Völler). Trainer: Franz Beckenbauer.
**Goals:** 1-0 José Luis Brown (23), 2-0 Jorge Alberto Francisco Valdano (56), 2-1 Karl-Heinz Rummenigge (72), 2-2 Rudolf Völler (84), 3-2 Jorge Luis Burruchaga (85).
**Cautions:** Diego Armando Maradona, Julio Jorge Olarticoechea, Héctor Adolfo Enrique, Nery Alberto Pumpido / Lothar Herbert Matthäus, Hans-Peter Briegel.

# WORLD CUP 1986 FINAL RANKING

| | | | | | | | | | |
|---|---|---|---|---|---|---|---|---|---|
| 1. | **Argentina** | 7 | 6 | 1 | 0 | 14 | - | 5 | 13 |
| 2. | West Germany | 7 | 3 | 2 | 2 | 8 | - | 7 | 8 |
| 3. | France | 7 | 4 | 2 | 1 | 12 | - | 6 | 10 |
| 4. | Belgium | 7 | 2 | 2 | 3 | 12 | - | 15 | 6 |
| 5. | Brazil | 5 | 4 | 1 | 0 | 10 | - | 1 | 9 |
| 6. | Mexico | 5 | 3 | 2 | 0 | 6 | - | 2 | 8 |
| 7. | Spain | 5 | 3 | 1 | 1 | 11 | - | 4 | 7 |
| 8. | England | 5 | 2 | 1 | 2 | 7 | - | 3 | 5 |
| 9. | Denmark | 4 | 3 | 0 | 1 | 10 | - | 6 | 6 |
| 10. | Soviet Union | 4 | 2 | 1 | 1 | 12 | - | 5 | 5 |
| 11. | Morocco | 4 | 1 | 2 | 1 | 3 | - | 2 | 4 |
| 12. | Italy | 4 | 1 | 2 | 1 | 5 | - | 6 | 4 |
| 13. | Paraguay | 4 | 1 | 2 | 1 | 4 | - | 6 | 4 |
| 14. | Poland | 4 | 1 | 1 | 2 | 1 | - | 7 | 3 |
| 15. | Bulgaria | 4 | 0 | 2 | 2 | 2 | - | 6 | 2 |
| 16. | Uruguay | 4 | 0 | 2 | 2 | 2 | - | 8 | 2 |
| 17. | Portugal | 3 | 1 | 0 | 2 | 2 | - | 4 | 2 |
| 18. | Hungary | 3 | 1 | 0 | 2 | 2 | - | 9 | 2 |
| 19. | Scotland | 3 | 0 | 1 | 2 | 1 | - | 3 | 1 |
| 20. | South Korea | 3 | 0 | 1 | 2 | 4 | - | 7 | 1 |
| 21. | Northern Ireland | 3 | 0 | 1 | 2 | 2 | - | 6 | 1 |
| 22. | Algeria | 3 | 0 | 1 | 2 | 1 | - | 5 | 1 |
| 23. | Iraq | 3 | 0 | 0 | 3 | 1 | - | 4 | 0 |
| 24. | Canada | 3 | 0 | 0 | 3 | 0 | - | 5 | 0 |

# WORLD CUP 1986 AWARDS

**GOLDEN BALL (best player of the World Cup final tournament)**
Diego Armando Maradona (Argentina)

**GOLDEN BOOT (best goalscorer)**
Gary Winston Lineker (England)

**FIFA FAIR-PLAY TROPHY**
Brazil

# GOALSCORERS

**6 goals:** Gary Winston Lineker (England)
**5 goals:** Diego Armando Maradona (Argentina)
Antônio de Oliveira Filho "Careca I" (Brazil)
Emilio Butragueño Santos (Spain)
**4 goals:** Jorge Alberto Francisco Valdano (Argentina)
Preben Elkjær-Larsen (Denmark)
Alessandro Altobelli (Italy)
Igor Belanov (Soviet Union)
**3 goals:** Jan Ceulemans, Nicolaas Pieter Claesen (Belgium)
Jesper Olsen (Denmark)
Rudolf Völler (West Germany)
**2 goals:** Jorge Luis Burruchaga (Argentina), Vincenzo Scifo (Belgium), Josimar Higino Pereira, Sócrates Brasileiro Sampaio Vieira de Oliveira (Brazil), Jean-Pierre Papin, Michel Platini, Yannick Stopyra (France), Fernando Quirarte Gutiérrez (Mexico), Abderrazak Khairi (Morocco), Roberto Cabañas González, Julio César Romero Insfrán (Paraguay), Ramón María Calderé Del Rey (Spain), Klaus Allofs (West Germany)
**1 goal:** Djamel Zidane (Algeria), José Luis Brown, Pedro Pablo Pasculli, Oscar Alfredo Ruggeri (Argentina), Stéphane Demol, Erwin Vandenbergh, Frank Vercauteren, Daniel Veyt (Belgium), Édino Nazareth Filho "Edinho" (Brazil), Plamen Getov, Nasko Sirakov (Bulgaria), John Eriksen, Michael Laudrup, Søren Lerby (Denmark), Peter Andrew Beardsley (England), Manuel Amoros, Luis Fernández, Jean-Marc Ferreri, Bernard Genghini, Dominique Rocheteau, Jean Amadou Tigana (France), Lajos Détári, Márton Esterházy (Hungary), Ahmad Radhi Amaiesh Al Salehi (Iraq), Luis Enrique Flores Ocaranza Manuel Negrete Arias Hugo Sánchez Márquez Raúl Servín Monetti (Mexico), Abdelkrim Merry (Morocco), Colin John Clarke, Norman Whiteside (Northern Ireland), Włodzimierz Smolarek (Poland), Carlos Manuel Correia dos Santos, Diamantino Manuel Fernandes Miranda (Portugal), Gordon David Strachan (Scotland), Choi Soon-Ho, Huh Jung-Moo, Kim Jong-Boo, Park Chang-Sun (South Korea), Oleg Blokhin, Vasiliy Ratz, Sergey Rodionov, Pavel Yakovenko, Ivan Yaremchuk, Aleksandr Zavarov (Soviet Union), Eloy José Olaya Prendes, Andoni Goikoetxea Olaskoaga, Julio Salinas Fernández, Juan Antonio Señor Gómez (Spain), Antonio Alzamendi Casas, Enzo Francéscoli Uriarte (Uruguay), Andreas Brehme, Lothar Herbert Matthäus, Karl-Heinz Rummenigge (West Germany)

Own goals:
**2** Cho Kwang-Rae (South Korea), against Italy
László Dajka (Hungary), against Soviet Union

Total number of goals scored: **132**
Average goals per match: **2.39**

# LIST OF REFEREES

| Name | DOB | Country | M |
|---|---|---|---|
| Luigi Agnolin | 21.03.1943 | Italy | 3 |
| Romualdo Arppi Filho | 07.01.1939 | Brazil | 3 |
| Carlos Alfonso Espósito | 04.11.1941 | Argentina | 2 |
| Jesús Díaz Palacio | 16.10.1954 | Colombia | 2 |
| Siegfried Kirschen | 13.10.1943 | East Germany | 2 |
| George Courtney | 04.06.1941 | England | 2 |
| Johannes Nicolaas Ignatius „Jan" Keizer | 06.10.1940 | Holland | 2 |
| Antonio Márquez Ramírez | 22.05.1936 | Mexico | 2 |
| Ioan Igna | 04.06.1940 | Romania | 2 |
| Erik Fredriksson | 13.02.1943 | Sweden | 2 |
| Jamal Al Sharif | 08.12.1956 | Syria | 2 |
| Ali Bennaceur | 02.03.1944 | Tunisia | 2 |
| Volker Roth | 01.02.1942 | West Germany | 2 |
| Zoran Petrović | 10.04.1952 | Yugoslavia | 2 |
| Christopher Francis Bambridge | 07.10.1947 | Australia | 1 |
| Horst Brummeier | 31.12.1945 | Austria | 1 |
| Alexis Ponnet | 09.03.1939 | Belgium | 1 |
| Bogdan Dochev | 26.06.1935 | Bulgaria | 1 |
| Hernán Silva Arce | 05.11.1948 | Chile | 1 |
| Berny Ulloa Morera | 05.08.1950 | Costa Rica | 1 |
| Vojtěch Christov | 16.03.1945 | Czechoslovakia | 1 |
| Joël Quiniou | 17.11.1950 | France | 1 |
| Romulo Méndez Molina | 21.12.1938 | Guatemala | 1 |
| Lajos Németh | 14.08.1944 | Hungary | 1 |
| Shizuo Takada | 05.08.1947 | Japan | 1 |
| Idrissa Marcel Traoré | | Mali | 1 |
| Edwin Sydney Picon-Ackong | 04.11.1940 | Mauritius | 1 |
| Alan Snoddy | 29.03.1955 | Northern Ireland | 1 |
| Efrain Gabriel González Roa | 18.03.1942 | Paraguay | 1 |
| Carlos Alberto Da Silva Valente | 25.07.1948 | Portugal | 1 |
| Fallaj Khuzam Al Shanar | 10.10.1947 | Saudi Arabia | 1 |
| Valeri Butenko | 16.07.1941 | Soviet Union | 1 |
| Victoriano Sánchez Arminio | 26.06.1942 | Spain | 1 |
| André Daina | 08.07.1940 | Switzerland | 1 |
| David Stanley Socha | 27.09.1938 | United States | 1 |
| José Luis Martínez Bazán | 11.02.1942 | Uruguay | 1 |

## WORLD CUP 1986 – THE SQUADS

### ALGERIA

| Nr | Name | DOB | Club |
|---|---|---|---|
| | **Goalkeepers** | | |
| 1 | Nacerdine Drid | 22.01.1957 | Mouloudia Club dOran |
| 21 | Larbi El Hadi | 27.05.1961 | Widad Adabi Boufarik |
| 22 | Mourad Amara | 19.02.1959 | JS de Kabylie Tizi-Ouzou |
| | **Defenders** | | |
| 2 | Mahmoud Guendouz | 24.02.1953 | Jeunesse Sportive dEl Biar |
| 3 | Fathi Chebal | 19.08.1956 | FC Rouen (FRA) |
| 4 | Nourredine Abdallah Kourichi | 12.04.1954 | Lille OSC (FRA) |
| 5 | Abdellah Medjadi Liegeon | 01.12.1957 | AS Monaco (FRA) |
| 15 | Abdelhamid Sadmi | 01.01.1961 | JS de Kabylie Tizi-Ouzou |
| 16 | Faouzi Mansouri | 17.01.1956 | Montpellier SC (FRA) |
| 19 | Mohammed Chaib | 20.05.1957 | Raed Chabab Kouba |
| 20 | Fodil Megharia | 23.05.1961 | AS Olympique de Chlef |
| | **Midfielders** | | |
| 6 | Mohamed Kaci Saïd | 02.05.1958 | Raed Chabab Kouba |
| 8 | Karim Maroc | 05.03.1958 | Montpellier SC (FRA) |
| 10 | Lakhdar Belloumi | 29.12.1958 | Ghali Club de Mascara |
| 14 | Djamel Zidane | 28.04.1955 | K Waterschei Thor (BEL) |
| 18 | Halim Ben Mabrouk | 25.06.1960 | Racing Paris FC (FRA) |
| | **Forwards** | | |
| 7 | Salah Assad | 30.08.1958 | FC Mulhouse (FRA) |
| 9 | Djamel Menad | 22.07.1960 | JS de Kabylie Tizi-Ouzou |
| 11 | Mustapha Rabah Madjer | 15.02.1958 | FC do Porto (ALG) |
| 12 | Tedj Bensaoula | 01.12.1954 | Le Havre AC (FRA) |
| 13 | Rachid Harkouk | 16.05.1956 | Notts County FC (ENG) |
| 17 | Faouzi Ben Khalidi | 03.02.1963 | Widad Adabi Boufarik |
| **Trainer:** | Rabah Saâdane | 03.05.1946 | |

### ARGENTINA

| Nr | Name | DOB | Club |
|---|---|---|---|
| | **Goalkeepers** | | |
| 15 | Luis Alberto Islas | 22.12.1965 | Club Estudiantes de La Plata |
| 18 | Nery Alberto Pumpido | 30.07.1957 | CA River Plate Buenos Aires |
| 22 | Héctor Miguel Zelada | 30.04.1957 | CF América Cdad. de México (MEX) |
| | **Defenders** | | |
| 5 | José Luis Brown | 10.11.1956 | CD Atlético Nacional Medellín (COL) |
| 6 | Daniel Alberto Passarella | 25.05.1953 | AC Fiorentina (ITA) |
| 8 | Néstor Rolando Clausen | 29.09.1962 | CA Independiente Avellaneda |
| 9 | José Luis Cuciuffo | 01.02.1961 | CA Vélez Sarsfield |
| 13 | Oscar Alfredo Garré | 09.12.1956 | Club Ferro Carril Oeste Buenos Aires |
| 16 | Julio Jorge Olarticoechea | 18.10.1958 | CA Boca Juniors Buenos Aires |
| 19 | Oscar Alfredo Ruggeri | 26.01.1962 | CA River Plate Buenos Aires |
| | **Midfielders** | | |
| 2 | Sergio Daniel Batista | 09.11.1962 | AA Argentinos Juniors Buenos Aires |
| 3 | Ricardo Enrique Bochini | 25.01.1954 | CA Independiente Avellaneda |
| 4 | Claudio Daniel Borghi | 28.09.1964 | AA Argentinos Juniors Buenos Aires |
| 7 | Jorge Luis Burruchaga | 09.10.1962 | FC Nantes (FRA) |
| 10 | Diego Armando Maradona | 30.10.1960 | SSC Napoli (ITA) |
| 12 | Héctor Adolfo Enrique | 26.04.1962 | CA River Plate Buenos Aires |
| 14 | Ricardo Omar Giusti | 11.12.1956 | CA Independiente Avellaneda |
| 20 | Carlos Daniel Tapia | 20.08.1962 | CA Boca Juniors Buenos Aires |
| 21 | Marcelo Antonio Trobbiani | 17.02.1955 | Elche CF (ESP) |
| | **Forwards** | | |
| 1 | Sergio Omar Almirón | 18.11.1958 | CA Newell's Old Boys Rosario |
| 11 | Jorge Alberto Francisco Valdano | 04.10.1955 | Real Madrid CF (ESP) |
| 17 | Pedro Pablo Pasculli | 17.05.1960 | US Lecce (ITA) |
| **Trainer:** | Dr. Carlos Salvador Bilardo | 16.03.1939 | |

## BELGIUM

| Nr | Name | DOB | Club |
|---|---|---|---|
| **Goalkeepers** | | | |
| 1 | Jean-Marie Pfaff | 04.12.1953 | FC Bayern München (GER) |
| 12 | Jacques Munaron | 08.09.1956 | RSC Anderlecht Bruxelles |
| 20 | Gilbert Bodart | 02.09.1962 | R Standard Liège |
| **Defenders** | | | |
| 2 | Eric Gerets | 18.05.1954 | PSV Eindhoven (NED) |
| 4 | Michel De Wolf | 19.01.1958 | KAA Gent |
| 5 | Michel Renquin | 03.11.1955 | R Standard Liège |
| 13 | Georges Grün | 25.01.1962 | RSC Anderlecht Bruxelles |
| 14 | Léo Albert Clijsters | 06.11.1956 | Thor Waterschei SV Genk |
| 15 | Léo Vander Elst | 07.01.1962 | Club Brugge KV |
| 19 | Hugo Broos | 10.04.1952 | Club Brugge KV |
| **Midfielders** | | | |
| 3 | Frank Richard Vander Elst | 30.04.1961 | Club Brugge KV |
| 6 | Frank Vercauteren | 28.10.1956 | RSC Anderlecht Bruxelles |
| 7 | René Vandereycken | 22.07.1953 | RSC Anderlecht Bruxelles |
| 8 | Vincenzo Scifo | 19.02.1966 | RSC Anderlecht Bruxelles |
| 10 | Philippe De Smet | 29.11.1958 | KSV Waregem |
| 11 | Jan Ceulemans | 28.02.1957 | Club Brugge KV |
| 17 | Raymond Mommens | 27.12.1958 | KSC Lokeren |
| 21 | Stéphane Demol | 11.03.1966 | RSC Anderlecht Bruxelles |
| 22 | Patrick Vervoort | 17.01.1965 | K Beerschot VAV Antwerpen |
| **Forwards** | | | |
| 9 | Erwin Vandenbergh | 26.01.1959 | RSC Anderlecht Bruxelles |
| 16 | Nicolaas Pieter Claesen | 01.10.1962 | R Standard Liège |
| 18 | Daniel Veyt | 09.12.1956 | KSV Waregem |
| **Trainer:** | Guy Thys | 06.12.1922 | |

## BRAZIL

| Nr | Name | DOB | Club |
|---|---|---|---|
| **Goalkeepers** | | | |
| 1 | Carlos Roberto Gallo | 04.03.1956 | SC Corinthians Paulista São Paulo |
| 12 | Paulo Victor Barbosa de Carvalho "Paulo Vítor" | 07.06.1957 | Fluminense FC Rio de Janeiro |
| 22 | Émerson Leão | 11.07.1949 | SE Palmeiras São Paulo |
| **Defenders** | | | |
| 2 | Édson Boaro | 03.07.1959 | SC Corinthians Paulista São Paulo |
| 3 | José Oscar Bernardi | 20.06.1954 | São Paulo FC |
| 4 | Édino Nazareth Filho "Edinho" | 05.06.1955 | Udinese Calcio (ITA) |
| 6 | Leovegildo Lins Gama Júnior "Júnior I" | 29.06.1954 | Torino Calcio (ITA) |
| 13 | Josimar Higino Pereira | 19.09.1961 | Botafogo de FR Rio de Janeiro |
| 14 | Júlio César da Silva | 08.03.1963 | Guarani FC Campinas |
| 16 | Mauro Geraldo Galvão | 19.12.1961 | SC Internacional Porto Alegre |
| 17 | Cláudio Ibrahim Vaz Leal "Branco" | 04.04.1964 | Fluminense FC Rio de Janeiro |
| **Midfielders** | | | |
| 5 | Paulo Roberto Falcão | 16.10.1953 | São Paulo FC |
| 10 | Arthur Antunes Coimbra "Zico" | 03.03.1953 | CR Flamengo Rio de Janeiro |
| 15 | Ricardo Rogério de Brito "Alemão" | 22.11.1961 | Botafogo de FR Rio de Janeiro |
| 18 | Sócrates Brasileiro Sampaio Vieira de Oliveira | 19.02.1954 | CR Flamengo Rio de Janeiro |
| 19 | Elzo Aloísio Coelho | 22.01.1961 | Atlético Mineiro Belo Horizonte |
| 20 | Paulo Silas do Prado Pereira | 27.08.1965 | São Paulo FC |
| 21 | Valdo Cãndido Filho "Valdo II" | 12.01.1964 | Grêmio Foot-ball Porto-Alegrense |
| **Forwards** | | | |
| 7 | Luís Antônio Corrêa da Costa "Müller" | 31.01.1966 | São Paulo FC |
| 8 | Wálter Casagrande Júnior | 15.04.1963 | SC Corinthians Paulista São Paulo |
| 9 | Antônio de Oliveira Filho "Careca I" | 05.10.1960 | São Paulo FC |
| 11 | Edivaldo Martins da Fonseca | 13.04.1962 | Atlético Mineiro Belo Horizonte |
| **Trainer:** | Telê Santana da Silva | 26.07.1931 | |

## BULGARIA

| Nr | Name | DOB | Club |
|---|---|---|---|
| | **Goalkeepers** | | |
| 1 | Borislav Mikhailov | 12.02.1963 | FK Vitosha Sofia |
| 22 | Ilia Valov | 29.12.1961 | Botev Vratsa |
| | **Defenders** | | |
| 3 | Nikolai Arabov | 21.02.1953 | FC Sliven |
| 4 | Petar Petrov | 20.02.1961 | FK Vitosha Sofia |
| 5 | Georgi Dimitrov | 14.01.1959 | CFKA Sredets Sofia |
| 13 | Aleksandar Markov | 17.08.1961 | DFS Spartak Pleven |
| 21 | Ilia Diakov | 28.09.1963 | Dobrudzha Tolbuchin |
| | **Midfielders** | | |
| 2 | Nasko Sirakov | 26.04.1962 | FK Vitosha Sofia |
| 6 | Andrei Jeliazkov | 9.07.1952 | RCP Strasbourg (FRA) |
| 8 | Aian Sadakov | 28.09.1961 | DFS Lokomotiv Plovdiv |
| 10 | Jivko Gospodinov | 6.09.1957 | JSK-Spartak Varna |
| 11 | Plamen Getov | 4.03.1959 | Spartak Pleven |
| 12 | Radoslav Zdravkov | 30.07.1956 | CFKA Sredets Sofia |
| 15 | Georgi Iordanov | 21.07.1963 | FK Vitosha Sofia |
| 17 | Hristo Kolev | 21.09.1964 | DFS Lokomotiv Sofia |
| 19 | Atanas Pashev | 21.11.1963 | AFD Trakia Plovdiv |
| | **Forwards** | | |
| 7 | Bojidar Iskrenov | 1.08.1962 | FK Vitosha Sofia |
| 9 | Stoicho Mladenov | 24.04.1957 | CFKA Sredets Sofia |
| 14 | Plamen Markov | 11.09.1957 | FC Metz (FRA) |
| 16 | Vasil Dragolov | 17.08.1962 | Beroe Stara Zagora |
| 18 | Boicho Velichkov | 13.08.1958 | Lokomotiv Sofia |
| 20 | Kostadin Kostadinov | 25.06.1959 | AFD Trakia Plovdiv |
| **Trainer:** | Ivan Vutsov | 14.12.1939 | |

## CANADA

| Nr | Name | DOB | Club |
|---|---|---|---|
| | **Goalkeepers** | | |
| 1 | Martino „Tino" Lettieri | 27.09.1957 | Minnesota Strikers (USA) |
| 21 | Sven Habermann | 03.11.1961 | *unattached* |
| 22 | Kenneth Paul Dolan | 16.04.1966 | Edmonton Brickmen |
| | **Defenders** | | |
| 2 | Robert Lenarduzzi | 01.05.1955 | Tacoma Stars (USA) |
| 3 | Bruce Alec Wilson | 20.06.1951 | *unattached* |
| 5 | Terence Moore | 02.06.1958 | Glentoran Belfast FC (NIR) |
| 6 | Ian Christopher Bridge | 18.09.1959 | FC La Chaux-de-Fonds (SUI) |
| 12 | Randolph Fitzgerald Samuel | 23.12.1963 | *unattached* |
| 20 | Colin Miller | 04.10.1964 | Glasgow Rangers FC (SCO) |
| | **Midfielders** | | |
| 4 | Randolph Lee Ragan | 07.06.1959 | *unattached* |
| 8 | Gerard Gray | 20.01.1961 | Chicago Sting (USA) |
| 11 | Mike Sweeney | 25.12.1959 | Cleveland Force (USA) |
| 13 | George Pakos | 14.08.1952 | Victoria Athletic Association |
| 15 | Paul John James | 11.11.1963 | CF Monterrey (MEX) |
| 16 | Gregory Stewart Ion | 12.03.1963 | *unattached* |
| 17 | David McDonald Norman | 06.05.1962 | Tacoma Stars (USA) |
| 18 | James Matthew Lowery | 15.01.1961 | *unattached* |
| 19 | Pasquale DeLuca | 26.05.1962 | Cleveland Force (USA) |
| | **Forwards** | | |
| 7 | Carl Howard Valentine | 04.07.1958 | Cleveland Force (USA) |
| 9 | Branko Segota | 08.06.1961 | San Diego Sockers (USA) |
| 10 | Igor Vrablic | 19.07.1965 | RFC Seraing (BEL) |
| 14 | Dale William Mitchell | 21.04.1958 | Tacoma Stars (USA) |
| **Trainer:** | Anthony Keith Waiters | | |

## DENMARK

| Nr | Name | DOB | Club |
|---|---|---|---|
| | **Goalkeepers** | | |
| 1 | Troels Rasmussen | 04.07.1961 | Aarhus GF |
| 16 | Ole Qvist | 25.02.1950 | Kjøbenhavns Boldklub |
| 22 | Lars Høgh | 14.01.1959 | Odense BK |
| | **Defenders** | | |
| 2 | John Sivebæk | 25.10.1961 | Manchester United FC (ENG) |
| 3 | Søren Busk | 10.04.1953 | MVV Maastricht (NED) |
| 4 | Morten Olsen | 14.08.1949 | RSC Anderlecht Bruxelles (BEL) |
| 5 | Ivan Nielsen | 09.10.1956 | Feyenoord SC Rotterdam (NED) |
| 12 | Jens Jørn Bertelsen | 15.02.1952 | FC Aarau |
| 17 | Kent Nielsen | 28.12.1961 | Brønshøj BK |
| 21 | Henrik Andersen | 07.05.1965 | RSC Anderlecht Bruxelles (BEL) |
| | **Midfielders** | | |
| 6 | Søren Lerby | 01.02.1958 | FC Bayern München (GER) |
| 7 | Jan Mølby | 04.07.1963 | Liverpool FC (ENG) |
| 8 | Jesper Olsen | 20.03.1961 | Manchester United FC (ENG) |
| 11 | Michael Laudrup | 15.06.1964 | FC Juventus Torino (ITA) |
| 13 | Per Frimann | 04.06.1962 | RSC Anderlecht Bruxelles (BEL) |
| 15 | Frank Arnesen | 30.09.1956 | PSV Eindhoven (NED) |
| 18 | Flemming Christense | 10.04.1958 | Lyngby BK |
| 20 | Jan Bartram | 06.03.1962 | Aarhus GF |
| | **Forwards** | | |
| 9 | Klaus Berggreen | 03.02.1958 | Pisa SC (ITA) |
| 10 | Preben Elkjær-Larsen | 11.09.1957 | Hellas Verona (ITA) |
| 14 | Allan Rodenkam Simonsen | 15.12.1952 | Vejle BK (DEN) |
| 19 | John Eriksen | 20.11.1957 | Feyenoord SC Rotterdam (NED) |
| **Trainer:** | Josef "Sepp" Piontek (GER) | 05.03.1940 | |

## ENGLAND

| Nr | Name | DOB | Club |
|---|---|---|---|
| | **Goalkeepers** | | |
| 1 | Peter Leslie Shilton | 18.09.1949 | Southampton FC |
| 13 | Christopher Charles Eric Woods | 14.11.1959 | Norwich City FC |
| 22 | Gary Richard Bailey | 09.08.1958 | Blackburn Rovers FC |
| | **Defenders** | | |
| 2 | Gary Michael Stevens | 27.03.1963 | Everton FC Liverpool |
| 3 | Kenneth Graham Sansom | 26.09.1958 | Arsenal FC London |
| 5 | Alvin Edward Martin | 29.07.1958 | West Ham United FC London |
| 6 | Terence Ian Butcher | 28.12.1958 | Ipswich Town FC |
| 12 | Vivian Alexander Anderson | 29.07.1956 | Arsenal FC London |
| 14 | Terence William Fenwick | 17.11.1959 | Queens Park Rangers FC London |
| 15 | Gary Andrew Stevens | 30.03.1962 | Tottenham Hotspur FC London |
| | **Midfielders** | | |
| 4 | Glenn Hoddle | 27.10.1957 | Tottenham Hotspur FC London |
| 7 | Bryan Robson | 11.01.1957 | Blackburn Rovers FC |
| 8 | Raymond Colin Wilkins | 14.09.1956 | Milan AC (ITA) |
| 11 | Christopher Roland Waddle | 14.12.1960 | Tottenham Hotspur FC London |
| 16 | Peter Reid | 20.06.1956 | Everton FC Liverpool |
| 17 | Trevor McGregor Steven | 21.09.1963 | Everton FC Liverpool |
| 18 | Stephen Brian Hodge | 25.10.1962 | Aston Villa FC Birmingham |
| 19 | John Charles Bryan Barnes | 07.11.1963 | Watford FC |
| | **Forwards** | | |
| 9 | Mark Wayne Hateley | 07.11.1961 | Milan AC (ITA) |
| 10 | Gary Winston Lineker | 30.11.1960 | Everton FC Liverpool |
| 20 | Peter Andrew Beardsley | 18.01.1961 | Newcastle United FC |
| 21 | Kerry Michael Dixon | 24.07.1961 | Chelsea FC London |
| **Trainer:** | Robert William Robson | 18.02.1933 | |

## FRANCE

| Nr | Name | DOB | Club |
|---|---|---|---|
| | **Goalkeepers** | | |
| 1 | Joël Bats | 04.01.1957 | Paris St. Germain FC |
| 21 | Philippe Bergeroo | 13.01.1954 | Toulouse FC |
| 22 | Albert Rust | 10.10.1953 | FC Sochaux-Montbéliard |
| | **Defenders** | | |
| 2 | Manuel AMoros | 01.02.1962 | AS Monaco |
| 3 | William Ayache | 10.06.1961 | FC Nantes |
| 4 | Patrick Battiston | 12.03.1957 | Girondins de Bordeaux |
| 5 | Michel Bibard | 30.11.1958 | Paris St. Germain FC |
| 6 | Maxime Bossis | 26.06.1955 | Racing Paris |
| 7 | Yvon Le Roux | 19.04.1960 | FC Nantes |
| 8 | Thierry Tusseau | 19.01.1958 | Girondins de Bordeaux |
| | **Midfielders** | | |
| 9 | Luis Fernández | 02.10.1959 | Paris St. Germain FC |
| 10 | Michel Platini | 21.06.1955 | Juventus FC Torino (ITA) |
| 11 | Jean-Marc Ferreri | 26.12.1962 | AJ Auxerre |
| 12 | Alain Giresse | 02.08.1952 | Girondins de Bordeaux |
| 13 | Bernard Genghini | 18.01.1958 | AS Monaco |
| 14 | Jean Amadou Tigana | 23.06.1955 | Girondins de Bordeaux |
| 15 | Philippe Vercruysse | 28.01.1962 | Racing Club Lens |
| | **Forwards** | | |
| 16 | Bruno Bellone | 14.03.1962 | AS Monaco |
| 17 | Jean-Pierre Papin | 05.11.1963 | Club Brügge KV (BEL) |
| 18 | Dominique Rocheteau | 14.01.1955 | Paris St. Germain FC |
| 19 | Yannick Stopyra | 09.01.1961 | Toulouse FC |
| 20 | Daniel Xuereb | 22.06.1959 | Racing Club Lens |
| **Trainer:** | Henri Michel | 29.10.1947 | |

## HUNGARY

| Nr | Name | DOB | Club |
|---|---|---|---|
| | **Goalkeepers** | | |
| 1 | Péter Disztl | 30.03.1960 | Videoton SC Székesfehérvár |
| 18 | József Szendrei | 25.04.1954 | Újpesti Dózsa SC |
| 22 | József Andrusch | 31.03.1956 | Budapesti Honvéd SE |
| | **Defenders** | | |
| 2 | Sándor Sallai | 26.03.1960 | Videoton SC Székesfehérvár |
| 3 | Antal Róth | 14.09.1960 | Pécsi MSC |
| 4 | József Varga | 09.10.1954 | Denizlispor Kulübü (TUR) |
| 6 | Imre Garaba | 29.07.1958 | Budapesti Honvéd SE |
| 12 | József Csuhay | 12.07.1957 | Videoton SC Székesfehérvár |
| 13 | László Disztl | 04.06.1962 | Videoton SC Székesfehérvár |
| 14 | Zoltán Péter | 23.03.1958 | Zalaegerszegi TE |
| 16 | József Nagy | 20.10.1960 | Szombathelyi Haladás VSE |
| | **Midfielders** | | |
| 5 | József Kardos | 22.03.1960 | Újpesti Dózsa SC |
| 8 | Antal Nagy | 17.10.1956 | Budapesti Honvéd SE |
| 10 | Lajos Détári | 24.04.1963 | Budapesti Honvéd SE |
| 15 | Péter Hannich | 30.03.1957 | Rába ETO Győr |
| 17 | Győző Burcsa | 13.03.1954 | AJ Auxerre (FRA) |
| | **Forwards** | | |
| 7 | József Kiprich | 06.09.1963 | Tatabányai Bányász SC |
| 9 | László Dajka | 29.04.1959 | Budapesti Honvéd SE |
| 11 | Márton Esterházy | 09.04.1956 | AEK Athína (GRE) |
| 19 | György Bognár | 05.11.1961 | MTK-VM Budapest |
| 20 | Kálmán Kovács | 11.09.1965 | Budapesti Honvéd SE |
| 21 | Gyula Hajszán | 09.10.1961 | Rába ETO Győr |
| **Trainer:** | György Mezey | 07.09.1941 | |

## IRAQ

| Nr | Name | DOB | Club |
|---|---|---|---|
| | **Goalkeepers** | | |
| 1 | Raad Hammoudi Salman | 20.04.1953 | Al Shorta Baghdad |
| 20 | Jassim Abdul-Fatah Nasif | 02.02.1951 | Al Jaish FC Baghdad |
| 21 | Ahmad Jassim Mohammed | 04.05.1960 | Al Rasheed Sport Club Karkh |
| | **Defenders** | | |
| 2 | Maad Ibrahim Majid | 30.06.1960 | Al Rasheed Sport Club Karkh |
| 3 | Khalil Mohammed Allawi | 06.09.1958 | Al Rasheed Sport Club Karkh |
| 4 | Nadhim Shaker Salim | 13.04.1958 | Al Tayaran Sport Club Baghdad |
| 5 | Samir Shaker Mahmoud | 29.02.1958 | Al Rasheed Sport Club Karkh |
| 15 | Natiq Hashim Abidoun | 15.01.1960 | Al Tayaran Sport Club Baghdad |
| 22 | Jassim Ghanim Oraibi Al Roubai | 16.08.1961 | Al Shabab Sport Club Baghdad |
| | **Midfielders** | | |
| 6 | Ali Hussein Shihab | 05.05.1961 | Talaba Sport Club Baghdad |
| 7 | Haris Mohammed Hassan | 03.03.1958 | Al Rasheed Sport Club Karkh |
| 12 | Jamal Ali Hamza | 02.02.1956 | Talaba Sport Club Baghdad |
| 13 | Karim Mohammed Allawi | 01.04.1960 | Al Rasheed Sport Club Karkh |
| 14 | Basil Gorgis Hanna | 06.09.1961 | Al Shabab Sport Club Baghdad |
| 16 | Mahmoud Hamza Shaker | 05.05.1960 | Al Shabab Sport Club Baghdad |
| 17 | Anad Abid Tweresh | 03.08.1954 | Al Rasheed Sport Club Karkh |
| 18 | Ismail Mohammed Sharif | 17.04.1962 | Al Shabab Sport Club Baghdad |
| 19 | Basim Qasim Hamdan | 22.03.1959 | Al Shorta Baghdad |
| | **Forwards** | | |
| 8 | Ahmad Radhi Amaiesh Al Salehi | 27.03.1964 | Al Rasheed Sport Club Karkh |
| 9 | Karim Saddam Minshid | 26.05.1960 | Al Jaish FC Baghdad |
| 10 | Hussein Saeed Mohammed | 21.01.1958 | Talaba Sport Club Baghdad |
| 11 | Abdul-Rahim Hamed Aufi | 23.05.1963 | Al Jaish FC Baghdad |
| **Trainer:** | Evaristo de Macedo Filho (BRA) | 22.06.1933 | |

## ITALY

| Nr | Name | DOB | Club |
|---|---|---|---|
| | **Goalkeepers** | | |
| 1 | Giovanni Galli | 29.04.1958 | AC Fiorentina Firenze |
| 12 | Franco Tancredi | 10.01.1955 | AS Roma |
| 22 | Walter Zenga | 30.04.1960 | Internazionale FC Milano |
| | **Defenders** | | |
| 2 | Giuseppe Bergomi | 22.12.1963 | Internazionale FC Milano |
| 3 | Antonio Cabrini | 08.10.1957 | FC Juventus Torino |
| 4 | Fulvio Collovati | 09.05.1957 | Internazionale FC Milano |
| 5 | Sebastiano Nela | 13.03.1961 | AS Roma |
| 6 | Gaetano Scirea | 25.05.1953 | FC Juventus Torino |
| 7 | Roberto Tricella | 18.03.1959 | Hellas Verona |
| 8 | Pietro Vierchowod | 06.04.1959 | UC Sampdoria Genova |
| | **Midfielders** | | |
| 9 | Carlo Ancelotti | 10.06.1959 | AS Roma |
| 10 | Salvatore Bagni | 25.09.1956 | SSC Napoli |
| 11 | Giuseppe Baresi I | 07.02.1958 | Internazionale FC Milano |
| 13 | Fernando De Napoli | 15.03.1964 | US Avellino |
| 14 | Antonio Di Gennaro | 05.10.1958 | Hellas Verona |
| 15 | Marco Tardelli | 24.09.1954 | Internazionale FC Milano |
| 16 | Bruno Conti | 13.03.1955 | AS Roma |
| | **Forwards** | | |
| 17 | Gianluca Vialli | 09.07.1964 | UC Sampdoria Genova |
| 18 | Alessandro Altobelli | 28.11.1955 | Internazionale FC Milano |
| 19 | Giuseppe Galderisi | 22.03.1963 | Hellas Verona |
| 20 | Paolo Rossi | 23.09.1956 | Milan AC |
| 21 | Aldo Serena | 25.06.1960 | FC Juventus Torino |
| **Trainer:** | Vincenzo „Enzo" Bearzot | 26.09.1927 | |

## MEXICO

| Nr | Name | DOB | Club |
|---|---|---|---|
| | **Goalkeepers** | | |
| 1 | Pablo Larios Iwasaki | 31.07.1960 | CDSC Cruz Azul Ciudad de México |
| 12 | Ignacio Rodríguez Bahena | 13.08.1959 | CF Atlante Ciudad de México |
| 20 | Carlos Olaf Heredia Orosco | 19.10.1957 | Tigres de la UA de Nuevo León |
| | **Defenders** | | |
| 2 | Mario Alberto Trejo Guzmán | 18.09.1961 | CF América Ciudad de México |
| 3 | Fernando Quirarte Gutiérrez | 17.05.1956 | CD Guadalajara |
| 4 | Armando Manzo Ponce | 16.10.1958 | CF América Ciudad de México |
| 14 | Félix Cruz Barbosa Ríos | 04.04.1961 | Club UNAM Ciudad de México |
| 17 | Raúl Servín Monetti | 29.04.1963 | Club UNAM Ciudad de México |
| 18 | Rafael Amador Flores | 16.11.1967 | Club UNAM Ciudad de México |
| | **Midfielders** | | |
| 6 | Carlos de los Cobos Martínez | 10.12.1958 | CF América Ciudad de México |
| 7 | Miguel España Garcés | 04.04.1961 | Club UNAM Ciudad de México |
| 8 | Alejandro Domínguez Escoto | 09.02.1961 | CF América Ciudad de México |
| 10 | Tomás Juan Boy Espinoza | 05.07.1953 | Tigres de la UA de Nuevo León |
| 13 | Javier Aguirre Onaindía | 01.12.1958 | CF América Ciudad de México |
| 16 | Carlos Eduardo Muñoz Remolina | 08.09.1962 | Tigres de la UA de Nuevo León |
| | **Forwards** | | |
| 5 | Francisco Javier Cruz Jiménez | 24.05.1966 | CF Monterrey |
| 9 | Hugo Sánchez Márquez | 11.07.1958 | CF Real Madrid (ESP) |
| 11 | Carlos Manuel Hermosillo Goytortúa | 24.08.1964 | CF América Ciudad de México |
| 15 | Luis Enrique Flores Ocaranza | 08.08.1962 | Club UNAM Ciudad de México |
| 19 | Javier Hernández Gutiérrez | 01.08.1961 | CF Estudiantes Guadalajara |
| 21 | Cristóbal Ortega Martínez | 25.07.1956 | CF América Ciudad de México |
| 22 | Manuel Negrete Arias | 15.05.1959 | Club UNAM Ciudad de México |
| **Trainer:** | Velibor „Bora" Milutinović (YUG) | 07.09.1944 | |

## MOROCCO

| Nr | Name | DOB | Club |
|---|---|---|---|
| | **Goalkeepers** | | |
| 1 | Ezaki Badou | 02.04.1959 | Wydad Athletic Club of Casablanca |
| 12 | Salahdine Hmied | 01.09.1961 | Forces Armées Royales de Rabat |
| 22 | Abdelfettah Mouddani | 30.07.1956 | Kénitra Athletic Club |
| | **Defenders** | | |
| 2 | Labid Khalifa | 1955 | Kénitra Athletic Club |
| 3 | Abdelmajid Lamris | 12.02.1959 | Forces Armées Royales de Rabat |
| 4 | Mustapha El Biyaz | 12.12.1960 | Kawkab Athletic Club of Marrakech |
| 5 | Noureddine Bouyahyaoui | 07.01.1955 | Kénitra Athletic Club |
| 14 | Lahcen Ouadani | 14.07.1959 | Forces Armées Royales de Rabat |
| 20 | Abdellah Bidane | 10.09.1965 | Club Omnisport De Meknès |
| | **Midfielders** | | |
| 6 | Abdelmajid Dolmy | 19.04.1953 | Raja Club Athletic of Casablanca |
| 7 | Mustapha El Haddaoui | 28.07.1961 | Lausanne-Sports (SUI) |
| 8 | Abdelaziz Bouderbala | 26.12.1960 | FC Sion (SUI) |
| 10 | Mohamed Timoumi | 15.01.1960 | Forces Armées Royales de Rabat |
| 15 | Mouncif El Haddaoui | 21.10.1964 | Association Sportive de Salé |
| 18 | Mohamed Sahil | 11.10.1963 | Kawkab Athletic Club of Marrakech |
| 19 | Fadel Jilal | 04.03.1964 | Wydad Athletic Club of Casablanca |
| 21 | Abdelaziz Souleimani | 30.04.1958 | Maghreb Association Sportive of Fez |
| | **Forwards** | | |
| 9 | Abdelkrim Merry "Krimau" | 13.01.1955 | AC Le Havre (FRA) |
| 11 | Mustapha Merry | 21.04.1958 | USVA Valenciennes (FRA) |
| 13 | Abdelfettah Rhiati | 25.02.1963 | Maghreb Association Sportive of Fez |
| 16 | Azzedine Amanallah | 07.04.1956 | Besançon RC (FRA) |
| 17 | Abderrazak Khairi | 20.11.1962 | Forces Armées Royales de Rabat |
| **Trainer:** | José Faria (BRA) | 26.04.1933 | |

## NORTHERN IRELAND

| Nr | Name | DOB | Club |
|---|---|---|---|
| | **Goalkeepers** | | |
| 1 | Patrick Anthony Jennings | 12.06.1945 | Tottenham Hotspur FC (ENG) |
| 12 | James Archibald Platt | 26.01.1951 | Coleraine FC |
| 13 | Philip Anthony Hughes | 19.11.1964 | Bury FC (ENG) |
| | **Defenders** | | |
| 2 | James Michael Nicholl | 28.12.1956 | West Bromwich Albion FC (ENG) |
| 3 | Malachy Martin Donaghy | 13.09.1957 | Luton Town FC (ENG) |
| 4 | John Patrick O'Neill | 11.03.1958 | Leicester City FC (ENG) |
| 5 | Alan McDonald | 12.10.1963 | Queens Park Glasgow FC (SCO) |
| 18 | John McClelland | 07.12.1965 | Watford FC (ENG) |
| 20 | Bernard Anthony McNally | 17.02.1963 | Shrewsbury Town FC (ENG) |
| | **Midfielders** | | |
| 6 | David McCreery | 16.09.1957 | Newcastle United FC (ENG) |
| 7 | Stephen Alexander Penney | 16.01.1964 | Brighton and Hove Albion FC (ENG) |
| 8 | Samuel Baxter McIlroy | 02.08.1954 | Manchester City FC (ENG) |
| 10 | Norman Whiteside | 07.05.1965 | Manchester United FC (ENG) |
| 15 | Nigel Worthington | 04.11.1961 | Sheffield Wednesday FC (ENG) |
| 16 | Paul Christopher Ramsey | 03.09.1962 | Leicester City FC (ENG) |
| 21 | David Anthony Campbell | 02.06.1965 | Nottingham Forest FC (ENG) |
| | **Forwards** | | |
| 9 | James Martin Quinn | 18.11.1959 | Blackburn Rovers FC (ENG) |
| 11 | Ian Edwin Stewart | 10.09.1961 | Newcastle United FC (ENG) |
| 14 | Gerard Joseph Armstrong | 23.05.1954 | West Bromwich Albion FC (ENG) |
| 17 | Colin John Clarke | 30.10.1962 | AFC Bournemouth (ENG) |
| 19 | William Robert Hamilton | 09.05.1957 | Oxford United FC (ENG) |
| 22 | Mark Caughey | 31.08.1960 | Linfield FC Belfast |
| **Trainer:** | William Laurence Bingham | 05.08.1931 | |

## PARAGUAY

| Nr | Name | DOB | Club |
|---|---|---|---|
| | **Goalkeepers** | | |
| 1 | Roberto Eladio Fernández Roa | 09.07.1957 | Asociación Deportivo Cali (COL) |
| 12 | Jorge Antonio Battaglia Méndez | 12.05.1960 | Club Sol de América Villa Elisa |
| 22 | Julián Coronel | 23.10.1958 | Club Guaraní Asunción |
| | **Defenders** | | |
| 2 | Juan Bautista Torales | 09.03.1956 | Club Libertad Asunción |
| 3 | César Zabala Fernández | 03.06.1961 | Club Cerro Porteño Asunción |
| 4 | Vladimiro Schettina Chepini | 08.10.1955 | Club Guaraní Asunción |
| 5 | Rogelio Wilfrido Delgado Casco | 12.10.1959 | Club Olimpia Asunción |
| 13 | Virginio Cáceres Villalba | 21.05.1962 | Club Guaraní Asunción |
| 14 | Luis Nery Caballero | 17.09.1962 | Club Guaraní Asunción |
| | **Midfielders** | | |
| 6 | Jorge Amado Núñez Infrán | 18.10.1961 | Asociación Deportivo Cali (COL) |
| 8 | Julio César Romero Insfrán | 28.08.1960 | Fluminense FC Rio de Janeiro (BRA) |
| 10 | Adolfino Cañete Azcurra | 13.09.1956 | CDSC Cruz Azul (MEX) |
| 15 | Eufemio Raúl Fernández Cabral | 21.03.1955 | Club Guaraní Asunción |
| 16 | Jorge Alberto Guasch Bazán | 17.01.1961 | Club Olimpia Asunción |
| 19 | Marciano Rolando Chilavert González | 22.05.1961 | Club Guaraní Asunción |
| | **Forwards** | | |
| 7 | Buenaventura Ferreira Gómez | 04.07.1960 | Asociación Deportivo Cali (COL) |
| 9 | Roberto Cabañas González | 11.04.1961 | CD América Cali (COL) |
| 11 | Alfredo Damián Mendoza Sulewski | 12.12.1963 | CD Independiente Medellín (COL) |
| 17 | Francisco Javier Alcaraz | 04.10.1960 | Club Nacional Asunción |
| 18 | Evaristo Isasi Colman | 26.10.1955 | Club Olimpia Asunción |
| 20 | Ramón Angel Hicks Cáceres | 30.05.1959 | Club Libertad Asunción |
| 21 | Faustino ALonso | 15.02.1961 | Club Sol de América Villa Elisa |
| **Trainer:** | Cayetano Ré Ramírez | 07.02.1938 | |

## POLAND

| Nr | Name | DOB | Club |
|---|---|---|---|
| **Goalkeepers** | | | |
| 1 | Józef Młynarczyk | 20.09.1953 | FC do Porto (POR) |
| 12 | Jacek Kazimierski | 17.08.1959 | KP Legia Warszawa |
| 19 | Józef Wandzik | 13.08.1963 | KS Górnik Zabrze |
| **Defenders** | | | |
| 2 | Kazimierz Przybyś | 11.07.1960 | Poland RTS Widzew Łódź |
| 3 | Władysław Żmuda | 06.06.1954 | US Cremonese (ITA) |
| 4 | Marek Ostrowski | 22.11.1959 | MKS Pogoń Szczecin |
| 5 | Roman Wójcicki | 08.01.1958 | RTS Widzew Łódź |
| 10 | Stefan Majewski | 31.01.1956 | 1.FC Kaiserslautern (GER) |
| 14 | Dariusz Kubicki | 06.06.1963 | KP Legia Warszawa |
| 18 | Krzysztof Pawlak | 12.02.1958 | Lech Poznań |
| **Midfielders** | | | |
| 6 | Waldemar Matysik | 27.09.1961 | KS Górnik Zabrze |
| 7 | Ryszard Tarasiewicz | 27.04.1962 | KS Śląsk Wrocław |
| 13 | Ryszard Komornicki | 14.08.1959 | KS Górnik Zabrze |
| 15 | Andrzej Buncol | 21.09.1959 | KP Legia Warszawa |
| 20 | Zbigniew Boniek | 03.03.1956 | AS Roma (ITA) |
| **Forwards** | | | |
| 8 | Jan Urban | 14.05.1962 | KS Górnik Zabrze |
| 9 | Jan Karaś | 17.03.1959 | KP Legia Warszawa |
| 11 | Włodzimierz Smolarek | 16.07.1957 | RTS Widzew Łódź |
| 16 | Andrzej Pałasz | 22.07.1960 | KS Górnik Zabrze |
| 17 | Andrzej Zgutczyński | 01.01.1958 | KS Górnik Zabrze |
| 21 | Dariusz Dziekanowski | 30.09.1962 | KP Legia Warszawa |
| 22 | Jan Furtok | 9.03.1962 | GKS Katowice |
| **Trainer:** | Antoni Piechniczek | 03.05.1942 | |

## PORTUGAL

| Nr | Name | DOB | Club |
|---|---|---|---|
| **Goalkeepers** | | | |
| 1 | Manuel Galrinho Bento | 25.06.1948 | Sport Lisboa e Benfica |
| 12 | Jorge Manuel Martins da Silva | 12.08.1954 | CF Os Belenenses Lisboa |
| 22 | Vítor Manuel Alfonso Damas de Oliveira | 08.10.1947 | Sporting Clube de Portugal Lisboa |
| **Defenders** | | | |
| 2 | João Domingos Silva Pinto | 21.11.1961 | FC do Porto |
| 4 | José Joaquim Pimentel Ribeiro | 02.11.1957 | Boavista FC do Porto |
| 5 | Álvaro Monteiro de Magalhães | 03.01.1961 | Sport Lisboa e Benfica |
| 8 | Frederico Nobre Rosa | 06.04.1957 | Boavista FC do Porto |
| 13 | António Maurício Farinha Henrique Morato | 06.11.1964 | Sporting Clube de Portugal Lisboa |
| 15 | António Henriques Fonseca de Jesus Oliveira | 08.06.1958 | Sport Lisboa e Benfica |
| 16 | José António Prudéncio Conde Bargiela | 29.10.1957 | CF Os Belenenses Lisboa |
| 20 | Augusto Soares Inácio | 01.02.1955 | FC do Porto |
| **Midfielders** | | | |
| 3 | António Augusto Gomes de Silva „Sousa" | 28.04.1957 | Sporting Clube de Portugal Lisboa |
| 6 | Carlos Manuel Correia dos Santos | 15.01.1958 | Sport Lisboa e Benfica |
| 7 | Jaime Moreira Pacheco | 22.07.1958 | Sporting Clube de Portugal Lisboa |
| 11 | Fernando Óscar Bandeirinha Barbosa | 26.11.1962 | Associação Académica de Coimbra |
| 14 | Jaime Fernandes Magalhães | 10.07.1962 | FC do Porto |
| 18 | Luís Fernando Peixoto Gonçalves Sobrinho | 05.05.1961 | CF Os Belenenses Lisboa |
| 21 | António dos Santos Ferreira André | 24.12.1957 | FC do Porto |
| **Forwards** | | | |
| 9 | Fernando Mendes Soares Gomes | 23.11.1956 | FC do Porto |
| 10 | Paulo Jorge dos Santos Futre | 20.02.1966 | FC do Porto |
| 17 | Diamantino Manuel Fernandes Miranda | 03.08.1959 | Sport Lisboa e Benfica |
| 19 | José Rui Lopes Águas | 28.04.1960 | Sport Lisboa e Benfica |
| **Trainer:** | José Augusto da Costa Séneca Torres | 08.09.1938 | |

## SCOTLAND

| Nr | Name | DOB | Club |
|---|---|---|---|
| | **Goalkeepers** | | |
| 1 | James Leighton | 24.07.1958 | Aberdeen FC |
| 12 | Andrew Lewis Goram | 13.04.1964 | Oldham Athletic FC (ENG) |
| 22 | Alan Roderick Rough | 25.11.1951 | Hibernian Edinburgh FC |
| | **Defenders** | | |
| 2 | Richard Charles Gough | 05.04.1962 | Dundee FC United |
| 3 | Maurice Daniel Robert Malpas | 03.08.1962 | Dundee FC United |
| 5 | Alexander McLeish | 21.01.1959 | Aberdeen FC |
| 6 | William Fergus Miller | 02.05.1955 | Aberdeen FC |
| 13 | Stephen Nicol | 11.12.1961 | Liverpool FC (ENG) |
| 14 | David Narey | 12.06.1956 | Dundee FC United |
| 15 | Arthur Richard Albiston | 14.07.1957 | Manchester United FC (ENG) |
| | **Midfielders** | | |
| 4 | Graeme James Souness | 06.05.1953 | UC Sampdoria Genova (ITA) |
| 7 | Gordon David Strachan | 09.02.1957 | Manchester United FC (ENG) |
| 8 | Robert "Roy" Sime Aitken | 24.11.1958 | Celtic Glasgow FC |
| 10 | James Bett | 25.11.1959 | Aberdeen FC |
| 11 | Paul Michael Lyons McStay | 22.10.1964 | Celtic Glasgow FC |
| 16 | Francis McAvennie | 22.11.1959 | West Ham United FC London (ENG) |
| 21 | David Cooper | 25.02.1956 | Glasgow Rangers FC |
| | **Forwards** | | |
| 9 | Eamonn John Peter Bannon | 18.04.1958 | Dundee FC United |
| 17 | Steven Archibald | 27.09.1956 | FC Barcelona (ESP) |
| 18 | Graeme Marshall Sharp | 16.10.1960 | Everton FC Liverpool (ENG) |
| 19 | Charles Nicholas | 30.12.1961 | Arsenal FC London (ENG) |
| 20 | Paul Whitehead Sturrock | 10.10.1956 | Dundee FC United |
| **Trainer:** | Alexander Chapman Ferguson | 31.12.1941 | |

## SOUTH KOREA

| Nr | Name | DOB | Club |
|---|---|---|---|
| | **Goalkeepers** | | |
| 1 | Cho Byung-Deouk | 26.05.1958 | Hallelujah FC |
| 21 | Oh Yeon-Kyo | 25.05.1960 | Yukong FC Kokkiri |
| | **Defenders** | | |
| 2 | Park Kyung-Hoon | 19.01.1961 | Posco Atoms Pohang |
| 3 | Chung Jong-Soo | 27.03.1961 | Yukong FC Kokkiri |
| 5 | Chung Yong-Hwan | 10.02.1960 | Pusan Daewoo Royals |
| 12 | Kim Pyung-Seok | 22.09.1958 | Ulsan Hyundai Horang-i |
| 14 | Cho Min-Kook | 05.07.1963 | Lucky-Goldstar FC Hwangso |
| 15 | Yoo Byung-Ok | 02.03.1964 | Hanyang University |
| | **Midfielders** | | |
| 4 | Cho Kwang-Rae | 19.03.1954 | Pusan Daewoo Royals |
| 8 | Cho Young-Jeung | 18.08.1954 | Lucky-Goldstar FC Hwangso |
| 9 | Choi Soon-Ho | 10.01.1962 | Posco Atoms Pohang |
| 13 | Noh Soo-Jin | 10.02.1962 | Yukong FC Kokkiri |
| 16 | Kim Joo-Sung | 17.01.1966 | Chosun University |
| 17 | Huh Jung-Moo | 13.01.1955 | Ulsan Hyundai Horang-i |
| 18 | Kim Sam-Soo | 08.02.1963 | Ulsan Hyundai Horang-i |
| | **Forwards** | | |
| 6 | Lee Tae-Ho | 29.01.1961 | Pusan Daewoo Royals |
| 7 | Kim Jong-Boo | 03.11.1965 | Korea University |
| 10 | Park Chang-Sun | 02.02.1954 | Pusan Daewoo Royals |
| 11 | Cha Bum-Kun | 21.05.1953 | TSV Bayer 04 Leverkusen (GER) |
| 19 | Byun Byung-Joo | 26.04.1961 | Pusan Daewoo Royals |
| 20 | Kim Yong-Se | 21.04.1960 | Yukong FC Kokkiri |
| 22 | Kang Deuk-Soo | 16.08.1961 | Lucky-Goldstar FC Hwangso |
| **Trainer:** | Kim Jung-Nam | 28.-01.1943 | |

## SOVIET UNION

| Nr | Name | DOB | Club |
|---|---|---|---|
| **Goalkeepers** | | | |
| 1 | Rinat Dasayev | 13.06.1957 | Spartak Moskva |
| 16 | Viktor Chanov | 21.07.1959 | Dinamo Kiev |
| 22 | Sergey Krakovskiy | 11.08.1960 | Dnepr Dnepropetrovsk |
| **Defenders** | | | |
| 2 | Vladimir Bessonov | 05.03.1958 | Dinamo Kiev |
| 3 | Aleksandr Chivadze | 08.04.1955 | Dinamo Tbilisi |
| 4 | Gennadiy Morozov | 30.12.1962 | Spartak Moskva |
| 5 | Anatoliy Demyanenko | 19.02.1959 | Dinamo Kiev |
| 6 | Aleksandr Bubnov | 10.10.1955 | Spartak Moskva |
| 10 | Oleg Kuznetzov | 22.03.1963 | Dinamo Kiev |
| 15 | Nikolay Larionov | 19.01.1957 | Zenit Leningrad |
| 21 | Vasiliy Ratz | 25.04.1961 | Dinamo Kiev |
| **Midfielders** | | | |
| 7 | Ivan Yaremchuk | 19.03.1962 | Dinamo Kiev |
| 8 | Pavel Yakovenko | 19.12.1964 | Dinamo Kiev |
| 9 | Aleksandr Zavarov | 24.04.1961 | Dinamo Kiev |
| 12 | Andrey Bal | 16.02.1958 | Dinamo Kiev |
| 13 | Gennadiy Litovchenko | 11.09.1963 | Dnepr Dnepropetrovsk |
| 17 | Vadim Evtushenko | 01.01.1958 | Dinamo Kiev |
| 20 | Sergei Aleynikov | 07.11.1961 | Dinamo Minsk |
| **Forwards** | | | |
| 11 | Oleh Blokhin | 05.11.1952 | Dinamo Kiev |
| 14 | Sergey Rodionov | 03.09.1962 | Spartak Moskva |
| 18 | Oleg Protasov | 04.02.1964 | Dnepr Dnepropetrovsk |
| 19 | Igor Belanov | 25.09.1960 | Dinamo Kiev |
| **Trainer:** Valeriy Lobanovskiy | | 06.01.1939 | |

## SPAIN

| Nr | Name | DOB | Club |
|---|---|---|---|
| **Goalkeepers** | | | |
| 1 | Andoni Zubizarreta Urreta | 23.10.1961 | Athletic Club de Bilbao |
| 13 | Francisco Javier González „Urrutikoetxea" | 17.02.1952 | FC Barcelona |
| 22 | Juan Carlos Iglesias Ablanedo | 02.09.1963 | Real Sporting Gijón CF |
| **Defenders** | | | |
| 2 | Pedro Tomás Reñones Grego | 09.08.1960 | Club Atlético de Madrid |
| 3 | José Antonio Camacho Alfaro | 08.06.1955 | Real Madrid CF |
| 4 | Antonio Maceda Francés | 16.05.1957 | Real Madrid CF |
| 8 | Andoni Goikoetxea Olaskoaga | 23.05.1956 | Athletic Club de Bilbao |
| 11 | Julio Alberto Moreno Casas | 07.10.1958 | FC Barcelona |
| 15 | Miguel Porlán Noguera „Chendo" | 12.10.1961 | Real Madrid CF |
| **Midfielders** | | | |
| 5 | Víctor Muñoz Manrique | 15.03.1957 | FC Barcelona |
| 6 | Rafael Gordillo Vázquez | 24.02.1957 | Real Madrid CF |
| 7 | Juan Antonio Señor Gómez | 26.08.1958 | Real Zaragoza CD |
| 14 | Ricardo Gallego Redondo | 08.02.1959 | Real Madrid CF |
| 17 | Francisco Javier López Alfaro | 01.11.1962 | Sevilla CF |
| 18 | Ramón María Calderé Del Rey | 16.01.1951 | FC Barcelona |
| 21 | José Miguel González Martín del Campo „Michel" | 23.03.1963 | Real Madrid CF |
| **Forwards** | | | |
| 9 | Emilio Butragueño Santos | 22.06.1963 | Real Madrid CF |
| 10 | Francisco José Carrasco Hidalgo | 06.03.1959 | FC Barcelona |
| 12 | Enrique Setién Soler „Quique" | 27.09.1958 | Club Atlético de Madrid |
| 16 | Hipólito Rincón Povedano | 28.04.1957 | Real Betis Balompié Sevilla |
| 19 | Julio Salinas Fernández | 11.09.1962 | Athletic Club de Bilbao |
| 20 | Eloy José Olaya Prendes | 16.07.1964 | Real Sporting Gijón CF |
| **Trainer:** Miguel Muñoz Mozún | | 19.01.1922 | |

## URUGUAY

| Nr | Name | DOB | Club |
|---|---|---|---|
| | **Goalkeepers** | | |
| 1 | Rodolfo Sergio Rodríguez | 20.01.1956 | Santos FC (BRA) |
| 12 | Fernando Harry Álvez Mosquera | 04.09.1959 | CA Peñarol Montevideo |
| 22 | Celso Otero Quintas | 01.02.1958 | Montevideo Wanderers FC |
| | **Defenders** | | |
| 2 | Nelson Daniel Gutiérrez Luongo | 13.04.1962 | CA River Plate Buenos Aires (ARG) |
| 3 | Eduardo Mario Acevedo Cardozo | 25.09.1959 | Defensor Sporting Club Montevideo |
| 4 | Víctor Hugo Diogo Silva | 09.04.1958 | SE Palmeiras São Paulo (BRA) |
| 6 | José Alberto Batista González | 06.03.1962 | CD Español Buenos Aires |
| 13 | César Javier Vega Perrone | 02.09.1959 | Danubio FC Montevideo |
| 14 | Alfonso Darío Pereyra Bueno | 19.10.1956 | São Paulo FC (BRA) |
| 15 | Eliseo Roque Rivero Pérez | 27.12.1957 | CA Peñarol Montevideo |
| | **Midfielders** | | |
| 5 | Miguel Angel Bossio Bastianini | 10.02.1960 | CA Peñarol Montevideo |
| 8 | Jorge Wálter Barrios Balestrasse | 24.01.1961 | SFP Olympiakos Peiraiás (GRE) |
| 10 | Enzo Francéscoli Uriarte | 12.11.1961 | CA River Plate Buenos Aires (ARG) |
| 11 | Sergio Rodolfo Santín Spinelli | 06.08.1956 | CD Atlético Nacional Medellín (COL) |
| 16 | Mario Daniel Saralegui | 24.04.1959 | CA Peñarol Montevideo |
| 17 | José Luis Zalazar Rodríguez | 26.10.1963 | CA Peñarol Montevideo |
| 18 | Rúben Walter Paz Márquez | 08.08.1959 | SC Internacional Porto Alegre (BRA) |
| | **Forwards** | | |
| 7 | Antonio Alzamendi Casas | 07.06.1956 | CA River Plate Buenos Aires (ARG) |
| 9 | Jorge Orosmán da Silva Echeverrito | 11.12.1961 | Club Atlético de Madrid (ESP) |
| 19 | Venancio Ariel Ramos Villanueva | 20.06.1959 | RC Lens (FRA) |
| 20 | Carlos Alberto Aguilera Nova | 21.09.1964 | Club Nacional de Montevideo |
| 21 | Wilmar Rubens Cabrera Sappa | 31.07.1959 | Valencia CF (ESP) |
| **Trainer:** | Omar Borrás | 15.06.1929 | |

## WEST GERMANY

| Nr | Name | DOB | Club |
|---|---|---|---|
| | **Goalkeepers** | | |
| 1 | Harald Schumacher | 06.03.1954 | 1.FC Köln |
| 12 | Ulrich Stein | 23.10.1954 | Hamburger SV |
| 22 | Eike Immel | 27.11.1960 | BV Borussia Dortmund |
| | **Defenders** | | |
| 2 | Hans-Peter Briegel | 11.10.1955 | Hellas Verona (ITA) |
| 3 | Andreas Brehme | 09.11.1960 | 1.FC Kaiserslautern |
| 4 | Karlheinz Förster | 25.07.1958 | VfB Stuttgart |
| 5 | Matthias Herget | 14.11.1955 | FC Bayer 05 Uerdingen |
| 6 | Norbert Eder | 07.11.1955 | FC Bayern München |
| 14 | Thomas Berthold | 12.11.1964 | SG Eintracht Frankfurt |
| 15 | Klaus Augenthaler | 26.09.1957 | FC Bayern München |
| 17 | Ditmar Jakobs | 28.08.1953 | Hamburger SV |
| | **Midfielders** | | |
| 8 | Lothar Herbert Matthäus | 21.03.1961 | FC Bayern München |
| 10 | Felix Magath | 26.07.1953 | Hamburger SV |
| 13 | Karl Allgöwer | 05.01.1957 | VfB Stuttgart |
| 16 | Olaf Thon | 01.05.1966 | FC Schalke 04 Gelsenkirchen |
| 18 | Uwe Rahn | 21.05.1962 | Borussia VfL Mönchengladbach |
| 21 | Wolfgang Rolff | 26.12.1959 | Hamburger SV |
| | **Forwards** | | |
| 7 | Pierre Littbarski | 16.04.1960 | 1.FC Köln |
| 9 | Rudi Völler | 13.04.1960 | SV Werder Bremen |
| 11 | Karl-Heinz Rummenigge | 25.09.1955 | Internazionale FC Milano (ITA) |
| 19 | Klaus Allofs | 05.12.1956 | 1.FC Köln |
| 20 | Dieter Hoeneß | 07.01.1953 | FC Bayern München |
| **Trainer:** | Franz Beckenbauer | 11.09.1945 | |